South of France

Provence & the Côte d'Azur

timeout.com

Penguin Books

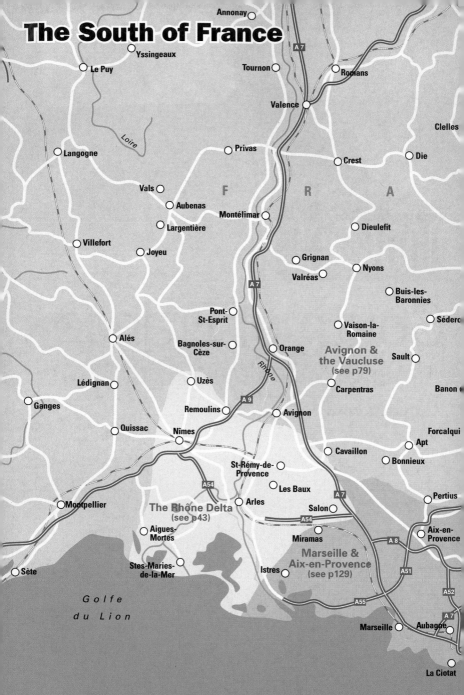

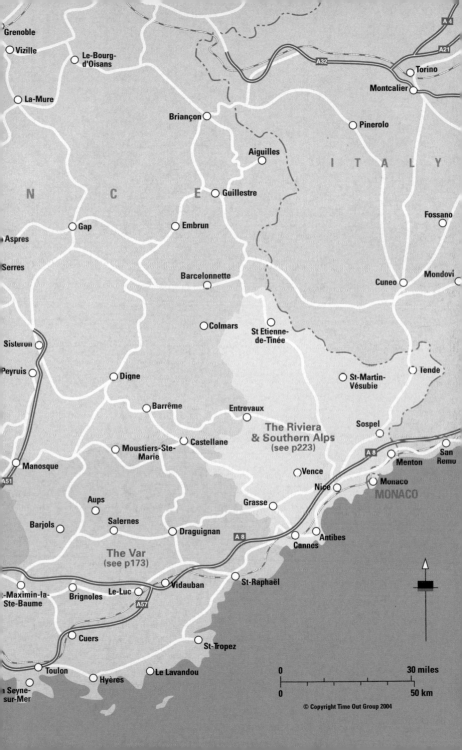

PENGUIN BOOKS

Published by the Penguin Group
Penguin Books Ltd, 80 Strand, London WC2R ORL, England
Penguin Books USA Inc, 375 Hudson Street, New York, New York 10014, USA
Penguin Books Australia Ltd, 250 Camberwell Road, Camberwell, Victoria 3124, Australia
Penguin Books Canada Ltd, 10 Alcorn Avenue, Toronto, Ontario, Canada M4V 3B2
Penguin Books (NZ) Ltd, cnr Rosedale and Airborne Rds, Albany, Auckland, New Zealand

Penguin Books Ltd, Registered Offices: 80 Strand, London WC2R ORL, England

First published 2000
Second edition 2002

Third edition 2004
10 9 8 7 6 5 4 3 2 1

Copyright © Time Out Group Ltd, 2000, 2002, 2004.
All rights reserved

Reprographics by Quebecor Numeric, 56 bd Davout, 75020 Paris
Cover reprographics by Precise Litho, 34-35 Great Sutton Street, London EC1
Printed and bound by Cayfosa-Quebecor, Ctra. de Caldes, Km 3 08 130 Sta Perpètua de Mogoda, Barcelona, Spain

**Edited &
designed by
Time Out Paris**
15-17 rue des Martyrs
75009 Paris
Tel: +33 (0)1.44.87.00.45
Fax:+33 (0)1.44.73.90.60
Email: editors@timeout.fr

**For
Time Out Guides Ltd**
Universal House
251 Tottenham Court Road
London W1T 7AB
Tel: +44 (0)20 7813 3000
Fax:+44 (0)20 7813 6001
www.timeout.com

Editorial

Editor Natasha Edwards
Production Editor Alison Culliford
Editorial Assistants Marie-Noëlle Bauer,
André Bittar, Joanna Brown, Clodagh Finn,
Elizabeth Guill, Fiona Johnson, Marie Thiel,
Anna Watson, Dora Whitaker

Managing Director Paris Karen Albrecht

Guides Editorial/Managing Director Peter Fiennes
Series Editor Ruth Jarvis
Deputy Series Editor Lesley McCave
Guides Co-ordinator Anna Norman

Design

Art Director Paris Richard Joy
Ad Design Philippe Thareaut
Art Director Mandy Martin
Acting Art Director Scott Moore
Picture Editor Jael Marschner

Advertising

Sales & Administration Manager Philippe Thareaut
Advertising Sales (Cannes) Carlos Pineda
Sales Director Mark Phillips
International Sales Manager Ross Canadé

Production

Guides Production Director Mark Lamond
Production Controller Samantha Furniss

Time Out Group

Chairman Tony Elliott
Managing Director Mike Hardwick
Group Financial Director Richard Waterlow
Group Commercial Director Lesley Gill
Group Marketing Director Christine Cort
Marketing Manager Mandy Martinez
Group General Manager Nichola Coulthard
Group Art Director John Oakey
Online Managing Director David Pepper
Accountants Sarah Bostock, Abdus Sadique

Features for the third edition were written or updated by: Introductions Natasha Edwards. **History**
Natasha Edwards (*August 1944* Fiona Johnson). **The South of France Today** John Laurenson (*Fire!* Natasha Edwards).
Provençal Food Natasha Edwards (*A cook's tour of Provence* Anna Watson). **Provençal Wine** Richard James.
The Creative South Natasha Edwards. **The Festive South** Anna Watson. **Nîmes & the Pont du Gard** Natasha Edwards.
St-Rémy & Les Alpilles Alexander Lobrano. **Arles** Stephen Mudge. **The Camargue** Stephen Mudge.
Avignon Isabel Pitman. **Orange & Châteauneuf-du-Pape** Stephen Mudge. **Carpentras & Mont Ventoux**
Stephen Mudge (*Bike ride* Isabel Pitman). **The Drôme Provençale** Isabel Pitman. **The Luberon** Natasha Edwards.
Marseille Richard James (*Read my lips* Isabel Pitman). **Cassis, the Calanques & La Ciotat** Inger Holland, Richard
James (*Calanques walk* Richard James). **Aix-en-Provence** Anna Watson. **Toulon & Western Côte** Inger Holland.
Hyères to Les Maures Natasha Edwards. **St-Tropez** Natalie Whittle (*How to do St-Tropez* Alexander Lobrano).
St-Raphaël & the Estérel Alison Culliford. **Brignoles & the Ste-Baume** Inger Holland. **Draguignan & the Central Var**
Inger Holland, Nicola Mitchell (*At home with the Beckhams* Toby Rose). **The Gorges du Verdon** Sarah Fraser. **Cannes**
Sarah Fraser (*How to crash Cannes Film Festival* Toby Rose). **Antibes to Cagnes** Tristan Rutherford. **Nice** Sarah Fraser
(*Nice snacks* Rosa Jackson, *Nice v Monaco, Winter warmer* Tristan Rutherford). **The Corniches** Tristan Rutherford.
Monaco & Monte-Carlo Tania Cagnoni. **Roquebrune to Menton** Tristan Rutherford. **Grasse & the Gorges du Loup**
Annie Sparks (*Napoléon's long march*) Natasha Edwards. **Vence & St-Paul** Tania Cagnoni. **Into the Alps** Sarah Fraser.
Directory Anna Watson. **Additional listings** Sarah Fraser, Alexander Lobrano. **Index** Marie-Noëlle Bauer, Fiona Johnson.

The Editor would like to thank Jean-Pierre Bordaz, Olivia Bordaz and all the contributors from previous editions.

Maps by JS Graphics – john@jsgraphics.co.uk, with revisions and extensions by Philippe Landry. Street plans are based on
material supplied by Thomas Cook Publishers. Toulon map drawn by Philippe Landry.

Photography Karl Blackwell. **Additional photography** François Delena, Adam Eastland, Pierre Domenech, Comité
Départemental du Tourisme, Les Ballets de Monte-Carlo.

Contents

Introduction

In the early days the right sort wintered on the Riviera and summered in the Alps. Things have switched around since then, but the British still continue to flock to a coast that, in many ways, they invented – after waves of Celts, Greeks, Romans, Saracens and Italians, not to mention Franks and Angevins (plus a few cavemen) had been here before. All these people, plus more recent Russians and Americans, *emigrés* and immigrants, have left their traces, but that undefinable *je ne sais quoi* has turned the result into something indisputably French: a land of food, wine, ancient history, modern mores and eye-goggling, ogling people-watching.

Indeed, Provençal prints, terracotta tommettes, wrought-iron belfries, sachets of lavender and vats of *tapenade*, all epitomise the age-old charms of Provence, but the South of France also remains a centre of the avant-garde. Picasso, Picabia and Mallet-Stevens made their mark last century and a new generation is embracing modernity today: the wildly conceptual Hi Hôtel has opened in Nice, far-from-rustic luxury farm hamlet 'maisons' have arrived in the Luberon and an old cinema is the place to stay in St-Rémy.

The Mediterranean climate and the Latin lifestyle give the South of France an enduring appeal, and now it is easier to get to than ever before, with cheap flights from the UK and fast trains from Paris. Come and explore.

ABOUT THE TIME OUT GUIDES

Time Out South of France is one of an expanding series of *Time Out* guides produced by the people behind London's and New York's successful listings magazines. With the first edition of *Time Out South of France* in 2000, the dynamic, critical approach of Time Out's city guide series was applied for the first time to a whole region. This third edition, thoroughly revised and updated by writers resident in France, contains even more on what to see and where to eat and stay, whether you're a regular or a first-time visitor, and up-to-the-minute information on arts and cultural events.

THE LIE OF THE LAND

The South of France is as much about an image and a lifestyle as technical boundaries. The main area we cover coincides with the southern portion of the modern French administrative region of Provence-Alpes-Côte d'Azur, taking in the *départements* of Bouches-du-Rhône, Vaucluse, Var, Alpes-Maritimes and the south of the Alpes de Haute-Provence. But we also spread west into the Gard *département* to Nîmes and Uzès, which fell within Roman Provincia, to Aigues-Mortes at the western boundary of the Camargue, and north to the south of the Drôme *département*, an area often dubbed 'the Drôme Provençale', where the characteristic vegetation of olives and herbs already augurs the South.

There is online information on over 40 international cities on www.timeout.com.

Our regional sections are arranged in a roughly west-east order. All the areas covered, from big cities to rural backwaters, start with the background history and sightseeing information, followed by where to eat, where to stay and visitor information, including the addresses of the relevant tourist offices. Listings for restaurants, bars and hotels are more detailed in larger conurbations. We give essential road and public transport information at the end of chapters, but sometimes suggested routes between villages are detailed in the main text. Bear in mind that public transport in inland rural areas is often extremely limited.

PRICES AND PAYMENT

The prices we've supplied should be treated as guidelines, not gospel. If you encounter prices that vary wildly from those we've quoted, ask whether there's a good reason. If not, go elsewhere. For hotels we have listed the price for a double room as the best indication for the price bracket within which a hotel falls (although these hotels may well equally have single rooms or, indeed, triples, quadruples or suites). The range for a double takes in different categories of room and/or variations between low- and high-season prices. French hotel prices generally do not include breakfast, although those for *chambres d'hôtes*, the French equivalent of B&B, generally do. For restaurants, we give the price range for set menus (referred to in French as *formule, menu* or *prix-fixe*); note that the lowest-priced *menu* is often available only on weekday lunches. Where no *menus* are served, we give an average for a three-course meal without drinks,

for one person. In main cities we note whether restaurants, hotels and cafés take credit cards – American Express (AmEx), Diners Club (DC), MasterCard (MC) and Visa (V). The most widely accepted credit card is Visa. Note that credit cards are often not accepted for less than €15.

TELEPHONE NUMBERS
All French phone numbers have ten digits. Numbers for the area covered in this guide (except Monaco, code 00 377) start with 04. From outside France, dial the country code (33) and leave off the zero at the beginning of the number. Numbers prefixed by 06 are mobile phones, 08.36 numbers are premium rate and 08.00 are freephone numbers (sometimes available from outside France at standard international rates).

POSTCODES
All addresses in France have a five-figure postcode, starting with the two figures that indicate the *département* (eg. 06000 Nice, 06400 Cannes). For questions of space and readability, we have not put postcodes in each address but, should you need to write to someone in a particular town or village, have included them in the address of tourist information offices.

THE LOWDOWN ON THE LISTINGS
Above all, we've tried to make this book as useful as possible. Addresses, phone numbers, transport information, opening details and admission prices are all included. Most French hotels and restaurants are small, family-run concerns and will close for annual holidays. We try to list seasonal and weekly closures for

restaurants, hotels and tourist attractions, although these can vary from year to year. Before you go out of your way, we advise you to phone ahead to check opening times and other particulars. While every effort has been made to ensure the accuracy of the information contained in this guide, the publishers cannot accept responsibility for any errors it may contain.

ESSENTIAL INFORMATION
For practical information, including emergency numbers, car hire and essential vocabulary, turn to the Directory at the back of this guide. For food terms, see the chapter on Provençal Food.

LET US KNOW WHAT YOU THINK
We hope you enjoy *Time Out South of France* and we'd like to know what you think of it. We welcome your tips for places that you consider we should include in future editions and we value and take notice of your criticisms of our choices. There's a reader's reply card at the back of this book – or you can simply email us on editors@timeout.fr.

In Context

Features

History

Friends, Romans, countrymen: everyone from Boney to the British Army has hit the beach in the Côte d'Azur.

Even before the last ice age, hunter societies had left animal paintings on the walls of the Grotte Cosquer in the Calanques. Later, Neolithic man took up residence in the fertile region around Nice and Monaco, as well as in the cave-pocked Verdon gorges.

Around 1200BC, the Gauls – a Celtic people – began to migrate from the Rhine Valley into France and Italy. The southernmost front of this advance developed into the Ligurian culture, which stretched from Spain into Italy. Skilled metal workers and stone carvers, the Ligurians lived in *oppidiums* – fortified villages such as that at Entremont, near Aix.

Western civilisation first came to Provence in the form of the Greeks from the Ionian city of Phocaea, who founded the colony of Massalia (modern-day Marseille) in about 600BC. By the beginning of the fifth century BC, Massalia had become so powerful that it was minting its own money and had begun to plant colonies along the coast at Nikaia (Nice), Olbia (Hyères), Taureontum (Les Lecques) and Agde, and inland at Arles. The Greeks planted vines and olives, and the pan-Mediterranean trade in wine, olive oil and other goods soon filtered through to neighbouring Celtic areas.

ROMAN 'PROVINCIA'

Marseille took the Roman side during the Carthaginian Wars, a smart move that stood it in good stead when Rome went annexing beyond the Alps towards the end of the second century BC. Called in by Marseille to help the city repulse a Celtic attack, the Romans stayed on, destroying the *oppidium* of Entremont and founding the city of Aquae Sextiae (Aix-en-Provence) in 122BC. In recognition of its support, Marseille was allowed to remain an independent state within Roman territory.

The main reason, however, for expansion into the south of France was the need to secure the land route to Spain. From around 120BC, Roman Consul Cneus Domitius Ahenobarbus created the Via Domitia (Domitian Way) with staging posts at Nîmes, Beaucaire, Cavaillon and Apt. By 118BC Rome controlled the whole coast westwards to the Pyrenees and a large swathe of the hinterland. The Romans subdued by colonisation: vast numbers of settlers were attracted by a promise of free land. The Celtic town at Vaison-la-Romaine became a semi-autonomous federated city. Narbonne, further west, became the capital of Gallia Narbonensis, also known, more simply, as 'Provincia'. After 115BC, the Celtic tribe of the Cimbri and the Germanic Teutons mounted a series of raids on Provence, culminating in a humiliating defeat for the Romans at Orange in 105BC.

'The aqueducts, baths, amphitheatres and temples often surpassed those of similar-sized Italian cities.'

Under the *pax romana*, Gallia Narbonensis became a model province. Provence became an important supplier of grain, olive oil and ships for the ever-hungry empire. In return, it was treated more as an extension of the motherland than a colonial outpost. The aqueducts, baths, amphitheatres and temples that serviced fine cities, such as Aix, Arles, Nîmes, Orange and Glanum (St-Rémy), often surpassed those of similar-sized Italian cities. Further east they constructed the major port of Fréjus (probable birthplace of the historian Tacitus), Cemenelum (Nice), and a ring of fortified settlements in what is now the eastern Var. Even after Julius Caesar had subdued the rest of Gaul in the Gallic Wars (58-51BC), this remained the most Roman of the empire's transalpine possessions.

Marseille was eclipsed after it supported Pompey against Caesar in the Civil Wars. Besieged in 49BC, its possessions were transferred to Arles, Narbonne and Fréjus – though it continued to be a centre of scholarship. The imperial connection with Provence was reinforced under Antoninus Pius (emperor 138-161 AD), whose family came from Nîmes; and with Constantine Arles became a favoured imperial residence in the fourth century.

MONKS AND INVADERS

The Christian community came into the open with the foundation of the monasteries of St-Honorat on the Iles des Lérins and St-Victor in Marseille in the early fifth century. The latter was the centre of a monastic diaspora that gave the South a generous sprinkling of abbeys from Le Barben to Castellane, ensuring the land was worked even in times of crisis – though the monks could be as tyrannical in exploiting the peasantry as any feudal landlord.

When the Roman empire finally fell apart in 476, the bishoprics maintained some semblance of order in the face of invasions by Visigoths and Ostrogoths. It was the Franks who eventually gained the upper hand, after a period of anarchy during which Roman embellishments fell into ruin and fields returned to swampland. The new rulers looked north rather than south, and the Mediterranean trade that had sustained cities like Arles or Marseille gradually dried up.

The three-way partition of the Carolingian empire between the sons of Louis 1er in the Treaty of Verdun in 843 made the Rhône a frontier and provided the basis for the later division between Provence and Languedoc. In 931 the kingdom of Provence – one of many fragments of Charlemagne's former empire – was allied with Burgundy. Over the next couple of centuries, imperial rule gave way to out-and-out feudalism, as local lords used brute force and taxes to subdue the territory around their castle strongholds. The Saracens terrorised the coast and launched raids on the surrounding countryside from their base at La Garde-Freinet in the Massif des Maures, until driven out by Guillaume 1er, Count of Arles, in 974, confirming the power of the kingdom of Arles, which became part of the Holy Roman Empire.

COUNTS AND CONSULATES

From the end of the 11th century more efficient agriculture, the revival of trade and the rise of the guilds provided the money for the construction of new religious foundations, such as the magnificent abbey of St Gilles in the Camargue, with its richly carved façade, and the restoration and embellishment of St-Trophime in Arles. A sober, pared-back style of Romanesque also evolved in the 12th century at the great Cistercian foundations of Silvacane, Senanque and Thoronet. Northern French Gothic (which had its beginnings at St-Denis in the 12th century) was slow to percolate South, where Romanesque continued to hold sway, though a few fine Gothic edifices were built, notably the Palais des Papes in Avignon, the Cathédrale St-Suffrein in Carpentras and the magnificent Basilique St-Maximin-la-Ste-Baume.

Sometime in the 11th century, a small local dynasty had felt confident enough to award itself the title of Counts of Provence. When the line died out in 1113, the title passed to the House of Barcelona, which became the nominal ruler of the area. However, the larger cities soon asserted their independence, setting up governments known as Consulates. In the country, local bosses such as the lords of Les Baux and count of Forcalquier put up fierce resistance to those claiming higher authority.

Barcelona's sway over Mediterranean France was helped along by language. Provençal, the eastern dialect of Occitan or *langue d'Oc*, was a close cousin of Catalan. Out of the apparent anarchy and the frequent shifts in the balance of power among the warring seigneuries, a distinctive local culture emerged, which reached its fullest expression in the poetry and ballads of the troubadours, or itinerant love poets.

ANJOU COUNTS, BABYLONIAN POPES

Provence was spared the destruction and slaughter visited upon south-western France during the Albigensian Crusade against the Cathars. But the crusade altered the balance of power in the south: the Counts of Toulouse were crushed, and Languedoc passed to the French crown in 1271, except for the Comtat Venaissin (including Avignon, Carpentras, Cavaillon and Fontaine-de-Vaucluse), which Philippe III of France gave to the Papacy in 1274.

The Counts of Provence emerged as sole rulers of the land between the Rhône and the Alps. The last Count of Provence, Raymond-Bérenger V, was also one of the shrewdest and most cultured. He gave his territories an efficient administration and dealt with the increasingly muscular power of France in a masterful piece of dynastic planning, marrying all four daughters to kings or future kings: the eldest Marguerite to Louis IX of France, Eleanor to Henry III of England, Sanchia to Richard of Cornwall and, in 1246, Béatrice to Charles d'Anjou, brother of Louis IX, thus bringing Provence under Angevin rule.

The Anjou princes ruled for two and a half centuries, bringing a new degree of stability, and making Aix their administrative capital, though they preferred to reside in Palermo or Naples until they were chased out of Sicily in 1282. Louis II of Anjou, however, founded the University of Aix in 1409. Good King René (1434-80) likewise concentrated first on Italy until he lost Naples to Aragon in 1442, thereafter dividing his time between Angers and Provence, where he established his court at Aix and built a lavishly furnished château at Tarascon. His reign was longer and more stable than most, and the poet-king encouraged a minor artistic revival from his court. The administrative reforms introduced by the last Count of Provence were continued with the establishment of the Etats généraux, a regional assembly that had the power to raise taxes and take over the reins of government in times of crisis. The last of the local warlords, the Baux family, retreated to Orange, setting off the dynastic daisy chain that would lead to the latter becoming a corner of Protestant Holland in the 16th century.

In 1306, French-born pope Clément V made good use of Papal bolthole the Comtat Vénaissin, transferring his whole court first to Carpentras and then to Avignon, and ushering in the papacy's 70-year 'Babylonian captivity'. When the Jews were expelled from France, first in 1306 by Philippe le Bel and again in 1394 under Charles VI, they found refuge in the Papal enclave, where fine synagogues survive at Carpentras and Cavaillon. The Black Death hit Provence in 1348, entering through the port of Marseille and decimating the population.

The Avignon Papacy spurred an economic, intellectual and cultural renaissance in the region, from new industries like glass-making, paper manufacture and melon growing to the rise of an artistic school, now known as the Provençal Primitives (*see right*). To the east, in the territory of Nice (grabbed by the House of Savoy in 1388) – and especially its mountainous hinterland – Niçois painter Louis Bréa and Piedmontese imports Giovanni Canavesio and Jean Baleison would found a distinctive school in the mid-15th to mid-16th centuries.

UNION WITH FRANCE AND THE WARS OF RELIGION

Charles du Maine, René's nephew, survived his uncle by only a year. Dying without an heir in 1481, he bequeathed Anjou, Maine and Provence (excluding Savoy, Monaco and the Comtat Venaissin) to portly King Louis XI of France. Not only Provence but Roussillon, Burgundy, Lorraine and parts of northern Italy came under the sway of this fat controller.

After trying strong-arm tactics for the first three years, France decided to allow Provence at least the illusion of independence for the time being, with the Act of Union (1486) granting the region substantial autonomy within the French state. A *parlement* was established at Aix in 1501, but there were still several pockets of autonomy – notably Marseille, which stoutly defended its republican traditions. François 1er subdued the city with the fort on the Ile d'If and used the Marseille shipyards in his Italian wars against his arch-enemy, the Holy Roman Emperor Charles V, who replied by besieging the city in 1523. He added similar fortifications on the Ile de Porquerolles and at St-Paul-de-Vence, where they survive pretty much intact.

On the ground the dominant issue became that of religious difference. Protestantism had achieved a firm foothold in Provence and eastern Languedoc, especially among the rural poor. Even before Luther, the Waldensian or Vaudois sect – whose tweaking of Catholic doctrine was more than enough to be branded heretical – had put down roots in the Luberon, where feudal landlords encouraged them to repopulate the land after the Black Death. The movement was brutally put down in April 1545, when Vaudois villages were pillaged and burned and their populations massacred. This

Enguerrand Quarton and the Provençal Primitives

At a crossroads of culture between northern and southern Europe, cosmopolitan Provence saw a flourishing of the arts in the late Middle Ages at its rival spheres of power: on one hand, the papal-owned Comtat Venaissin, centred on Avignon; on the other the burgeoning court of the Counts of Provence at Aix-en-Provence under René d'Anjou or 'Good King René', Renaissance man, wine-loving poet and artistic patron. The Popes had brought with them talented Italian artists such as the Sienese Simone Martini when they moved to Avignon in the early 14th century and, despite the return of the Pope to Rome in 1417, a wealthy and independent elite persisted at Avignon. Rich bankers and merchants, often of Italian origin, plus clergy and local aristocracy, meant plenty of opportunities for artists from the battle-torn north of France and Flanders. Within this highly international milieu, a distinct Provençal school emerged: a fusion of meticulous Flemish-style detail with the intense southern light that encouraged the simplification of forms and strong shadows.

Works by the Provençal Primitives are rare today. Many disappeared with the destruction of churches and monasteries during the French Revolution and the artists have only really been rediscovered since an exhibition at the Louvre in Paris in 1904.

In Aix, Nicolas Froment painted the *Buisson Ardent* (Mary and the Burning Bush), today in

Aix cathedral, for René of Anjou, depicting the king and his queen (who he also painted in a meticulous double portrait) flanking the Virgin. Froment was succeeded around 1447-72 as court painter by Flemish artist Barthélémy van Eyck, who had painted another masterpiece of the Provençal school, the *Annunciation* (today in the Eglise de la Madeleine in Aix), the central panel of a larger altarpiece commissioned in 1445 by a local draper for the church of St-Sauveur. Van Eyck worked for the king at his splendid new Château de Tarascon and travelled with him to Angers.

But the artist who stands out most in the Provençal School is the mysterious Enguerrand Quarton, whose rare works are some of the masterpieces of 15th-century European art. Little is known about Quarton himself, except that he was probably born in Laon in Picardy and possibly trained in Flanders before heading south. Quarton seems to have arrived in Aix in 1444, where he collaborated with Van Eyck on manuscripts, then Arles, where he practised stained glass making as well as painting. Moving to Avignon in 1447, he was kept busy working for a clientele of clergy, notables and corporations until his death in around 1466, possibly from the Plague.

Fortunately, two of Quarton's paintings can be seen in Provence today: the extraordinary *Coronation of the Virgin (pictured)*, painted in meticulous detail for the Chartreuse in Villeneuve-lès-Avignon (now in the Musée Pierre de Luxembourg). Here, in a symbolic representation of the universe, the Virgin is flanked by Jesus, God and the Holy Spirit, floating above the crucifixion and a minutely depicted view of the earth and hell below. The other is the earlier *Virgin and Child with an Apple* in the Musée du Petit Palais in Avignon. Quarton's third great masterpiece, the *Pietà d'Avignon*, discovered by writer Prosper Mérimée in an Avignon church in 1834, is today in the Louvre. With its elongated figures, the resigned stoic suffrance and sensitively rendered features of the Virgin, Mary Magdalen and St John bowed over the gaunt, angular body of the dead Christ, the *Pietà*, which has since inspired artists as varied as Mondrian and Giacometti, is a masterpiece of sheer, tragic power.

August 1944: Provence liberated

Over time, the beaches of Cavalaire, St-Raphaël and Le Lavandou have become more synonymous with the garish than the 'guerre'. However, in August 1944, they were the stage upon which unfolded a dramatic and intense battle to restore the battered French national pride and, eventually, its freedom.

Operation Dragoon, a 250,000-strong wave of Allied manpower, hit the Provençal shores between Toulon and Cannes on 15 August. The forces significantly included the 1st French Army under General de Lattre de Tassigny. This was the military representation of Charles de Gaulle's alternative French government, a body teeth-grittingly recognised by the British and American establishments despite a deep and mutual repulsion between Roosevelt and de Gaulle ('prima donna!' sneered Roosevelt; 'corpse!' muttered our Frenchman). As American forces, airdropped inland at Le Muy, barrelled up the Rhône valley in the direction of Lyon and Grenoble, General de Lattre's forces landed on the coast at Pramousquier and Cap Nègre to take care of the strategic ports of Toulon and Marseille, while 20,000 GIs from the 36th Texan Division landed on the Plage du Dramont. Taking full advantage of German disarray, the Allies moved quickly to encircle the cities. After just over a week of intense fighting and high casualties, Marseille fell on 23 August, Cannes on the 25th, Toulon on the 27th, ecstatically echoing the liberation of Paris on the 25th. Although, in British memory, the Provence landings seem an afterthought to the Normandy triumph in June, the events in Provence are still tied up with the euphoria of the liberation of Paris and the wider sense of the French recapturing their country. In this case, many of the 'French' liberating France came from the colonies of Algeria, Morocco, Senegal and Cameroon (a fact ungracefully forgotten by the Toulonnois in 1995, when they voted for Le Pen's Front National at local election time). De Lattre's army apparently also caused related concerns to de Gaulle, who ordered that it should be 'whitened' with restless throes of exiled Resistance fighters.

Sixty years on, the memorials that pepper the coast are easily missed amid the crush of a Côte d'Azur summer. For quieter reflection, there are national cemeteries at Boularis, Rayol-Canadel and Luynes. The main memorial-museum is on Mont Faron in Toulon; you can also visit the Musée de la Libération at Le Muy (one of the first villages liberated thanks to the American soldiers parachuted in) and the US war cemetery outside Draguignan. A more general history of the occupation and *maquis* resistance can be found at Le Musée d'Histoire 1939-45 in Fontaine de Vaucluse. Ceremonies, concerts, marches and displays commemorating the 60th anniversary will take place across the region in 2004 (Var Tourist Board 04.94.50.55.50); Le Muy is hosting two days of films, parades and Glenn Miller tributes (Le Muy Office du Tourisme, 04.94.45.06.67).

Yank Magazine's 1944 liberation issue.

was only the opening salvo of the Wars of Religion, which really kicked in when French Calvinism – or Huguenotism – spread throughout France in the 1550s. There were Protestant enclaves in Orange, Haute Provence and the Luberon, but the main seedbed of the new faith lay west of the Rhône: in Nîmes, three-quarters of the population became

'The Baron des Adrets specialised in throwing Catholic prisoners from the top of the nearest castle.'

Huguenot. The 1560s saw atrocities on both sides. Most of the Huguenots of Orange were massacred in 1563; in reprisal, the Baron des Adrets, who had converted from Catholicism only the year before, went on the rampage; he specialised in throwing Catholic prisoners from the top of the nearest castle (two years later he reconverted and retired to the family estate).

In 1593, first Bourbon monarch, the Protestant Henri de Navarre (Henri IV) converted to Catholicism to assure power in Paris, and issued the Edict of Nantes in 1598 to reconcile the warring factions. The Edict guaranteed civil and religious liberties to Protestants. In the South its main effect was to reconfirm the Rhône split (*see p7*) – this time as a religious rather than political frontier.

Under Louis XIII and his minister Cardinal Richelieu, the Catholic Counter-Reformation reached its apogée. Flamboyant Baroque churches were built at L'Isle-sur-la-Sorgue, Martigues and in Italian-ruled Nice; sculptor and architect Pierre Puget built his masterpiece La Vieille Charité in Marseille. The Royals made a few trips down south. In 1638 queen Anne of Austria, still childless after 22 years of marriage to Louis XIII, made a pilgrimage to Cotignac to pray for a son – later visiting Apt in 1660 in gratitude for the birth of Louis XIV.

In 1685 Louis XIV, encouraged by his fervently Catholic mistress Madame de Maintenon, revoked the Edict of Nantes, leading to massacres of Protestants in Nîmes and Arles; Protestant churches were demolished and schools closed. The main effect, though, was to deprive Nîmes and Uzès of their industrious Huguenot manufacturers, who emigrated in their thousands (though a few converted and stayed on to make silk and the blue linen 'de Nîmes' that English merchants called 'denim').

DICTATORSHIP AND ENLIGHTENMENT

By the 17th century, the history of the South had become bound up with that of France. Of use to Paris mainly as a source of fruit, olive oil,

Henri IV, who ended the Wars of Relgion.

wine, textiles and taxes, and as a builder of ships for royal wars, the Midi was drained of funds and, at the same time, kept firmly in line by the increasingly centralised State and absolutist rule of the Sun King ('*l'état c'est moi*') Louis XIV. When restless Marseille dared to set up a rebel council in 1658, Louis XIV turned the town's cannons on itself and built an additional fort designed above all to keep an eye on the unruly citizens. The port of Toulon was expanded and turned into the main base of the Mediterranean fleet, busy waging war against the Spanish. Louis XIV's military architect Vauban added his characteristic star-shaped defences in both Toulon and Antibes.

Marseille took a further body blow in 1720, when a visiting Syrian ship caused one of the last big outbreaks of plague in the West, which killed 50,000 people in the city alone. A plague wall was built that stretched as far as the Luberon to try and restrict the disease but it spread all the same.

The 18th century was also a time of increasing prosperity. A wealthy bourgeoisie developed in the main industrial centres – textiles around Nîmes, salt at Aigues-Mortes and Hyères, furniture at Beaucaire (site of the most important fair in the South), faïence in Marseille and Moustiers, perfumery and tanning in Grasse. In the 'parliamentary' city of Aix (capital of the *Etats généraux* administrative area of Provence), a caste of politicians with plenty of time on their hands built themselves sumptuous townhouses and lavish country *bastides*.

REVOLUTIONS AND RESTORATIONS

Resentment of Paris and its taxes continued to simmer, fuelled by bad harvests and rising unemployment. When the Revolution broke out in 1789, Provence was swift to join in. Among its primary movers was the Comte de Mirabeau, elected as *député* of Aix when the Third Estate was finally convened in 1789. The dockers of Marseille were particularly active, taking the Forts of St-Jean and St-Nicolas in an echo of the Bastille – though the republic's battle-hymn *La Marseillaise*, was in fact written by Alsatian Rouget de l'Isle, and only associated with Marseille when adopted by its Jacobin national guard (*les Féderés*) marching to Paris in 1792.

'St-Maximin-la-Ste-Baume was saved by an organ rendition of *La Marseillaise* by Napoléon's brother.'

The Revolution was anti-clerical as well as anti-royal. Religious foundations and churches became state property and religious festivals were replaced by the cult of the Supreme Being. There were some lucky escapes: Toulon cathedral survived as an arms depot, St-Maximin-la-Ste-Baume was saved by an organ rendition of *La Marseillaise* by Napoléon's brother Lucien. The papal enclave of the Comtat Venaissin was reincorporated into France in 1791 and in 1792 Revolutionary forces took Nice (subsequently handed back to Italy in 1814). Anarchy soon set in all over France, with counter-revolutionary uprisings brutally put down by Robespierre's Terror of 1793, notably in Marseille and Toulon. The British took advantage of the confusion to occupy Toulon in 1793; they were sent packing by artillery commanded by a rising military star, 24-year-old Napoléon Bonaparte. In 1799, after a military coup, Napoléon became First Consul and in 1804 declared himself Emperor.

Perhaps the main legacy of the Revolution was a further weakening of regional autonomy with the abolition of the *Etats généraux* and the carve-up of France in 1790 into centrally administered *départements*. Under his rule, Napoléon gave France the *lycée* educational system and the Napoleonic Code of civil law.

Though he had served his military training in Antibes and Toulon, Bonaparte had little affection for Provence, and the feeling was mutual. Defeated in 1814, Napoléon's return from exile on Elba and flight north to Paris through the Alps are today commemorated by the Route Napoléon (*see p293*). Napoléon's return was brief and, after Waterloo, the Bourbon monarchy was restored under Louis XVII.

FROM RESTORATION TO REPUBLIC

The radical spirit endured, nurtured in the shipyards of Toulon and Marseille, and most of the South threw its weight behind the 1848 Revolution, which saw the monarchy again overthrown and Louis-Napoléon Bonaparte, the nephew of Napoléon I, elected first Président and later, in 1852, Emperor Napoléon III. The glittery Second Empire was a period of colonial and industrial expansion. The opening of the Suez Canal in 1869 and the spread of colonial France quadrupled Marseille's port traffic, and long boulevards, a new cathedral, the Bourse Maritime and Palais de Longchamp were all built. Toulon expanded beyond its walls and gained a glamorous opera house. Steamships poured out of the shipyards of La Ciotat and La Seyne-sur-Mer, and the coastal railway, an engineeering feat with its tunnels and viaducts, had reached Nice by 1865, Monaco by 1868.

The last of the major territorial reshuffles took place in 1860, when Napoléon III received Nice and its mountainous hinterland from the House of Savoy in return for his diplomatic neutrality during the unification of Italy. Monaco was now a one-town state, having lost Roquebrune and Menton in 1848 when the inhabitants revolted against the Grimaldis' exorbitant taxes. Ironically, it was his principality's increasing isolation and threatened bankruptcy that spurred Charles III to reinvent Monaco as the gambling capital of Europe.

In parallel with the arrival of the industrial revolution, tourism arrived in the south, initially an aristocratic stop-off for the winter season in Hyères and Nice. In 1822, the Promenade des Anglais, then a picturesque footpath, was laid out by the English colony in Nice. In 1834, Lord Brougham wintered in Cannes. Russians and English, including Queen Victoria, flocked to the Riviera. Provence's ancient heritage was also rediscovered in the late 19th-century: the Arènes were cleared in Arles, Viollet-le-Duc restored the ramparts of Avignon and excavations began at Vaison-la-Romaine.

The centralised administrative and education system meant that Provence was more part of France than ever before, and the Provençal language largely died out except in remote rural communities. At the same time, an ever-present current of Catholic fundamentalism created a reactionary minority that would take different forms, from the revival of the Provençal language and traditions promoted by Frédéric Mistral – author of epic Provençal poem *Mirèio* (Mireille) and one of the seven young poets who founded the Félibrige movement in 1854 in Avignon – to the proto-Fascist Action Française movement founded in Paris in 1899 by Southerner Charles Maurras.

In Context

THE TWENTIETH CENTURY TO TODAY

The early 20th century was the era of the great waterfront hotels, built in response to a surge in tourism: between 1890 and 1910 the number of foreigners visiting Nice grew almost sixfold to over 150,000. Amused by these eccentric milords, the French bourgeoisie continued to winter in the country; only in the 1920s did French artists, designers and socialites begin to descend on Le Midi in any great number: American railroad magnate Frank Jay Gould opened up the summer season in Juan-Les-Pins and built the Palais de la Méditerranée in Nice. The artistic avant-garde came too and Modernist architects put up radical new villas.

World War I was a distant, rain-soaked northern affair, although it took its toll of Provençal conscripts and Fréjus played a curious role as acclimatisation zone for colonial troops. In the 1930s, France saw its first socialist government under Léon Blum's Front Populaire, enthusiastically supported in the south – and the arrival of paid holidays for all.

World War II did mark the South. After the fall of Paris in June 1940, and nominal rule of France transferred to Maréchal Petain in Vichy, the South became part of the *zone libre* or free France (except Menton, occupied by Mussolini's Italian army) – not that this prevented the creation of a number of internment camps for aliens, notably at Les Milles, just outside Aix; Marseille served as an important escape route. From autumn 1942, the South was occupied by German troops. Hardest hit were the strategic naval ports of Marseille and Toulon, ravaged both by Allied bombing raids and by the retreating Germans in 1944. Groups of *maquis*, or resistants, hid out in the hills. The Alpes-Maritimes was occupied by Italian troops until the fall of Italy in September 1943 when they were replaced by Germans. The liberation of Provence by Allied forces based in North Africa came on 15 August, in a two-pronged attack centred on the Var (*see p10*).

Post-war reconstruction was responsible for some of the architectural horrors that dog the South; lax or corrupt planning departments did the rest, suffocating the Côte d'Azur in concrete – a combination of the arrival of mass tourism and the urban housing shortage in main towns. Heavy industry, too, has done its share of environmental damage, especially west of Marseille where the salt marsh of the Etang de Berre became a huge oil dump.

Since the 1980s – when Mitterrand granted the regions a limited form of autonomy – the centralising impetus of the previous two centuries has begun to be reversed. The regional assembly is largely about a degree of economic power, and the South of France with its large number of expat second-homers and immigrés from both outside and within France has less of a sense of Provençal identity than in the fiercely maintained cultures of the Pays Basque and Brittany, although Provençal lessons are now available in schools and dual-language street signs have appeared.

The southern economy remains highly skewed, with great disparities between rich and poor, the highest property prices outside Paris, above-national-average unemployment and a population that soars in summer and plummets in winter. Hi-tech industry poles in Aix and Sophia Antipolis, biotechnology in Nîmes, and the petro-chemicals of the Etang de Berre are the counterparts to the largely agricultural interior (important producer of fruit and veg), while international conventions and congresses bolster the economies of Nice and Cannes, although much of the south remains heavily dependent on tourism.

In the 21st century, there are signs of new confidence. Marseille, France's second urban agglomeration, is bypassing its reputation of dodgy dealing and gangsters (though mafia-style killings are still not unknown) and trading in the image of strike-torn docks for one of dynamism and service industry. The arrival of the TGV in 2001 and the ambitious Euroméditerranée development have both boosted the regional economy and brought the South closer than ever to Paris.

Watching the **Monaco Grand Prix.**

Key events

c25,000BC cave paintings in Calanques.
5000BC-2500BC rock engravings in Vallée des Merveilles.
c600BC Phocaean Greeks found Massalia (modern-day Marseille).
122BC Romans defeat Oppidium of Entremont and found Aquae Sextiae (Aix-en-Provence).
120BC Romans build Via Domitia to Spain, with staging posts at Apt, Beaucaire, Nîmes.
105BC Romans defeated by Celts at Orange.
49BC Caesar besieges Marseille, founds Fréjus.
6BC Trophée des Alpes at La Turbie.
c90AD construction of Pont du Gard.
476 Fall of Roman Empire.
843 Treaty of Verdun – former Carolingian Empire divided into three.
974 Saracens' last stronghold at La Garde-Freinet in the Maures
1113 Provence passes to house of Barcelona; Languedoc to Toulouse.
1160 construction of Abbaye de Thoronet.
1195 Comtés of Forcalquier and Provence united.
1240 Louis IX founds Aigues-Mortes.
1246 Béatrice of Provence marries Charles d'Anjou, brother of French King Louis IX.
1274 Comtat Venaissin given to papacy.
1295 Charles II founds Basilique of St Mary Magdalene at St-Maximin-la-Ste-Baume.
1297 Grimaldi family come to power in Italian city state of Monaco.
1306 Jews expelled from France by Philippe le Bel.
1306-1417 Avignon Papacy.
1348 Black Death decimates population.
1372 Raymond de Turenne, Lord of Baux.
1409 Louis II d'Anjou founds Université d'Aix.
1471 Good King René moves court to Aix.
1481 Provence bequeathed to Louis XI.
1486 Act of Union between France and Provence; Parlement de Provence held at Aix.
1503 Nostradamus born in St-Rémy.
1523 Emperor Charles V besieges Marseille.
1538 François 1er signs peace treaty with Charles V in Château de Villeneuve-Loubet.
1540s-90s Wars of Religion.
1545 Massacre of Mérindol.
1563 Huguenots massacred in Orange.
1567 Catholics massacred in Nîmes.
1598 Henri IV issues Edict of Nantes granting religious tolerance to Protestants.
1608 Henri IV buys Antibes from Grimaldis.
1637 Battle of St-Tropez; royal troops beat off Spanish galleys.
1649 Cours Mirabeau laid out in Aix.

1671 Vieille Charité begun in Marseille.
1680 Darse Neuve naval docks at Toulon.
1685 Louis XIV revokes Edict of Nantes.
1690s Louis XIV's military architect Vauban builds forts in Marseille, Toulon, Entrevaux.
1720 Plague spreads from Marseille.
1789 French Revolution begins.
1791 Avignon & the Comtat Venaissin incorporated into France.
1792 Nice taken by revolutionary forces.
1793 Napoléon captures royalist Toulon.
1799 Coup d'Etat by Napoléon.
1804 Bonaparte proclaimed Emperor.
1815 1 March: Napoléon lands at Golfe Juan.
1822 Bauxite found at Les-Baux-de-Provence.
1822 Promenade des Anglais laid out in Nice.
1834 Lord Brougham settles in Cannes.
1848 Revolution; Louis-Philippe overthrown.
1853 Joliette port opens in Marseille.
1854 Félibrige movement founded.
1860 Nice, Roquebrune, Menton join France.
1863 Casino de Monte-Carlo opens.
1888 Van Gogh settles in Arles and then St-Rémy (1889-90).
1892 Queen Victoria stays in Hyères.
1906 Matisse, Braque and Derain spend the summer at L'Estaque.
1936 Front Populaire introduces paid summer holidays.
1940 Fall of France in World War II; south becomes zone libre.
1942 South occupied by German troops.
15 Aug 1944 Liberation of Provence.
1946 First Cannes film festival.
1947 Roya and Bevera valleys become part of France; first Avignon theatre festival.
1947-51 Matisse Chapelle du Rosaire.
1952 Le Corbusier's Cité Radieuse, Marseille.
1956 Brigitte Bardot stars in Vadim's *Et Dieu Créa la femme* in St-Tropez.
1960s Ecole de Nice art movement.
1962 Algerian independence: thousands of *pieds-noirs* settle in South of France.
1969 Creation of Sophia Antipolis.
1974 Toulon replaces Draguignan as Préfecture of the Var.
1982 Death of Princess Grace of Monaco.
1992 Flooding at Vaison-la-Romaine kills 37.
1993 Carré d'Art opens in Nîmes.
2001 TGV Méditérranée high-speed train between Paris and Marseille and Nîmes.
2002 Front National candidate Jean-Marie Le Pen gets through to second round in Presidential elections.
2003 Summer fires destroy 20% of Maures.

The expulsion of *pieds-noirs* from Algeria in 1962.

The South of France Today

The current social and political situation in the South reflects the legacy of the Algerian War.

What with the sunbeds and seafood platters, the sea scooters and the Provençal-print napkins, it's difficult to imagine war on the Côte d'Azur. But the conflict that began five decades ago on the other bank of the Mediterranean and continued until Algerian independence in the summer of 1962 was one of the cruellest of the 20th century, and its effects long-lasting.

Today, cities such as Marseille, home town of Zinedine Zidane and France's best rap group, the *black-blanc-beur* (black-white-Arab) IAM, are good examples of a new, multicultural France. There are even signs of the entrepreneurial success of a new generation of French-Algerians. But half-decent race relations have been a long time coming. The South of France has an unenviable reputation as heartland of the extreme right and one reason has been resentment of the French-Algerian community following the Algerian War.

Jean-Marie Le Pen, leader of the extreme-right Front National, chose to run in Provence-Alpes-

Côte-d'Azur in the 2000 regional elections (and is planning to do so again for the 2004 regional elections). Three in ten people voted for him in the 2002 presidential elections when he made it to the run-off against Jacques Chirac. It's here that the extreme right got its first taste of real power, controlling at one time or another the towns of Toulon, Orange and Vitrolles. One of the reasons for this is that the Front National has close links with the biggest losers of the Algerian War: those who were forced to flee the country of their birth along with the French army when Charles de Gaulle agreed to grant Algeria independence. Many 'returnees' from French Algeria now live in the South of France.

Half a century ago the hills behind Nice and St Raphaël resonated to blasting car horns as motorists sounded their support for 'Al-gér-ie Fran-çaise!' The Interior Minister at the start of the war, a certain François Mitterrand, declared that 'Algeria is France and the Mediterranean separates France as the Seine separates Paris.'

Administratively speaking, he was right. Although the Algerians did not have French citizenship (which would have allowed them to move to France), they had French nationality. Also, unlike any other French colony, Algeria had been colonised not just militarily and economically but physically. Over a million white settlers, the *pieds-noirs* (literally 'black-feet' – from the leather boots worn by the French soldiers), ruled the Algerian roost on behalf of the *Métropole* (mainland France).

'If they could no longer be on "their" bank of the Mediterranean, at least they could live on the other.'

It was the *pieds-noirs* who gave De Gaulle a hero's welcome in Algiers in June 1961 when the president appeared on a balcony draped in the *tricolore* and proclaimed 'Je vous ai compris!' (I have understood you.) As De Gaulle raised his long arms in his trademark V-for-victory, an ecstatic crowd was convinced that the president, symbol of resistance, would never abandon them. Less than a year later he had. Some 10,000 *pieds-noirs* were massacred after De Gaulle decided to stop the war.

Many of the 1.2 million *pieds-noirs* who fled across the Mediterranean with the retreating French army settled in the south of France. Much of the cheap, 1960s housing in port towns such as Toulon or Nice was built to accommodate them. To this day, the *pieds-noirs* bear De Gaulle a grudge, which is one reason many of them support Le Pen rather than the Gaullist President Chirac and his current government.

For most of these refugees, if they could no longer be on 'their' bank of the Mediterranean, at least they could live on the other. The *pieds-noirs* were consummate Mediterraneans; a good number were of Italian stock. Many North African Jews became to-all-intents-and-purposes *pieds-noirs* as well. If you visit the Arab neighbourhoods of some big French cities, the shops selling North African cloth and braid are, more often than not, run by Arabic-speaking Jews called Maurice or Jean.

The most celebrated *pied-noir* was the writer Albert Camus. For him, Algeria was not only his subject matter, it was a cause. Once the war had started, he struggled, vainly, to stop the slide towards terrorism of the nationalists and the pro-French *ultras*. The colonial condition of being at home abroad clearly contributed to the existentialist philosophy he helped to develop. Things were considerably less complicated for most *pieds-noirs*, for whom

the word designates a people who are more demonstrative, closer to their families and more charming and considerate towards women than the rest of the French. And usually they are.

Many *pieds-noirs*, and the Jews first among them, wouldn't touch the Front National with a bargepole. But along with the hastily packed baggage they brought back from Algeria, there was, for many, a burning resentment against the Algerians who had driven them out and the French who'd abandoned them.

Half a million people died in the Algerian War. 15,000 French troops were killed. The Algerian Liberation Army lost five times more. In addition to the professional soldiers, hundreds of thousands of Frenchmen were sent to Algeria to do their military service. These include Chirac, who served as an officer during the first three years of the war and was wounded in action. France's North African war veterans' association, the FNACA, has over a third of a million members. The number of people living in France today who were directly affected by the Algerian War are to be counted in their millions.

But the conflict was much nastier than even these figures suggest. The Algerian FLN (National Liberation Front) were Communists and Islamists united in their hatred of French rule. The French had brought them the best – Haussmannian architecture, Delacroix and, albeit in a strange, French form, rock 'n' roll. It had also brought them the worst – the brutal disdain with which much of the governing class dealt with the 'natives', *les indigènes*. The FLN used terror bombing against both French and Algerian civilians in attacks that barely differed from those carried out by Islamic extremists today. They also carried out massacres of civilians, of *pieds-noirs* but also of Algerians who refused to join them. The French armed forces – an army built around the resistance heroes of De Gaulle – responded with the widespread use of torture, the scale of which has only recently been established. Le Pen, who was also in Algeria (though, unlike Chirac, he was there as a professional soldier in the parachute regiment), won a libel case against the French satirical journal *Le Canard Enchaîné* for accusing him of using torture in Algeria. It is safe to say that for many of his supporters it would have mattered little if he'd lost.

The Côte d'Azur also has more than its fair share of surviving members of the OAS (Organisation de l'Armée Secrète). This secret terror organisation was set up by disaffected generals and *pied-noir* politicians who suspected De Gaulle was planning to pull France out of Algeria. The group made several attempts on De Gaulle's life (inspiring the

British novelist Frederick Forsyth to write *The Day of the Jackal*) and helped co-ordinate a failed generals' putsch in April 1961. During March 1962, the month of the Evian Agreement which granted Algerian independence, OAS operatives set off an average of 120 bombs a day. They targeted not only Muslims but the army, police and civilians, schools and hospitals. In France proper, OAS-métro, which had contacts high up in the French political establishment, waged a parallel terror war against FLN activists and 'defeatist' politicians. One of the founders of the OAS, Jean-Jacques Susini, was sentenced to death and later amnestied for his part in an attempt to assassinate De Gaulle in Toulon in 1964. He has long been a personal friend of Le Pen and is one of the FN's regional councillors.

When they were in charge in Algeria, many *pieds-noirs* believed the 'natives' were an inferior race. Their racism towards ethnic Algerians would even shock visitors from mainland France. But the *pieds-noirs* nevertheless identified with the country. For those starting new lives in France, the bitterness of war, (what they saw as) betrayal and exile would have been bad enough. Post-war Algerian immigration – that Algerians

Pieds-noirs adopted Algerian customs and dress.

should kick them out only to come and live in France – angered them even more.

For a significant part of the population of the South of France, the Algerian War is un-finished business. And none more so than for the Algerians who fought for France, the *harkis*. The *harkis*, so-called because many of them formed mobile army units called *harkas*, were far more numerous than the Algerians who fought against France for the FLN (by the end of the war there were some 150,000 *harkis* fighting in French uniforms compared to 20,000 FLN fighters). They usually came from poor, rural communities and considered military service as a legal obligation to the government. That the government could or should be anything other than French was not obvious to many of them.

What awaited the *harkis* was one of the great hidden tragedies of the 20th century. The Evian Agreement, which resulted in an immediate ceasefire between the French army and the Algerian nationalists, did not explicitly mention the *harkis* but it did include an FLN pledge not to take revenge upon its former enemies. The *pieds-noirs* were to be allowed to settle in the *Métropole*. But France did not want the *harkis*. One of De Gaulle's most distinguished biographers quotes the General as describing them as 'Ce magma qui n'a servi à rien' ('those dregs that served no purpose'). Unmarried *harkis* were offered the choice between being paid off or coming to France as part of the French army. *Harkis* with families were offered no choice at all. The result was that most stayed, re-assured perhaps by the continuing presence of the French army in the country.

Shortly after the ceasefire, the slaughter started. Over the following six months some 70,000 *harkis* were killed, often in the most barbaric way, by local populations encouraged to take their revenge on these 'traitors'. Evidence from official archives released in 1999 shows that, while some elements in the French army tried to help their former comrades-in-arms, they were countermanded by the French government. Two ships that tried to dock at Marseille with *harki* refugees on board were sent back to Algeria. About 20,000 *harkis* were eventually allowed to come to France but, considered unsuitable for integration in (white, Christian) French society, they were hidden away in rural detention camps. Many others were put to work building 'forest hamlets' in the hills above Nice.

Even when they got out of the camps – and the last camp wasn't closed until 1990 – the *harkis*' troubles weren't over. Cold-shouldered by the French, they often found themselves living on the same housing estates as Algerian immigrants who regarded even their sons and daughters as traitors. Today, *harki* families still suffer alarmingly high rates of unemployment, alcoholism and suicide.

The current government has created a remembrance day for the *harkis* (25 September) and started paying a 'recognition payment' to them and their widows. For their sons and daughters it is not nearly enough. They are campaigning not only for more compensation but for an apology for their 'internment' in France and an admission that France shares the guilt for the massacre of *harkis* in Algeria.

The first stone of a Musée National de l'Outre Mer (National Museum of Overseas Territories) will be laid in Parc Chanet in Marseille in 2004. The government says that this museum and research centre will start to put the record straight about the *harkis* as well as other episodes, both positive and negative, to do with France's colonial history.

Along the beach at the Mourillon, a peaceful seaside suburb of Toulon, there's a jetty. Walk to the end, with the waves crashing under your feet, and there's a plaque. It reads, 'On the 5 May 1830, on the orders of the King, Charles X, a fleet... of 103 war ships and 500 merchant vessels crewed by 20,000 sailors and transporting 38,000 troops set sail for Algiers in order to... make Algeria a land of progress that, after a century of work and war in common, would be linked to France by ties of brotherhood.' Until they build the museum, this is as a good a place as any to ponder the extraordinary and terrible Algerian adventure and the impact it still has in France today.

Fire!

In the summer heatwave of 2003 over 400 fires wreaked havoc on the South of France, especially in the Massif des Maures where there were seven deaths and 24,000 hectares of the St-Tropez hinterland destroyed. Other fires ravaged the Estérel, La Motte near Draguignan, parts of the Bouches-du-Rhône and the Alpes-Maritimes around Eze.

Fire spread quickly, helped by the tinder-dry conditions of the summer drought and strong winds. The noise of Canadair fire-fighting planes overhead and the sight of blackened trees, burnt-out cars and columns of smoke became familiar. Evacuated holidaymakers camped on the beach at a Ste-Maxime encircled by flames, and a halo of fire glowed red behind the port at St-Tropez.

Driving through the blackened landscape after the fires, it didn't take phenomenal powers of observation to notice that areas where there were vineyards and olive groves had suffered much less than adjacent woodland. So how much has the disappearance of traditional methods of land husbandry and the parcelling up of woodland for holiday villas been responsible for the spread of fires? The introduction of exotic species has also been blamed, with eucalyptus and mimosa burning more rapidly than the native oaks and pines.

Sadly, almost all the fires seem to have been caused by man. Personal grudges and copycat actions saw vast tracts of land disappear under smoke, possibly started by molotov cocktails. A cigarette stub burned patches of land along the A8 motorway and a former volunteer fireman was accused of starting fires around Les Arcs. But the south also seems incapable of instituting fire prevention and water-sprinkling systems – unlike the heavily forested Landes in the southwest. Despite a 1995 law aiming to define the areas most at risk, not one municipality in the Var had set up a prevention plan by 2003. The south seems to prefer to maintain a large and expensive fire service – not large enough, as it turned out, when help had to be brought in from as far away as Russia. Rumours persist, too, of property developers with a financial interest in burning.

Optimistically, after only a couple of weeks the cork oaks around La Garde Freinet were sprouting green again, proof of the miraculous powers of regeneration and the natural burn cycle of the Mediterranean. Forest fires have probably always been a part of the ecosystem here, though without the same pressures of population as there are today. Perhaps next time round a controlled clearing of the undergrowth and a return to the olive should be on the programme.

Provençal Food

Colourful, seasonal and beautifully healthy – the food of the South is worth luxuriating in.

Garlic, olive oil and plentiful herbs are at the heart of Provençal cuisine, imbuing with flavour the cornucopia of local fish, vegetables and game. The celebrated Provençal sauces and condiments – *aïoli, pistou, rouille* and *tapenade* – work variations on these basic ingredients. Green or black olive *tapenade* is often served as an appetiser spread on toast, but can accompany salads or be cooked with fish. Chopped raw vegetables, and perhaps hard-boiled eggs and potatoes, are dipped into tangy *anchoïade*, a boat of warm anchovy and olive oil purée, while *aïoli*, mayonnaise with lashings of pounded garlic, can be served with *crudités*, stirred into soup or served as the celebratory *grand aïoli* with cooked vegetables, salt cod and snails that often appears as a special weekly market dish in cafés. *Pistou* is a seasoning of basil, garlic and oil that adds its tang to a minestrone-like soup. Thyme, rosemary, bay leaves, lavender and honey find their way as flavourings on everything from lamb or rabbit to crème brûlée and ice cream.

MEAT AND FISH

As with anywhere in France, you'll always be able to find a *steak-frites*, but in the Camargue look out in particular for dark, tender bull's meat (*taureau*), simply grilled or stewed in hearty *boeuf à la gardiane*, similar to Provence's other beef classic, *daube de boeuf*. Sheep raised in Les Alpilles, the Crau plain and the Alpine foothills produce tender lamb, perhaps roast with rosemary, summer savory or whole heads of garlic. Game includes rabbit, hare and wild boar from the *garrigue* (brush hillsides) and woodland, which find their way into rich stews and *saucissons*. Rabbit is stewed with white wine, herbs and tomatoes. Thrift is at the heart of Provençal cooking and the less noble parts are used, too, as in the *pieds et paquets* of Marseille (stuffed tripe and sheep's feet stewed in wine).

Along the coast, Provence has developed a splendid battery of fish and shellfish dishes. Over-fishing of the Mediterranean means that

LA TERRASSE A MOUGINS
RESTAURANT

L'HOTEL DU VILLAGE

Enjoy a simple and authentic stay at L'Hôtel du Village in the heart of Mougins. The two suites and two bedrooms of the Villa Lombarde retain all the charm of this Provençal village, to make a heaven of peace!

La Terrasse à Mougins is a new-style restaurant with its old-style rotisserie and an outstanding view of the bay of Cannes.

a lot of the fish actually comes from Brittany, but there is still an often-pricey local catch, seen in the fish markets of Marseille and St-Tropez or delivered direct to seashore restaurants. The celebrated fish soup *bouillabaisse* is found all along the coast, though Marseille is its

> **'A group of restaurants has even signed a *bouillabaisse* charter to defend the authentic recipe.'**

acknowledged home; a group of restaurateurs has even signed a *bouillabaisse* charter to defend the authentic recipe. *Bouillabaisse* is traditionally served in two courses, first the saffron-tinted soup, accompanied by toasted baguette, fiery *rouille* and a sprinkling of gruyère, then the fish. Purists insist on 12 varieties of fish and shellfish, but the three essentials are *rascasse* (scorpion fish), *grondin* (red gurnet) and *congre* (conger eel). Mussels are generally included too, though langouste or lobster are often considered a false luxury touch.

Less well-known but equally delicious is *bourride*, a creamy garlic-spiked fish soup made from one or more of john dory, sea bass and monkfish liaised with *aïoli*. If you're lucky, you may find *poutargue*, the pressed, salted grey mullet roe that is a speciality of Martigues. Mussels are raised in the bay of Toulon and are popular on the Var coast, *à la marinière* (with white wine, onions and shallots), *à la provençale* (with white wine, tomatoes, onion and garlic) or gratinéed. Other fish preparations include marinated sardines, *loup au fenouil* (sea bass baked with fennel) and red mullet with basil. *Brandade de morue*, salt cod soaked in milk and puréed with olive oil, is a speciality of Nîmes. Some of the best meals consist of just-out-of-the-sea fish, chosen at table, then grilled on charcoal at a beachside restaurant. Expect to pay by weight (allow roughly 400g-500g per person).

FRUIT AND VEGETABLES
The quality and variety of the vegetables and fruit in Provence is superb, whether they come from fields and orchards along the Durance and Var rivers or tiny coastal gardens. This part of France is thus a paradise for vegetarians – although specifically vegetarian restaurants and menus are rare. As well as *ratatouille*, other favourites include *barigoule d'artichauts*, *tomates provençales* (slow-baked tomatoes with a scattering of garlic and breadcrumbs on top) and courgette-flower fritters. There are all manner of stuffed vegetables and baked *tians* (gratins named after the earthenware dish in which they are cooked). And what could be

simpler – or more delicious – than grilled red peppers, served cold and drizzled with olive oil?

In spring, the region produces some of the best asparagus in France, followed by a summer abundance of aubergines, courgettes (look out for yellow and round varieties) and tomatoes. Artichokes are usually of the violet, almost chokeless, variety. Humbler chickpeas, broad beans and fennel also feature in traditional recipes, as do *blettes* – swiss chard, braised and served with cream as a vegetable or in the curious sweet-savoury *tourte* that is a speciality of Nice. Epeautre, a type of wild wheat grown on Mont Ventoux, is also making a comeback, while rice is grown in the Camargue. Autumn brings wild mushrooms, pumpkins and squash, while *mesclun*, that distinctly Provençal salad of mixed leaves and herbs, is available all year round. Winter truffle hunting is a serious affair in the Drôme (*see p113*), Luberon and the Var.

The delicious orange-fleshed melon de Cavaillon has been grown here since being introduced by the Avignon papacy in the 14th century. Other fruit includes early strawberries from Carpentras, cherries, apricots and table grapes, citrus fruits from Menton, and a sumptuous glut of figs in late summer.

CHEESE
Dairying is limited, but you'll find plenty of farmhouse goat cheeses at markets. Look out for unctuous banon, made with goat's milk in the area around Forcalquier, wrapped in a chestnut leaf and aged to a pungent runniness; picodon, a small, young, tangy goat's cheese from north Provence; pelardon, similar to picodon, but aged and very firm; and brousse de Rove, a ricotta-like soft, mild, fresh cheese made from goat's or ewe's milk and used to fill ravioli or eaten drizzled with olive oil or honey.

MARKETS
Even in the most touristy village or most glamorous resort, markets remain a vital aspect of Provençal life and stands selling scented candles and lavender sachets remain squarely outnumbered by stalls laden with goat's cheeses, fresh herbs, ripe tomatoes and glossy aubergines. You'll also find stalls specialising in *saucisson sec*, olives and *tapenades*, jams and honey – often with opportunities to taste. In larger towns, there are daily markets; in smaller towns and villages they're often held once or twice a week, usually in the morning. A growing trend is for farmers' markets, sometimes in the evening, where you buy direct from the producer.

RESTAURANT LORE
The South of France is heaven for the restaurant junkie, offering meals to suit all moods, from celebrated haute cuisine temples

A cook's tour of Provence

Cooking schools are booming in Provence. Styles vary from homely farmhouse to grandiose château but most involve selecting the raw ingredients at market, via chopping and mixing, frying or baking to the final eating, with insights into local produce and cooking techniques. Classes range from a half-day to a week, all include food and wine, some include accommodation and excursions – but be prepared to pay as much, or more, to cook it yourself as to dine at a good restaurant. All the courses below are available in English, unless stated.

The Atelier Culinaire Provençale at **Château de Clapier** (Mirabeau, 04.42.93.11.80, www.acp-aix.com, 1-day from €65; 1wk from €750) is on a wine estate in the Luberon. Chef Daniel Peyraud guides the group through Aix market, letting seasonal produce inspire his menus. His style is a light, modern take on regional produce: think roast red mullet with a lemon-caper sauce and raspberry sorbet. Both one-day and week-long classes include a wine tasting at the estate.

The Ecole de Cuisine at Côtes de Provence wine producer **Château de Berne** (Lorgues, 04.94.60.48.88, www.chateauberne. com, 1-day €100; 3-days from €916) is run by chef Jean-Louis Vosgien in a house overlooking pool and vineyards. The surroundings are gorgeous and facilities excellent, but the feel is that of a crisp, luxury resort and perhaps less relaxed than other schools.

The atmosphere is more domestic with **Ghislaine Daniel** (06.20.66.06.80, class €15, in French only), who offers simple, hands-on classes in her home in Aix-en-Provence. Students cook, clean up and eat their creations together – and you're encouraged to have seconds.

The Ecole de Cuisine at **Mas de Cornud** (04.90.92.39.32, www.mascornud.com, half-day from €130, 1wk from €2,000) is in a

stone farmhouse B&B near St-Rémy. Chef Nito Carpitas draws dual inspiration from her Egyptian background and Provençal cuisine. These intensive courses are ideal for experienced cooks wanting to hone their skills.

In Arles, **Cuisine et Tradition School of Provençal Cuisine** (04.90.49.69.20, www.cuisine provencale.com, 5-days from €895) is led by French chef Erick Vedel and his wife Madeleine. Hands-on classes are held in their ancient stone kitchen, but also include visits to the market and local artisans, such as a goat-cheese maker and beekeeper. Erick's recipes for Provençal mussels and Etruscan duck are delicious.

In a 16th-century stone farmhouse in the Drôme Provençale, **Ecole Culinaire Tuillières** (Pont de Barret, 04.75.90.43.91, 1wk from €1,300) is both cooking school and rustic guesthouse. Classes, with Austrian chef Hermann Jenny and his wife Susan, are thorough, entertaining and cater to all levels, as budding cooks learn to prepare dishes such as chicken terrine, lamb stew and the authentically Provençal *tarte aux pignons*.

Kathie Alex's **Cooking with Friends in France** (04.93.60.10.56, www.cookingwith friends.com, 1wk from €2,450) combines cooking technique with 'cultural experience' in the former house of Julia Child near Grasse. At **Haute Provence** (www.georgeannebren nan.com, 1 wk approx €2,750), US cookbook author Georgeanne Brennan gives courses in a restored farmhouse outside Aups. Shorter options are lunch or dinner classes taught by a professional chef at Avignon hotel **La Mirande** (04.90.85.93.93, www.lamirande.fr, half-day from €100), and **Les Petits Farcis** (06.81.67.41.22, www.petitsfarcis.com, one-day €165), where Rosa Jackson offers market visits followed by a cooking class in a renovated flat in Vieux Nice.

and showbiz *spectacles* to the inimitable village bar-cum-*tabac*-cum-café-cum-restaurant where all sorts pile in for a *pastis*, gossip and, often, a surprisingly good *menu du jour*.

At the grandest establishments with famous chefs, you'll eat sublime food and pay sublimely ridiculous prices. The local French population tends to patronise these places only on special occasions, or for lunch, when many renowned kitchens offer relatively affordable menus. The locals are more likely to seek out good-value establishments, where there may be less silverware on the table and only one waiter or waitress, but the cooking can still be spot on.

The Provençal diet with its emphasis on vegetables, olive oil and fish perfectly matches the health concerns of today, but the southern restaurant scene is not standing still. If many restaurants delight in dyed-in-the-wool Provence, with print cloths and the comforting reassurance of age-old *daubes* and *tians*, other restaurants are renewing southern cuisine with creative use of seasonal, regional produce or cosmopolitan touches from the Mediterranean and beyond. Outside influences are not new: the Italian kitchen had a strong impact in Nice, long part of the kingdom of Genoa, where as well as all sorts of local snacks (*see p259*), Italianate gnocchi and ravioli (the latter often filled with *daube*) are common. Marseille cuisine goes well beyond *bouillabaisse*; the city boasts a superb selection

> **'Seaside destinations can be distinctly glitzy (gold jewellery and tans, real or fake, required).'**

of ethnic restaurants, reflecting the kaleidoscopic variety of people who've settled there from all over the Mediterranean. The city has large Italian, Spanish, North African, Greek and Armenian communities, and these cuisines have also made their mark on many chefs.

A whirlwind of chefs at the top has seen Alain Lorca officially annointed dauphin to Roger Vergé, one of the inventors of modern Provençal cooking, at the **Moulin de Mougins** and succeeded at the **Negresco** by Paris star Michel del Burgo, while Daniel Hébert formerly at **La Mirande** in Avignon has moved to the chic **Domaine des Andéols** in the Luberon.

The trend of super-chefs opening bistro annexes and rural retreats continues. Alain Ducasse's southern antennae take in Monte-Carlo, Moustiers, La Celle and St-Tropez; the Pourcel twins of Montpellier have an outlet in Avignon. But there is also a legion of chefs, many of them trained at the best restaurants,

who have gone out on their own and opened good-value restaurants worth discovering, such as Olivier Gouin at **Maison Gouin** in the Luberon, Luc Andreu at **Ail Heure** in Beaucaire, Gil Renard at **La Tonnelle** in Bormes-les-Mimosas and Jean-Marc Delacourt at **Le Parcours** in Nice, to name a few.

Restaurants are generally relaxed in France. Although you shouldn't come to the table in a bathing costume unless you're right on the beach, ties are rarely required and T-shirts and shorts are usually fine. However, the French are generally well-dressed (think smart-casual), especially in the evening. Seaside showbiz destinations can be distinctly glitzy (gold jewellery and tans, real or fake, required), while haute cuisine establishments, even in a village, can be as dressy as Paris – if not more so.

By law, the menu, with prices, must be posted outside the restaurant. Depending on the establishment, there is usually a choice of one or more *prix-fixe* menus, ranging from a basic, inexpensive, two- or three-course *formule*, sometimes including wine, via the classic *entrée*, *plat*, cheese and dessert, to the *menu dégustation*, an extravagant gastronomic splurge of the chef's party pieces. The *menu-carte* is an increasingly popular formula, with all *entrées*, *plats*, *desserts* at the same price. Here we list the range of *menu* prices rather than average *à la carte* prices, as the former are a pretty accurate indication of the latter – though in the gourmet temples, a meal *à la carte* may cost significantly more than the priciest menu; note that the cheapest menu may well be available only on weekday lunchtimes. Note that bread is always included free with a meal in France and French tap water is perfectly drinkable – it's perfectly acceptable to ask for a *carafe d'eau* if you don't want to buy mineral water. By French law, service is included in the price of a meal: it's customary, however, to leave some change, up to around 5% of the bill.

Most restaurants serve from around noon or 12.30pm until around 2pm. Dinner service usually runs from 7.30pm (though if you arrive before 8.30pm you're likely to find only foreigners) to 10.30pm or 11pm, when the last orders are taken. If you've missed lunch, you can usually get a salad or a sandwich in a café. Many cafés also serve good lunchtime *plats du jour* or even full menus, while brasseries in larger towns are good bets for a late meal, often serving until midnight or later.

For most upmarket places, reservations are recommended; some top restaurants ask clients to reconfirm on the day. Even in simpler bistros, especially during the peak season, it's always worth ringing ahead to reserve a table, even if only for the same evening.

Provençal menu lexicon

Agneau lamb. **aiglefin** haddock. **ail** garlic. **aïoli** garlic mayonnaise. **airelle** cranberry. **alouettes sans têtes** literally headless skylarks, actually small stuffed beef parcels. **amande** almond; **– de mer** small clam. **ananas** pineapple. **anchoïade** anchovy and olive sauce, served with raw vegetables. **anchois** anchovy. **andouillette** sausage made from pig's offal. **anguille** eel. **artichauts à la barigoule** small purple artichokes braised in white wine. **anis** aniseed. **asperge** asparagus. **aubergine** aubergine (GB); eggplant (US).

Bar sea bass. **barbue** brill. **baudroie** coastal monkfish. **bavarois** moulded cream dessert. **bavette** beef flank steak. **béarnaise** sauce of butter and egg yolk. **beignet** fritter or doughnut; **– de fleur de courgette** courgette flower fritters. **betterave** beetroot. **biche** venison. **bifteak** steak. **bisque** shellfish soup. **blanc** white; **– de poulet** chicken breast. **blanquette** 'white' stew, usually veal, made with eggs and cream. **blette** swiss chard; **tourte de –** swiss chard pie with pine nuts and raisins. **boudin noir/blanc** black (blood)/ white pudding. **boeuf** beef; **– à la gardiane** (Camargue) bulls' beef stewed with carrots and celery; **– gros sel** boiled beef with vegetables. **bouillabaisse** (Marseille) Provençal fish soup. **bourride** thick garlicky fish soup. **brandade de morue** (Nîmes) purée of salt cod, milk, garlic and olive oil (often with potato, too). **brébis** ewe's milk cheese. **brochet** pike. **brouillade** scrambled egg; **– aux truffes** scrambled egg with with truffles. **brousse** soft, mild white cheese. **bulot** whelk.

Cabillaud fresh cod. **caille** quail. **caillette** pork terrine with herbs and spinach or chard cooked in caul. **calmar** squid. **calisson d'Aix** (Aix-en-Provence) diamond-shaped sweet of almonds, sugar and preserved fruit. **canard** duck. **cannelle** cinnamon. **cardon** cardoon (edible thistle). **câpre** caper. **carrelet** plaice. **cassis** blackcurrants, also blackcurrant liqueur. **cassoulet** stew of haricot beans, sausage and preserved duck. **catégau d'anguilles** (Camargue) eels cooked with red wine and garlic. **céleri** celery; **–rave** celeriac. **cèpe** cep mushroom. **cerise** cherry. **cervelle** brains. **champignon** mushroom. **charlotte** moulded cream dessert with biscuit edge. **châtaigne** chestnut. **chateaubriand** thick fillet steak. **cheval** horse. **à cheval** with an egg on top. **chèvre** goat's cheese. **chevreuil** young roe deer. **chichis** deep-fried dough sticks. **chou** cabbage. **choucroute** sauerkraut, usually served *garnie* with cured ham and sausages. **chou-fleur** cauliflower. **ciboulette** chive. **citron** lemon. **– vert** lime. **citronnelle** lemongrass. **civet** game stew. **clafoutis** baked batter dessert filled with fruit, usually cherries. **cochon de lait** suckling pig. **colin** hake. **confit de canard** preserved duck. **congre** conger eel. **contre-filet** sirloin steak. **coquille** shell; **– st-jacques** scallop. **côte** chop; **– de boeuf** beef rib. **crème chantilly** whipped cream. **crème fraîche** thick, slightly soured cream. **cresson** watercress. **crevette** prawn (GB), shrimp (US). **croquant** crunchy; **croquante de Nîmes** hard nut biscuit. **croque-monsieur** toasted cheese and ham sandwich. **en croûte** in a pastry case. **cru** raw. **crudités** assorted raw vegetables. **crustacé** shellfish.

Daube meat (beef or lamb) braised slowly in red wine with lardons, onions, garlic and herbs. **daurade** sea bream. **désossé** boned. **dinde** turkey.

Echalote shallot. **écrevisse** freshwater crayfish. **endive** chicory (GB), Belgian endive (US). **entrecôte** beef rib steak. **entremêts** milk-based dessert. **épeautre** wild wheat. **épices** spices. **épinards** spinach. **escabèche** sautéed, marinated fish, served cold. **escargot** snail. **espadon** swordfish. **estocafinado** (Nice) salt cod stewed with garlic and tomato. **estouffade** beef, braised with carrots, onions, garlic and orange zest.

Faisan pheasant. **farci** stuffed. **farcis niçois/petits farcis** (Nice) vegetables stuffed with meat or mushrooms and herbs. **fenouil** fennel. **faux-filet** sirloin steak. **feuilleté** 'leaves' of (puff) pastry. **fève** broad bean (UK), fava bean (US). **filet mignon** tenderloin. **flageolet** small green kidney bean. **flambé** flamed in alcohol. **flétan** halibut. **foie** liver; **foie gras** fattened goose or duck liver. **forestière** with mushrooms. **fougasse** flat bread made with olive oil, flavoured with lardons or olives, also sweet versions. **au four** baked. **fraise** strawberry. **framboise** raspberry. **frisée** curly endive. **fromage** cheese; **– blanc** smooth cream cheese. **fruit** fruit. **fruits de mer** shellfish. **fruits rouge** red summer berries.

Galette flat flaky pastry cake, potato pancake or buckwheat savoury *crêpe*. **galinette** tub gurnard fish. **gardiane de boeuf** Camargue beef stew. **garni(e)** garnished. **gésiers** gizzards. **gibier** game. **gigot d'agneau** leg of lamb. **gingembre** ginger. **girolle**

chanterelle mushroom. **glace** ice cream. **glacé(e)** frozen or iced. **gras** fat. **gratin dauphinois** sliced potatoes baked with cream and garlic. **grenouille** frog; **cuisses de –** frogs' legs. **grondin** red gurnet. **groseille** redcurrant; **– à maquereau** gooseberry.

Haché minced. **hachis Parmentier** shepherd's pie. **hareng** herring. **haricot** bean; **– vert** green bean. **homard** lobster. **huile** oil. **huître** oyster.

Ile flottante poached whipped egg white floating in vanilla custard.

Jambon ham; **– cru** cured raw ham. **jarret de porc** ham shin or knuckle. **joue** cheek.

Langouste spiny lobster. **langoustine** Dublin bay prawn/scampi. **langue** tongue. **lapin** rabbit; **– à la provençale** rabbit in white wine with tomato and herbs. **lard** bacon. **lardon** small cube of bacon. **laurier** bay leaf. **légume** vegetable. **lentilles** lentils. **lieu** pollock. **lièvre** hare. **limande** lemon sole. **lotte** monkfish.

Mâche lamb's lettuce. **magret** duck breast. **maquereau** mackerel. **marcassin** wild boar. **mariné** marinated. **marmite** small cooking pot. **marquise** mousse-like cake. **marron** chestnut. **merguez** spicy lamb/ beef sausage. **merlan** whiting. **merlu** hake. **mesclun** salad of tiny leaves and herbs. **miel** honey. **mirabelle** tiny yellow plum. **moelle** bone marrow; **os à la –** marrow bone. **morille** morel mushroom. **moules** mussels. **morue** dried, salted cod. **mulet** grey mullet. **mûre** blackberry. **muscade** nutmeg. **myrtille** bilberry (UK), blueberry (US).

Navarin lamb and vegetable stew. **navet** turnip. **navette** boat-shaped biscuit flavoured with orange flower water. **noisette** hazelnut; small round portion of meat. **noix** walnut; **– de coco** coconut. **nouilles** noodles.

Oeuf egg; **– en cocotte** baked egg; **– en meurette** egg poached in red wine; **– à la neige** see *Ile flottante*. **oie** goose. **oignon** onion. **onglet** cut of beef, similar to *bavette*. **oseille** sorrel. **oursin** sea urchin.

Pageot pandora, similar to sea bream. **pain** bread; **– perdu** French toast. **palombe** wood pigeon. **palourde** type of clam. **pamplemousse** grapefruit. **pan bagnat** (Nice) bread roll filled with tuna, tomatoes, onions, egg, olive oil. **panais** parsnip. **en papillote** cooked in a packet. **pastèque** water melon. **pâte** pastry. **pâtes** pasta. **paupiette** slice of meat or fish, stuffed and rolled. **pavé** thick steak. **pêche** peach. **perdrix** partridge. **persil** parsley. **petits farcis** (see farcis niçois). **petits pois** peas. **petit salé** salt pork. **pied** foot (trotter). **pieds et paquets** (Marseille) stew of stuffed tripe and sheep's feet. **pignon** pine kernel. **piment** hot pepper or chilli. **pintade** guinea fowl. **pissaladière** pizza-like onion and anchovy tart. **pistou** pesto-like basil and garlic sauce served with vegetable soup. **pleurotte** oyster mushroom. **poire** pear. **poireau** leek. **pois chiche** chickpea. **poisson** fish. **poivre** pepper. **poivron** red or green (bell) pepper. **pomme** apple. **pomme de terre** potato. **porc** pork. **potage** soup. **potiron** pumpkin. **poulet** chicken. **poulpe** octopus. **poutargue** (Martigues) preserved grey mullet roe. **pressé** squeezed. **prune** plum. **pruneau** prune.

Quenelle light, poached fish dumpling. **quetsche** damson. **queue de boeuf** oxtail.

Rabasse truffle. **raie** skate. **raisin** grape; **– sec** raisin. **rascasse** scorpion fish. **ratatouille** Provençal stew of onion, aubergine, courgette, tomato and peppers. **réglisse** liquorice. **reine-claude** greengage plum. **ris de veau** veal sweetbreads. **riz** rice. **rognon** kidney. **romarin** rosemary. **roquette** rocket. **rouget** red mullet. **rouille** spicy red pepper, garlic and olive oil sauce, served with *bouillabaisse*.

Sablé shortbread biscuit. **St-Pierre** John Dory. **salade niçoise** (Nice) salad of tuna, lettuce, green beans, egg and anchovies. **salé** salted. **sandre** pike-perch. **sanglier** wild boar. **sarde** bream-like Mediterranean fish. **saucisse** sausage. **saucisson sec** small dried sausage. **saumon** salmon. **seiche** squid. **socca** (Nice) thin pancake made with chickpea flour. **souris d'agneau** lamb knuckle. **stockfisch** dried cod. **supion** small squid.

Tapenade Provençal olive and caper paste. **tartare** raw minced steak (also tuna or salmon). **tarte Tatin** caramelised apple tart cooked upside-down and served warm. **taureau** (Camargue) bull's meat. **tête de veau** calf's head jelly. **thon** tuna. **thym** thyme. **tian** vegetable gratin baked in an earthenware *tian*. **topinambour** Jerusalem artichoke. **tourte** covered pie or tart, usually savoury. **travers de porc** pork spare ribs. **tripoux** dish of sheep's tripe and feet. **tropézienne** (St-Tropez) sponge cake filled with custard cream. **truffe** truffle. **truite** trout.

Vacherin dessert of meringue, cream, fruit and ice cream; a soft, cow's milk cheese. **veau** veal. **velouté** stock-based white sauce; creamy soup. **viande** meat. **violet** sea potato. **volaille** poultry.

Château de Berne

Château de Berne is a magnificent estate set in Provence. Rich in history, culture and charm, it invites guests to tour its working vineyards and cellars, stay at the finest of luxury French hotels, dine on its haute cuisine and indulge in its many sporting, leisure and cultural activities and courses.

Original shows

Inspired by its rich cultural heritage, the estate offers an impressive and varied programme of events. From jazz evenings and dinner dances to themed carnivals, concerts, food fairs and art exhibitions. Our events afford visitors a genuine insight into the

Provencal way of life. Alternatively, try your hand at quad bike riding or a 4x4 tour of the vineyards.

Art de Vivre courses

In addition to a variety of wine tours and tastings, a range of inspired courses and workshops are available at the estate, including the introduction to the art of perfume and watercolour painting, where pupils are taught by well-known teachers. Golf can also be arranged for your pleasure.

New cookery school

For those with a passion for cuisine, the school invites you to capture the essence of Provencal cooking and enjoy the fruits of your labour amongst the rosemary and thyme.

L'Auberge ★★★★

L'Auberge is quite simply a unique and charming hotel in an immaculately restored château that offers a handful of guests the finest things in life in one of the most captivating corners of the world.

Château de Berne - Chemin de Berne - 83510 LORGUES
Tel: +33 (0)4.94.60.43.60 - Fax: +33 (0)4.94.60.43.58
e-mail: info@chateauberne.com - www.chateauberne.com

Provençal Wine

Taste your way around the South of France and you'll find a rosy future lies ahead.

Southeast France is home to a bewildering array of wine appellations: from minuscule Palette just east of Aix and Nice's bijou Bellet to the huge sweeping Côtes de Provence and Coteaux d'Aix; up and coming Costières de Nîmes, Côtes du Ventoux, Cairanne and Rasteau to established royalty like Châteauneuf-du-Pape, Gigondas and Bandol. And if the Provence Côte d'Azur region currently seems less dynamic than the Languedoc-Roussillon, there's still plenty of good wine to be found amid the plonk. The relatively hot and dry climate favours red grape varieties, although certain appellations, such as Cassis, are rated for their whites.

There's a long tradition of making dry rosés in the Mediterranean. Ideal for summer drinking, they have the fullness of a red to go with local food yet retain the refreshing edge of a chilled white. Provence is quintessentially the land of rosé (it makes up 70 per cent of some appellations). The best – and alas the dearest – are from Bandol and Les Baux, made from free-run juice drained or 'bled' off (hence the French term *saignée*) shortly after crushing, having macerated on the skins of the (red) grapes for a few hours. The juice is then fermented fairly cool to preserve fresh aromas and fruit – thus it is made like a white wine. Only the heartiest, more expensive styles will improve in bottle, so make sure you buy the youngest possible.

TOUR 1: LES BAUX-DE-PROVENCE

This youthful sub-region, which was given a separate AOC (*appellation d'origine contrôlée*) only in 1995, centres on the historic hilltop village of Les Baux-de-Provence in Les Alpilles. The appellation encompasses just 12 growers spread over 330 hectares, thus making it ideal for a compact tour to discover rich individual reds, full dry rosés and beautiful wild countryside. Here syrah and cabernet sauvignon – ironically perceived as an Australian blend – harmoniously collide with grenache and mourvèdre. The best reds do age well and may justify the high prices

Les Baux commands, but some should be more convincing at this level. The AOC white wines are currently classified as Coteaux d'Aix-en-Provence but the growers are lobbying for Les Baux status, which could be seen as a cynical attempt to boost the prices of generally average whites. However, they want to base it on the marsanne and roussanne varieties (not permitted for appellation whites at the moment) and sémillon. Tasting the complex, barrel-fermented *vins de pays* made from these grapes confirms their potential, and they are an admirable improvement on grenache blanc, rolle and clairette.

The majority of estates in Les Baux are farmed organically and one, **Château Romanin** (St-Rémy-de-Provence, 04.90.92.45.87), near the airfield, is run on biodynamic principles (with homeopathic methodology, taking account of astronomical and atmospheric conditions). Owners Colette and Jean-Pierre Peyraud have successfully followed this philosophy since they bought the property in 1990. Back towards St-Rémy is the **Domaine Hauvette** (Quartier de la Haute Galine, St-Rémy, 04.90.92.03.90), which makes a rich oaky white and highly rated reds. Heading east again, off the D99 before the turning for Eygalières, is the **Domaine de Terres Blanches** (04.90.95.91.66).

A few kilometres south along the D24, you'll come across **Domaine de la Vallongue** (Quartier de la Vallongue, Eygalières, 04.90.95.91.70), which makes a fab rosé and traditional reds. South of here and east of Le Destet you'll spot the vineyards of **Domaine de Lauzières** (Mouriès, 04.90.47.62.88), but there's no cellar – Jean-André Charial of the luxurious Oustau de Baumanière hotel (*see p60*) makes his wines from this estate's grapes. **Mas de Gourgonnier** (Mouriès, 04.90.47.50.45) is situated on the other side of Le Destet.

Moving back towards Les Baux via Maussane on the D5, **Mas de la Dame** (04.90.54.32.24, www.masdeladame.com) is where Anne Poniatowski and Caroline Missoffe make their award-winning wines, including the elegant Cuvée La Stèle red and creamy Coin Caché white. Not far from the ancient Bauxite city along the D27 is **Mas Ste-Berthe** (Les Baux, 04.90.54.39.01), whose lovely 1995 red shows the wines' ageing potential. Heading west, the Auge valley is home to **Olivier Penel** (Fontvieille, 04.90.54.62.95, www.olivierdauge.com) and his 'new wave'-leaning but good reds. Further along this road towards Fontvieille, stop off at **Château d'Estoublon** (rte de Maussane, Fontvieille, 04.90.54.64.00) before travelling north again via St-Etienne-du-Grès to **Château Dalmeran** (St-Etienne-du-Grès, 04.90.49.04.04). Hopefully you'll be able to buy a bottle of its superb 1997 red.

TOUR 2: BANDOL

'Le Rond-Point des mourvèdres' stands at exit 11 off the A50, La Cadière-Le Castellet to the north of Bandol. A roundabout dedicated to the mourvèdre grape variety lets you know who's boss around here. Majestic mourvèdre shapes not only the heart of the region but the hearts and minds of the growers too. This beefy, late-ripening red grape needs plenty of sunshine and intimate handling to control its yield and tannins, thus producing structured, complex yet rounded wines suited to barrel ageing.

> ### 'A roundabout dedicated to the mourvèdre grape variety lets you know who's boss around here.'

Elsewhere in the south, winemakers use only a small proportion of mourvèdre as they struggle to coax a fine performance out of it. Here, at least 50 per cent is required in the red wines to qualify as AOC Bandol. And the best rosés, which are serious, full-bodied and dry, also contain quite a lot of mourvèdre along with cinsault and/or grenache. Bandol's reputation stems from its reds yet it produces two-thirds rosé (plus 5 per cent often overpriced white); at the leading estates, however, the focus is firmly on reds.

AOC Bandol, totalling 1,400 hectares – less than half the area of Châteauneuf-du-Pape – also

Mourvèdre grapes shape **Bandol** wines.

takes in Sanary, Le Castellet, La Cadière d'Azur and parts of St-Cyr-sur-Mer, Le Beausset, Evenos and Ollioules, in a sweeping amphitheatre around Bandol itself. The rosés go well with local food such as anchovies, sea urchin, mullet and also ethnic cuisine; red Bandol is a good match for pigeon or duck.

Heading south briefly on the D82 from the rond-point towards Le Plan du Castellet, you'll find **Domaine Tempier** (1082 chemin des Fanges, 04.94.98.70.21, www.domainetempier. com), owned by the Peyraud family. Back in the early days, Lucien pushed for mourvèdre to become the main variety (re)planted and hence the backbone of the appellation. Its rosé develops nicely in bottle and two reds are excellent: La Migoua – a single vineyard comprising mourvèdre, syrah, cinsault and grenache – and La Tourtine, made up of 80 per cent mourvèdre, and therefore very sturdy and concentrated.

Follow the D559b south out of Le Plan then take the lane on the right under the motorway. **Moulin des Costes** (La Cadière d'Azur, 04.94.98.58.98, www.bunan.com), resting on steep terraces laden with flat stones, is one of four estates that collectively create Domaines Bunan (also including Château la Rouvière and Mas de la Rouvière). Château la Rouvière red, the pinnacle of the range, is enriched with over 90 per cent mourvèdre and a little syrah. Its full-bodied Blanc de Blancs is made from clairette pointue and the lovely intense rosé half mourvèdre, with gutsy 14 per cent alcohol.

The vineyards of celebrated **Château de Pibarnon** (Chemin de la Croix des Signaux, La Cadière, 04.94.90.12.73) border the Bunans but the only way there is to wind back on the D559b south to the right and up the hill again. Laidback aristos Eric de Saint Victor and his father Henri, the Comte, cultivate the highest slopes of Bandol at 300m. Here the soil is particularly chalky, which they believe tames mourvèdre. As Eric put it: 'It's very macho, on this soil we manage to make something quite fine.'

TOUR 3: COTES DE PROVENCE – MASSIF DES MAURES

Getting to grips with the Côtes de Provence as a whole isn't easy. A region on this scale – the appellation extends across the Var over 19,000 hectares from within the Bouches-du-Rhône to the edge of Alpes-Maritimes – naturally bears very diverse terrain, producers and personalities. The result is wines ranging from rough, harmless but cheap, through very drinkable to serious and pricey, all officially wearing the same AOC badge. So it's worth concentrating on a specific area, and selecting the best within it.

The coastal strip between Hyères and St-Tropez bordering the Massif des Maures offers scenic touring and some high-quality estates. La Londe-les-Maures provides a good place to start and a *terroir* particularly successful for white wines – not the norm in rosé country. Take a left at the main lights in the town, heading north over the N98, and follow the signs for **Château Ste-Marguerite** (Le Haut Pansard, 04.94.00.44.44, www.chateausainte marguerite.com). This peaceful spot surrounded by handsome vines is owned by Jean-Pierre Fayard, whose Cru Classé (an ancient, unofficial classification) wines include a fine white made from low-yielding rolle, sémillon and ugni blanc, and smoky-textured red from syrah and cabernet sauvignon.

Rejoin the D559 in La Londe then turn right just out of town. Follow this twisty lane until you reach a mini-roundabout where another right takes you to **Clos Mireille** (rte de Brégançon, 04.94.01.53.53, www.domaines-ott.com), signposted Domaines Ott, which owns this and other properties in Côtes de Provence and Bandol. Clos Mireille, also a Cru Classé, is unusual in that it currently only produces white wines: the floral citrussy Blanc de Blancs and richer oak-aged L'Insolent.

'Wines ranging from rough to serious and pricey all wear the same AOC badge.'

Turn right back on to the country lane and follow the signs for Brégançon; a quarter of an hour or so later you'll come across the aristocratic **Château de Brégançon** itself (639 route de Léoube, Bormes-les-Mimosas; 04.94.64.80.73, www.chateaudebregancon.com), appropriately another Cru Classé. Recommended tastings include its Prestige rosé and limited edition Cuvée Hermann Sabran red, with one third cabernet sauvignon lending a Bordeaux-like finesse and power.

A further 30-40 minutes (depending on traffic) towards St-Tropez on the winding D559 coastal road will eventually bring you to Gassin, home of one of the grandest Cru Classé estates, **Château Minuty** (rte de Ramatuelle, 04.94.56.12.09) with its smart gardens and cute Napoléon III chapel. To find it, either turn right on to the D89 and climb almost to the village but go left just before the top, descend a little and take a right into the side entrance; or circle around and approach from the Ramatuelle road via the main gate. Its Cuvée Réserve rosé and red are pretty special. You could finish the tour by visiting **Château Barbeyrolles** (04.94.56.33.58) next door, where you can also taste wines from the owners' other property, Château la Tour de l'Evêque.

Deschamps and Makeieff's *Les Etourdis* at the Théâtre de Nîmes. *See p33.*

The Creative South

A fresh crop of new artists, designers and choreographers are renewing the creative tradition.

Beyond the South of France's renowned summer festivals, there's a dynamic all-year cultural scene that is renewing dance and questioning artistic creation, from the princely establishment of Monte-Carlo to the underground hub of Marseille.

ART

The South of France's phenomenal modern art legacy (*see p31* **Bathers and odalisques**) is a difficult act to live up to and has tended to spawn a morass of sub-Picasso potters and neo-impressionist daubers. Yet a number of important older-generation artists who marked the 1960s and 70s are still active here today, including Support-Surface founder **Claude Viallat** in Nîmes, sculptor **Bernard Pagès**

and Fluxus artist **Ben**. There's also a dynamic, conceptually based, emerging young art scene, centred in particular on Marseille.

Among the young artists who are making their mark in France and internationally is **Gilles Barbier**, whose installations composed of multiple wax clones of himself in different vaguely sinister situations suggest questions of identity, science and belonging, fiction and reality. **Natacha Lesueur**'s elaborately set-up glossy photos deal with issues of femininity, fetishism and food. Extravagant cocktail headdresses, chignons with cucumber curls and caviar dreadlocks comment on food, ceremony, glamour and fashion, while mouths replaced by vegetable teeth tread a neat line between attraction and repugnance. **Francesco**

Finizio creates tragi-comic situations using video, soundworks and installation to treat issues related to consumer society.

The perpetual issue of the revival (or not) of painting is present too. Nice-based **Pascal Pinaud** works with the motifs and structures of abstraction. One series uses car paint and titles such as *Volkswagen* and *Porsche*, others use acrylic gel and even knitting or aluminium. The stripy, lacquer paintings and installations of **Cédric Tesseire** (like Lesueur part of La Station collective in Nice in the late 90s) similarly play with and break the rules of Pop Art and minimalism. **Anne Pesce**'s paintings derive from photographs and voyages to Greenland and the Antarctic, as well as the view of the sea from where she lives in Vence.

'La Friche La Belle de Mai is wilfully pluridisciplinary and experimental.'

A number of public institutions and artist-run spaces play an important role on the contemporary art scene. As well as the **Frac** (Fonds Régional d'Art Contemporain), based in Marseille but organising events all over the region, and the two modern art museums **MAC** in Marseille and **MAMAC** in Nice, **La Friche La Belle de Mai** and the **Villa Arson** in Nice act as artistic hothouses. The commercial gallery scene is smaller, but led by **Galerie Roger Pailhas** in Marseille and **Galerie Catherine Issert** in Vence.

Occupying some 45,000m² of an old tobacco factory, and place of exchange for over 300 artists, dancers, performers, musicians, graphic and web designers, puppeteers and street acts, **La Friche La Belle de Mai** is wilfully pluridisciplinary and experimental – a melting pot of art, music, theatre, performance and dance, as well as an umbrella for several artist-run organisations. According to director Philippe Foulquié, 'La Friche's mission is to make the artist the centre of a system of socialisation founded on the dual necessity of creating works and interaction with the public.'

Within the Friche, associations like Astérides and the Triangle organise artists' residencies and temporary exhibitions, nourished by exchanges with similar outfits, such as Triangle Arts at the Gasworks in London, the Tramway in Glasgow or the Hangar in Barcelona. Astérides, run by a group of artists including Gilles Barbier, invites mainly young artists for studio residencies of up to six months, but has also included well established names like Tony Cragg or international up-and-comers such as Tatiana Trouvé, Hugues Reip and Virginie

Bathers and odalisques

In the inter-war period as the avant-garde mixed with the jet set, the daring new beach society of the Riviera became the playground for equally daring modern art, exploring Surrealism, abstraction and new forms of representation. Picabia was both satirist of jet set society and part of it with his passion for cars (he owned 127) and the extravagant fancy-dress balls that he organised in the Casino at **Cannes**. In 1925 he designed himself a house at **Mougins**, the Château de Mai, which he constantly transformed, adding terraces, a swimming pool, turrets and an atelier as he moved away in his paintings from the machine-like inventions to a dreamy mythology. Giacometti, Picasso, Man Ray, Stravinsky, Poulenc and Buñuel were among those who holed-up at the avant-garde **Villa Noailles** in Hyères (*see p182*).

In 1917 Matisse, who had spent summers with Braque and Derain at L'Estaque in 1906, paid his first visit to **Nice**. From 1919 on he spent half the year there, finding both light and calm, but fed also by Classical and Oriental art and visits to North Africa. Despite his long friendship with Bonnard and Picasso, Matisse essentially remained isolated on the hill of Cimiez, developing in his interiors, still lifes and odalisques his interest in colour and pattern and combining southern light with the textile background of the north.

Picasso was less interested in southern light than in people and his output was ever linked to his life and lovers. As early as the 1910s, he spent summers in the South. Bathers and the human body became a recurrent subject, from simple oil sketches on cardboard to the elongated bronze sculptures and tin cut-outs of the 50s. His *Baigneuses regardent un avion*, painted in 1920 at **Juan-les-Pins**, or his curious sand-covered tableaux-reliefs of the 30s (done at much the same time as André Masson's automatic sand paintings produced in Antibes) show his affinities with the Surrealists, in parallel with his classical period. Other works celebrate the Mediterranean and and local fishermen as well as mytholgical themes such as Pan, centaurs and the Minotaur.

Barré. Triangle similarly organises exhibitions, residencies and the Action-Man-Oeuvres pluridisciplinary performances.

In Nice, the **Villa Arson**, which comes under the aegis of the Ministry of Culture, has a more institutional edge, but its combination of art school, residencies and international exhibitions and cultural programmes also make it an important forum for debate.

ARCHITECTURE AND DESIGN

From his agency in Bandol, with the sound of cicadas screeching outside the window, Rudy Ricciotti is a rare architect outside the Paris power-base to have made it on the international scene. A *grande gueule* (big mouth) not afraid to speak out against the establishment or architectural mediocrity, Ricciotti has become known, on the one hand, for his radical, often

> **'There is no difference between working with a historic building or designing a contemporary one.'**

sculptural and minimalist modern buildings and, on the other, for his subtle adaptation of historic buildings for new cultural use.

The latter include the **Abbaye de Montmajour** near Arles and the **Collection Lambert** in Avignon. Ricciotti sees no contradiction between the two: 'There is no difference between working with a historic building or designing a contemporary one: in both cases we are talking about the urban. There is no break between history and modernity.' After the **Centre Chorégraphique National** currently under construction in Aix-en-Provence – 'a spidery, complex and fleeting structure in concrete and glass' – the conversion

of the semi-derelict Grands Moulins de Paris into a new university faculty in Paris and the Nikolaisaal concert hall in Potsdam, Germany, Ricciotti has just been named as the winner of the competition for the new Musée National des Civilisations de l'Europe et de la Méditerranée in Marseille. He also works for private clients in the south, where he has almost single-handedly revived the tradition of the avant-garde seaside villa. Minimalist constructions, such as the Villa Le Goff in Marseille and the Villa Lyprendi in Toulon, are both radical interventions and camouflaged into the natural landscape – literally in the case of Villa Le Goff's, whose glass facade, opening on to a long, narrow swimming pool, is hung with a curtain of camouflage netting that provides a dialogue between interior and exterior.

On the design front, **Fred Sathal**, who recently returned to live in her birthplace Marseille, is one of select group of young designers invited to show at the haute couture *défilés*, and in 2003 featured in a solo show at the Musée de la Mode in Marseille. Her clothes are typically colourful, favouring wafty, multi-layered, asymmetric cuts and mixing different fabrics and textures from sequins to felt.

Marseille-based design group **Cooked in Marseille** uses silicone to create the funky Expres'soft espresso cup, the brilliantly simple silicone Oeugy ring egg cup and silicone lightbulb shades, or colourful neo-60s pouffes and modulable seats in pvc or foam. Then there's the more extravagant style of **David Emery**, based in the Gard between Nîmes and Avignon, whose tendril-like crushed velvet chandeliers and vegetation-inspired iron and velvet sofas and chairs are Baroque yet contemporary, seen in modish Paris restaurants Rue Balzac and Dada and Avignon's Numéro 75.

DANCE AND THEATRE

The Ballet National de Marseille (BNM) was in crisis at the beginning of 2004, when artistic director **Marie-Claude Pietragalla** was forced to resign following a strike by 80% of the personnel of the company and its dance school. The strikers complained that Pietragalla, an acclaimed dancer in her own right, spent too much of the budget on her own productions at the expense of prestigious touring engagements. In her defence, Pietragalla claimed she had been left with zero repertoire when celebrated choreographer Roland Petit retired in 1990, taking his creations with him. She had renewed the classical ballet programme, invited guest choreographers such as William Forsythe and Jeri Kylian, toured in China and Thailand and pulled in more than 303,000 spectators.

Ballets de Monte-Carlo.

Rudy Ricciotti's **Villa Lyprendi** above Toulon.

Following in the footsteps of Petit, who had created the ballet company in 1972 and whose name was as intrinsically linked with it as Diaghilev's with the Ballets Russes, was never going to be easy and whoever takes on the job next still has a tough act to follow.

Since he arrived in Monaco in 1993, **Jean-Christophe Maillot**, previously at the Centre National Chorégraphique de Tours, has rejuvenated the Ballets de Monte-Carlo and brought them to the forefront of the dance scene with his slimmed down updatings of the classics. 'I want to transmit an emotion to the audience and propose other solutions to the classics, which no longer correspond to what the audience wants.' Maillot's updating of *Cendrillon* keeps Prokofiev's music but gives a high-energy, modern psychological gloss to the Cinderella fairytale, in which the key element is the relationship between Cinderella and the fairy godmother, alias her mother. Other creations include *La Belle*, an audacious reworking of Tchaikovsky's *Sleeping Beauty*, and a stripped-back version of *Roméo et Juliette* with a sexy postmodern Juliette.

Angelin Preljocaj, previously at the CNCDC in Châteauvallon and now in Aix-en-Provence, similarly creates a bridge between contemporary dance and ballet. As well as creating a repertoire for his own company, he has choreographed pieces including Le Parc for the Opéra National de Paris.

More strictly contemporary **Georges Appaix** and his La Liseuse company (again based at La Friche La Belle de Mai) often starts from a poem or philosophical essay. He works closely with jazz and popular Mediterranean music.

In theatre, Marseille's Théâtre de la Criée continues to play a major role, along with more alternative outfits and experimental circus pioneers **Archaos**. There is also new blood at the Théâtre de Nîmes where **Macha Makeieff and Jérôme Deschamps** have recently been appointed artistic directors. Deschamps and Makeieff, famous for the over-the-top Deschiens clan who made it from the stage to a prime spot on Canal+ TV station, create theatre that is at once radical and accessible. They are likely to spend the next few years hopping between Paris and the South, using Nîmes as a platform for new work and a meeting point for other directors and southern companies. Their latest piece, *Les Etourdis* (which translates roughly as 'the scatterbrains'), premiered at Nîmes in December 2003, takes a typically Makeieff and Deschamps perspective of socially downtrodden and confused non-conformists, innocents in the modern world.

Nice Jazz Festival. *See p39.*

The Festive South

The South of France loves to have fun, whether it's hosting international jazz greats, opera stars or a festival of melons.

Festivals are a way of life for the South of France, providing a star-studded roster of entertainment. Most, especially those dedicated to music, dance and theatre, fall in the summer, when tourists descend upon the South to soak up the sun and a little culture while they're at it.

However, in 2003, France's prestigious summer festival season went bottoms-up and the habitual culture flood fizzled out, as France's *intermittents du spectacle* – non-salaried actors, backstage staff and broadcasting technicians – went on strike in a row with the Ministry of Culture over planned changes to their unemployment benefit scheme. After protests and disruption, one by one, the Festival de Marseille, Festival d'Avignon (*see p90*) and Festival International d'Art Lyrique at Aix-en-Province were ignominiously cancelled; only the Chorégies d'Orange survived as the *intermittents* decided that cancelling would be playing into the hands of the Front National-led local council. Those events that did go ahead were generally prefaced by leaflets and speeches from actors and stage staff campaigning for their cause.

Despite last year's strikes, 2004 promises to be an excellent festival year. Though the theatre, dance and music festivals are top-notch, be sure to check out some of the more obscure village celebrations, where you may see a bull-fight, ancient dances, medieval processions,

independent film screenings or a fireworks display. Foodies have plenty of options as well, with festivals celebrating everything from lemons to crêpes, wines to chestnuts.

INFORMATION

Tourist offices are good sources for concert leaflets and the comprehensive free booklet *Terre de Festivals* (also on www.cr-paca.fr, www.festivals.laregie-paca.com), covering summer arts festivals in the Provence-Alpes-Côtes d'Azur region. Tickets can often be bought at tourist offices, at branches of book and record chain **Fnac** (www.fnac.fr) or at agencies, including **France Billet** (08.92.69.26.94/ www.francebillet.com) and **Globaltickets** (01.42.81.88.98/ www.globaltickets.com).

Spring

Transhumance

Throughout rural Provence, including St-Remy-de-Provence, La Garde-Freinet, St-Etienne-de-Tinée, Riez. **Information** local tourist offices. **Date** May or June. The traditional moving of flocks between winter and summer pastures occurs in late spring. Thousands of sheep, accompanied by dogs, carts and donkeys, are driven through the villages to the sound of flutes and tambourines. In St-Rémy on Pentecost Monday, flocks parade twice around the town centre.

carnival floats in the streets of Cavaillon; similar *corsos* (processions) are held in Apt and Pertuis.

Fête de la Vigne et du Vin
Avignon, Châteauneuf-du-Pape, Gigondas & other villages. **Information** 04.90.84.01.67/
www.fetedelavigneetduvin.com. **Date** May.
On Ascension weekend, the southern Côtes du Rhône wines are celebrated with a wine village in front of the Palais des Papes, plus open-houses and tastings at many producers and wine cellars.

Marseille & Aix

Art Dealers
Marseille. **Information** 04.91.54.02.22/
www.rogerpailhas.com. **Tickets** free. **Date** end May.
At the contemporary art fair organised by Marseille art dealer Roger Pailhas, eight international galleries each feature a promising young artist.

The Var

Festival de la Mode
Villa Noailles, Hyères. **Information** 04.94.65.22.72/
www.festival hyeres.com. **Tickets** free, but by advance reservation only. **Date** Apr.
Young, international fashion designers showcase ideas, plus fashion photography exhibitions.

La Bravade
St-Tropez. **Information** Office de Tourisme (04.94.97.45.21). **Date** mid-May.
A colourful procession evokes the arrival of headless Christian martyr Torpes (alias Tropez) in 68 AD.

The Riviera & southern Alps

Le Printemps des Arts
various venues, Monte-Carlo. **Information** 00.377-92.16.24.2). **Tickets** €15. **Date** Apr.
Monte Carlo celebrates the arts with concerts, operas and ballets by local and international groups. 2004's festival featured the premiere of Jean-Christophe Maillot's *Miniatures* by the Ballets de Monte-Carlo.

Tennis Master Series Monte-Carlo
Monte-Carlo Country Club. **Information** 04.93.41.72.00/www.mccc.mc. **Tickets** €10-€135.
Date mid-Apr.
International men's hard-court tournament.

Cannes Film Festival
Cannes. **Date** mid-May.
The world's most-hyped film festival attracts stars, movie moguls and hangers-on (*see also p230*).

Grand Prix de Monaco
Monaco. **Information** 00.377-93.15.26.00/
www.acm.mc. **Tickets** €35-€420. **Date** May or June.
Formula One cars tear around the city-state's tight bends, often with spectacular pile-ups. Book ahead.

The Rhône Delta

Feria Pascale
Arènes, Arles (04.90.96.03.70/www.arenes-arles.com). **Date** Easter Sat to Easter Mon. **Tickets** €12-€86.
Three spirited days of Spanish-style bull-fighting in the Roman arena with international toreadors.

Fête des Gardians
Arènes, Arles, & around town. **Information** Office de Tourisme (04.90.18.41.20). **Date** 1 May.
The Queen of Arles is crowned, accompanied by *gardians* and equine bravado in the Roman arena.

Feria de Pentecôte
Arènes, Nîmes (04.66.02.80.80/www.arenesdenimes.fr). **Date** late May or early June. **Tickets** €38-€90.
The biggest of Nîmes *ferias* convenes bull-fighting stars, music and art, with partying all over town. Smaller *ferias* in September and February.

Pèlerinage de Mai
Stes-Maries-de-la-Mer. **Information** 04.90.97.82.55.
Date 23-25 May.
Gypsies from across Europe converge on tiny Stes-Maries-de-la-Mer in honour of gypsy chief Black Sarah who, according to legend, met the three apocryphal Marys (Mary Magdalene, Mary Jacob and Mary Salome) here on their arrival by boat from Palestine. On 23 May Sarah's relics are lowered from the church that houses them. On 24 May the relics are carried down to the sea, flanked by gypsies, *Arlésiennes* in costume and *gardians* on horseback. The relics of Marys Jacob and Salome follow on 25 May to be blessed by a bishop in a fishing boat.

Avignon & the Vaucluse

Ascension Day
Cavaillon. **Information** Office de Tourisme (04.90.71.32.01). **Date** May.
A parade of bands and flamboyantly decorated

Summer

Fête de la Musique

Throughout France. **Information**
(www.fetedelamusique.culture.fr). **Date** 21 June.
The longest day of the year sees free concerts all
over France, taking in all types of music; from string
quartets and Johnny Hallyday covers to hip-hop.

Bastille Day (le Quatorze Juillet)

Throughout France. **Date** 14 July.
The French national holiday commemorates the
storming of Bastille prison in Paris 1789 and the
start of the French Revolution. *Bals* and fireworks
are usually in the evening of 13 and/or 14 July.

The Rhône Delta

Festival de la Nouvelle Danse

Uzès. **Information** 04.66.22.51.51/www.uzesdanse.fr.
Box office (from mid-May) Office de Tourisme
(04.66.22.68.88). **Tickets** €8-€40. **Date** June.
Uzès aims to introduce unknown dance talents. 2004
promises companies from Israel, Romania and
Belgium, and the prestigious Ballets de Monte-Carlo.

Garlic Fair

Uzes. **Information** Office de Tourisme
(04.66.22.68.88). **Date** 24 June.
In a festival dating back to 1524, the town centre is
piled high with bulbous, purple cloves of garlic.

Fête de la Tarasque

Tarascon. **Information** Office de Tourisme
(04.90.91.03.52/www.tarascon.org). **Date** end June.
Tarascon celebrates St Marthe's miraculous victory
over an amphibious Rhône-dwelling beast. A model
of the monster is paraded and there are tributes to
Good King René, who founded the fête in 1474, and
Daudet's fictional adventurer Tartarin of Tarascon,
along with four days of music, bull-running and food.

Rencontres Internationales de la Photographie

Musée Réattu & other venues, Arles. **Information**
04.90.96.76.06/www.rip-arles.org. **Tickets** €5; *soirées*
€12-€17. **Date** early July to mid-Aug.
The RIP is a major gathering for contemporary art
photography, with the 2004 edition curated by
Martin Parr. Themed shows, retrospectives and special commissions are accompanied by debates and
workshops. There's also a fringe festival, *Voies Off.*

Suds à Arles

Théâtre Antique and other venues, Arles.
Information 04.90.96.06.27/www.suds-arles.com.
Tickets €8-€22. **Date** July.
World music from Latin America and Africa to the
Balkans. Look out for free concerts, brass bands,
dance classes, outdoor film screenings and mint tea.

Nuits Musicales d'Uzès

Uzès. **Information** Office de Tourisme

(04.66.22.68.88). **Tickets** €8-€35. **Date** July.
Concerts in historic buildings played by renowned
Baroque ensembles such as Musica Antiqua Köln.

La Feria Provençale

St-Rémy-de-Provence. **Information** Office de
Tourisme (04.90.92.74.92). **Date** mid-Aug.
Three days of bull races, parades and mounted
abrivado (herding bulls into the ring) and *bandido*
(taking them back out again).

Avignon & the Vaucluse

Festival d'Avignon

Avignon. **Information** Bureau du Festival
d'Avignon, 20 rue Portail Bocquier (04.90.27.66.50/
reservations 04.90.14.14.14/www.festival-
avignon.com). **Date** July. **Tickets** €10-€33.
Avignon's performing arts extravaganza was
founded in 1947, cramming international theatre,
dance, music and visitors into the historic city, with
pride of place to the courtyard of the Palais des
Papes. After strike-hit 2003, a new directorial team
hopes to make its mark in 2004 (*see also pp90-91*).

Avignon Public Off

Avignon. **Information** Maison d'Off Bureau
d'Accueil, Conservatoire de Musique, pl du Palais
(www.avignon-off.org). **Date** July. **Tickets** €9-€13.
Avignon's fringe festival is on a very different wavelength. Anyone can perform in 'Le Off', provided
they can find enough space and get through local-
authority red tape. Impromptu stagings range from
fire-eatings to vaudevillian comedy and music.

Festival Provençal

Palais du Roure & other venues, Avignon &
surrounding area. **Information** 04.90.86.27.76/
www.nouvello.com. **Date** July.
This festival promotes Provençal language and folklore with plays and debates.

Festival de la Correspondance

Grignan. **Information** 04.75.46.55.83/
www.festivalcorrespondance-grignan.com.
Date early July.
Celebrate letter-writing with readings and dramati-
sations of epistles by noted scribblers. Past editions
featured Colette, Madame de Sévigné and Jean
Genet's prison correspondence. There are calligra-
phy workshops to brush up your handwriting.

Festival de la Sorgue

L'Isle-sur-la-Sorgue. **Information** Office de Tourisme
(04.90.38.04.78). **Date** July.
Folklore, street theatre, exhibitions, a floating market and a *corso nautique*, in which flower-laden
punts battle on the island's canals, plus concerts in
L'Isle and Fontaine-de-Vaucluse.

L'Eté de Vaison

Théâtre Antique, Vaison-la-Romaine. **Information**
04.90.28.84.49/www.vaison-festival.com. **Tickets**
€15-€38. **Date** July.

Menton sucks lemons in the **Fête du Citron**. *See p40.*

Ballet, tango and flamenco have all featured at this stomping dance and theatre festival.

Les Estivales de Carpentras

Théâtre de Plein Air, Carpentras. **Information** (04.90.60.46.00). **Tickets** €26. **Date** July.
A multidisciplinary array of music, dance and theatre staged in an open-air auditorium.

Les Chorégies d'Orange

Théâtre Antique, Orange. **Information** Bureau des Chorégies d'Orange, 18 pl Sylvain (04.90.34.24.24/ www.choregies.asso.fr). **Tickets** €5-€180. **Date** mid-July to early Aug.
Orange's Roman amphitheatre provides a sublime setting for lyric opera and has miraculous acoustics. 2004 features Verdi's *Nabucco* and Bizet's *Carmen*.

Festival de Melon

Cavaillon. **Information** 04.90.71.73.02. **Date** July.
Cucurbitaceous fun as the melon mafia, alias the 'Brotherhood of the Knights of the Order of the Melons of Cavaillon' are solemnly enthroned.

Festival International de Quatuors à Cordes

Luberon. **Information** 04.90.75.89.60. **Tickets** €8-€20. **Date** July-Aug.
Europe's best string quartets perform in the Abbaye de Silvacane, and churches at Cabrières d'Avignon, Fontaine-de-Vaucluse, Goult, L'Isle-sur-la-Sorgue and Roussillon. Tickets on the door only.

Marseille & Aix

Fête de la St-Pierre

Martigues. **Information** Office de Tourisme (04.42.42.31.10). **Date** end June.
The statue of St-Pierre, patron saint of fishermen, is carried to the port for nautical parades and blessing of boats. Also in La Ciotat, Cassis and Marseille.

Argilla, Fêtes de la Céramique Aubagne

Aubagne. **Information** Office de Tourisme (04.42.03.49.98). **Date** mid-Aug.
The biennial (the next is in 2005) ceramics market is France's biggest and emphasises art pottery.

Festival de Marseille

Marseille. **Information** Bureau d'accueil, 6 pl Sadi Carnot (04.91.99.00.20/box office 04.91.99.02.50/ www.festivaldemarseille.com). **Tickets** €4-€32. **Date** July.
This festival of experimental dance, theatre and music has a growing reputation, although 2003 was cancelled due to the *intermittents'* strikes.

Festival International d'Art Lyrique

Aix-en-Provence. **Information** Boutique du Festival, 11 rue Gaston de Saporta (04.42.17.34.34/ www.festival-aix.com). **Tickets** €25-€185. **Date** July.
The prestigious international opera festival attracts innovative directors and international divas. Mozart

is always featured and the festival has broadened to include early and contemporary opera. 2004 premieres *Hanjo*, based on a No drama by Mishima.

Festival Danse à Aix
Aix-en-Provence. **Information** Danse à Aix, 1 pl Joan Rewald, Espace Forbin (04.42.96.05.01/box office from June 04.42.23.41.24/www.danse-a-aix.com). **Tickets** €10-€26. **Date** mid-July to mid-Aug.
Contemporary dance performances from the movers and shakers of the French scene.

Festival International de Piano
La Roque d'Antheron. **Information** 04.42.50.51.15/ www.festival-piano.com). **Tickets** €12-€75. **Date** mid-July to mid-Aug.
Top concert pianists perform in the château garden and other venues, with some crossover into jazz.

Musique à l'Empéri
Château de l'Empéri, Salon-de-Provence. **Information** 04.42.92.73.88/www.musique-emperi.com. **Tickets** €10-€20. **Date** early Aug.
The Château de l'Empéri's courtyard is the setting for chamber music from Mozart to Dusapin.

The Var

Festival Medieval
pl de la République, Hyères. **Information** Office de Tourisme (04.94.00.79.74). **Date** July.
Jugglers, fire eaters, musicians, acrobats and storytellers go carousing in Hyères' old streets, inspired by Louis IX's landing in 1254.

Draguifolies
Draguignan. **Information** Théâtres en Dracenie, bd Georges Clemenceau (04.94.50.59.50). **Date** July-Aug.
Free concerts, theatre and dance performances in numerous open-air sites around town.

Mosaïque des Suds
Théâtre du Pont d'Olive, Brignoles (04.94.72.08.27). **Tickets** €21. **Date** late July.
This festival mixes dance, art, music and theatre of 'southern' cultures, from the Middle East to Spain.

Festival de Théâtre de Ramatuelle
Ramatuelle. **Information** Bureau d'Accueil (04.94.79.20.50/www.ticketnet.fr/ramatuelle). **Tickets** €37. **Date** early Aug.
Founded by French thesp Jean-Claude Brialy in 1985, this festival promoting *bonne humeur* brings a cultural slant to the St-Trop' summer scene.

Jazz Festival de Ramatuelle
Ramatuelle. **Infomation** Bureau d'Accueil (04.94.79.10.29/www.jazzfestivalramatuelle.com). **Tickets** €29. **Date** mid-Aug.
A week of jazz in an outdoor amphitheatre.

The Riviera & southern Alps

Voiles d'Antibes
Port Vauban, Antibes. **Information** 04.92.91.60.00. **Date** June.
Classy classic yacht regatta sees four days of inshore racing between classic and modern yachts, followed by plenty of partying for landlubbers.

Marseille celebrates its musical melting pot in the **Fiesta des Suds**.

Les Baroquiales

Roya and Bévéra valleys. **Information** 04.93.04.12.55/
www.lesbaroquiales.org. **Tickets** €8-€20. **Date** end
June to early July.
Baroque musicians play in Alpine valley churches.

Biennale de Céramique Contemporaine

Musée de la Céramique, Vallauris (04.93.64.16.05).
Tickets €2-€4. **Date** end June to Sept.
This biennial potters' mecca (the next is in 2004)
features contemporary ceramics from Europe.

Jazz à Juan

Juan-les-Pins. **Information** 04.92.90.53.00/
www.antibesjuanlespins.com. **Tickets** €30-€65.
Date mid-July.
This beachside jazz festival has secured legends on
its line-up ever since its 1960 debut with Count
Basie, Miles Davis and Ella Fitzgerald. Nowadays,
it is an umbrella for pop, Latin and fusion, as well
as jazz. The fringe, Jazz Off, is more affordable.

Nice Jazz Festival

Jardins de Cimiez, Nice. **Information** Office de
Tourisme (04.92.14.48.00/box office 04.92.09.75.56/
www.nicejazzfest.com). **Tickets** €25. **Date** July.
Less serious than Jazz à Juan and enjoyably unpre-
dictable – Kool and the Gang have played here, as
has Gil Scott-Heron. The Roman arena setting creates a rather sophisticated Woodstock atmosphere.

Festival International d'Art Pyrotechnique de Cannes

La Croisette, Cannes. **Information** 04.92.59.41.20.
Tickets free. **Date** July.
International pyrotechnicians set off fireworks.

Musiques au Coeur

Chantier Naval Opéra, Port Vauban, Antibes.
Information 04.92.90.53.00. **Tickets** €13-€50.
Date early July.
Choral and orchestral works at a small but glossy
open-air music festival.

Les Nuits du Sud

pl du Grand Jardin, Vence. **Information** 04.93.58.06.3).
Tickets €13 **Date** mid-July to mid-Aug.
Life in sleepy Vence speeds up for four weeks of
raunchy Latin, salsa, raï and dance in the open air.

Festival de Musique

parvis St-Michel, Menton. **Information** 04.92.41.76.95/
www.villedementon.com. **Tickets** €19-€48. **Date** Aug.
Founded in 1950, this festival regularly features a
mix of classical music greats and the up-and-coming, in the church square overlooking the old port.

Autumn

Journées du Patrimoine

Throughout France (www.culture.gouv.fr). **Date** 3rd
weekend in Sept.
Architectural heritage weekend, when historic and
official buildings around France open to the public.

The Rhône Delta

Fêtes des Prémices du Riz

Arles. **Information** (04.90.93.19.55). **Date** mid-Sept.
Camargue's rice harvest is marked by a *corso*, led
by the Ambassadrice du riz on a Camargue pony.

Avignon & the Vaucluse

Fête de la Veraison

Châteauneuf-du-Pape. **Information** (04.90.83.71.08)
Date 3 days early Aug.
In a festival dating back to medieval times, wine-
makers set up tasting stalls amid costumed actors,
craft and food vendors and much revelry – as a €3
verre de Veraison buys you unlimited refills.

Marseille & Aix

Fête du Livre

Cité du Livre, Aix-en-Provence. **Information**
04.42.26.16.85. **Date** Oct.
Literary festival invites big-name guests (Toni
Morrison and V S Naipaul have both featured) for
bookish debates, plus film, art and music events.

Fiesta des Suds

Docks des Suds, Marseille. **Information**
(04.91.99.00.00/reservations 08.25.83.38.33/www.dock-
des-suds.org). **Tickets** €5-€32. **Date** Oct.
A musical melting pot from rock and electro to salsa
reflects Marseille's multiracial population.

The Var

Rencontres Internationales du cinéma des Antipodes

St-Tropez. **Information** (01.47.97.45.98/
www.festivaldesantipodes.org). **Date** Oct.
Film buffs feast on shorts, feature films and documentaries from Australia and New Zealand.

La Fête des Châtaignes

Collobrières. **Information** Office de Tourisme
(04.94.48.08.00/www.collotour.com). **Date** Oct.
France's *marrons glacés* capital goes chestnut-crazy
with street entertainment, exhibitions and all manner of chesnut products to buy and eat.

The Riviera & southern Alps

Festival Mondial de l'Image Sous-Marine

*Palais des Congrès, Antibes-Juan-Les-Pins
(04.93.61.45.45/www.underwater-festival.com).*
Tickets €10-€12 **Date** Oct.
Divers, artists, film-makers and photographers congregate to discuss all things underwater.

Monaco Fête Nationale

Monaco (00.377-93.15.28.63). **Date** 18-19 Nov.

The Rocher's national day is celebrated with a fun fair, fireworks at the port (18 Nov), a Te Deum in the cathedral, cinema and outdoor concert (19 Nov).

Winter

Avignon & the Vaucluse

Messe des truffes
Chapel Notre-Dame, Richerenches. **Information** Office de Tourisme (04.90.28.05.34/ www.richerenches.fr) **Date** 3rd Sun in Jan.
Truffle worship climaxes with a mass to honour St Antoine, patron saint of *trufficulteurs*, headlined by the Chevaliers du Diamont Noir; fresh truffles are later auctioned off to repair the church roof.

Les Hivernales
Avignon and Vaucluse. **Information** 04.90.82.33.12/ box office 04.90.82.10.66/www.hivernales-avignon.com. **Tickets** €4-€26. **Date** Feb.
Cutting-edge contemporary dance; Mark Tompkins and Georges Appaix were recent highlights.

Marseille & Aix

La Chandeleur
Basilique St-Victor, Marseille. **Information** 04.96.11.22.60. **Date** 2 Feb.
A candlelit procession behind the black virgin of the Basilique St-Victor marks the end of Christmas.

The Var

Fêtes de la Lumière à St-Raphaël
St-Raphaël. **Information** Office de Tourisme 04.94.19.52.52/www.saint-raphael.com. **Date** Dec.
For two weeks St-Raphaël is decked in lights, while street theatre groups and musicians fill the town to bursting. New Year's Eve is a blaze of fireworks.

Le Corso Fleuri
Bormes-les-Mimosas. **Information** Office de Tourisme (04.94.01.38.38). **Date** 3rd Sun in Feb.
Spring blooms in a colourful parade of floral floats in myriad forms, from fairy gowns to steam trains.

The Riviera & southern Alps

Festival International de la Danse
Palais des Festivals & other venues, Cannes. **Information** 04.92.99.33.83/www.cannes-on-line.com. **Tickets** €10-€28. **Date** Nov.
The dance biennial (next in 2005) reflects the dynamic dance scene in Europe and the Mediterranean.

Rallye Automobile Monte-Carlo
Monaco. **Information** Office de Tourisme (00.377-92.16.61.16). **Date** Jan.
Since 1911, rally drivers have careered over snow-bound passes and down into the principality.

Festival International du Cirque de Monte-Carlo
Espace Fontvieille, Monaco. **Information** 00.377-92.05.23.45. **Tickets** €7-€114. **Date** late Jan.
The cream of international circus artistes compete in avant-garde acrobatics and daredevil stunts.

Carnaval de Nice
Nice. **Information** 04.93.92.80.73/ www.nicecarnaval.com. **Tickets** €10-€20. **Date** month before Lent.
The Carnaval parade marks the period of excess leading up to Lent (*see p256*).

Fête du Citron
Menton. **Information** Office de Tourisme (04.92.41.76.76) **Date** 2wks in mid-Feb.
Menton piles the yellow fruit into giant sculptures in kitsch floats – the theme in 2004 is Walt Disney.

Napoléon à Golfe-Juan
Vallauris-Golfe-Juan. **Information.** Office de Tourisme (04.93.63.82.52) **Date** 1st weekend in Mar.
The canny Corsican's landing from Elba and north-wards march is re-created in period dress, including a 400-strong Napoleonic army with horses and arms.

Christmas cheer

Winter sees residents dig deep into their larders, as Christmas takes on a distinct Provençal slant. Early in December families and churches get out their *santons*, the terracotta crib figures that feature all the trades and pastimes of rural Provence from fishwives and bakers to shepherds, as well as the Holy family. Handmade *santons* remain a big industry, especially in Marseille and Aubagne, and not just for tourists. In Arles the Salon International des Santonniers (Cloître St-Trophime, 04.90.96.47.00) gathers French *santons* and their international counterparts, and there's a Foire aux Santons in Marseille. Many villages perform La Pastorale, a ritualised staging of the announcement of Christ's birth to the shepherds.

Christmas itself is a foodie affair. Mass on Christmas Eve is preceded by a lavish dinner spread, culminating in the *Treize Desserts* that symbolise Christ and the 12 apostles: the *pompe à l'huile* (a type of biscuit made with olive oil and orange flower water), white nougat, dark nougat, *les quatre mendiants* (hazelnuts, figs, almonds, walnuts for the monastic orders), dates, prunes, mandarins, apples, pears and grapes, with local variants such as *calissons d'Aix*, melon or candied fruit.

The Rhône Delta

Introduction

A wet and wonderful land awaits you at the mouth of the Rhône. Get set for flamingos, crocodiles and a load of bull.

The River Rhône has always defined this area, bringing early prosperity from river trade, or dammed and channelled to irrigate the fertile flood plain and keep out the sea from the flat marshes of the Camargue, while the **Pont du Gard** aqueduct was an early feat of engineering bringing water across the dry limestone plateau to nourish Nîmes. But water also remains a perpetual battle: flash floods severely hit the area in the autumns of 2002 and 2003, destroying bridges in the Gard in 2002 and flooding large areas of Arles, Beaucaire and the Camargue in 2003, when a dam was breached.

The Roman past continues to mark the area. **Arles** and **Nîmes** boast some of the best preserved Roman remains in the world, so that you can really get a feel of what life in the ancient cities must have been like (and death in the extraordinarily atmospheric Les Alyscamps). Yet these two cities, despite all their tourist attractions, remain living, workaday towns with year-round populations and busy cultural programmes. At **St-Rémy-de-Provence**, the remains of Glanum present centuries of successive occupation in a glorious rural setting, yet St-Rémy itself epitomises Provençal chic with a rich Renaissance heritage, fashionable café society and memories of two famous former residents, Nostradamus and Van Gogh. Quiet **Beaucaire** and **Tarascon** point to a wealthy Provençal past, while mysterious **Aigues-Mortes** is a unique, planned city.

If the **Camargue** and the **Grande Crau** are eerie flatlands with exceptional birdlife and gigantic skies, then the jagged **Alpilles** hills, although not high, still present dramatic mountain scenery and bizarre perspectives, especially secretive **Les Baux-de-Provence**, part-medieval stronghold and part bauxite mining village, while the surrounding hills with their olive groves and vineyards hide some of France's choicest gastronomic destinations.

Pretty much everywhere in the Rhône Delta area is united by a passion for bull-fighting and gentler **Course Camargaise**, but there are also more rustic festivities, such as the Transhumance moving of flocks in St-Rémy, the garlic fair of Uzès or the Fête de la Tarasque in Tarascon, and the gypsy gathering at **Stes-Maries-de la Mer**.

Don't miss The Rhône Delta

Les Alyscamps, Arles
Fashionable Dark Ages cemetery. *See p65.*

Les Arènes
Arles (*see p66*) or Nîmes (*see p46*) for bull-fighting, Course Camargaise or a concert.

Ateliers de l'Image
St-Rémy style hotel for photo buffs, complete with a tree house. *See p56.*

Bull-fighters' haunts
Toreros' faves: Hôtel Imperator, Nîmes (*see p51*), Grand Hôtel Nord Pinus, Arles (*see p71*).

La Chasagnette
Fashionable dining in the Camargue. *See p73.*

Château des Baux
Eerie feudal eyrie of the powerful Lords of Baux. *See p59.*

Flamingos
Pink birds and sunsets to match in the Camargue. *See p72.*

Jardins de la Fontaine
18th-century garden splendour of terraces and marble nymphs in Nîmes. *See p47.*

Moulin Jean-Marie Cornille
Stock up on extra virgin olive oil. *See p59.*

Musée du Bonbon, Uzès
Sweet treat for kids. *See p52.*

Romanesque wonders
Richly carved doorways at St-Trophime, Arles (*see p66*) and St-Gilles-du-Gard (*see p72*).

Strange brews
Roman wine at the Mas de Tourelles, thyme liqueur at St-Michel de Frigolet. *See p61.*

Nîmes & the Pont du Gard

Far from resting on its (awe-inspiring) Roman laurels, Nîmes combines classical and contemporary, with the added spice of *feria*.

Dubbed the Rome of France (a title it disputes with nearby Arles), Nîmes wears its antique treasures with nonchalance and cleverly marries its wealth of architectural heritage with daring modern interventions. Its two most imposing Roman remains, the Maison Carrée and the Arènes, form part and parcel of everyday life – even the crocodile and palm tree emblem, brought here by Roman legionnaires who had previously served in Egypt, crops up everywhere, from the nickname of Nîmes football team (les Crocos) to traffic bollards and a bronze sculpture by Martial Raysse. Nîmes is also the most Spanish of the cities of the south, with its tapas bars, bullfights and late-night dining. At *feria* time, especially the Feria de Pentecôte in May, the party spirit takes over the whole town, as cafés serving paella and sangria spill out on to the pavement.

It was a Celtic tribe that first discovered the great spring – Nemausus – that gave the city its name. Such a convenient stop on the Via Domitia between Italy and Spain was bound to attract Roman attention and by 31 BC they had moved in, building roads and ramparts, a forum and a temple, the amphitheatre, baths and fountains, as well as the Pont du Gard aqueduct to supply water to the metropolis of 25,000 people.

After the collapse of the Roman empire, Nîmes declined in importance, wracked by war and religious squabbles. It has always been non-conformist, welcoming the 12th-century Cathar heretics and becoming a major centre of Protestantism in the 16th century, which saw the town heavily embroiled in the Wars of Religion. After the revocation of the Edict of Nantes in 1685, many Protestants emigrated or converted to Catholicism. The town prospered in the 17th and 18th centuries from dye-making and textiles, processing the wool and silk of the region. Its tough local cotton of white warp and blue weft – already referred to as 'denim' (de Nîmes) in London by 1695 – became a contemporary icon after Levi Strauss used it to make trousers for Californian gold-diggers.

Nîmes' dusty image took a fashionable turn in the 1980s when flamboyant right-wing mayor

Jean Bousquet, founder of the Cacharel fashion house, commissioned several ambitious projects, including a Jean Nouvel housing estate (cours Nemausus, av Général Leclerc), the Carré d'Art art museum, a Philippe Starck bus stop and works of art all over the city. Dynamism continues today – the railway station was magnificently refurbished for the arrival of the TGV in 2001, and has given impetus to a new development south of the station.

Sightseeing

The centre of Nîmes is small enough to visit on foot, with most of the sights inside the triangle, (called 'l'Ecusson' or shield, after its shape) formed by three 19th-century boulevards: Gambetta, Victor Hugo and Amiral Courbet.

Facing each other across the north end of boulevard Victor Hugo, the **Maison Carrée**, a superbly preserved Roman temple surrounded by a marble-paved open space on the site of the Roman forum, is daringly echoed by the glass and steel **Carré d'Art**, modern art museum and library, designed by Norman Foster.

To the east lies the heart of Nîmes, the partially pedestrianised old town, which is slowly being refurbished. Here shops and cafés are tucked within Romanesque arches, walls are half-stripped of modern accretions to reveal the ancient stonework beneath, and many 17th- and 18th-century mansions have been beautifully restored. Rue Nationale, on the trace of the Via Domitia, leads between the covered Halles and the **Porte Auguste**, one of the original Roman gates of the city. On rue de l'Aspic, the **Hôtel Fontfroide** has a 17th-century double spiral staircase, while there are three early Christian sarcophagi embedded in the porch of the **Hôtel Meynier de Salinelles**. On rue de Fresque look out for an intact medieval stone shopfront. The **place du Marché**, where Nîmes' corn market used to be held, is adorned with a fountain by Martial Raysse, a modern take on the crocodile tied to a palm tree theme, while on the Grand'Rue, the elegant Hôtel Rivet, now the art school, has a floor by artist Bernard Pagès. On place des Herbes stands the much-altered

Cathédrale de Notre-Dame et St-Castor.
Next door, the elegant former bishop's palace
contains the **Musée de Vieux Nîmes**, a
collection of local curiosities and decorative
arts. On boulevard Amiral Courbet, the
Muséum d'Histoire Naturelle and **Musée
d'Archéologie** are both housed in an old
Jesuit college. The adjoining chapel is used for
temporary exhibitions. West of Les Halles near
the Office du Tourisme, the **Ilot Littré**, once
the dyers' and spinners' district, has been well-
restored with cleaned 17th- and 18th-century
facades and hidden courtyards.

At the southern tip of the shield stand the
monumental **Arènes**, the beautifully preserved
Roman amphitheatre that could accommodate
20,000 visitors for gladiatorial combat or
chariot races. Today it's perfectly suited to
bullfights and concerts. If you don't agree with
the bloodshed of the full-blown Spanish-style
Feria, then try the gentler Course Camargaise

(*see p51* **Tauromania**). Nearby, the **Musée
des Cultures Taurines** gives further insights
into the art of bullfighting. The elegantly
restored **Musée des Beaux-Arts**, which has
a good collection of French, Dutch and Italian
paintings, lies a few streets south of the broad
rue de la République.

West of the city centre from place Antonin,
elegant 17th- and 18th-century patricians'
houses line the canal along Quai de la Fontaine
leading to the **Jardin de la Fontaine**, a
beautiful 18th-century formal garden. Needless
to say, this favourite local promenade contains
its fair share of ancient remains, too: on one
side, the ruined Temple de Diane; at the top of
the hill, the **Tour Magne**, a vital component of
the original pre-Roman ramparts.

Also to the north of the central triangle, in
rue de la Lampèze, is the **Castellum**, recently
discovered remnants of a Roman water tower
that was the original arrival point for the water

The Rhône Delta

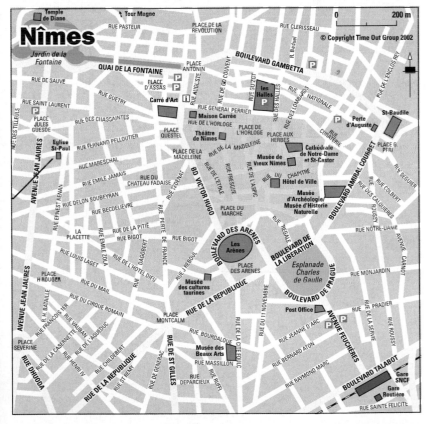

Ancient and modern: the rooftop terrace of the **Carré d'Art** museum and gallery...

supply from the Pont du Gard, distributed across the city through thick lead pipes from ten holes still visible in the basin wall.

Les Arènes

bd des Arènes (04.66.76.72.95/www.nimes.fr/ feria box office 4 rue de la Violette 04.66.02.80.80/ www.arenesdenimes.fr). **Open** *mid-Mar to mid-Oct* 9am-7pm daily. *mid-Oct to mid-Mar* 10am-5pm daily (but call ahead as the arena is closed on feria and concert days). **Admission** €4.65; €3.40 10-16s; free under-10s. **No credit cards**.

Encircled by two tiers of 60 stone arcades, this is a standard-issue Roman arena of perfect classical proportions: smaller than Arles but better preserved. The arcades surround the corridors and *vomitoria* (exits) and the great oval 'arena' (from the *arènes* or sands that were spread to soak up the blood). On the exterior look out for the small carvings of Romulus and Remus, the wrestling gladiators and two bulls' heads supporting a pediment over the main entrance on the north side. The arena is an amazing piece of engineering, constructed out of vast blocks of stone by teams of slaves. You can still sit on the original stone benches and see the podium for the president of the games and sockets for the poles that held a huge awning to shelter the crowd. For the best view, climb to the top tier of seats, traditionally reserved for slaves and women. The original games included gladiator fights, as well as slaves and criminals thrown to animals. Dogs were set on porcupines to get the blood flowing and the crowd excited. There

were also chariot races and even mock sea battles when the arena was flooded with water. After the departure of the Romans, the amphitheatre was made into a fortress. By the Middle Ages it was a huge tenement block; when it was finally cleared in the early 19th century, centuries of rubbish had added over six metres to the ground level. The first *corrida* took place in 1853. The *feria* today is a key event in the social calendar. The arena is covered in winter by a clever hi-tech glass-and-steel structure allowing it to be used for events all year round.

Carré d'Art

pl de la Maison Carrée (04.66.76.35.80/library 04.66.76.35.50/http://musees.nimes.fr). **Open** 10am-6pm Tue-Sun. **Admission** €4.70; €3.40 10-16s; free under-10s. **No credit cards**.

Opened in 1993, the Foster-designed Carré d'Art is a masterful play of transparency and space, giving a fascinating perspective of the Maison Carrée. It houses the Musée d'Art Contemporain and the Bibliothèque Carré d'Art, a vast library and media centre. The art gallery is constructed around a light-filled atrium strung with glass staircases. The museum gives an excellent representation of French art since 1960, including works by Raysse, Boltanski, Klein, Frize and Lavier, as well as arte povera and German and British currents, plus a strong line-up of temporary exhibitions (June-Sept 2004 Contre-Images; Oct-Jan Olivier Mosset). The public library also contains an important collection of early manuscripts. The chic café at the top has great views.

and, opposite, the Corinthian columns of the **Maison Carrée**.

Cathédrale de Notre-Dame et St-Castor

pl aux Herbes (04.66.67.27.72). **Open** 8.30am-6pm Mon-Sat. **Admission** free.

Nîmes' cathedral is not what it was. Although founded in 1096, like much of the town it was wrecked during the 16th-century Wars of Religion, and the current building is mainly a 19th-century reconstruction. The remains of a Romanesque frieze, sculpted with Old Testament scenes, are visible on the facade.

Jardin de la Fontaine + Tour Magne

quai de la Fontaine (04.66.67.65.56). **Open** *gardens Apr to mid-Sept* 7.30am-10pm daily; *mid-Sept to Mar* 7.30am-7pm daily. *Tour Magne* 9am-7pm (July, Aug until 10pm). **Admission** *gardens* free; *Tour Magne* €2.40; €1.90 10-18s; free under-10s. **No credit cards.**

The spring that bubbles up at the heart of these lovely gardens was the reason the Romans named the city Nemausus after the Roman river-god. In the 18th century, formal gardens were laid out by Jacques Philippe Mareschal, director of fortifications for Languedoc. They provided a complex system of reservoirs and distribution of the clean water that was sadly lacking after the Pont du Gard aqueduct was abandoned. Now the canals and still green pools, with balustraded stone terraces and marble nymphs and cupids, provide a retreat from the summer heat. On one side stand the ruins of the so-called Temple of Diana, part of the Roman sanctuary whose function remains uncertain. Behind the canals, terraces and footpaths climb up the hill. High up Mont Cavalier on the edge of the garden, the octagonal Tour Magne was part of Nîmes' pre-Roman ramparts. Its viewing platform 140 steps up provides a good view over the city, the garrigue landscape and Les Alpilles.

Maison Carrée

pl de la Maison Carrée (04.66.36.26.76). **Open** *Apr-Sept* 9am-7pm daily. *Oct-Mar* 10am-5pm daily. **Admission** free.

Not *carré* (square) at all but rectangular, this astonishingly well-preserved Roman temple was built in the first century BC and dedicated to Augustus' deified grandsons. With a great flight of stone steps leading up to finely fluted Corinthian columns adorned with a sculpted frieze of acanthus leaves, it has always inspired hyperbole. Arthur Young, an 18th-century British traveller, called it 'the most light, elegant and pleasing building I have ever beheld', and Thomas Jefferson, after failing to import it to America, had it copied as the model for the Virginia state capitol. It has remained in almost constant use, its functions ranging from legislative seat to tomb, church to stables to fine art museum. Today it contains drawings and photos relating to similar temples around Roman Gaul and a splendid fresco, only unearthed in 1992 when the Carré d'Art was being built. Against a blood-red background sits a mythical hunter surrounded by a border of pagan frolics, most discernibly Cassandra being dragged by her hair, and two louche-looking dwarves. Lovely as it is, the temple could do with a clean-up, and suffers from constant traffic pollution.

Musée d'Archéologie & Muséum d'Histoire Naturelle

13bis bd Amiral Courbet (04.66.76.74.54/ http://musees.nimes.fr). **Open** 10am-6pm Tue-Sun. **Admission** €4.45; €3.20 10-16s; free under-10s. **No credit cards**.

Housed in the old Jesuit college, the archaeology museum has a magnificent collection of Roman statues, sarcophagi, entablatures, coins, mosaics and some gorgeous Roman glass. Pottery includes a rare pre-Roman statue, the Warrior of Grezan. Upstairs is a treasure trove of everyday items, from oil lamps to kitchen equipment, tools and cosmetic jars. The natural history museum includes some important Iron Age menhirs, a good anthropological collection and plenty of stuffed bears, tigers and crocodiles.

Musée des Beaux-Arts

rue Cité Foulc (04.66.67.38.21/http://musees.nimes.fr). **Open** 10am-6pm Tue-Sun. **Admission** €4.45; €3.20 10-16s; free under-10s. **No credit cards**.

The imposing facade of this early 20th-century building leads straight into a beautiful restoration by architect Jean-Michel Wilmotte. Seven paintings illustrating the story of Anthony and Cleopatra by Nîmes-born 18th-century painter Natoire hang in the skylit central atrium around the Roman mosaic *The Marriage of Admetus*. Elsewhere the eclectic collection includes Jacopo Bassano's *Susanna and the Elders*, Rubens' *Portrait of a Monk* and the *Mystic Marriage of St Catherine* by Giambono.

Musée des Cultures Taurines

6 rue Alexandre Ducros (04.66.36.83.77/ http://musees.nimes.fr). **Open** 10am-6pm Tue-Sun. **Admission** (with Musée de Vieux Nîmes) €5.55; €3.30 10-16s; free under-10s. **No credit cards**.

Further your knowledge of bull-fighting culture at this new museum not far from the Arènes. The collection goes from torreadors' costumes and bull-fighting posters to eight plates designed by Picasso.

Musée de Vieux Nîmes

pl aux Herbes (04.66.76.73.70/http://musees.nimes.fr). **Open** 11am-6pm Tue-Sun. **Admission** (with Musée des Cultures Taurines) €5.55; €3.30 10-16s; free under-10s. **No credit cards**.

This museum, housed in the 17th-century bishop's palace, was established in 1920 to preserve the tools of local industries and artefacts of regional life. The collection, much of it displayed as reconstructed interiors, comprises furniture, pottery and fabrics including some early denim, shawls and silks.

Arts & entertainment

For local entertainment listings, pick up the freebies *Nîmescope* and regional *César* or check out www.sortiranimes.com.

Le Sémaphore

25 rue Porte de France (04.66.67.88.04). **Tickets** €5.50; €4.60 12-25s; €3.50 under-12s. **Credit** MC, V.

The Roman **Arènes** in all their splendour. *See p46.*

Le Sémaf, as it is affectionately known, offers an excellent programme of original-language (*version originale*) films and themed weeks.

Théâtre de l'Armature

12 rue de l'Ancien Vélodrome (04.66.29.98.66/ www.larmature.org). **Box office** 9am-noon, 2-6pm Mon-Fri. **Shows** 9pm Thur-Sat. **Tickets** €6-€9. **No credit cards.**

This alternative theatre acts as a showcase for touring companies, staging works by contemporary writers such as Philippe Minyana.

Théâtre de Nîmes

1 pl de la Calade (04.66.36.65.00/box office 04.66.36.65.10). **Box office** 11am-1pm, 2-6pm Tue-Fri; 2-6pm Sat. **Shows** 8.30pm Tue-Sat; 6pm Sun. **Tickets** €6-€30. **Credit** AmEx, DC, MC, V.

This pretty vintage theatre is now in the hands of Macha Makeieff and Jérôme Deschamps, creators of the hilarious Deschiens clan. It also hosts opera, dance and short runs by top visiting directors, such as Peter Brook, Julie Brochen and Stanislas Nordey.

Restaurants

See also p51, **Hôtel Imperator**.

Le Chapon-Fin

3 rue du Château Fadaise (04.66.67.34.73). **Open** noon-2.30pm, 7.30-10.30pm Mon-Fri; 7.30-10.30pm Sat. Closed Aug. **Average** €30. **Credit** AmEx, DC, MC, V.

This Nîmois institution has walls cluttered with old Bardot posters and paintings by grateful clients. Food is warming and generous, ranging from local *brandade* to cassoulet and Alsatian *choucroute*.

L'Esclafidou

7 rue Xavier Sigalon (04.66.21.28.49). **Open** noon-2pm, 7.30-10pm Tue-Sat. **Menus** €14-€19. **Credit** AmEx, MC, V.

A charming restaurant with a shady summer terrace on a square. The Provençal cuisine includes fish and salads, with lashings of olive oil, garlic and spices.

La Fontaine du Temple

22 rue de la Curaterie (04.66.21.21.13). **Open** noon-2pm, 7-11pm Mon-Sat. Closed last wk of Aug. **Average** €25. **Credit** AmEx, DC, MC, V.

This neighbourhood restaurant and bar serves local specialities like *taureau* with anchovy sauce, lamb with thyme, *brandade* with lobster sauce and snails.

La Grande Bourse

2 bd des Arènes (04.66.36.12.12). **Open** noon-midnight daily. **Menus** €10.50-€17. **Credit** MC, V.

This celebrated café-brasserie was recently repainted in Pompeian red and gold and has a terrace overlooking the arena. Brasserie dishes include *taureau* steaks and squid provençale. Service can be slow.

Le Jardin d'Hadrien

11 rue de l'Enclos de Rey (04.66.22.07.01). **Open** *July, Aug* noon-2pm, 7.30-10pm Mon-Sat (dinner only Mon, Wed). *Sept-June* noon-2pm, 7.30-10pm daily (lunch only Tue, Sun). **Menus** €18-€24. **Credit** AmEx, MC, V.

Sitting under the plane trees behind this dignified 19th-century house is restful after battling the throngs around the arena. Chef Alain Vinouze prepares seasonal dishes with a local bent, such as *brandade* and roast pigeon with olives.

Lisita

2 bd des Arènes (04.66.67.29.15). **Open** noon-2pm, 8-10pm Tue-Sat. **Menus** €26-€39. **Credit** AmEx, DC, MC, V.

Chef Olivier Douet's stylish restaurant (not related to the hotel upstairs) is a hit, with his modern, market-inspired southern cooking. Sit in the colourful dining rooms, the outdoor summer courtyard or on the veranda which overlooks the arena.

Magister

5 rue Nationale (04.66.76.11.00). **Open** 7.30-9.30pm Mon, Sat; noon-2pm, 7.30-9.30pm Tue-Fri. Closed July. **Menus** €30-€45. **Credit** AmEx, MC, V.

One of Nîmes' top restaurants for smooth service and perfectly judged cooking. Try the *brandade*, stuffed pigeon or lamb braised in red wine with mint. The wine list offers the best of local vintages.

Restaurant Nicolas

1 rue Poise (04.66.67.50.47). **Open** noon-2pm, 7-10.30pm Tue-Fri, Sun; 7.30pm Sat. **Menus** €12.50-€21. **Credit** DC, MC, V.

One of the few places in Nîmes open on a Sunday, this friendly, family-run establishment next to the Musée Archéologique has exposed stone walls, sleek lighting, all the requisite bullfighting photos and generously served home cooking.

Vintage Café

7 rue de Bernis (04.66.21.04.45). **Open** noon-2pm, 8-10pm Tue-Thur; noon-2pm, 8-10.30pm Fri; 8-10pm Sat. **Menus** €14-€24.10. **Credit** MC, V.

This friendly bistro, adorned with colourful paintings, is tucked into a quiet corner of the old town. Try the oysters in anchovy *jus* or Camargue bull steak.

Wine Bar chez Michel

11 sq de la Couronne (04.66.76.19.59/ www.winebarchezmichel.com). **Open** 7pm-midnight Mon, Sat; noon-2pm, 7pm-midnight Tue-Fri. **Menus** €12-€20. **Credit** AmEx, DC, MC, V.

Local wines are the norm round here, so this is a rare chance to eat and sample wines from France and beyond. Despite the 60s steakhouse decor, the food – fish, shellfish and beef – is reliably fresh.

Bars, cafés & nightlife

La Bodeguita

3 bd Alphonse Daudet (04.66.58.28.27). **Open** noon-2.30pm, 5.30pm-midnight Mon-Sat. **No credit cards.** The tapas bar of the Royal Hôtel has a terrace, and serves tapas (€3-€15), lunchtime *plats* and wine, both local and Spanish, by the glass. There are themed flamenco, tango, jazz and poetry evenings.

Le Café Olive

22 bd Victor Hugo (04.66.67.89.10). **Open** 9am-1am
Mon-Sat. **Credit** MC, V.
Old stone and contemporary furniture meet in this
renovated café which offers pan-Mediterranean cuisine, margaritas and evening concerts and revues.

La Casa Don Miguel

18 rue de l'Horloge (04.66.76.07.09). **Open** 11am-
3pm, 6pm-1am daily (Oct-Apr closed Mon). **Average**
€12. **Credit** AmEx, MC, V.
Lurking under low brick vaults, this buzzing tapas
bar serves good food, both hot and cold (tapas
around €4 each), plus live music (flamenco, jazz,
world, folk) on Friday and Saturday evenings.

Gilbert Courtois

8 pl du Marché (04.66.67.20.09). **Open** *July, Aug*
8am-midnight daily. *Sept-June* 8am-7.30pm daily.
Credit AmEx, MC, V.
This *belle époque* café with comfortable terrace is a
Nîmes institution for tea, coffee, hot chocolate and
cakes. Simple meals are also available.

Haddock Café

13 rue de l'Agau (04.66.67.86.57). **Open** 11am-3pm,
7pm-1am Mon-Fri; 7pm-1am Sat. **Credit** AmEx, MC, V.
This popular café serves food until late (menus
€12.50-€18.50) and has a busy agenda of live music
and debates.

O'Flaherty's

2 bd Amiral Courbet (04.66.67.22.63). **Open** 11am-
2am Mon-Fri; 5pm-2am Sat, Sun. **Credit** AmEx, DC,
MC, V.
This popular Irish pub draws throngs for whisky
and Guinness, plus free live music on Thursday.

Lulu Club

10 impasse de la Curaterie (04.66.36.28.20). **Open**
11pm-late Tue-Sun. **No credit cards.**
Lulu is a long-standing gay bar and disco, where
straights are also welcome.

Le Mazurier

9 bd Amiral Courbet (04.66.67.27.48). **Open** 7am-
midnight daily. **Credit** MC, V.
Take advantage of this good old-fashioned *belle
époque* brasserie for leisurely morning coffee over a
newspaper on the terrace, or a *pastis* at the zinc bar.

Le Pelican

54 rte de Beaucaire (04.66.29.63.28). **Open** 6.30pm-
2am Tue-Sun. **No credit cards.**
Recently opened venue offering music from jazz to
cajun and food from Languedoc to Louisiana.

Shopping

The best shopping is in the old town where,
amid the expected rash of chain stores, you can
still find splendid local stores and produce. For
food, the covered market of **Les Halles** (rue
des Halles, 7am-1pm daily) can't be beat (Daniel

Pause for contemplation beside the **Arènes**.

for olives, Durand for *brandade*). There is also a
flea market Mondays on boulevard Jean Jaurès.
F Nadal (7 rue St-Castor, 04.66.67.35.42) is a
tiny shop selling olive oil from vats, handmade
soaps, herbs, honey, coffee, spices and jars of
brandade. **L'Huilerie** (10 rue des Marchands,
04.66.67.37.24, closed Mon) has spices, herbs,
tisanes and beautifully packaged honeys,
mustards and olive oil. Long-established
boulangerie-pâtisserie **Villaret** (13 rue de la
Madeleine, 04.66.67.41.79, closed Sun) is the
place to buy Nîmes other speciality, jaw-
breaking *croquants*. For regional wines, visit
the **Espace Costières** (19 pl Aristide Briand,
04.66.36.96.20, closed Sat, Sun).

Although it has now delocalised, fashion
group **Cacharel** (2 pl de la Maison Carrée,
04.66.21.82.82, closed Sun) was founded in
Nîmes by former mayor Jean Bousquet and still
has a smart showcase facing the Maison Carrée.

Streets near the arena abound in bullfighting
memorabilia, some of it tack, from full regalia to
vintage prints. **Marie Sara Création** (40 bis
rue de la Madeleine, 04.66.21.18.40, closed Mon,
Sun) is the place to buy your complete toreador
outfit. Marie Sara was famous in her day as a
bullfighter. **L'Oeil du Taureau** (4 rue
Fresque, 04.66.21.53.28, closed Mon, Sun) is a
good second-hand bookshop. If too many
southern prints are getting you down, check out

the cool contemporary furniture from Cassina, Kartell et al at Philippe Starck-designed **RBC Nîmes** (1 pl de la Salamandre, 04.66.67.62.22, closed Sun), or the well-chosen mix of ethnic and funky furniture, ceramics and decorative items at **Galerie Béa** (4 pl d'Assas, 04.66.21.19.34, closed Sun).

Where to stay

Acanthe du Temple Hôtel

1 rue Charles Babut (04.66.67.54.61/www.hotel-du-temple.com). **Double** €32-€60. **Credit** MC, V.
The fussy decoration isn't for all tastes (shame they crazy-paved the stairwell), but it's spotlessly clean, friendly and well placed.

Hôtel de l'Amphithéâtre

4 rue des Arènes (04.66.67.28.51). Closed Jan.
Double €39-€64. **Credit** AmEx, MC, V.
Surprisingly smart for the price, this well restored 18th-century building has a lovely staircase, antique furniture and large, white-tiled bathrooms.

Hôtel Imperator

quai de la Fontaine (04.66.21.90.30/www.hotel-imperator.com). **Double** €99-€183. **Credit** AmEx, DC, MC, V.
Nîmes' top hotel is smart but unstuffy and a favourite rendezvous for toreadors and their entourages. It has a lovely garden, 1930s lift and luxurious, air-conditioned rooms. Its gourmet restaurant, L'Enclos de la Fontaine serves specialities like fish *escabèche* or lacquered duck with peaches.

Hôtel de la Mairie

11 rue des Greffes (04.66.67.65.91). **Double** €30-€45. **Credit** AmEx, MC, V.
This budget hotel is very simple but friendly and the maze-like old building has undeniable charm; cheaper rooms don't have bathrooms.

New Hôtel la Baume

21 rue Nationale (04.66.76.28.42/www.new-hotel.com). **Double** €120. **Credit** AmEx, DC, MC, V.
A 17th-century mansion with a beautiful stone staircase. Rooms are spacious and well decorated, and bathrooms are smart. There is also a restaurant.

L'Orangerie

755 rue de la Tour Évêque (04.66.84.50.57/www.orangerie.fr). **Double** €62-€115. **Credit** AmEx, DC, MC, V.
This charming hotel just beyond the centre has a garden, small pool, gym and good restaurant (menus €13-€49). Some rooms have private terraces.

Le Royal Hôtel

3 bd Alphonse Daudet (04.66.58.28.27). **Double** €60-€85. **Credit** AmEx, DC, MC, V.
This fashionable little hotel is studiously casual with artfully distressed walls, a palm-filled lobby, leather club chairs and friendly proprietors. Rooms vary in size but all are light and tasteful.

Resources

Hospital

Hôpital Caremeau, 246 chemin du Carreau de Lanes.

Internet

Netgame, 25 rue de l'Horloge (04.66.36.36.16).
Open 10am-11pm daily.

Police station

1 av Feuchères (04.66.28.33.00).

Post office

1 bd de Bruxelles (04.66.76.69.50).

Tourist information

Office de Tourisme, 6 rue Auguste, 30000 Nîmes (04.66.58 38.00/www.ot-nimes.fr). **Open** *July, Aug* 8am-8pm Mon-Fri; 9am 7pm Sat; 10am-6pm Sun. *Sept-June* 8.30am-7pm Mon-Fri, 9am-7pm Sat, 10am-6pm Sun.

Tauromania

If you're not into the full blood-and-guts drama of Spanish-style *corrida* but still want to see the Arènes in action, then go for the gentler Course Camargaise, held periodically – often in the week before *feria* (tickets can be bought on the door). Somewhere between comedy and a test of agility, Course Camargaise pits the small, black Camargue bulls against nimble white-clad *raseteurs* who try to grab the *cocardes*, rosettes and other 'attributes' hung from the bull's lyre-shaped horns and forehead. Course Camargaise has an honourable history in the area. Early games, using all sorts of animals from lions to dogs to fight bulls, were recorded in 1402 in Arles, before being codified in the 19th century into the less violent entertainment enjoyed today. A typical spectacle starts with a parade of Arlésiennes (women dressed in the traditional long skirts and shawls of Arles), then the *capelado*, the parade of *raseteurs* to the inevitable toreadors' march from *Carmen*. When the bull is released into the ring, *tourneurs* distract the bull and get him into a good position to charge; the *raseteurs* begin to run, followed by the bull, and attempt to grab the attributes, leaping over the barriers in the nick of time to avoid being spiked by the sharp horns. The most dangerous Course Camargaise usually gets is when a bull tosses away the ringside and charges round the outer passageway, to the alarm of nearby spectators.

North of Nîmes

Pont du Gard

'As I humbled myself, suddenly something lifted up my spirits, and I cried out, "Why am I not a Roman?"' First-time visitors to the extraordinary triple-decker aqueduct of Pont du Gard – the highest the Romans ever built – are wont to come over all rhapsodic, just like Jean-Jacques Rousseau. What is more astonishing still is that the limestone arches, rising to a height of 49m, have resisted both the erosion of time and the interference of man.

The aqueduct originally carried drinking water from the springs at the Fontaine d'Eure in Uzès across the Gardon river to Nîmes, along a 50km route, much of it through underground channels dug out of solid rock. Fragments of water channels and lost aqueduct arches still litter the entire area and the trail has recently been clearly signposted.

The bridge itself is built from gigantic blocks of stone, some weighing as much as six tons, which were hauled into place by pulleys, wheels... and huge numbers of slaves. It was built with a slight bow to enable it to withstand great water pressure; during devastating floods in 1988 and 2002, the Pont du Gard stood firm while several other bridges collapsed. Although walking across the bridge is now forbidden, you can get up next to it on the 18th-century bridge built alongside. There is a little beach where you can swim, and canoes can be hired (Kayak Vert, 04.66.22.84.83, open Apr-Oct, €17-€36).

In an attempt to capitalise on the millions of people who visit the bridge (for free) each year, the **Public Information Centre** was opened in 2001, providing a film and exhibition and a 600m² interactive space for children.

Public Information Centre

Concession Pont du Gard, Vers-Pont-du-Gard (04.66.37.50.99). **Open** *May-Sept* 9.30am-6pm daily. *Oct-Apr* 10am-5pm daily. Closed Jan. Film in English 3pm daily. *Car park* 7am-1am daily. **Admission** €10; €9 6-21s; free under-6s. **Credit** MC, V.

Uzès & the Gardon

Charming, Italiante **Uzès** is often dubbed the Tuscany of France. Beautifully restored since being designated a *ville d'art* in 1962, the restored local pale, soft limestone has already taken on a time-worn look, making Uzès a favourite location for historical films such as *Cyrano de Bergerac*. Its revival of fortunes is seen in a proliferation of antique shops and restaurants. Uzès offers a variety of colourful festivals ranging from a truffle day in January and garlic fest on 24 June, via summer wine, dance and Baroque music, to the national day of the donkeys of Provence on 13 October.

A powerful medieval bishopric and later a major centre of Protestantism, Uzès prospered in the 17th and 18th centuries from linen, serge and silk. It was also an important ducal seat and still calls itself the first duchy of France.

Within the ring of boulevards along the former ramparts, the arcaded **place aux Herbes** sums up Uzès, coming alive for the market (Wed morning, all Sat), which is a great source of olives, baskets, Provençal fabric and pottery. Behind here a web of small streets and squares leads through to the **Duché d'Uzès**, where the duke lives on, Republicanism notwithstanding. A guided tour includes a visit to the dungeons, complete with hologram ghost. Beyond the ramparts on a promenade offering views of the surrounding countryside, the 17th-century **Cathédrale St-Théodorit** (open 9am-6pm Mon-Sat) contains a superb 18th-century organ. The earlier **Tour Fenestrelle**, an arcaded round bell tower reminiscent of Pisa, is the only part of the Romanesque cathedral to survive the Wars of Religion (it made a handy watchtower). Next door, the late 17th-century bishop's palace houses the **Musée Georges Borias** with local pottery and paintings, as well as a tribute to novelist André Gide, who was born here in 1869. Take a look also at the elegant neo-classical Hôtel du Baron de Castille on place de l'Evêché, now an antiques shop. In impasse Port Royal, the **Jardin Medieval** contains a remarkable collection of carefully labelled local plants and medicinal and culinary herbs. The recently excavated **Fontaine d'Eure**, the spring which originally carried water to Nîmes via the Pont du Gard, is a short walk from Uzès town centre (take chemin André Gide out of town to the Vallée de l'Alzon). At Pont des Charettes, 1km south of Uzès, the **Musée du Bonbon**, belonging to sweet manufacturer Haribo, is a nostalgia trip for adults and sheer sticky heaven for kids.

Between Uzès and Nîmes, the **Gorges du Gardon** are the most spectacular of a series of deep river gorges; they are visible from Pont St-Nicolas on the D979, where a fine, seven-arched medieval bridge spans the chasm. To walk along them, detour through Poulx, taking the D135 then the D127, to pick up the GR6 footpath through the depths; at the north-east end, the village of **Collias** provides wonderful views.

The area is famous for its fine white clay; **St-Quentin-la-Poterie**, north of Uzès, is a must for pottery junkies. Over the centuries it churned out amphorae, roof tiles and bricks by the ton.

Pont du Gard.

The last large-scale factory closed down in 1974, but craft potters have returned; their work, often in the local green or blue glazes, can be seen in the Galerie Terra Viva adjoining the **Musée de la Poterie Méditerranéenne**. The village is a delight, its crumbling ochre houses with loggias and carved columns festooned with washing.

Duché d'Uzès
pl de Duché, Uzès (04.66.22.18.96). **Open** *June-Aug* 10am-1pm, 2-6.30pm daily. *Sept-May* 10am-noon, 2-6pm daily. **Admission** €11; €8 students, 12-16s; €4 7-11s; free under-7s. **No credit cards**.

Jardin Medieval
impasse Port Royal, off rue Port Royal, Uzès (04.66.22.38.21). **Open** *Apr-June, Sept* 2-6pm Mon-Fri; 10.30am-12.30pm, 2-6pm Sat, Sun. *July, Aug* 10.30am-12.30pm, 2-6pm daily. *Oct* 2-5pm daily. Closed Nov-Mar. **Admission** €2; free under-16s. **No credit cards**.

Musée du Bonbon
Pont des Charettes (04.66.22.74.39/www.haribo.com). **Open** *July-Sept* 10am-7pm daily. *Oct-June* 10am-1pm, 2-6pm Tue-Sun. Closed 3wks Jan. **Admission** €4; €3 students; €2 5-15s; free under-5s. **No credit cards**.

Musée de la Poterie Méditerranéenne
6 rue de la Fontaine, St-Quentin-la-Poterie (04.66.03.65.86/www.musee-poterie-mediterranee.com). **Open** *Apr-June, Oct-Dec* 2-6pm Wed-Sun. *July-Sept* 10am-1pm, 3-7pm daily. **Admission** €3; €2.30 students, 12-18s; free under-12s. **No credit cards**.

Musée Georges Borias
Palais de l'Evêché, pl de l'Evêché, Uzès (04.66.22.40.23). **Open** *Feb, Nov, Dec* 2-5pm Tue-Sun. *Mar-June* 5-6pm Tue-Sun. *July, Aug* 10am-noon, 3-6pm Tue-Sun. *Sept, Oct* 3-6pm Tue-Sun. Closed Jan. **Admission** €2; €1 students, 5-15s; free under-5s. **No credit cards**.

Where to stay & eat

In Uzès, family-run **La Taverne** (9 rue Sigalon, 04.66.22.47.08, www.lataverne.uzes.fr, closed end Nov, menus €20-€27) does a refined, modern take on regional cuisine, and has a simple, but tasteful air-conditioned hotel across the street (No.4, 04.66.22.13.10, double €52-€57). The **Hôtel du Général d'Entraigues** (pl de l'Evêché, 04.66.22.32.68, www.lcm.fr/savry, double €55-€122) mixes antiques and modern in a 15th-century building and has a swimming pool unnervingly suspended over the dining room (menus €22-€49).

In Arpaillargues, 4km from Uzès, **Château d'Arpaillargues** (Hôtel Marie d'Agoult, 04.66.22.14.48, closed Nov-Mar, double €76-€229) has gardens, pool, tennis courts and barbecues in summer (menus €26-€40). In Collias, the **Hostellerie le Castellas** (Grande

Rue, 04.66.22.88.88, www.lecastellas.fr, closed Jan & Feb, double €72-€187, menus €43-€60) consists of several houses converted into a hotel, with palmy garden, pool and restaurant. The acclaimed **Table d'Horloge** (pl de l'Horloge, 04.66.22.07.01, closed lunch July-Sept, Wed & Thur Sept-June and all Feb, menu €40) in St-Quentin-la-Poterie has a weekly-changing market menu. In St-Maximum, **Château de St-Maximum** (rue du Château, 04.66.03.44.16, www.chateaustmaximin.com, double €145-€230) is a stylish B&B in a galleried Renaissance château where Racine sometimes stayed.

Resources

Market day in Uzès is Wednesday morning and all day Saturday, in St-Quentin Friday morning.

Tourist information
St-Quentin-la-Poterie *Office Culturel, Maison de la Terre, rue de la Fontaine, 30700 St-Quentin-la-Poterie (04.66.22.74.38)*. **Open** 9am-noon, 2-5pm Mon, Tue, Thur, Fri.
Uzès *Office de Tourisme, Chapelle des Capucins, pl Albert 1er, 30700 Uzès (04.66.22.68.88/www.ville-uzes.fr)*. **Open** *June-Sept* 9am-6pm Mon-Fri; 10am-1pm, 2-5pm Sat, Sun. *Oct-May* 9am-noon, 1.30-6pm Mon-Fri; 10am-1pm Sat.

Getting there & around

By air
Aéroport de Nîmes-Arles-Camargue (04.66.70.49 49) is 10km SE of Nîmes. A shuttle bus links the airport to the town centre and train station (€4.30).

By car
For Nîmes coming S from Lyon/Orange or NE from Montpellier, take A9 autoroute, exit no.50. West from Arles: A54 autoroute, exit no.1. For Uzès, take the D979 from Nîmes. Pont du Gard is 14km SE of Uzès on the D981, 20km NE of Nîmes on the N86 (take the Remoulins exit from the A9); from Avignon take the N100 then the D19.

By train/bus
Nîmes is on the Paris-Avignon-Montpellier line, with TGV direct to Paris in around 3hrs. Nîmes *gare routière* is just behind the train station. **STD Gard** (04.66.29.27.29) runs several buses a day Mon-Sat between Nîmes and Avignon and Nîmes and Uzès (some Uzès buses stop at Remoulins for the Pont du Gard and a few continue to St-Quentin-la-Poterie), plus 3 buses daily to Avignon via Remoulins for the Pont du Gard (none Sun) and 3 buses between Uzès and Avignon. **Cars de Camargue** (04.90.96.36.25) runs a service between Nîmes and Arles, four a day Mon-Sat, two on Sun.

Though all the main sights in Nîmes are walkable, **TCN** (04.66.38.15.40) runs the useful little La Citadine bus, which runs in a loop from the station passing many of the principal sights. Individual tickets cost €0.36 and are valid 30mins.

St-Rémy & Les Alpilles

The craggy Alpilles hills provide a surreal backdrop to super-chic St-Rémy, an improbable feudal fortress and France's only designer hay.

In the triangle created by the Rhône and Durance rivers south of Avignon, the mysterious Alpilles hills harbour some of Provence's most fashionable destinations.

St-Rémy-de-Provence

Stylish (too stylish?) St-Rémy-de-Provence sits in a dramatic setting at the foot of the jagged Alpilles hills. Birthplace of Nostradamus (1503-66) and home to Van Gogh in 1889-90, today St-Rémy is a bolthole for many of Paris' creative elite, which has earned it a reputation as the St-Germain-des-Prés of the south.

Circular boulevards Victor Hugo, Marceau, Mirabeau and Gambetta, following the old ramparts, are the liveliest part of town, shaded by plane trees and crammed with cafés, restaurants and boutiques. Watch the parade of soigné Parisians dressed for *la vie campagnarde* from the terrace of the Café des Arts (30 bd

St-Rémy-de-Provence: mind your head.

Victor Hugo), open since the 1950s and a favourite with the *pastis*-swilling in-crowd. At 8 boulevard Mirabeau, estate agent to the stars Emile Garcin (04.90.92.01.58) is anxious to sell only to those he feels will respect the 'soul' of the region, and is capable of freezing dubious candidates out of his office. If it's the aromas of Provence that draw you, follow your nose to the **Musée des Arômes et des Parfums**. Here you'll find antique perfume stills and all kinds of heady potions made from essential oils.

On boulevard Marceau, the august **Collégiale St-Martin** church was rebuilt in 1820 after the original structure caved in, and has a renowned 5,000-pipe modern organ, used for concerts each summer. Follow the street to the right of the church into the old town, where narrow streets, squares with burbling fountains and Renaissance *hôtels particuliers* give a sense of St-Rémy's illustrious past. Nostradamus was born on rue Hoche. On place Favier, the 15th-century Hôtel de Sade, built during the Renaissance on the site of Roman baths, was the family mansion of the Marquis de Sade; today it's the **Musée Archéologique**, showing fragments found at Glanum (*see p56* **Glanum and Les Antiques**). Most distinctive are the pre-Roman sculptures, and a stone lintel with hollows carved to hold the severed heads of enemies. Across the square, the **Musée des Alpilles Pierre-de-Brun** (closed for renovation until summer 2004) presents furniture, clothing, documents and objects from a long-gone Provence in a handsome, 16th-century galleried courtyard house, once the home of the Mistral de Mondragon family. The 18th-century Hôtel Estrine is now the **Centre d'Art Présence Van Gogh** and has many reproductions of Van Gogh's work, along with letters from Vincent to his brother Théo and exhibitions of contemporary art.

For a year from May 1889 Van Gogh was cared for by nuns in the psychiatric asylum adjoining the pretty **Monastère St-Paul-de-Mausole**, just south of the town, which has a Romanesque chapel and a cloister, where there is a permanent exhibition of art brut produced by mental patients at the hospital. During his stay, Van Gogh produced more than 150 paintings, including *Olive Groves* and *Starry Night*. Just past here, you come upon St-Rémy's impressive archaeological sites Les Antiques and Glanum (*see below*). Normally this would be an excuse for a pleasant country stroll but, given the speed of the traffic hurtling past, prepare for a dusty 15-minute sprint.

Centre d'Art Présence Van Gogh

Hôtel Estrine, 8 rue Estrine (04.90.92.34.72). **Open** 10.30am-12.30pm, 2.30-6.30pm Tue-Sun. Closed Jan-Mar. **Admission** €3.20; €2.30 students; free under-12s. **No credit cards.**

Monastère St-Paul de Mausole

Centre d'Art Valetudo, Maison de Santé St-Paul (04.90.92.77.00). **Open** *Apr-Oct* 9.15am-7pm daily. *Nov-Mar* 10.15am-4.45pm daily. **Admission** €3.40; €2.40 students; free under-16s. **No credit cards.**

Musée des Alpilles Pierre-de-Brun

Hôtel Mistral de Mondragon, 1 pl Favier (04.90.92.70.14). **Open** reopening summer 2004.

Apr-Sept 10am-6pm Tue-Sun. *Oct-Mar* 10am-5pm Tue-Sun. **Admission** €3; €2 students; free under-18s, all 1st Sun of mth. **No credit cards.**

Musée Archéologique

Hôtel de Sade, rue du Parage, (04.90.92.64.04). **Open** *July-Aug* 11am-6pm daily. *Sept-Apr* 11am-5pm Tue-Sun. **Admission** €2.50; free under-18s. **No credit cards.**

Musée des Arômes et des Parfums

34 bd Mirabeau (04.90.92.48.70). **Open** *Apr to mid-Sept* 10am-12.30pm, 2.30-7pm Mon-Sat. Closed mid-Sept to Mar. **Admission** free.

Where to stay & eat

The talk of St-Rémy in terms of lodgings is the new wing of the **Hôtel Les Ateliers de l'Image** (traverse de Borry, 5 av Pasteur,

Glanum and Les Antiques

The fascinating mishmash of remains at Glanum and Les Antiques is one of the most impressive traces of the Roman presence in Provence. Sitting in a field on the southern edge of St-Rémy, Les Antiques consists of a wonderfully preserved mausoleum (*pictured*), carved with lively reliefs, put up in tribute (some experts believe) to the grandsons of Augustus, and a Roman triumphal arch that once marked the entrance to Glanum – superimposed layers of Celtic, Greek and Roman city, long buried under river silt until excavations began in the 1920s.

The sheer extent of the ruins of Glanum (entrance just up the road from Les Antiques) gives a sense of the urban buzz that reigned here in ancient Gaul. Glanum began as a pilgrimage site with a sanctuary visited by the Glaniques, a Celtic-Ligurian people, in the fifth and sixth centuries BC. The ancient Greek masonry style of many of the oldest buildings – huge blocks of precisely cut stone fitted without mortar – indicates contact with the Hellenistic world during the second century BC, but Glanum really grew after the Roman legions occupied Provence in 49 BC, building forum, basilica, public baths and theatre. Models and plans (and a visit to the Musée Archéologique) help make sense of the visit, as do some facsimile temple columns.

The south end of the site is like a corner of ancient Greece, all white limestone rocks and olive trees; you can see the sacred spring and sanctuary of the original settlers, with a deep water basin from the second century BC. The

central area is the most complex, dominated by Roman temples. The site's surprisingly good café-restaurant La Taverna Romana (open lunch May-Sept) serves tasty dishes inspired by ancient Roman food.

Glanum

rte des Baux (04.90.92.23.79). **Open** *Apr-Aug* 9am-7pm daily. *Sept-Mar* 10.30am-5pm Tue-Sun. **Admission** €6.10; €4.10 18-25s, students; free under-18s. **Credit** MC, V.

04.90.92.51.50, www.hotelphoto.com, closed Jan-Feb, double €150-€600, menus €15-€69). To his existing hotel in an old cinema, young but deep-pocketed Lyonnais photographer Antoine Godard has created this annexe from the legendary Hôtel de Provence and has invented a surprising but pleasant hybrid of Scandinavia and Provence. For a splurge, reserve the tree-house suite which has a private tree house. The garden, with two swimming pools, was done by Godard's landscape-architect wife. In the restaurant Chez L'Ami, Japanese chef Masao Ikeda sends out dishes like leek soup with langoustine gyoza and soy-lacquered lamb with Japanese aubergines. There are also photo exhibitions and courses and a cocktail bar.

Le Castelet des Alpilles (6 pl Mireille, 04.90.92.07.21, closed Nov-Mar, double €36.60-€78.50) is rustic but comfortable, with rooms looking on to a garden. Another simple but welcoming option is the Hôtel du Cheval Blanc (6 av Fauconnet, 04.90.92.09.28, closed mid-Nov to Mar, double €40-€46) in the heart of town, where Mme Maguy Ramon has been welcoming guests for 30 years. The intimate Mas des Carassins (1 chemin Gaulois, 04.90.92.15.48, closed Jan to mid-Mar, double €120), has 14 newly renovated rooms in a converted 19th-century farmhouse. Just outside St-Rémy on the road to Tarascon, the Château de Roussan (04.90.92.11.63, double €73-€89.50) is set in a breathtakingly romantic park. The estate belonged to Nostradamus' brother before being transformed by his grandson-in-law, a royal official. Bedrooms have antique furniture; bathrooms are a little spartan.

Tucked behind the Café des Arts' buzzing bar, the Restaurant des Arts (30 bd Victor Hugo, 04.90.92.08.50, closed 10 Jan-10 Mar, double €32-€54, average €18) is the oldest in St-Rémy and riddled with atmosphere. It specialises in rich, traditional dishes such as daube de taureau. There are 15 rooms upstairs. The straightforward decor of Alain Assaud (13 bd Marceau, 04.90.92.37.11, closed 15 Nov-15 Dec, 5 Jan-15 Mar, menus €24-€37) belies the renowned chef's very sophisticated seasonal cuisine. Good-value La Gousse d'Ail (6 bd Marceau, 04.90.92.16.87, closed 10 Jan-10 Mar, menu €12-€30) has recently moved to larger premises and added a jazz night; specialities include bouillabaisse, snails and taureau with garlic cream. La Maison Jaune (15 rue Carnot, 04.90.92.56.14) occupies a handsomely restored 18th-century townhouse and is favoured by locals for François Perraud's modern take on Provençal cooking, seen in dishes like sardines grilled with fennel and saffron, and roast pigeon on a bed of cabbage with hazelnut oil. For delicious fruit tarts and a Provençal-style cuppa, maybe seasoned with aniseed, fig or rosemary, stop by Charmeroy (51 rue Carnot, 01.32.60.01.23) tearoom.

Shopping

St-Rémy boasts plenty of sophisticated shops. Two not to miss are stunningly inventive chocolatier Joël Durand (3 bd Victor Hugo, 04.90.92.38.25), whose lavender chocolates make brilliant gifts, and Le Petit Duc (7 bd Victor Hugo, 04.90.92.08.31), where talented Dutch-born pastry chef Hermann Van Beek and his French wife Anne Daguin have resurrected a variety of ancient biscuit recipes, including pine nut 'pignolats', found in the Traité des Fardements et des Confitures, written in 1552 by local lad Michel de Notre-Dame, aka Nostradamus. Fabienne Villacreces (10 rue Jaume Roux, 04.90.94.45.45) has beautifully cut, very feminine fashions. NM Déco (9 rue Hoche, 04.90.92.57.91) offers sophisticated cashmere, silk and linen for swanning around your converted mas. At Terre d'Art (16 rue Jaume Roux, 04.90.92.41.21) you'll find no-fuss Provençal tableware. The danger at Vent d'Autan (49 rue Carnot, 04.32.60.06.54) is that the modern furniture and Provençal antiques will make you want to go house hunting.

Resources

Market day in St-Rémy is Wednesday.

Internet

Café des Variétés, 32 bd Victor Hugo (04.90.92.42.61). Open 8.30am-10.30pm Mon, Wed-Sun.

Tourist information

Office de Tourisme, pl Jean Jaurès, 13210 St-Rémy-de-Provence (04.90.92.05.22). Open summer 9am-noon, 1-7pm Mon-Sat; 9am-noon Sun. winter 9am-noon, 2-6pm Mon-Sat.

Les Alpilles, Les Baux-de-Provence & La Grande Crau

The craggy bone-white limestone outcrop of the Alpilles is one of the more recent geological formations to be thrust up from the earth's crust, and it shows: there are no smooth, time-worn edges here, just dramatically barren rock stretching south from St-Rémy. On a spur dominating the range, its surreal rock forms accentuated by centuries of quarrying, is the bizarre eyrie of Les Baux: not, as it appears from below, a natural phenomenon but a fortified village complete with ruined château.

The medieval Lords of Baux were an independent lot, swearing allegiance to no one

Les Baux-de-Provence – not just any old mining village. *See p57.*

and only too ready to resort to bloodshed. Their court, however, was renowned for its chivalry: only ladies of the highest birth and learning were admitted, and quibbles over questions of gallantry were often referred here. In 1372, the sadistic Raymond de Turenne became guardian of Alix, the last princess of Les Baux. Dubbed 'the scourge of Provence', he terrorised the countryside for miles around, making his prisoners leap to their death from the castle walls. On Alix's death, a subdued Baux passed to Provence, then France, only to raise its head again as a Protestant stronghold in the 17th century. Cardinal Richelieu ordered the town to be dismantled and fined it into submission.

The village lay deserted for centuries, picking up again in 1822 when bauxite – named after the place and main source of aluminium – was discovered there, and subsequently when the wild and windswept became fashionable among travellers. Beneath the ruins of the castle, the winding streets, cottages and noble mansions of the old town have been restored and are visited by two million people a year. The **Chapelle des Pénitents-Blancs** on place de l'Eglise is decorated with frescoes by Yves Brayer. The **Musée Yves Brayer** contains many of the artist's vigorous oil paintings of the region, and the **Fondation Louis Jou** houses the presses, wood blocks and manuscripts of a typographer. By the

château, the 14th-century Tour de Brau houses the **Musée d'Histoire des Baux**, with huge models of siege engines and battering rams outside. Within the ruins of the **Château des Baux**, you can clamber over masonry and walk along the battlements, discovering remnants of towers and windows, a dovecote, Gothic chapel, a leper's hospital and breathtaking sheer drops to the plateau below.

From the edge of the escarpment, there are views across the savage, unearthly rocks of the Val d'Enfer (Hell Valley), said to have inspired Dante's *Inferno* and the backdrop for Cocteau's *Le Testament d'Orphée*. Walkers can follow GR 6 footpath through the valley (access from D27) and along the crest of Les Alpilles. The **Cathédrale d'Images**, a vast old bauxite quarry, makes a dramatic setting for audiovisual shows with thousands of images projected on to the 20-metre-high walls. The theme changes each year, with Alexandria in 2004. Note that the quarries are cool (16°C) so bring a jumper.

The lower slopes of Les Alpilles are covered with vineyards producing increasingly renowned Les Baux-de-Provence reds and rosés and Coteaux d'Aix-en-Provence whites. In the heart of Les Alpilles, the tiny village of **Eygalières** is really too pretty for its own good, now filled with overpriced interior design shops and restaurants. However, its delightful

12th-century **Chapelle St-Sixte**, which dominates a spartan, luminous hillside speckled with olive and almond trees, lifts the spirits. Pagan rites involving spring water from Les Alpilles were performed on the hill. Indeed, one ritual still remains: on the day of a couple's engagement the future husband drinks spring water from his fiancé's hands. If they don't marry within a year legend has it that he'll die.

Heading west from Eygalières, many foodies (including Sir Terence Conran, who has a house in the area) consider a stop at the pretty little town of **Mausanne-les-Alpilles** *de rigueur* if for no other reason than to buy the fruity, green olive oil at the **Moulin Jean-Marie Cornille** (rue Charloun Rieu, 04.90.54.32.37).

To the south-west, **Fontvieille** boasts a literary landmark, the **Moulin de Daudet**. Alphonse Daudet's *Letters from my Windmill* (1860) captures the essence of life in the South, though he was accused of caricaturing the locals. Daudet never actually lived in his windmill, preferring a friend's château nearby, but the view from the pine-scented hilltop is delightful and the display on milling informative. Just outside town are the remains of a Roman aqueduct.

Further along the road towards Arles stands the important medieval sanctuary of the **Abbaye de Montmajour**, founded by the Benedictines on a great rock surrounded by marshland. The 12th-century church, crypt and cloisters have been painstakingly pieced together over the past century by the sensitive souls of Arles. The interior, renovated by Rudi Ricciotti and used for exhibitions, is plain and serene; it's at its most human in the tiny 11th-century chapel of St Peter, with hermits' cells and an altar gouged out of a cave.

Extending eastwards around the market town of St-Martin-de-Crau is the Grande Crau, the arid, rocky limestone 'desert' of Provence. Part of the expanse is cultivated, producing, among other things, France's only hay to be awarded an *appellation contrôlée*.

French Air Force flying school jets and hard-sell Nostradamus heritage make an unlikely couple at the sprawling commercial crossroads of **Salon-de-Provence** on the eastern edge of the Crau. In the **Maison de Nostradamus**, where the astrologer and doctor wrote his *Centuries* and lived from 1547 until his death in 1566, a CD-guided visit talks you through kitsch waxwork tableaux: little Michel being schooled in cabalism by his uncle; the Plague; and the consecratory visit from a busty, satin-clad Catherine de Médicis. More atmospheric is Nostradamus' tomb – a simple tablet set into the wall in the Gothic **Collégiale de St-Laurent**, beyond the city wall. The Romano-Gothic church of St-Michel in the old town is

also worth a look, as are two surviving gateways: Tour de Bourg Neuf, guarded by a black Virgin, and Porte de l'Horloge, topped by a wrought-iron belfry. Looming over Salon is the **Château de l'Emperi**, built between the tenth and 13th centuries for the bishops of Arles, and today home to a military museum and Napoleonic memorabilia. Modern town life centres around the Hôtel de Ville and the shops of cours Gimon, and the cafés of place Croustillat. Around 1900, the arrival of the railway made Salon a boomtown. Prosperous soap barons (much of what is called *savon de Marseille* is actually made here) built themselves fanciful faux-châteaux, some of which remain, especially around the station.

Abbaye de Montmajour

rte de Fontvieille, Fontvieille (04.90.54.64.17). **Open** *Apr-Sept* 9am-7pm Mon, Wed-Sun. *Oct-Mar* 10am-5pm Mon, Wed-Sun. **Admission** €6.10; €4.10 students; free under 18s. **Credit** V.

Cathédrale d'Images

Val d'Enfer, Petite rte de Maillane, Les Baux-de-Provence (04.90.54.38.65/www.cathedrale-images.com). **Open** *mid-Feb to Sept* 10am-7pm daily. *Oct to mid-Jan* 10am-6pm. Closed mid-Jan to mid-Feb. **Admission** €7; €4.10 8-18s; free under-8s. **Credit** DC, MC, V. **Wheelchair access.**

Château des Baux

(04.90.54.55.56/www.chateau-baux-provence.com). **Open** *spring* 9am-6.30pm daily. *summer* 9am-8.30pm daily. *autumn* 9am-6pm daily. *winter* 9am-5pm daily. **Admission** €5.50; €3.50 7-18s, students; free under-7s. **Credit** MC, V.

Château de l'Emperi

Montée du Puech, Salon-de-Provence (04.90.56.22.36). **Open** 10am-noon, 2-6pm Mon, Wed-Sun. **Admission** €3.05; €2.30 7-15, students; free under-7s. **No credit cards.**

Fondation Louis Jou

Hôtel Jean de Brion, Grande Rue, Les Baux-de-Provence (04.90.54.34.17). **Open** *Apr-Dec* 11am-1pm, 2-6pm Mon, Thur-Sun. *Jan-Mar* by appointment. **Admission** €3; €1.50 7-18s; free under-7s. **No credit cards.**

Maison de Nostradamus

rue Nostradamus, Salon-de-Provence (04.90.56.64.31). **Open** 9am-noon, 2-6pm Mon-Fri; 2-6pm Sat, Sun. **Admission** €3.05; €2.30 7-18s, students; free under-7s. **No credit cards.**

Moulin de Daudet

Allée des Pins, Fontvieille (04.90.54.60.78). **Open** *Apr-Sept* 9am-7pm daily. *Oct-Mar* 10am-noon, 2-5pm

> ▶ For a tour of Les Baux-de-Provence's acclaimed vineyards, *see p27*.

The Rhône Delta

daily. Closed Jan. **Admission** €2; €1 6-12s; free under-6s. **No credit cards.**

Musée d'Histoire des Baux

Hôtel de la Tour de Brau, rue de Trencart, Les Baux-de-Provence (04.90.54.55.56). **Open** *June-Aug* 9am-8pm daily. *Apr-May* 9am-6.30pm daily. *Sept-Mar* 9am-5pm daily. **Admission** €7; €5.50 students; €3.50 7-17s; free under-7s. **Credit** MC, V.

Musée Yves Brayer

Hôtel des Porcelets, rue de l'Eglise, Les Baux-de-Provence (04.90.54.36.99). **Open** *Apr-Sept* 10am-12.30pm, 2-6.30pm daily. *Oct-Mar* 10am-12.30pm, 2-5.30pm Mon, Wed-Sun. Closed Jan. **Admission** €4; €2.50 15-18s; free under-15s. **No credit cards.**

Where to stay & eat

In Les Baux, the **Mas d'Aigret** (04.90.54.20.00/ www.masdaigret.com, closed Jan, double €95-€170), right below the fortress on the D27A, has recently renovated rooms with balconies and a swimming pool. The **Reine Jeanne** (04.90.54.32.06, closed 2wks Nov, 3wks Jan, double €47-€63, menus €21-€30) has bedrooms and apartments, some with views across the valley, and serves reliable regional dishes. Tucked away amid fig trees just off the main road leading up to Les Baux, **L'Oustau de Baumanière** (Val d'Enfer, 04.90.54.33.07, www.oustaudebaumaniere.com, closed Jan & Feb, double €260, restaurant closed Wed & Thur Oct-May, menus €82-€128) is perhaps the most quietly glamorous country inn in France. Chef Jean-André Charial produces luxurious classical cooking, and there's even a seven-course vegetable menu from the hotel's own gardens. He also owns the **Cabro d'Or** (Mas Carita, rte d'Arles, 04.90.54.33.21, www.lacabrodor.com, closed Nov to mid-Dec, double €130-€340, restaurant closed lunch Mon & Sun, menus €45-€70) with plush farmhouse chic, where exquisitely prepared food is served inside or on a serene garden terrace. Deep in the Alpilles, the **Domaine de Valmouriane** (Petite rte des Baux, 04.90.92.44.62, double €125-€160, menus €35-€65) is a luxurious *mas* surrounded by woods, with a pool and a restaurant offering stylish regional cooking.

L'Oustaloun (pl de l'Eglise, Mausanne-les-Alpilles, 04.90.54.32.19, closed 3wks Feb, 3wks Nov, double €55, menus €20-€25) has eight rooms in a 16th-century abbey and a restaurant serving regional cuisine. One of the trendiest restaurants in Mausanne is **Centre Ville** (65 av de Vallée des Baux, 04.90.54.23.31, menus €20-€28), which is run by Jean-Pierre Demery, former owner of fabric company Souleiado; tellingly, it is done in soothing greys and beiges with nary a Provençal print in sight. In an old farmhouse on the edge of town, **Le Bistrot du** **Paradou** (04.90.54.32.70, closed Sun, dinners Oct-May and 2wks in Nov, menus €38-€43) is hardly a find but still manages to serve very good Provençal food in a changing daily menu.

To make the most of Eygalières, stay at the **Hôtel Le Mas du Pastre** (04.90.95.92.61, closed mid-Nov to mid-Dec, double €105-€160), a charming converted farmhouse with a pool. Bistro is a misnomer for smart **Bistrot d'Eygalières** (rue de la République, 04.90.90.60.34, closed mid-Jan to mid-Mar, double €115-€160, menus €64-€114), where hot young Belgian chef Wout Bru draws a showbiz clientele. Book well ahead.

Towering above its rivals in Fontvieille is the **Auberge La Régalido** (rue Frédéric Mistral, 04.90.54.60.22, double €188-€210, menus €38-€58), which offers old-fashioned haute cuisine and accommodation in an ancient *moulin à huile*. Among these casual bistros, **Le Patio** (117 rte du Nord, 04.90.54.73.10, menus €16-€27) has a loyal following for its all-inclusive menus featuring delicious, local home-style cooking; it has a pleasant interior courtyard and small garden for al fresco dining. A fine choice if you're travelling with children, or don't want anything fussy and formal, is **La Peiriero** (34 av des Baux, 04.90.54.76.10, closed mid-Nov to Apr, double €84-€120), a friendly hotel with a delightful pool built into a former quarry.

In Salon, the **Hôtel Vendôme** (34 rue Maréchal Joffre, 04.90.56.01.96, double €40-€48) has a small garden. The grandest place to stay is the **Abbaye de Ste-Croix** (rte du Val de Cuech [D16], 04.90.56.24.55, closed 5 Nov-end Mar, double €170-€453, restaurant closed lunch Mon & Thur, menus €77-€108), 5km out of town in the Crau. The rooms in former monks' cells mostly have private gardens or roof terraces, there's a pool, and the restaurant draws local bigwigs. Far better value is the **Hostellerie Domaine de La Reynaude** in Aurons (04.90.59.30.24, double €55-€112, menus €20-€36), a converted coaching inn in a pretty valley. Bedrooms are modern and comfortable, but the chief draw in summer is the large pool.

Resources

Morning markets are Wednesday in Salon, Friday in Fontvielle and St-Martin-de-Crau.

Tourist information

Les Baux *Office du Tourisme, Maison du Roi, 13520 Les Baux-de-Provence (04.90.54.34.39/ www.lesbauxdeprovence.com).* **Open** *Mar-Sept* 9am-7pm daily. *Oct-Apr* 9.30am-1pm, 2-6pm daily.
Salon *Office de Tourisme, 56 cours Gimon, 13300 Salon-de-Provence (04.90.56.27.60).* **Open** *15 June-15 Sept* 9am-12.30pm, 2.30-7pm Mon-Sat, 10am-4pm Sun. *16 Sept-14 June* 9am-noon, 2-6pm Mon-Sat.

Beaucaire, Tarascon & La Petite Crau

Midway along the Roman road that linked Italy with Spain, **Beaucaire** (known to the Romans as Ugernum) was the locale of one of the great medieval fairs of Europe, when thousands of merchants would sail their vessels up the Rhône each July to sell silks, spices, pots, skins, wines and textiles on the expanse of land between river and castle. Later the town became known for its finely made furniture and mirrors. Today, shabby streets conceal Beaucaire's former prosperity; but closer examination reveals intricate architectural details in sculpted windows and doorways. Dominating the town, the **Château de Beaucaire** is now a picturesque ruin. It's off-limits to the public except during afternoon falconry displays (daily except Wed Mar-June, daily July-Nov). The surrounding garden contains the **Musée Auguste-Jacquet**, where odds and ends from Roman Beaucaire are beautifully displayed.

On the opposite bank of the Rhône, **Tarascon** is dominated by its great white-walled 15th-century **Château**, the favourite castle of Good (as in good-living) King René, with its ornately carved grand courtyard. To satisfy the King's love of material comforts, the castle was lavishly decorated with spiral staircases, painted ceilings and tapestries. Snuggled around the castle is the old town. The rue des Halles has covered medieval arcades and the 15th-century Cloître des Cordeliers, used for exhibitions. The **Musée Souleiado** offers a history of the local textile industry – Tarascon was once a major production centre for 'Les Indiennes', the printed cottons inspired by imported Indian designs that have become an emblem of Provence. These prints fall in and out of fashion and, for the moment, are down for the count from too many garish imitations.

To the French, Tarascon is synonymous with its fictional resident Tartarin, Alphonse Daudet's character who confirmed Parisians' preconceptions about bumbling provincials. The town is also inseparable from the Tarasque, a mythical river-dwelling beast that reputedly used to devour the odd human until St Martha happened along in the ninth century. St Martha's bones are in the **Collégiale Ste-Marthe**. On the last weekend of June, a model of the dreaded beast is paraded through the streets amid fireworks and bullfights.

Four kilometres north-west of Beaucaire, the **Abbaye St-Roman** is an extraordinary fifth-century abbey with chapels, cells, altars and 150 tombs hewn out of sheer rock. **Mas des Tourelles**, 4km south-west on the D38, is a copy of an ancient Roman winery, and makes wine the way the Romans did – not very well. The CNRS state science research institute was involved in the recreation of the recipes, adding ingredients such as fenugreek, honey and seawater, which makes ordinary Costières de Nîmes taste like nectar in comparison. South towards Arles, **Le Vieux Mas** is a faithful reconstruction of an early 1900s Provençal farmhouse, with farm animals, original equipment and regional products.

North of Tarascon, La Montagnette hill is famous for its herbs, made into a medicinal-tasting liqueur by monks at the 19th-century **Abbaye St-Michel-de-Frigolet** (04.90.95.70.07) – *férigoulo* being the Provençal word for thyme. East of here, between St-Rémy and Avignon, is the fertile Petite Crau plain, important for market gardening. Stop off at sleepy **Graveson**, which has a Romanesque church and the **Musée Chabaud**, dedicated to the powerful landscape paintings and disturbing portraits of Auguste Chabaud (1882-1955). Pleasant **Maillane** is the birthplace of Frédéric Mistral, revered founder of the Félibrige movement (*see p12*), whose house and garden (now **Museon Mistral**) have been preserved as he left them. **Châteaurenard**, the traffic-choked main town, is best known for its vast, mostly wholesale, fruit and vegetable

Château de Tarascon, done up by King René.

market. Two ruined towers are all that remain of the medieval castle, which came a cropper during the Revolution.

Abbaye St-Roman

D99 (04.66.59.52.26/www.abbaye-saint-roman.com). **Open** *Apr-Sept* 10am-6pm daily. *Oct-Mar* 2-5pm Sat, Sun & school holidays. **Admission** €5; €2 students; free under-12s. **No credit cards.**

Château de Tarascon

bd du Roi René, Tarascon (04.90.91.01.93). **Open** 10.30am-5pm daily. **Admission** €6.10; €3.05 12-18s; free under-12s. **No credit cards.**

Mas des Tourelles

4294 rte de Bellegarde (04.66.59.19.72/ www.tourelles.com). **Open** *Apr-June, Sept, Oct* 2-6pm daily. *July-Aug* 10am-noon, 2-7pm Mon-Sat; 2-7pm Sun. *Nov-Mar* 2-6pm Sat. **Admission** €4.60; €1.50 under-6s. **Credit** AmEx, MC, V.

Musée Auguste-Jacquet

In the château gardens, Beaucaire (04.66.59.47.61). **Open** *Apr-Oct* 10am-noon, 2-6pm Mon, Wed-Sun (July, Aug until 7.15pm). *Nov-Mar* 10am-noon, 2-5.15pm Mon, Wed-Sun. Closed 1wk Christmas. **Admission** €2.20; €0.60 under-14s. **No credit cards.**

Musée Auguste Chabaud

cours National, Graveson (04.90.90.53.02). **Open** *June-Sept* 10am-noon, 1.30-6.30pm daily. *Oct-May* 1.30-6.30pm daily. **Admission** €4; free under-12s. **No credit cards.**

Musée Souleiado

39 rue Proudhon, Tarascon (04.90.91.08.80). **Open** *May-Sept* 10am-6pm daily. *Oct-Apr* 10am-5pm Tue-Sat. **Admission** €6.10; €3.05 12-18s; free under-12s. **No credit cards.**

Museon Mistral

11 av Lamartine, Maillane (mairie 04.90.95.74.06). **Open** *Apr-Sept* 9.30-11.30am, 2.30-6.30pm Tue-Sun. *Oct-Mar* 10-11.30am, 2-4pm Tue-Sun. **Admission** €3.50; €1 students; free under 11s. **No credit cards.**

Le Vieux Mas

rte de Fourques (04.66.59.60.13). **Open** *Apr-Sept* 10am-7pm daily. *Oct-Mar* 10am-12.30pm, 1.30-6pm Wed, Sat, Sun & school holidays. Closed Jan. **Admission** €5.50; €3.05 5-16s; free under-5s. **Credit** MC, V.

Where to stay & eat

The **Hôtel des Doctrinaires** (quai du Général de Gaulle, 04.66.59.23.70, double €51-€69, menus €16-€38) in Beaucaire is probably the best hotel of the two towns. Set in a 17th-century doctrinal college, dowdy but spacious guest rooms do not live up to the vaulted reception; its trad cuisine is popular with locals. A cheaper option is the **Hôtel Napoléon** (4 pl Frédéric Mistral, 04.66.59.05.17, double €30,

average €15), in a square near the river; it has a restaurant offering pizzas and simple local fare. Book ahead to snag a table at **L'Ail Heure** (46 rue du Château, 04.66.59.67.75, menus €15-€31), the most fashionable bistro in Beaucaire where chef Luc Andreu has rapidly won a crowd of regulars with dishes such as red mullet in pistou jus and grilled squid with rocket.

In Tarascon, the small **Hôtel Provençal** (12 cours Aristide Briand, 04.90.91.11.41, double €38-€44, menus €16-€24) has a restaurant serving regional specialities; it is not to be confused with the **Hôtel de Provence** (7 bd Victor-Hugo, 04.90.43.58.13, double €38-€50), a stylishly decorated hotel (no restaurant). Opposite the castle, **Rue du Château** (24 rue du Château, 04.90.91.09.99, double €75) is a charming *chambres d'hôte*.

Resources

Market day is Thursday in Beaucaire, and Sunday in Tarascon and Châteaurenard.

Tourist information

Beaucaire *Office de Tourisme, 24 cour Gambetta, 33000 Beaucaire (04.66.59.26.57/www.ot-beaucaire.fr).* **Open** *Apr-Sept* 8.45am-noon, 2-6pm Mon-Fri, 9.30am-12.30pm, 2.15-6.15pm Sat (plus 9am-noon Sun July). *Oct-Mar* 8.45am-noon, 2-6pm Mon-Fri. **Châteaurenard** *Office de Tourisme, 11 cours Carnot, 13160 Châteaurenard (04.90.24.25.50).* **Open** *July-Sept* 9am-noon, 3-7pm Mon-Sat, 10am-noon Sun. *Oct-June* 9am-noon, 2-6pm Mon-Sat. **Tarascon** *Office de Tourisme, 59 rue des Halles (04.90.91.03.52/www.tarascon.org).* **Open** *Apr-Sept* 9am-12.30pm, 2-6pm Mon-Sat, 10am-noon Sun. *Oct-Mar* 9am-noon, 2-5pm Mon-Sat.

Getting there & around

By car

For St-Rémy, A7 exit 25, then D99 between Tarascon and Cavaillon. Or south of Avignon on the N570 and D571, via Châteaurenard. Les Baux is 8km south of St-Rémy by D5 and D27. Tarascon and Beaucaire are reached by N570 and D970 from Avignon or D999 from Nîmes. Salon is at the junction of the A7 (exit 27) and A54 (exit 14/15) or by N113 from Arles.

By train

Frequent TGVs serve Avignon and Nîmes. Local trains stop at Tarascon on the Avignon Centre-Arles line. Salon-de-Provence has several trains a day from Avignon; for Marseille or Arles, change at Miramas.

By bus

Cartreize (08.00.19.94.13, www.lepilote.com) is an umbrella organisation for buses within the Bouches du Rhône, including services between Avignon and Les Baux via Châteaurenard and St-Rémy, St-Rémy and Tarascon (Mon-Sat), Arles and St-Rémy, Arles and Marseilles via Salon de Provence, Avignon and Maillane via Châteaurenard and Graveson.

Arles

From bullfighting to flamenco, photography to the rice harvest, Arles loves an excuse to party. At other times its ancient ruins are reason enough to linger.

The ancient town of Arles continues to throw up its secrets. As recently as October 2003, remains of a fourth-century cathedral were unearthed on the site of the future Médiapôle in the south-east of the old town centre, providing a vital link in the puzzle between Roman Arles and the city of today. Once excavations are complete – probably in 2005 – the site will be opened to the public. Straddling the river Rhône, Arles was badly hit by 2003's floods but it was recent residential areas rather than the historic centre that were affected. The town wears its history with ease; its ancient monuments are not museum pieces but part of the urban fabric. The great Roman arena is encircled by the old town like a snail in its shell, while newer buildings snuggle up to the walls of the cathedral of St-Trophime.

The medieval centre of Arles was built over the Roman ruins and happily incorporates earlier vestiges, such as the column embedded in the Grand Hôtel Nord Pinus on the site of the original forum. It has an intimate feel; narrow streets providing protection from the chilly blasts of the mistral, cobbled alleys and hidden courtyards concealing centuries of history.

Arles was a Greek trading port as early as the sixth century BC, but its importance grew by leaps and bounds in 104 BC when the Romans constructed a canal to facilitate river navigation between the city and the sea. In 49 BC, the city backed Julius Caesar in his victorious bid to break Marseille's stranglehold on not only sea trade but the Domitian Way land route from Rome to Spain. Arles' moment of glory had arrived, and it began to acquire its rich heritage of no-expense-spared monuments. The city was home to a roaring trade in everything the Orient produced, as well as its own flourishing output of textiles and silverware.

Dark Ages battles took a relatively minor toll on the town and, by the Middle Ages, Arles had regained its clout, becoming a major centre of religious and temporal power. At its height, the kingdom of Arles included Burgundy and part of Provence. The kingdom was so influential that in 1178 Holy Roman Emperor Frederick Barbarossa pitched up and was crowned King of Arles in the newly finished cathedral.

Gradually, as the sea retreated, Marseille took over as the most important port and in the 19th century railway traffic replaced river traffic.

Les Alyscamps. See p65.

Though Frédéric Mistral and his Félibrige freedom fighters (see p12) fought tooth and nail to restore the area's prestige, Arles has never really regained its lost glory.

This fact has failed to dent the Arlésian attachment to local traditions. Long-running festivals, especially the exciting climax of the bullfight *ferias* in April and July, prompt the most colourful displays of local pride when everyone from middle-aged matrons to teenagers appears in full Arlésienne fig (lace *fichus*, shawls, bonnets and all). But just about any event will bring Arles' citizens out en masse: the **Rencontres Internationales de la Photographie**, which sees photo exhibitions all over town; **Les Suds à Arles** world music festival; **Mosaïque Gitane**, a flamenco festival in July and August; the **Fêtes des Prémices du Riz** rice harvest in September (*see pp34-40*).

Arles is irrevocably linked with Van Gogh, who arrived here in February 1888 in search of southern light and colour, only to discover the city covered in thick snow. Undaunted, he rented

the 'Yellow House' and began working furiously. In the space of 15 months, punctuated by the occasional stay in the town asylum, a dispute with Gauguin and the lopping off of his own ear, he produced some 300 canvases of startling colours and contours. In truth the good citizens of Arles, like everybody else, rejected the unbalanced Dutchman, who in April 1889, terrified that he was losing his artistic grip, checked himself into the asylum at nearby St-Rémy-de-Provence (see p55). Somewhat embarrassed by not owning a single one of the artist's works, the city makes do with a mock-up of one of his most famous subjects, the **Café de la Nuit**, and the **Espace Van Gogh** bookshop and arts centre. The **Fondation Van Gogh**, however, pays the right sort of homage to the misunderstood genius. Its superb collection of works by contemporary masters would have pleased Van Gogh, who so much wanted to establish a community of artists here.

Sightseeing

The best view of Arles is from the top tier of the **Arènes** (Roman amphitheatre), looking across terracotta roofs and ochre walls to the River Rhône. Adjacent to the Arènes are the crumbling remains of the **Théâtre Antique** (Roman theatre), described by Henry James as 'the most touching ruins I had ever beheld'. Today they provide an atmospheric backdrop for an outdoor theatre season in June and July. Further down the hill on place de la République stands the great Romanesque **Cathédrale St-Trophime**. The magnificent 12th-century sculpture around the doorway on the newly scrubbed facade is equalled only by the superb cloisters next door. At the centre of the square is a fountain and an Egyptian granite obelisk, moved here from the Roman circus in the 17th century, on one side, the Hôtel de Ville with its 17th-century classical facade and celebrated vestibule vaulting. Accessible from the vestibule is the Plan de la Cour, a small medieval square with several historic municipal buildings, the 13th-century Palais des Podestats with its Romanesque doorway and windows and, next to it, a lovely 15th-century maison commune. Extending beneath the Hôtel de Ville are the **Cryptoportiques** (entry on rue Baize), an underground gallery of obscure purpose dug out by the Romans below the forum.

A block away is Frédéric Mistral's pet project, the **Museon Arlaten**, which has a vast collection devoted to Provençal folklore, crafts and particularly costumes, all housed in a 16th-century mansion with a courtyard built round the columns of the original Roman forum. At every turn is intriguing evidence of Arles'

many layers, such as the Corinthian columns (themselves a reference to the Romans) of a 12th-century cloister door on rue du Cloître, the antique bas-reliefs on the Hôtel des Amazones in rue des Arènes, or the 18th-century bulls' heads sculpted on the facade of the Grande Boucherie in rue du 4 Septembre.

Place du Forum, next to the original forum site, is the centre of Arles life today, buzzing with cafés and restaurants, notably the Van Gogh-pastiche **Café de la Nuit** and hip **Grand Hôtel Nord Pinus**, where bullfighters and their acolytes congregate. All is watched over by a statue of Frédéric Mistral, leaning on his stick and looking, as he himself complained, as if he's waiting for a train. From here it is a short stroll to the banks of the Rhône, where you can walk along the quays, visit the partly excavated **Thermes de Constantin** baths complex or browse through the collections of Picasso and other modern masters in the **Musée Réattu**, housed in a lovely old priory with a facade that was once part of the city walls.

At the southern end of rue de l'Hôtel de Ville and the Jardin d'Eté, the shady, café-lined **boulevard des Lices** is the best place to observe le tout Arles, especially on Saturday mornings, when the market held there offers southern colours and smells. Local cheeses, olives, hams and sausages – donkey is the local speciality – are generally good buys, as are the pottery and olive-wood bowls.

Further south, the necropolis of **Les Alyscamps** lies on the ancient Aurelian Way from Rome. The avenue of marble sarcophagi is a wonderfully melancholy place to stroll. The best of the tombs and sculptures, however, have been transferred to the **Musée de l'Arles Antique**, west of the old centre. Spanking new and purpose-built for the city's collection of old marbles, the museum lies on the banks of the Rhône by the site of the Roman circus, itself under excavation.

Before leaving Arles, spare a thought for another ancient monument: the Jeanne Calment retirement home is named after the woman who held the title of world's oldest person (able to remember Van Gogh in her mother's boulangerie) before she died aged 120 in 1997.

Les Alyscamps

av des Alyscamps. **Open** Mar, Apr, Oct 9-11.30am, 2-5.30pm daily. May-Sept 9-11.30am, 2-5.30pm daily. Nov-Feb 10-11.30am, 2-4.30pm daily. **Admission** €3.50; €2.60 12-18s; free under-12s. **No credit cards**. From its beginnings as a pre-Christian necropolis until well into the Middle Ages, Les Alyscamps (the name means the Elysian Fields) was one of the most fashionable places in Europe to spend eternity. Corpses from up-country were parcelled up and floated down the Rhône with the burial fee in their

The Rhône Delta

Cathédrale St-Trophime.

mouths, to be fished out by gravediggers' assistants on the Trinquetaille bridge. By the Renaissance, many of the magnificent stone sarcophagi had been stolen or presented to distinguished visitors; in the 19th century the railway cut through one end of the cemetery. But the remaining avenue of tombs is still as wonderfully atmospheric as when Van Gogh painted it and at one end you can still visit the tiny ruined church of St-Honorat, with its Romanesque tower, and the marks where St Trophime is said to have kneeled to bless the spot.

Les Arènes

rond-point des Arènes (04.90.49.36.86/box office 04.90.96.03.70/www.arenes-arles.com). **Open** *Oct-Feb* 10am-4.30pm daily. For summer opening times please call. Closed during events. **Admission** €4; €3 12-18s; free under-12s. **No credit cards.**
This amphitheatre is one of the oldest in the Roman world, built in the first century AD to accommodate 21,000 spectators, with tunnels at the bottom through which wild beasts were released into the arena. Like Nîmes, it had three storeys of 60 arcades each, but the top floor here was plundered for building stone in the Middle Ages (the rest is in remarkably good shape because it was fortified for defensive purposes). The rabble that constructed a slum within its walls a couple of centuries later was not cleared out until 1825, when restoration began.

For a true taste of Roman-style bloodlust, come for a bullfight, when the arena echoes to the sound of the spectators and the persecuted animal. It is used for both classic Spanish-style bullfighting and the more humorous, less bloodthirsty local variant,

course Camargaise. The season gets underway with the April *feria* and the *gardian* festival on 1 May, when the Queen of Arles is crowned; it culminates in early July when the coveted Cocarde d'Or is awarded. Tickets are usually available on the gate, but book ahead for the *feria* and Cocarde d'Or. In summer, the arena also hosts concerts and films.

Cathédrale St-Trophime

pl de la République (04.90.96.07.38). **Open** *church* 8.30am-6.30pm daily. *cloister* 10am-5.30pm daily. **Admission** *church* free. *cloister* €3.50; €2.06 12-18s; free under-12s. **No credit cards.**
A church has stood on this site since the fifth century. The current, stunning Romanesque cathedral was built in the 12th century to house the relics of St Trophimus, a third-century bishop of Arles. Its austere nave is impressively tall, hung with Aubusson tapestries and dotted with Roman sarcophagi and 17th-century Dutch paintings. It is the portal, however, that really takes your breath away. Recently restored, its vivid carving is clearly visible: the tympanum shows Christ in glory, with life-size apostles accommodated in the columns below. The frieze – its style perhaps inspired by Roman sarcophagi – depicts the Last Judgement, with souls being dragged off to hell in chains or handed over to saints in heaven. The cloister sculptures are Romanesque in the north and east arcades and 14th-century Gothic in the south and west; the two styles form a surprisingly harmonic whole. The carved columns and capitals feature a profusion of Biblical characters and stories. Above the cloister, a walkway offers good views of the bell tower and the town.

Cryptoportiques

rue Baize. **Open** *Mar, Apr, Oct* 9-11.30am, 2-5.30pm daily. *May-Sept* 9-11.30am, 2-6.30pm daily. *Nov-Feb* 10-11.30am, 2-4.30pm daily. **Admission** €3.50; €2.60 12-18s; free under-12s. **No credit cards.**
These mysterious, horseshoe-shaped Roman underground galleries were originally constructed to support the hillside foundations of the forum and may also have been used as a religious sanctuary or for grain storage. During World War II they provided refuge for Resistance members and they still exude a chill and sinister atmosphere.

Fondation Van Gogh

Palais de Luppé, 24bis rond-point des Arènes (04.90.49.94.04). **Open** *Apr to mid-Oct* 10am-7pm daily. *mid-Oct to mid-Mar* 9.30am-noon, 2-5.30pm Tue-Sun. Closed 1wk Mar. **Admission** €7; €5 students, 8-18s; free under-8s. **Credit** MC, V.
Work by contemporary artists in tribute to Van Gogh include a Hockney chair, a Rauschenberg sunflower in acrylic yellow and blue on steel, plus works by Bacon, Rosenquist, Lichtenstein and Viallat, and photos by Doisneau and Cartier-Bresson. The catalogue explains how Vincent inspired each artist.

Musée de l'Arles Antique

presqu'île du Cirque Romain (04.90.18.88.88/ www.arles-antique.org). **Open** *Mar-Oct* 9am-7pm daily. *Nov-Feb* 10am-5pm daily. **Admission** €5.50; €4 students; free under-18s, all 1st Sun of month. **Credit** MC, V.

On the fringes of the Roman circus, this modern blue triangle designed by Henri Ciriani houses the many antiquities once scattered throughout Arles' museums and archaeological sites. The well-displayed collection includes statues, capitals, pottery, jewellery, glass and villa mosaics along with maps, models and town plans. Best of all are the beautifully carved sarcophagi from Les Alyscamps, many dating from the fourth century AD or earlier.

Musée Réattu

10 rue du Grand Prieuré (04.90.49.38.34). **Open** *Mar-Apr* 10am-12.30pm, 2-5.30pm daily. *May-Sept* 10am-12.30pm, 2-7pm daily. *Oct-Feb* 1-5.30pm daily. **Admission** €4; €3 students, 12-18s; free under-12s; special exhibitions more. **No credit cards.**

Housed in a 15th-century priory, this museum contains works by its founder, Provençal artist Jacques Réattu, along with a collection of more modern work

by Léger, Dufy, Gauguin and others. Most notable are the 57 drawings made by Picasso in 1971 and donated to the museum by the artist a year later to thank Arles for amusing him with its bullfights. Also by Picasso is a delicious rendering of Lee Miller as an Arlésienne painted in Mougins in 1937.

Museon Arlaten

29 rue de la République (04.90.93.58.11). **Open** *Apr, May* 9.30am-12.30pm, 2-6pm Tue-Sun. *June-Aug* 9.30am-1pm, 2-6.30pm daily. *Sept* 9.30am-1pm, 2-6pm daily. *Oct-Mar* 9.30am-12.30pm, 2-5pm Tue-Sun. Last entry 1hr before closing. **Admission** €4; €3 12-18s; free under-12s. **No credit cards.**

Frédéric Mistral used the money from his Nobel Prize for Literature in 1904 to set up this museum to preserve the traditions of Provence, thus establishing an enduring fashion for collections of regional memorabilia. Attendants wear Arlésien costume and captions come in French and Provençal only. Despite the stuffiness, this is a worthwhile and authentic collection of humble domestic and rural

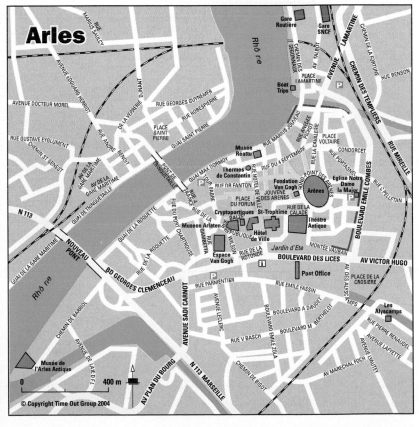

objects: furniture, tools, kitchen equipment, shoes and clothing. Best of all is a bizarre haul of traditional talismans: a fig branch burned to encourage maternal milk, a ring fashioned from the third nail of a horseshoe to ward off haemorrhoids and large quantities of toothache-prevention equipment. There are large tableaux, too: a home birth; a Christmas scene with the traditional 13 desserts of Provence; and a Camargue *gardian*'s cabin.

Le Pont Van Gogh

rte de Port-St-Louis.
Van Gogh's famous Pont du Langlois has recently been restored (after being bombed during World War II) and moved to the southern outskirts of Arles.

Théâtre Antique

rue de la Calade (04.90.49.36.25). **Open** *Mar, Apr, Oct* 9-11.30am, 2-5.30pm daily. *May-Sept* 9-11.30am, 2-6.30pm daily. *Nov-Feb* 10-11.30am, 2-4.30pm daily. **Admission** €3; €3 students, 12-18s; free under-12s. **No credit cards.**
The Roman theatre, dating from the first century BC and ransacked for building stone from the fifth century on, once seated over 10,000 but today is a mess of tumbledown columns and fragments of carved stones. Its forlorn glory makes it a particularly romantic setting for summer theatre and music performances. Vestiges of the original tiers of stone benches remain, along with two great Corinthian columns of the stage wall, once used as a gallows. It was here in 1651 that the Venus of Arles, now in the Louvre, was dug up.

Thermes de Constantin

rue du Grand Prieuré. **Open** *Mar, Apr, Oct* 9-11.30am, 2-5.30pm daily. *May-Sept* 9-11.30am, 2-6.30pm daily. *Nov-Feb* 10-11.30am, 2-4.30pm daily. **Admission** €3; €2.20 students, 12-18s; free under-12s. **No credit cards.**
At the fourth-century Roman baths, once part of a larger complex of baths on the banks of the Rhône, you can still see the vaulted caldarium, warm bath, and the bricks of the underfloor heating system.

Arts & entertainment

See also *p68* **Les Arènes**. For entertainment listings, pick up fortnightly freebie *César* in shops and the tourist office.

Actes Sud

23 quai Marx Dormoy. **Open** *bookshop* 9am-7pm Mon-Fri. *cinema* (04.90.93.33.56) films 6.30pm, 9pm Mon-Sat; 3pm, 6pm Sun. *Hammam Chiffa* (04.90.96.10.32) *men* 5.30-10pm Mon, Wed, Thur; *women* 9am-5pm Mon, Sat, Sun; 9am-10pm Tue-Fri.
This arts complex by the Rhône houses its own publishing house, arts cinema, hamman and L'Entrevue restaurant (*see p71*).

Espace Van Gogh

pl du Dr Félix Rey (04.90.49.37.53). **Open** 6am-9pm daily. **Admission** free.
A library, bookshop and exhibition space set around a garden courtyard in the hospital where the painter was treated, restored to look as it did in his time.

Les Arènes. *See p66.*

Théâtre d'Arles

bd Georges Clemenceau (04.90.52.51.51). **Box office** 11am-1pm, 1-6.30pm Tue-Sat and 1hr before performance Sat. **Tickets** €20. **Credit** MC, V.

Restored and re-opened in 2001, this splendid old theatre offers music and lectures as well as plays.

Théâtre de la Calade

Le Grenier à Sel, 49 quai de la Roquette (04.90.93.05.23/www.theatredelacalade.voici.org). **Box office** 10am-12.30pm, 2-6pm Mon-Fri. **Tickets** €6.50-€17. **No credit cards.**

Based in a former salt warehouse, this theatre company offers its own performances, opera, visiting companies and workshops.

Restaurants

Au Bryn du Thym

22 rue du Dr Fanton (04.90.49.95.96). **Open** noon-2pm, 7-10pm Mon, Thur-Sun; 7-10pm Wed. **Menu** €17. **Credit** MC, V.

Tucked behind place du Forum, this intimate restaurant – all white beams, white tablecloths, tiled floor and bunches of lavender – serves Provençal-based cuisine with a rich touch: *gambas à la crème de whisky*, pumpkin soup with scallops, duck with figs, *taureau* steak with mirabelles. The restaurant also has an adjoining Provencal gift shop.

La Charcuterie Arlésienne

51 rue des Arènes (04.90.96.56.96). **Open** noon-1.30pm, 7.30-9.30pm Tue-Sat. Closed Aug. **Menus** €15-€22. **Credit** MC, V.

This old charcuterie serves some of the best pork produce in Arles. The authentic Lyonnaise bistro cooking comes as something of a surprise in a Provençal stronghold, but in cooler months could provide a welcome change from local specialities.

L'Entrevue

pl Nina Berberova (04.90.93.37.28). **Open** 9.30am-3pm, 7-11pm daily. Closed Sun lunch Oct-Apr. **Menu** €25. **Credit** V.

Part of the Actes Sud complex, this couscous restaurant has a terrace overlooking the river, drawing young intellectuals who appreciate the lively atmosphere, and the well-prepared Moroccan food.

La Gueule du Loup

39 rue des Arènes (04.90.96.96.69). **Open** 7.45-9.45pm Mon; 12.30-1.30pm, 7.45-9.45pm Tue-Sat. **Menus** €25. **Credit** DC, V.

You get to this first-floor, beamed restaurant through the deliciously scented kitchen where madame busily chops shallots in a big white apron. Try the *charlotte d'agneau* with aubergines and red pepper coulis, a tarte Tatin of deliciously sweet turnips with foie gras, scallop and sorrel terrine and chestnut mousse with almond milk. Book ahead.

Le Jardin de Manon

14 av des Alyscamps (04.90.93.38.68). **Open** *summer* noon-1.30pm, 7-9.30pm Mon, Tue, Thur-Sun. *winter* 1.30pm, 7-9.30pm Mon, Tue, Thur, Sat; noon-1.30pm Fri, Sun. Closed 2wks Nov, 2wks Feb. **Menus** €18.50-€36. **Credit** AmEx, MC, V.

There are not a great number of restaurants down by the Alyscamps, and as its name suggests Manon has a delightful garden for al fresco dining. The interior, like the menu, features local colour combined with contemporary touches.

Lou Caleu

27 rue Porte de Laure (04.90.49.71.77). **Open** noon-2pm, 7-10pm Tue-Sat. Closed 15 Jan-15 Feb. **Menus** €17-€25. **Credit** AmEx, DC, MC, V.

The best of several restaurants on a street near the Roman theatre brings a light touch to Provençal cooking in dishes such as chicken with herbs and honey, tomato stuffed with aubergine or pork *daube*.

Le Malarte

2 bd des Lices (04.90.96.03.99). **Open** noon-3pm, 7-9.30pm daily. **Menu** €15. **Credit** MC, V.

At some point during your visit you are sure to find yourself on the busy boulevard des Lices, with its slightly tacky brasseries and cafés, but you can have an enjoyable meal at the Malarte, including excellent *petits farcis*, all served with a smile.

La Mule Blanche

9 rue du Président Wilson (04.90.93.98.54). **Open** noon-2.30pm, 8-10pm Mon-Sat. **Average** €20. **Credit** AmEx, MC, V.

Be prepared to wait for a seat on the palm-shaded terrace of this useful and popular address in the centre of town. The long menu provides a good selection of simple grilled fish and meat, big salads and pasta, all prepared to a decent standard.

Bars & cafés

Andalucia Café

14 bd des Lices (04.90.96.40.72). **Open** *summer* 9am-2am daily. *winter* 10am-3pm, 6-11.30pm daily. **Average** €15. **Credit** DC, MC, V.

The old Grande Brasserie of Arles has metamorphosed into a celebration of southern Spain, with fountains, columns and the inevitable bullfighting theme. Good for coffee, *tapas* or a cooling gaspacho on the terrace at the height of summer.

Café de la Nuit

pl du Forum (04.90.96.44.56). **Open** *summer* 9am-2am daily. *winter* 9am-11.30pm daily. **Credit** MC, V.

This fun café has a great people-watching terrace, a lofty interior painted in vibrant Van Gogh colours and a bar decorated to look like his painting of the same name. Try the very good tagliatelle or bull *daube* with an inexpensive carafe of regional wine.

Clubs & music venues

Cargo de Nuit

7 av Sadi Carnot (04.90.49.55.99/ www.cargodenuit.com). **Open** 8pm-5am Thur-Sat,

The Rhône Delta

some Sun. Closed July, Aug, mid-Dec to mid-Jan.
Admission €7-€10. **Credit** MC, V.
Listen to world music, rock, electronic and jazz (live
and canned). Food is also served.

El Patio de Camargue
chemin de Barriol (04.90.49.51.76/www.chico.fr).
Open 8pm-late Sat, by reservation only. **Average**
€45. **Credit** AmEx, MC, V.
This Spanish restaurant on the banks of the Rhône
serves tapas and paella, accompanied by gypsy gui-
tar, songs and dancing from Chico et les Gypsies,
led by a founder member of the Gypsy Kings.

Shopping

Arles' markets take place on boulevard des Lices
on Saturdays and on boulevard Emile Combes
on Wednesdays. Both offer local fruit, vegetables
and fish, and a vast array of nuts, spices, herbs,
charcuterie and bric-a-brac. More bric-a-brac can
be found on the boulevard des Lices on the first
Wednesday of the month.

The streets of the old town, west of the Arena
from rue de la République to the river, are
pleasant for shopping (all open Mon-Sat unless
stated). Best buys are local products, such as
perfumes, incense, soaps and candles, with a
good range at upmarket chain **L'Occitane**
(58 rue de la République, 04.90.96.93.62) and
Fragrances (53 rue de la République,
04.90.18.20.64). At **Santons Chave** (14 rond-
point des Arènes, 04.90.96.15.22), you can buy
Provençal crêche figures and see them being
made. **L'Arlésienne** (12 rue de la République,
04.90.93.28.05) is the place to buy Provençal
fabrics, waistcoats, frilly skirts, *gardian* cowboy
shirts and even a complete Arlésienne costume
by the designer who dresses the assistants in the
Museon Arlaten. **Souleiado** (4 bd des Lices,
04.90.96.37.55), the Tarascon-based Provençal
fabric producer, has a huge range of colourful
patterns for clothing and furnishing, as well as
ready-to-wear garments. **Christian Lacroix**
(52 rue de la République, 04.90.96.11.16) is a
native of Arles, and his exuberant style screams
South of France; gorgeous clothes and jewellery
plus childrenswear, porcelain and table linen fill
this, his original shop.

Food, too, is worth seeking out. **Boitel** (4 rue
de la Liberté, 04.90.96.03.72, closed three weeks
Feb) sells regional delicacies, from handmade
chocolates to cakes, biscuits and nougat, and
also has a small tearoom. **La Charcuterie
Arlésienne** (51 rue des Arènes, 04.90.96.56.96,
closed Sun & Mon, *see also p71*) supplies the
cognoscenti with sausages, charcuterie and a
good choice of wine. **La Maison des
Gourmands** (28 rond-point des Arènes,
04.90.93.19.38) is the place for Provençal nougat,
biscuits, olive oil and honey.

The best bookshop is run by Arles-based
publisher **Actes Sud** (*see p70*), which has a
branch and children's bookshop in the Espace
Van Gogh. **Forum Harmonia Mundi** (3 rue
du Président Wilson, 04.90.93.38.00) is another
institution. Now a France-wide chain, the
classical, jazz and world music specialist began
here in 1958. Near the Musée Reattu and the
banks of the Rhône is a small antiques enclave
with, notably, **Antiquités Maurin** (4 rue de
Grille, 04.90.96.51.57, closed Mon morning &
all Sun), a large shop crammed with Provençal
furniture, paintings and objets d'art. **Livres
Anciens Gilles Barbero** (3 rue St-Julien,
04.90.93.72.04) is a bookshop stuffed full of
antiquarian books, maps, photos and postcards,
wonderful for browsing for original gifts.

Where to stay

Hôtel de l'Amphithéâtre
5 rue Diderot (04.90.96.10.30/
www.hoteldamphitheatre.fr). **Double** €45-€127.
Credit AmEx, DC, MC, V.
Set in a restored 17th-century building on a tiny
street, this is a gem, with warm old tiles, yellow
walls and original wrought-iron banisters. Rooms
are small but charmingly decorated, and bathrooms
well designed with big mirrors. Garage available.

Hôtel l'Arlatan
26 rue du Sauvage (04.90.93.56.66/www.hotel-
arlatan.fr). Closed Jan to early-Feb. **Double** €85-€153.
Credit AmEx, DC, MC, V.
This Provençal mansion is built over part of the
Roman basilica (you can see the excavations under
glass) and has a medieval Gothic tower among other
period details, carved ceilings and antiques. There
is an elegant salon with vast fireplace, an enclosed
garden courtyard and a pool.

Hôtel Le Calendal
5 rue Porte de Laure (04.90.96.11.89/
www.lecalendal.com). Closed 3wks in Jan. **Double**
€45-€97. **Credit** AmEx, DC, MC, V.
This romantic hotel occupies several cleverly linked
old buildings around a large, shady garden with
tables and palm trees. Sunny coloured rooms, each
different, look over either the Théâtre Antique or the
garden. The *salon de thé* serves good light meals.

Hôtel Le Cloître
16 rue du Cloître (04.90.96.29.50/
www.members.aol.com/hotelcloitre). Closed Nov to
mid-Mar. **Double** €43-€63. **Credit** AmEx, MC, V.
A good-value hotel in a narrow street near the
Roman theatre, with a Romanesque vaulted dining
room and exposed stone walls in the bedrooms.

Hôtel Le Galoubet
18 rue du Dr Fanton (04 90.93.18.11). Closed Nov-
Feb. **Double** €45-€55. **Credit** AmEx, V.
Arles has an above-average number of architec-

Closed Nov to mid-Mar. **Double** €54-€56. **Credit** AmEx, MC, V.
For cheap and cheerful accommodation just across the Rhône, this traditional building does a good job and includes a solarium for sun worshippers eager to escape the confines of the old city.

Hôtel St-Trophime
16 rue de la Calade (04.90.96.88.38). Closed mid-Nov to Feb. **Double** €50-€70. **Credit** AmEx, DC, MC, V.
Housed in an atmospheric old building in the centre of Arles, this hotel boasts a stone-arched lobby, carved ceilings and a courtyard.

Resources

The Pass Monuments and Circuit Arles Antique passes are available at the tourist office, museums and sights.

Hospital
Hôpital Général Joseph Imbert *quartier Haut de Fourchon (04.90.49.29.29).*

Internet
Le Cyber Espace *10 bd Gambetta (04.90.52.51.30).* **Open** 9am-10pm daily.

Police station
1 bd des Lices (04.90.18.45.00).

Post office
5 bd des Lices (04.90.18.41.00).

Tourist information
Office de Tourisme *esplanade Charles de Gaulle, bd des Lices, 13200 Arles (04.90.18.41.20/www.ville-arles.fr).* **Open** *Apr-Sept* 9am-5.45pm Mon-Sat; 10.30am-2.15pm Sun. *Oct, Nov* 9am-5.45pm Mon-Sat; 10.30am-2.15pm Sun. *Dec-Mar* 9am-4.45pm Mon-Sat; 10.30am-2.15pm Sun.

Getting there & around

By air
Arles is about 20km from Nîmes-Arles-Camargue airport. A taxi takes half an hour and costs about €30.

By car
The A54 goes through Arles; exit 5 is nearest the centre, or take the N570 from Avignon.

By train
Arles is on the main coastal rail route, and connects with Avignon for the TGV to Paris.

By bus
Cars de Camargue (04.90.96.36.25) runs buses between Nîmes and Arles 3 times daily Mon-Fri, twice on Sat (none Sun), and 4 buses Mon-Fri, between Arles and Stes-Maries-de-la-Mer. The **SNCF** (08.92.35.35.35) runs 3 or 4 buses daily (Mon-Sat) to Avignon. **Cartreize** (08.00.19.94.13, www.lepilote.com) runs buses between Arles and Marseille. It's best to walk around Arles town centre, but **STAR** runs a free bus 'Starlette', which follows a circuit taking in most of the museums and monuments until 6.30pm.

Café de la Nuit celebrates Vincent. *See p69.*

turally interesting hotels, including this reasonably priced fine old town house.

Grand Hôtel Nord Pinus
17 pl du Forum (04.90.93.44.44/www.nord-pinus.com). Closed Nov-Jan. **Double** €137-€275. **Credit** AmEx, DC, MC, V.
The bullfighters' favourite, opened in the 19th century, is dramatically decorated with heavy carved furniture, Peter Beard's giant black-and-white photos, *feria* posters and mounted bulls' heads. It has an elegant bar and the slightly pretentious Brasserie Nord Pinus. Book well ahead at *feria* time.

Hôtel du Musée
11 rue du Grand Prieuré (04.90.93.88.88/ www.hoteldumusee.com.fr). Closed Jan. **Double** €46-€61. **Credit** AmEx, DC, MC, V.
The rooms of this small hotel in a 16th-century mansion have been recently restored and elegantly decorated with Provençal antiques. Breakfast is served in a leafy inner courtyard.

L'Hôtel Particulier
4 rue de la Monnaie (04.90.52.51.40/www.hotel-particulier.com). **Double** €139-€229. **Credit** AmEx, DC, MC, V.
For the ultimate aristocratic high life, set up home in the *hôtel particulier*, a majestic mansion impressively converted into an exclusive hotel, including a Roman-style swimming pool in the walled gardens.

Hôtel Portes de Camargue
15 rue Noguier (04.90.96.17.32/www.portecamargue.com).

The Camargue

The eerily beautiful Rhône delta yields its best secrets to those willing to take to the saddle. So give rein to the cowboy in you.

Nestling in the delta between the Grand and Petit Rhône, the great flat region of marsh, pasture, salt-water *étangs* (ponds) and sand dunes of the Camargue is one of Europe's major wetlands, a vast protected area of 140,000 hectares. Eerily beautiful, it is a wonderland of flora and fauna: purple herons and pink flamingos; black bulls and grey ponies, wild boar; the beavers that thrive again here after reaching the verge of extinction; wintering egrets; bulrushes and samphire, pastures and paddy fields; not to mention dense clouds of France's most bloodthirsty mosquitoes. It is a fragile balance: if the Rhône floods, as in 2003, the salt level in the lagoons is lowered, disturbing flora and fauna; the reverse happens if the sea breaks through the dykes.

It was not until the Middle Ages that the marshes were settled by Cistercians and Templars. Salt was harvested as a commodity, as it still is, in vast quantities, today. With the decline of religious establishments in the 16th century, the Camargue passed into the hands of cattle- and horse-raising *gardians*, descendants of whom, dressed in black hats, high leather boots and velvet jackets, still herd small black fighting bulls on horseback. The area is dotted with white, thatched *gardians'* cabins, with one semi-circular end, set against the Mistral.

In 1970, 85,000 hectares of the Camargue, including the town of **Stes-Maries-de-la-Mer** (*see p74*), became a regional nature reserve, protecting the area from rapacious developers. The reserve centres on the Etang de Vaccarès, a body of brackish water covering 6,500 hectares. Boat trips can be taken on the canals on **Tiki III** (Le Grau d'Orgon, 04.90.97.81.68, closed mid-Nov to mid-Mar) and with **Aventure en Camargue** (Aigues-Mortes, 06.03.91.44.63).

The **Musée Camarguais**, in a converted sheep ranch between Arles and Stes-Maries-de-la-Mer, explains the region's history, produce and people, and provides information on nature trails. Further along by the small Etang de Ginès, the **Maison du Parc** gives information on riding and ecology and has a good view of avian antics from upstairs. For a closer brush with birdlife, visit the **Parc Ornithologique de Pont de Gau**, which replenishes stock in its aviaries and gives access to birdwatching trails along the Ginès lagoon.

The 20km walk from Stes-Maries-de-la-Mer to the salt-processing town of **Salin-de-Giraud** along the dyke built in 1857 to protect the wetlands from the sea allows extensive views across the reserve. The dyke is off limits to cars, though mountain bikes are tolerated. If you don't wish to part with your vehicle, various points on the D37 and C134 roads allow glimpses of herring gulls and blackheaded gulls, herons, avocets and egrets as well as the slender-billed gull and the red-crested pochard, which breed nowhere else in France. 20,000 flamingos roost on the Vaccarès lagoon, filtering plankton through big, hooked beaks.

East of the Etang de Vaccarès, the hamlet of **Le Sambuc** is home to the **Musée du Riz**, dedicated to the vital role played by rice in the agriculture of the Camargue: not only is it an important cash crop, but it also absorbs the salt in the soil, enabling other cereals to grow. For solitude strike out along the sea wall walk at the Pointe de Beauduc or the vast empty beach of Piémanson at the mouth of the Grand Rhône.

Across the salt lagoons, west of Arles, **St-Gilles-du-Gard** was an important medieval port forced to turn to agriculture when the sea receded. The village is dominated by its 12th-century abbey church, founded by Cistercian monks as a rest stop on the pilgrimage route to Compostela. All that remains of the original Romanesque building after Huguenot forces wreaked havoc during the Wars of Religion is the facade and the rib vaulting of the crypt; the rebuilt 17th-century version was half the size, but the elaborate carving on the three portals rivals that of St-Trophime in Arles. Opposite, the Maison Romane is a superb 12th-century house, now home to the medieval sculpture and local memorabilia of the **Musée de St-Gilles**.

Maison du parc naturel et régional de Camargue

Pont de Gau, rte d'Arles, Stes-Maries-de-la-Mer (04.90.97.86.32). **Open** *Apr-Sept* 10am-6pm daily. *Oct-Mar* 9.30am-5pm Mon-Thur, Sat, Sun.

Musée Camarguais

Mas du Pont de Rousty, D570 (04.90.97.10.82). **Open** *Apr-Sept* 9.15am-5.45pm daily (until 6.45pm July & Aug). *Oct-Mar* 10.15am-4.45pm Mon, Wed-Sun. **Admission** €4.60; €2.30 10-18s; free under-10s. **Credit** AmEx, MC, V.

Musée du Riz

rte de Salin-de-Giraud, Le Sambuc (04.90.97.29.44).
Open 9.30am-5.30pm daily (closed Sun Dec-Mar).
Admission €3.50; free under-12s. **No credit cards.**

Musée de St-Gilles

Maison Romane, St-Gilles-du-Gard (04.66.87.40.42).
Open *June* 9am-noon, 2-6pm Mon-Sat. *July, Aug*
9am-noon, 3-7pm Mon-Sat. *Sept-May* 9am-noon,
2-5pm Mon-Sat. Closed Jan. **Admission** free.

Parc Ornithologique de Pont de Gau

*rte d'Arles, 4km from Stes Maries de la Mer
(04.90.97.82.62/www.parc-ornitho.com).* **Open** *Apr-
Sept* 9am-sunset. *Oct-Mar* 10am-sunset. **Admission**
€6.50; €3.50 4-10s; free under-4s. **No credit cards.**

Where to stay & eat

Just outside Stes-Maries-de-la-Mer begins a long
succession of ranch-style hotels, all of which are
pleased to organise horse riding or 4WD trips.
Pride of place goes to the luxurious **Mas de la
Fouque** (rte du Bac du Sauvage, 04.90.97.81.02,
www.masdelafouque.com, closed 3wks Dec-Jan,
double €280-€450), whose large, stylish rooms
have wooden balconies overlooking a lagoon.
Even the ornothologically challenged will be
impressed, and the boss cooks a mean leg of
local lamb to enjoy after swimming in the
large pool. **Mangio Fango** (rte d'Arles,
04.90.97.80.56, www.hotelmangio fango.com,

closed Jan, double €63-€110) is a friendly
hotel with a luxuriant garden, pool, large rooms
and a restaurant, which offers an outstanding
half-board deal in summer (€139-€191). **Le
Pont des Bannes** (rte d'Arles, 04.90.97.81.09,
www.pontdesbannes.com, double €130) is a
converted hunting lodge with a certain rustic
chic, while **Le Boumian** (rte d'Arles,
04.90.97.81.15, www.leboumian.camargue.fr,
double €115) is a friendly ranch hotel with pool
and horse riding. The restaurant at
Hostellerie du Pont de Gau (rte d'Arles,
5km NW of Stes-Maries-de-la-Mer,
04.90.97.81.53, closed Wed mid-Nov to Easter,
closed Jan to mid-Feb, menus €18-€47) has
serious Provençal cookery and good service.
The **Lou Mas Dou Juge** (rte du Bac du
Sauvage, Pin Fourcat, 04.66.73.51.45, double
€92-€122) is a *chambres d'hôtes* with seven
rooms in a working farm on the Petit Rhône,
and offers horse-riding. East of the Etang de
Vaccarès, **Le Mas de Peint** (Le Sambuc,
04.90.97.20.62, closed mid-Nov to mid-Dec, mid-
Jan to mid-Mar, double €197-€254, restaurant
closed Wed, menus €34-€43) is the last word in
Camargue chic: stone floors, linen sheets, beams
and log fires, presided over by an owner happy
to show you his bulls and let you ride his horses
(€40/2hrs). Hip restaurant of the moment is **La
Chassagnette** (rte de Sambuc, 04.90.97.26.96,
closed Tue, Wed, menu €52). Sometimes the

Monsters and angels vie for attention at **St-Gilles-du-Gard**'s abbey church.

beauty of the concept is everything: a minimalist menu, which proposes starters, meat or fish, cheese and pudding may sound like any French transport café, but here the menu is served in a sleekly modernised barn, and as you sip an apéritif you can wander around the organic kitchen garden. The sight of fashionably dressed diners standing in hushed wonder in front of a row of courgettes is to be treasured, but fashion aside the talented chef provides a gargantuan country feed at a substantial, but extras-free, price. The **Authentiques Cabanes de Gardian de la Grand Mar** (04.90.97.00.64, minimum two days stay, weekend €150-€200, week €385-€537) sleep four adults and two children in real (or well-faked) self-catering *gardian* cabins. In St-Gilles, **Le Cours** (10 av François Griffeuille, 04.66.87.31.93, www.hotel-le-cours.com, closed mid-Dec to mid-Mar, double €40-€66, menus €10-€28.50) is a friendly and simple Logis de France; its restaurant is a local favourite.

Resources

St-Gilles market is Thursday and Saturday.

Tourist information

St-Gilles *Office de Tourisme, 1 pl Frédéric Mistral. 13800 St-Gilles-du-Gard (04.66.87.33.75/www.ot-saint-gilles.fr).* **Open** *May, June, Sept* 9am-noon, 2.30-6pm Mon-Sat. *July, Aug* 9am-12.30pm, 3-7pm Mon-Sat; 10am-noon Sun. *Oct-Apr* 9am-noon, 2-5pm Mon-Sat.

Stes-Maries-de-la-Mer

Each May gypsies from all over Europe and the Middle East converge on Stes-Maries-de-la-Mer for an exuberant three-day pilgrimage, during which the streets throb with flamenco, horse races and bullfights. Soon after the death of Christ, the legend goes, Mary Magdalene (*see also p203*), Mary Salome (mother of James and John) and Jesus' aunt Mary Jacob fled Palestine by sea and washed up on the shores of Provence, where they were met by Black Sarah the gypsy (who may, according to another version, have travelled from the Holy Land with the three Marys as their maid). The local populace converted *en masse* and Sarah was adopted by the gypsies as their patron saint. The Church came up with some convenient relics in 1448: three sets of bones that may indeed be those of Middle Eastern women of the first century AD. The vast, fortified 12th-century church still dominates the present town, its crypt hot with hundreds of candles burning around an effigy of Black Sarah. But Stes-Maries is primarily a seaside resort, with a long sandy beach, cheap cafés and too many shops for picking up that essential Provençal

cowboy shirt. The low-rise hacienda-style second homes mean that you will not want to linger long, but take the time to head off down the road which follows the *plage est* (€3 in a car), the further you go the fewer tourists you see and the impressive salt marshes and vast deserted beaches provide the real Camargue. The **Musée Baroncelli** has exhibits on bullfighting and other traditions, plus the odd stuffed flamingo donated by the Marquis Folco de Baroncelli, a 19th-century aristocrat who became a Camargue cowboy.

Musée Baroncelli

rue Victor Hugo (04.90.97.87.60). **Open** *May to mid-Nov* 10am-noon, 2-6pm daily, alternate weeks. Closed mid-Nov to Apr. **Admission** €2; €1.30 6-12s; free under-6s. **No credit cards**.

Where to eat

For seaside-resort atmosphere head for the **Brasserie de la Plage** (1 av de la République, 04.90.97.84.77, menu €16). The **Brûleur de Loups** (67 av Gilbert Leroy, 04.90.97.83.31, closed Tue dinner, Wed and mid-Nov to Dec, menus €23-€37.50) has a sea view and specialities including bull carpaccio and *bourride*.

Resources

Market is Monday and Friday morning.

Tourist information

Office de Tourisme, 5 av Van Gogh, 13700 Stes-Maries-de-la-Mer (04.90.97.82.55/ www.saintesmaries.com). **Open** *Apr-June, Sept* 9am-7pm daily. *July, Aug* 9am-8pm daily. *Oct* 9am-6pm daily. *Nov-Feb* 9am-5pm daily.

Aigues-Mortes

On the western edge of the Camargue, the medieval walled city of Aigues-Mortes (from the Latin 'dead waters') rises up from the gloomy salt marshes and acres given over to the cultivation of Listel Gris wine. This would surely be nobody's first choice for urban development but Louis IX wanted to set out on crusade from his own port rather than using then-Provençal Marseille. Realising that the take-up for his new town would be low, he offered generous tax and commercial incentives. The town thrived through the Hundred Years War, when the Burgundians seized it, only to have it snatched back by the Armagnacs, who after slaughtering their enemies stored the salted corpses in the **Tour des Bourguignons**. Receding sea and silting-up of the canals led to the town's decline in the 15th century. The monumental ramparts, punctuated by massive

The Pèlerinage de Mai at **Stes-Maries-de-la-Mer.**

towers, make for a great walk. The most spectacular tower is the **Tour de Constance**. Built 1240-49, and containing a small chapel, it doubled as cells for political or religious prisoners. Once within the ramparts, the town has more than its share of tacky souvenir shops and in summer becomes overrun with day-trippers. **Eglise Notre-Dame-des-Sablons** has suffered from too many refits, but its wood-framed nave has an austere charm. The **Chapelle des Pénitents Blancs** and **Chapelle des Pénitents Gris** are interesting Baroque buildings that would benefit from more regular opening (ask at the tourist office). Place St-Louis, the main square, is a lively hub, with exhibitions in the town hall in summer.

You can also visit the **Caves de Listel** to swig some of the flinty rosé or learn all about salt production at the **Salins du Midi**. Northeast of Aigues-Mortes, the **Château de Teillan** was the former priory of the Abbaye de Psalmody, which sold the land for Aigues-Mortes to Louis IX; later additions include a Renaissance facade and 18th-century orangery.

Urban development of the 20th-century kind has expanded the ports of Le Grau-du-Roi and Port Camargue into ugly resorts whose toytown architecture provides a strange backdrop for flocks of pink flamingos.

Caves de Listel
Domaine de Jarras (04.66.51.17.00/www.listel.fr). **Open** *Apr-Sept* 10am-6pm daily. *Oct-Mar* 10am-noon, 2-5pm Mon-Fri. **Admission** €3; free under-15s. **Credit** MC, V.

Château de Teillan
Aimargues (04.66.88.02.38). **Open** *mid-June to mid-Sept* 2-6pm Tue-Sun. **Admission** €4. *Park only* €3; €2.50 12-15s; free under-12s.

Salins du Midi
(04.66.51.17.10). **Open** 9am-6.45pm daily. Closed Nov-Feb. **Admission** €6.80; €5 4-12s; free under-4s.

Tour de Constance & Ramparts
Logis du Gouverneur, pl Anatole France (04.66.53.61.55). **Open** *May* 9.30am-1pm, 2-6pm daily. *June-Aug* 9.30am-8pm daily. *Sept* 9.30am-7pm. *Oct* 10am-6pm. *Nov-Apr* 10am-1pm, 2-5pm daily. **Admission** €6.10; €4.10 18-25s; free under-18s. **Credit** MC, V.

Where to stay & eat

Restaurants on the main square are fun for an apéritif, but locals prefer frantic bistro-pizzeria **Coco** (19 rue Jean Jaurès, 04.66.53.91.83, menu €12). More upmarket **Dit Vin** (6 rue du 4 septembre, 04.66.53.52.76, www.ditvin-divine.com, menus €11-€25) is a reliable address with a nice interior terrace. **Hôtel Les Templiers** (23 rue de la République, 04.66.53.66.56, doubles €90-€125) has been restored with just the right dose of distressed elegance. A more old-fashioned atmosphere reigns at **Hôtel-Restaurant St-Louis** (10 rue Amiral Courbet, 04.66.53.72.68/ www.lesaintlouis.fr, closed end-Nov to mid-Mar, doubles €79-€102), but the garden terrace is very attractive. **Hôtel Tour de Constance** (1 bd Diderot, 04.66.53.83.50, closed mid-Nov to

Feb, double €42) is clean and practical. There is a lively row of portside fish restaurants at Port Grau-du-Roi, but don't expect sophistication.

Resources

Market is on Wednesday and Sunday mornings.

Tourist information

Office de Tourisme, pl St-Louis, 30220 Aigues Mortes (04.66.53.73.00/www.ot-aiguesmortes.fr). **Open** *June-Sept* 9am-6pm daily. *Oct-May* 9am-noon, 1-6pm Mon-Fri; 10am-noon, 2-6pm Sat, Sun.

Getting there

By car

Leave the A54 at exit 4 and take the D570 to Stes-Maries-de-la-Mer. For Aigues-Mortes take the D570 from Arles or Stes-Maries and then the D58.

By train/bus

The nearest SNCF station is Arles, from which **Voyages Telleschi** (04.42.28.40.22) runs several buses a day to Stes-Maries-de-la-Mer. From Nîmes TGV station, you can get to Aigues-Mortes by train or by bus with **STDG** (04.66.29.52.00).

White horses...

Finding a mount in the Camargue would seem an easy proposition. As you enter the region, ranches line the sides of the road, proposing rides of all sorts. In the summer of 2003, with the sun beating down providing temperatures into the mid-forties and mosquitoes forming into special, fine weather battalions, honest brokers rightly explained that it was too hot for the horses, while less reputable types were quite willing to see us gallop off to certain heat exhaustion – a B-movie cowboy scenario with canteens of water and fond farewells to favourite nag. There is nothing like choice to confuse the eager punter, so head to the Office de Tourisme de Stes-Maries-de-la-Mer, which separates trusty professionals (*see below*) from more unscrupulous operators.

If you're a beginner, head to the outstandingly helpful **Les Chevaux du Vent**, (rte d'Arles, 06.09.50.42.36), a government-approved riding school, which takes its role seriously. Even an hour on a white horse in the relative cool of the evening is a more enjoyable experience when you are not being bounced along like a sack of potatoes, and the view across the Camargue is magical with pink flamingos and assorted bird life, glimpses of grazing horses and a cautious sighting of distant bulls. Part of the appeal of riding is the extra height a horse gives you, allowing panoramic views across the salt marshes, which from a car can seem bleak and uniform. The white horses seem quiet and immune to tourist chatter and incompetent riding, but look as handsome as on the postcards.

If you've got some experience, it's better to opt for one of the longer trips, especially in a slightly cooler season. Exciting possibilities include a whole-day hack, which allows you to cross the ponds and paddy fields of the Camargue, cross the Petit Rhône by ferry, and pause for a lunchtime picnic on the beach of the Grand Radeau. For the real Western fantasy you can head off across the plains for several days, staying in authentic *cabanes*, traditional small white washed cottages, €80-€115 per day depending on the quality of your cowboy or girl accommodation and food.

Riding stables

Based at Stes-Maries-de-la-Mer, the following all cater for both beginners and experienced riders. Expect to pay €26-€28 for two hours, €70-€100 for a day (including lunch).

Brenda-Centre de Tourisme Equestre *Mas St-Georges, Astouin, (04.90.97.52.08/ www.brendatourismeequestre.com).*
Cabanes de Cacharel *Hôtel Mas des Aliscornes, rte d'Arles (04.90.97.83.41/ www.camargueacheval.com). Closed mid-Dec to mid-Mar.*
Promenades à Cheval du Pont de Gau *rte d'Arles, (04.90.97.89.45/ www.pontdegau.com). Closed mid-Nov to early-Feb, except Christmas.*
Le Tamaris *rte d'Arles (04.90.96.94.87/ www.promenade-tamaris.com). Closed Jan.*
Lou Simbèu *Le Clos du Rhône, Tiki III (06.76.77.61.82/www.lou-simbeu. camargue.fr). Closed 15 Nov-15 Feb.*
Mas de Pioch *rte d'Arles (04.90.97.55.51/ www.manadecavallini.com). Closed mid-Oct to mid-Mar, except Christmas.*
Promenade à Cheval du Boumian *rte d'Arles (04.90.97.93.12/ www.leboumian.camargue.fr).*
Promenade des Rièges *rte de Cacharel, (04.90.97.91.38/ www.promenadedesrieges.com). Closed mid-Nov to Apr.*

Avignon &
the Vaucluse

Introduction

Beyond the cultural treats of Avignon, the verdant Vaucluse is for those who appreciate great wine, great food and the great outdoors.

Unlike most French *départements*, which are named after rivers, the land-locked Vaucluse, taking in Avignon and the hilly lands spreading north and east of the Rhône, gets its name from a mystery: the *val clausa* or closed valley, where water bubbles out of a deep pool at **Fontaine de Vaucluse**. The area was strongly marked both by the Avignon papacy, which injected the Papal court as a centre of scholarship and artistic production in the 14th century, and by the Wars of Religion that set village against village. Until 1793, **Avignon** remained part of a prosperous independent enclave, known as the Comtat Venaissin, also taking in Cavaillon, Carpentras, Fontaine de Vaucluse and L'Isle-sur-la-Sorgue. This period left not only the majestic Palais des Papes, worthwhile museums and cardinals' palaces of Avignon, but also a Jewish heritage unique in France, with beautiful synagogues at **Carpentras** and **Cavaillon**, and unsuspected industrial relics that include paper mills and ochre-processing.

Today, though, the **Luberon** is at the forefront of the new rural chic. Lovely scenery, attractive villages that have stayed largely within their historic limits, imposing châteaux, remote abbeys and plenty of old farmhouses ripe for conversion are combined with the worldly social gloss of villages like **Gordes** or **Lourmarin**, all within easy reach of a cultural fix in Avignon or Aix. The less-known, lower-key, truffle-packed **Drôme Provençale** (the southern part of the Drôme *département*) is strongly tipped to follow. On the eastern edge of the Luberon, in the sparsely populated Alpes de Haute-Provence *département*, **Forcalquier** has a more provincial feel with traces of a once-powerful past as an independent Comté while, north of Avignon, **Orange** and **Vaison-la-Romaine** offer impressive Roman remains and some of the best southern Côtes du Rhône wines, notably **Châteauneuf-du-Pape**.

The Luberon massif, the ragged **Dentelles de Montmirail**, the **Baronnies** and the astonishing, bleak **Mont Ventoux** all offer plentiful opportunities for walking, riding, cycling and rock-climbing, making these places feel healthy and outdoorsy, but not too wild – after all you're never far from a vineyard or a sophisticated restaurant.

Don't miss Avignon & the Vaucluse

Chambre de Séjour avec Vue
Arty guesthouse in the Luberon. *See p117.*

Collection Lambert, Avignon
Mansion full of contemporary art. *See p84.*

Colorado de Rustrel
The ochre landscape colour shock. *See p117.*

Coronation of the Virgin
Enguerrand Quarton's Medieval masterpiece in Villeneuve-lès-Avignon. *See p94.*

Hôtel La Mirande, Avignon
Papal treatment, views and decor. *See p93.*

Institut du Monde de l'Olivier
Olive oil lessons in Nyons. *See p110.*

Lacoste
Romantic village ruins. *See p114.*

Mont Ventoux
Astonishing bald-headed, windy mountain. *See pp103-6.*

Notre-Dame de Salagon
Medieval kitchen garden and rural crafts in a Romanesque priory. *See p126.*

L'Opéra Café
For watching Avignon's gay fauna. *See p89.*

Synagogues
Rococo pretty at Carpentras (*see p101*) and Cavaillon (*see p120*).

Théâtre Antique, Orange
The perfect setting for opera. *See p96.*

Village des Bories
Drystone shepherd life from Gordes' less-chic ancestors. *See p123.*

Paris on a platter with Time Out

Now in its 12th edition, the annual *Time Out Paris Guide* is truly the critic's choice, with up-to-the-minute picks of the city's coolest places, plus shopping, sightseeing and the best spots to lay your head in style and comfort.

For the first time in book form, Time Out's honest, authoritative reviews of 850 top Paris tables. Discover refined haute cuisine, classic bistros, bustling cafés and brasseries, plus the best bars, clubs, boutiques, wine and cookery classes.

On sale now at good bookshops or on www.timeout.com/shop

Avignon

Despite being left stranded in greasepaint in 2003, Avignon retains its *joie de vivre*, carried by a lively café culture under the shadow of its papal palace.

Avignon's recent dramas, when its prestigious Festival was cancelled abruptly in 2003 (*see p90*, **Avignon Festival RIP?**), could never eclipse its centuries of papal glory. The spectacular Palais des Papes is fossilised in a state of indelible splendour, and no wholesale party-pooping can tarnish its weather-beaten crown.

The city is still contained within its 14th-century walls: 4km of beautifully preserved ramparts, crenellated in the 19th century by ubiquitous 'improver' Viollet le Duc, who filled in the moat. Looming from within is the fairytale centrepiece of the Palais des Papes and the golden Virgin gleaming at the top of Cathédrale Notre-Dame-des-Doms. At its feet, the stubby remains of the Pont d'Avignon grind abruptly to a halt in the middle of the Rhône.

Only recently, the city has been re-styling itself in response to the theatre crowds and the new arrivals from the TGV station opened in 2001. A surge of new bars, cafés, restaurants, hotels and shops pander to hefty wallets, with students and the thriving gay community leading the way in hip hang-outs. Even Malcolm McLaren, ageing harbinger of cool, has moved in, and the Collection Lambert has added contemporary art to the city's heritage.

Yet beneath the grandeur is another Avignon: a town of gloomy, twilit streets, chill with autumn river damps and pummelled by the howling mistral. Huge parts of Avignon remain shabby and unrestored, and once the festival hysteria has packed up, it descends into an austere, cultural graveyard where theatre companies battle to remain open all year. Futhermore, Avignon has long cultivated a stuffy, bourgeois reputation that hides squalor behind a 'see and be seen' Sunday best. Today, the capital of the Vaucluse is reputed to be one of France's most crime-ridden cities, with the suburbs turning increasingly into a barren, inter-racial gangsterland.

HISTORY

Avignon started life as a neolithic settlement on the Rocher des Doms. Under the Romans, it flourished as a river port, but it was not until the 12th century, when Avignon's clergy became a power to be reckoned with, that the village started to think big, building towers, the Romanesque cathedral and St-Bénezet bridge.

In 1306, French Pope Clément V brought his court from turmoil-wracked Rome to the safety of the independent Vatican-owned Comtat Venaissin. After his death in 1314 six further French popes saw no reason to relocate to Rome. Their 68-year 'Babylonian captivity', as furious Italians branded it, utterly transformed the quiet provincial backwater. The population soared and artists, scholars, architects, weavers and jewellers flocked to find patronage. The virtue industry fostered vice in equal measure: 'a sewer,' sniffed Petrarch, 'the filthiest of cities'.

Gregory XI, elected in 1370, was badgered by the persuasive St Catherine of Siena into returning to the Holy See. He took her advice, went back, and promptly died in 1378. The Italians elected a Roman pope, but the French were loath to lose their hold on the reins of power and swiftly elected Clement VII in Avignon. The rival popes excommunicated each other, sparking the Great Schism, which finally ended when all sides agreed on the election of Martin V in 1417.

Even after the popes returned to Italy, Avignon remained papal territory. Without French censorship, and far enough from Rome to escape Vatican checks, the town flourished as an artistic, religious and publishing centre, which continued when the town was returned to France in 1791: it was to Avignon that the Félibrige turned in the 19th century to get its Provençal revival works into print (*see p12*).

Sightseeing

The terraced gardens of the Rocher des Doms, perched above the Rhône, is where Avignon started, and it's also a good place to begin a visit (although if you arrive by train the Centre Ville station is at the opposite side of the old town). A miniature vineyard sloping down the northern side signals Avignon's role as capital of Côtes du Rhône, with an example of every grape variety represented: the full gamut is harvested during the Ban des Vendanges festival in September. From the Rocher, the view ranges over the whole city – 'its closely knitted roofs of weathered tile like a pie crust fresh from the oven', as Lawrence Durrell wrote – and takes in a great sweep of the Rhône and Villeneuve-lès-Avignon on the opposite bank.

Avignon & the Vaucluse

Jutting into the river below the Rocher des Doms stand the four remaining arches of the **Pont St-Bénezet**. It can be reached by walking along the only section of the city walls open to the public. Between the Dom and the bridge, the **Musée du Petit Palais**, a former

cardinal's palace, has a superb collection of early Italian and Provençal paintings, and sculptures rescued from Avignon churches.

The massive bulk of the **Palais des Papes**, more like an ogre's castle than pontiff's palace, shares its square with **Cathédrale Notre-**

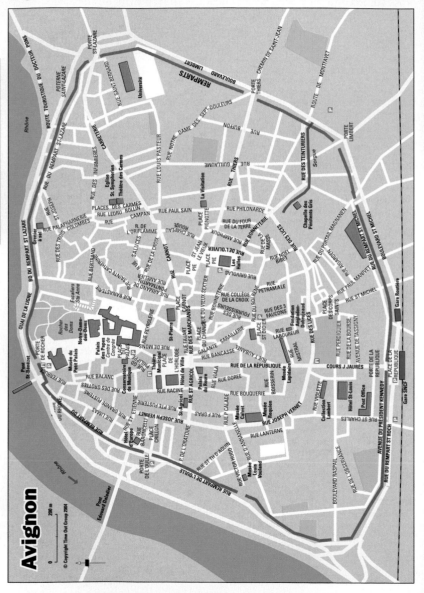

Avignon

0   200 m

© Copyright Time Out Group 2004

Dame-des-Doms and the swagged and
furbelowed former Hôtel des Monnaies (mint),
now the Conservatoire de Musique. Before
entering the Palais, get a sense of its solidity by
walking along rue de la Peyrollerie to see its
towers, embedded in sheer rock.

A little further south, **place de l'Horloge** is
the centre of town life, with its cafés, **Théâtre
Municipal** and grand 19th-century Hôtel de
Ville. The square gets its name from the Gothic
clock tower, Tour du Jacquemart, although the
painted wooden figurines of Jacquemart and his
wife have taken retirement from ringing the
hour. At festival time the square is home to a
whirling carousel of musicians and minstrels.

South of here rue de la République is
Avignon's main shopping thoroughfare. To
the west lies the smart part of town, its streets
packed with fashionable restaurants and
beautifully restored mansions. On rue St-
Agricol, the 15th-century carved doorway of
Église St-Agricol (open for services only,
5pm Sat) has been newly restored, as has its
16th-century painting of the Assumption by
Avignon artist Simon de Châlons. An alley off
rue Agricol leads to the 15th-century **Palais
du Roure** (3 pl du Collège du Roure,
04.90.80.80.88, guided tours 3pm Tue), where
the aristocratic *gardian* (Camargue cowboy)
poet Folco Baroncelli was born, and where
Frédéric Mistral edited *Aïoli*, his journal in
Provençal. Today it is a literary archive and
headquarters of the Festival Provençal in July,
putting on plays in the local *félibrige* dialect.

Rue Joseph Vernet, which curves round to
join busy rue de la République, is a shopaholic's
dream of designer stores and handmade
chocolates in a parade of 17th- and 18th-century
hôtels particuliers. Off its northern end, the
Hôtel d'Europe on rue Baroncelli has long
been a favourite with visiting foreign lovers,
among them the eloping Brownings and John
Stuart Mill and Mrs Taylor (Harriet Hardy).
When Harriet died there, Mill was so distraught
that he bought a house overlooking the
cemetery where she was buried, furnishing it
with the contents of their last hotel room.

Further south on rue Victor Hugo, the
Musée Vouland is a lavishly decorated
private house, full of 18th-century French
furniture and faïence. Back on rue Joseph
Vernet, the **Musée Calvet** displays sculpture
and paintings in the elegant colonnaded
galleries of an 18th-century palace. In another
wing is the **Muséum Requien**, an old-
fashioned natural history museum. Nearby,
another renovated 18th-century *hôtel* contains
the cutting-edge contemporary art of the
Collection Lambert. On rue Portail Boquier,
check out the mixture of historic and modern, at

the **Hôtel Cloître St-Louis**, a former
monastery. On one side of the cloister, the
Espace St-Louis is used for art exhibitions
and becomes a box office during the festival.

East of rue de la République, on a spacious
paved square, the lovely church of **St-Didier**
was built in the simple, single-aisled Provençal
Gothic style. Nearby, the **Médiathèque
Livrée Ceccano**, a 14th-century cardinal's
palace, is now the municipal library and
multimedia centre. Around the corner in rue
Laboureur is the **Fondation Angladon-
Dubrujeaud**, a worthwhile private art
museum; the **Musée Lapidaire** collection of
ancient sculpture is housed nearby in a former
Jesuit chapel. Across rue des Lices, not far from
the tourist office, lies shady place des Corps-
Saints. Stretched in front of the 14th-century
Chapelle de St-Michel et Tous-les-Saints, it
becomes a sea of café chairs in summer.

Heading east out of place St-Didier, rue du
Roi René has several fine 17th- and 18th-
century mansions; at No.22 a plaque records
that this was where Italian poet Petrarch first
set eyes on Laure in 1327, the woman he was to
idolise for the rest of his life. At the far end, the
cobbled, boho rue des Teinturiers is one of
Avignon's most atmospheric streets, winding
along beside the river Sorgue, where the water
wheels of the dye works that gave the street its
name are still visible. Production of the
patterned calico known as *indiennes* thrived
here until the end of the 19th century. Now the
street is home to cafés under spreading plane
trees, second-hand bookshops and art galleries.
At No.8 the **Chapelle des Pénitents Gris**
(open 2-5pm Tue, Sat), crouched at the end of a
tiny bridge, was founded in the 13th century.
The chapel is believed to have had its own, mini
version of the 'parting of the Red Sea': during
the floods of 1433, the waters are said to have
curled back either side of the aisle, allowing the
consecrated host to be carried out safe and dry.

The partly pedestrianised streets north of
place St-Didier are the heart of the medieval
town. Most of this district is surprisingly
shabby, dimly lit at night, with empty statue
niches and pigeon-daubed churches. At the
Hôtel de Rascas on rue des Fourbisseurs, the
corbels of a projecting upper storey point to a
cardinal's demands for extra airspace. Place Pie
is home to Avignon's covered food market
(7am-1pm Tue-Sun). In place St-Pierre to the
north, the Gothic church of **St-Pierre** (open for
services only; 6.30pm Fri, Sat) has finely carved
walnut doors and a handsome belfry.

The winding streets behind the Palais des
Papes lead to rue Banasterie and the **Chapelle
des Pénitents Noirs**, which has a sumptuous
Baroque interior painted to the last inch with

gold leaf and cherubs, but is rarely open. Round the corner on rue des Escaliers Ste-Anne, the **Utopia** arts cinema is one of Avignon's liveliest cultural centres. Just inside the northern ramparts lies **Le Grenier à Sel**, a restored salt house, newly reawakened as an arts venue and auction house. Opposite, the Porte de la Ligne gateway emerges beside the Rhône, close to the jetty where you can catch a new, free ferry service that nips you across to the grassy Ile de la Barthelasse every 15 minutes in summer.

Back inside the ramparts and down a warren of murky backstreets, the **Mont-de-Piété** is birthplace to the modern French savings bank: a pocket-sized museum recalls the building's philanthropic past. Further east on place des Carmes, **Eglise St Symphorien** (04.90.82.10.56, open Mon & morning Sun), originally a Carmelite convent, has a 15th-century Gothic facade and some lovely polychrome wooden statues inside. Its 14th-century cloisters now rub shoulders with one of Avignon's oldest theatre companies, the **Théâtre des Carmes**. This is the university district, packed with bars, cafés and second-hand bookstores. Past the Porte St-Lazare, avenue Stuart Mill leads to **Cimetière St-Véran** (04.90.80.79.95, open 8.30am until dusk daily) where Harriet Hardy and Mill are buried.

Cathédrale Notre-Dame-des-Doms

pl du Palais (04.90.82.12.24). **Open** Feb-Oct 7am-6pm daily. *Nov-Jan* 7am-5pm daily. *Treasury Apr-Nov* 9am-noon, 2-7pm daily. *Dec-Mar* by appointment. Despite its imposing position, this is a surprisingly unspiritual church. Apart from the Romanesque porch and a fine marble throne, most vestiges of its 12th-century origins have been obliterated by subsequent alterations: a Baroque gallery, a rebuilt tower and a tacky golden statue of the Virgin perched on its pinnacle. Even the Simone Martini frescoes have been moved to the Palais des Papes.

Collection Lambert

Hôtel de Caumont, 5 rue Violette (04.90.16.56.20/ www.collectionlambert.com). **Open** *July* 11am-7pm daily. *Aug* 11am-7pm Tue-Sun. *Sept-June* 11am-6pm Tue-Sat. **Admission** €5.50; €4 students, 12-16s; free under-12s. **Credit** MC, V.
Parisian art dealer Yvon Lambert has loaned his formidable contemporary art collection to Avignon for 20 years. Housed in an 18th-century *hôtel particulier*, the 850 pieces, spanning the late 1950s to the present, are interwoven with temporary exhibitions and new commissions. Particularly strong on conceptual and minimalist art, the collection takes in painting, sculpture, installation, video and photography by names such as Nan Goldin, Douglas Gordon, Thomas Hirschhorn, Jean-Michel Basquiat, Cy Twombly and Jonathan Monk. The collection is presented in two changing exhibitions a year, with an adventurous, guest-curated exhibition each summer. There is a good bookshop, and a courtyard café.

Eglise St-Didier

pl St-Didier (04.90.86.20.17). **Open** 8am-7pm daily.
This pretty example of Provençal Gothic has delicate 14th-century Italian frescoes in the north chapel. In the Chapelle St-Bénezet are relics of the bridge-building saint himself, or his skull at least; experts have established that he was only 25 at his death.

Fondation Angladon-Dubrujeaud

5 rue Laboureur (04.90.82.29.03/www.angladon.com). **Open** *June-Sept* 1-6pm Tue-Sun. *Oct-May* 1-6pm Wed-Sun, **Admission** €6; €3 students; €1.50 7-14s; free under-7s. **No credit cards.**
Arranged like a period home, this 18th-century mansion is decorated with the collection left by 19th-century Paris couturier Jacques Doucet to local artist-couple Jean and Paulette Angladon-Dubrujeaud. In the upper rooms, each painting, piece of furniture and *objet d'art* is hung with an eye to the right setting. Dutch oils are complemented by oak chests, *armoires* and faïence, while 18th-century French portraits occupy a lavish gilt and brocade salon. The celebrity line-up of paintings on the ground-floor covers Degas, Picasso, Cézanne, Modigliani and Sisley, and boasts the only Van Gogh in Provence.

Le Grenier à Sel

2 rue du Rempart St-Lazare (04.90.27.09.09/ www.grenieraselavignon.com). **Open** 9am-noon, 2-6pm Mon-Fri (plus Sat, Sun during exhibitions). **Admission** €5; €3 students, 12-18s, over-60s; free under 12s. **No credit cards.**
This award-winning renovation of a 16th-century salt warehouse acts as a part-time auction house for Jacques Desamais and an arts venue. Its opening show was a retrospective of Gaston Chaissac, and to come are Balthus (mid-Aug to mid-Nov 2004) and the Fauves in 2005. The split-level stone structure with wooden beams is a listed historic monument, shot through with metal and glass in an open, austere conversion by architect Jean-Michel Wilmotte.

Médiathèque Livrée Ceccano

2 bis rue Laboureur, (04.90.85.15.59). **Open** 1-6pm Mon; 10am-6pm Tue-Sat. **Admission** free.
The public library is grandly housed in the former palace of 14th-century Cardinal Annibal Ceccano, extended in the 18th-century by the Jesuits. The two main halls retain their original frescoes and painted wooden ceilings. The faded canopy of heraldic motifs featuring Ceccano's spread-eagle coat of arms has survived the building's multiple reincarnations as a barracks and then a lycée, albeit wasted above the 1970s bookcases and strip lighting.

Mont-de-Piété

6 rue Saluces, (04.90.86.53.12). **Open** 8.30-11.30am, 1.30-5pm Mon-Fri. **Admission** free
The current municipal archives are a monument to good works and cunning business plans. It was here that France's first church-owned pawnbroker was

The formidable **Palais des Papes**. *See p87.*

set up as a charitable mission in 1610, with the aim of distributing loans to, and subsequently 'de-shaming', the region's poor. Silk conditioning works were later introduced as an enterprising ruse to boost capital after the Revolution. A curious 'museum' in the former chapel makes a brief but engaging visit.

Musée Calvet

65 rue Joseph Vernet (04.90.86.33.84/ www.fondation-calvet.org). **Open** 10am-1pm, 2-6pm Mon, Wed-Sun. **Admission** €6; €3 12-18s; free under-12s. **No credit cards**.

The beautifully restored fine art museum displays its collection in elegant, colonnaded rooms around a courtyard. The ground floor has Gobelins tapestries and medieval sculpture. 18th- and 19th-century French paintings include works by the Avignon-based Vernet family and David's *La Mort du jeune Bara*. There is a good modern section with works by Bonnard, Vuillard, Sisley, Manet and Dufy, and Camille Claudel's head of her brother Paul, who had her sent to a mental asylum near Avignon when her relationship with Rodin became too scandalous.

Musée Lapidaire

27 rue de la République (04.90.85.75.38/ www.fondation-calvet.org). **Open** 10am-1pm, 2-6pm, Wed-Mon. **Admission** €2; €1 12-18s; free under-12s. **No credit cards**.

Avignon's archaeological collection is superbly displayed in a 17th-century Jesuit chapel. As well as Greek, Gallo-Roman and Etruscan sculpture, mosaics and glass, it is rich in Egyptian sculpture, stele

and shabti. The Gallo-Roman selection has a depiction of the Tarasque of Noves, the local man-eating monster immortalised by Daudet.

Musée Louis-Vouland

17 rue Victor Hugo (04.90.86.03.79/ www.vouland.com). **Open** *May-Oct* 10am-noon, 2-6pm Tue-Sat; 2-6pm Sun. *Nov-Apr* 2-6pm Tue-Sun. **Admission** €4; €2.50 12-18s; free under-12s. **No credit cards**.

A 19th-century *hôtel particulier* with *trompe-l'oeil* ceilings houses the largely 18th-century decorative arts collection of former resident Louis Vouland. A preserved meat salesman, Vouland spent 50 years acquiring furniture and porcelain, including faïence from Les Moustiers, Montpellier and Marseille, Ming porcelain and intricate inlaid writing-desks. 19th-century paintings from the Avignon school include works by Claude Firmin and Pierre Grivolas.

Musée du Petit Palais

pl du Palais-des-Papes (04.90.86.44.58). **Open** *June-Sept* 10am-1pm, 2-6pm Mon, Wed-Sun. *Oct-May* 9.30am-1pm, 2-5.30pm Mon, Wed-Sun. **Admission** €6; €3 12-18s; free under-12s. **No credit cards**.

First constructed in 1308 for a cardinal, the Petit Palais had its Renaissance facade and decorative tower added in the late 15th century by Cardinal Giuliano della Rovere, the future Pope Julius II. Today, the series of atmospheric rooms, with original stone fireplaces and *trompe-l'oeil* ceilings, house magnificent medieval paintings, frescoes and sculpture, many rescued from churches destroyed in the

Never heard of a balcony bra? A cheeky sculpture lends a hand on **place de l'Horloge**. *See p83.*

Revolution. Note the sarcophagus of Cardinal Jean de Lagrange, with its anatomically realistic depiction of a decaying corpse, and his brutally mutilated tomb effigy. The bulk of the paintings were assembled by Gian Pietro Campana di Cavelli, a 19th-century Italian collector who went bankrupt, allowing Napoléon III to snap up his entire estate. It provides a fine introduction to the International Gothic style brought to Avignon by the mostly Sienese artists patronised by the popes, and clung to long after it had gone out of fashion elsewhere.

Muséum Requien d'Histoire Naturelle

67 rue Joseph Vernet (04.90.82.43.51). **Open** 9am-noon, 2-6pm Tue-Sat. **Admission** free.

An old-fashioned natural history museum, packed with rocks, minerals, stuffed animals and fossils. Buried in the archives is John Stuart Mill's collection of dried flowers and herbs. Temporary exhibitions hold a magnifying glass up to regional themes such as local insects and mushrooms.

Palais des Papes

pl du Palais (04.90.27.50.73/www.palais-des-papes.com). **Open** *Apr-July* 9am-7pm daily; *Aug, Sept* 9am-8pm; *Nov-Mar* 9.30am-5.45pm daily. **Admission** *mid-Mar to Oct* €9.50; €7.50 students, 8-17s; free under-8s. *Nov to mid-Mar* €7.50; €6 students, 8-17s; free under-8s. **Credit** MC, V.

More of a fortress than the palace of God's representative on earth, the Palais des Papes is a brutal power statement. The interior is strangely empty after the devastation wreaked during the Revolution, when 60 pro-papal prisoners were flung into the Tour des Latrines. During the palace's subsequent use as a prison and barracks soldiers chipped off bits of fresco to sell but many exquisite fragments remain. The Palais is a complicated labyrinth with two interlocking parts: the forbidding Palais Vieux, built in the 1330s for the austere Cistercian monk Pope Benedict XII, and the more showy Palais Neuf, tacked on a decade later by Clément VI. You can wander at will (an audio guide is included in the entry fee), or join a guided tour (some are in English). Across the main courtyard from the ticket office is the Salle de Jésus, the antechamber of the papal council room or Consistoire, where frescoes from the cathedral are displayed. The Chapelle St-Jean next door has delightful frescoes (c1346) by Matteo Giovanetti, Clément VI's court painter. Upstairs, the ceiling of the Grand Tinel banqueting hall was once coloured blue and dotted with gold stars to resemble the sky. Next door, the kitchens with their huge pyramid-shaped chimney could feed 3,000 guests. There are more Giovanetti frescoes, lavish with lapis lazuli and gold, in the Chapelle St-Martial. Beyond the Salle de Parement (robing room), Benedict XII's tiled study was only discovered in 1963. The papal bedchamber is followed by the Chambre du Cerf, Clement VI's study, with some delightful frescoes that exude the spirit of courtly love. Vast as it is, the Chapelle Clémentine, which you come to next, was

barely large enough to hold the college of cardinals when it gathered in conclave to elect a new pope. Through the Chamberlain's Room, whose raised stone slabs mark the spot where papal treasure was discovered, stairs lead up to the battlements, with a dramatic view over the city. Back on the ground floor, the Grande Audience hall has a bevy of Biblical prophets frescoed by Giovannetti. The palace's empty spaces are put to good use with occasional art exhibitions, and the *cour d'honneur* is a key venue for festival productions. At weekends, a 'backstage' tour, Palais Secret (€21.50, including Provençal brunch and wine tasting) reveals unrestored rooms, terraces and gardens usually unseen by the public, including the steamrooms, storerooms and the garden of Benoît XII. On your way out, stock up on Côtes du Rhône at La Bouteillerie, former wine cellar to the papal banquets.

Pont St-Bénezet

rue Ferruce (04.90.27.51.16/www.palais-des-papes.com). **Open** *mid-Mar to June, Oct* 9am-7pm daily. *July-Sept* 9am-8pm daily. *Nov to mid-Mar* 9.30am-5.45pm daily. **Admission** *mid-Mar to Oct* €3.50; *Nov to mid-Mar* €3; free under-8s. **Credit** MC, V.

The original pont d'Avignon was begun in 1185 by a divinely inspired shepherd boy from the Ardèche who became St Bénezet. He lifted the first massive stone, convincing the sceptical populace that construction was possible. When completed, the bridge was 22 arches and nearly a kilometre long, and contributed greatly to the development of Avignon, although in 1660, after a huge flood, the *avignonnais* finally gave up the unequal maintenance struggle. Today, only four arches and a tiny Romanesque fisherman's chapel remain; a small museum in the reception area explains the history. Despite the song, it seems unlikely that anyone ever danced on the narrow, traffic-packed structure. It is more likely that people danced 'sous le pont' (under the bridge): the Ile de la Barthelasse, which the bridge used to cross, was a favourite R&R spot during the Middle Ages.

Arts & entertainment

La Galerie MMB

20 rue de la Balance, (04.90.85.17.21). **Open** 10am-noon, 2-6pm Tue-Sat. **Admission** free.

Marie-Marguerite Buhler recently opened this contemporary art space behind the place du Palais. She shows French sculptors and painters with a taste for sobre, architectural forms.

L'Hélicon

23 rue Bancasse (04.90.16.03.99). **Open** noon-2pm Mon-Wed; noon-2pm, 7-11pm Thur, Fri; 7-11pm Sat (noon-2pm, 7-11pm daily in July). Musical evenings Fri, Sat. Closed Jan. **Menus** €18-€25. **Credit** MC, V.

A jovial local knees-up as *chanson française* is performed by guest stars, or Freddy the owner himself. A surprisingly young clientele heckles for more Piaf and Brassens as they munch good, hearty fare.

The **Théâtre Municipal** offers a year-round feast of music and theatre.

Piscine de la Barthelasse

Ile de la Barthelasse (04 90 82 54 25). **Open** *May-Aug* 10am-7pm daily. **Admission** €4.70; €3.20 after 5pm; €2.50 2-5s. **Credit** MC, V.
Olympic-sized open-air pool for when the city gets too hot to bear.

Théâtre des Carmes

6 pl des Carmes (04.90.82.20.47). **Box office** 9am-4pm Mon-Fri. **Tickets** €10-€15. **Credit** MC, V.
Avignon's oldest theatre company (also claiming the title of foundation-stone to the 'Off' festival) is firmly committed to radical theatre.

Théâtre du Chien qui fume

75 rue des Teinturiers (04.90.85.25.87/www.chienqui fume.com). Closed Aug. **Box office** one hour before show. **Shows** 8.30pm some Thur, Fri. **Tickets** €10-€25; free last Fri of the month. **No credit cards.**
Director Gérard Vantaggioli keeps the theatre buoyant throughout the year with new productions, exhibitions, and *chanson française* sung by his May '68 buddies. A free show on the last Friday of the month welcomes new theatre, song, dance and circus acts.

Théâtre Municipal

20 pl de l'Horloge (04.90.82.81.40). **Box office** 11am-6pm Mon-Sat; 11am-12.30pm Sun. **Tickets** €5-€60. **Credit** MC, V.
The main permanent house in Avignon stages official festival productions in July and opera, ballet, comedy, chamber and symphony music all year.

Utopia

La Manutention, 4 rue des Escaliers Ste-Anne (04.90.82.65.36). **Box office** 11am-11pm daily. Tickets €4-€5; €40 ten-show pass. **No credit cards.**
Avignon's main *version originale* (original language) cinema is a cultural hub with a packed programme and good bistro-bar. It has a smaller offshoot at 5 rue Figuière. Free information sheet *La Gazette* is available city-wide for listings and reviews.

Restaurants

Le Caveau du Théâtre

16 rue des Trois Faucons (04.90.82.60.91). **Open** noon-2pm, 7-10pm Mon-Fri; 7-10.30pm Sat. **Menus** €10.60-€18. **Credit** MC, V.
This friendly bistro with background jazz looks like a wine cellar in one room and a theatre backstage in the other. Theatre-going couples come here for good-value dishes such as pork *filet mignon* in garlic and honey sauce, and lemon purée with verbena coulis.

La Compagnie des Comptoirs

83 rue Joseph Vernet (04.90.85.99.04/www.la compagniedescomptoirs.com). **Open** noon-2pm, 7.30-11pm Tue-Sat; noon-2pm Sun. **Average** €30. **Credit** AmEx, V.
The celebrated Pourcel twins of Montpellier have awakened Avignon to the ways of hip, urban concept dining. So far, it is the middle-aged who appear most curious to sample the fusion cuisine, blending

the Mediterranean with India, Italy and Morocco. The bamboo lounge bar has good cocktails and late-night DJs, its clientele decamping in summer to the designer 'souk' outside.

L'Epicerie

10 pl St-Pierre (04.90.82.74.22). **Open** 12.30-2.30pm, 7-10pm Mon-Sat. Closed Nov-Mar. **Average** €20. **Credit** MC, V.

Fashionable, picture-perfect L'Epicerie hides in a tiny cobbled square. Relaxed staff serve a vegetable-strong Mediterranean menu.

Hiely–Lucullus

5 rue de la République, (04.90.86.17.07). **Open** noon-2pm, 7-10pm daily. **Menus** €24-€38. **Credit** MC, V.

Tradition on a plate, here is where to find dainty feasting for the civilised. Amid hushed conversation the cuisine blends a delicate balance of southern flavours: light tapenade crêpes, calf's liver with roast figs, and home-made pâtisseries.

Le Grand Café

La Manutention, 4 rue des Escaliers Ste-Anne (04.90.86.86.77). **Open** noon-midnight Tue-Sat (meals noon-2pm, 7.30-10pm). Closed Jan. **Menus** €16.50-€30. **Credit** AmEx, DC, MC, V.

Avignon goes all 'designer dining room' in this converted army supplies depot next to the Utopia cinema. There's a small lunch menu and afternoon tea, while in the evenings the acoustics swell with well-to-do patter as waiters serve inventive Med cuisine.

Maison Nani

29 rue Théodore Aubanel (04.90.82.60.90). **Open** 11.30am-2.30pm Mon-Thur; 11.30am-2.30pm, 7-11pm Fri, Sat. **Average** €15. **No credit cards.**

This relaxed café is preserved in a permanent, lazy weekend mode. Select from imaginative salads to accompany seafood *choucroute*, entrecôte steak and foie gras, followed by chocolate and chestnut gateau.

Le Mesclun/Brunel

48 rue de la Balance (04.90.86.14.60). **Open** noon-3pm Tue-Sat (and 7.30-11pm Mon-Sat in July). Closed mid-Dec to mid-Jan. **Menus** €20. **No credit cards.**

This comely little bistro churns out good, quick Provençal lunches, including fish, salads, and aïoli on Fridays. Brunel, its more contemporary parent at No.26 (04.90.85.24.83), lets you enjoy the same lunch menu seated in Philippe Starck chairs, with more sophisticated fare at night (Tue-Sat).

La Mirande

4 pl de la Mirande (04.90.85.93.93/www.la-mirande.fr). **Open** 12.30-2pm, 7.30-10pm Mon, Thur-Sun. Closed Jan. **Menus** €49-€82. **Credit** AmEx, DC, MC, V.

Under chef Jérôme Verrière the restaurant of Hôtel de la Mirande remains fit for a pope, proffering foie gras with peach salad, lobster ravioli, and a raft of elaborate desserts. Eat in the rose garden or in the 15th-century dining room. Tuesday and Wednesday nights see an informal *table d'hôte* in the old kitchens, where cookery courses are held by guest chefs.

Numéro 75

75 rue Guillaume Puy (04.90.27.16.00). **Open** noon-2.15pm, 7.30-10pm Mon-Sat. **Menus** €20-€30. **Credit** MC, V.

Brunel's restaurant empire reaches its most decadent expression in the stylishly converted former *hôtel particulier* of the Pernod family with a lush, walled garden. Wealthy young lovers and families crunch over the gravel to try pork tagine, gambas a la plancha and other Mediterranean flavours.

Piedoie

26 rue des Trois Faucons (04.90.86.51.53). **Open** 7.15-9.30pm Mon; noon-1.30pm, 7.15-9.30pm Tue-Sun. Closed 2wks Feb & Aug. **Menus** €18-€52. **Credit** MC, V.

Chef Thierry Piedoie's cooking is light and well-balanced and the €18 lunch menu is excellent value – on our visit it gave us delicate herb ravioles, monkfish on a bed of leeks with dill and a strawberry gratin. The service and setting are quite formal.

Woolloomooloo

16 bis rue des Teinturiers (04.90.85.28.44/ www.woolloo.com). **Open** 11.45am-2.10pm, 7.30-11pm Tue-Sun (9am-2am daily in July). **Menus** €11-€24. **Credit** MC, V.

The funky, candlelit HQ to Avignon's boho crowd is permanently buzzing with brooding students and playwrights in the making, fuelling their genius on its 'world food' menu.

Bars & cafés

Le Café de la Comédie

15 pl Crillon (04.90.85.74.85). **Open** 7am-1am Mon-Sat (7am-3am during festival). Closed 1wk in Feb & Aug. **Credit** DC, MC, V.

In a calm, spacious square, dotted with restaurants, Café de la Comédie attracts late-twentysomethings who huddle under a plane tree, looking out on the Renaissance facade of Avignon's first theatre.

Le Café-Lavoir

101 rue Bonnetterie (04.90.27.91.06). **Open** 10am-8pm Mon Sat (till 1am daily in July). **No credit cards.**

Fit in a coloured wash while you relax over coffee or herbal tea at this new multi-tasking café-cum-launderette, a friendly landing stage with pavement terrace, monthly art exhibitions, jazz concerts and lively debate led by owner-author Réné Soler.

Le Cid Café

11 pl de l'Horloge (04.90.82.30.38/www.lecidcafe.com). **Open** 7am-1am daily. **Credit** MC, V.

Often dolling itself up in camp 'themed' disguises, the Cid remains queen of the café parade on place de l'Horloge. The laidback crowd is pleasantly mixed by day, gay by night, when there are DJs: disco on Monday, Latino on Wednesday, house at weekends.

L'Opéra Café

24 pl de l'Horloge (04.90.86.17.43). **Open** 9am-1am daily (meals served noon-2.15pm, 7-11pm). **Menu** €13-€32. **Credit** DC, MC, V.

A flamboyant, purple-clad posing parlour, this is the latest amethyst in the crown of place de l'Horloge. The terrace chairs are full all day with an often gay crowd, enjoying the decorative spectacle of young 'demoiselles d'Avignon' and their persistant suitors.

Simple Simon Tea Lunch

26 rue Petite Fusterie (04.90.86.62.70). **Open** noon-7pm Mon-Sat. Closed Aug. **Average** €10. **Credit** MC, V.

A slice of Britain complete with beams, English china and swirly carpets, this tea room has a permanent stream of sweet-toothed visitors. The spotlit cake table is piled with cheesecake, shortbread and scones, while savoury staples like fish pie and Irish stew are served all day.

Clubs & live music

Le Bokao's

9bis quai St-Lazare (04.90.82.47.95). **Open** 10pm-5am Wed-Sat. **Admission** free Wed-Fri; €10 incl 1st drink Sat. **Credit** AmEx, DC, MC, V.

This converted barn beside the Rhône has just been elevated from bar to full-blooded nightclub, pumping disco, house and techno. A good freebie boogie on weekdays, it is worth the hike beyond the ramparts, but only if staff like the look of you.

Delirium

1 rue Mignard (04.90.85.44.56/www.ledelirium.net). **Open** 8.30pm-1am Thur-Sat (daily in July). **Admission** €2 inscription **No credit cards**.

Avignon Festival RIP?

The Avignon Festival put on its most tragic performance to date in summer 2003. For the first time in its 57-year history, the pacemaker of the French theatre scene skipped a beat and was cancelled at the eleventh hour. The city was already dressed in full costume – stage waiting in the Cour d'Honneur, posters papering the lampposts and 74,000 seats sold in advance – but gone was the festive buzz that usually electrifies the streets for three weeks each July, turning Avignon into an international showcase for theatre and dance. Only two days after the official 'In' festival was due to open, its outgoing artistic director, Bernard Faivre d'Arcier (BFA), solemnly declared it cancelled. In its place was a morbid *tableau vivant*: performers and stagehands lying silent and crying on the streets, dressed in mourning, their mouths gagged with black tape and the words 'En Grève': the cast and crew of Avignon 2003 were on strike.

For a short prologue it was costly: the festival made a loss of almost €2 million, and local trade was strangled by hotel cancellations and empty restaurant tables. Avignon lost a predicted €40 million, its Chamber of Commerce declaring it a 'cultural catastrophe zone'. The town-theatre divide widened, with the hotel trade blaming 'dandies' nostalgic for May 68 for 'spoiling the party'.

Yet this suicidal damper was part of a wider national drama, as one by one festivals across France were cancelled when the *intermittents du spectacle* (performing artists, backstage staff and broadcasting technicians) went on strike in protest against a reform to their previously rather generous unemployment benefit scheme. The untimely political bombshell, announced by culture minister Jean-Jacques Aillagon, brought 'l'exception culturelle' into the spotlight. The big question: how much is France, so-called protector of the arts, prepared to pay to keep its culture alive? Avignon switched roles and became a high-profile platform for the national debate. The 'In' and fringe 'Off' festivals joined forces for the first time, with many who had opted to strike staying behind to create an alternative programme of debates and improvised plays to address the culture crisis.

Avignon's catastrophic fall was not just a sacrifice to the higher cause of French art. It was a sign that the festival was already rotting inside. Cast in the role of the villain is Bernard Faivre d'Arcier, blamed by many for having lost the original democratic spirit of the festival that Jean Vilar created in 1947 with his Théâtre National Populaire. Under BFA's 16-year tenure, the heavily subsidised 'In' has grown into an institutionalised elite citadel, its soaring ticket prices and exclusive sales system putting it out of reach to the wider audience. At the same time, theatre companies accuse him of pushing 'the masses' a bit too far and turning the fringe 'Off' into a flabby, low-brow theme park, opening the floodgates to an uncensored circus of talentless 'artists', who sap audiences and dilute the festival's creative pedigree. Ushered offstage by the new right-wing government, his final year made for an ignominious exit. 'Perhaps the end of an era, but not the end of the festival,' were his hopeful words on the unprecedented cancellation. Is this the nail in the coffin, or will Avignon live to see the curtain rise again?

This relaxed, new members' club is a modern-day cultural salon with exhibitions and performance art. The space unrolls like a furniture showroom, murmuring with the beautiful and bohemian who sip inspiration from the melonjaja cocktail.

Pub Z

58 rue Bonneterie (04.90.85.42.84). **Open** noon-1.30am Mon-Sat. Closed Aug. **No credit cards.**
A lifesize zebra welcomes you into the striped bar popular with rockers and students. There's a happy hour (7.30-8.30pm), art shows and weekend DJ.

The Red Lion

21-23 rue St-Jean-le-Vieux (04.90.86.40.25). **Open** 10am-1am daily. **Credit** AmEx, MC, V.

This butch British pub is popular with students for its long happy hour (5-8pm). Guinness, Strongbow and McEwan's are on tap and the pub-grub includes fish 'n' chips. There's live rock and blues (10pm-1am) on Tuesday, Wednesday and Sunday, and a free-for-all jam session on Monday.

The Red Zone

25 rue Carnot (04.90.27.02.44). **Open** 10pm-3am Mon, Sun; 9pm-3am Tue; 6.30pm-3am Wed-Sat. **Credit** AmEx, DC, MC, V.
Very red and very popular, this bar-club near the university is where Avignon youth comes after a night's drinking on place Pie. Varied dance nights include funk, house and salsa. On Wednesday, the ladies are invited to run the bar.

The festival organisers are adamant that the show must go on. Bailed out by a government recovery package, they announced business as usual for 2004. All eyes are on new artistic director Vincent Baudriller and administrative sidekick Hortense Archambault, both hoped to pump young blood into the Avignon machine. Baudriller was BFA's right-hand man as artistic advisor, and behind the introduction of a new generation of radical international directors including Rodrigo García and Frédéric Fisbach. Baudriller's plans so far are

to approach the festival from scratch, and continue the public forum opened in 2003, keeping the political temperature on high with the artistic support of German director Thomas Ostermeier.

What is certain is that without an 'In', the 'Off' can't stand alone. In the post-cancellation chaos, its ranks split over whether to join the strikes in solidarity. A quarter of the 540 theatre troupes did. For the 'treacherous' remainder it was a question of trying to salvage as much as they could to recover costs from venue hire, costumes, accommodation and unread flyers. Avignon can make or break a theatre act, with at least half staggering home bankrupt. Those who soldiered on put on a brave face despite a heatwave and the media's failure to mention that the fringe was peforming at all. The red badge 'Vive le Off' was paraded around town, echoing the words of Avignon's mayor Marie-José Roig that 'the Off must go ahead'.

But the theatrical punch was missing. Actors bombarded the few, remaining tourists with discount ticket offers, and prowled the streets in a predatory charade. Behind the burlesque, the air was taut with a frightening desperation. Although the fringe may have gained market clout over the years, it could never lead a one-man show and the crisis exposed its fragility.

But the city itself was possibly left the most shocked, forced to question whether it can survive without its festival. The devastation to the local economy was a sobering reminder that the Avignon should not rely on July to carry the show, but develop a thriving arts scene throughout the year. So watch centre stage: the drama has only just began.

Avignon & the Vaucluse

Shopping

The indoor Les Halles market in place Pie is open from 7am to 1pm Tuesday to Sunday. The place des Carmes holds a flower market on Saturday morning, and a flea market on Sunday morning. All shops open Mon-Sat unless stated.

Rue de la République is the commercial centre, with high-street names such as Zara, H&M and Fnac. Peeling off down the pedestrian rue des Marchands is a maze of street-wear clothes shops and boutiques; **Les Olivades** (No.28, 04.90.86.13.42) sells Provençal fabrics by the metre and clothes, **Mouret** (No.20, 04.90.85.39.38), Avignon's oldest shop, is an enchanting hatter frozen in the 1860s. Further east down rue Bonneterie, **Liquid** (No.37, 04.90.85.19.89) is a modern, design-led drinks shop in which to discover the region's Côtes du Rhône. **Hermès** has upgraded to grander premises on place de l'Horloge (No.2, 04.90.82.61.94), heralding the cross-over west down rue St Agricol with Parisian designers such as **Christian Lacroix** (No.10, 04.90.27.13.21). **La Tropézienne** (No.22, 04.90.86.24.72/www.latropezienne.net) is a Provençal food paradise, selling calissons, nougat and the local speciality, papaline, a pink, spiky-coated oregano liqueur chocolate. Opposite, ice-cream shop **Deldon** (No.35, 04.90.85.59.41) is a good summer heat buster.

Rue Joseph Vernet is the city's elegance capital, with **Cacharel** (No.8, 04.90.86.19.19), **Comptoir des Cotonniers** (No.27, 04.90.14.63.84) and **Ventilo** (No.28, 04.90.85.26.51). **Chocolatier Puyricard** has an outpost at No.33 (04.90.85.96.33). Parallel rue Petite Fusterie is a home decoration hotbed with **Galerie 5, 6, 7** (No.17, 06.10.25.76.69) selling 1950s-70s furniture, while more traditional antiques and garden furniture are found at **Hervé Baume** (No.19, 04.90.86.37.66). Second-hand books in English can be found at **Shakespeare** (155 rue Carreterie, 04.90.27.38.50, closed Mon, Sun), which also doubles as a tearoom.

Where to stay

Auberge de Cassagne

450 allée de Cassagne, Le Pontet (04.90.31.04.18/ www.hotelprestige-provence.com). Closed Jan. **Double** €110-€580. **Menus** €50-€88. **Credit** AmEx, DC, MC, V.

A ten minute escape by car from the bustle of the town centre is this luxury, Provençal-style hotel, set around a peaceful garden with a tennis court and small swimming pool. Philippe Boucher's gastronomic restaurant is filled with serious foodies.

La Bastide des Papes

352 Chemin des Poiriers, Ile de la Barthelasse (04.90.86.09.42). Closed 1wk in Jan & June. **Double** €90-€110. **Credit** MC, V.

Sweet sensations at Provençal *épicerie* **La Tropézienne**.

This pretty 14th-century *chambres d'hôtes*, set in orchards with a pool, is a tasteful rural retreat on the Ile de la Barthelasse (take the No.20 bus or go it alone on their selection of mountain bikes). A *table d'hôtes* is offered alongside free use of the spacious kitchen.

Camping du Pont d'Avignon

Ile de la Barthelasse (04.90.80.63.50/www.camping-avignon.com). Closed Nov-Mar. **Rates** two-person tent €9.60-€20; four-person bungalow €189-€420 per week. **Credit** AmEx, MC, V.

A Rhône-side campsite on Ile de la Barthelasse (take Pont Edouard Daladier), with an outdoor swimming pool and mountain bike hire.

Hôtel de Blauvac

11 rue de la Bancasse (04.90.86.34.11/www.hotel-blauvac.com). Closed Jan. **Double** €51-€76. **Credit** AmEx, DC, MC, V.

A 17th-century building overlooking a quiet, winding street leading to the place de l'Horloge. The de Blauvac is very reasonably priced, with large, well-designed rooms and friendly service.

Hôtel Colbert

7 rue Agricol Perdiguier (04.90.86.20.20/www.lecolbert-hotel.com). Closed Nov-Feb. **Double** €45-€77. **Credit** DC, MC, V.

Part of a cluster of budget hotels on a tiny street in the middle of town, Le Colbert has clean and attractive rooms, newly redecorated, with air-conditioning. You can breakfast in the fountain courtyard.

Hôtel Cloître St-Louis

20 rue Portail Boquier (04.90.27.55.55/www.cloitre-saint-louis.com). **Double** €100-€315. **Credit** AmEx, DC, MC, V.

A 16th-century cloister, chapel wing and fountain courtyard of a former monastery have been grafted with a contemporary steel and glass extension by Jean Nouvel, with a walled garden and rooftop pool.

Hôtel de Garlande

20 rue Galante (04.90.80.08.85/www.hoteldegarlande.com). Closed Jan. **Double** €60-€110. **Credit** AmEx, DC, MC, V.

Don't be put off by the shady location down a side-street: it belies the simple elegance and motherly welcome found within this discreet, newly decorated hotel, with several family-sized rooms.

Hôtel d'Europe

12 pl Crillon (04.90.14.76.76/www.hotel-d-europe.fr). **Double** €129-€410. **Credit** AmEx, DC, MC, V.

Napoléon, Victor Hugo, John Stuart Mill, Tennesse Williams and Jackie Onassis are just some of the past guests at this 16th-century mansion, set in an attractive garden. The rooms and suites are spacious and tastefully decorated with antiques.

Hôtel Innova

100 rue Joseph Vernet (04.90.82.54.10). **Double** €30-€47. **Credit** MC, V.

This no-frills, homely stop-off offers cut-price kipping, and is remarkably cheap for its elegant setting

in a *hôtel particulier*. Rooms are basic and clean, and by spring 2004 will all contain bathroom facilities.

Hôtel de la Mirande

4 pl de la Mirande (04.90.85.93.93/www.la-mirande.com). **Double** €280-€450. **Credit** AmEx, DC, MC, V.

This 18th-century cardinals' palace turns sleeping into a sumptuous history lesson. Aubusson tapestries, antique furniture, Pierre Frey fabrics and Venetian chandeliers transport you back in time, all packaged in 21st-century luxury and service. It also has one of Avignon's best restaurants (*see p89*).

Hôtel Mignon

12 rue Joseph Vernet (04.90.82.17.30/www.hotel-mignon.com). Closed last 2wks Dec. **Double** €38-€45. **Credit** AmEx, MC, V.

A sweet little hotel with small but good-value rooms, comedy tiger-print wall carpeting and extremely welcoming staff. The breakfast room is so small that, to cater for the overspill, some lucky volunteers get breakfast in bed.

Hôtel de Mons

5 rue de Mons (04.90.82.57.16/www.hoteldemons.com). Closed Nov. **Double** €52-€73. **Credit** AmEx, DC, MC, V.

This quaintly converted 13th-century chapel is an eccentric, budget choice off place de l'Horloge. Some of the rooms are a little too squeezed into its nooks and crannies, so insist on seeing them first.

Hôtel du Palais des Papes

3 pl du Palais (04.90.86.04.13). **Double** €75-€184. **Credit** MC, V.

The 15th-century former papal stables has just redecorated, introducing a more modern, North African elegance. The restaurant terrace, serving southern cuisine, looks on to place de l'Horloge, while the smaller Lutrin restaurant offers scenic lunches.

Hôtel du Parc

18 rue Agricol Perdiguier (04.90.82.71.55). Closed 20 Dec-5 Jan. **Double** €35-€45. **Credit** MC, V.

A few doors up from the Colbert, the Parc's balconies cascade with greenery and views on to flower-filled square Agricol Perdiguier. The modest, rustic, beamed, stone-walled interior is cosy and clean.

Hôtel Le Splendid

17 rue Agricol Perdiguier (04.90.86.14.46/www.avignon-splendid-hotel.com). Closed mid-Nov to mid-Dec. **Double** €48-€65. **Credit** AmEx, MC, V.

Cheerful owners the Lemoines run a simple, neat hotel just opposite the Parc, and have recently given all rooms en suite facilities.

Le Limas

51 rue du Limas, (04.90.14.67.19). Closed 2wks Aug. **Double** €76-€159. **No credit cards.**

Starck bathroom fittings and Le Corbusier furniture contrast with the period features in this *chambres d'hôtes* in an 18th-century mansion. Dynamic owner Marion Wagner serves breakfast on the roof terrace in summer and Sunday supper in winter.

Resources

The free Avignon-Villeneuve 'Passion' Passport gives 20-50% reductions (after the first ticket) on most museums and sights. Two mini tourist trains make circuits of Avignon (10am-6pm daily, till 7.30pm July & Aug) from place du Palais. One gives a 30-minute tour of the main sites (€6), the other runs to the Rocher des Doms (€2). Bikes can be hired from Aymard (80 rue Guillaume Puy, 04.90.86.32.49, closed Mon, 2wks in Aug).

Hospital

Centre Hospitalier Général, 305 rue Raoul Follereau (04.32.75.33.33).

Internet

Webzone Cybercafé, 3 rue St-Jean le Vieux (04.32.76.29.47). **Open** 10am-11.30pm daily (9am-3am July).

Police

Police municipale, pl Pie (04.90.85.13.13/Lost property 04.32.76.01.73).

Post office

La Poste, cours Président Kennedy (04.90.27.54.00). **Open** 8am-7pm Mon-Fri; 8am-noon Sat.

Tourist information

Avignon Office de Tourisme, 41 cours Jean Jaurès, 84008 Avignon (04.32.74.32.74/www.ot-avignon.fr). **Open** *Apr-June, Sept, Oct* 9am-6pm Mon-Sat; 10am-5pm Sun. *July* 9am-7pm daily. *Nov-Mar* 9am-6pm Mon-Fri; 9am-5pm Sat; 10am-noon Sun.

Villeneuve-lès-Avignon

West of the Rhône in the Gard *département* lies hot competition for the cultural limelight: the historic skyline and gentle tourism of Avignon spills over across the Ile de la Barthelasse into Villeneuve-lès-Avignon (take Pont Edouard Daladier, bus 11 or the summer Bâteau Bus from allée de l'Oulle). This small settlement centred on the tenth-century **Abbaye St-André** came into its own in 1307, when King Philippe le Bel decided it was a prime location for keeping an eye on Papal goings-on across the river. A heavily fortified 'new town' (*villeneuve*) sprang up, plus a watchtower, the **Tour Philippe le Bel**, which grew higher as Avignon became more powerful. Its heights are now used for exhibitions. Unjustifiably upstaged by its brasher neighbour, Villeneuve offers some stunning architecture, a superb view and one matchless work of art.

For the view, head for the west tower of the **Fort St-André**, the fortress built around the abbey in the 14th century, and climb along the massive ramparts. Inside are the remains of the Abbaye St-André: bewitching terraced gardens

leading to a tiny Romanesque chapel, a ruined 13th-century church and a moving graveyard with sarcophagi laid out like little beds.

Below the fort, the **Chartreuse du Val de Bénédiction** was once the largest Carthusian monastery in France. The charterhouse has been painstakingly restored, removing all signs of the depredations suffered during the Revolution, when to add insult to injury the Gothic tomb of Pope Innocent VI, who founded the monastery in 1352, was converted into a white marble rabbit hutch. There are monks' cells resembling little terraced cottages off two pale stone cloisters, as well as a laundry, kitchen, prisons and a herb garden funded by beauty company Yves Rocher. A small chapel off the Cloître du Cimetière (an enchanting open-air theatre venue during the festival), has exquisite frescoes by Matteo Giovanetti. 'Chocolat' guided tours on winter Sundays culminate in a fireside tea of hot chocolate and cake. The Chartreuse now acts as a state-funded centre for playwrights, whose recorded voices can be heard echoing through the buildings, reading aloud the fruits of their work.

The **Musée Pierre de Luxembourg** is a former cardinal's residence today bursting with four floors of art, including a delicately carved ivory Virgin and Child and 16th- and 17th-century religious paintings by Mignard and de Champaigne. The collection's masterpiece is the extraordinary *Coronation of the Virgin* (1453-54) by Enguerrand Quarton, a leading light in the Avignon school (*see p8*). The entire medieval world view is represented in detailed landscape and human activity.

Just south of the museum, the 14th-century **Collégiale Notre-Dame** has works by Mignard and Levieux, a lavish 18th-century altarpiece, and a copy of Enguerrand Quarton's *Pietà* (the original is in the Louvre).

Chartreuse du Val de Bénédiction

58 rue de la République (04.90.15.24.24/ www.chartreuse.org). **Open** *Apr-Sept* 9am-6.30pm daily. *Oct-Mar* 9.30am-5.30pm daily. **Admission** €6.10; €4.10 18-25s; under-18s free. **Credit** (€10 minimum) AmEx, DC, MC, V.

Eglise Notre-Dame

pl du Chapître. **Open** *Apr-Sept* 10am-12.30pm, 3-7pm daily. *Oct-Mar* 10am-noon, 2-5pm daily. Closed Feb. **Admission** free.

Fort St-André & Abbaye St-André

montée du Fort (fort 04.90.25.45.35/abbey 04.90.25.55.95). **Open** *Fort Apr-Sept* 10am-1pm, 2-6pm daily. *Oct-Mar* 10am-1pm, 2-5pm daily. *Gardens Apr-Sept* 10am-12.30pm, 2-6pm Tue-Sun. *Oct-Mar* 10am-12.30pm, 2-5pm Tue-Sun. *Abbey* by appointment. **Admission** *Fort* €4.60, €3.10 18s-26s; free under-18s. *Abbey & gardens* €4, €3 under-18s. **No credit cards.**

Avignon & the Vaucluse

Terrace-sitting in **Villeneuve-lès-Avignon**.

Musée Pierre de Luxembourg

rue de la République (04.90.27.49.66). **Open** *Apr-Sept* 10am-12.30pm, 3-7pm daily. *Oct-Mar* 10am-noon, 2-5pm Tue-Sun. Closed Feb. **Admission** €3; €2 students; free under-18s. **No credit cards.**

Tour Philippe le Bel

rue Montée de la Tour (04.32.70.08.57). **Open** *Apr to mid-June* 10am-12.30pm, 1.30-7pm Tue-Sat. *mid-June to Sept* 10am-12.30pm, 1.30-7pm daily. *Oct-Nov, Mar* 10-noon, 2-5pm Tue-Sun. Closed Dec-Feb. **Admission** €1.60; free under-18s. **No credit cards.**

Where to stay & eat

Villeneuve's hotels absorb the overflow from the Avignon festival, but are also worth considering in their own right. The luxury option is **Le Prieuré** (7 pl du Chapitre, 04.90.15.90.15, www.leprieure.fr, closed Nov to mid-Mar, double €120-€295, restaurant closed Sept to June, Tue-Wed), an exquisitely restored, if slightly retro, 14th-century archbishop's palace with library, garden, pool and gourmet restaurant. A homelier, designer option is the 17th-century **Hôtel de l'Atelier** (5 rue de la Foire, 04.90.25.01.84, www.hoteldelatelier.com, closed Nov-Dec, double €45-€90), tastefully redecorated by set designer Dominique Baroush as an airy modern-rustic guest house. On the banks of the Rhône, **Le Vieux Moulin** (5 rue du Vieux Moulin, 04.90.25.00.26, www.avignon-vieuxmoulin.com, closed Mon & Tue except

July, and all Jan, menus €25-€30) was an old stone grain depot for the trade boats, today serving southern staples with a fruity twist, such as magret de canard with a white peach gratiné. **Aubertin** (1 rue de l'Hôpital, 04.90.25.94.84, closed Sun, Mon and last 2wks Aug, menus €35-€49) is the distinguished dining choice, offering inventive cuisine by chef Jean-Claude Aubertin; hot lobster pâté with morels and Camargue bull steak with honeyed carrots. In next-door village Les Angles, **C'est la Lune** (270 montée du Valadas, 04.90.25.40.55, open daily July-Aug, rest of year Thur, Fri only, plus lunch on Wed & Sat, average €30) is a North African fusion bar-restaurant, where hip Avignon and Villeneuve congregate to eat lamb couscous, swimming it off in the outdoor pool by day, or dancing it off to the lounge DJ at night. The two salons are redecorated virtually every week by globetrotting owner Georges, also the force behind Woolloomooloo in Avignon (*see p89*).

Resources

A €6.86 passport gives entrance to Villeneuve's five main monuments. Thursday is market day, held outside the Tourist Office, with a flea market on Saturday.

Villeneuve Office du Tourisme

1 pl Charles David, 30400 Villeneuve-lès-Avignon (04.90.25.61.33/www.villeneuvelesavignon.fr/tourisme). **Open** *Sept-June* 9am-12.30pm, 2-6pm Mon-Sat. *July* 10am-7pm Mon-Fri, 10am-1pm, 2.30-7pm Sat-Sun. *Aug* 9am-12.30pm, 2-6pm daily.

Getting there & around

By car

From the A7 autoroute, exits 23 (Avignon Nord) and 24 (Avignon Sud) link with the outer ring road.

By train

Avignon is at the junction of the Paris-Marseille and Paris-Montpellier lines. The Gare Centre Ville has frequent links to Arles, Nîmes, Orange, Toulon and Carcassonne. The new Gare TGV (08.92.35.35.35, www.tgv.com) is 4km south of Avignon. A bus service leaves from the station at the arrival of each train, taking passengers to the Gare Centre Ville, and leaves from the centre for the Gare TGV every 15mins. From May to October, a Eurostar weekly service travels direct from London to Avignon in six and a half hours, leaving Waterloo on Saturday mornings, with a return journey in the afternoon.

By bus

The bus station (04.90.82.07.35) is on av Montclar, next to the Centre Ville train station with buses from Avignon to Carpentras, Cavaillon, St-Rémy, Orange, Nîmes, Arles, Aix, Marseille, Nice and Cannes. Town buses are run by **TCRA** (04.32.74.18.32).

Orange & Châteauneuf-du-Pape

The Romans left theatres and bridges, the Popes left vines: Orange and the bulbous banks of the Rhône are an operatic treat.

The baking Rhône flood plain north of Avignon is home to some of the most prestigious appellations of the southern Côtes du Rhône, just part of a legacy going back to the Romans and the area's Papal past.

Orange

Orange sits somewhat uneasily around its glorious antique theatre. Long under foreign domination, first by the Romans, later the house of Orange, it is now a fief of the Front National. The extreme right council dislikes the Chorégies, Orange's venerable and prestigious opera festival (*see p37*), and is rumoured to cancel the visits of artists coming from sexual or ethnic minorities, but this shouldn't put you off from visiting the town's shady squares and this magnificent relic of the Roman city of Arausio, which at its peak was four times as large as today's town. Orange declined sharply in the Dark Ages, but picked up in the 12th century, as an enclave governed by troubadour-prince Raimbaut d'Orange. In 1530 the town passed to a junior branch of the German house of Nassau, and gave its name to Nassau's Dutch principality 14 years later. Thereafter, Orange became a sort of Protestant buzzword (finding its way into Ulster's Orange Order and the Orange Free State) and the town itself attracted Protestant refugees from all over Provence during the Wars of Religion.

The Dutch Nassaus held on to their little piece of France against the odds, and in 1622 Maurice de Nassau built an impressive château and fortifications. Unfortunately he used stones from the remaining Roman monuments not previously destroyed by the Barbarians, and only the Arc de Triomphe and the Théâtre Antique survived the pillaging. In 1673, as he was embarking on another war with Protestant Holland, Louis XIV ordered the destruction of the château. The Treaty of Utrecht in 1713 finally gave the principality to France, but the proudly independent town has not forgotten its roots, and Queen Juliana of the Netherlands was back in 1952 planting an oak tree on the site of the château. Tourism apart, the town is home to

the cavalry regiment of the French Foreign legion, who stroll around the town in uniform.

Geographically and emotionally, the **Théâtre Antique** dominates the town. Quite simply, this is the best-preserved Roman theatre anywhere. What sets it apart is the unrivalled state of preservation of the stage wall, a massive, sculpted sandstone screen 36m high which Louis XIV referred to as 'the finest wall in my kingdom'. The amphitheatre was a multifunctional space, which hosted everything from political meetings to concerts, sporting events and plays. In the fourth century the theatre was abandoned and makeshift houses were built within the auditorium. It was not until the 19th century that restoration began and the Chorégies d'Orange was born. The Roman statue of Augustus, which presides over the stage from a niche, was placed here in 1951.

In a 17th-century building opposite the main entrance to the theatre, the **Musée Municipal** houses an interesting collection of Roman artefacts, including a unique series of cadastres. These engraved marble tablets map the streets, administrative divisions and geographical features of the Orange region in Roman times in the course of three successive surveys (the earliest dates from 77AD). On the top floor is an unsuspected curiosity: a selection of post-Impressionist paintings by Welsh artist Frank Brangwyn. The local tradition of the printed cotton cloth known as *indiennes* is celebrated in series of paintings by 18th-century artist GM Rossetti. Modern-day *indiennes* can be tracked down next door at **La Provençale** (5 pl Sylvain, 04.90.51.58.86, closed Mon, Sun, and Nov to mid-Feb, open afternoons in Dec).

On top of the hill of St-Eutrope, into which the curve of the seats was dug, is a pleasant park with the ruins of Maurice de Nassau's château and the **Piscine des Cèdres** (04.90.34.09.68, open end June-end Aug), an open-air swimming pool which is a temptation in hot, dusty summers. It is also the scene of important recent archaeological excavations.

The old town, in front of the theatre, is a tight knot of twisting streets that liven up at festival

Théâtre Antique: where opera singers check out the Roman art of perfect acoustics.

time, but provide little architectural competition for the towering classical monuments, although they abound in attractive shady squares, ideal for a pre-dinner *pastis*. The best and liveliest cafés and the majority of the town's eating places are in front of the Roman theatre.

Out of the centre, on the northern edge of the town, the **Arc de Triomphe** is Orange's other great Roman monument. The triumphal arch spanning the former Via Agrippa, which linked Lyon to Arles, was built in 20BC, is the third largest of its kind in the world, the north side is a riot of well-preserved carving, with military paraphernalia arranged in abstract patterns.

Théâtre Antique/Musée Municipal
rue Madeleine Roch (04.90.51.17.60). **Open** *Mar, Oct* 9.30am-6pm daily. *Apr, May, Sept* 9am-7pm daily. *June-Aug* 9am-8pm daily. *Nov-Feb* 9.30am-5pm daily. **Admission** €7.50; €5.50 7-17s; free under-7s. **Credit** MC, V.

Where to stay & eat

The most comfortable hotel in the town centre is the renovated **Hôtel Arene** (pl de Langes, 04.90.11.40.40, closed 3wks in Nov, double €77-€92), which has 30 personalised, air-conditioned rooms on a paved square. Pretty in pink on the edge of the arena, the **Hôtel St-Jean** (1 cours

Pourtoules, 04.90.51.15.16, closed Jan to mid-Feb, double €38-€70) is an attractive budget choice, while the unprepossessing **Glacier** (46 cours Aristide Briand, 04.90.34.02.01, www.le-glacier.com, closed 19 Dec-5 Jan, double €47-€70) has outstandingly helpful staff. In summer a pool is important, which condemns you to a chain hotel of which the air-conditioned modern **Hôtel Mercure Orange** (rte de Caderousse, 04.90.34.24.10, double €95-€125) is the best, or the out-of-town **Mas des Aigras** (towards Gap, 04.90.34.81.01, closed 20 Dec to 20 Jan, Tue & Wed Oct to Mar, doubles €70-€106) which slightly overplays the Provençal card.

The best restaurant in town is the **Parvis** (55 cours Portoules, 04.90.34.82.00, menu €22.50-€41) where Jean-Michel Berengier's imaginative cuisine takes its cue from the local produce, eaten on a sunny terrace or in the beamed interior. Authentic local cuisine can be had at **Le Forum** (3 rue Mazeau, 04.90.34.01.09, closed Mon & lunch Sat and 2wks end Feb & end Aug, menus €17-€52), including a fine *lièvre à la royale* (hare) for game lovers. The **Café du Théâtre** (pl des Frères Mounet, 04.90.34.12.39) is the liveliest place in town for a quick drink. If you have overdosed on the indigenous cuisine, **Le Saigon** (20 pl Sylvain, 04.90.34.18.19, average €25) is a decent

Vietnamese restaurant just beside the Théâtre Antique. For an out-of-town gastronomic treat try the **Pré du Moulin** in the quiet village of Sérignan du Comtat (04.90.70.14.55, closed Feb, menus €29-€85), where the outstanding €29 lunch menu provides chef Pascal Alonso ample scope for his considerable talent.

Resources

Market day in Orange is Thursday morning.

Tourist information

Office de Tourisme, 5 cours Aristide Briand, 84100 Orange (04.90.34.70.88/www.provence-orange.com). **Open** *Apr-Sept* 9-7pm Mon-Sat, 10am-6pm Sun. *Oct-Mar* 10am-1pm, 2-5pm Mon-Sat.

Châteauneuf-du-Pape

Châteauneuf-du-Pape – like Sancerre or Roquefort – is one of those places that says exactly what it does. Just to reinforce the point, the road south from Orange has vines growing right to the edge of the tarmac, their grapes destined not only for the princely red that takes its name from the village, but also Côtes du Rhône and Côtes du Rhône Villages. As every second farm is a wine estate, invitations to taste and visit are thick on the ground (though it takes a certain nerve to resist buying when you have sniffed, sipped and slurped every vintage for the last ten years); the tourist office has a comprehensive list of vineyard visits. The

original vineyards were planted at the initiative of the Avignon popes (commemorated in the village's name) who summered here in the castle built by wine-lover John XXII in 1316. The tight rules regarding yield and grape varieties laid down in 1923 were far-sighted blueprints for France's *appellation d'origine contrôlée* regulations, and sealed the reputation of the local red, which is a complex blend of at least eight varieties, dominated by grenache. The alluvial soil, sprinkled with heat-absorbing pebbles, the widely spaced vines and the cloud-dispersing mistral all contribute to the muscular alcoholic content (12.5 per cent) and complex nose of the wine. Recently, white Châteauneuf-du-Pape (a minimum five-grape blend) has made a name for itself, too.

All that wine money has at least been put to good use. **Châteauneuf-du-Pape** is an outstandingly beautiful village, tastefully restored, with a characterful town centre. Little remains of the Château des Papes itself, destroyed in the Wars of Religion, but the views are exceptional. One winemaker, the Père Anselme, has had the clever idea of opening a museum to celebrate the area's winemaking tradition: the **Musée des Outils de Vignerons**. The baskets, pruners and suchlike are interesting enough, but the shop and tasting-room at the end is what this is all about. If you need a sugar rush to get out of here, there is also a good chocolate-maker, **Castelain** (rte d'Avignon, 04.90.83.54.71).

Temptation galore at **Châteauneuf-du-Pape**.

Musée des Outils de Vignerons

Le Clos (04.90.83.70.07/www.brotte.com). **Open** July-Sept 9am-1pm, 2-7pm daily. Oct-June 9am-noon, 2-6pm daily. **Admission** free.

Where to stay & eat

Châteauneuf is a good base if you want to avoid drinking and driving. **La Garbure** (3 rue Joseph Ducos, 04.90.83.75.08, www.la-garbure.com, closed Mon & Sun from Nov-Apr & 1wk in Jan, double €55-€77, menus €20-€45) in the main street is an attractive choice, both for local cuisine and its comfortable rooms. For something more elaborate, the **Hôtellerie Château des Fines Roches** (rte de Sorgues, 04.90.83.70.23, double €155-€200, menus €30-€75), a 19th-century pile set in a vineyard, has a good though pricey restaurant. At Courthezon, 7km NE, **Lou Pequelet** (pl Edouard Daladier, 04.90.70.28.96, closed Mon, menus €18-€25) offers home-cooking in an unspoilt village.

Resources

Market day is Friday morning.

Tourist information

Office de Tourisme, pl Portail, 84103 Châteauneuf-du-Pape (04.90.83.71.08). **Open** July, Aug 9.30am-7pm Mon-Sat, 10am-1pm 2-5pm Sun. Sept-June 9am-12.30pm, 2-6pm Mon-Sat.

Pont-St-Esprit & Bagnols

The 'Bridge of the Holy Spirit' spans the Rhône just where it enters Provence. Built 1265-1319 by a brotherhood inspired by one Jéhan de Thianges, who was 'led by divine inspiration', the bridge was originally a more elaborate affair with bastions and towers. It remains an impressive curved structure, with 19 of the 25 arches still in their original state. The town of **Pont-St-Esprit** itself was badly bombed in World War II and was at the centre of a scandal in 1951, when its bread became mysteriously poisoned. Pretty rue St-Jacques is named after the pilgrims who stayed here on their way to Santiago de Compostela. The religious paintings and artefacts in the **Musée d'Art Sacré du Gard** may not set your pulse on fire, but the beautiful building is a well-preserved medieval merchant's house that was inhabited by the same family for six centuries. More odds and ends, including early 20th-century painting and 220 18th-century pharmacy jars, are displayed in the **Musée Paul Raymond** in the old town hall.

Bagnols-sur-Cèze, 11km south, has one of the best markets in the region, and one of the most satisfying small museums. Outside town by the Rhône, it also offers the Centre atomique de Marcoule nuclear processing plant, which has quadrupled the town's working population. The old town is full of character, particularly on Wednesday market day, when most of the centre is given over to produce of all sorts. This is the place to stock up on local gastronomic products or good-quality Provençal fabrics. Rue Crémieux, which runs up to the place Mallet, is filled with fine townhouses dating from the 16th to the 18th centuries. Look up at the riotous gargoyles of No.15, and browse in the organic food shop housed in the courtyard. On the second floor of the town hall, a 17th-century mansion in place Mallet, is the town's big cultural draw, the **Musée Albert André**. In 1923, a fire destroyed the museum's patchy and parochial collection of daubs. Painter Albert André, who was standing in as curator, launched an appeal – with the help of his friend Renoir – to the artists of France, to help him fill the empty walls. They responded in force, and today the museum provides a frozen snapshot of early 20th-century living art, with works by Renoir, Signac, Bonnard, Matisse, Gauguin and others. Memories of the rich archaeological past of the town, both Celtic-Ligurian and Gallo-Roman, are housed in the **Musée d'Archéologie Léon Alègre**.

Perched above the river Cèze, 10km west of Bagnols, **La Roque-sur-Cèze** is a picture-postcard village with a fine Romanesque church, approached by an ancient single-track bridge. Just downstream, the Cèze cuts through the limestone to form the spectacular **Cascade de Sautadet**. Bathers should beware for this stretch of the river is a frequent scene of tragic drownings. North of La Roque, in the middle of an oak forest that would not be out of place in a medieval romance, is the 13th-century **Chartreuse de Valbonne** monastery, now a hospital for tropical diseases, which produces its own Côtes du Rhône wine. You can visit the richly decorated Baroque church, cloisters and (for an extra fee) a reconstituted monk's cell.

Chartreuse de Valbonne

St-Paulet-de-Caisson (04.66.90.41.24/vineyard 04.66.90.41.00). **Open** May-Aug 9am-6.30pm daily. Sept-Apr 9am-noon, 1.30-5.30pm Tue-Sun. **Admission** €4; €2.50 10-16s; free under 10s. **Credit** AmEx, DC, MC, V.

Musée Albert André

pl Mallet, Bagnols (04.66.50.50.56). **Open** 10am-noon, 2-6pm Tue-Sun. Closed Feb. **Admission** €4.20; under-16s free. **No credit cards**.

Musée d'Archéologie Léon Alègre

24 av Paul Langevin, Bagnols (04.66.89.74.00). **Open** 10am-noon, 2-6pm Tue, Thur, Fri. **Admission** €4.20. **No credit cards**.

Musée d'Art Sacré du Gard

2 rue St-Jacques, Pont-St-Esprit (04.66.39.17.61).
Open *July, Aug* 10am-7pm Tue-Sun. *Sept-June* 10am-
noon, 2-6pm Tue-Sun. **Admission** €3; €2 10-16s;
free under-10s. **No credit cards.**

Musée Paul Raymond

pl de l'Hôtel de Ville, Pont-St-Esprit (04.66.39.09.98).
Open *July, Aug* 10am-7pm Tue-Sun. *Sept-June* 10am-
noon, 2-6pm Tue-Sun. **Admission** €3; €2 10-16s;
free under-10s. **No credit cards.**

Where to stay & eat

In Pont-St-Esprit, the **Auberge Provençale**
(rte de Nîmes, 04.66.39.08.79, closed 24 Dec-
2 Jan, double €30, restaurant closed dinner Sun
Oct-Mar, menus €10-€20) has simple
accommodation and a popular restaurant.
Typical Provençal fare is served at **Lou Recati**
(6 rue Jean Jacques, 04.66.90.73.01, closed Mon,
Tue lunch & 2wks in Oct, menus €12-€21).

The luxurious **Château de Montcaud**
(5km W of Bagnols, rte d'Alès Combe, Sabran,
04.66.89.60.60, www.relaischateaux.com/
montcaud, closed Nov-Mar, double €165-€325,
restaurant closed lunch, menus €45-€75, bistro
closed Sat & Sun, menus €25-€30) is a 19th-
century pile with shady wooded grounds, a nice
swimming pool, rose garden, tennis courts and
a Turkish bath. Special breaks are available
with half-board and tickets for Les Chorégies.
Its restaurant, Les Jardins de Montcaud offers
fine country cooking in a stone *mas* with tables
on the patio in summer. The **Château du Val
de Cèze** (rte d'Avignon, 04.66.89.61.26, double
€98-€107) has a set of comfortable bungalows
in its grounds, while right in the centre of
Bagnols, the **Hôtel-Bar des Sports** (3 pl Jean
Jaurès, 04.66.89.61.68, double €44) has
convenient and reliable rooms. For a quick
snack, the **Crêperie/Saladerie Clémentine**
(12 pl Mallet, 04.66.89.42.26, closed Sat, Sun,
average €12) has a terrace overlooking a
pretty square. At La Roque-sur-Cèze, **Le Mas
du Bélier** (04.66.82.21.39, closed Mon & Tue
from Oct to Mar, menus €12.50-€36) is a
romantic waterside inn, and at the entrance to
the village, **La Tonnelle** (pl des Marronniers,
04.66.82.79.37, closed Nov-Mar, double €70) is a
good-value *chambres d'hôtes*.

Resources

The market is on Saturday morning in Pont-St-
Esprit and Wednesday in Bagnols-sur-Cèze.

Tourist information

Bagnols-sur-Cèze *Office de Tourisme, Espace
St-Gilles, av Léon Blum, 30200 Bagnols-sur-Cèze
(04.66.89.54.61/www.ot-bagnolssurceze.com).*
Open *July-Aug* 9am-7pm Mon-Fri; 9am-6pm Sat;

Châteauneuf-du-Pape. *See p98.*

10am-1pm Sun. *Sept-June* 9am-noon, 2-6pm
Mon-Fri; 9am-noon Sat.
Pont-St-Esprit *Office de Tourisme, Résidence
Welcome, 30130 Pont-St-Esprit (04.66.39.44.45/
www.ot-pont-saint-esprit.fr).* **Open** *June-Aug* 9am-
12.30pm, 1.30-6.30pm Mon-Fri; 9am-12.30pm, 3-6pm
Sat; 9am-noon Sun. *Sept-May* 8am-noon, 2-5.30pm
Mon-Fri; 9am-noon Sat.

Getting there & around

By car

Orange (A7 exit 21) is 30km N of Avignon. For Pont
St-Esprit and Bagnols-sur-Cèze take A7 exit 19 and
N86. For Châteauneuf-du-Pape take the D68 from
Orange or N7 and D17 from Avignon.

By train

Orange station (av Frédéric Mistral, 04.90.11.88.00) is
on the main Paris-Avignon-Marseille line, but only a
few TGVs stop here, so a change is often inevitable.

By bus

Rapides du Sud-Est (04.90.34.15.59) runs 12 buses
a day, Mon-Sat, between Avignon and Orange.
Cars Auran (04.66.39.10.40) runs buses daily
between Avignon, Pont-St-Esprit and Bagnols-sur-
Cèze. **Sotra Ginaux** (04.75.39.40.22) runs daily
buses, Mon-Fri (less in school holidays), between
Orange and Pont-St-Esprit, Avignon to Aubernas via
Pont-St-Esprit, and Aubernas to Bagnols.

Carpentras & Mont Ventoux

Roman remains, vertiginous hill towns and a challenge for the Lycra-clad:
it takes a lot of will to suck olives round here.

For more than 500 years after it was ceded to the Holy See in 1274, Carpentras and its surroundings, including Mont Ventoux, Vaison-La Romaine, Avignon and Cavaillon, were part of the Comtat Venaissin, a papal enclave inside French territory, a sort of huge, rural Vatican City.

Carpentras

Carpentras, a bustling town with a population of 30,000, is a good provincial antidote to tourist fatigue. Though there are no must-see monuments, the place is full of character, with an independent spirit and a great market, which takes over the spacious, tree-lined outer avenues on Friday. The name comes from the Gallic for a two-wheeled chariot, whose construction was the ancient speciality. Of the city walls only the crenellated 14th-century **Porte d'Orange** remains, but the congested town centre follows a walled city plan and it is virtually compulsory to leave your car and explore on foot.

The **Musée Comtadin-Duplessis** concentrates on the customs and history of the region, with a floor dedicated to local primitive painting. More charming is the **Musée Sobirats**, a well-preserved and evocatively furnished, pre-Revolutionary nobleman's house in a typical 18th-century street.

The **Cathédrale St-Siffrein** (pl St-Siffrein, open 8.30am-noon, 2-6pm daily) combines an extraordinary mish-mash of styles and epochs, ranging from 15th-century Provençal Gothic to an early 20th-century bell-tower. The 15th-century door on the south side is known as the Porte des Juifs. When Philippe le Bel expelled the Jews from France, many of them fled to the papal-controlled Comtat Venaissin, only to be blackmailed or bullied into a Catholic baptism. The chained Jews passed through this door on their way to conversion. Note the carved rats gnawing on a globe above the door; explanations are as numerous as they are unconvincing. The cathedral's interior is rather gloomy but the Treasury is worth a look for its wonderful 14th-century wooden statues, and an important relic, the St-Mors, made from two nails taken from the cross. This symbol has

appeared in the town's crest since the 13th century. Just behind the cathedral is an unobtrusive Roman triumphal arch. It lacks the grandeur and state of preservation of its big brother in Orange, but features some good carving, notably the chained prisoners on the east side. Next door, the 17th-century **Palais de Justice** has frescoes from the 17th and 18th centuries (the tourist office can arrange a visit). This is the spiritual hub of the old town and it is here, on a specially erected outdoor scaffold, that the intermittently interesting arts festival, Les Estivales, takes place in the second fortnight of July. From here one can explore the smart shops of the **Passage Boyer**, the result of a mid-18th-century job creation scheme and based on the Parisian covered passages.

Opposite the Hôtel de Ville is France's oldest surviving **Synagogue**, dating from the 14th century, though largely rebuilt in the 18th. You can visit the lower floor, where there are ovens for baking unleavened bread and a piscina for women's purification rites, and the sanctuary (men must wear a copal). Today, the Jewish community in Carpentras numbers just 122, but the culture remains strong. The Jewish cemetery just outside town was desecrated in the 1990s, an event which gained widespread national attention, although the true identity of the perpetrators is still uncertain.

South of the centre, the **Hôtel Dieu** is a splendid 18th-century hospital, which now houses the tourist office. Take a look at the rich collection of earthenware pharmacy jars, exemplifying the French dedication to all things medical, and a Baroque chapel containing the tomb of Bishop d'Inguimbert, the hospital's founder. The hospital has now moved and there are plans to transform the building into a cultural centre, housing museums and giving a badly needed cultural focus to the town.

For huntin', shootin' and fishin' types, the town is also famous for its decoys. If you're visiting between December and February, look out for black truffles, while the sticky, brightly coloured, locally made humbugs, *berlingots*, are available all year.

Musées Comtadin-Duplessis

234 bd Albin Durand (04.90.63.04.92). **Open** *Apr-Oct* 10am-noon, 2-6pm Mon, Wed-Sun. *Nov-Mar* 10am-noon, 2-4pm Mon, Wed-Sun. **Admission** €2 (with Musée Sobirats); free under-12s. **No credit cards**.

Musée Sobirats

rue du Collège (04.90.63.04.92). **Open** *Apr-Sept* 10am-noon, 2-6pm Mon, Wed-Sun. *Oct-Mar* 10am-noon, 2-4pm Mon, Wed-Sun. **Admission** €2 (with Musée Comtadin-Duplessis); free under-12s. **No credit cards**.

Synagogue

pl de l'Hôtel de Ville (04.90.63.39.97). **Open** *June-Sept* 10am-6pm Mon-Fri; 9.30am-1pm Sun. *Oct-May* 10am-6pm Mon-Fri. Closed Jewish holidays. **Admission** free but small donation welcome.

Where to stay & eat

The liveliest restaurant in town is **Chez Serge** (90 rue Cottier, 04.90.63.21.24, www.chez-serge.com, closed Sun, menus €12.80-€25), which has an attractive terrace and an enthusiastic chef. The **Atelier de Pierre** (30 pl de l'Horloge, 04.90.60.75.00, closed Sun & Mon and 2-17 Jan; menus from €23) is set in a delightful courtyard in the shadow of an ancient belfry. The only other serious gastronomic restaurant in town is **Le Vert Galant** (12 rue

Carpentras: squares made for chariot races.

de Clapiès, 04.90.67.15.50, closed lunch Mon, dinner Sun Oct-Mar & all Sun Apr-Sept, menus €28-€46), which offers a special truffle option in season, but service can be stretched in the cramped room. Hotels in the town centre are a pretty dull collection, but the recently renovated **Le Fiacre** (153 rue Vigne, 04.90.63.03.15, double €50-€120) is set in a characterful old townhouse. For a real treat head out of town to Monteux, where the **Domaine de Bournereau** (579 chemin de la Sorguette, Monteux, 04.90.66.36.13, www.bournereau.com, double €110-€170, closed 7 Nov-25 Jan) is a beautifully restored farmhouse with a pool overlooking Mont Ventoux. Hermann and Klaus are warm and welcoming hosts. The village has an amusingly decorated bistro, **Les Tremas** (29-31 bd Trewey, Monteux, 04.90.66.30.97, closed dinner Mon-Wed & all Sun, menus €15.80-€26), and the nearby **Saule Pleureur** (145 chemin de Beauregard, Monteux, 04.90.62.01.35, closed all Mon, lunch Sat, dinner Sun, 3wks in March, 2wks in Nov, menus €32-€66) offers perfect classical French cuisine; chef Michel Philibert runs truffle 'galas' in February. Marquis de Sade devotees will be excited to know that one of his former châteaux, 15km from Carpentras in Mazan, is now a luxury hotel, **Château de Mazan** (pl Napoléon, 04.90.69.62.61, www.chateaudemazan.fr, closed Jan & Feb, double €90-€255, menus €30-€62) with only slight financial sadism involved. The gloriously restored building is more grand townhouse than traditional château, but the subtle mix of ancient stone walls and contemporary design has been skilfully managed, with chef Iris Enrich offering cuisine that matches the cool sophistication of the dining room and the splendid summer terrace.

Resources

Internet

Wooxnext, 284 av du Comtat Venaisson, (04.90.67.13.54). **Open** 8am-8pm Mon-Sat.

Tourist information

Office de Tourisme, Hôtel Dieu, pl Aristide Briand, 84200 Carpentras (04.90.63.00.78/www.tourisme.fr/carpentras). **Open** *June-Sept* 9am-7pm daily. *Oct-May* 9.30am-12.30pm, 2-6pm Mon-Sat.

Pernes-les-Fontaines

The 37 fountains that give Pernes its name and fame date from the mid-18th century. Pernes is a good place to while away an afternoon, with its fine old houses, chapels and towers. The 16th-century **Porte Notre-Dame** – a remnant of the city walls – incorporates the chapel of

Cathédrale St-Siffrein: drunken Provençal Gothic. *See p101.*

Notre-Dame-des-Grâces. Nearby is the most striking of Pernes' fountains, the Fontaine du Cormoran, crowned by an open-winged cormorant and featuring the town's emblem of a pearl and the sun. The **Eglise Notre-Dame-de-Nazareth** nearby has sections dating from the 11th century. Pernes' artistic jewels are the 13th-century frescoes that decorate the upper floors of the **Tour Ferrande** (contact the tourist office to visit), which depict lively Biblical stories and scenes from the life of Charles of Anjou. The tower overlooks the fontaine Guillaumin or *du gigot*, so called because of its resemblance to a leg of lamb. The town's other tower, **Tour de l'Horloge** (rue du Donjon, open 9am-7pm in summer, 9am-5pm in winter) is all that remains of the château of the counts of Toulouse, who ruled Pernes from 1125 to 1320, when it was the capital of the Comtat Venaissin.

Locals will tell you that if you drink from the fontaine de la Lune at the base of the Porte St-Gilles, you'll go quite mad. Should the water have no effect, celebrate with pastries from the excellent boulangerie in place Aristide Briand.

Where to stay & eat

Au Fil du Temps (73 pl Louis Giraud, 04.90.66.48.61, closed Tue & Wed, 1wkOct,

2wks Dec, 2wks Feb, menus €45-€65) is presided over by young chef Frédéric Robert, offering market-fresh dishes and delicious desserts. Nearby Le Beaucet, which holds an annual pilgrimage in honour of St Gentius, patron saint of Provençal farmers, is home to one of the region's best restaurants **Auberge du Beaucet** (04.90.66.10.82, closed Mon & Sun, all Dec & Jan, menu €30), which offers local wines and cuisine, goat's cheeses produced in the village and a spectacular country view.

Resources

Market day in Pernes-les-Fontaines is Saturday.

Tourist information

Office de Tourisme, pl Gabriel Moutte, 84210 Pernes-les-Fontaines (04.90.61.31.04). **Open** *mid-June to mid-Sept* 9am-12.30pm, 2.30-7.30pm Mon-Sat. *mid-Sept to mid-June* 9am-12.30pm, 2-5pm Mon-Fri.

Mont Ventoux

When the Italian poet Petrarch reached the summit of Mont Ventoux in 1336, he 'remained immobile, stupefied by the strange lightness of the air and the immensity of the spectacle'. He has been credited with inventing the sport of mountain climbing – it had never occurred to

Avignon & the Vaucluse

Bike ride Mont Ventoux challenge

Considered to be the most tortuous stage of the Tour de France, Mont Ventoux is a mythical pilgrimage for cyclists. When the snow melts, its slopes swarm with thousands of little piston legs, pumping away on razor-sharp wheels in the agonising quest for victory. Barthes called it a 'god of evil', a superior hell in which heroes are made and men called to sacrifice. When a hunk of limestone gets this kind of PR from a leading philosopher, who wouldn't turn up to try their luck?

Theoretically, anyone can make it up Mont Ventoux. But it is not the type of thing to do on a last minute 'visit olive oil factory or cycle up a mountain' whim. It is over 20km of pure ascent, covering up to 1,610m in altitude. The feat takes on average two hours for the properly trained, 50 minutes for the Lance Armstrong clones, and six hours for the determined who push the bike all the way. You need to be relatively fit.

Be prepared for the meteorological beating you might get along the course. The 'vent' of Ventoux hints at winds that can reach 250km/hr when the Mistral throws a tantrum. Don't even consider going up if gusts are already strong down below. The temperature generally drops by 10ºC as you gain altitude, but the weather can change dramatically, bolting from heatwave to thunder, fog, hail or even snow in the time it takes to reach the finish. Check the weather forecast in advance (Metéo France 08.92.68.02.84).

The route There are three possible routes of attack: the toughest is the southern slope from Bédoin (D974), with a 22km scale and the gradient reaching 10.7% at its steepest. Malaucène, 21km north (D974), offers more merciful, and even flat stretches on which to recover dead legs. Sault is the sissy option (D164), at 26km on the end of the eastern tail, it makes for the gentlest ride through lavender fields, cruising at a 4.7% incline.

What to wear Frankly, it is big, bad Bédoin or nothing. So dress the part. Wear thin, blister-busting gloves and wraparound shades to keep oncoming flies from blinding you. Forget dignity and succumb to padded lycra leggings: the shammy leather gusset is hideous, but your nether regions will be forever grateful.

Bike hire Racing bikes (*vélos de course*), complete with helmet and bike repair kit can be hired at **Bédoin Location** (Chemin de la Ferraille, 04.90.65.94.53, www.bedoin-location.com, day €19, half €12),

AcScycles in Malaucène (av de Verdun, 04.90.65.15.42, closed Mon morning, Sun afternoon, day €12, half €9) or **Albion Cycles** in Sault (rte Ste-Trinité, 04.90.64.09.32, closed Mon, full day €12, half €10).

When to go Human traffic runs from May to October, and is thickest in the summer when the heat fails to discourage the keenos from sweating it up through the melting tarmac. It is best to get a 6am start to use the morning cool and see the view before the haze arrives.

What to carry Stuff your pockets with tissues (cycling makes your nose run), wedges of nougat and pain d'épices to keep you fuelled.

The ride The beginning is the worst bit. From Bedoin, you warm up slowly through the Côtes du Ventoux vineyards, sussing out the mighty contours of the damage ahead. The route is at its tamest here, but startled muscles and the enormity of the task mean your enthusiasm is at zero. Don't be discouraged when a bevy of svelte grandpas free-wheel past you on their way down: the Ventoux is crawling with people in extremely active retirement. Similarly, don't get miffed when you are overtaken by the pros, who slice past in silence like killer wasps. Watch their leg muscles, as corrugated as Cadbury's flakes, and dream of how toned you'll look at the top.

After 6km, beyond the village of Ste-Estève, the gradient starts to get silly. The fields thicken into forest and the real whipping begins as you enter the steepest section of the mountain. Bollards every kilometre indicate the remaining distance until the peak, plus the approaching incline. Turns become less frequent and the route straightens into corridors of sheer rise that put your sense of humour into spasm. A few minutes into this phase and you may start veering the wheels back down towards a hot bath and a regenerating glass of rosé. Don't give in. Think champion: finishing lines, sponsorship deals and launching your own sports deodorant. In these conditions, you have to dig deep to find motivation.

It is best to have a support car creeping along ahead, full of water bottles, clothing and a willing friend to cheer you along. Even if rent-a-crowd are booked out, you are not alone. Everyone is on a shared, ludicrous mission, and greets one another with a punchy 'Courage!', or a victorious fistwag. Many offer food and drink to the visibly fading; if not, their wives (or husbands) are on the side of

The end is in sight...

the track on video duty distributing advice and biscuits. None of this kindliness can hide the pain. By the halfway mark the slope eases off but your palms are grated to pulp and your thighs feel bludgeoned by the exertion. So pace yourself. Remember this is not a race: there is no shame, only glory on Mont Ventoux.

To distract you from the torment, the road provides a good read. 'Go Ruby and Bill' and 'Courage Cassandre et Sébastian' painted out in crooked capitals, transform the surface into an international messageboard. If it all gets too much, take a break and admire the plant life. The oak, beech and pine forests, best seen in autumn, are replaced by rare arctic flowers higher up, such as the Greenland poppy which blooms in July.

Once you get above the tree line, where the Chalet Reynard restaurant (04.90.61.84.55, closed Tue) is joined by the road from Sault, vegetation and air thin to a lunar landscape just waiting to be cast in a Bond movie: folds of white crumbled rock, scudding clouds and the stripy red mast lording at the top. You have the easiest 6km to go, and are short of breath and in need of extra jumpers.

The ominous memorial to British Olympic cyclist Tommy Simpson, who died of heart failure only 1km from the summit in the 1967 Tour de France, lies close to the end, smothered in cycling club stickers, empty isotonic drink bottles and stones scribbled with mournful messages. Don't be put off – after all Tommy was cruising on a cocktail of amphetamines and Cognac when he met his end. Helpful 'Pacmen' painted on the road gobble balls the length of the home straight, and help you along to the finishing line.

At the pinnacle, the euphoria and relief are intoxicating. With the onrush of triumph, vigorous winds and the endless views (if it's cloudy, guess the sight from the display panels) you can't stop grinning along with all the other cyclists and their families. Look out and marvel, as the peak itself is pretty uneventful. A giftshop welcomes you with souvenirs and Le Vendran bar stamps your postcards to authenticate 'I woz ere' bragging.

The fun is not yet over. The descent north to Malaucène offers more open views, so you can travel with the backdrop of Mont Blanc. But if you think free-wheeling all the way down is as easy as it looked on the way up, think again. This is the dangerous bit: as you gather speed, the cold bites harder, your hands strain from constant braking. Take the hairpins too fast and you risk impaling yourself on a tree. Ride slowly, or better still, have a short go down to the Mont Serein ski resort, hop in the car for the remainder, and then jump out again for the grand finale at Malaucène, spinning along, arms in the air and heading straight for a massage.

This is the official version. The sly will find further shortcuts. Hitching is not encouraged, but Bédoin Location will drive you to the summit, and leave you to meander down on mountain bikes for the criminal fee of €63.

anybody before to do such a thing just for the hell of it. Nowadays, the summit is easily reached by a hairpin, graffiti-daubed road built in the 1930s, though in summer crowds of cyclists make the job as difficult as possible for themselves by panting up to the Air Force radar station and TV masts which scar the otherwise bare summit (*see p104* **Bike ride: The Mont Ventoux challenge**). In 1994 UNESCO designated Mont Ventoux a biosphere reserve. As you climb, the vegetation changes noticeably, as does the temperature. Winds can howl across Mont Ventoux ('windy mountain') at up to 250km per hour. At 1,909m, the barren summit is snow-capped in winter and often shrouded in mist in summer. On a clear day the view is spectacular.

The main D974 summit route forks off from the Vaison-Carpentras road at **Malaucène**. Just beyond Malaucène the source du Groseau spring may have been venerated by ancient Celtic inhabitants; the Romans certainly thought highly of it, channelling its waters down to quench thirst in Vaison (*see right*). The unusual octagonal chapel of **Notre-Dame-de-Groseau** was part of an 11th-century monastery, all other traces of which have disappeared. Just below the summit is the small ski resort of **Mont Serein** (chalet d'accueil 04.90.63.42.02)., a riot of shell suits and four-wheel-drives in winter.

An alternative approach to the summit is to take the quieter D19, which runs past the remains of a 17th-century aqueduct to the Belvedere du Paty above Crillon-le-Brave, with fine views towards Carpentras. To the east, **Bédoin** with its fine church is the last village of any size before the long haul to the top and starting point for a direct four-hour hike (information available at the tourist office). Mont Ventoux is famous for *épeautre*, or wild barley. Previously known as the poor man's wheat, it has been revived as a local gastronomic treat, to be washed down with the local red wine, Côtes du Ventoux. East of Mont Ventoux, **Sault** is one of main centres for lavender production.

Where to stay & eat

The centuries-old **Hostellerie de Crillon-le-Brave** (pl de l'Eglise, 04.90.65.61.61, www.crillonlebrave.com, closed Jan to mid-Mar, double €155-€560, menus €45-€65), in the southern lee of Ventoux, has been tastefully restored using natural fabrics and tiles. The atmosphere is welcoming and the cooking is sophisticated with a Provençal twist. Tiny Crillon-le-Brave also has the delightful **Restaurant du Vieux Four** (04.90.12.81.39, menu €23.50), an old bakery with magical views.

East of Bédoin **Le Mas des Vignes** (04.90.65.63.91; closed Mon, lunch Tue, lunch

Harvest time at **Sault**, Mont Ventoux's pungent lavender capital.

July & Aug, and mid-Oct to mid-Mar, menu €30) has fine food and spectacular views over the Dentelles de Montmirail. For comfort-seekers there is the **Hôtel L'Escapade** in Bédoin (pl Portail l'Olivier, 04.90.65.60.21, closed Nov-Apr, double €43-€45). The **Hôtel Pins** (1km out of Bédoin on chemin des Crans, 04.90.65.92.92, closed Nov-Mar, double €55-€75), in a beautiful position and the bonus of a pool. For the full outdoorsy experience, pitch up at the **Camping Municipal** in Sault (04.90.64.07.18, closed Oct-Apr, €3.10/person, tent pitch €2.70).

Resources

Market day in Bédoin is Monday.

Tourist information

Bédoin *Office de Tourisme, Espace Marie-Louis-Gravier, pl du Marché, 84410 Bédoin (04.90.65.63.95).* **Open** *mid-June to Aug* 9am-6pm Mon-Sat; 9.30am-12.30pm Sun. *Sept to mid-June* 9am-12.30pm, 2-6pm Mon-Fri; 9am-12.30pm Sat.

Les Dentelles de Montmirail

Dentelle means lace, and the curious limestone formations of these peaks certainly present an intricate and arresting pattern on the skyline. Jurassic limestone strata pushed upwards then eroded by the elements, the Dentelles draw walkers, rock-climbers and landscape artists and are surrounded by some pretty villages which turn out eminently quaffable wines.

Malaucène, on the road separating the Dentelles from Mont Ventoux, is the jumping-off point for both. The village perches on a hill and is dominated by the 14th-century fortified church of **St-Michel-et-Pierre**. At **Le Barroux**, south of here, the ruined 12th-century castle (04.90.62.35.21) offers fine views.

Terraced **Beaumes-de-Venise** is famous for its sweet dessert wine, made from the muscat grape. You can see Beaumes' olive oil being pressed at the **Moulin à Huile La Balméenne** (04.90.62.94.15, open Mon-Sat, plus afternoon Sun May-Aug & Dec).

On the western flank of the Dentelles, the tiny village of **Gigondas** gives its name to the famous grenache-based red wine. Above Gigondas is the **Col du Cayronis** pass, a challenge for rock-climbers. A little to the north, the hill village of **Séguret**, car-free and oozing charm, gets more tourist attention than is good for it, with its 12th-century church, old houses and great views. Above Séguret, **Le Crestet** has a pretty arcaded square and 11th-century church. Climb up to the 12th-century castle (not open to the public) and enjoy the view. Taking the GR footpath at the top of the village you can

also see through the trees the striking white, cube-shaped Modernist former studio of sculptor François Stahly.

Where to stay & eat

Restaurant-hotel Les Florets (rte des Dentelles, Montmirail, 04.90.65.85.01, closed Jan to mid-Mar, restaurant closed Wed Apr-Oct and Mon-Wed Nov, Dec, double €80-€85, menus €22-€32) is set in a vineyard 2km outside Gigondas; outstanding local dishes are served accompanied by the family's own wine. In Montmirail, **Montmirail Hôtel** (04.90.65.84.01, www.hotelmontmirail.com, closed mid-Oct to mid-Mar; double €60-€84) has a pool and garden. A sporty alternative is the basic **Gîte d'Etape des Dentelles** in Gigondas (04.90.65.80.85, closed mid-Jan to Mar, dormitory €12-€13), which provides courses and information on climbing, mountain biking and walking in the mountains. For elegant living among the vines, the **Domaine de Cabasse** (between Séguret and Sablet, 04.90.46.91.12, www.domaine-de-cabasse.fr, closed Dec-Apr, double €85-€128), provides cosseting, a good-sized pool and its own wine. If you're cycling up Mont Ventoux, **Les Ecuries du Ventoux** (Quartier des Grottes, Malaucène, 04.90.65.29.20, €13 dormitory) is a stable converted into a clean, efficient *gîte d'étape*, though the beds are ear-bud thin.

Resources

Market day in Malaucène is Wednesday.

Tourist information

Gigondas *Office de Tourisme, pl du Portail, 84190 Gigondas (04.90.65.85.46).* **Open** *Apr-Nov* 10am-noon, 2-6pm daily (until 7pm July & Aug). *Dec-Mar* 10am-noon, 2-5pm Mon-Sat.
Malaucène *Syndicat d'Initiative, pl de la Mairie, 88340 Malaucène (04.90.65.22.59).* **Open** *Apr* 10am-noon, 3-5pm Mon-Sat; *July-Aug* 9am-12.30pm, 3-6pm Mon-Sat; *Oct-Mar* 10am-noon Mon-Sat.

Vaison-la-Romaine

A proudly independent, prosperous town since Roman times, Vaison-la-Romaine's sprawls over both banks of the Ouvèze river with its pale, red-roofed houses. On 22 September 1992, swollen by heavy rains, the Ouvèze turned into a raging torrent, sweeping away houses, a campsite and an entire industrial estate, and killing 37 people. Incredibly, of the town's two bridges, it was the modern road bridge that was destroyed; the 2,000-year-old **Pont Romain** lost its parapet – since rebuilt – but otherwise held up. Vaison has picked itself up and gone back to being a neat, discreet small town, appreciated by the Parisians who converge here in summer. The old town, perched on a cliff and dominated by the 12th-century château of the Comtes de Toulouse, is a web of twisting medieval streets. It is some distance from the modern town built up from the 18th century on across the river. But it is this modern town which covers the original Roman nucleus of Vaison. Beneath the houses, banks and cafés are the forum and associated temples. By the time excavations began in earnest in 1907, only the suburbs of the Roman town were left to explore. Two slices of ancient life were exposed (the ticket gives admission to both *quartiers*, the museum and the cathedral cloister).

Start at the museum in the **Quartier de Puymin**. Admirably organised, the collection features statues, mosaics and domestic objects found in and around Vaison. Especially striking is a marble family group, dating from 121 AD, showing a stark-naked Emperor Hadrian standing proudly next to his elaborately dressed wife Sabina, who is clearly trying to humour her husband. Pride of place goes to a third-century AD silver bust, and charming floor mosaics from the Peacock villa. Behind the museum is the Roman amphitheatre, which hosts a summer music and theatre festival, L'Eté de Vaison.

Head out past the tourist office to the **Quartier de la Villasse**. The colonnaded main street, with its huge paving stones and monumental scale, evokes the prosperity of Roman Vaison better than any other single sight. On either side are remains of shops, baths and villas, including the one where the silver bust was found. Whoever owned this property was in the money; the 5,000m^2 *domus* had its own baths and an extensive hanging garden.

Cathedral Notre-Dame-de-Nazareth, a ten-minute walk away on avenue Jules Ferry, is an unusual example of Provençal Romanesque, with fine carving and pure lines. Recent excavations have revealed that it was built on the ruins of an important Roman building. Inside, the most notable feature is the 11th-century high altar on four delicate marble columns. Up the hill north of the cathedral, the curious Romanesque **Chapelle de St-Quenin** (currently closed for restoration) has a unique triangular apse, based on an earlier Roman temple – for centuries the good citizens of Vaison thought it *was* Roman.

Quartiers de Puymin & de la Villasse

Open *Mar-May* 10am-12.30pm, 2-6pm. *June-Sept Puymin* 9.30am-6.30pm. *La Villasse* 9.30am-noon, 2.30-6.30pm. *Cloister* 9.30am-12.30pm, 2-6.30pm. *Oct-Dec, Feb* 10am-noon, 2-5pm daily. Museum closed Tue mornings. All closed Jan. **Admission** €7; €3.50 12-18s. **No credit cards**.

Where to stay & eat

The **Hostellerie le Beffroi** (rue de l'Evêché, 04.90.36.04.71, www.le-beffroi.com, closed Feb-Mar, double €68-€85) has fine views from its charming 16th-century building; the restaurant (closed Tue, lunch Mon-Fri and dinner Sat & Sun, menus €25.50-€41) is good value for high-class fare. The **Logis du Château** (Les Hauts de Vaison, 04.90.36.09.98, closed Oct-Mar, double €46-€76, restaurant closed lunch Mon-Fri, menus €17.50-€30.80) offers simple modern rooms and a traditional restaurant, plus pool and tennis court. Near the Roman ruins, the **Brin d'Olivier** (4 rue du Ventoux, 04.90.28.74.79, closed 2wks in Dec, Jan, Mar & June, double €61-€84, restaurant closed all Wed, lunch Sat, menus €23-€50) is an attractive small hotel with interesting Provençal food. The **Hôtel Burrhus** (1 pl de Montfort, 04.90.36.00.11, www.burrhus.com, closed mid-Dec to Feb, double €47-€69) is on the liveliest square in town and has some original art in the public rooms and bedrooms, while **Le Bateleur** (1 pl Théodore Aubanel, 04.90.36.28.04, closed all Mon & dinner Sun, menus €15-€34) is a serious family restaurant. The place for a treat, though, is **Le Moulin à Huile** (quai Maréchal Foch, 04.90.36.20.67, www.moulin-huile.com, closed all Mon, dinner Sun, menus €40-€70), where master-chef Robert Bardot serves up a heavenly feast in a garden by the Pont Romain.

Resources

Market day in Vaison-la-Romaine is Tuesday, plus Thursday and Saturday June to September.

Tourist information

Office de Tourisme, pl Chanoine Sautel, 84110 Vaison-la-Romaine (04.90.36.02.11/www.vaison-la-romaine.com). **Open** 9am-noon, 2-5.45pm daily (closed Sun from mid-Sept to mid-Mar).

Getting there & around

By car

Take A7 (exit 21) and the D950 to Carpentras. The D938 goes south to Pernes, north to Mont Ventoux and Vaison, D7 to Beaumes-de-Venise and Gigondas.

By train/bus

The TGV runs to Avignon, with some services stopping at Orange. **Arnaud** (04.90.63.01.82) runs two buses a day from Marseille to Carpentras, via Pernes-les-Fontaines, four buses a day from Orange to Carpentras and four a day from Avignon to Carpentras. **Cars Comtadins** (04.90.67.20.25) operates services between Carpentras and Vaison-la-Romaine (also serving Malaucène) and Bédoin. Orange to Vaison via Sablet, north of Gigondas, is served by **Cars Lieutaud** (04.90.36.05.22).

The Drôme Provençale

Long punned as 'Midi moins le quart', the verdant, northern tip of Provence has now been officially outed as the (so far) unspoilt, new playground of the South.

History left a trail of Roman bridges, Romanesque churches, and medieval-to-Renaissance châteaux; nuclear energy contributed the power station at Pierrelatte, an unfortunate backdrop to this pocket of exceptional natural beauty.

The Tricastin & Grignan

Baptised by the Gaul tribe of the Tricastanii, this Rhône-side plain of vineyards, lavender and oak today bathes in its venerated AOC Coteaux du Tricastin wines, and its claim to be France's leading truffle producer (*see p113* **Digging for diamonds**). St-Paul-Trois-Châteaux, the ancient capital, boasts a grand total of zero châteaux, but it is home to the textbook Romanesque, 12th-century Ancienne Cathédrale. Next door, the **Maison de la Truffe et du Tricastin** has a permanent truffle exhibition and tastings.

The **Château de Grignan** is splendidly ladylike, befitting Madame (or Marquise) de Sévigné, who immortalised it through her gushy letters to her daughter, Comtesse de Grignan. Reclining on a hillock, the original 12th-century feudal fort was retouched into one of the finest examples of Renaissance architecture in south-east France. Furnished apartments provide an elegant venue for exhibitions, theatre and concerts. Madame de Sévigné is buried in the 16th-century Collégiale St-Sauveur, and the village is exhaustingly themed in her name with the Festival de la Corréspondence in July, a **Musée de la Typographie** and the new 'Women in Literature' festival in September, which attracts international stars such as Muriel Spark.

Visit the 19th-century columned *lavoir* in place du Mail – the Tuesday market-place. For an idle oak-shaded stroll, the Grotte de Rochecourbière, 1km south beyond the public swimming pool, is a rock shelter cocooning the round stone table where the Marquise allegedly penned many of her letters. The valley leading west towards the Rhône passes by the charming village of **Valaurie** (8km, D451) with its Romanesque church.

South of Grignan, past the lollipop-thin medieval tower at Chamaret, hovers the medieval hill village of **Suze-la-Rousse**. On the west bank of the river Lez, Suze's name is derived from the Celtic 'uz', meaning high place and, allegedly, the auburn mane of one of the ladies of **Château de Suze**. The fortified château began as a 12th-century hunting lodge for the Princes of Orange, before being lined with an Italianate grand courtyard which forms the backdrop each summer for art installations by the likes of Daniel Buren and Félice Varini, and chamber music in July. Inside, the château houses the Université du Vin. Created in 1978, this bastion of higher education and research has its own vineyard, with 70 different grape varieties. The local harvest is kick-started with wine tastings and dancing at the Ban des Vendanges in September; the **Caves Coopératives** (04.75.04.48.38) is a good year-round filling station for Coteaux du Tricastin.

Château de Grignan
Grignan (04.75.91.83.55). **Open** 9.30-11.30am, 2-5.30pm daily (closed Tue Nov-Mar). **Admission** guided visits 5.10; €3.10 11-18s; free under-11s; gardens €1.50; free under-11s. **Credit** V.

Château de Suze-la-Rousse
Suze-la-Rousse (04.75.04.81.44). **Open** 9.30-11.30am, 2-6.30pm daily (closed Tue Nov-Mar). **Admission** €3.10; €2.10 11-18s, students; free under-11s. **Credit** AmEx, DC, MC, V.

Maison de la Truffe et du Tricastin
rue de la République, St-Paul-Trois-Châteaux (04.75.96.61.29). **Open** *summer* 9am-noon, 3-7pm Tue-Sat; 10am-noon, 3-7pm Sun. *winter* 9am-noon, 2-6pm Tue-Sat; 10am-noon, 2-6pm Sun. **Admission** €3.50; €1.80 7-11s; free under-7s. **No credit cards.**

Musée de la Typographie
Maison du Bailli, pl St-Louis, Grignan (04.75.46.57.16). **Open** *July-Aug* 10am-6.30pm daily. *Sept-June* 10am-12.30pm, 2-6pm Tue-Fri; 11am-6.30pm Sat, Sun. **Admission** €3; €2.30 10-18s, students; free under-10s. **Credit** MC, V.

Where to stay & eat

In season, truffles permeate the menus of local restaurants, notably **L'Esplan** in St-Paul-Trois-Châteaux (15 pl de l'Esplan, 04.75.96.64.64, closed lunch & end Dec, menus €20-€42, all-truffle menu €70). In Grignan, the **Café de Sévigné** (pl Sévigné, 04.75.46.51.82) facing the town hall is good for a scenic beer, although many locals have now defected to the reborn **Hôtel Sévigné** at the foot of the château (15 pl Castellane, 04.75.46.50.97, double €43-€53, restaurant closed Mon & dinner Tue, menus €19.50-€25) with its hearty Provençal food. Roses adorn the gardens and curtains of 19th-century **Manoir de la Roseraie** (rte de Valréas, 04.75.46.58.15, www.manoirdela roseraie.com, closed early Jan to mid Feb & early Dec, double €155-€330, menus €32-€61). Despite a pool, tennis court and lawns, its luxuriance just misses good taste, though chef Freddy Trichet keeps up the gastronomic tradition. **Le Clair de la Plume** (pl du Mail, 04.75.91.81.30, www.chateauxhotels.com/ clairplume, double €85-€120), off the market-place, is a tasteful rural-chic hotel, with trellised garden and English tearoom. Monique at **L'Eau à la Bouche** (rue St-Louis, 04.75.46.57.37, closed Mon & Tue Nov-June, Mon July-Aug, average €25) serves homely *plats* in a dining room crammed with flowers. 18th-century **L'Autre Maison** (rue du Grand Faubourg, 04.75.46.58.58, www.lautremaison.com, closed Nov to mid-Dec, double €69-€76) is a bright, modern-rustic guesthouse, with homemade jam for breakfast. About 3km west towards Valaurie, **La Maison du Moulin** (quartier petit Cordy, 04.75.46.56.94, www.maison dumoulin.com, double €75-€120), an old water mill, has a pool, library and rooms decorated in glossy magazine style, and holds lavender and truffle cookery weekends. For B&B in a more authentic mill, **Le Moulin de l'Aulière** (4km south of Colonzelle, 04.75.91.10.49, double €55) is a 19th-century family home, preserved in a time warp with the old schoolroom and children's books still in place. Towards Suze, **Campsite Les Truffières** (lieu-dit Nachony, 04.75.46.93.62, www.lestruffieres.com, closed Oct-Apr) has an outdoor swimming pool.

In Suze-la-Rousse, the vine-clad terrace of **Pizzeria de la Fontaine** (pl du Champ de Mars, 04.75.98.28.67, average €12) offers down-to-earth replenishment, while elegant rest, homely suppers and a pool can be found at the new **Les Aiguières** guesthouse (rue de la Fontaine d'Argent, 04.75.98.40.80, www.les-aiguieres.com, double €76). Further south, the luxury option is the **Château de Rochegude** (Rochegude, 04.75.97.21.10, www.chateau rochegude.com, double €170-€350, closed beg Nov, restaurant closed Nov-Apr lunch Sun-Tue, menus €35-€85), in a grandiose castle with restaurant, park, pool and tennis court.

Resources

Market day is Tuesday in Grignan, Friday in Suze-la-Rousse.

Tourist information

Grignan *Office de Tourisme, pl du Jeu de Ballon, 26230 Grignan (04.75.46.56.75/www.guideweb.com/ grignan).* **Open** *May-Sept* 10am-12.30pm, 2.30-7pm daily. *Oct-Apr* 10am-12.30pm, 2-5.30pm Mon-Sat.
Suze-la-Rousse *Office de Tourisme, av des Côtes-du-Rhône, 26790 Suze-la-Rousse (04.75.04.81.41).* **Open** 9am-noon, 3-6pm Mon; 9am-noon, 2.30-6pmTue-Fri; 9am-noon Sat.

Nyons

Dubbed Petit Nice, Nyons crouches in a bowl of mountains at the opening of the Eygues valley. With its own regenerative wind, the 'Pontias', perennial sun and a halo of olive groves, Giono called it 'paradise on earth'. The retired and their multiplying pink villas seem to agree. Visit the medieval place des Arcades, the vaulted rue des Grands Forts, the remains of the feudal château and the 13th-century Tour Randonné. Once a prison, reconstructed in the 19th century as a chapel, its neo-Gothic crest dominates Nyons. The Thursday morning market sprawls over much of the town.

Nyons is the most northerly olive growing area in Europe, and its emblematic black *tanche* – giving a mild, fruity oil – was the first variety in France to be awarded an *appellation d'origine contrôlée*. **L'Institut du Monde de l'Olivier** has exhibitions and oil-tasting workshops. Olive-pressing history tours are given at the **Musée de l'Olivier** and the family-run **Les Vieux Moulins** on the banks of the Eygues (also containing the perfumed remains of an 18th-century soap factory). Olives are now pressed next door at the new **Moulin Autrand-Dozol** (04.75.26.02.52) and olive-related products and local wines are available year round at the **Vignolis Coopérative du Nyonsais** (pl Olivier de Serres, 04.75.26.95.00, closed morning Sun) and from the producers that dot the surrounding countryside. **La Scourtinerie** is the last workshop in France to handmake natural-fibre olive-pressing mats, now sold as doormats.

Next to the Vieux Moulins, the 'Roman' donkey bridge, an elegant single arch actually built in the 13th and 14th centuries, is enveloped in summer by the scent of lavender distilling downstream at the **Distillerie Bleu Provence**, where you can buy essential oils from local plants, or even make your own eau de toilette in group workshops.

For a novel dip, the **Nyonsoldeïado** outdoor water world (promenade de la Digue, 04.75.26.06.92) is refreshingly tame, despite its waterfalls and Jacuzzis. On the road in from Grignan, peel off down the lime-tree avenue towards Venterol, a radiant, picture-postcard village tumbling down the hillside, with a 17th-century bell tower. For scenic walks, the Sentier

'Wish you were here': Mme de Sévigné's view from **Château de Grignan**. *See p109.*

Avignon & the Vaucluse

des Oliviers takes you up through the olive groves. The more challenging forest path along the Garde-Grosse mountain to the south joins part of the GR9 and enjoys a soaring panorama.

Distillerie Bleu Provence
58 promenade de la Digue (04.75.26.10.42). **Open** 9.30am-12.30pm, 2.30-6.30pm (June-Sept until 7.30pm). **Admission** €2.50; €1.50 students; free under-12s. **No credit cards.**

Institut du Monde de l'Olivier
40 pl de la Libération (04.75.26.90.90). **Open** 8.30am-12.30pm, 1.20-5.30pm Mon-Fri (till 4.30pm Fri). Tastings Thur afternoons during school holidays. **Admission** free; tastings €5.50; €4.40 students; €2 8-16s; free under-8s. **No credit cards.**

Musée de l'Olivier
allée des Tilleuls (04.75.26.12.12). **Open** 10-11.30am, 2.30-5.30pm daily. **Admission** €2; €1 7-18s, students; free under-7s. **No credit cards.**

La Scourtinerie
36 rue de la Maladrerie (04.75.26.33.52). **Open** 9.30am-noon, 2.30-6.30pm Mon-Sat (until 7pm June-Sept). Workshop closed Sat. **Admission** free. **Credit** (shop) MC, V.

Les Vieux Moulins
4 promenade de la Digue (04.75.26.11.00). **Open** *July-Aug* 10am-noon, 2.30-6pm Mon-Sat; 10am-noon Sun. *Sept-June* 10am-noon, 2.30-6pm Tue-Sat. Closed Jan to early Feb. **Admission** €4; free under-12s. **Credit** AmEx, DC, MC, V.

Where to stay & eat

Whet your appetite at one of the many café terraces on place de la Libération, or visit the friendly new **Brasserie Artisanale du Sud** (69 av Frédéric Mistral, 04.75.26.95.75, www.la-grihete.com). Part of a revival of Provençal micro-breweries, it produces original, aromatic beer using local ingredients such as fig and lime-blossom. Locals and their artwork fill the **Resto des Arts** (13 rue des Déportés, 04.75.26.31.49, closed Wed, lunch Tue & Sat, 15 Dec-15 Jan, menus €13-€25). Foodies can sample whole-roast Baronnies lamb at **Le Petit Caveau** (9 rue Victor Hugo, 04.75.26.20.21, closed Mon & dinner Sun, Oct-Apr dinner Thur, menus €29-€45), now under new ownership. Three sisters run the cheap and cheerful **Hôtel au Petit Nice** (4 av Paul-Laurens, 04.75.26.09.46, closed Nov & beg July, restaurant closed Mon dinner & Sun, double €41.20-€44.30), helped by its decent €13 weekday menu. **Une Autre Maison** (pl de la République, 04.75.26.43.09, closed Nov-Dec, double €115-€155, menu €42) is the design choice, with a walled garden, pool and lithe guests in hotel dressing-gowns, limbering up for the massage and truffle cookery weekends. The restaurant has well-chosen wines and a speciality chicken bouillabaisse. Heading out west on the D94, **La Bastide des Monges**

(rte d'Orange, 04.75.26.99.69,www.bastidedes
monges.com, closed mid Oct-mid Apr, double
€69-€124) is a farmhouse conversion with a pool
and vineyard views.

Resources

Tourist information

*Office de Tourisme, pl de la Libération, 26110 Nyons
(04.75.26.10.35/www.nyonstourisme.com).* **Open**
June, Sept 9.30am-noon; 2.30-6pm Mon-Sat; 10am-
1pm Sun. *July, Aug* 9am-12.30pm, 2.30-7pm Mon-Sat;
10am-1pm, 2-5pm Sun. *Oct-May* 9.30am-noon, 2.30-
5.45pm Mon-Sat.

Buis-les-Baronnies

The precipitous limestone Baronnies mountains
swell southeast of Nyons. Popular for rock-
climbing, hiking and riding, the heady landscape
is known for its rich variety of aromatic plants.

Sheltered beside the river Ouvèze under the
jagged Rocher St-Julien, sleepy **Buis-les-
Baronnies** was the medieval capital of the
Barons of Mévouillon. With the Renaissance
facade of the **Couvent des Ursulines**, used
for art exhibitions, as its backdrop, the village
enjoys a tranquillity interrupted only by the
constant thud of *pétanque* under the plane trees.
Since the 19th century, Buis has produced
almost all of France's world-class lime-blossom:
the avenues of 'yellow gold' which line the
valleys are hand harvested for Europe's largest
tilleul fair in July. Aromatic and medicinal herbs
are available at the Wednesday market in place
des Arcades, at herborist Bernard Laget (pl des
Herbes, 04.75.28.16.42) or the new **Maison des
Plantes Aromatiques et Médicinales**
above the tourist office. Built into the medieval
ramparts, with its own herb garden, it presents
a small, fragrant display of the history and
distillation of the blossom.

An hour-long, cricket-screaming walk
through terraced olive groves takes you up to
the hillside village of **La Roche-sur-le-Buis**,
where the Chapelle des Pénitents is now a
micro-museum of traditional farm instruments,
and its tiny graveyard has been cultivated into
an enchanting 'symbolic plant garden'. Further
afield, climb north to the Gorges d'Ubrieux or
follow the foot of Mont Ventoux east towards
the **Montbrun-les-Bains** spa village.

Maison des Plantes Aromatiques et Médicinales

*14 bd Eysseric, (04.75.28.04.59/www.maisondes
plantes.com).* **Open** *July, Aug* 9am-noon, 3-7pm Mon-
Sat; 10am-12.30pm, 4-7pm Sun. *Sept-June* 9.15am-
noon, 2-5.30pm Mon-Sat; 10am-12.30pm, 2.30-5.30pm
Sun. **Admission** €3.50; €1.50 12-18s; free under-12s.
No credit cards.

Where to stay & eat

La Fourchette (pl des Arcades, 04.75.28.03.31,
closed lunch Mon in July & Aug, plus dinner
Sun from Sept-June, menus €14-€34) serves
refined regional cuisine. Further along, the
rambling **Hôtel les Arcades Le Lion d'Or**
(pl des Arcades, 04.75.28.11.31, www.hotel
arcades.fr closed Dec-Jan, double €44-€53)
boasts a garden, new outdoor swimming pool
and gentle wake-up calls from the fountain in
the square. For ecclesiastical pomp **L'Ancienne
Cure** opposite the church (2 rue du Paroir,
04.75.28.22.08, www.ancienne-cure.com, closed
Dec-Mar, double €55-€90) was the 15th-century
holiday home of the bishop of Valence, and is
now a gracious *chambres d'hôte* lavishly
decorated with Oriental antiques and historical
detail – the former chapel is the TV room, and a
cosy family room under the eaves was the old
servant's quarter. **Bar des Passions** (allée des
Platanes, 04.75.28.12.32, double €35, no
reservations) is a shrine to the Renault Alpine
and Johnny Hallyday – owner Michel has his
own Johnny museum; rooms are basic but
welcoming. **La Terrasse** (La Roche-sur-le-
Buis, 04.75.28.23.94, average €15) welcomes you
after the climb to La Roche-sur-le-Buis with
bistro classics, bric-a-brac and vertiginous views.

Resources

Tourist information

*Office de Tourisme, 14 bd Eysséric, 26170 Buis-les-
Baronnies (04.75.28.04.59/www.buislesbaronnies.com).*
Open *July-Aug* 9am-noon, 3-7pm Mon-Sat; 10am-
12.30pm, 4-7pm Sun. *Sept-June* 9.15am-noon,
2-5.30pm Mon-Sat; 10-12.30pm, 2.30-5.30pm Sun.

Getting there & around

By car

Leave the A7 autoroute at exit 18 and take D133 and
D541 for Grignan, or exit 19 and D994 for Suze-la-
Rousse. Nyons is 20km from Grignan by D941 and
D538, and 30km from Buis by D5, D46 and D538.

By bus/train

Nearest train stations are Avignon, Orange and
Montélimar. **Cars Lieutaud** (04.90.36.05.22,
www.cars-lieutaud.fr) runs 2 buses a day, Mon-Sat,
between Nyons and Avignon via Vaison-la-Romaine,
and between Avignon and Buis-les-Baronnies. **Cars
Dunevon** (04.75.28.41.54) runs 2 buses a day, Mon-
Fri, between Nyons and Buis, fewer during the school
holidays. **Cars Teste** (04.75.00.27.90) runs 5 buses a
day between Montélimar and Nyons via Grignan
(three the other way), plus buses between Grignan
and Nyons via Valréas. **Autocars Petit Nice**
(04.75.26.35.58) runs 5 buses a day, Mon-Sat, from
Nyons to Vaison, with 3 return journeys; fewer buses
run during school holidays.

Digging for diamonds

Black, warty and resembling something between a dog's nose and donkey dung, the *tuber melanosporum* appears an unlikely candidate for a gourmet delicacy. But the sought-after Périgord truffle or *rabasse* of Provence, dubbed the *diamant noir* (black diamond) by gastronome Brillat-Savarin in 1826, is a pungent culinary pin-up. Today its principal hiding place extends beneath the Drôme Provençale and the Enclave des Papes, a shard of the Vaucluse wedged below Grignan, which holds the truffle capital of Richerenches.

The 3,300 hectares of *truffières* (oak woods) that streak the region provide 'host' trees, their roots clutched by the fungus, which develops underground, cushioned by the chalky soils and Mediterranean climate. In mid-November, the hunting season begins. Lasting till mid-March, this winter ritual is cloaked in secrecy as *trufficulteurs* forage for the buried lump of luxury, helped by their furry friends in a Provençal take on *One Man and his Dog*. Eschewing the more greedy and boisterous pig (too likely to scoff the booty), the Tricastin uses trained dogs, often Labradors, to sniff out the odour penetrating the earth (and claim their reward of biscuits, gruyère or saucisson), while the *trufficulteur* wades in with a metal claw, the *fouji*, or a

makeshift instrument, such as a screwdriver, to extract the loot. The truffles vary from mere pellets up to whopping 45g grenades. Early finds are dark brown, with white, marbled interiors; by mid-December, the winners emerge, blackened to full maturity.

More than just an extravagant sandwich-filler, the truffle represents a natural myth. Believed to have been a gift from Zeus, born of a bolt of lightning, a plateful was the price for strangers to win citizenship into ancient Athens. The Romans sussed out that it was an aphrodisiac, and Napoléon, hungry for an heir, was later advised to feed his wife Empératrice Marie-Louise on the stuff. Such refinement comes at a price. No longer the 'gem of the poor' – free game to medieval peasants in wild woodlands – nor mined in bulk as in its 19th-century heyday, the truffle is now a precious rarity, retailing on average at €450/kg, and peaking at a record €1,060/kg. Values creep up for the Christmas rush, with heatwaves and media hype helping to boost figures along the way.

The price is fixed at the truffle market held in Richerenches every Saturday morning in season since 1924. A furtive ceremony, layered in codes, this is bulk buying, cash-in-hand for the professionals, and the interests of France's leading chefs (their names furiously protected) lie behind the *courtiers* brokers – who line the pavements with their Mercs, waiting for play. At around 9am, the *rabassiers* start shopping around the car boots with their sacks of wares, still caked in earth, bargaining away, heads bowed and backs turned. With much peering into filthy carrier bags, smelling, weighing and stabbing at calculators, there is little sign of the truffle itself or its value. This is a closed affair, muffled by discretion.

Local producers will give you a truffle-hunting demonstration and tasting if you kindly agree to buy their goods. Visit Joël Barthélemy every Sunday in Suze-la-Rousse, (04.75.04.87.13), André Férraud in Réauville (04.75.98.52.82), the Domaine de Bramarel south of Grignan (04.75.46.52.20), or join a Saturday tasting with the Maison de la Truffe et du Tricastin (*see p109*). The public can buy fresh and preserved truffles at markets throughout the Tricastin in winter, with the biggest market on Friday down in Carpentras, and a pre-Christmas truffle and wine fair in Grignan in mid-December.

Avignon & the Vaucluse

The Luberon

The heart of posh Provence, the Luberon offers antiques and gastronomic tables aplenty, plus an ochre lunar landscape painted by man.

First impressions of the Luberon depend a little on where and when one arrives. On one hand there is the worldly buzz of Parisians in Provence, hiding out in designer *mas* and exchanging *bisous* at café tables. On the other, near deserted age-old stone streets and local farmers sipping *pastis* at the bar.

Hill villages, fortresses and Renaissance châteaux testify to a proudly unconventional land that was heavily embroiled in the Wars of Religion. The area was declared a Parc Régional in 1977 and, despite the arrival of Champagne socialists and Brits on the trail of *A Year in Provence*, it remains – mostly – unspoiled. Incomers renovate decrepit *bastides,* and there is a limit on new construction, but rising property prices are forcing locals out. The Luberon remains a major grower of fruit and veg, while locals work to keep smaller-scale olive oil and lavender production alive and to improve the quality of the Côtes de Luberon, Côtes de Ventoux and Coteaux de Pierrevert wines.

At the heart of the Parc Régional is the rocky limestone massif of the Montagne du Luberon, cut in two by the Aiguebrun valley which divides the Petit Luberon to the west and the Grand Luberon, rising to the 1,125m Mourre Nègre, to the east. The Luberon remains pleasantly green even in high summer and offers plenty of opportunities for walking, riding and cycling. Footpaths include the *grandes randonnées* GR6, 9, 92 and 97. 'Le Luberon en vélo' is a 100km bike route running partially along disused railway tracks; arrows are in green and white in the direction Cavaillon-Apt-Forcalquier and green and orange in the opposite direction, with a new southern route that completes the loop via Manosque, Lourmarin and Lauris.

North Luberon: from Taillades to Saignon

Once important for stone quarrying, the rugged northern flank of the Montagne du Luberon is punctuated by a string of picturesque hill villages. At the western edge of the ridge, tranquil **Taillades** is the village that best recalls the stone quarrying past. Houses seem to sit on blocks of cut rock and the remains of two châteaux – one fortified, one Renaissance –

face each other across a ravine. A path climbs to a chapel perched over one former quarry, now an atmospheric outdoor theatre.

Hugging the N100, inconspicuous **Coustellet**'s main attraction is its summer farmers' market (Wednesday evening, Sunday morning from April to November), but you might also want to visit the **Musée de la Lavande**, where a film explains how the tiny purple flowers are distilled and a smelling machine demonstrates the difference between true lavender and the hybrid *lavindin*. It is run by a family that still cultivates lavender high up on Mont Ventoux.

Oppède-le-Vieux, reached through narrow country lanes to the south, perfectly symbolises the rebirth of the Luberon. The old village was abandoned during the 19th century and has been resettled since the 1960s by artists, potters and writers; it is still romantically overgrown. At the top are the recently restored Romanesque **Collégiale Notre Dame d'Alidon**, with a gargoyle-adorned belltower, and the ruined castle of notorious baron Jean de Meynier, behind the brutal 1545 massacre of the Vaudois (or Waldensian) heretics, a proto-Protestant sect who populated many of the Luberon villages. Below the village, the **Sentier vigneron** follows quiet lanes amid vineyards, with discreet panels signalling grape varieties.

Just east of here, **Ménerbes** remains a clock-stopped stone village where fine doorways point to a prosperous past. At the top, the turreted former château (not open to the public) was once a Vaudois stronghold. On the plain below the village, you can visit the state-of-the-art cellars of the **Domaine de la Citadelle**, where Yves Rousset-Rouard, producer of the *Emmanuelle* films, has established himself as one of the most respected wine-makers of the area. The visit also takes in the corkscrew collection of the **Musée du Tire-Bouchon**. On the scenic D109 between Ménerbes and Lacoste, a bumpy track leads to the isolated **Abbaye St-Hilaire**, the remains of a 13th-century Carmelite priory, whose owners have restored the cloister, chapel and garden.

With its fortified medieval gateways and cobbled streets, the tiny, semi-deserted village of

Return to the source at **L'Isle-sur-la-Sorgue** and **Fontaine-de-Vaucluse**. *See p122.*

Going for old

Antiques dealers began settling in L'Isle-sur-la-Sorgue after a first *foire à la brocante* was held here in 1962, and there are now an estimated 300 dealers, concentrated along avenue de la Libération, avenue des Quatre Otages and around the station, many of them in picturesque canalside locations. Each Sunday, the antiques shops and arcades (open 10am-7pm Mon, Sat, Sun) are joined by squadrons of junkier *brocanteurs* who line avenue des Quatre Otages, while at Easter and on 15 August major antiques fairs flow over into nearby fields. Merchandise ranges from high-quality antiques and garden statuary to pedal cars and quirky collectibles, including many Provençal items, such as gilt mirrors, *armoires*, carved buffets and openwork bread cabinets, printed fabrics, and Apt, Moustiers and Marseille faïence. There are also architectural salvage specialists offering old zinc bars, bistro fittings and hotel reception booths.

The different arcades have different characters: two-storey **Quai de la Gare** is the most upmarket, with plenty of fine 18th-century furniture, paintings and porcelain, **Village des Antiquaires de la Gare**, in a former carpet factory, is more ramshackle and boho, **Hôtel Dongier** is set up as a series of smart interiors, while **Isle-aux-Brocantes** is reached across a canal and abounds in vintage garden furniture and 20th-century items.

Even if there are few true bargains (some shops seem to pack up entire crates of furniture for shipping direct to stores in the USA, and it's not uncommon to hear sums being discussed in dollars), prices are noticeably lower than in Paris, where a fair number of the goods end up. Needless to say, the usual bargaining rules apply. Should you succumb, transport firms can ship your buys around the world.

Antiques arcades

Hôtel Dongier *9 esplanade Robert Vasse (04.90.38.63.63)*.
L'Isle aux Brocantes *7 av des Quatre Otages (04.90.20.69.93)*.
Village des Antiquaires de la Gare *2bis av de l'Egalité (04.90.38.04.57)*.
Le Quai de la Gare *4 av Julien Guigue (04.90.20.73.42)*.

Lacoste should not be missed. The ruined castle at the top was the home of the scandalous Marquis de Sade on and off for 30 years until his imprisonment in 1786, and it has recently been acquired by global fashion magnate Pierre Cardin, who puts on an opera festival each summer. From here the road zigzags up the ramparts of **Bonnieux**. Inhabited since Neolithic times, Bonnieux became a Templar commanderie and later a papal outpost, until reunited with France in 1793. A 12th-century church on the hilltop is reached up cobbled steps from rue de la République; the newer parish church in the lower village contains four 15th-century panel paintings. The tiny **Musée de la Boulangerie** recounts the process of breadmaking. North of Bonnieux on the way to the Roman **Pont Julien**, the **Château de Mille** (D3, rte de Bonnieux, 04.90.74.11.94, closed Sun) is the oldest wine château in the Luberon and a former summer residence of the Avignon papacy.

In the less-known eastern half of the Luberon above Apt, the remarkably unspoiled village of **Saignon** stretches along a craggy escarpment between a square-towered Romanesque church and cemetery and a rocky belvedere. Its remote location and mountain site made the nearby hamlet of **Buoux** an important refuge during the Wars of Religion: high on the hillside are ruins of the **Fort de Buoux** demolished by Louis XIV to deter Huguenots from taking refuge here. A little further, at the end of the secluded Aiguebrun valley, rock climbers pepper the overhanging crags and assorted footpaths lead to Sivergues and the Mourré Nègre.

Abbaye St-Hilaire

Menerbes (04.90.75.88.83). **Open** *summer* 9am-6pm daily. *winter* 10am-5pm daily. **Admission** free.

Collégiale Notre-Dame d'Alidon

Oppède-le-Vieux. **Open** *Apr-Nov* 10.30am-6pm Sat, Sun (or by appointment with the Mairie 04.90.76.90.06).

Fort de Buoux

Buoux (04.90.74.25.75). **Open** dawn to dusk daily. Closed in bad weather. **Admission** €3; €2 7-16s, students; free under-12s. **No credit cards**.

Musée de la Boulangerie

12 rue de la République, Bonnieux (04.90.75.88.34). **Open** *Apr-June, Sept, Oct* 10am-12.30pm, 2.30-6pm Mon, Wed-Sun. *July, Aug* 10am-1pm, 3-6.30pm Mon, Wed-Sun. Closed Nov-Mar. **Admission** €3.50; €1.50 students, 12-16s; free under-12s. **No credit cards**.

Musée de la Lavande

rte de Gordes, Coustellet (04.90.76.91.23/ www.museedelalavande.com). **Open** *1-14 Feb, 16 Sept-Dec* 10am-noon, 2-6pm daily. *15 Feb-June, 1-15 Sept*-10am-noon, 2-7pm daily. *July, Aug* 10am-7pm daily. Closed Jan. **Admission** €4; free under-15s. **Credit** AmEx, DC, MC, V (shop only).

Musée du Tire-Bouchon

Domaine de la Citadelle, Le Chataignier, chemin de Cavaillon, Ménerbes (04.90.72.41.58/www.musee dutirebouchon.com). **Open** *Apr-Sept* 9am-noon, 2-7pm daily. *Oct-Mar* 9am-noon, 2-6pm Mon-Fri. **Admission** €4; free under-15s. **Credit** MC, V.

Where to stay & eat

At Robion, **Lou Luberon** (av Aristide Briand, 04.90.76.65.04, closed Sun & some evenings, menus €11.50-€26) looks like a simple roadside bar but serves delicious salads and carefully prepared regional dishes. At Coustellet, haute-cuisine trained Olivier Gouin took over the old family butcher **Maison Gouin** (pl du Marché Paysan, 04.90.76.90.18, closed Wed & Sun and 15 Nov-6 Dec & Feb-beg Mar, menus €11.50-€31) and turned it into a restaurant combined with butcher and upmarket deli. There's an informal inexpensive menu at lunch and a more dressed up affair in the evening.

Sadist connections abound in Lacoste. Try simple *café-tabac* **Café de Sade** (rue Basse, 04.90.75.82.29, café all year except mid-Jan to Feb, restaurant closed mid-Nov to mid-Mar, menus €12.50-€20) for a drink, *plat du jour* and local gossip. In an old bakery in Bonnieux, the semi-troglodyte **Le Fournil** (5 pl Carnot, 04.90.75.83.62, closed Mon & Tue and Dec-Jan, menus €25-€35) – John Malkovich's favourite – is the very definition of low-key Provençal style, with great service and an inventive menu using local produce. The 18th-century **Hostellerie de la Prieuré** (rue Jean-Baptiste Auvard, 04.90.75.80.78, closed Nov-Mar, restaurant also closed lunch Tue-Fri, double €53-€98, menus €19-€33.50), on the descent to Lacoste, has a chapel and vast fireplaces as reminders of its priory past; bedrooms overlook a walled garden or ramparts. On the garrigue covered plateau above the village, the upmarket **La Bastide de Capelongue** (1.5km east on D232, 04.90.75.89.78, closed mid-Nov to mid-Dec, mid-Jan to mid-Mar, double €183-€259 incl dinner, menus €46-€69) is a tastefully decorated modern *bastide* with a pool. Off the D194 **Les Trois Sources** (chemin de la Chaîne, Bonnieux, 04.90.75.95.58, www.lestroissources.com, double €60-€130) is a lovely *chambres d'hôtes* in an ancient building surrounded by mulberry trees.

The remote **Auberge des Seguins** (Buoux, 04.90.74.16.37, double €65-€85, half-board available), under the crags at the end of a valley, is a popular choice with walkers and rock climbers, and has a small *buvette* where walkers can stop for a drink. In Saignon, the **Auberge du Presbytère** (pl de la Fontaine, 04.90.74.11.50, closed 15 Nov-mid-Feb except

Christmas, double €52-€115, restaurant closed Wed, menus €21.50-€34) overlooks the village square. **Chambre de Séjour avec Vue** (04.90.04.85.01, www.chambreavecvue.com, double €75) is an old house that has been transformed with a remarkable eye for colour and design by Kamila Regent; she invites artists in residence to work and exhibit in the house, while letting out three bedrooms and an apartment. Evening meal on request (€25).

Resources

Tourist information

Bonnieux *Office de Tourisme, 7 pl Carnot, 04480 Bonnieux (04.90.75.91.90).* **Open** 2-6pm Mon; 9.30am-12.30pm, 2-6pm Tue-Sat.

Lourmarin & the south Luberon châteaux

The southern edge of the range is known for its trio of Renaissance châteaux. One of the largest and liveliest Luberon villages, **Lourmarin**, with its cluster of grey-shuttered stone houses, belfry and medieval church, is the *de facto* gastronomic capital of the area. Despite all the antiques and gift shops, estate agents and a fabulous kitchen shop, tourism here remains civilised, with action centred on the main street where **Café Gaby** and **Café de l'Ormeau** enjoy a friendly rivalry. Lourmarin was settled by Vaudois peasants and suffered in the merciless massacre of April 1545, when much of the village was temporarily abandoned. Rebuilt, it thrived in the 17th and 18th centuries as a centre of silk production. The Protestant temple now stands at the exterior of the village. From here rue du Temple leads to the 15th-to-16th-century **Château de Lourmarin**, which presents a a fortified medieval aspect from one side and the large windows of the Renaissance on the other. The château narrowly escaped destruction in the Revolution; it was restored in the early 1900s and since 1925 has hosted artists and writers in residence and chamber music concerts (summer only). Don't miss the cantilever staircase and an extraordinary Renaissance fireplace which combines classical Corinthian capitals with native Indian figures from the newly discovered Americas. Albert Camus lived on the edge of the village and is buried in the cemetery alongside his wife.

West of Lourmarin, **Mérindol** is worth a visit not so much for its second homes of today as for the moving evocation of what used to be. Climb the waymarked route des Vaudois to the ruined village that is witness to the massacre of 1545, when Jean de Meynier, president of the

Parlement d'Aix, sent in his troops to implement the Decree of Mérindol, which condemned the Vaudois as heretics. Within six days 22 villages were pillaged and burned and an estimated 2,500 were dead. Mérindol was razed to the ground and its ruined citadel, now bearing the plaque of the Mémorial des Vaudois remains a potent symbol. Only one large villa spoils the sense of abandon and there are hilltop views as far as the Alpilles, Montagne Ste-Victoire and the Ste-Baume massif.

West of Mérindol, the **Gorges de Regalon** (parking €2.30), where the river has sculpted out a narrow gorge (dry in summer, but apt to flood after heavy rain), provide a welcome breath of cool air: pleasant for a stroll amid wild rosemary and shrubs or the start of a more ambitious walk to Oppède across the range.

More workaday than chic Lourmarin, **Cadenet** has some charming stepped streets and ancient houses, as well as the small **Musée de la Vannerie**, devoted to basketmaking, once one of the town's principal activities. The main square features a statue of the drummer boy of Arcole, born in the village, who saved French troops in the war against Austria in 1796. Only foundations remain of the château that once towered above the village.

East of Lourmarin on the D27, lovely, still partly walled **Cucuron** is a tangle of narrow streets. On place de l'Horloge, a fortified bell-tower gateway leads to a ruined keep. The surprisingly large **Eglise Notre-Dame-de-Beaulieu** contains a fine Baroque altarpiece and Gothic side chapels. Below, sunk into a rock, the **Moulin à Huile Dauphin** olive press (04.90.77.26.17, press open Nov-Dec, shop all year) is a favourite with some of the super-chefs. On the square where the market is held on Tuesday morning, the plane-tree-shaded **Bassin de l'Etang** is a large stone water tank built in the 15th century to supply local flour mills. From here footpaths lead up the **Mourre Nègre**, the Luberon's highest point. Further east, the Luberon is quieter and less-populated and tiny authentic villages Cabrières d'Aigues and La Motte d'Aigues slumber in the sunshine.

Ansouis is dominated by its Renaissance château whose ramparts wind up around the mound. It is still inhabited by the Sabran-Pontevès family, who sometimes conduct the tours themselves. The visit takes in baronial halls and massive kitchens, but the highlight is the terraced gardens. The Romanesque church is built into the edge of the ramparts.

Towards **Pertuis**, today dull and traffic-clogged (but useful if you need a supermarket or a train), the **Château Val Joanis** combines wine growing with beautifully planted terraced gardens. Further east at **La Tour-d'Aigues**,

amid rolling vineyards, are the remains of what was once the finest of all the Renaissance châteaux, destroyed by fire in 1792. Across ample defensive ditches, the pedimented entrance and part of the wings survive. In its heyday it had a park, orangerie and exotic menagerie. Two museums, the **Musée des Faïences** and **Musée de l'Histoire du Pays d'Aigues**, are housed in the cellars.

In an area of vineyards, oak and pine forests lie the fortified village of **Grambois** (where part of *La Gloire de mon père* was filmed) and **La Bastide de Jourdans**, founded in the 13th century but now much smaller than when it was a centre of silk production.

Château d'Ansouis

rue Cartel, Ansouis (04.90.09.82.70). **Open** *guided tours mid-Feb to Apr, Oct to mid-Nov* 2.30-5.30pm Mon, Wed-Sun. *May-Sept* 2.30-5.30pm daily. *mid-Nov to mid-Feb* 2.30-4.30pm Sat, Sun. **Admission** €6; €3 6-18s; free under-6s. **No credit cards**.

Château de Lourmarin

Lourmarin (04.90.68.15.23). **Open** *guided tours Mar, Apr, Oct* 11am, 2.30pm, 3.30pm, 4.30pm Mon, Wed-Sun. *May-Sept* 10am, 11am, 2.30pm, 3.30pm, 4.30pm, 5.30pm daily (more in July, Aug). *Nov-Feb* 11am, 2.30pm, 4pm Mon, Wed-Sun (Sat, Sun only in Jan). **Admission** €5; €2 10-16s; free under-10s. **No credit cards**.

Château Val Joanis

rte de Cavaillon (D973), Pertuis (04.90.79.88.40/www.val-joanis.com). **Open** *Apr-Oct* 10am-7pm daily. *Nov-Mar* 2-6pm Tue-Sat. **Admission** free.

Musée des Faïences

Château de la Tour-d'Aigues (04.90.07.50.33/www.chateau-latourdaigues.com). **Open** *Apr-Oct* 10am-1pm, 2.30-6.30pm daily. *Nov-Mar* 2-5pm Mon, Sun; 10am-noon Tue; 10am-noon, 2-5pm Wed-Sat. **Admission** €4.50; €2 8-16s, students; free under-8s. **No credit cards**.

Musée de la Vannerie

La Glaneuse, av Philippe de Girard, Cadenet (04.90.68.24.44). **Open** *Apr-Oct* 10am-noon, 2.30-6.30pm Mon, Thur-Sat; 2.30-6.30pm Wed, Sun. Closed Nov-Mar. **Admission** €3.50; €1.50 students; free under-16s. **No credit cards**.

Where to stay & eat

Lourmarin has become the gourmet capital of the Luberon thanks in part to Reine Sammut at **La Fenière** (D945 rte de Cadenet, 04.90.68.11.79, www.reinesammut.com, closed mid-Nov to Jan, double €138-€200, restaurant closed Mon & lunch Tue, menus €45-€100). Housed in a stylish modern *mas*, she's particularly good at starters, often using produce from her vegetable garden. There are some attractive rooms upstairs. Sammut is rivalled by young Edouard Loubet

Lourmarin, built on silk farming, is now a gastronomic draw. *See p117.*

at **Le Moulin de Lourmarin** (rue du Temple, 04.90.68.06.69, closed mid-Jan to mid-Feb, double €190-€490, restaurant closed Tue & Wed, menus €91-€152) in a controversially converted but very comfortable water mill. He concocts sublime dishes with herbs and wild plants, although can come unstuck when too complicated. When not in the mood for haute-gastronomie, locals enjoy laidback **l'Antiquaire** (9 rue du Grand Pré, 04.90.68.17.29, closed Mon & lunch Tue, dinner Sun in winter, 3wks Nov-Dec & 3wks Jan-Feb, menus €18-€28) or the pan-Mediterranean flavours at **Maison Ollier Michel-Ange** (pl de la Fontaine, 04.90.68.02.03, closed Wed, and Tue Oct-Easter, all mid-Nov to mid-Dec, menus €20-€50). Well-hidden in the heart of the village **Chambres d'Hôtes de la Cordière** (impasse de la Cordière, rue Albert Camus, 04.90.68.03.32, double €45-€70) has four characterful rooms (tiled floors, rolltop baths) in an ancient house with courtyard and vaulted kitchen. Amid vineyards 2km east of Lourmarin, **Le Mas de Guilles** (rte de Vaugines, 04.90.68.30.55, www.guilles.com, closed mid-Nov to Mar, double €80-€150, restaurant dinner only, menu €38) is a cleverly converted *mas* with swimming pool and tennis courts. Under the combe de Lourmarin a short walk from the village, friendly **Hostellerie du Paradou** (rte d'Apt, 04.90.68.04.05, www.leparadou-lacascade.com, closed mid-Nov to Jan, double €57-€90, restaurant closed Thur & lunch Fri, menus €22-€35) is a stone *mas*

with spacious lawns and nine simple rooms; the restaurant serves regional food and wines.

At the top of Cadenet, **La Tuilière** (chemin de la Tuilière, 04.90.68.24.45, www.latuiliere.com, double €61-€76) offers five rooms in a big old house, with ramshackle terraced garden, small pool and billiard table. The **Camping Val de Durance** (Les Routes, Cadenet, 04.90.68.37.75, www.homair-vacances.com, closed Oct-Mar, pitch €12 and €5-€7/person) has well-spaced pitches, screened by trees. It overlooks a small lake open to the public, which has been arranged for swimming with a small sandy beach (May-Sept 9am-8pm daily).

In scenic Cucuron, good-value **L'Horloge** (55 rue Léonce Brieugne, 04.90.77.12.74, closed Wed and Feb school holidays, €14.50-€21) is housed in vaulted cellars, a cool retreat for some quietly creative Provençal cooking. **L'Arbre de Mai** (rue de l'Eglise, 04.90.77.25.10, closed mid Jan to Feb, double €64-€68, restaurant closed Mon & Tue, menus €15-€23) is a basic but comfortable hotel and restaurant serving traditional Provençal cooking. Nearby at Vaugines, the **Hostellerie du Luberon** (cours St-Louis, 04.90.77.27.19, www.hostellerie duluberon.com, closed Nov-Feb, double €105-€118 incl dinner, menus €15-€25) is a modern *mas* overlooking a pool and vineyards. Specialities include *caillettes*, fish and local lamb.

There are fewer options on the eastern slopes of the Luberon, but the well-presented regional fare at **Restaurant de la Fontaine** (pl de la

Fontaine, 04.90.07.72.16, closed Mon-Wed, dinner Sun in winter, and 10 Dec-10 Jan, 2wks in Feb, menu €26) at St-Martin-de-la-Brasque is justifiably popular.

Tourist information

Morning markets are Thursday and Saturday in Ansouis, Tuesday in Cucuron and La Tour d'Aigues, Monday in Cadenet, Friday in Lourmarin, Wednesday in Mérindol.

Tourist information

Ansouis *Office de Tourisme, pl du Château, 84240 Ansouis (04.90.09.86.98/ www.ansouis.fr).* **Open** *Apr-Sept* 10am-noon, 2-6pm daily. *Oct-Mar* 10am-noon, 2-5pm. Closed Jan.
Cucuron *Office de Tourisme, rue Léonce Brieugne, 84160 Cucuron (04.90.77.28.37).* **Open** *July, Aug* 9am-noon, 2.30-6.30pm Mon-Sat. *Sept-June* 9am-noon, 2-4pm Tue-Sat.
Lourmarin *Office de Tourisme, 17 av Philippe de Girard, 84160 Lourmarin (04.90.68.10.77/ www.lourmarin.com).* **Open** *Apr-Oct* 9.30am-1pm, 3.30-7pm Mon-Sat; 9.30am-noon Sun. *Nov-Mar* 9.30am-12.30pm, 2.30-4pm Mon-Sat.
Mérindol *Office de Tourisme, rue du Four, 84360 Mérindol (04.90.72.88.50).* **Open** 9am-12.30pm, 2-5.30pm Tue-Sat.

Cavaillon

Cavaillon is the melon capital of France: the juicy globes are celebrated in a festival in July, and crop up in everything from jam to chocolates. The town injects a dose of real life into the Luberon – housing estates, lounging youths and an absurd number of roundabouts – but compensates with an all-year arts scene thanks to a Scène Nationale theatre and the **Grenier à Sons** (157 av du Général de Gaulle/ 04.90.06.44.20) weekly music venue. In recent years Cavaillon has been more associated with militant farmers than with sightseeing, but past the anonymous periphery is an old town with relics from what was once an important medieval diocese. The big market is wholesale only, but on Monday there is a lively food and general goods market.

The earliest visible reminder of Cavaillon's past is the spindly first-century **Arc Romain** (pl du Clos), bearing traces of sculpted flowers and winged victories. Behind it, a footpath zigzags up the cliff to the medieval **Chapelle St-Jacques** offering panoramic views. At the foot of the Arc, peer into the time-capsule **Fin de Siècle** café. The raggedy old town is presided over by the Romanesque **Cathédrale Notre-Dame et St-Véran**, with its damaged cloister, octagonal tower and sundial. A relief on one altar refers to local melon cultivation, introduced by the Avignon popes. Outside, tree-

shaded place Philippe de Cabassole has some fine 18th-century houses. The Baroque facade of the Grand Couvent reflects church power during the Comtat Venaissan; in the **Musée de l'Hôtel Dieu**, archaeological finds from a Neolithic settlement on St-Jacques hill are displayed in the former hospital and chapel.

Like nearby Carpentras (*see p101*), Cavaillon had a sizeable Jewish community, and its beautiful, light-filled **Synagogue** (built 1772-4) is one of the finest in France. The baby pink and blue upper level has bronze chandeliers, rococo tabernacle and delicate ironwork. The lower level doubled as a bakery. It was a bit of a last gasp: in 1791, the Comtat Vénaissin was integrated into France and French Jews were given their liberty, marking the end of Cavaillon's ghetto. The town's Jewish population today is mainly of North African origin. The synagogue now contains the **Musée Juif Comtadin**, housing the tabernacle doors from the earlier synagogue, and possessions that had belonged to the community; there are plans to expand into the former rabbi's house next door.

Musée de l'Hôtel Dieu

Grand-Rue (04.90.76.00.34). **Open** *June-Sept* 9.30am-12.30pm, 2.30-6.30pm Mon, Wed-Sun. **Admission** (incl Synagogue) €3; €1.05 12-18s, free under-12s. **No credit cards**.

Synagogue/Musée Juif Comtadin

rue Hébraïque (04.90.76.00.34). **Open** *Apr-Sept* 9am-12.30pm, 3-6.30pm Mon, Wed-Sun. *Oct-Mar* 9am-noon, 2-5pm Mon, Wed-Fri. **Admission** (incl Musée de l'Hôtel Dieu) €3; €1.05 12-18s; free under-12s. **No credit cards**.

Where to stay & eat

Cavaillon's hotels leave quite a lot to be desired, though old-fashioned **Hôtel du Parc** (183 pl François Tourel, 04.90.71.57.78, double €56-€66) near the tourist office offers traditional style and a garden. Culinary prospects are more promising. Upmarket, old-fashioned **Prévot** (353 av de Verdun, 04.90.71.32.43, closed Sun and 2wks Aug, menus €25-€70) is famed for its inventive summer melon menu. **Le Pantagruel** (5 pl Philippe de Cabassole, 04.90.76.11.98, closed Mon & Sun, menus €14-€35) has a striking high-ceilinged dining room with a huge open fire on which meat is grilled in winter. In summer, start with the gigantic *anchoïade* before roast lamb with herbs and honey. **Côté Jardin** (49 rue Lamartine, 04.90.71.33.58, closed Sun, and Mon & Tue dinners in winter, 3wks Jan, menus €13-€23) has tables around a courtyard fountain and good-value Provençal cooking, especially fish. The *belle époque* café **Le Fin de Siècle** (46 pl du Clos, 04.90.71.12.27, closed Tue & Wed, menus €12-€27) has kept its mosaic frontage and large mirrors; upstairs is a restaurant. Outside town, the **Mas du Souléou** (5 chemin St-Pierre des Essieux, 04.90.71.43.22, www.souleou.com, doubles €81) is a lovely B&B in a 19th-century *mas* restored with enormous taste, where Mr Lepaul concocts dinner (€24) in the kitchen.

Resources

Market day is Monday. Internet is available at the tourist office.

Tourist information

Office de Tourisme, pl François Tourel, 84300 Cavaillon (04.90.71.32.01/www.cavaillon-luberon.com). **Open** 9am-12.30pm, 2-6.30pm Mon-Sat (and 10am-noon Sun July, Aug).

Apt

At first sight there is not much going on in Apt, with its industrial outskirts, plane trees and sleepy squares along the Calavon river. But it comes alive on Saturday morning with the largest market for miles around.

Place de la Bouquerie is the main access point for the old town, via the narrow main street, rue des Marchands. The **Ancienne Cathédrale Ste-Anne** throws an arch across the street. Now demoted to the status of parish church, it is a curious mix of Gothic and Baroque with crypts

Cavaillon: real life in the Luberon.

dating from the fourth and 11th centuries. In 1660 Anne of Austria visited on pilgrimage to St Anne in thanks for the birth of Louis XIV and gave money to complete the Chapelle Royale. A Roman sarcophagus harks back to the town's foundation as a staging post on the Via Domitia.

Nearby, the **Maison du Parc** informs about the flora, fauna and geology of the Parc Régional du Luberon, and contains the child-oriented **Musée de la Paléontologie**. Next door, the new **Musée de l'Aventure Industrielle**, which opened in July 2003 in an old candied fruits confectionary, traces the three industries that brought Apt prosperity in the 18th and 19th centuries: candied fruits, cream-glazed and marbled earthenware, and the extraction of ochre. Today, although plenty of pottery can be picked up at market, only **Faïence d'Apt** (286 av de la Libération, 04.90.74.15.31, closed Mon morning & Sun) continues the traditional marbleware. If all this mind-candy whets your appetite for the real thing, head for **Aptunion**, the town's biggest manufacturer of candied fruits.

Ancienne Cathédrale Ste-Anne

rue de la Cathédrale (04.90.04.85.44/www.apt-cathedrale.com). **Open** 10am-noon, 3-6pm Tue-Fri (2-4pm Oct-June); 10am-noon Sat, Sun. *Treasury July-Sept* guided tours only 11am, 5pm Mon-Sat, 11am Sun. **Admission** free.

Aptunion

on N100, quartier Salignan (04.90.76.31.43). **Open** *factory* by appointment; *shop* 9am-noon, 2-6pm Mon-Sat.

Maison du Parc & Musée de la Paléontologie

60 pl Jean Jaurès (04.90.04.42.00). **Open** 8.30am-noon, 1.30-6pm Mon-Sat. **Admission** €1.50; free under-18s. **No credit cards**.

Musée de l'Aventure Industrielle

14 pl du Pastal (04.90.74.95.30). **Open** 10am-noon, 2-5.30pm Wed-Sat (and 2-5.30pm Sun July-Sept). **Admission** €4; €2 students, over-60s; free under-12s. **No credit cards**.

Where to stay & eat

At the **Auberge du Luberon** (8 pl du Fbg Ballet, 04.90.74.12.50, double €52-€82, restaurant closed Mon & lunch Tue, plus dinner Sun Nov-Apr, menus €26-€54), chef Serge Peuzin offers a special *menu aux fruits confits* in which Apt's speciality features in every course; there are also 14 bedrooms. Apt's new designer eat is **Le Carré Gourmand** (pl St-Martin, 04.90.74.74.00, closed lunch Mon, average €45), set in a renovated 17th-century *hôtel particulier*. It has a less formal café in summer, a gourmet bakery and a wine bar open in the evenings. With the **Domaine des Andéols** (Les Andéols, St-Saturnin-les-Apt, 04.90.75.50.63, www.domaine desandeols.com, house for two €370-€407) just north of Apt, the Luberon has gained a stunning boutique hotel. Olivier Massart created nine 'maisons' from the buildings of the family farm, where encaustic, tile and oak finishes become high-voltage with modern furniture classics, contemporary art and comforts like plasma screen TVs. The grounds are a tour-de-force with a fibreoptic lit staircase leading to the restaurant where chef Daniel Hebert (ex-La Mirande in Avignon) does a different market menu nightly. The low-key spa has sauna, hammam and indoor pool, while an infinity pool overlooks the olive groves.

Resources

Tourist information

Office de Tourisme, 20 av Philippe de Girard, 84400 Apt (04.90.74.03.18/www.ot-apt.fr). **Open** *mid-June to mid-Sept* 9am-7.30pm Mon-Sat; 9am-12.30pm Sun. *mid-Sept to mid-June* 9am-noon, 2-6pm Mon-Sat.

L'Isle-sur-la-Sorgue & Fontaine-de-Vaucluse

L'Isle-sur-la-Sorgue is known as the 'Venise Comtadin' for its double (in places triple) ring of canals. Dripping wheels recall a past when water powered a silk industry and later paper mills. What makes the town tick today is France's largest concentration of antiques dealers outside Paris, strung out along the canals (*see p116* **Going for gold**). In the old town, star sight is the **Collégiale Notre-Dame-des-Anges**, which has a Baroque interior with heavens full of cherubim. Outside, place de la Liberté contains the pretty *belle époque* **Café de France**, galleried houses and the tourist office in the old public granary. The former Musée Donadeï de Campredon, an elegant 18th-century *hôtel particulier*, is now the **Maison René Char**, recreating the study of the Surrealist poet who lived in the town. It also has temporary modern art exhibitions.

Upstream (7km by D25), **Fontaine-de-Vaucluse** clusters around the source of the Sorgue river. Water mysteriously gushes out of a sheer cliff face into a jade-green pool, giving the name Vallis Clausa (closed valley) or Vaucluse to the whole *département*. Numerous divers, including the late Jacques Cousteau, have attempted without success to find the source; their exploits, and the geological wonders of the area, are explained in the underground museum **Le Monde souterrain de Norbert Casteret**. Above the village is a

The precipitous village of **Gordes**.

ruined castle, originally built by monks to protect pilgrims to the tomb of dragon-slayer St Véran. Abandoned factories hint at Fontaine's more industrial past, notably paper-making for the Comtat Venaisson. The pretty Romanesque church has a painting of St Véran and an 11th-century open altar table. Outside, a column commemorates Petrarch. Across the river, the **Musée Pétrarque** stands on the site where Italian Renaissance scholar Petrarch (1304-74) wrote his famous *Canzoniere*. Further up, past the mill, the **Musée d'Histoire 1939-1945 'L'Appel de la Liberté'** contains exhibitions on daily life during the Occupation.

Between April and December, the Sorgue can be navigated by canoe between Fontaine-de-Vaucluse and Partage des Eaux. Canoes can be hired at **Canoë Evasion** (on D24 at Pont de Galas, 04.90.38.26.22, closed Jan-Mar).

Collégiale Notre-Dame-des-Anges

pl de la Liberté, L'Isle-sur-la-Sorgue **Open** 10am-noon, 3-5pm Tue-Sat. **Admission** free.

Maison René Char

20 rue du Dr Tallet, L'Isle-sur-la-Sorgue (04.90.38.17.41/www.campredon-expos.com). **Open** 10am-noon, 3-6pm Tue-Sun. **Admission** €6; €5 students; free under-14s. **No credit cards.**

Le Monde souterrain de Norbert Casteret

chemin de la Fontaine, Fontaine-de-Vaucluse (04.90.20.34.13). **Open** *Feb-May, Sept-Nov* 10am-noon, 2-5pm Tue-Sat. *June-Aug* 10am-noon, 2-5pm daily. Closed Dec-Jan. **Admission** €4; €3.25 under-18s. **No credit cards.**

Musée d'Histoire 1939-1945 'L'Appel de la Liberté'

chemin du gouffre, 84800 Fontaine-de-Vaucluse (04.90.20.24.00). **Open** *Mar, Nov-Dec* 10am-noon, 2-5pm (till 6pm in Mar) Sat, Sun. *Apr, May, Oct* 10am-noon, 2-6pm Mon, Wed-Sun (till 5pm last 2wks Oct). *June-Sept* 10am-6pm Mon, Wed-Sun. Closed Jan, Feb. **Admission** €3.50; €1.50 12-18s; free under-12s (€4.60, €2.80 with Musée Pétrarque). **No credit cards.**

Musée Pétrarque

quai du Château Vieux, Fontaine-de-Vaucluse (04.90.20.37.20). **Open** *Apr to 14 Oct* 10am-noon, 2-6pm Mon, Wed-Sun (15-30 Oct until 5pm). Closed Nov-Mar. **Admission** €3.50; €1.50 12-18s; free under-12s (€4.60, €2.80 with Musée d'Histoire). **No credit cards.**

Where to stay & eat

Hungry antiques browsers are served by a rash of restaurants along the canals of L'Isle-sur-la-Sorgue. One of the best is stylish bistro **Le Carré des Herbes** (13 av des Quatres Otages, 04.90.38.62.95, closed Tue & Wed, and Jan or Feb, menus €12-€28), now under the wing of Paris chef Bernard Pacaud. The stylish **Café du Village**, within the Village des Antiquaires de la Gare (04.90.20.72.31, open lunch Mon, Sat, Sun, menu €18), serves imaginative, modern market-inspired cooking. The **Rendezvous des Marchands** (91 av de la Libération, 04.90.20.84.60, open Mon, Sat, Sun 10am-7pm) is part-*brocante*, part-waterside café, offering grilled kebabs and salads. If you want to maximise every minute of antiques hunting, the **Hôtel Araxe** (rte d'Apt, 04.90.38.40.00; double €51-€111, menus €21-€28.50) is a functional central option. For calm and character try the **Mas de Cure Bourse** (carrefour de Velorgues, 04.90.38.16.58, double €75-€115), a comfortable 18th-century coaching inn, with vaulted hallway, rooms *à la provençale*, large garden and pool, set in orchards 3km from town.

Fontaine-de-Vaucluse is strong on snacks and ice cream, as well as river trout. The **Hostellerie Le Château** (quartier du Château Vieux, 04.90.20.31.54, closed lunch in winter, menus €25-€35) has a veranda restaurant in a waterside setting. The new **Hôtel du Poète** (04.90.20.34.05, www.hoteldupoete.com, closed Jan & early Feb, double €70-€260) has added a comfortable new air-conditioned option, with 23 neo-Provençal rooms in an imaginatively landscaped garden with pool, beside the river.

Tourist information

L'Isle-sur-la-Sorgue market is Thursday and Sunday.

Tourist information

L'Isle-sur-la-Sorgue *Office de Tourisme, pl de l'Eglise, 84800 L'Isle-sur-la-Sorgue (04.90.38.04.78/ www.ot-islesurlasorgue.fr).* **Open** 9am-12.30pm, 2.30-6pm Mon-Sat; 9am-12.30pm Sun.
Fontaine-de-Vaucluse *Office de Tourisme, chemin de la Fontaine, 84800 Fontaine-de-Vaucluse (04.90.20.32.22).* **Open** 10am-6pm Mon-Sat.

Gordes & the Plateau de Vaucluse

Fiefdom of the *gauche caviar*, France's Champagne socialists (or the *gauche tapenade* as some dub them here), **Gordes** is almost too pretty for its own good, with a spectacular hillside setting, dominated by the turrets of its château, drystone walls and steep, stepped alleys. Tasteful shops sell the usual Provençal crafts and produce, while the **Château de Gordes** has a semi-permanent exhibition by the Belgian painter Pol Mara (don't believe the old posters you still see mentioning Vasarely).

West of Gordes, the **Village des Bories** is a group of restored drystone, beehive-shaped huts, inhabited between the 16th and 19th centuries and probably much earlier. An attempt has been made to reconstruct the rural lifestyle of *borie* dwellers, with *borie* houses, stables and sheepfolds dotted over the hillside, and a photo exhibition shows similar drystone structures in other countries.

North of Gordes, at the base of a wooded valley, the **Abbaye Notre-Dame-de-Sénanque**, founded in 1148, is one of the great triumvirate of Provençal Cistercian monasteries (with Silvacane and Thoronet). Set in lavender fields, the beautifully preserved Romanesque ensemble still houses a monastic community.

Surrounded by strangely eroded outcrops of ochre-red rocks, **Roussillon** is among the most picturesque of all the Luberon villages, although it can get suffocatingly full of tourists. The houses are painted in an orange wash, which makes the entire village glow. Walk past the belfry-sundial of the **Eglise St-Michel** to an orientation table, and note the 18th-century facades on place de la Mairie. To the left of the village cemetery, above car park 2, the **Sentier des Ocres** (closed Nov-Mar, €2, free under-10s), a footpath with information panels, offers spectacular views amid peculiar rock formations, the result of ochre quarrying. On the D104 towards Apt, the former ochre works have reopened as the **Conservatoire des**

Avignon & the Vaucluse

Ocres et Pigments Appliqués. Guided tours show how the rock was made into pigment.

Reached by small lanes south of the D22 towards Rustrel from Apt, undulating green countryside suddenly gives way to the vibrantly coloured **Colorado de Rustrel**, a valley littered with rocks long exploited for ochre pigment in colours that vary from pale cream via yellows and orange to deep, russet red. Near the car park, a path descends to a picnic site and *buvette* and relics of disused ochre works. Wear decent shoes and do stick to the *sentiers* – colour-coded waymarked paths of varying lengths – which lead you round some of the most spectacular turrets, chimneys and banks.

Abbaye Notre-Dame-de-Sénanque
3km N of Gordes on D177 (04.90.72.05.72/ www.senanque.fr). **Open** guided visits generally 10.45am, 2.20pm, 3.20pm, 4.45pm Mon-Sat. Closed Sun morning, 2nd & 3rd wks of Jan. **Admission** €6; €5 students; €2.50 6-18s; free under-6s. **No credit cards**.

Château de Gordes
Gordes (04.90.72.02.89). **Open** 10am-noon, 2-6pm daily. **Admission** €4; €3 10-17s; free under-10s. **No credit cards**.

Conservatoire des Ocres et Pigments appliqués
Usine Mathieu, D104, Roussillon (04.90.05.66.69). **Tours** 11am, 3pm, 4pm (plus noon, 5pm in July, Aug). **Admission** €5; free under-11s. **Credit** MC, V.

Village des Bories
Les Savournins, Gordes (04.90.72.03.48). **Open** *June-Sept* 9am-8pm daily. *Nov-May* 9am-5pm daily. **Admission** €5.50; €3 10-17s; free under-10s. **No credit cards**.

Where to stay & eat

In Gordes, **La Bastide de Gordes** (rte de Combe, 04.90.72.12.12, closed Nov to mid-Dec, Jan to mid-Feb, double €140-€498) is an upmarket hotel built into the ramparts, with spectacular views. The **Domaine de l'Enclos** (rte de Sénanque, 04.90.72.71.00, closed mid-Nov to mid-Mar, double €80-€180, restaurant open Mon-Sat dinner only by reservation, menu €45) offers all mod cons; ground-floor rooms have private gardens. Adjoining the château, **Café-Restaurant La Renaissance** (pl du Château, 04.90.72.02.02, menus €11.50-€30) has tables out on the square and very hip waitresses.

In Roussillon, **David** (pl de la Poste, 04.90.05.60.13, closed Wed all year, dinner Sun except mid-June to mid-Sept, and all Jan to mid-Feb, menus €29.50) is the most reliable of several bistros and snack bars. On the edge of the village, the ochre-washed **Sables d'Ocre** (on D104, Roussillon, 04.90.05.55.55, double

€55-€75, closed Nov to mid-Mar) is a friendly family-oriented modern hotel with pool.

In Goult, just north of the N100 Avignon-Apt road, the **Café de la Poste** (pl de la Libération, 04.90.72.23.23, lunch only, closed Mon and Nov-Feb, menu €10) gained fame in Mayle's *A Year in Provence* and Jean Becker's film *L'Eté meurtrier*. Join locals and chic second-homers for gossip and home cooking. British couple Nick and Maggie Denny treat their guests like old friends at **La Fontaine de Faucon** (chemin de la Fontaine de Faucon, Quartier Ste-Anne, 04.90.09.90.16, www.fontainedefaucon.com, double €100-€120, menu €28), a *chambres d'hôtes* in a gorgeous old farmhouse just outside the village; dinner can be served on request.

Resources

Market is Tuesday morning in Gordes, Thursday morning in Roussillon.

Tourist information
Gordes *Office de Tourisme, Le Château, 84220 Gordes (04.90.72.02.75/www.gordes-village.com).* **Open** *July, Aug* 9am-12.30pm, 2-6.30pm Mon-Sat. *Sept-June* 9am-noon, 2-6pm Mon-Sat.
Roussillon *Office de Tourisme, pl de la Poste, 84220 Roussillon (04.90.05.60.25/www.roussillon-provence.com).* **Open** *July, Aug* 10am-noon, 2-6pm Mon-Sat. *Sept-June* 1.30-5.30pm Mon-Fri.

Manosque

Though it nestles at the eastern edge of the Luberon range, Manosque is very much a Durance Valley town – the largest in the sparsely populated *département* of Alpes de Haute-Provence. Housing and industrial parks now sprawl over the hillside, but for a long time the town remained within the city walls, where the not-yet-tarted-up network of narrow streets, squares and covered passageways gives an interesting perspective on what the Luberon must have been like before it became so hip. Manosque is positively moribund on a Sunday out of season and liveliest on a Saturday, when a market takes over the centre.

Porte Saunerie leads into **rue Grande**, Manosque's main shopping street. At No.14, a plaque marks the house where novelist Jean Giono (1895-1970), son of a shoemaker, was born. At No.21 is a branch of **Occitane**, the phenomenally successful Manosque-based cosmetics and skincare company that is now the town's main employer. Note also the fine 18th-century balcony at No.23. There are two historic churches, **St-Sauveur**, which features in Giono's swashbuckler *Le Hussard sur le Toit*, and **Notre-Dame-de-Romigier** on place de

Follow the yellow rock road: Roussillon's **Sentier des Ocres**. *See p123.*

l'Hôtel de Ville, which has a fine Renaissance doorway and a black Virgin inside.

The Giono link is exploited to the full with literary competitions and walks on the theme of 'Jean Giono, poet of the olive tree' (Haute-Provence olive oil gained an *appellation contrôlée* in 1999). The **Centre Jean Giono**, in an 18th-century *hôtel particulier*, has exhibitions and a permanent display about the writer's life and work. His own house, **Lou Paraïs** (montée des Vraies Richesses, 04.92.87.73.03), north of the old town, is open for guided visits on Friday afternoons (ring ahead).

Centre Jean Giono

3 bd Elémir Bourges (04.92.70.54.54). **Open** *Apr-June* 9.30am-12.30pm, 2-6pm Tue-Sat. *July-Sept* 9.30am-12.30pm, 2-6pm daily. *Oct-Mar* 2-6pm Tue-Sat. **Admission** €4; €2 12-18s; free under-12s. **No credit cards.**

Where to stay & eat

The best-placed hotel is the **Grand Hôtel de Versailles** (17 av Jean Giono, 08.00.10.05.38; double €26-€61), a simple, former coaching inn. Manosque's top chef is **Dominique Bucaille** (43 bd des Tilleuls, 04.92.72.32.28, closed dinner Wed, all Sun & mid-July to mid-Aug, menus €15-€61), who offers refined seasonal cooking. In

the old town, go for regional fare at **Le Luberon** (21bis pl du Terreau, 04.92.72.03.09, closed Mon, dinner Sun & 3wks Oct, menus €12.50-€48).

Resources

Market day in Manosque is Saturday.

Tourist information

Office du Tourisme, pl du Dr Joubert, 04100 Manosque (04.92.72.16.00/www.ville-manosque.fr). **Open** *July, Aug* 9am-7pm Mon-Sat; 10am noon Sun. *Sept-June* 9am-12.15pm, 1.30-6pm Mon-Sat.

Pays de Forcalquier

In the early Middle Ages, the counts of Forcalquier rivalled those of Provence. The two were united in 1195 when Gersande, Comtesse de Forcalquier, married Alphonse, Count of Provence; their son Raymond Bérenger V craftily succeeded in marrying all four daughters to future kings. Today Forcalquier is light years from its illustrious past but still a lively local centre, with a big market on Monday mornings.

The sober Romano-Gothic **Cathédrale Notre Dame du Bourguet** is almost as wide as it is long, with triple nave and impressive organ loft. The former Couvent des Visitandines now contains the **Cinématographe** cinema, the Mairie, and the **Musée Municipal** where archaeological finds include a fine Roman head from nearby Lurs. Narrow streets next to the cathedral lead into the old town, where there are fine houses on rue Béranger and a fancy Gothic fountain on place St-Michel. Climb past the carrillon up the wooded mound where the citadel was replaced in 1875 by the octagonal **Chapel Notre-Dame de Provence**, with its neo-Gothic musician angels. Forcalquier's other main sight is its **cemetery**, north-east of the centre, with striking landscaped walls of yew.

At **Mane**, once a market halt on the Via Domitia, houses climb up in concentric curtain walls around the feudal castle (closed to public). On the edge of the village, the former monastery **Notre-Dame de Salagon** combines fascinating botanical gardens with an ethnographical museum. The 12th-century Romanesque chapel has traces of medieval frescoes and modern red stained-glass by abstract painter Aurélie Nemours, while assorted priory buildings contain exhibits on sage growing, bee-keeping and a reconstructed forge. The highlight is the medieval garden, which reveals that turnips, parsnips and pulses were then staples rather than what we now think of as Provençal cuisine. Other gardens are planted with herbs, aromatic plants and flowers used in popular remedies.

A colony of white domes erupting out of the hillside above St-Michel-l'Observatoire belong to the **Observatoire de Haute-Provence**, a site chosen for the national astronomical research laboratory for the purity of its air and clear skies. The **Centre d'Astronomie** tries to make astronomy accessible to the public and runs observation evenings in July and August.

Centre d'Astronomie

plateau du Moulin à Vent, St-Michel-l'Observatoire (04.92.76.69.69/www.astrosurf.com/centre.astro). **Open** *July, Aug* observation nights 9.30pm-12.30am Tue-Fri. *Sept-June* ring for details. **Admission** €8.75; €7 6-16s; free under-6s. **No credit cards.**

Prieuré Notre Dame de Salagon

Musée-Conservatoire ethnologique de Haute-Provence, Mane (04.92.75.70.50). **Open** *May-Sept* 10am-noon, 2-7pm daily. *Oct* 2-6pm daily. *Nov-Apr* 2-6pm Sat, Sun and school holidays. **Admission** €5; €2.60 12-18s; free under-12s. **No credit cards.**

Musée Municipal

pl du Bourguet, Forcalquier (04.92.75.91.19). **Open** *Apr-Sept* 3-6pm Wed-Sat. Closed Oct-Mar. **Admission** €2; free under-18s. **No credit cards.**

Observatoire de Haute Provence

St-Michel l'Observatoire (04.92.70.64.00/www.obs-hp.fr). **Open** *Apr-Sept* 2-4pm Wed. *Oct-Mar* 3pm sharp Wed. **Admission** €2.30; €1.50 10-18s; free under-10s. **No credit cards.**

Where to stay & eat

Hotels are low-key and unflashy in Forcalquier. On the main street, not far from the cathedral, the no-longer-so-grand **Grand Hôtel** (10 bd Latourette, 04.92.75.00.35, double €36-€45) offers dubious wallpaper, but spacious, clean rooms. There are several café-brasseries on place du Bourguet and around place St-Michel in the old town. Olive oil emporium **Oliviers & Co** (3 rue des Cordeliers, 04.92.75.05.70, closed Tue from Nov-Mar) has a café attached.

Resources

Market in Forcalquier is Monday morning.

Tourist information

Office de Tourisme, 13 pl du Bourguet, 04300 Forcalquier (04.92.75.10.02/www.forcalquier.com). **Open** *June-Sept* 9am-noon, 2-7pm Mon-Sat; 10am-1pm Sun. *Oct-May* 9am-noon, 2-6pm Mon-Sat.

Getting there & around

By car

From A7, exit 25 for Cavaillon. D2 runs from Cavaillon to Taillades and joins the N100, the Avignon-Apt-Forcalquier road, which rings the Montagne de Luberon. L'Isle-sur-la-Sorgue is on the N100 or by D938 from Cavaillon. To the south, the D973 runs along the Durance from Cavaillon via Mérindol and Lauris to Cadenet and Pertuis. The only road across the range is the D943 from Cadenet via Lourmarin, which then forks to Apt (D943) and Bonnieux (D36). Manosque can be reached by D973 and N96 or A51 from Aix-en-Provence. For Cadenet from Aix, take the N7 and D543/D943 via Rognes.

By train

TGV to Avignon with shuttle buses to L'Isle-sur-la-Sorgue and Cavaillon or TGV Aix-en-Provence with three shuttles a day to Manosque. Several local trains a day run from Avignon Centre Ville to Cavaillon and L'Isle-sur-la-Sorgue. Both Pertuis and Manosque are on the branch line from Marseille to Gap via Aix (Manosque-Gréoux-les-Bains station is 1.5km S of the centre, with occasional buses Mon-Sat).

By bus

Cars Sumian (04.91.49.44.25) runs 2 buses daily between Marseille and Apt, via Cadenet, Lourmarin and Bonnieux, and 2 buses daily between Aix and Apt, via Cadenet and Lourmarin. **Cars Arnaud** (04.90.38.15.58/www.voyages-arnaud.fr) runs buses between L'Isle-sur-la-Sorgue and Fontaine de Vaucluse or Avignon, none on Sun. **Barlatier** (04.32.76.00.40) runs 8 buses a day between Avignon and Apt, 3 a day between Cavaillon and Avignon and once daily between Cavaillon and Apt and Cavaillon and Forcalquier, all Mon-Sat, none on Sun. **Express de la Durance** (04.90.71.03.00) runs two buses a day between Cavaillon and Gordes. There are no bus services to Roussillon.

Marseille & Aix

Introduction

Marseille and Aix-en-Provence are Provence at its most urban – and urbane – and neither of them gives a toss about flowery fabrics.

Despite their contrasting images – rough and ready Marseille versus elegant, civilised Aix-en-Provence – both cities have an independent spirit that helped fuel the French Revolution, and both boast historic and well-respected universities and thriving year-round cultural scenes. In addition to Aix's prestigious Festival International d'Art Lyrique and Marseille's growing Festival de Marseille, Marseille boasts dynamic theatres and the most adventurous contemporary art scene in the South.

As France's oldest city, with a history going back 2,600 years, **Marseille** has plenty to offer tourists but can also do very well without them, thank you. Its love-us-or-leave-us attitude is refreshing after the hard-sell tourism of much of the coast: Marseille belongs to the Marseillais, and like any self-respecting *citadins* in summer they go on holiday. Some of the best restaurants close in August, but it's a great place to come

out of season, and is currently at the centre of an enormous urban renewal.

Just as life in Marseille focuses on its Vieux Port, that in **Aix-en-Provence** centres on the Cours Mirabeau and its stretch of pavement cafés. With its beautifully preserved *hôtels particuliers* and countless fountains, Aix, former capital of Provence, is a shopping magnet. You can follow a Cézanne trail from his *atelier* in Aix-en-Provence to the **Montagne Ste-Victoire** and the port at **L'Estaque**.

Despite all Marseille's gritty urban edge, you are never far from the sea: boats bob in the Vieux Port and every other corner gives a glittering vista of the sparkling Med. To the east the town gradually fizzles out into the scrub-covered limestone **Calanques**. Less-known are the **Côte Bleue**, the pretty stretch of coast west of Marseille, and the old fishing town of **Martigues**.

Don't miss **Marseille & Aix**

Baie des Singes, Marseille
Fish and famous faces in a landscape straight out of the Greek islands. *See p143.*

Cassis Services Plongée
Calanque-diving with the master. *See p153.*

Café society
'Les Deux Gs' on Aix's Cours Mirabeau (*see p165*) or Bar de la Marine and chilled-out Le Crystal on Marseille's Vieux Port (*see p146*).

La Cité Radieuse
Le Corbusier's experiment in modern living for Marseille. *See p141.*

Docks de la Joliette
Renovated docks that symbolise the new Marseille. *See p138.*

L'Epuisette, Marseille
Testing-ground for wonderchef Guillaume Sorrieu. *See p144.*

Fresh fish, Marseille
Straight off the boat on to the quai. *See p134.*

La Friche La Belle de Mai
Marseille cultural laboratory of art, theatre, dance and music. *See p142.*

Hôtel Cardinal, Aix
Period dwelling in Quartier Mazarin. *See p168.*

Montagne Ste-Victoire
Where Cézanne found inspiration. *See p170.*

Musée de la Mode de Marseille
Imaginatively presented fashion. *See p136.*

Notre-Dame de la Garde
Give thanks to Marseille's Bonne Mère. *See p140.*

place Richelme
Aix's daily fruit and veg market. *See p157.*

Site Mémorial des Milles, Aix
Sober reminder of World War II. *See p162.*

Zoo de la Barben
Roaming hippos and big cats with a château backdrop. *See p170.*

Marseille

France's oldest city is also its feistiest: come here for secluded beaches, Baroque cathedrals, the best pizza outside Naples and a *bouillabaisse* of cultures.

'When Parisians come here they're a bit afraid,' a Marseille hotel owner said, poking fun a little. '…Now it's the TGV, the second city and all that.' The TGV phenomenon – the extension of the high-speed train line in 2001 that brought Marseille to three hours from Paris – is widely quoted, and by all accounts has been a huge success. Some are quietly delighted by an increasing flow of visitors from the capital and boost to the economy; others seem more reticent. For the downside of this new influx of interest and money has been a noticeable rise in property and restaurant prices.

Popular myths and the fishy reputation surrounding Marseille are as widespread in France as abroad. If the *French Connection* movies and more recently Robert Guédiguian's *La ville est tranquille* haven't exactly painted a pretty *bouillabaisse*-suffused picture of the city; then other images suggest a lively and upbeat side: the omnipresent blue-and-white of football team OM, Luc Besson's *Taxi* films packed with local humour and colour, the bold Euroméditerranée redevelopment project.

As is so often the case here, there is no simple truth: the oldest city in France is one of fascinating contradictions. The sun almost always shines but the ferocious Mistral chills the bones in winter. The rocky coastline is breathtaking but sought-after beaches call for a map and hiking boots. The architecture can be stunning but, despite much restoration in hand, many buildings are crumbling and Marseille has its share of modern eyesores. Some of the neighbourhoods behind the Vieux Port remain relatively poor while the Corniche, the coastal road to the south, is peppered with grand stucco villas. A dangerous reputation lingers but the crime rate is no higher than in other major French cities and continues to drop.

Bouillabaisse, méchoui, pizza and nems may illustrate the ethnic mix here, but France's second-largest city offers so much more. The Marseillais will vigorously defend their city and will tell you, in their endearingly loud way, that it doesn't give itself over easily.

HISTORY

Life in Marseille has revolved around the Vieux Port ever since a band of Phoenician Greeks sailed into this strategically located natural harbour in 600BC. On that very day a local chieftain's daughter, Gyptus, was to choose a husband and the Greeks' dashing commander Protis clearly fitted the bill. The bride came with a donation of land and a hill near the mouth of the Rhône, where the Greeks founded a trading post named Massalia, a name that still crops up in modern Marseille – one of the city's best known bands is called Massilia Sound System.

Legend aside, the history of Marseille is irrevocably linked to its development as a port. By 500 BC, Massalia's Greeks were trading throughout Mediterranean Europe and from Cornwall to the Baltic. Caesar besieged the city in 49 BC, seizing almost all its colonies, and Massalia's Greeks were left with little more than their famous university and much-vaunted independence, which they were to lose and regain several times over the years.

Louis XIV ushered in the first great transformation since the arrival of the Greeks: he pulled down the city walls in 1666 and expanded the port to the Rive Neuve. The city was devastated by plague in 1720, losing more than half its population of 90,000. By the Revolution, however, its industries of soap manufacturing, oil processing and faïence were flourishing. The demand for labour sparked a wave of immigration from Provence and Italy.

Marseille supported the Revolution enthusiastically, only to turn monarchist under the First Empire and republican under the Second. By the time of Napoléon III, Algeria had become a French *département*, leading to a huge increase in trans-Mediterranean shipping. The emperor initiated the construction of an entirely new port, La Joliette, which was completed in 1853. In 1869, when the Suez Canal opened, Marseille became the greatest boomtown in Europe. Between 1851 and 1911, the population rose by 360,000. As immigrants arrived from all over southern Europe, it acquired the astonishingly cosmopolitan population that it maintains to this day.

Marseille's heyday was soon to come to an abrupt halt. In 1934, King Alexander of Yugoslavia and Louis Barthou, the French foreign minister, were assassinated on La Canebière. In 1939, the city was placed under national guardianship when widespread corruption in local government was revealed.

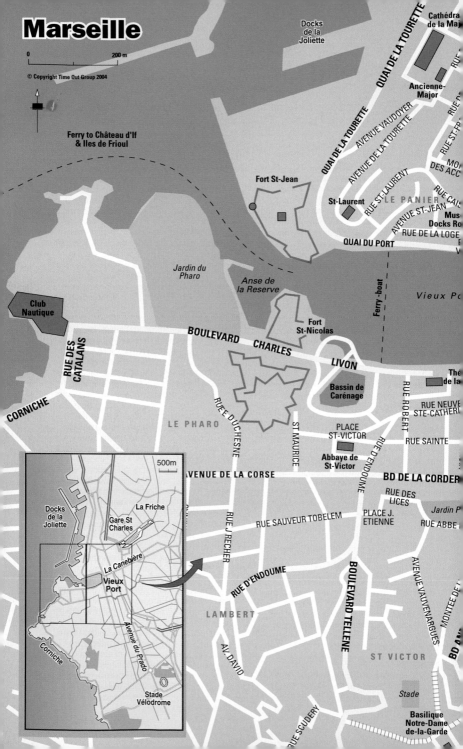

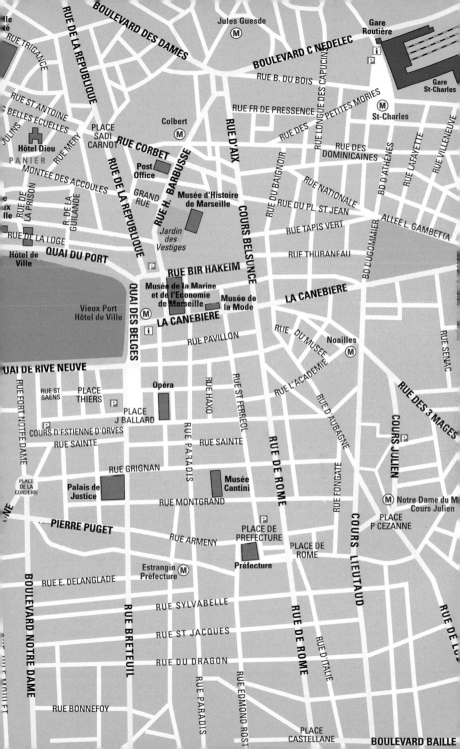

Following the independence of Tunisia in 1956 and Algeria in 1962, Marseille received a mass exodus of French colonials, North African Jews and North Africans who had been involved in colonial administration. At the same time, the loss of these colonies hit Marseille's shipping trade. From 1954 to 1964, the population grew by 50%, creating a severe housing shortage. New neighbourhoods were rapidly constructed to cope with the influx; areas of high unemployment throughout the 1970s and 80s, these neighbourhoods were infamous for drug dealing and crime.

Significantly, however, while Jean-Marie Le Pen and his 'France for the French' extreme-right politics have gained ground elsewhere in the region, Marseille is one place where the melting pot seems to work. The city elected a socialist council continuously from 1953 to 1995, but Jean-Claude Gaudin, the conservative mayor of Marseille since 1995, easily won the 2001 municipal elections. Gaudin wisely put an optimistic spin on the city's unemployment rate, which did actually drop from 17% to 14.7% in June 2003 (nationally it's around 9.6%).

Marseille is repositioning itself as a service and research centre, and is fast learning to capitalise on its spectacular setting and cultural facilities. If they are really serious about tourism – and indeed enhancing the feel-good factor for its 800,000 inhabitants – the authorities need to get more serious about cleaning, and not just around the Vieux Port. Suffice it to say the good citizens appear fonder of their ubiquitous dogs – and haphazardly-parked cars – than the people who walk the pavements.

Sightseeing

Marseille takes in 57km of seafront, from L'Estaque in the north to the Calanques in the south and is laid out in 16 arrondissements moving clockwise from the Vieux Port, then anticlockwise in an outer semi-circle.

Vieux Port & La Canebière

If you think of Marseille as a gritty city, you'll be surprised by the beauty of the Vieux Port. Fashionable bars and avant-garde theatres rub shoulders with boat merchants; luxury yachts bob alongside fishing trawlers, which deliver the day's catch at quai des Belges (officially renamed quai de la Fraternité) to one of France's most photogenic markets. Here, you don't need to ask if the fish is fresh: the octopuses are still slithering and sea bream try valiantly to hop out of the tub. This eastern quay is the departure point for ferries to Château d'If, the Iles de Frioul (*see p142*) and the Côte Bleue (*see p151*).

From this vantage point the two forts guarding the entrance to the port come into view: **Fort St-Jean** (which will form part of the future Musée des Civilisations de l'Europe et de la Méditerranée) on the north bank and Fort St-Nicolas (closed to the public) on the south. The former, which provides a popular suntrap, was built in the 12th century and the latter under Louis XIV. Tellingly, their guns used to face towards, rather than away from, the city: the Marseillais are still proud of this display of the king's doubts about their allegiance.

The quai du Port, to the north, is the quieter side and offers pleasant strolling towards the sea. The Nazis – aided by the Vichy regime – were responsible for brutally reshaping this corner of the city, the historic St-Jean district, which was dynamited in February 1943, razing 1,500 old apartment buildings to the ground. The ancient church of St-Laurent, reached by a flight of steps, is all that remains today. The 25,000 inhabitants of the north bank were cleared out of their homes in under 48 hours, events commemorated by an annual ceremony, when wreaths are laid in nearby place du 23 janvier 1943, and in the **Mémorial des Camps de la Mort** around the corner. The 1950s apartment blocks that now line the *quai*, designed by architect Fernand Pouillon, look proud and elegant in their way.

They are offset by the fine 17th-century **Hôtel de Ville**, currently surrounded by a massive building site until early 2005, when a grand new public space costing €45 million will be unveiled. Remains of much earlier shipping activity can be seen just near here in the **Musée des Docks Romains**, while the **Maison Diamantée** evokes the prosperous merchants' houses that stood here in the 16th century. Behind this, steps lead up to the ancient, and gradually gentrifying, Le Panier district.

The quai de Rive Neuve on the opposite bank houses some of the city's hippest bars and clubs, including the **Bar de la Marine** and the **Trolleybus**, and the **Théâtre de la Criée**, created from the city's old fish market in the 1970s. Further along where it turns into boulevard Charles Livon, the busy road leading past **Palais du Pharo** towards the Corniche, is faster-paced and less pedestrian-friendly. Behind quai de Rive Neuve, a thriving restaurant and café district has sprung up on place Thiars, cours d'Estienne d'Orves and place aux Huiles. A small ferry runs (if not undergoing maintenance) from Hôtel de Ville on the north side of the port to place aux Huiles on the south (8am-6.30pm, €0.50), but it's just as quick to walk.

Climb up behind and follow rue Sainte all the way to the ancient **Abbaye de St-Victor**, a fascinating double-decker church and once one of the most powerful abbeys in the south. On

Surprisingly graceful: the **Vieux Port**.

foot from here, there is a steep yet rewarding route up to Notre-Dame de la Garde (*see p140*).

Running east from the Vieux Port, **La Canebière** (from *canèbe*: hemp in Provençal, after a rope factory once located here), the city centre's formerly glorious main drag, long served as the dividing line between the 'poor' north and the 'rich' south of Marseille. It's now rather shabby in parts and dominated by chain stores. However, the Canebière still makes for an interesting walk with its faded 19th-century wedding-cake facades, lively multicultural atmosphere and plenty of cheap places to eat. At the Vieux Port end, near the Office du Tourisme, a landscaped square leads to the colonnaded facade of the **Opéra de Marseille**. Across the street, the Bourse et Chambre de Commerce, decorated with ship carvings alluding to the importance of the port, now contains the **Musée de la Marine**. Nearby a modern cubic building houses the dynamic **Musée de la Mode** and a fashion-industry trade centre. At the top end of La Canebière, you can't miss the tall, imposing **Eglise des Réformés**.

To the north of La Canebière stretches the North African neighbourhood of **Belsunce**, known for its handsome 18th-century residences and as the most likely place to be mugged. This may be unfair, but best be wary of loitering lads in quiet back streets. It's also home to the tremendous new municipal library designed by Adrien Fainsilber. At the end of the Cours Belsunce in place Jules Guesde stands the imperial **Porte d'Aix**, a triumphal arch built 1825-33. The surrounding streets offer a vibrant experience of Marseille today: corner-shop mosques, boutiques selling cheap fabrics and gadgets, and sweetmeats of every kind. It's just minutes from the Vieux Port, but so different in mood you might have spent 24 hours on a ferry.

Abbaye de St-Victor

3 rue de l'Abbaye, 7th (04.96.11.22.60). M° Vieux-Port; bus 55, 61, 54, 81. **Open** 9am-7pm daily. **Admission** free. *Crypt* €2, free under-12s. **No credit cards.**

This spectacular, fortified medieval church was built on the remains of an ancient necropolis. The earlier church, founded in the fifth century by St Jean Cassian, was the city's first basilica and heart of a powerful abbey complex. Destroyed by Saracens in the 11th century, it was rebuilt and fortified in the 14th century. Chunks of the earlier church remain in its convoluted crypt, where sarcophagi include the tomb of St Victor, ground to death between two millstones by the Romans.

Eglise des Réformés

1 rue Barbaroux, 1st (04 91 48 57 45). M° Réformés-Canebière. **Open** 4-6pm daily. **Admission** free. This handsome neo-Gothic church got its 'nickname' from an order of reformed Augustine monks, whose chapel stood on this site; its actual name is St-

Vincent-de-Paul. Founded in 1852, it was conse-crated only in 1888 due to lack of funds. The two spires, one of which houses four bells, are 69m high.

Fort St-Jean/Musée National des Civilisations de l'Europe et de la Méditerranée

quai du Port, 2nd (04.96.13.80.90/www.musee-europemediterranee.org). M° Vieux-Port. **Open** (during exhibitions) 10am-noon, 2-7pm Mon, Wed-Sun. **Admission** €2; €1.50 students; free under-18s. **No credit cards.**

The imposing walled fortress begun by the Knights Hospitaliers is currently used for temporary exhibi-tions, which prefigure the Musée National des Civilisations de l'Europe et de la Méditérranée (due to open 2008), based around the folk art collection of the former Musée National des Arts et Traditions Populaires in Paris, as well as diverse recent acqui-sitions from olive oil to graffiti.

Jardins des Vestiges/Musée d'Histoire de Marseille

Centre Bourse, 1 sq Belsunce, 1st (04.91.90.42.22). M° Vieux-Port. **Open** noon-7pm Mon-Sat. **Admission** €2; €1 10-16s; free under-10s. **No credit cards.**

While the foundations for the Centre Bourse shop-ping centre were being dug in the 1970s, remains of Marseille's original Greek walls and a corner of the Roman port were unearthed, preserved here in a sheltered enclave. The adjoining Musée d'Histoire de Marseille has an exhibition of urban art, Portraits d'Industrie (until 28 Aug 2004), part of the 19th- and 20th-century collection due to go on show in 2005.

Mémorial des Camps de la Mort

esplanade de la Tourette, 2nd (04.91.90.73.15). M° Vieux-Port or Joliette, bus 83. **Open** *June-Sept* 11am-6pm Tue-Sun. *Oct-May* 10am-5pm Tue-Sun. **Admission** free.

In January 1943 following orders from Hitler, Karl Oberg, head of Gestapo in France, declared: 'Marseille is the cancer of Europe. And Europe can't be alive as long as Marseille isn't purified… That is why the German authorities want to cleanse the old districts and destroy them with mines and fire.' These chilling words resonate in a series of haunt-ing and fascinating pictures that capture subsequent vile events, on display in a former bunker.

Musée Cantini

19 rue Grignan, 6th (04.91.54.77.75). M° Estrangin-Préfecture. **Open** *June-Sept* 11am-6pm Tue-Sun. *Oct-May* 10am-5pm Tue-Sun. **Admission** €3; €1.50 10-18s, students; free under-10s. **No credit cards.**

This 17th-century mansion houses one of France's foremost Fauve and Surrealist art collections togeth-er with some fine post-war works. Highlights include a Signac of the port, Dufy from his early Cézannesque neo-Cubist phase and paintings by Camoin, Kupka, Kandinsky, Léger and Ernst. Upstairs focuses on Surrealism and abstraction, including Arp, Brauner and Picabia, plus works by Dubuffet, Balthus and Bacon.

Musée des Docks Romains

pl Vivaux, 2nd (04.91.91.24.62). M° Vieux-Port, or bus 83. **Open** *June-Sept* 11am-6pm Tue-Sun. *Oct-May* 10am-5pm Tue-Sun. **Admission** €2; €1 10-16s, students; free under-10s. **No credit cards.**

During post-war reconstruction in 1947, the remains of a first-century Roman shipping warehouse were uncovered. This museum preserves the site intact, and documents maritime trade through terracotta jars, amphorae and coins.

Musée de la Marine et de l'Economie de Marseille

9 La Canebière, 1st (04.91.39.34.76/www.marseille-provence.cci.fr/patrimoine). M° Vieux-Port. **Open** 10am-6pm Mon-Fri. **Admission** €3; €1.50 12-18s; free under-12s. **Credit** MC, V.

This grandiose building housing the city's Chamber of Commerce was inaugurated by Napoléon III in 1860. The museum charts the maritime history of Marseille from the 17th century with paintings, mod-els, old maps and engravings, and celebrates ports of the world from Liverpool to Montevideo.

Musée de la Mode de Marseille

11 La Canebière, 1st (04.96.17.06.00/ www.espacemodemediterranee.com). M° Vieux-Port. **Open** *June-Sept* 11am-6pm Tue-Sun. *Oct-May* 10am-5pm Tue-Sun. **Admission** €3; €1.50 10-16s; free under-10s. **No credit cards.**

The fashion museum adjoining the Espace Mode Méditérranée has more than 3,000 accessories and

Le Panier: on its way up.

outfits, from the 1920s to the present, displayed in well-presented, changing exhibitions, ranging from thematic shows (fashion mags until Sept 2004) to young southern designers, such as Fred Sathal.

Musée du Vieux Marseille (Maison Diamantée)

2 rue de la Prison, 2nd (04.91.55.28.68). Mº Vieux-Port, bus 83 & 49B. **Open** *June-Sept* 10am-7pm Tue-Sun. *Oct-May* 10am-5pm Tue-Sun. **Admission** €3; €1.50 10-16s; free under-10s. **No credit cards.**
Reopened for temporary exhibitions only following painstaking renovation, the Maison Diamantée, so named because of its diamond-faceted Renaissance facade, was built in 1570 by wealthy merchant Pierre Gardiolle. Exhibitions give an impression of daily life in Marseille since the 18th century including furniture, photographs and Provençal costume.

Le Panier, La Joliette & Les Carmes

Le Panier, rising between quai du Port and grimy (but improving) rue de la République, has been the traditional first stop for successive waves of immigrants and today is at the top of the tourist itinerary. It's hard to resist the charm of its narrow, hilly streets, steep stairways and semi-crumbling pastel-coloured houses – think Italy-meets-Tunisia. Certain Marseillais (the ones who don't live here) still think of Le Panier as a dodgy area to be avoided at night, but nowadays there is little evidence to support such fears. Its population is changing as teachers, students and arty professionals renovate flats, and chic boutiques selling pottery and soap attest to its aspirations; it remains to be seen whether Le Panier will become the Marais of Marseille.

Whether you take one of the stairways up from the Vieux Port or any of the roads leading to rue Caisserie, the striking **Hôtel Dieu** above catches your eye. Designed in 1753 by the nephew of Jules Hardouin-Mansart (of place Vendôme in Paris fame), its arcaded facade is typical of hospital architecture of the time, though it was modified during the Second Empire. At the foot of the punishing Montée des Accoules, the **Eglise Notre-Dame des Accoules** has a remarkable spire and 13th-century bell tower.

After it has peaked, the Montée des Accoules runs down to gently animated place de Lenche (also reached from avenue St-Jean), which is edged by a few bars, restaurants and shops. Peaceful place des Moulins is located roughly in the middle of the sector. On the north side is the stunning **Vieille Charité**, built as a poorhouse but now home to two museums and a pleasant café. West of the Vieille Charité, with an unimpeded line to God and sea (despite the

motorway roaring by alongside), is the huge, kitsch 19th-century **Cathédrale de la Major** and its predecessor l'Ancienne Major.

Behind Le Panier, the up-and-coming La Joliette area, centred around the 1860s **Docks de la Joliette**, is not so much a tourist destination as focus of the Euroméditerranée project, anticipated as playing a key role in stimulating the city's economy. Cargo ships and a frenetic motorway make it a distinctly unpleasant place to visit, but this should change in 2006, when a tunnel replaces the flyover with an impressive esplanade. By 2008, the whole 2.7km expanse from Fort St-Jean to Arenc should be transformed into the Cité de la Méditerranée. The bold plans, overseen by architects Yves Lion and François Kern, embrace public housing, a museum and aquarium, restaurants, theatre, offices and two hotels.

Stretching from place de la Joliette to the Vieux Port runs traffic-laden rue de la République, the main Haussmann-style artery of the 2nd arrondissement, and a good place to find good-value ethnic restaurants, snack joints and bakeries. This area is undergoing a makeover too, as evidenced by glossy done-up apartments and offices dotted among the rather grimier whole. This refit, another phase of the EM redevelopment, is set to continue.

Heading left down rue Jean Trinquet, some unobtrusive, smelly steps just past rue Cathala lead up to place des Grands Carmes and an undiscovered gem **Eglise Notre-Dame du Mont-Carmel**, currently undergoing restoration to preserve its 300-plus statues, Baroque interior and many paintings. This spot offers a respite and urban views across to Le Panier and the imposing residential block on place Sadi Carnot, once infamous as Nazi headquarters, attacked by the Résistance on 19 August 1944.

Cathédrale de la Major

pl de la Major, 2nd (04.91.90.53.57). Mº Joliette. **Open** 10am-noon, 2-5.30pm Tue-Sun. **Admission** free.
The largest cathedral built in France since the Middle Ages, the neo-Byzantine Nouvelle Major was started in 1852 and completed in 1893 with Oriental-style cupolas and a lustrous mosaic. The remains of the 11th-century Ancienne Major, parts of which go back to Roman times, lie in a state of disrepair.

Centre de la Vieille Charité

2 rue de la Charité, 2nd (04.91.14.58.80). Mº Joliette or Vieux-Port. **Open** *June-Sept* 11am-6pm Tue-Sun. *Oct-May* 10am-5pm Tue-Sun. **Admission** *each museum* €2; €1 10-16s, free under-10s, all Sun morning. *exhibitions* €3; free under-10s, all Sun morning. **No credit cards.**
Constructed from 1671-1749 as a poorhouse, this ensemble designed by Pierre and Jean Puget has beautiful open loggias on three storeys around a

courtyard, which is dominated by a magnificent chapel with an oval-shaped dome. It was renovated and reopened as a cultural complex in 1986. The former chapel now houses temporary exhibitions; around the sides are the Musée d'Archéologie Méditerranéenne and the Musée des Arts Africains, Océaniens and Amerindiens (MAAOA). The former has a superb collection of archaeological finds from Provence and the Mediterranean and the most important Egyptian collection in France outside Paris. MAAOA displays tribal art and artefacts from Africa, the Pacific and the Americas, including tastefully engraved human skulls.

Docks de la Joliette

10 pl de la Joliette, 2nd (04.91.14.45.00/ www.euromediterranee.fr). M° Joliette. **Open** *9am-6pm Mon-Sat.* **Admission** free.

The handsome stone warehouses of this 19th-century industrial port run along the waterfront for almost a mile and were modelled on St Katharine's Dock in London. They were state of the art when opened in 1866, but as traffic declined and cargo shifted to containers, the buildings fell into disuse and there were plans to demolish them. However, they have been brilliantly renovated into office space by architect Eric Castaldi as centrepiece of the Euroméditerranée redevelopment. The Docks are now occupied by a diverse mix of companies, bars and restaurants, and employ over 3,500 people. An information centre in atrium 10.2 displays designs and models of the entire scheme.

St-Charles, Longchamp & the northeast

Northeast of Belsunce is the main station, the **Gare St-Charles**, with its majestic staircase guarded by two sombre lions and colonial statues. The immediate area is a sprawling building site until an underpass connecting to the A7 motorway is finished at the end of 2004.

In the working-class neighbourhood of Belle de Mai behind the station, a former squat in a disused tobacco factory has become the thriving cultural centre **La Friche la Belle de Mai**. The surrounding area is hardly appealing on foot, although the southeast corner of Belle de Mai has also been targeted as the focus of an innovative media complex.

At the far end of boulevard Longchamp stands the grandiose **Palais Longchamp**, which holds the **Musée des Beaux-Arts** and **Muséum d'Histoire Naturelle**. Behind the palace are attractive landscaped gardens, which stay open later than the museums.

Much further out in the 13th arrondissement, heading past the bright blue Hôtel du Département (seat of the Bouches-du-Rhône Conseil Général) designed by British architect Will Alsopp, is the Château-Gombert district.

Home to a technopôle (technological research and business centre) as well as the delightful **Musée du Terroir Marseillais**, this is a charming little suburban village of winding roads where property is now sought-after.

Musée des Beaux-Arts & Muséum d'Histoire Naturelle

Palais Longchamp, bd de Longchamp, 4th. M° Longchamp-Cinq Avenues. **Open** *Musée des Beaux-Arts (04.91.14.59.30) June-Sept* 11am-6pm Tue-Sun. *Oct-May* 10am-5pm Tue-Sun. *Muséum d'Historie Naturelle (04.91.14.59.50)* 10am-5pm Tue-Sun. **Admission** *Musée des Beaux-Arts* €2; €1 10-16s; free under-10s. *Muséum d'Histoire Naturelle* €3; €1.50 10-16s; free under-10s. **No credit cards.**

No other monument expresses the ebullience of 19th-century Marseille better than the Palais Longchamp. This ostentatious complex, inaugurated in 1869, was built to celebrate the completion of an 84km aqueduct bringing the waters of the Durance to the drought-prone port. A massive horseshoe-shaped classical colonnade, with a triumphal arch at its centre and museums in either wing, crowns a hill landscaped around fountains. On the ground floor of the fine art museum are works by Marseille sculptor and architect Pierre Puget (1620-94); on the first floor is a superior collection of 16th- and 17th-century French, Italian and Flemish paintings. The second floor is devoted to French 18th- and 19th-century works and old master drawings. The natural history museum has zoological and prehistoric artefacts.

Musée du Terroir Marseillais

5 pl des Héros, 13th (04.91.68.14.38). M° La Rose then bus 5. **Open** *9am-noon, 2-6.30pm Tue-Fri; 2.30-6.30pm Sat, Sun.* **Admission** €4; €1.60 6-14s; free under-6s. **No credit cards.**

Founded in 1928, the museum offers a charming insight into Provençal culture: hand-painted 18th-century dressers, faïence, dolls and ancient kitchen gadgets such as a fig-drier.

Musée Grobet-Labadié

140 bd de Longchamp, 1st (04.91.62.21.82). M° Longchamp-Cinq-Avenues. **Open** *June-Sept* 11am-6pm Tue-Sun; *Oct-May* 10am-5pm Tue-Sun. **Admission** €2; €1 10-16s; free under-10s. **No credit cards.**

The intimate Musée Grobet-Labadié houses the private art collection of a wealthy 19th-century couple. Their 1873 mansion, scrupulously renovated, offers an intriguing glimpse into cultivated tastes of the time, ranging from 15th- and 16th-century Italian and Flemish paintings to Fragonard and Millet, medieval tapestries and 17th- and 18th-century Provençal furniture and faïence.

Notre-Dame, Cours Julien & Castellane

Stretching south and southeast of the Vieux Port, the densely populated 6th arrondissement

Notre-Dame-de-la-Garde. *See p140.*

is interestingly varied in terms of architecture and people. Its southern and western parts, along with the neighbouring 7th and 8th arrondissements, are considered the chic districts of Marseille. The city's most famous – and audaciously stand-out – landmark, the stripey neo-Byzantine basilica of **Notre-Dame de la Garde**, rises on a peak to the south of the Vieux Port (a pleasant sign-posted climb). It can also be reached from the other side, via twisting streets and steps from the quiet Vauban district or the serene Jardin Puget.

Perched on another hill south of Noailles leading to Notre-Dame du Mont, is the bohemian – if that means tastefully graffitied – Cours Julien, site of the former central food market (it still has a flower market Wed and Sat mornings and organic food Fri mornings). An eclectic collection of fashion boutiques, bookshops, French and ethnic restaurants, cafés with sun-soaked terraces, theatres and music venues make for a slightly uncomfortable contrast with less well-off locals, who also like to chill out here.

It's very different in mood to the fine 19th-century apartment blocks, strung with wrought iron balconies, that line rue de Rome in the area around the **Préfecture**. The regal police headquarters is fronted by cascading fountains, wide pavements much loved by skateboarders, and an attractive square, which borders the top of trendy rue St-Ferréol. South of here, place Castellane with its elegant Cantini fountain (1911-13) marks the beginning of the broad avenue du Prado, which has the grace of the Champs-Elysées without the megastores or overpriced cafés. It's also worth venturing to the **Parc du XXVI Centenaire** a little to the east.

Notre-Dame de la Garde

rue Fort du Sanctuaire, 6th (04.91.13.40.80). Bus 60 from Vieux Port or Petit Train de la Bonne Mère. **Open** 7am-7pm daily. **Admission** free.
Balancing on a 162m-high peak, 'La Bonne Mère', topped by a massive gilded statue of the Virgin Mary and Child, is the emblem of Marseille and the most visited tourist site in Provence. Building began in 1853 and the interior decoration was completed in 1899. Deeply loved by Marseillais (and rightly so), its Byzantine-style interior is filled with remarkable ex votos, including one for Olympique de Marseille. The mosaic floors were made in Venice, and alternating red and white marble pillars add to the richness of the surprisingly intimate chapel. Outside, the esplanade offers spectacular vistas in all directions.

Parc du XXVI Centenaire

sq Zino Francescatti, 8th. M° Castellane/Périer, or bus 42 or 50. **Open** *Mar-Apr, Sept-Oct* 8am-7pm daily; *May-Aug* 8am-9pm daily; *Nov-Feb* 8am-5.30pm daily. **Admission** free.
This agreeable 10-hectare park is a recent and as yet unfinished addition in honour of Marseille's 26

Putting the city in perspective.

centuries of history. Stemming from the site of the former Gare du Prado, it combines paved walkways, lawns and a stream between the old platforms, and is mercifully dog-free. At the main entrance a growing list of patrons' names is engraved in stone.

La Corniche, Prado & the southwest

The Corniche Président Kennedy – known simply as La Corniche – carves along the coast from just beyond the Vieux Port to where the 8th begins near the Centre de Voile. Vantage points, craggy coves and little beaches along the way offer stunning views of the rocky coastline, offshore islands and spooky Château d'If. The sheltered and sandy **Plage des Catalans**, encircled by cafés and restaurants, looks tempting but costs €5 per two hours. Further along, the chic little **Vallon des Auffes** inlet has a bijou harbour and a couple of upmarket restaurants. Equally sought-after, sticking out on the exposed westerly tip, is the pretty Malmousque district. It has several rocky bays and a quay, which offer refreshing although unsupervised bathing points (the most popular are in front of the Foreign Legion base down from rue de la Douane, and Anse de Maldormé and Anse Fausse Monnaie around the corner).

Following the road south, the ominously named Plage du Prophète is a quite attractive, larger beach. All of these sunspots can be reached by strolling down through the smart residential areas of Bompard and (hilly) Roucas Blanc, occasionally a challenging up-and-down walk. The No.73 bus offers a fun rollercoaster ride from Castellane via Périer down to Vallon de l'Oriol on the seafront. In addition the less reliable 83 runs (or rather crawls) along the Corniche between the Vieux Port and Prado.

In the 8th arrondissement, past the Rond-Point du Prado, stands the **Stade Vélodrome**, proud home to the city's worshipped football team Olympique de Marseille. Further along boulevard Michelet you can also stop in for a drink at Le Corbusier's landmark **Cité Radieuse**. Heading southwest between Ste-Anne and Mazargues on avenue d'Haïfa – just before César's gigantic bronze sculpture of a thumb – the **Musée d'Art Contemporain** contains an adventurous collection of contemporary art. The avenue du Prado ends at the Plage du Prado in front of a bold marble copy of Michelangelo's *David*. Along this broad recreational stretch of beach (Parc Balnéaire), you'll see David-like windsurfers being tossed about on the waves, as they brave Marseille's fearsome Mistral. Facing another elongated beach, the 17-hectare **Parc Borély**, with its horseracing track, botanical gardens, lake and château, is a haven for families, joggers and *pétanque* players.

Continuing on through Bonneveine and Vieille Chapelle, this stretch of coast, with its series of sand and shingle beaches, shows Marseille at its most sporty and Californian; but the picturesque ports of Pointe Rouge and Madrague de Montredon remain typically Marseillais. La Madrague also has an unofficial gay 'beach', or rather an isolated patch of rocks accessed from bd Mont-Rose. **Les Goudes** is located 1.7km beyond here, a seemingly remote village surrounded by barren outcrops yet still within the city limits. With its small stone houses blending into the orangey rock, it attracts fishing enthusiasts, divers and hikers; it's a great place to feast on fresh fish or wood-fired pizza. Even further along at the end of the road is the timeless village of Callelongue, which is dominated by the forbidding Massif de Marseilleveyre and too many cars at weekends.

La Cité Radieuse

280 bd Michelet, 8th (hotel 04.91.16.78.00). M° Rond-Point du Prado then bus 21 or 22. **Guided tours** ask at hotel or at Office de Tourisme.
La Maison de Fada (Madman's House), as Marseille folk once scornfully but now affectionately call Le Corbusier's 1952 reinforced-concrete apartment block (or just 'Le Corbu'), is where the architect tried out his prototype for mass housing. The vertical garden city became the model for countless urban developments. Perched on stilts, the complex contains 340 balconied flats plus a shopping floor that serves as a 'village street'. On the roof are an open-air theatre, a gym and a nursery school, offering panoramic views. The flats are mostly duplexes, in which the architect designed every detail. The Cité also contains a hotel (*see p151*).

Musée d'Art Contemporain (MAC)

69 av d'Haïfa, 8th (04.91.25.01.07). Bus 23 or 45. **Open** *June-Sept* 11am-6pm Tue-Sun. *Oct-May* 10am-5pm Tue-Sun. **Admission** €3; €1.50 10-16s; free under-10s. **No credit cards.**
Marseille's dedicated contemporary art museum is located in a hangar-like space. Its contents, which change regularly, range from perplexing to hilarious, such as Parant's *La Voiture Rouge*. In the garden are sculptures by César, Absalon and Dietman.

Musée de la Faïence

157 av de Montredon, 8th (04.91.72.43.47). M° Castellane or Prado then bus 19. **Open** *June-Sept* 11am-6pm Tue-Sun; *Oct-May* 10am-5pm Tue-Sun. **Admission** €2; €1 10-16s; free under-10s. **No credit cards.**
Surrounded by a magnificent park at the foot of the Marseilleveyre, Château Pastré was constructed in 1862 by a rich trading family. Today it houses the Musée de la Faïence, recalling the pottery industry that thrived in Marseille in the late 17th and 18th centuries, as well as other Provençal production.

Stade Vélodrome (Olympique de Marseille)

3 bd Michelet, 8th. M° Rond-Point du Prado. Club office: 25 rue Negresco, 8th (04.91.76.56.09/ www.olympiquedemarseille.com). **Open** *shop & museum (www.madeinsport.com)* 2.30-7pm Mon-Sat.
L'Olympique de Marseille commands the sort of fervour that separatist movements might elsewhere. OM needed plenty of fighting spirit in 1993, when saviour-president Bernard Tapie, a former socialist minister, set up their victory over Valenciennes. The club clawed its way back from disgrace thanks to a crop of international talent, even though Zidane has since departed for Madrid. Tapie bounced back as 'sporting director', although in 2002 OM was again under investigation for dodgy transfer deals. The Stade Vélodrome is the largest stadium in the country after Paris' Stade de France, with 60,000 seats. The best (€70) are in the Jean-Bouin stand, but the Ganay (max €60) also offers a relatively quiet viewpoint. Tickets can be bought from the stadium on match day, in advance from L'OM Café (3 quai des Belges, Vieux Port) or ring 32 29 Allo OM.

L'Estaque

The faded industrial district of L'Estaque, hugging the coast on the northwest of the city, looks like an unlikely place to have swayed the history of modern art, but it did. When Paul

Cézanne first visited it in 1870, the little fishing village was already evolving into a working-class suburb living off its tile factories and cement works. The transition clearly intrigued him, because his most famous painting of the town, *Le Golfe de Marseille vu de L'Estaque* (now in the Art Institute of Chicago), has a factory chimney smoking in one corner.

The main attraction for Cézanne (and Derain, Braque, Dufy and the other artists who came here in their wake) – the remarkable light and diverse shapes of the landscape – survives today. It's not easy to pick out the locations the painters immortalised, but you can stroll around the village and up to Cézanne's favourite viaduct or take the Circuit des Peintres walking tour organised by the Marseille tourist office.

The seafront road along the so-called Plage de l'Estaque (for the most part a fenced-off private harbour) has been improved to provide better pedestrian access, although the proper beach, Plage de Corbières, is a couple of kilometres out the other side.

Ile d'If & Iles de Frioul

The Ile d'If, a tiny islet of sun-bleached white stone 20 minutes from the Vieux Port, is today inhabited by salamanders and seagulls. Its two most famous residents – Edmond Dantès and Abbé Faria, the main characters of Alexandre Dumas' *The Count of Monte Cristo* – never existed. To keep Marseille under control, François 1er had a fortress built here in 1524 so formidable that it never saw combat and was eventually converted into a prison. Thousands of Protestants met grisly ends here after the Edict of Nantes was revoked in 1685. But it was Dumas who put If on the map by making it the prison, from which Dantès escaped: wily administrators soon caught on and kept tourists happy by hacking out the very hole through which Edmond slid to freedom in the story. The Château is quickly visited, so bring a picnic and enjoy the clean seawater. Off-season the one café is likely to be closed.

It's easy to combine a visit to the Chateau d'If with the **Iles de Frioul**, a collection of small islands, two of which – Ile Ratonneau and Ile Pomègues – were joined by the digue de Berry in the 18th century. Aside from a few holiday flats by the marina, they consist largely of windswept rock, wonderfully isolated beaches and fragrant clumps of thyme and rosemary. Ratonneau is also the home of the impressive Hôpital Caroline, constructed 1824-28 as a quarantine hospital to protect Marseille from epidemics. Today it is a curious historic site with spectacular views well worth a visit (and the slog up the hill). In June

and July, it hosts the Nuits Caroline – a series of night-time events ranging from live jazz to open-air theatre (€23, including boat, 04.96.11.04.61).

Château d'If
Ile d'If, 1st (04.91.59.02.30). **Open** *May-Sept* 9.30am-6.30pm daily. *Oct-Apr* 9.30am-5.30pm Tue-Sun. **Admission** €4.60; €3.10 18-25s; free under-18s.

Ferries
GACM (04.91.55.50.09, www.answeb.net/gacm) runs regular crossings (less frequent Oct-May), many of which stop at If and Iles de Frioul. **Return ticket** *one island* €9; €4 3-6s; free under-3s; *both islands* €15; €6.50 3-6s; free under-3s. **No credit cards**.

Arts & entertainment

For information, pick up weekly *L'Hebdo* from kiosks or freebies *Métro* and *Marseille Plus*.

Frac Provence-Alpes-Côtes d'Azur
1 pl Francis Chirat, 2nd (04.91.91.27.55). M° *Joliette.* **Open** 10am-12.30pm, 2-6pm Mon-Sat. **Admission** free.

The Fonds régional d'art contemporain has a wide-ranging collection of contemporary art, from inter-national names to young artists, exhibited, along with special commissions, at its own gallery in Le Panier and in schools, museums and cultural centres across the PACA region.

La Friche la Belle de Mai
41 rue Jobin, 3rd (04.95.04.95.04/www.lafriche.org). M° *Gare St-Charles, buses 49a & 49b.* **Open** 9am-7pm Mon-Sat. **Admission** free.

A disused tobacco factory in the scruffy (but increasingly trendy) Belle de Mai quarter, La Friche started life as an artists' squat but is now home to numerous artistic, musical, theatrical and media outfits, as well as putting on regular art exhibitions. These include Aide aux Musiques Innovatrices, Théâtre Massalia, Radio Grenouille and Georges Appaix's La Liseuse dance company.

Galérie Roger Pailhas
20 quai Rive Neuve, 7th (04.91.54.02.22/ www.rogerpailhas.com). M° *Vieux-Port.* **Open** 11am-1pm, 2-6pm Tue-Sat. Usually closed Aug. **Admission** free.

In a massive first-floor space by the Vieux Port, Roger Pailhas is one of France's rare contemporary art galleries outside Paris which counts. Over the years Pailhas has collaborated with major international artists including Dan Graham and Daniel Buren, but he also picks up young local talents, such as Corinne Marchetti who addresses contemporary culture and sexuality in witty embroidered scenes.

Gyptis Théâtre
136 rue Loubon, 3rd (04.91.11.00.91/www.theatre online.com). Bus 31, 32, 33, 34. **Box office** 1-6.30pm Mon-Fri. **Tickets** €8-€19. **Credit** MC, V.

Run by director-actors Chatôt and Vouyoucas, the

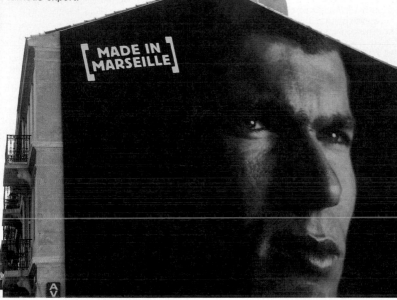

Marseille's most famous export.

Gyptis' varied programme is dedicated to giving young directors, writers and artists their first break.

Opéra Municipal

2 rue Molière, 1st (04.91.55.11.10/www.mairie-marseille.fr). M° Vieux-Port. **Box office** 10am-5.30pm Tue-Sat. **Tickets** €8-€60. **No credit cards.**
The original opera was one of the city's great 18th-century buildings. Partially burnt down in 1919, it was rebuilt in art deco style preserving the original facade. Today it holds performances of opera and the Ballet National de Marseille, whose creative director Marie-Claude Pietragalla was forced to resign in early 2004.

Théâtre National de la Criée

30 quai Rive Neuve, 7th (04.91.54.70.54/ www.theatre-lacriee.com). M° Vieux-Port. **Box office** 10am-7pm (in person 1-7pm) Tue-Sat; limited summer opening. **Tickets** €10-20. **Credit** MC, V.
This celebrated theatre was created from the former fish market in 1981. Director Jean-Louis Benoit, in partnership with producer and artistic consultant Frédéric Bélier-Garcia, have put an international slant on the 2004 season.

Théâtre du Gymnase

4 rue du Théâtre Français, 1st (04.91.24.35.24). M° Noailles. **Box office** noon-6pm Tue-Sat (phone 08.20.00.04.22 11am-6pm). **Tickets** €20-€30. **Credit** MC, V.
This candy-box of a theatre dating from 1834 was restored in 1986. Directed by Dominique Bluzet, it's one of the best-attended, most innovative theatres in France, staging its own take on everything from classics to contemporary drama.

Restaurants

Bouillabaisse – which Marseillais say can only be authentically made here – is a must for any visitor: seek out a well-reputed restaurant such as **Le Miramar** and be prepared to pay at least €40 per person. Pizza is another speciality , thanks to a history of immigration from Italy.

Les Arcenaulx

25 cours d'Estienne d'Orves, 1st (04.91.59.80.30/ www.les-arcenaulx.com). M° Vieux-Port. **Open** noon-2pm, 8-11pm Mon-Sat. Closed 1wk in Aug. **Menus** €28-€49.50. **Credit** AmEx, DC, MC, V.
In a strikingly converted former Arsenal building, this restaurant amid an antiquarian bookshop, publisher and kitchen shop-cum-épicerie has become the dinner rendezvous of Marseille's chattering classes. Typical of the modern southern cooking are mesclun with pine kernels, sea bass with asparagus, and *brousse* cheese with honey and berries.

Baie des Singes

Cap Croisette, Les Goudes, 8th (04.91.73.68.87). **Open** ring for details. Closed Oct-Mar. **Average** €40. **Credit** MC, V.

Even though getting here involves arriving by boat or scrabbling over a rocky promontory, you won't be the first: President Chirac and a host of TV personalities have already done it. And you can see why – the bare white rock and blue seas could be a Greek island. The speciality is dead simple, fresh fish, presented in a basket for you to choose from before being grilled (priced by the 100g). There's a sunbathing terrace and you can swim from the rocks.

Le Bistrot du Livon

42 quai de Rive Neuve, 7th (04 91 55 02 27). Mº Vieux-Port, bus 83. **Menus** €16-€18. **Credit** DC, MC, V.

This elegant bistro is done out with a tasteful wood interior. Set menus offer no choice, so it's better to pick from the *à la carte* selection, such as fried monkfish and a spectacular dark chocolate soufflé.

Chez Michel

6 rue des Catalans, 7th (04.91.52.30.63). Bus 54, 83. **Open** daily noon-2pm, 7.30-10pm. **Average** €55. **Credit** AmEx, MC, V.

This Marseille institution, looking across the Anse des Catalans, is a failsafe choice for *bouillabaisse* or *bourride*; the fish are expertly de-boned by sea-weathered waiters and served with a garlicky *rouille*.

Chez Vincent

25 rue Glandèves, 1st (04.91.33.96.78). Mº Vieux-Port. **Open** noon-2pm, 8-11pm Tue-Sat; 8-11pm Sun. **Average** €25. **No credit cards.**

In the mini red-light district near the Vieux Port, this old-fashioned Italian place has many night-owl regulars, including singers from the nearby Opéra. Try the spaghetti with tiny clams, lasagne or a pizza.

Le Clou

24 cours Julien, 6th (04.91.48.08.63/ 04.91.92.46.22). Mº Notre-Dame du Mont or Noailles. **Open** noon-2.30pm, 7-11pm Mon-Thur; noon-2.30pm, 7-11.30pm Fri, Sat; 7-11pm Sun. Closed two wks in Dec. **Menu** €18. **Credit** MC, V.

At the quieter end of 'Cours Ju' but compensated by a splendid garden terrace, Le Clou serves generous portions of authentic Alsatian fare. Highlights include *salade paysanne* with lardons & croutons, *coq au Riesling* with creamy *spätzle* noodles and pork-laden *choucroute garnie*.

Country Life

14 rue Venture, 1st (04.96.11.28.00). Mº Vieux-Port or Estrangin-Préfecture. **Open** 11.30am-2.30pm Mon-Fri; *shop* 9am-6.30pm Mon-Thur, 9am-3pm Fri. **Average** €6. **Credit** MC, V.

This vegetarian self-service has uprooted from Paris. The cook turns out a tempting array of vegetable tarts and quiches: the Petite/Grande Assiette (€3.95/€6.95) is good value.

L'Epuisette

Anse du Vallon des Auffes, 7th (04.91.52.17.82). Bus 83. **Open** 12.15-2pm, 7.45-10pm Tue-Sat. **Menus** €42-€82. **Credit** AmEx, DC, MC, V.

Baie des Singes restaurant. *See p143.*

Young wonder-chef Guillaume Sourrieu continues to astonish, offering up mouthwatering delights at this seafood restaurant, dramatically located on a craggy stone finger surrounded by the Med. Try the shellfish risotto with violet and coriander fritter, or the caramelised scallops with bacon and lime confit. The chocolate brownie with marinated bananas and Indian pepper ice cream is a little piece of heaven.

L'Escale

2 bd Alexandre Delabre, rte des Goudes, 8th (04.91.73.16.78). Bus 19, 20. **Open** *summer* 7.30-10.30pm Mon, Tue; noon-2pm, 7.30-10.30pm Wed-Sun; *winter* noon-2pm, 7.30-10.30pm Wed-Sun. Closed Jan. **Average** €50. **Credit** AmEx, MC, V.
The sleepy fishing village of Les Goudes is only 30 minutes (if you're lucky with traffic) from the centre of Marseille. Former fishmonger Serge Zaroukian does a delicious sauté of baby squid and perfectly cooked monkfish served with ratatouille and onion gratin. Ideal for Sunday lunch – but it's very popular, so book ahead.

La Kahena

2 rue de la République, 1st (04 91 90 61 93). M° Vieux-Port. **Open** noon-2.30pm, 7-10.30pm daily. **Average** €15. **Credit** MC, V.
This is one of the best North African restaurants in the centre, as evidenced by its popularity (book at the weekend), and you'll struggle to eat three courses. To start, try the *chorba* (spicy chickpea broth), calamari or a substantial salad. The *merguez* are good, as is the fish couscous.

Lemon Grass Restaurant

8 rue Fort Notre Dame, 7th (04.91.33.97.65/ www.lemon-grass-marseille.com). M° Vieux-Port. **Open** 8-10.30pm Mon-Sat. Closed 1 15 Jan and last week of Aug. **Menus** €25-€32. **Credit** MC, V.
Contemporary interior and ambient soundtrack provide a relaxed setting for Florent Saugeron's modern fusion cooking at this restaurant on a side street off the Vieux Port. Dishes such as sea bass with a spice and nut crust, lamb with spices and couscous, rice stewed in a banana leaf, plus a veggie option, borrow from Europe, Asia and the Med.

Des Mets de Provence Chez Maurice Brun

18 quai de Rive Neuve, 7th (04.91.33.35.38). M° Vieux-Port. **Open** 8-10.30pm Mon; noon-2pm, 8-10.30pm Tue-Fri; 8-10.30pm Sat. Closed 1-15 Aug. **Menus** €38 (lunch), €52 (dinner). **Credit** MC, V.
Founded in 1936, this place proudly perpetuates traditional Provençal cuisine. Having ascended the wonky old steps, you'll discover a big rotisserie in the fireplace. The proprietor recites the daily offerings on the substantial, delicious prix-fixe.

Le Miramar

12 quai du Port, 2nd (04.91.91.10.40/ www.bouillabaisse.com). M° Vieux-Port. **Open** noon-2pm, 7.15-10pm Tue-Sat. Closed two wks Jan, three wks Aug. **Average** €60. **Credit** AmEx, DC, MC, V.

This 1950s-vintage portside restaurant is one of the best places to sample the city's fabled *bouillabaisse*. Young star chef Christian Buffa took over in 2003. Since *bouillabaisse* is always a two-course meal – the soup, then the fish – don't order a starter.

L'Orient Exploré

9 rue Dejean, 6th (04.91.33.54.15). M° Estrangin-Préfecture. **Open** 11.30am-2pm, 7-11pm Mon-Fri; 7-11pm Sat. Closed Aug. **Menu** €14.50. **No credit cards.**
The loud rug on the ceiling doesn't distract you from the well-rendered versions of familiar Egyptian and Middle Eastern dishes, including felafel, kefta and chicken kebab. The Oriental cakes are tasty.

Le Peron

56 Corniche J F Kennedy, 7th (04.91.52.15.22). Bus 83. **Open** noon-2.15pm, 8-10.15pm Mon-Sun. **Menus** €43-€57. **Credit** AmEx, MC, V.
One of Marseille's most fashionable addresses, so you'll need to book. The dark-wood decor is sleek and modern, the sea view one of the very best in town and the cooking inventive (such as crisp-skinned hake served with mustard-dressed lentils).

Pizzaria Etienne

43 rue Lorette, 2nd (no phone). M° Vieux-Port. **Open** 7.30-11pm Mon-Sat. **Average** €22. **No credit cards.**
Owner Stéphane Cassaro is a legendary Panier personality. Pizza is considered a starter here and main courses are enormous. Pasta can be disappointingly mushy, so go for meat, or fried squid with garlic.

Une Table au Sud

2 quai du Port, 2nd (04.91.90.63.53). M° Vieux-Port. **Open** noon-2pm, 7.30-10.30pm Tue-Thur; noon-2pm, 7.30pm midnight Fri, Sat. **Menus** €39-€65. **Credit** AmEx, MC, V.
After working for Alain Ducasse, chef Lionel Lévy opened this relaxed, contemporary restaurant and has quickly won a reputation for his modern French cooking. He also holds wine and food evenings featuring top-flight producers.

Toinou Dégustation

3 Cours St-Louis, 1st (04.91.33.14.94 / www.toinou.com). M° Vieux-Port. **Open** 11.30am-2.30pm, 6.30-10.30pm Mon-Thur, Sun; 11.30am-2.30pm, 6.30pm-midnight Fr, Sat. **Menus** €11.80-€41. **Credit** V.
A good choice for raw seafood; the shuckers have won prizes for speed if not necessarily precision. A meal here is fun, festive and fast, and the good-value *plateau du pirate* (€11.80) includes a glass of wine.

Zé

19-20 quai de Rive Neuve, 7th (04 91 55 08 15). M° Vieux-Port. **Open** noon-2pm, 8-11pm daily. **Menu** €28. **Credit** MC, V.
The fusion cooking is respectable at this new-ish, self-consciously designy place located on a buzzing stretch of *quai*. Expect silver-metal and black-and-white minimalism with square lines and cube stools.

Cafés & bars

Le Bar de la Marine
15 quai de Rive Neuve, 7th (04.91.54.95.42). M°
Vieux-Port. **Open** 7am-2am daily. **Credit** AmEx, V.
This quayside bar has a fading, slightly raffish air
and attracts a diverse crowd.

La Boutique du Glacier
1 pl Général de Gaulle, 1st (04.91.33.76.93).
M° Vieux-Port. **Open** 7.45am-7.15pm Mon-Sat,
7.45am-1pm & 3.30-7.15pm Sun. **Credit** MC, V.
With a snappy new wood-and-marble decor, this tea
room thankfully continues to attract nice old dears,
who come for the decadent cakes and ice creams.

Café Parisien
1 pl Sadi Carnot, 2nd (04.90.05.77). M° Colbert or
Vieux-Port. **Open** 6am-9pm Mon-Wed; 6am-1am
Thur-Sat. **Credit** V.
Drinks are quite pricey at this handsome 1901 *belle*
époque café but the atmosphere is stylish. This is
where night people come for breakfast when the
clubs close. Tapas are served in the evening and Le
Papou's Italian cuisine Thur-Sat from 7.30pm.

La Caravelle
34 quai du Port, 2nd (04.91.90.36.64). M° Vieux-
Port. **Open** 7am-2am daily. **Credit** AmEx, MC, V.
Hidden up a flight of stars inside the Hôtel Belle-Vue
(*see p149*), la Caravelle serves breakfast and lunch
but is above all a (pricey) boho cocktail bar. A handful of coveted tables on the narrow balcony offer an
idyllic view of the Vieux Port.

Le Crystal
148 quai du Port, 2nd (04.91.91.57.96). M° Vieux-
Port, bus 83. **Open** *May-Sept* 9am-2am daily. *Oct-Apr*
Mon, Sun 9am-6pm; Tue-Sat 9am-2am. **Credit** MC, V.
This groovy café has 1950s-diner appeal with red
leatherette banquettes and Formica tables, but in
sunny weather the foliaged terrace will lure you outside. Brunch is served at weekends; also a few main
dishes, frozen cocktails (€6.10) and chill-out music.

Les Danaïdes
6 sq Stalingrad, 1st (04 91 62 28 51). M° Réformés-
Canebière. **Open** 7am-9pm Mon-Sat. **Credit** MC, V.
In a tranquil square enclosed by hectic roads, this
'gay friendly' café has a large terrace out front. Busy
at lunch, it offers stress-free drinking in the evening.

M P Bar
10 rue Beauvau, 1st (04.91.33.64.79). M° Vieux-Port.
Open 5pm-dawn nightly. **Credit** MC, V.
Though it's just behind the Vieux Port, don't expect
rum-toting sailors at the bar. The regulars here are
gay-scene Marseillais; midweek it's quiet, the atmosphere always friendly.

O'Cours Jus
67 cours Julien, 6th (04.91.48.48.58). M° Notre-
Dame-du-Mont-Cours-Julien. **Open** 6.30am-7pm Mon-
Sat. Closed Aug, 25 Dec-2 Jan. **No credit cards.**

This is one of the more bohemian cafés along Cours
Julien, and its small terrace attracts a big crowd for
coffee, beer and snacks.

La Part des Anges
33 rue Sainte, 1st (04.91.33.55.70). M° Vieux-Port.
Open 9am-2am Mon-Sat; 9am-1pm, 6pm-2am Sun.
Credit MC, V.
This smart wine bar and shop hunts down wines
from all over France, including undiscovered off-the-
wall growers, and sells many by the glass to a mixed
crowd of oenophiles. Food includes cheese, charcuterie and a few hot dishes.

Plauchut
168 La Canebière, 1st (04.91.48.06.67).
M° Réformés-Canebière. **Open** 7am-8pm Tue-Sun.
Closed July or Aug. **Credit** MC, V.
This celebrated yet down-to-earth pâtisserie and tea
room has an art nouveau interior by Rafaël Ponson,
whose swirls and flourishes rival those of the towering cakes, ice cream and chocolates.

Clubs & music venues

Most venues don't have box offices; tickets are
available from Fnac and ticket agencies.

L'Affranchi
212 bd St-Marcel, 11th (04.91.35.09.19/
www.l-affranchi.com). Buses 40, 15. **Admission** €8.
No credit cards.
L'Affranchi is a showcase for Marseille rap and
reggae. It also occasionally hosts special eventssuch
as a celebration of Algerian music and cinema.

Dock des Suds
12 rue Urbain V, 2nd (04.91.99.00.00/
08.25.83.38.33/www.dock-des-suds.org).
M° National. **Admission** varies.
The 5,000m² dock hosting the Fiesta des Suds each
autumn is now programming music with a world
and salsa bias all year round.

Dôme-Zénith
48 av St-Just, 4th (04.91.12.21.21/www.le-dome.com).
M° St-Just-Hôtel du Département; buses 41, 53, 81 &
Fluobus at night. **Admission** varies.
A big modern venue for international rock acts and
stars of French variété.

Espace Julien
39 cours Julien, 6th (04.91.24.34.10/infoline
04.91.24.34.19/www.espace-julien.com). M° Notre-
Dame-du-Mont-Cours-Julien. **Admission** varies.
This long-standing, very active venue on the boho
'Cours Ju' hosts music ranging from international
pop and blues to local electro; small bands and DJs
play in the Café Julien.

L'Intermédiaire
63 pl Jean Jaurès, 6th (04.91.47.01.25). M° Notre-
Dame-du-Mont-Cours-Julien. **Open** 6.30pm-2am Mon,
Tue; 5.30pm-2am Wed-Sat; 6.30pm-2am first Sun of
mth. **Admission** free. **No credit cards.**

It's always *pastis*-time at the **Bar de la Marine**.

The hippest venue for jazz, blues and rock is crowded but friendly. Concerts at 10.30pm Wed-Sat, jam session Tue and live jazz first Sun of the month.

Le Moulin
47 bd Perrin, 13th (04.91.06.33.94/ www.concertandco.com/lemoulin). Mº St Juste.
Box office 7.30pm on day or through agencies.
Admission €10-€22. **No credit cards**.
This converted cinema has become one of Marseille's main venues for visiting French and international rock, reggae and world music bands.

The New Cancan
3 rue Sénac-de-Meilhan, 1st (04.91.48.59.76). Mº Réformés-Canebière. **Open** 6pm-6am daily; disco from 11pm. **Admission** free Mon-Fri, Sun; 8pm before midnight, €11 after Sat. **Credit** AmEx, MC, V.
Marseille's largest gay club has changed little since the 70s. Stage shows enliven the atmosphere as does the backroom. Friendly, mixed, uninhibited crowd.

Le Trolleybus
24 quai Rive Neuve, 7th (04.91.54.30.45/ www.letrolley.com). Mº Vieux-Port. **Open** 11pm-dawn Wed-Sat. **Admission** free Wed-Fri; €10 Sat.
Credit MC, V.
This sprawling club is the ground zero of Marseille nightlife and was given a facelift in 2003. Different zones offer techno, salsa, funk… and *pétanque*. An equally heterogeneous crowd goes from young bankers to rappers in tracksuits.

Le Vinyl
40 rue Plan Fourmiguier, 7th (04.91.33.04.34). Mº Vieux-Port. **Open** 11pm-dawn Thur-Sun. **Admission** free; €13 after midnight Sat (plus men on Fri). **Credit** AmEx, DC, MC, V.
This club has an underground air and leans towards Afro-Caribbean music.

Shopping

Rue St-Ferréol is lined with shops including **Galeries Lafayette** department store (No 40, 04.96.11.35.00) and fashion chains. Several chic designer places, interspersed with tempting food stores, have also sprung up on rues Francis Davso, Grignan and Paradis. For a quirkier selection, head to Cours Julien or rue Thubaneau. The **Centre Bourse** (04.91.14.00.50) near the Vieux Port is the main shopping centre, with a Fnac store on the second floor. Marseille has some 30 markets, the most famous of which are fresh fish daily on quai des Belges (quai de la Fraternité), Cours Julien (flowers Sat and Wed mornings, organic food Fri morning) and avenue du Prado (every morning, flowers Fri). The flea market (av du Cap Pinède, 15th, bus 35 & 70) is worth a visit, with antiques sold Friday-Sunday.

Ad Hoc Books
8 rue Pisançon, 1st (04.91.33.51.92/ www.adhocbooks.fr). Mº Vieux-Port. **Open** 10am-7pm Mon-Sat. **Credit** MC, V.
English-language bookshop opened in 2001 by Adrian Simmonds, who used to work at Foyles.

Arterra
3 rue du Petit Puits, 2nd (04.91.91.03.31). Mº Colbert or Joliette. **Open** 9am-1pm, 2-6pm Mon-Sat. **Credit** MC, V.
This workshop in Le Panier shows that santons (Christmas crib figures) can be artful, not cloying.

G Bataille
25 pl Notre-Dame-du-Mont, 6th (04.91.47.06.23/ www.g-bataille.com). Mº Notre-Dame-du-Mont-Cours-Julien. **Open** 8am-8pm Mon-Sat. **Credit** MC, V.
This magnificent *traiteur* (deli) is the perfect place to shop for a picnic of delicious cheeses, prepared salads, cold meats, pastries, wines and olive oil.

La Compagnie de Provence
1 rue Caisserie, 2nd (04.91.56.20.94). Mº Vieux-Port. **Open** 10am-1pm, 2-7pm Mon-Sat. **Credit** MC, V.
This is the place to come for cubes of Marseille soap. The classic is non-perfumed olive-oil green, but vanilla, jasmine and honey are also on offer.

Four des Navettes
136 rue Sainte, 7th (04.91.33.32.12). Mº Vieux-Port, bus 55 & 61. **Open** 7am-8pm Mon-Sat; 9am-1pm, 4-7.30pm Sun. **Credit** MC, V.
Founded in 1781, this bakery is famous for its boat-shaped *navettes*, orange-scented biscuits.

Read my lips: Marseille-speak

Feeling confused, stupid and picked upon in Marseille? Don't be alarmed, you are not alone. The sing-song Marseillais patois is an international mystery. Thick, ebullient and constantly reinventing itself, it is an ethnic cross-breed that even other French struggle to comprehend. Phrases bounce up and down like a bobbing ship. Every vowel is pulled out on long elastic, and then twanged back at the end, with a liberal distribution of the sound 'eu' to round off. *Pain* becomes 'Paaaygne,' *mer* becomes 'Maaayreu' and *une fille* is puffed up into 'uuna feeeeyeu.'

The Marseillais mouth is a nimble instrument that makes the most of every syllable, sucking each word dry to the bone, and spitting out letters on the way. *Avec* gets robbed of its c ('*viens avé' moi*') and the usually closed *quand* is ejected from a grimace with a yelping 'Caai?' Even before a Marseillais gets angry, chirpy greetings tend to sound like heavy-duty artillery.

Most complicated of all is the minefield of colloquial phrases and slang that have been layered on top of the original Occitan (Provençal language). This is the voice of a cosmopolitan port: a linguistic recycling depot, evolving daily, that attests to Marseille's immigrant history.

This pungent slang cocktail, made fashionable by groups like IAM and Massilia Sound System, varies from street to street, but can be best heard booming from the bars and fishwives around the Vieux Port and in the northern *quartiers*. Its unofficial spokesperson is the garish *cagole*, seen strutting her stuff down La Canebière.

Gross exaggeration is the key, with limbs joining in to punctuate mere banalities with furious gesturing. For the full gym display, watch the crowds at an OM match at the Stade Vélodrome (preferably versus PSG). Clenched fists and pulling of guns, however, have the same implications as back home.

The Marseillais don't exactly use their famous soap to wash their mouth out. They just say what they think. So here is a useful guide to knowing if you are in the process of making a new friend, or about to get punched.

Aggoun Arabic for deaf and dumb: an insult to anyone incompetent – 'T'i es un aggoun!'
Aller à dache to go far off, which for a Marseillais means a short way up the A7.
Arrête de me crier! stop shouting! – the city's emblematic refrain.

Bombasse a good-looking woman: 'Bombasse atomicasse!' – atomically fit.
Cacou from the Spanish 'caco' (thief) and the Provençal 'cacoua' (youngest) a flashy, extravagant lad who dresses up to get in with the ladies, but rarely succeeds.
Cagole the female equivalent: foul mouthed, intellectually challenged and vulgar, she talks loudly and wears skimpy clothing.
Cafi full, as in a heaving bar, or someone loaded with money – 'cafi de fric.'
Cagadou loo.
Cagnard beating sunlight, heatwave.
T'y as craqué! 'You've gone mental!' A regular reaction to most mild behaviour.
Degun Provençal for no-one – 'Y'a degun ici', means 'there is no-one in here,' often used on storming in and out of a bar.
Dormiasse as in *dormir* (to sleep) – a lazy person who takes all-day siestas.
Esquicher to run over, to squish.
Estoumagade from *estomac* (stomach): a fight or shocking, stomach-turning event.
Estranger foreigner, that is someone who isn't from Marseille, namely you.
Estrasse Provençal for old rag – used to insult someone who lets themselves go, by getting drunk or dressing like a sack.
Fada mad, or an empassioned enthusiast.
Figure de dépression moody-chops: *figure* (face) or *face/facha/tetou* plus any word is a way of describing someone's appearance.
Fille bien tanquée as in 'tank'– a girl well armed with 'tits 'n arse.'
Gadjie, Gadjo Gypsy words for boy and girl.
Gari pronounced 'gaaaaaari': Provençal for rat, but used as in 'mate'. 'Oh gaaaaari, tu manges la pizza!' means 'Oi mate, you're not looking so chipper!'
Mon vié! from the Occitan for penis, here it means a fatalistic 'oh shit!'
O moune! 'Oi mate cooeeee, over'ere!' Or 'love': a favourite with the fishwives.
Payot (otte) originally meaning a non-Gypsy, then a little rich kid, and now the dweeb at the top of the class.
Putayne! the warcry of the disgruntled Marseillais: *Putain*, literally prostitute, here means 'oh shit!' The more 'a's the more shitty.
Stoquefiche stockfish, known for being flat – a skinny or flat-chested woman.
Va te gratter avec un oursin! literally, 'go scratch yourself with a sea urchin!' and here meaning 'f**k off!'

Librairie Internationale Maurel

95 rue de Lodi, 6th (04.91.42.63.44). M° Baille or Castellane, bus 54 & 74. **Open** Mon-Fri 9am-12.15pm, 2-6.45pm; Sat 9am-noon, 3-6pm. **Credit** MC, V.

The jovial eponymous proprietor specialises in English- and Italian-language books but also has Russian, German and Spanish material.

Madame Zaza de Marseille

74 cours Julien, 6th (04.91.48.05.57). M° Notre-Dame-du-Mont-Cours-Julien. **Open** 10am-1pm, 2-7pm Mon-Fri; 10am-7pm Sat. **Credit** AmEx, MC, V.

Fashion and costume jewellery with a baroque yet alternative edge.

La Maison du Pastis

108 quai du Port, 2nd (04.91.90.86.77./ www.lamaisondupastis.com). M° Vieux-Port, bus 83. **Open** *school holidays* 10am-7.30pm daily; *term time* 10am-2pm, 4-7.30pm Tue-Sat. **Credit** MC, V.

This smart little shop specialises in small-production *pastis*, *anisette* and absinthe. It opened l'Heure Verte, the absinthe café next door, in January 2004.

Manon Martin

10 rue de la Tour, 1st (04.91.55.60.95). M° Vieux-Port. **Open** 10am-7pm Mon-Sat. **Credit** AmEx, MC, V.

This short, pedestrianised street behind the Vieux Port has become a focus for local designers, led by flamboyant hat stylist Manon Martin.

Pâtisserie d'Aix

2 rue d'Aix/1 rue Nationale, 1st (04.91.90.12.50). M° Colbert. **Open** 5am-8pm Tue-Sun. **No credit cards.**

This famous Tunisian pastry shop is stacked high with pyramids of honey-drenched delights.

Rive Neuve

30 cours d'Estienne d'Orves, 1st (04.96.11.01.01). M° Vieux-Port. **Open** 10.30am-7.30pm Mon-Sat. **Credit** MC, V.

Indicative of the designer boutiques now colonising Marseille (a huge Agnès b is opposite), Rive Neuve has a cutting-edge selection of men's and women-wear that includes Alberta Ferretti, Paul Smith, Coast, Camarlinghi and shoes by Alain Tondowski.

Where to stay

Auberge de Jeunesse de Marseille Bonneveine

Impasse du Dr Bonfils, 8th (04.91.17.63.30/www.fuaj.net/ homepage/marseille). M° Rond-Pont du Prado then bus 44. Closed mid-Dec to Feb. **Rates** 1st night €13.35; further nights €11.45 per person. **Credit** DC, MC, V.

Just 200m from the sea and very near the Calanques, this comfortable youth hostel is a good bet if you're looking for a holiday in nature.

La Cigale et la Fourmi

19-21 rue Théophile Boudier, Mazargues, 9th (04.91.40.05.12/www.cigale-fourmi.com). M° Rond-Point du Prado then bus 22. **Rates** €19-€25 per person. **No credit cards.**

These boho budget studios are popular with students and backpackers and feel a little different to standard city lodgings. Each will sleep two to four.

Etap Hôtel Vieux Port

46 rue Sainte, 1st (08.92.68.05.82). M° Vieux-Port. **Double** €48.50. **Credit** AmEx, MC, V.

The Cours d'Estienne d'Orves facade of this old arsenal building is gorgeous, even if the rooms of this budget chain hotel feel a bit like prison cells. Still, you can't beat the location or the price.

Hôtel Alizé

35 quai des Belges, 1st (04 91 33 66 97/www.alize-hotel.com). M° Vieux-Port. **Double** €63-€80. **Credit** AmEx, DC, MC, V.

Admire the panorama from one of 16 rooms (of 39) that face the Vieux Port. The other rooms don't have much of a view. All have recently been redecorated in Impressionist-inspired autumnal colours.

Hôtel Belle-Vue

34 quai du Port, 2nd (04 96 17 05 40). M° Vieux-Port. **Double** €99-€122. **Credit** AmEx, MC, V.

This historic hotel above La Caravelle bar has 18 tastefully renovated rooms with immaculate bathrooms. Try to get one facing the port. Pictures by local artists adorn the stairs.

Hôtel Edmond Rostand

31 rue Dragon, 6th (04.91.37.74.95/ www.hoteledmondrostand.com). M° Estrangin-Préfecture. **Double** €49-€54. **Credit** AmEx, DC, MC, V.

This clean, friendly place is reasonable value and has adequate (though not spacious) air-conditioned bedrooms and an airy breakfast room.

Hôtel Hermès

2 rue Bonneterie, 2nd (04.96.11.63.63/ www.hotelmarseille.com). M° Vieux-Port. **Double** €45-€76. **Credit** AmEx, DC, MC, V.

Though its rooms are small, this simple hotel just steps from the Vieux Port is good value. Three rooms on the top floor have small terraces with superb views of the harbour and Notre-Dame de la Garde. There's a roof-top sundeck too.

Hôtel Le Corbusier

280 bd Michelet, 8th (04.91.16.78.00/ www.hotellecorbusier.com). M° Rond-Point du Prado + bus 21 or 22. **Double** €45-€105. **Credit** MC, V.

Fans of modern architecture, or those looking for something unusual, won't want to miss the opportunity to stay in the famous Cité Radieuse. Rooms are basic but the new owners (since July 2003) are touching up the flyworn bathrooms, while keeping the Le Corbusier spirit. Pricier rooms are large and there are two studios with terrace, sea view and original Le Corbusier kitchens (not for use).

Mercure Beauvau Vieux Port

4 rue Beauvau, 1st (04.91.54.91.00/ www.mercure.com). M° Vieux-Port. **Double** €121-205. **Credit** AmEx, DC, MC, V.

Marseille & Aix

This historic hotel, where Chopin and George Sand once stayed, overlooks the Vieux Port. Due to reopen in April 2004 following extensive renovation.

Mercure Prado

11 av de Mazargues, 8th (04.96.20.37.37/ www.mercure.com). Mº Rond-Pont du Prado. **Double** €66-€115. **Credit** AmEx, DC, MC, V.
This new-ish Mercure has post-modern design with furniture by Marc Newson, Ingo Maurer and Philippe Starck. Internet access in rooms on request. A good choice for business travel, yet within walking distance of the beach and Parc Borély.

New Hôtel Bompard

2 rue des Flots-Bleus, 7th (04 91 99 22 22/www.new-hotel.com). Bus 61. **Double** €91-€108. **Credit** AmEx, MC, V.
This neat, walled hotel in a quiet residential area near the Corniche has 46 air-conditioned rooms in the old wing and extension, family apartments with kitchen, and four sumptuous Provençal-style *mas* (€170-€200), plus swimming pool and gardens.

Hôtel Peron

119 Corniche JF Kennedy, 7th (04.91.31.01.41/ www.hotel-peron.com). Bus 83. **Double** €66. **Credit** AmEx, MC, V.
This eccentric, family-run hotel is a study in kitsch – Moroccan, Oriental, Dutch and Breton rooms were decorated in the 60s (it's beginning to show) when it was the first hotel in Marseille to install small yet charming baths. Most have stunning sea views.

Le Petit Nice – Passédat

Anse de Maldormé, Corniche JF Kennedy, 7th (04.91.59.25.92/www.petitnice-passedat.com). Bus 83. **Double** €275-€810. **Credit** AmEx, DC, MC, V.
Sitting on its own little promitory off the Corniche, this luxurious villa, with 13 sumptuous air-conditioned rooms, swimming pool and restaurant, is the address of choice for visiting stars.

Hôtel Résidence du Vieux Port

18 quai du Port, 2nd (04.91.91.91.22/ www.hotelmarseille.com). Mº Vieux-Port. **Double** €115.50-€150. **Credit** AmEx, DC, MC, V.
This 1950s building features antique furniture, balconies (except on the second floor) and unbeatable views from every room across the Vieux Port to Notre-Dame de la Garde. Book well in advance.

Hôtel Le Rhul

269 Corniche Kennedy, 7th (04.91.52.01.77/ www.bouillabaissemarseille.com). Bus 83. **Double** €80. **Credit** AmEx, MC, V.
Though it doesn't have the character of Le Peron, the slightly pricier Rhul has the advantage of a few spacious terraces with jaw-dropping sea views and a restaurant renowned for its *bouillabaisse*.

Sofitel Palm Beach

200 Corniche J.F. Kennedy, 7th (04.91.16.19.00/ www.sofitel.com). Bus 83. **Double** €235-€465. **Credit** AmEx, DC, MC, V.

Re-opened in May 2002, this sleek hotel offers up stunning 260° views of the bay and islands. Open spaces, huge windows, and giant plants join with cutting-edge designs by Starck, Zanotta, Emu and Gervasoni to create a surprisingly warm feel. The salt-water pool is fed by a natural spring.

Getting there

From the airport

Aéroport Marseille-Provence (04.42.14.14.14) is 25km northwest of Marseille near Marignane. 'La Navette' coaches (04.42.14.31.27/04.91.50.59.34) run every 20 mins 6.10am-10.50pm to Gare St-Charles; and from the station to the airport 5.30am-9.50pm. The trip takes about 25 mins and costs €8.50. A taxi to the Vieux Port costs around €40.

By car

Marseille is served by three motorways. The A7-A51 heads north to the airport, Aix and Lyon; A55 runs west to Martigues; and A50 runs east to Toulon. The Prado-Carénage toll tunnel links the A55 to A50.

By train

The main station is the Gare St-Charles on the TGV line, with frequent trains from Paris, the main coast route east to Nice and Italy, and west via Miramas and Arles. Branch lines run to Miramas via Martigues and the Côte Bleue, and to Aix and Gap. In the station **SOS Voyageurs** (04.91.62.12.80, open 9am-7pm Mon-Sat) helps with children, the elderly and lost luggage.

By bus

The **Gare Routière** is by the station on on pl Victor Hugo, 3rd (04.91.08.16.40, Mº St-Charles). **Cartreize** (08.00.19.94.13, www.lepilote.com) is the umbrella organisation for all coach services in the Bouches-du-Rhône. **Eurolines** (04.91.50.57.55, www.eurolines.fr) operates coaches between Marseille and Avignon, Nice via Aix-en-Provence and daily coaches to Venice, Milan and Rome, Barcelona and Valencia.

By boat

SNCM (61 bd des Dames, 2nd, Mº Joliette) is the primary passenger line from the Gare Maritime de la Joliette; call 08.91.70.18.01 for Sardinia, Corsica or Italy; 08.91.70.28.02 for Algeria, Tunisia or Morocco.

Getting around

By bus & Métro

RTM (Espace Infos, 6 rue des Fabres, 1st (04.91.91.92.10/www.rtm.fr); open 7am-6pm Mon-Fri, 9am-5.30pm Sat) runs a comprehensive network of over 80 bus routes, two Métro lines (5am-9pm Mon-Thur; 5am-12.30am Fri-Sun & OM match nights) and a tram (closed in 2004 for extension work). The same tickets are used on all three and can be bought in Métro stations, on the bus (singles only) and at tabacs and newsagents displaying the RTM sign. A single ticket costs €1.50 and entitles the user to one hour's travel. The Carte Libertés (€7.50 or €15.25) offers 5 or 11 journeys depending on the price you pay, each also lasting up to an hour. For unlimited travel, a one-day

Martigues: the Venice of Marseille. Really.

ticket is €4, weekly pass €10 and monthly €40. At night, a network of Fluobuses run between the Canebière (Bourse) and outer districts.

By taxi
There are cab ranks on most main squares or call: **Marseille Taxi** (04.91.02.20.20), **Taxi Blanc Bleu** (04.91.51.50.00), **Taxi Plus** (04.91.03.60.03), **Taxi Radio Tupp** (04.91.05.80.80)). Pick-up fare is €1.70, then €1.24/km in the day, €1.64/km at night.

Resources

Hospital
Hôpital de la Conception *147 bd Baille, 5th (04.91.38.30.00). M° Baille.*
Hôpital Militaire Lavéran *34 bd Lavéran, 13th (04.91.61.70.00/www.hia-laveran.fr). M° Malpassé then bus 38.*

Internet
Escaliq Cyber Café *3 rue Coutellerie, 2nd (04.91.91.65.10/www.escaliq.net). M° Vieux-Port.* **Open** 11am-8.30pm Mon-Fri; 4-8.30pm Sat, Sun.
Info-Café *1 quai Rive Neuve, 1st (04.91.33.74.98/ www.info-cafe.com). M° Vieux-Port.* **Open** 9am-10pm, 2.30-7.30pm Sun.

Police
28 rue Nationale, 1th (04.91.14.29.50). M° St-Charles.

Post office
Hôtel des Postes, rue Henri Barbusse, 1st (04.91.15.47.00). M° Colbert or Vieux-Port.

Tourist information
Office du Tourisme, 4 La Canebière, 1st (04.91.13.89.00/www.marseille-tourisme.com). M° Vieux-Port. **Open** 9am-7pm Mon-Sat, 10am-5pm Sun. **Branch:** Gare St-Charles, 1st (04.91.50.59.18). **Open** June-Aug 11am-6pm Mon-Sat; Sept-May 10am-1pm, 1.30-5pm Mon-Fri.
A City Pass (€16 one day, €23 two days) offers free access to museums, Château d'If, tourist trains, guided tours and public transport.

Around Marseille

Martigues & the Côte Bleue

Beyond L'Estaque towards Carro is the relatively neglected Côte Bleue, much loved by Marseillais at weekends with its sheer cliffs, small fishing ports and rocky beaches. For once this is an area as easy to reach by train as by car – while the D5 meanders between inlets and over the red hills of the Chaine de l'Estaque, a landscape prone to fires in summer, the railway chugs scenically over a series of viaducts along the coast (the *découverte* day ticket allows as many stops as you like). Tiny coves like Niolon and La Madrague-de-Gignac give stunning views of the Marseille cityscape across the bay. The main resorts are **Sausset-les-Pins**, very popular with families, and **Carry-le-Rouet,** with its crowded beach. At **Carro** there is a picturesque fishing port and is a favourite with windsurfers. It's worth making a stop too at **La Redonne**'s peaceful little harbour.

Inland, **Martigues** is a pretty, though traffic-cluttered, old town of pastel houses built alongside canals, on the edge of the heavily industrialised (and polluted) Etang de Berre; a lagoon that is surrounded by one of the largest petrochemical and oil refining complexes in Europe. The railway station is some way out towards Lavera, which means a rather long walk along main roads or waiting for an infrequent bus. An alternative is to take the coach from Marseille or Aix to the bus station (pl des Aires) in the centre. The town is the result of a merging of three villages in 1581: Jonquières, Ferrières and L'Ile Brescon, linked by a series of bridges reminiscent of Amsterdam or Venice. In Jonquières, the main sight is the bijou and wildly colourful Baroque **Chapelle de l'Annonciade**, built 1664-71, which adjoins the church of St-Geniès. From here follow the road down to place Gérard Tenque and stroll around the many relaxed shops and cafés. On the Ile, the **Eglise de la Madeleine** is another fine Baroque edifice with ornately carved façade. Over in Ferrières, the modern **Théâtre des Salins** contrasts starkly with colour-washed fishermen's cottages. The **Musée Ziem** is a pleasant surprise containing works by Félix Ziem, Manguin, Loubon and Dufy, as well as the statue of St-Pierre, patron saint of fishermen, which is paraded from here to the port for the Fête de St-Pierre every June. The historic **Eglise St-Louis d'Anjou** on nearby rue Colonel Denfert was the site of the signing of the 1581 act of union between Provence and France.

Musée Ziem

bd du 14 Juillet (04.42.41.39.60). **Open** *July-Aug* 10am-noon, 2.30-6.30pm Mon, Wed-Sun. *Sept-June* 2.30-6.30pm Wed-Sun. **Admission** free.

Where to eat & stay

In Sausset-les-Pins locals delight in the imaginative cooking at **Les Girelles** (rue Frédéric Mistral, 04.42.45.26.16, closed Mon & Tue lunch in July & Aug, all Wed & dinner Sun Sept-June, and Jan; menus €28-38), which holds jazz evenings in summer. The harbour is lined with diverse restaurants and cafés – and boat hire shops – all in hot competition. In Carro friendly, family-oriented **Le Chalut** (port de Carro, 04.42.80.70.61, closed dinner Mon & all Tue, menus €15-€25) specialises in fish and shellfish. The **Auberge de la Calanque** (port de la Redonne, 04.42.45.95.01) does appetising pizzas (€9-€12.50). In Martigues, try the

flavoursome roast guinea fowl or delicate fish kebabs at **Le Miroir** (4 rue Marcel Galdy, 04.42.80.50.45, closed Mon, lunch Sat, dinner Sun & all Sun July-Aug, one wk Nov, 2wks Dec, two wks Easter; menus €14.50-€30). The **Hôtel Cigalon** (37 bd du 14 Juillet, 04.42.80.49.16 www.lecigalon.fr, double €34-€55, menus €11-€33) is a simple, cheerfully painted hotel.

Resources

Tourist information

Martigues *Maison du Tourisme, Rond-point de l'Hôtel de Ville, 13500 Martigues (04.42.42.31.10 www.ville-martigues.fr).* **Open** 9am-7pm Mon-Sat; 10am-1pm, 3-6pm Sun & public holidays.

Aubagne

Aubagne, 17km east of Marseille, is an active commercial centre. Its *vieille ville* is pleasant, dotted with tree-lined squares and a market on Tuesday and Sunday. Writer and filmmaker Marcel Pagnol was born here, and the shop facades and houses have retained (or have rather brazenly recreated) a nostalgic feel. You can visit the **Maison Natale de Marcel Pagnol** where he was born in 1895 and spent his first 18 months. The tourist office also runs a 9km hiking tour in French (from €30.50), or can provide directions for the Circuit Pagnol.

Aubagne is known for its ceramics industry, with a dozen santon workshops and the biennial Argilla fair and pottery market (next in August 2005). Aubagne's other claim to fame is as the home of the French Foreign Legion.

Maison Natale de Marcel Pagnol

16 cours Barthélémy (04.42.03.49.98). **Open** 9am-12.30pm, 2.30-6pm daily. **Admission** €3; €1.50 5-12s; free under 5s. **No credit cards.**

Musée de la Légion Etrangère

rte de la Thuilière, west of Aubagne on D44 (04.42.18.82.41). **Open** *June-Sept* 10am-noon, 3-7pm Tue-Thur, Sat, Sun; *Oct-May* 10am-noon, 2-6pm Wed, Sat, Sun. **Admission** free.

Where to eat

La Farandole (6 rue Martinot, 04.42.03.26.36, closed dinner Mon and two wks in Feb, menus €11-€22.50) serves typical Provençal cooking and is well located for quiet dining outdoors.

Resources

Tourist information

Office de Tourisme du Pays d'Aubagne, av Antide Boyer, 13400 Aubagne (04.42.03.49.98/ www.aubagne.com). **Open** 9am-noon, 2-6pm Mon-Sat.

Cassis, the Calanques & La Ciotat

The Calanques, the Mediterranean equivalent of fjords and lochs, offer stunning natural beauty and cute little fishing ports.

The Calanques

These spectacular gashes in the limestone cliffs between Marseille and Cassis were formed during the Ice Age when the deep valleys flooded as the sea level rose, leaving cavernous inlets and strange rock formations. The Calanques forge the rugged seaboard of a 5,000-hectare national reserve, where bushes, rare flowers, ferns and occasional trees cling to dry rocks, lined with trails to explore underwater, up cliffs and across mountain passes. Eagles and falcons share the skies with seagulls, and cliff colonies of puffins and stormy petrels.

The Calanques closest to Marseille are flatter and wider than those towards Cassis. The most well-known (and most visited in summer) are

Morgiou's tiny port.

Sormiou and **Morgiou**, which are dotted with *cabanons*: run-down, century-old holiday huts, built from recycled driftwood and scrap and so cherished by Marseille families that they are passed from generation to generation, and are now listed buildings. There is no electricity on either Calanque and only one telephone booth on Sormiou for emergencies. The setting is, however, perfect for lazy swims, diving or climbing. From the Cassis side, only the first Calanque, **Port-Miou**, is fully accessible by car. Boats sail to the other inlets. The best rock-climbing is up the 'finger of God' rock spur in **En-Vau**, which has a secluded beach, or, for hardened professionals, the cliffs of **Devenson**.

Human presence in the Calanques goes back into prehistory. In 1991, Henri Cosquer, a diver from Cassis, swam into a narrow tunnel 37m below sea level between Sormiou and Morgiou, emerging into a huge grotto. On the walls, he found the oldest-known cave paintings – bison, horses, handprints and penguins over 27,000 years old. The cave was sealed up, but Cosquer still accompanies divers into less artistic grottos on his boat *Cro-Magnon, see below*.

Activities

Diving & watersports

The Calanques offer some of the best diving in France. Maestro Henri Cosquer at **Cassis Services Plongée** (3 rue Michel Arnaud, Cassis, 04.42.01.89.16, www.cassis-services-plongee.fr, closed mid-Nov to mid-Mar) organises daily dives, weather permitting.

Walking & rock-climbing

For ecologically-minded guided nature walks, rock-climbing lessons, diving and kayaking, contact **Naturoscope** (3 impasse du Meunier, Marseille 9th, 04.91.40.20.11) or to climb, cave or scramble over (and under) the cliffs **Massilia Sport Adventure** (06.12.39.59.59, www.massilia-adventure.com).

Where to stay & eat

A meal at the spectacularly located **Le Lunch** in Sormiou (04.91.25.05.37, closed Oct to mid-Mar, average €35) is as close as you're likely to get to the local lifestyle. *Bouillabaisse* has to be ordered in advance; otherwise, opt for excellent grilled fish and a bottle of Cassis white. **Le Nautic** (04.91.40.06.37, closed Mon, dinner Sun, & Jan-Feb, menus €23-€34.50) is a decent bar-restaurant on the port at Morgiou. In Callelongue, **La Grotte** (1 av des Pebrons, 04.91.73.17.79, average €35) serves pizzas and grilled fish, but service is slow at weekends. The only place to stay in the Calanques is **La Fontasse** hostel (04.42.01.02.72, closed Jan to mid-Mar, dormitory €10 for YHA members) an hour's walk from Cassis; bring food and drinking water.

Getting there

By boat

From Marseille, boats leave from quai des Belges on the Vieux Port (GACM 04.91.55.50.09, www.answeb.net/gacm) at 2pm daily July & Aug and Wed, Sat & Sun the rest of the year. A round trip to Cassis, taking in the Marseilleveyre, calanques and islands with commentary, costs €25 and lasts about four hours (a stop-off is possible at the Iles du Frioul). From Cassis, regular boats (04.42.01.90.83, €11; €6.50 2-10s) leave 9.30am-5.30pm (10.30am in winter) from the eastern end of the port for the Circuit des trois Calanques and at set times for further afield. You can be dropped off or picked up at En-Vau or Morgiou. In July and August, there is a Spectacle Son et Lumière boat trip that leaves nightly at 10.30pm (€10).

By car

The single-track fire-roads to Sormiou and Morgiou are closed Easter-15 Sept, 7am-8pm, but cars are let in for those with lunch reservations.

By bus

Marseille bus 19 from Prado or Castellane runs to La Madrague de Montredon to reach the Calanques by footpath GR98; buses 21 and 21s go to the Université de Luminy for footpath 6a (*see below*), buses 22 and 23 from Prado to Beauvallon or Les Beaumettes lead to Sormiou and Morgiou.

Calanques walk Luminy to Sugiton

For hiking in the Calanques, IGN map 3615 is a must. The *grande randonnée* GR98, the 'balcony of the Mediterranean', twists high above the sea, stretching for 28km from La Madrague de Montredon in Marseille to Cassis (around a 12-hour hike). You can also reach the Calanques by pleasant shorter walks from Université de Luminy or Les Baumettes in the south-east of Marseille.

The fire risk here is enormous: there are no refuges in the national park, no tents nor campfires allowed at any time, although hikers can pitch sleeping bags under the stars from October to May. Be sure to bring food and water if you're exploring the interior. The GR98 remains open all year, but smaller inland paths are closed from mid-June to mid-September.

The walk From the terminus of bus 21 at Luminy, take the path straight up, following the sign for Sugiton Massif des Calanques Marseille – Cassis. This obvious trail ascends through a dry forested area twitching with crickets and leads to a crossroads. The route to the left, signposted Mont Puget – Gardiole,

is a fairly serious uphill climb, eventually ending up in the same place via a difficult descent down a gorge. To the right, the Belvedere is a picturesque vantage point reached by a gentle ascent. Sugiton and Candelle are to be found straight towards the sea by means of the path marked in yellow and green. The easier but longer way is by bearing off on the right fork, which heads down and around and turns back on itself. If you're feeling fit, climb directly down the rougher shortcut through shrubs and over rocks (ironically, it's perhaps easier to clamber back up this way on the return).

Both routes come out on to a civilised, if not exactly pretty, concrete path that winds its way down to another track, marked by red and white flashes. 'Red' is the tougher one, stemming from the Puget route already mentioned; the 'white' path, still quite steep and rocky, leads down to a couple of cute little coves below the Calanque de Sugiton sign. Reward yourself with a swim and a picnic (if you brought one). This walk is completed within a leisurely hour.

Cassis

A quiet fishing village out of season, awash with muscle boys and sun-worshippers in summer, Cassis (pronounce the last 's') is best known for its delicate white wines and dazzling calanques. The colourful, café-lined port attracted early 20th-century artists including Dufy, Matisse and Vlaminck, though sadly none of their works have made it into the **Musée Municipal**, a meagre display of town history and bad southern art. Cassis offers two beaches – the Plage de la Grande Mer on the sea side of the breakwater and Plage du Bestouan in a sheltered bay west of the port.

Cassis wines can best be tasted at **La Ferme Blanche** (rte de Marseille, 04.42.01.00.74), the oldest AOC Cru Classé, or **Le Clos Ste-Magdeleine** (av du Revestel, 04.42.01.70.28, closed Sat, Sun), whose vines thrive on the sunny slopes of Cap Canaille, the highest coastal cliff (416m) in Europe. The route des Cretes (D141) climbs with panoramic views across Cap Canaille to La Ciotat.

Musée Municipal Méditerranéen d'Arts et Traditions de Cassis

rue Xavier d'Authier (04.42.01.88.66). **Open** *Apr-Oct* 10.30am-12.30pm, 3.30-6.30pm Wed-Sat. *Nov-Mar* 10.30am-12.30pm, 2.30-5.30pm Wed-Sat. **Admission** free.

Where to stay & eat

The pink **Hôtel-Restaurant Le Jardin d'Emile** (23 av Amiral Ganteaume, 04.42.01.80.55, www.lejardindemile.fr, closed mid-Nov to mid-Dec, double €80-€130, restaurant closed Wed, menu €24-€34) stands in a tropical garden against the old city walls and serves the best Provençal cuisine in town. Winston Churchill learned to paint while staying at **Les Roches Blanches** (rte des Calanques, 04.42.01.09.30, www.roches-blanches-cassis.com, closed Nov-Mar except Christmas, double €110-€175, restaurant dinner only except July & Aug, menu €36) with its view of Cassis port and Cap Canaille. On the port, pleasant **Hôtel du Golfe** (3 pl Grand Carnot, 04.42.01.00.21, closed Nov-Mar, double €58-€89) has a brasserie that serves lunch, apéritifs and ice creams morning to night. Fish shop **La Poissonnerie Laurent** (6 quai Barthélémy, 04.42.01.71.56, closed Mon, lunch Thur & Jan, winter lunch daily, menu €20) was opened 65 years ago by Laurent Cinque and his wife Marie, now 85. She joins her grandson Laurent at their restaurant, where the morning's catch lies on icy counters. Order fig pie with lavender ice cream, then thyme liqueur.

Tomatoes ripe for the tasting in **Cassis** market.

Marseille & Aix

Resources

Market is on Wednesday and Friday mornings.

Tourist information

Office du Tourisme, quai des Moulins, 13260 Cassis (04.42.01.71.17/www.cassis.fr). **Open** *Mar-May, Oct* 9.30am-12.30pm, 2-6pm Mon-Fri; 10am-noon, 2-6pm Sat; 10am-noon Sun. *June-Sept* 9am-12.30pm, 2-7pm Mon-Fri; 9am-12.30pm, 3-6pm Sat, Sun. *Nov-Feb* 9.30am-12.30pm, 2-5pm Mon-Fri; 10am-noon, 2-5pm Sat; 10am-noon Sun.

La Ciotat & St-Cyr-sur-Mer

When the Krupp dockyard closed in 1989, 10,000 people in a town of 30,000 lost their jobs. 15 years later, mourning is decreed over, and the town is coming alive thanks to a new generation of industrious citizens. The graffitied dockyard factories are growing chic: 18 yacht maintenance companies have moved in and the Yacht Club (*see p156*) has opened as a giant entertainment complex. From the port, ferries peddle trips to the Calanques and the **Musée Ciotaden** presents the town's maritime history.

Since the mid-19th century, La Ciotat has doubled as a genteel summer residence. Among its illustrious visitors were Auguste and Louis Lumière who made the world's first film. It showed the Toulon-Marseille train pulling into La Ciotat station and thrilled the Parisians invited to the first Champagne projection in September 1895 at the Eden Théâtre, which still stands on the seafront boulevard Anatole France. The **Espace Lumière** continues the theme with photos, posters and a film archive.

Sandy white beaches curve around the Baie de la Ciotat to **St-Cyr-sur-Mer**, which boasts café life and a market on Sunday under a gilded replica of the *Statue of Liberty*, donated by sculptor Bartholdi. Its seaward extension **Les Lecques** is a wild clutter of shops and eateries and the promenade is family-friendly. Les Lecques claims to have been the Greek trading post of Taureontum, and to prove it, the **Musée de Taureontum** displays Greek and Roman artefacts. Past the museum, a 9km footpath (waymarked in yellow) clings to the coast through old pines and oaks to La Madrague (2hrs to Port d'Alon) and Bandol (3hrs 30min).

Espace Lumière

20 rue Maréchal Foch, La Ciotat (04.42.08.94.56). **Open** *July-Sept* 10am-noon, 4-7pm. *Oct-June* 3-6pm Tue-Sat. **Admission** free.

Musée Ciotaden

Ancien Hôtel de Ville, 1 quai Ganteaume, La Ciotat (04.42.71.40.99). **Open** *June-Sept* 4-7pm Mon, Wed-Sat. *Oct-May* 3-6pm Mon, Wed-Sat. **Admission** €3.20; €1.60 12-18s, students; free under-12s. **No credit cards.**

Musée de Taureontum

131 rte de La Madrague, St-Cyr-sur-Mer (04.94.26.30.46). **Open** *June-Sept* 3-7pm Mon, Wed-Sun. *Oct-May* 2-5pm Sat, Sun. **Admission** €3; €1 12-18s, students; free under-7s. **No credit cards.**

Where to stay, eat & drink

Las Vegas in La Ciotat? Why not ? At the **Yacht Club La Ciotat** (quai Port Vieux, 04.42.08.14.14, www.yclc.com, menus €26-€50), a giant entertainment complex with panoramic port views, boasts a restaurant serving fusion food, concerts at weekends, dancing, movies, comedy reviews and speed-dating soirées. For a more traditional lasagne, ravioli and the freshest seafood, head to **La Mamma** (Vieux Port, 04.42.08.30.08, closed Oct to mid-Nov and 2wks Feb, average €35). For wild beauty, the rustic bungalows and restaurant of **Chez Tania** (04.42.08.41.71, www.figuerolles.com, double €37-€128, menus €19-€53) lie in the nature reserve of the Calanque de Figuerolles.

Grand Hôtel des Lecques (24av du Port, 04.94.26.23.01, www.grandhotelsaintcyr.com, closed Nov to mid-Mar, double €69-€189, menus €26-€60) has old-world charm, an exotic garden, plus a pool and a slightly boring

restaurant. **Hôtel Petit Nice** (11 allée du Dr Seillon, 04.94.32.00.64, www.hotelpetitnice.com, closed Jan, double €47-€59) has a shady pool near the beach. For sports enthusiasts, **Hôtel-Golf Dolce Frégate** (04.94.29.39.39, www.dolce.com/fregate, rte de Bandol, St-Cyr-sur-Mer, double €175-€285) has an 18-hole course within the Domaine de Frégate vineyards (golf fees €48-€60) and two restaurants **Mas des Vignes** (04.94.29.39.39, menus €29-€47) and **La Restanque** (menu €26.50). On the coast path past La Madrague to Bandol (or by car D559, C6), beach restaurant **Calanque Port d'Alon** (04.94.26.20.08, closed dinner in Apr & Oct and all Nov-Jan; menus €27-€39) grills fish on an open fire. **Riviera del Fiori** on the new port of Les Lecques (04.94.32.18.20, closed dinner Tue, all Wed & Feb, menus €12.50-€23) grills fish hand-caught by divers and simmers the local catch of rock fish in its *bouillabaisse* (best to reserve).

Resources

La Ciotat has markets on Tuesday on place du Marché, Sunday on the port, and a farmers' market on Friday afternoon. Les Lecques' farmers' market is Wednesday and Saturday mornings in summer, with a market at St-Cyr on Sunday morning.

Tourist information

La Ciotat *Office de Tourisme, bd Anatole France, 13600 La Ciotat (04.42.08.61.32/ www.laciotatourisme.com).* **Open** *June-Sept* 9am-8pm Mon-Sat; 10am-1pm Sun. *Oct-May* 9am-noon, 2-6pm Mon-Sat.
Les Lecques *Office de Tourisme, pl de l'Appel du 18 Juin, 83270 Les Lecques (04.94.26.73.73/ www.saintcyrsurmer.com).* **Open** *July, Aug, Dec* 9am-7pm Mon-Sat; 10am-1pm, 4-7pm Sun. *Sept-Nov, Jan-June* 9am-6pm Mon-Fri; 9am-noon, 2-6pm Sat.

Getting there & around

By car

Leave the A50 from Marseille at exit 8 for Cassis, 9 and 10 for La Ciotat and St-Cyr. The D559 Marseille to Cassis is dramatically scenic, continuing along the coast via Les Lecques to Toulon. The D141 route des Crêtes climbs from Cassis to La Ciotat.

By train

Hourly trains between Marseille and Toulon stop at Cassis, La Ciotat and St-Cyr but stations are each about 3km from the centre.

By bus

Cartreize (04.42.08.41.05) runs buses between Aix-en-Provence, Marseille, Cassis and La Ciotat stations and La Ciotat to Les Lecques. **Transport St-Cyr Tourisme** (04.94.26.23.71) runs from St-Cyr station to Les Lecques and La Madrague.

Aix-en-Provence

Elegant and intellectual, Aix has been a restful place to take the waters since Roman times.

Rich with stately mansions, leafy streets lined with cafés, bustling markets and bubbling fountains, Aix serves as a contrast to its rougher southern rival Marseille. Aix's origins go back to Roman times. Aquae Sextiae was founded in 122 BC by Roman consul Sextius after he had defeated the Celto-Ligurian Oppidium at Entremont, the remains of which lie outside the city (see p162). Aix declined with the Roman empire but remained important enough to have a cathedral in the fifth century.

In the 12th and 13th centuries, the independent Counts of Provence held court in Aix, but it was in the 15th century that the city saw a true resurgence. In 1409, the university was founded by Louis II of Anjou, and under Good King René (1409-80), poet and patron of the arts, the city flourished and the court drew artists such as Nicolas Froment and Barthélémy van Eyck. After its absorption into France in 1486, Aix became the capital of the Parlement de Provence – the southern arm of a centralised administration. The city boomed again in the 1600s, when the newly prosperous political and merchant class began building elegant townhouses in a new district, the Quartier Mazarin, south of the vielle ville. This virtually doubled the city's size. A ring of boulevards, the cours, replaced the ramparts. Aix elected the radical, and hypnotically ugly, Comte de Mirabeau as député to the Etats généraux in 1789. A brilliant orator, he played an important role in the early days of the Revolution.

In the 19th century, Aix was bypassed by the main railway line and lost out to Marseille, but remained an important university and legal city with the creation of arts and law faculties and the new Palais de Justice.

Aix has expanded rapidly in the past 20 years, as new housing, business and university districts swallowed up rural villages and the grandiose agricultural bastides built by the nobility outside the city. Aix is home to a hi-tech industry pole that rivals Sophia Antipolis, numerous research institutes and France's biggest appeals court outside Paris.

Despite a reputation as the haughty bastion of the bourgeoisie, and its highbrow Festival International d'Art Lyrique every summer, Aix is a surprisingly young city, with some 40,000 students and a thriving café society.

Sightseeing

Vieil Aix

At the heart of the city – both physical and psychological – is the **Cours Mirabeau**, a broad avenue lined with plane trees and elegant stone houses. Although several of these are now banks or chain restaurants, the cours Mirabeau remains every bit as important for its place in café society as the boulevard St-Germain does in Paris. At one end is place Charles de Gaulle, better known as La Rotonde, marked by an elaborate 19th-century fountain in black and white marble, with lions at the base and figures of Justice, Agriculture and Fine Art on the top.

North of cours Mirabeau lies Vieil Aix, the oldest part of the city, a remarkably well-preserved maze where elegant squares and smart mansions alternate with more secretive, winding *ruelles*. Fountains splash in almost every square, statues peer out of niches on street corners and the whole place is buzzing with small bistros, cafés and shops.

Parallel to cours Mirabeau runs rue Espariat, where the early-18th-century Baroque church of **St-Esprit** and the belfry of a former Augustinian monastery nestle amid cafés and shops. Continue along rue Espariat into rue Fabrot, home to smart designer boutiques, via the glorious, cobbled place d'Albertas, a U-shape of classical façades with Corinthian pilasters, built in 1745 as a speculative venture by the powerful Albertas family. Almost opposite is the elegant 1672 Hôtel Boyer d'Eguilles, now part pharmacy, part school and part **Muséum d'Histoire Naturelle**.

Busy shopping streets rue Aude and rue Maréchal Foch lead to place Richelme, which comes alive every morning with a fruit and vegetable market under the plane trees. The door of the late-17th-century Hôtel Arbaud (7 rue Maréchal Foch) is framed by two muscular male slaves. In beautiful place de l'Hôtel de Ville, the Gothic belfry with astrological clock and rotating figures of the seasons mark a former town gateway. The grandiose **Hôtel de Ville** was the historic Provençal assembly. Even the post office next door occupies a magnificent 18th-century former grain market, whose pediment, an allegory of the Durance and Rhône rivers by Chastel, is given a wonderful spark of life by a leg dangling lasciviously out of the frame.

Running north from Hôtel de Ville, rue Gaston de Saporta contains some of Aix's finest *hôtels particuliers*: Hôtel Etienne de St-Jean (No.17) contains the **Musée du Vieil Aix**; Hôtel de Châteaurenard (No.19), where Louis XIV stayed in 1660, has a staircase painted with trompe l'oeil by Daret (it now houses the city's social services, but you can visit the entrance hall); Hôtel Maynier d'Oppédé (No.23), with a fine 1757 facade, belongs to the university. The street leads into the historic core of the university with the former law faculty, now the Institut des Etudes Politiques. Opposite is the composite structure of the **Cathédrale St-Sauveur**, with its sculpted portals and fortified towers. Next door, the Baroque Palais de l'Archevêché

contains the **Musée des Tapisseries** (tapestries) and hosts courtyard productions during the Festival International d'Art Lyrique.

West of the town hall, place des Cardeurs is lined with ethnic restaurants. Underground car park aside, it looks as ancient as any of the other squares but in fact was created only in the 1960s, when an area of slums, historically the Jewish quarter, was demolished. From here, narrow streets lead to the **Thermes Sextius** (thermal baths), some fragments of medieval city wall on rue des Etuves, as well as the last surviving tower on boulevard Jean Jaurès. Just west of the baths, the **Pavillon Vendôme** still stands in its formal gardens.

South-east of the town hall, the colonnaded mass of the Palais de Justice was built in the 1820s on the site of the former Comtal palace.

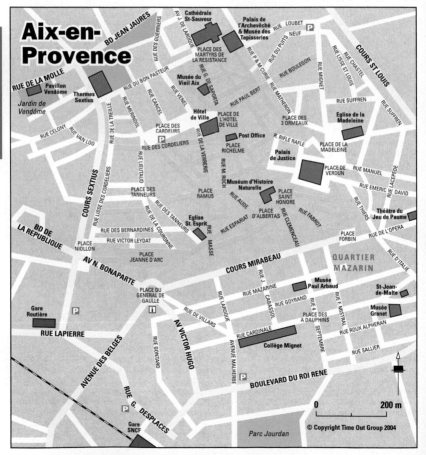

Aix-en-Provence

0   200 m

© Copyright Time Out Group 2004

Marseille & Aix

In front, place de Verdun (also reached from Cours Mirabeau by the covered passage Agard) fills with bric-a-brac and book stalls on Tuesday, Thursday and Saturday mornings. Its continuation, place des Prêcheurs and place de la Madeleine, resound to the city's main food market on the same days, with a flower market on other days, in the shadow of the neo-classical-fronted **Eglise de la Madeleine**. Further east from the Palais de Justice lies the Villeneuve quartier, which replaced the royal gardens in the late 16th century. Several ornate *hôtels particuliers* remain on rue Emeric David and rue de l'Opéra: Cézanne was born at No.25; at No.17 is the Jeu du Paume, a real tennis court built in 1660 and transformed into the **Théâtre du Jeu de Paume** a century later.

Cathédrale St-Sauveur

pl de l'Université (04.42.23.45.65). **Open** 7.30am-noon, 2-6pm Mon-Sat; 9am-noon, 2-6pm Sun (closed during services). *cloister* 9.30am-noon, 2-6pm Mon-Sat. **Admission** free.

Aix cathedral is a hotchpotch of Romanesque, Gothic, Renaissance and Baroque, reflecting its long on-off construction from the fifth to 18th centuries, with a semi-fortified exterior and rather damaged Gothic central door. At first sight the interior looks unremarkable, with three curiously linked naves, Gothic vaults and classical domes. But it has two jewels. The first is off the right-hand nave: a polygonal, fifth-century Merovingian baptistry, with crisply carved capitals and traces of frescoes (the hole in the ground is a throwback to the days of total immersion baptism). Further along to the right is a cloister, with paired capitals carved with mysterious beasts and foliage. In the central nave is the second treasure. Nicolas Froment's symbolically loaded 15th-century triptych of *Mary in the Burning Bush*, with King René and Queen Jeanne praying in the wings. At the end of the left nave, the 17th-century Corpus Domini chapel has a fine wrought-iron grille and a painting by Jean Daret.

Cours Mirabeau

Dubbed the 'Champs-Elysées of the south', stately, tree-lined cours Mirabeau was laid out in 1649 as a broad carriageway on the trace of the old ramparts, becoming the frontier between the old town of the Counts of Provence and the brand new Quartier Mazarin. Soon it became the favoured spot for local nobility to construct their mansions, notably Nos.20 and 38 on the southern side, where there was space to have a showoff facade on the street side and extensive gardens on the other. Cours Mirabeau is still the place to see and be seen today, whether you opt to promenade or simply sit and observe from a café table. In warmer months, street musicians stroll up and down, serenading diners and passers-by. The wide avenue contains mostly cafés down the sunny side (odd numbers), and banks and businesses in the shade (even). At No.53, the legendary

Deux Garçons (*see p165*) still plays out its role as artistic and intellectual meeting place. There are three fountains on the cours: the Fontaine des neuf canons, the Fontaine d'eau chaude, a mossy lump bubbling out water at 34°C, and the Fontaine du Roi René, with a statue by David d'Angers of the wine-loving king holding a bunch of grapes.

Eglise de la Madeleine

pl des Prêcheurs. **Open** 8-11.30am, 3-5.30pm daily. **Admission** free.

This former Dominican convent was rebuilt in the 1690s in the Baroque style. A neo-classical facade, busy with swags and garlands, was added in the 19th century. Inside there are several Baroque altarpieces by Carlos Van Loo and an *Annunciation* (1444) with plunging Gothic architectural perspective, attributed to Flemish painter Barthélemy Van Eyck. The church is used for classical concerts.

Hôtel de Ville

pl de l'Hôtel de Ville (04.42.91.90.00). **Open** Salle des Etats de Provence 10am-noon, 3-4.30pm Mon-Fri. **Admission** free.

The town hall was built in 1655-78 by Pierre Pavillon. A wrought-iron gateway leads into an elegant cobbled courtyard. At the back, a double stairway leads up to the Salle des Etats de Provence, the regional assembly room where taxes were voted. It is hung with portraits and mythological subjects.

Muséum d'Histoire Naturelle

6 rue Espariat (04.42.27.91.27/www.museum-paca.org). **Open** 10am-noon, 1-5pm daily. **Admission** €2; free students, under-25s. **No credit cards**.

Mineralogy and palaeontology collections, including hundreds of dinosaur eggs discovered on the Montagne Ste-Victoire, in a fine 17th-century *hôtel.*

Musée des Tapisseries

pl des Martyrs de la Résistance (04.42.23.09.91). **Open** 10am-12.30pm, 1.30-5pm Mon, Wed-Sun. **Admission** €2, free under-25s. **No credit cards**.

On the first floor of the former bishop's palace, the tapestry museum houses 17th- and 18th-century tapestries discovered in situ in the 19th century. There's a particularly lively series of scenes from *Don Quixote*, made at Beauvais 1735-44 after cartoons by Natier, along with costumes and model sets from opera productions from the Aix festival. Temporary exhibitions are related mainly to contemporary textile art.

Musée du Vieil Aix

17 rue Gaston de Saporta (04.42.21.43.55). **Open** *Apr-Sept* 10am-noon, 2.30-6pm Tue-Sun. *Oct-Mar* 10am-noon, 2.30-5pm Tue-Sun. **Admission** €4; free under-14s. **No credit cards**.

This small but worthwhile collection focuses on folk art, with *santons* (Christmas crib figures) and puppets from a mechanical crèche, plus some fine lacquered furniture and faïence. Two folding wooden screens and a fragile line of mechanical puppets depict the Fête-Dieu (Corpus Christi) procession that

Marseille & Aix

was a feature of Aix life every June until the beginning of the 20th century. The house, with its fine entrance hall, frescoes and a tiny painted *cabinet* with ornately carved and gilded domed ceiling, gives a glimpse of 17th-century aristocratic life.

Pavillon Vendôme

32 rue Célony or 13 rue de la Molle (04.42.21.05.78).
Open *Mar-Sept* 10am-noon, 2-6pm Mon, Wed-Sun.
Oct-Jan 10am-12.30pm, 1.30-5.30pm Mon, Wed-Sun.
Admission €2; free students, under-25s.
No credit cards.
This perfect pleasure dome was built by the aptly named Pierre Pavillon for the Duc de Vendôme in 1665. Set in formal gardens, the pavilion was later extended to three storeys following the classical hierarchy of Doric, Ionic and Corinthian orders. Giant Atlantes hold up the balcony and the interior is adorned with 17th- and 18th-century furniture.

Thermes Sextius

55 cours Sextius (08.00.63.96.99/www.thermes-sextius.com). **Open** 8.30am-7.30pm Mon-Fri; 8.30am-1.30pm, 2.30-6.30pm Sat. **Treatments** from €22.70.
Credit V.
Behind a wrought-iron grille and classical façade, the Thermes now house the glass and marble pyramids of an ultra-modern health spa. You can wander in and look at the small fountain, which still marks the original warm spring of the fashionable 18th-century establishment. To the right of the entrance are the remains of first-century BC Roman baths fed by the Source Imperiatrice.

Quartier Mazarin

Laid out on a strict grid plan in 1646, the Quartier Mazarin was conceived as a speculative venture and sold off in lots masterminded by Mazarin, Archbishop of Aix and brother of Louis XIV's powerful minister Cardinal Mazarin. It gradually became the aristocratic quarter and still feels very refined today. There are few shops or restaurants, other than classy *antiquaires* and select designer fashion names, but plenty of fine doorways, balustrades and wrought-iron balconies. The **Musée Paul Arbaud** occupies a townhouse on rue du 4 Septembre, the quarter's main thoroughfare, which leads into place des Quatre Dauphins, with a Baroque fountain depicting four dolphins splashing in the water. On the square, at the rear of an arcaded courtyard, is the beautiful 1650 Hôtel de Boisgelin, while nearby, on rue Cardinale, is the Collège Mignet (formerly Bourbon), where Cézanne and Zola went to school. Look also at the grandiose Hôtel Bonnet de la Baume on 2 rue Goyrand.

At the far end of rue Cardinale stands the **Eglise St-Jean de Malte**, built by the Knights of Malta (note the Maltese cross on the fountain in front) outside the city walls at the

end of the 13th century. One of the earliest Gothic structures in Provence, it has a wide nave and side chapels but no transept. The church once served as the burial place of the Counts of Provence. Beside it, the Commanderie of the Knights of Malta now houses the Musée Granet, the city's fine art and archaeology collection, currently closed for renovation.

Musée Granet

pl St-Jean de Malte. **Open** closed until 2006. Ring tourist office for details.
Aix's fine art museum is at the centre of an ambitious expansion project that should eventually quadruple the exhibition area. As well as an important collection of 17th-century Provençal painters and Flemish masters, there are several small Cézannes, a huge Ingres and works by the museum's founder, François Granet. The archaeological collection includes statues and other finds from Entremont and Roman Aix.

Musée Paul Arbaud

2a rue du 4 Septembre (04.42.38.38.95). **Open** 2-5pm Mon-Sat. **Admission** €2.50, free under-10s.
No credit cards.
Old masters from the Mirabeau family hang amid Provençal faïence and manuscripts collected by scholar Paul Arbaud. Fine pieces of Marseille and Moustiers faïence, from early monochrome grotesque style based on the designs of Berain to later polychrome examples, are light years from most of the tourist production made today.

Further out

Circling the old town, the busy peripheral boulevards follow the former ramparts. Beyond here lies 'new Aix', a post-war sprawl that includes an entire new district, Quartier Sextius Mirabeau. This is home to the dynamic **Cité du Livre**, a former match factory that is fast becoming the focus of a new cultural pole. The **Centre National Chorégrapique** is expected to open in 2005 next door and the Salle de Spectacles du Pays d'Aix will be built alongside.

The Aix suburbs are still dotted with former country villas and *bastides*. These include the Pavillon Lenfant (now part of the University of Aix); Jas de Bouffon, a country residence bought by Cézanne's father in 1859, and now at the centre of a redevelopment zone near the **Fondation Vasarely** (2km west of centre by the A8/A51); and **Château de la Pioline**, now a hotel (*see p168*). Nearby, at Les Milles, is a brick factory turned prison camp where numerous German and Austrian intellectuals, among them Surrealists Max Ernst and Hans Bellmer, were interned during World War II, and from which nearly 2,000 Jews were deported, many to Auschwitz. The refectory is now the

Mémorial National des Milles which is painted with murals by prisoners. Further south, beneath the perched village of Bouc-Bel-Air, the **Jardins d'Albertas**, terraced, 18th-century formal gardens with extravagant fountains, are a testimony to the power of the Albertas family.

North of Vieil Aix, past the pyramidal **Mausoleum of Joseph Sec** – a rare example of Revolutionary architecture dating from 1792, a period when there were more pressing things to do than build – a steep hill climbs to the Lauves, where Cézanne built his last studio, the **Atelier Cézanne**. If you continue climbing, you will come to a roundabout with the remains of an ancient city gate. Continue climbing up avenue Paul Cézanne (follow signs) to the spot where Cézanne painted many of his famous scenes of Montagne Ste-Victoire: a bit of a hike, but the view is definitely worth it. The remains of the Celto-Ligurian **Oppidium d'Entremont**, site of Sextius' victory in the second century AD, lie just outside the city to the north-west.

Atelier Cézanne

9 av Paul Cézanne (04.42.21.06.53/www.atelier-cezanne.com). Bus 1. **Open** *Apr, May* 10am-noon, 2.30-6pm daily. *June-Sept* 10am-6pm daily (till 6.30pm in July). *Oct-Mar* 10am-noon, 2.30-5pm daily. **Admission** €5.50; €2 students; free under-16s. **Credit** AmEx, MC, V.

Cézanne built this studio in 1902, and worked here until his death in 1906. Then outside the town, with views of the rocky ravines of the Montagne Ste-Victoire, it now overlooks post-war housing developments. The first-floor studio is a masterpiece of artistic clutter, with Cézanne's easels and palettes and many of the props – fruit, vases, a broken cherub statue – that are familiar from his still lifes.

Fondation Vasarely

1 av Marcel Pagnol, Jas de Bouffan (04.42.20.01.09). Bus 4. **Open** 10am-1pm, 2-6pm Mon-Fri; 10am-6pm Sat. **Admission** €7; €4 7-18s, students; free under-7s. **Credit** AmEx, MC, V.

At the 'centre architectonique', Hungarian-born abstract artist Victor Vasarely (1906-97) put his theories of geometrical abstraction and kinetic art into practice on a truly architectural scale. The building itself is composed of hexagonal structures of black and white squares and circles that reflect off water. Within, the hexagonal volumes are hung with large-scale paintings, tapestries and reliefs reflecting different periods of his work. Even if Vasarely's brand of kinetic art today seems strangely out of sync with contemporary art concerns, it remains an interesting 70s timewarp. The Fondation also owns thousands of drawings explaining his theories.

Jardins d'Albertas

N8, Bouc-Bel-Air (04.42.22.29.77). **Open** *May, Sept, Oct* 2-6pm Sat, Sun, public holidays. *June-Aug* 3-7pm daily. Closed Nov-Apr. **Admission** €3.50, €2.50 7-16s, free under-7s. **No credit cards.**

Jean-Baptiste Albertas, president of the Cour des Comptes, dreamed of constructing a lavish rural retreat, but he was assassinated on 14 July 1790, the château was never built and only the gardens, laid out with terraces and pools containing water-gushing sea beasts, were ever completed.

Oppidium d'Entremont

3km north-west of Vieux Aix via av Solari (D14), direction Puyricard (04.42.21.97.33/www.entremont. culture.gouv.fr). Bus 20. **Open** 9am-noon, 2-5.30pm Mon, Wed-Sun. **Admission** free.

This Celto-Ligurian hilltop settlement developed sometime around the second century BC on the site of an earlier sanctuary and was destroyed by Romans in the second century AD at the request of the land-hungry Marseillais. Excavated sections reveal a grid plan with residential zone, plus traces of shops, warehouses and workshops.

Site Mémorial des Milles

Les Milles (04.42.24.34.68). Bus 16. **Open** 9am-noon, 12.45-5pm Mon-Thur; 9am-noon, 12.45-4pm Fri. **Admission** free.

Between 1939 and 1943, this brick factory had a quite different role that for a long time lay, if not actively concealed, quite simply ignored. Les Milles was the sole French camp that served for internment, transit and deportation. Requisitioned as early as 1939 (before the German occupation), in a period of growing xenophobia and nationalism, it was used to round up 'enemy subjects' in France, both refugees from the Spanish Civil War and German and Austrian intellectuals, many of them Jewish, who had fled the Nazi regime. Among them were two Nobel prizewinners and the Surrealist painters Max Ernst and Hans Bellmer. After June 1940, although Provence at this time was part of Free France administered by Vichy, Les Milles became a transit camp; nearly 2,000 Jews were deported from here to Auschwitz via Drancy, a transit camp near Paris. Since 1997, the former warders' refectory has become the Mémorial. In the entrance, documents and archive photos relate the history of Les Milles and other internment camps, but it is the refectory that is the most telling witness, decorated with murals by prisoners that seem to take a subtly satirical slant in the form of a caricatural row of warders and a parody of Leonardo's *Last Supper*. Across the road, at the former Gare des Milles, a railway wagon recalls those who were transported to Auschwitz via Drancy.

Arts & entertainment

Pick up *Le Mois à Aix*, monthly listings magazine published by the tourist office (also available at www.aix-en-provence.com), and regional freebie weekly *César*, distributed in hotels and bars.

Rue Espariat: student central. *See p157.*

3BisF

Hôpital Montperrin, 109 av du Petit Barthélémy (04.42.16.17.75). **Open** 9am-6pm Mon-Fri. **Admission** *exhibitions* free. *theatre/dance* €9; €4.50 under-15s. **No credit cards.**
Artists' studios, exhibition space, contemporary dance, theatre productions and workshops within a hospital complex not far from the Cité du Livre.

Centre National Chorégraphique

rue des Allumettes (04.42.3.48.00). **Open** from Mar 2005. **Tickets** €8-€20.
Choreographer Angelin Preljocaj is based in the Cité du Livre but due to move next door into a new hi-tech dance centre in 2005. Bandol architect Rudy Ricciotti's spider's-web-like glass and concrete building plays on transparency. Albanian-born Preljocaj, who brings classical ballet into the 21st century, moved to Aix as a refugee from Châteauvallon when Toulon went Front National in the 1990s.

Cité du Livre

8-10 rue des Allumettes (04.42.91.98.65).
Open noon-6pm Tue, Thur, Fri; 10am-6pm Wed, Sat. **Admission** free.
Despite the name and the gigantic book that marks the entrance, this converted match factory covers not just literature but is a multi-disciplinary arts centre. As well as hosting an annual literary festival in October and housing the historic Bibliothèque Méjanes library, it is also the home of the Institut de l'Image (art cinema, video screenings and December short film festival), the Fondation St-John Perse (04.42.91.98.85), which is an exhibition space with a collection of manuscripts by the poet, as well as the Ballet Angelin Preljocaj *(see above)*, plus a library of opera on video.

Espace Musical Chapelle Ste-Catherine

20 rue Mignet (04.42.91.37.11). **Concerts** 7pm Tue. **Tickets** €3, free under-12s.
Former church used for classical concerts, essentially chamber music with a festival in Holy Week.

Galerie d'Art du Conseil Général

21bis cours Mirabeau (04.42.93.03.67). **Open** 10.15am-12.45pm, 1.30-6.30pm daily. **Admission** free.
The exhibition space of the Conseil Général des Bouches du Rhône shows modern and contemporary art and photography.

Théâtre des Ateliers

29 pl Miollis (04.42.38.10.45). **Box office** 10am-noon, 2-8pm Mon-Sat. Closed Aug. **Shows** 9pm. **Tickets** €11.50; €5.50 children. **No credit cards.**
A smallish theatre that works on co-productions of new work with other subsidised theatre venues.

Théâtre du Jeu de Paume

17-21 rue de l'Opéra (04.42.99.12.00/box office 04.42.99.12.12). **Box office** 11am-6pm (in person noon-6pm) Tue-Sat. **Tickets** €20-€35. **Credit** MC, V.
This beautiful vintage theatre was founded in 1756

Place de l'Hôtel de Ville. *See p157.*

on the site of the city's old real tennis court and reopened in 2000 after major renovation. Director Dominique Bluzet (of the Théâtre du Gymnase in Marseille) brings in successful Paris plays and visiting companies from Marseille and elsewhere. It is also one of the venues for the Festival d'Art Lyrique.

Restaurants & brasseries

Antoine Côté Cour

19 cours Mirabeau (04.42.93.12.51). **Open** 7.30pm-midnight Mon; noon-2.30pm, 7.30pm-midnight Tue-Sat. **Average** €25. **Credit** DC, MC, V.
The fashionable folk of Aix come to this stylish, lively Italianate restaurant, which serves veal dishes, gnocchi and pasta. An ornate entrance off the cours Mirabeau leads to a beautiful courtyard perfect for summer al fresco dining.

Bistro Latin

18 rue de la Couronne (04 42 38 22 88).
Open noon-2.30pm, 7.30-10.30pm Tue-Sat. **Menu** €21. **Credit** MC, V
This charming restaurant boasts an intimate setting and nouvelle cuisine at remarkable prices. The *prix fixe* includes such delights as mussels and spinach in saffron sauce, roasted pork loin with honey and garlic, lamb stew, and fresh cod with fennel sauce.

Brasserie des Deux Garçons

53 cours Mirabeau (04.42.26.00.51/www.les2 garcons.com). **Open** 6am-2am daily (meals noon-3pm, 7-11.30pm daily). **Menus** €20.10. **Credit** AmEx, MC, V.

Alias 'les 2 G', the legendary Deux Garçons café, founded in 1792 and named after the two waiters who bought it in 1840, still has its original canopied entrance and consulaire period interior with tall mirrors, chandeliers, old-fashioned cashier's desk and a salon off the side where you can read the papers or write your novel. It was the hangout of Cézanne, Zola and a long list of famous names from Piaf and Picasso to Churchill. The food is proficient brasserie fare, but it's the elegant café buzz that counts.

Café La Chimère

15 rue Brueys (04.42.38.30.00). **Open** 6.30pm-midnight Mon-Sat. **Menus** €21.50. **Credit** V.

If food is considered an art form, then La Chimère takes its art seriously. Whimsical concoctions of local, fresh ingredients are vertically arranged on platters with drizzles of sauce and garnishes such as shaved fennel or spun sugar. The decor is a rococo mix of gilt and crimson, with angels throughout. The prices are fantastic and cuisine excellent, making this an altogether fun place to spend an evening with friends.

Clos de la Violette

10 av de la Violette (04.42.23.30.71/www.closde laviolette.fr). **Open** noon-2pm, 7-9.30pm Tue-Sat (7-9.30pm in summer). Closed 2wks Feb & 2wks Aug. **Menus** €54-€117. **Credit** AmEx, MC, V.

In a spacious garden under ancient chestnut trees, chef Jean-Marc Banzo displays a knack for producing food that is at once light, healthy and unmistakably Provençal. Dishes like grilled red mullet with cabbage stuffed with squid, or a sublime croustillant of raspberries, spotlight his style. The service can be erratic, and the welcome cool.

Le Grillon

49 cours Mirabeau (04.42.27.58.81/www.cafele grillon.com). **Open** 6am-2am daily (meals noon-3pm, 7pm-1am daily). **Menus** €12.20-€32. **Credit** MC, V.

Sit on the terrace or in the deliciously pretty, pastiche-18th-century upstairs dining room. Plenty of Aixois eat here, as do tourists. Roast lamb with herbs and daily fish dishes are simple but proficient (the pasta is best forgotten), service affable and wines by the carafe affordable.

Le Petit Verdot

7 rue d'Entrecasteaux (04.42.27.30.12/www.lepetit verdot.com). **Open** 7-11pm Mon-Sat. **Menus** €13.50, €17. **No credit cards.**

Filled with wine barrels and an assortment of bottles, this charming wine bar and restaurant near to place des Tanneurs is the perfect setting for an intimate *dîner à deux*. The jovial German owner and her dog make delightful hosts and the traditional regional cooking and wine are excellent. The *prix-fixe* menus are a steal.

Student Aix

With over 40,000 students and a thriving café scene, historic Aix is an ideal place to live and study. The town attracts a large proportion of foreign students, not just because of its setting but because the Université d'Aix-Marseille III boasts one of the best French-language teaching centres in the country. **L'Institut d'Etudes Françaises pour Etudiants Etrangers** (www.univ-aixmarseille.fr) allows students to learn French at any level in programmes that last a term, academic year or summer. Optional classes can be taken on subjects ranging from literature to film, politics to cooking, and many classes are held in gorgeous ancient *hôtels particuliers* in Vieux Aix.

Some rooms on campus and furnished studios are available, though most of the town's students live in shared apartments or with French families. Accommodation ads are posted at l'Institut or at various bookstores.

Apart from Sciences-Po (political sciences) students, most of the French university students take their classes in the large campus-like Cité Universitaire on avenue Jules Ferry, south of the centre. It is easily accessible by bus and also offers libraries, the CROUS (student services), gym and lodgings.

Extra-curricular activities aren't as multitudinous as in Paris or Marseille, but there are plenty of trendy bars, clubs, cinemas and restaurants to keep you busy. If you want to meet other International students, check out **Book in Bar** or **The Red Clover** (*see p167*). **IPN** and **Le Mistral** are the places to dance, **Bar le Sextius** draws a crowd for its reggae night and other live musical events.

For students on a budget, street food is cheap, plentiful, and usually fairly tasty. For paninis and pizza, try **Pizza Napoli** on place Richelme. For an excellent cup of freshly roasted coffee, try **La Brûlerie Richelme** just off the square.

The only difficulty about studying French in Aix is that it is so international, it can be hard to find opportunities to speak French. Look for conversation-exchange partners posted at the university.

Studying in Aix is the perfect excuse to live in a beautiful city in Provence… no wonder students dub it 'Aix-en-vacances'.

Marseille & Aix

La Pizza

3 rue Aude (04 42 26 22 17). **Open** noon-2pm,
7.30-11.30pm daily. **Average** €13. **Credit** AmEx,
DC, MC, V.
Probably the most romantic pizzeria you'll ever have
seen, 'La Pizza' comes alive every night with tables
spilling onto the cobblestones overlooking the gorgeous place d'Albertas. A wide variety of wood-fired
pizzas are available as well as pastas and risottos.
Try the salmon risotto or gorgonzola gnocchi.

La Vieille Auberge

63 rue Esparjat (04.42.27.17.41). **Open** 7.15-10pm
Mon; noon-2pm, 7.15-10pm Tue-Sun. Closed Jan.
Menus €15-€38. **Credit** MC, V.
A beamed, pink-washed dining room with a giant
fireplace is the setting for chef Jean-Marie Merly's
sophisticated cooking, seen in dishes such as pepper
stuffed with *brandade* and red mullet stuffed with
aubergine and parmesan on a red-pepper *pain perdu.*

Yamato (Koji & Yuriko)

4 rue Lieutaud (04.42.38.00.20). **Open** noon-2pm,
7-10pm Mon-Thur, Sun; 7pm-10.30pm, Fri, Sat.
Menus €27-€43. **Credit** MC, V.
Staff glide around in kimonos at this Japanese
restaurant adorned with Nô masks. As well as excellent sushi and sashimi and crisp, light tempura
you'll find good grilled fish and rarer specialities like
uoroke and *sukiyaki* (strips of beef simmered at table
over a flame with vegetables and noodles).

Yôji

7 av Victor Hugo (04.42.38.48.76). **Open** 7-11pm
Mon; noon-2pm, 7-11pm Tue-Sat. **Menus** €20-€32.50.
Credit AmEx, MC, V.
This Korean-Japanese restaurant has a touch of
cosmopolitan glamour. The long basement is a
clever mixture of al fresco dining in a courtyard, plus
an elegant room with water features. Refined
Japanese cuisine is paired with the chance to indulge
in a sumptuous Korean barbeque thanks to cun-
ningly designed tables.

Bars & music venues

For a people-watching apéritif, cours Mirabeau
and rue Esparjat are the obvious choices,
beginning with the **Deux Garçons** (*see p165*)
and **Le Festival** (*see below*). For a light lunch
after the market, try **Le Pain Quotidien** on
place Richelme. For live music, several small
venues cater to the student population, but for
big-name bands head to Marseille.

Bar le Sextius

2 cours Sextius (04.42.26.78.20). **Open** 5-11pm daily.
No credit cards.
This casual bar with affordable drinks, a good wine
selection and a small dance floor is a popular student
spot to hear live music or meet friends. Every
Tuesday is reggae night.

Cours Mirabeau: café society for generations. *See p159.*

Le Bistrot Aixois

37 cours Sextius (04.42.27.50.10). **Open** 6.30pm-2am
Tue-Sat. **Credit** AmEx, MC, V.
Newly renovated and reopened after a fire, the
Bistrot has the BCBG (the French equivalent of
sloanes) student set queuing to get in. Once inside,
there are drinks, billiards and a small dance floor.

Le Divino

*Mas des Auberes, rte de Venelles (5 km from town)
(04.42.99.37.08/www.divino.fr).* **Open** *restaurant*
8pm-2am Tue-Sat. *club* 11pm-5am Thur-Sat.
Admission club €16. **Credit** MC, V.
More like a hip club in New York or Paris, Le Divino
attracts Aix's fashion victims with its trendy decor
and thumping music. Lounge at the bar or dance the
night away to house hits amid a beautiful crowd.

Le Festival

67bis rue Espariat (04.42.27.21.96). **Open** 7.30am-
2am daily. **Credit** MC, V.
Facing the fountain at La Rotonde, this café provides
an ideal spot in which to grab an outdoor table for
a drink on a sunny afternoon. Sit back here and
watch the world walk by.

Hot Brass Jazz Club

rte d'Eguilles, 04.42.21.05.57). **Open** 10.30pm-dawn
Fri, Sat. **Admission** €16-€19. **Credit** MC, V.
5km out of town, the Hot Brass offers live funk, soul,
rock, blues and Latin bands, mainly local outfits.
Reserve on the answerphone.

IPN

23 cours Sextius (04.42.26.25.17). **Open** 11.30pm-
4am Thur-Sat. **Admission** €4 (members); €6 (non-
members). **Credit** MC, V.
Always packed with students, this very popular
dance spot is conveniently located in an ancient
cellar in the centre of town. Great ambiance and
music, reasonable drink prices.

Mediterranean Boy

6 rue de la Paix (04.42.27.21.47). **Open** 8.30pm-2am
daily. **Credit** AmEx, DC, MC, V.
Upstairs is a classic gay bar tended by an avuncu-
lar fiftysomething patron. Downstairs is a cellar
with tables, chatting groups and the opportunity for
heavy petting. More twilight zone than dark room.

Le Mistral

*3 rue Frédéric Mistral (04.42.38.16.49/
www.mistralclub.com).* **Open** 11.30pm-5am Tue-Sat.
Admission €11-€15. **Credit** MC, V.
Behind a discreet entrance is this long-established
haunt of the BCBG student set. This chic club is
popular with international students, as it is one of
the few places open for dancing past 2am. The music
is a mix of pop, house, and techno.

L'Orienthé

5 rue du Félibre Gaut (06.62.16.48.25). **Open** 3pm-
1am Mon-Thur; 4pm-2am Fri, Sat; 3pm-midnight
Sun. Closed Sun in July, first 2wks of Jan.
No credit cards.

Leave your shoes at the door and relax over one of
50 varieties of tea and a delectable pastry at this
exotic tea salon/lounge. You sit on pillows around
low tables amid candles and incense.

The Red Clover

30 rue la Verrerie (04.42.23.44.61). **Open** 8am-2am
Mon-Sat. **Credit** MC, V.
The friendly, boisterous Red Clover pub is *the* spot
to meet international students in Aix and serves a
wide variety of beers and Irish whiskies. Don't
expect to speak much French here.

Book in Bar

*1bis rue Joseph Cabassol (04.42.26.60.07/
www.bookinbar.com).* **Open** 9am-7pm Mon-Sat.
Credit MC, V.
This cosy Anglophone bookshop and café near the
cours Mirabeau is a great spot not only to buy and
read books, but to meet other English speakers and
to search for jobs and housing on the bulletin board.

Shopping

Aix offers some of the most sophisticated
shopping territory in Provence (all open
Mon-Sat unless stated). Undoubted leader of the
fashion brigade is **Gago** (18, 20, 21 rue Fabrot,
04.42.27.60.19) with up-to-the-minute men's and
women's designer wear and accessories,
including Prada, Helmut Lang, YSL and Gucci.
But you'll also find **Yohji Yamamoto** (No.3,
04.42.27.79.15) and **Max Mara** (No.12,
04.42.26.80.85, closed Mon morning) on this
street. For simpler, casual wear **Sugar** (4 rue
Maréchal Foch, 04.42.27.48.33, closed Mon
morning) is worth a look. **Agnès b** (2 rue
Fernand Dol, 04.42.38.44.87, closed Mon
morning) is across the cours Mirabeau. A clutch
of good children's wear shops include **Catimini**
(9 pl des Chapeliers, 04.42.27.51.14, closed Mon
morning), colourful **Marese** (4 rue Aude,
04.42.26.67.00), and the excellent value **Du
Pareil au Même** (14 rue Maréchal Foch,
04.42.26.48.49, closed Mon morning), and
toddlers will love the traditional wooden toys at
Le Nain Rouge (47 rue Espariat, 04.42.93.50.05,
closed Mon morning).

Aix's culinary speciality is the *calisson d'Aix*,
diamond-shaped sweets made out of almonds,
sugar and preserved melon; some of the best
come from **Leonard Parli** (35 av Victor Hugo,
04.42.26.05.71) who has been producing them at
the rear of a pretty old shop since 1874, along
with little chocolate-covered nut biscuits.

There are numerous antique and interior
design shops on place des Trois Ormeaux and
neighbouring rue Jaubert. **La Maison
Montigny** (5 rue Lucas de Montigny,
04.42.27.74.56, closed Mon morning) has two
floors of high-tech kitchen equipment and

stained, restored furniture, tasteful grey linen and burnished stainless steel. **Scènes de Vie** (3 rue Jaubert, 3 rue Granet, 04.42.21.13.90, closed Mon morning) stocks sophisticated Provençal pottery. Upmarket antique and fabric shops also congregate in the Quartier Mazarin, especially along rues Cardinale and Granet. For details of regular brocantes and antiques fairs call (04.42.52.97.10).

Of Aix's bookshops, the **Librairie de Provence** (31 cours Mirabeau, 04.42.26.07.23, closed Sun) has a good fine art section, while **Librairie Paradox** (15 rue du 4 Septembre, 04.42.26.47.99, closed Sun) stocks books, videos and CD-Roms in English.

Where to stay

Château de la Pioline
260 rue Guillaume du Vair, La Pioline (04.42.52.27.27/www.chateauxdelapioline.fr). **Double** €150-€330. **Credit** AmEx, DC, MC, V.
5km out of the centre, this 16th-century château (downstairs is listed) has a graceful stairhall, elegant dining room (menus €35-€60) and formal garden, plus a pool. Too bad the motorway's in earshot.

Grand Hôtel Nègre Coste
33 cours Mirabeau (04.42.27.74.22/www.hotelnegre coste.com). **Double** €59-€125. **Credit** AmEx, MC, V.
The hospitable Hôtel Nègre Coste has a prime location and plenty of old-fashioned style, with period furniture and chandeliers downstairs and colourful bedrooms upstairs featuring antique wardrobes. Bedrooms at the front look over cours Mirabeau; quieter ones at the back have a view across rooftops to the cathedral.

Hôtel Aquabella
2 rue des Etuves (04.42.99.15.00/www.aquabella.fr). **Double** €155. **Credit** AmEx, DC, MC, V.
This modern 110-room hotel adjoining the revamped Thermes Sextius may lack the character of Aix's older hotels but compensates with spacious, comfortable rooms, helpful staff and a good location for exploring Vieil Aix. There's an airy reception area and a glass-walled restaurant, L'Orangerie. Special spa treatment packages are available.

Hôtel Artea
4 bd. de la République (04.42.27.36.00). **Double** €59-€68. **Credit** AmEx, MC, V.
A perfect spot for budget travellers wanting a central location. Rooms are simple and comfortable; larger ones easily accommodate groups. All the rooms are equipped with bathrooms *en suite*.

Hôtel des Augustins
3 rue de la Masse (04.42.27.28.59). **Double** €95-€230. **Credit** DC, MC, V.
On a sidestreet off the cours Mirabeau, this very appealing hotel was part of an Augustine convent

until the Revolution, becoming a hotel in the 1890s. The reception has been inserted into a spectacular vaulted space. Rooms are comfortable even if the Provençal-style furnishings don't quite live up to the promise of the lobby. Supposedly stayed in by many famous guests, including Martin Luther.

Hôtel Cardinal
24 rue Cardinale (04.42.38.32.30). **Double** €58. **Credit** MC, V.
Much loved by writers, artists and musicians here for the Aix festival, this little hotel in the Quartier Mazarin has bags of charm. Several rooms have stucco mouldings, a couple have original 18th-century painted overdoor panels, all have been recently redecorated with quality fabrics, old furniture, oil paintings and new bathrooms. Suites in the annexe by Musée Granet have a kitchenette.

Hôtel de France
63 rue Espariat (04.42.27.90.15). **Double** €54-€62. **Credit** AmEx, MC, V.
An inexpensive option in a town that has fewer central hotels than you might expect. Most rooms are a good size; those at the front overlook the cafés of a busy shopping street in Vieil Aix.

Hôtel Mercure Paul Cézanne
40 av Victor Hugo (04.42.91.11.11). **Double** €118-€160. **Credit** AmEx, DC, MC, V.
A stone's throw away from the train station and a short walk from cours Mirabeau, it's hard to find a more conveniently located hotel in Aix. Rooms are air-conditioned and simply decorated *à la provençale*.

Hôtel Paul
10 av. Pasteur (04.42.23.23.89). **Double** €35-€45. **Credit** V.
A rather dated lobby and drab rooms nonetheless provide a fantastic bargain for travellers on a budget at this hotel just north of the old town and down the hill from Cézanne's atelier. A shaded garden offers respite on hot afternoons.

Hôtel Le Pigonnet
5 av du Pigonnet (04.42.59.02.90/www.hotel pigonnet.com). **Double** €210-€380. **Credit** AmEx, DC, MC, V.
1 km from the town centre, this beautiful 19th-century mansion is a secluded, relaxed haven surrounded by flowers, cypress trees, and bubbling fountains. Relax by the swimming pool and soak up the sunshine. The restaurant 'La Riviera' (menus €38-€46) features excellent Provençal cuisine.

Hôtel des Quatre Dauphins
54 rue Roux Alphéran (04.42.38.16.39). **Double** €65-€85. **Credit** MC, V.
The 'four dolphins' has 12 simple but tastefully decorated – and newly air-conditioned – rooms in a 17th-century building on a corner of one of the most pleasant streets of the Quartier Mazarin. Most guests are returnees, so make sure you that you book well in advance.

Sunflowers, west of Aix.

Hôtel St-Christophe

2 av Victor Hugo (04.42.26.01.24/www.hotel-saintchristophe.com). **Double** €73-€109. **Credit** AmEx, DC, MC, V.
Located just off La Rotonde, the St Christophe has comfortable modern rooms behind a 19th-century façade, done up either 'art deco' or '*à la provençale*', suites have views of the Montagne Ste-Victoire. Downstairs is the big Brasserie Léopold.

Villa Gallici

10 av de la Violette (04.42.23.29.23/www.villa gallici.com). **Double** €200-€600. **Credit** AmEx, DC, MC, V.
Slightly out of the centre in an elegantly renovated *bastide*, luxurious Villa Gallici offers plush comfort, with Italianate trimmings. Some rooms have private gardens, and there's a swimming pool. It also has an excellent restaurant (average €76, closed Mon & lunch Tue & Wed in winter), where chef Christophe Gavot specialises in fish.

Getting there & around

By car

Leave the autoroute A8 at exit 29-31. Take the N7 from Avignon or St-Maximin-la-Ste-Baume. From Marseille, take the A51, which continues north towards Gap.

By train

Aix TGV station is 10km west of the city, served by regular shuttle buses. The old Aix station is on the slow Marseille-Sisteron line, with trains roughly every hour from Marseille-St-Charles.

By bus

Aix is served by six to ten buses daily to Avignon and an hourly shuttle to Marseille airport (gare routière 04.42.91.26.80). Aix is also a stop on the Marseille to Nice airport service (three daily) operated by Phocéen Cars (04.93.85.66.61).
   Although the centre of Aix is best explored by foot, there is also an extensive network of local buses serving outlying areas. Most leave from La Rotonde in front of the Office du Tourisme, where there is an information/ticket desk (04.42.26.37.28). Take No.1 to Atelier Cézanne, No.20 for the Oppidum d'Entremont, No.16 for La Pioline and Les Milles, No.4 from the old casino to the Fondation Vasarely.

By bike

Bikes can be hired from Cycles Zammit (27 rue Mignet, 04.42.23.19.53, closed Mon).

Resources

Hospital

Centre Hospitalier du Pays d'Aix Urgences, av Tamaris (04.42.33.50.00).

Internet

Pl@net Web, 20 rue Victor Leydat (04.42.26.83.01). **Open** 9am-11pm Mon-Thur; 9am-midnight Fri, Sat; 1-11pm Sun.

Police

av de l'Europe (04.42.93.97.00).

Post office

pl de l'Hôtel de Ville (04.42.17.10.40).

Tourist information

Office de Tourisme, 2 pl du Général de Gaulle (04.42.16.11.61/hotel reservations 04.42.16.11.84/ www.aixenprovencetourism.com). **Open** *June, Sept* 8.30am-7pm Mon-Sat; 10am-1pm, 2-6pm Sun. *July, Aug* 8.30am-90pm Mon-Sat; 10am-1pm, 2-6pm Sun. *Oct-Mar* 8.30am-7pm Mon-Sat; 10am-1pm, 2-6pm Sun. *Ticket office (04.42.16.11.70)* 9am-noon, 2-6pm Mon-Sat.

Around Aix

Montagne Ste-Victoire

The Montagne Ste-Victoire is inextricably linked with Paul Cézanne and if you are at all interested in art, you will want to see this mountain range which at once appears both familiar and much more massive than in his paintings. The Montagne also offers rugged villages, wild landscapes for walking and the changing colours that so obsessed Cézanne, who painted it in over 60 canvases and countless watercolours as he sought out the underlying geometrical structure in the landscape.

Cézanne was born into a wealthy Aixois family in 1839 (his father had a hat business on the cours Mirabeau before founding the Banque Cézanne et Cabassol) and even while at school would go for long walks on the mountain with his friend Emile Zola (curiously Cézanne is said to have excelled at literature and Zola at drawing). Their friendship came to an end in 1886 when Cézanne was bitterly wounded by the description of struggling painter Claude Lantier in Zola's *L'Oeuvre*, which he perceived as a portrait of him (although it also contains elements of Manet).

The best way to approach the Montagne Ste-Victoire is in a loop, taking a detour on the way out of Aix to the **Pont des Trois Sautets**, now a rather urban traffic junction, also painted by the artist. Cézanne rented a room to paint in at the **Château Noir**, just before Le Tholonet, from 1887 and later a hut at the **Carrière de Bibemus** quarry – before building his own Atelier on the Lauves hill, with a view of the mountain (*see p162*).

At Le Tholonet, the **Moulin Cézanne** has an exhibition on local history, the *barrage Zola* (built by Emile's dad) and the friendship between Cézanne and Zola. Upstairs are temporary exhibitions of painting and sculpture. The D17 follows the southern edge of the mountain, from where a footpath leads to the hermit's chapel of St-Ser, and through the village of Puyloubier, although the easiest access for walkers is from the north off the D10.

Another artist, Picasso, is buried in the grounds of the Château de Vauvenarges (private), which he bought in 1958. Note that it's easiest to travel by car, but, in season, the tourist office at Aix-en-Provence organises weekly bus tours to the main Cézanne sites (Apr-Nov 2-7pm Thur, €26).

Moulin Cézanne

rte Cézanne, Le Tholonet (04.42.66.90.41). **Open** May-Oct 3-6pm daily. **Admission** free.

West & North of Aix

Overlooking the lush plain west of Aix, sleepy **Lambesc** boasts a neo-classical church, an old *lavoir* and some fine houses, which hint at the village's 14 decades of fame (1646-1786), when it was the seat of the regional assembly. West of Lambesc, **Château de la Barben** was originally a fortress belonging to the Abbaye de St-Victor in Marseille, before becoming a residence of King René. Later it was home to the powerful Forbin family, who brought in André Le Nôtre to redesign the gardens. The adjoining **Zoo de la Barben** is a popular family attraction, where wild beasts including Siberian tigers roam in the beautiful grounds.

Across the Chaîne de la Trévaresse, through rolling oak woods and Coteaux d'Aix vineyards, the D15 (or N7 and D543 from Aix) leads to the **Abbaye de Silvacane**. The third of Provence's great Cistercian Romanesque abbeys (with Sénanque and Thoronet), it was begun in 1144 on swampy lands near the Durance. It has a sober church, impressive vaulted chapter house and a refectory with contemporary stained glass by artist Sarkis. Just to the west, the small town of **La Roque-d'Anthéron** has a famous summer piano festival, with concerts at Silvacane and in the grounds of the Château de Florans.

North of Aix by N96, the fortified **Château de Meyrargues** (04.42.63.49.90) on a strategic hilltop is now an upmarket hotel and restaurant, with views over fragments of a Roman aqueduct. 6km on is sleepy **Peyrolles-en-Provence**. This area lacks the cachet of the Luberon on the other side of the Durance, which means fewer tourists but also that you might arrive here and find the cafés shut and the streets deserted. A pity, because Peyrolles was once the residence of good king René. A rather grand gateway leads into what looks like a farmyard but is, in fact, the courtyard of the former royal château, now the *mairie* (town hall). On the other side of the village, on a rocky hillock amid some gloomy public housing and derelict industrial buildings, is the beautifully austere Chapelle de la St-Sépulcre, built on a Greek-cross plan (call the Mairie 04.42.57.80.05, to visit Mon-Fri).

Abbaye de Silvacane

La Roque d'Antheron (04.42.50.41.69). **Open** *Apr-Sept* 10am-6pm daily. *Oct-Mar* 10am-1pm, 2-5pm Mon, Wed-Sun. **Admission** €6.10, free under-17s. **Credit** V, MC

Château & Zoo de la Barben

D572/D22 La Barben (château 04.90.55.25.41/ zoo 04.90.55.19.12). **Open** *château* 10am-noon, 2-5.30pm daily. *zoo* 10am-6pm daily. Closed Jan. **Admission** *château* €7; €4 3-13s; free under-3s. *zoo* €12; €6 3-13s; free under-3s. **Credit** MC, V.

The Var

Introduction

Much of the Var has been colonised by the English and you can see why: perched villages, people-watching and the best beaches in the South of France.

From glamorous St-Tropez to troubled Toulon, the Var suffers from a schizophrenic image. But with large areas devoted to the vineyards of Bandol and the Côtes de Provence or to military training grounds, this area has suffered less from the over-development of the coast. If there are still undiscovered stretches of coast, many of them are to be found here, down steep *caps* accessible only by foot or boat.

Over the centuries, **St-Tropez** has been raided by Saracens, Signac, Brigitte Bardot and Johnny Hallyday, but you shouldn't let its showbiz reputation and appalling traffic jams scare you off. It masters its celebrity(ies) with a certain irony and still retains an undeniable fishing village charm. There are plenty of pleasant, quieter family resorts, too, like **Sanary-sur-Mer**, **Bormes-les-Mimosas** and **Le Lavandou**, while **Fréjus** boasts an impressive Roman heritage, often unjustly neglected against brasher neighbour **St-Raphaël**. Just inland, you soon find yourself in the wooded and remote-feeling Maures or the brick-red Estérel massifs; even Toulon sits at the foot of an impressive mountain terrain.

The Green Var around Brignoles is renowned for canoeing, walking and organic produce, but also leads to the mysterious cave in the Ste-Baume massif where the Magdalene is said to have lived out 30 years in solitude, and the pilgrimage site of **St-Maximin-la-Ste-Baume**.

In the mountainous interior, perched villages, like **Tourtour**, **Aups**, **Salernes**, **Cotignac** and **Bargemon**, with steep, narrow streets and wrought-iron belfries, have barely changed for centuries. Here, ever-so-Provençal tiles and pottery meet a cosmopolitan sheen, while the dramatic **Gorges du Verdon** provide breathtaking landscape vistas and challenging walking and rafting.

Don't miss — The Var

Abbaye de Thoronet
For cloistered calm. See p211.

Basilique Ste-Marie Madeleine
The Magdalene's last resting-place. See p203.

Café Le Senequier
Director's chair view of St-Trop. See p191.

Château de Trigance
For medieval castle living. See p215.

Chapelle Notre-Dame-de-Jérusalem, Fréjus
Cocteau's crusader chapel. See p198.

Cours Lafayette, Toulon
Toulon's fabulous street market. See p175.

Domaine de Rayol
A botanical world tour from the Med to Mexico. See p185.

Fontaine d'Ampus
Inspirational seasonal cooking in a mountain village. See p208.

Grand Canyon du Verdon
Jaw-dropping natural beauty. See p215.

Grottes troglodytes
Fashionable cave homes at Villecroze. See p207.

Ile de Porquerolles
The inspiration for Treasure Island. See p182.

Nikki Beach
Four-posters and party atmosphere on the beach at St-Tropez. See p191.

Le Papagayo, St-Tropez
Dark den of misdemeanours. See p192.

Plage de l'Estagnol
Golden sand, sheltering pines, child-friendly water and charcoal-grilled fish. See p184.

Téléphérique de Mont Faron
Cable car ride above the rade de Toulon. See p176.

Villa Noailles, Hyères
Mallet-Stevens' cubic wonder. See p181.

The Var

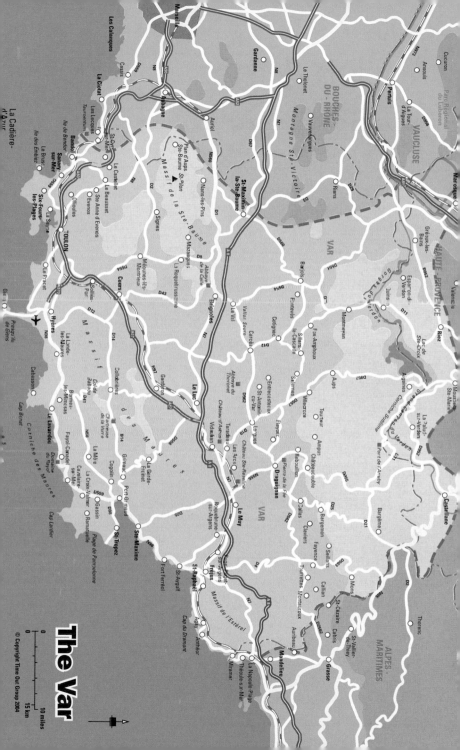

The Var

© Copyright Time Out Group 2004

0   10 miles
0   15 km

Toulon & the Western Côte

If you're tired of all the glamour and the gentrification, workaday Toulon, with its military port and feisty markets, can be a breath of fresh air.

France's leading Mediterranean naval base was largely flattened in World War II. Some soulless reconstruction, a couple of motorways dumping right into the centre of town, a tough urban reputation and some frankly dodgy nightlife don't put Toulon high on most tourist itineraries, but on the plus side it offers a busy port, fabulous market and atmospheric old town.

The Greeks and Romans knew about the impressive natural harbour, and exploited the local deposits of murex shells to make purple dye. But only after 1481, when Toulon became part of France, did the port become strategically important, with the construction of the arsenal and a ring of forts. Louis XIV's military architect Vauban expanded the docks, fortified the town with star-shaped bastions, and built the Fort St-Louis in Mourillon, which saw off Anglo-Spanish battleships during the War of the Spanish Succession in 1707.

In 1789, as the Revolution spread, Toulon chose the royal camp. In the subsequent uprising, it fell to an unknown young officer called Napoléon Bonaparte in 1793 and narrowly escaped being razed to the ground. The royalists scuppered their own ships and blew up the shipyards so the Revolutionaries couldn't get their hands on them. In a remarkable re-run, the French scuttled their Mediterranean fleet to blockade the harbour in 1942 as German forces advanced, and much of the old town was destroyed in 1944 by Allied bombs and retreating Germans. In 1995, when extreme-right Front National candidate Jean-Marie Le Chevallier was elected mayor, the town was again put into purgatory, and boycotted by many artists and performers, such as choreographer Angelin Preljocaj, who moved to Aix-en-Provence. A city of contrasts, where the military remains the biggest direct and indirect employer alongside a substantial immigrant population, Toulon has since come back into the fold, electing moderate right-wing mayor Hubert Falco in 2001, and as France's 14th largest city is trying to assert its identity independent of Marseille or Nice.

Sightseeing

One of the most curious aspects of post-War reconstruction was the massive avenue de la République housing project that slices through the city between the port and the old town. Walk through the ghastly housing bar, however, and you discover the lively, café-lined yachting marina, from where you can take boat trips to the Iles de Hyères or around the port (the only way to see the otherwise strictly off-limits military port). At the town hall annexe on quai Cronstadt, two 1657 atlantes by Pierre Puget around the door embody the agonising

Med colours in the port of **Toulon**.

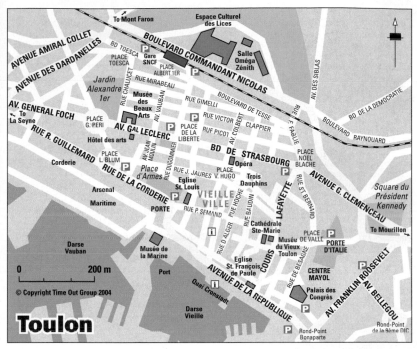

Toulon

labour of early dock-workers. The **Musée de la Marine** juts out into the westerly Darse Neuve, the 'new dock' built in 1680, and houses figureheads, ship models and marine paintings. Its ornate doorway with figures of Mars and Minerva is the former dockyard entrance. Nearby are the heavily guarded gates of the military port. Inside, an ancient wall is all that remains of the gruesome Le Bagne penal colony, described by Victor Hugo in *Les Misérables*, where prisoners lodged on hulks in the bay worked as galley slaves.

Back from the port lies a gritty red-light district, with its sex shops, no-star mariners' hotels and 'American bars' (read fleshpots). The neighbourhood, known locally as Le Petit Chicago (and getting smaller) is currently undergoing a massive renovation programme.

In the heart of the *vieille ville*, café-filled place Puget was the site of a daily grain market in the 17th century (now a book and flea market Fri mornings); Victor Hugo lived at No.5. The Fontaine des Trois Dauphins, installed in 1780, has been growing ever since due to calcium deposits and a tiny jungle of sprouting trees. Amid tenements to the south, contemporary and historic photography exhibitions are put on in the new **Maison de la Photographie** on

place du Globe. With a Baroque facade and Gothic interior, the **Cathédrale Ste-Marie** on place de la Cathédrale (open 9am-noon, 2.30-5.30pm) was built between the 11th and 17th centuries and was used as an arms depot during the Revolution. One block east, Cours Lafayette becomes a vast and colourful market every morning except Monday. Amid stalls overflowing with fruit and veg, you can try local snacks *la cade* (a fat chickpea crêpe) or sweet *chichi freigi* (doughnuts). Halfway along the street, the **Musée du Vieux Toulon** documents Toulon's history.

East of the old town, remnants of Vauban's ramparts and the fortified Porte d'Italie are squashed behind the modern Centre Mayol shopping centre and the Stade Mayol, home of Toulon's much-loved rugby team. Near the station, the sleek mirror-and-steel **Zénith Oméga** (bd du Commandant Nicolas, 04.94.22.66.77) hosts all manner of rock groups.

West of the *vieille ville* lies what's left of the 18th- and 19th-century new town. On place Victor Hugo, the **Opéra de Toulon** has an opulent red and gilt Second Empire auditorium. At 51 bd de Strasbourg, across from Galeries Lafayette, a plaque marks where the actor Raimu was born, though his statue has gone missing from behind the opera. Restaurant owners on the square insist new centrist Mayor Falco had him removed to spite extreme-right Mayor Le Chevallier, who put him up.

Further west, the lovely 19th-century former Var assembly building is now the **Hôtel des Arts**, which puts on exhibitions of contemporary art. Across the boulevard, the **Musée des Beaux-Arts** has a hodge-podge running from Fragonard and marine paintings by Vernet up to postwar abstraction and the cartoon-influenced *nouvelle figuration* of Combas and the Di Rosa brothers.

Rising above the town and lit nightly like a beacon, **Mont Faron** provides a wonderful escape from summer heat. It can be reached by car, a 9km drive up the winding Corniche du Mont Faron, or more directly by **Téléferique** cable car from boulevard Amiral Vence (04.94.92.68.25, about every 20mins, closed noon-2pm & Mon except July-Sept, and all Dec, Jan, return €5.80; €4 4-10s, free under-4s), which offers spectacular views as you rise over the Rade and naval docks. At the summit is the **Zoo du Mont Faron**, with big cats and monkeys, and a 19th-century fortress in which the **Musée-Mémorial du Débarquement** commemorates the 1944 liberation of Provence. Billed as the 'green lung' of Toulon, the pine woods and limestone outcrops of Mont Faron are criss-crossed with footpaths and dotted with picnic tables; there are two open-air restaurants.

Along the western shore in depressing, industrial **La Seyne-sur-Mer** (best access by boat from Toulon port to avoid the traffic jams), Fort Balaguier is where Napoléon captured Toulon in 1793, honoured in the fort's **Musée Naval**. Nearby, the 1890s neo-Mauresque **Villa Tamaris Pacha** displays contemporary art. Just south on the wooded St-Mandrier peninsula, the tiny fishing port of St-Mandrier-sur-Mer is lined with lively restaurants. A coastal path heads southward to the broad sandy beaches of Les Sablettes, Mar Vivo and Les Fabregas, which has a nudist stretch at one end.

Jutting out into the Rade, **La Tour Royale**, a fortress built for Louis XII in 1514, is today an annexe of the naval museum. East of here, **Le Mourillon** is Toulon's upmarket beach suburb, with colourful old houses and tiny streets packed with shops, restaurants and bars, plus a morning market (pl Emile Claude). Beyond the Fort St-Louis, built in the 1690s, the long sandy beaches of Le Mourillon with lawns, play areas and car park are defiantly urban and multicultural. A Sentier du Littoral footpath, once patrolled by Napoléon's customs agents, leads to several small beaches around Cap Brun, where handsome new white apartments give way to the stately villas of Ste-Marguerite.

From the open greenery of **Le Pradet**, a footpath leads to some sandy beaches accessible only to hikers and boaters. The path continues into the woods of Le Bauo Rouge and the **Musée de la Mine du Cap Garonne**, where you can descend a shaft to experience conditions in the mine where copper was extracted between 1862 and 1917.

Hôtel des Arts

236 bd du Maréchal Leclerc (04.94.91.69.18/ www.cg83.fr). **Open** (during exhibitions) 11am-6pm Tue-Sun. **Admission** free.

Maison de la Photographie

pl du Globe (04.94.93.07.59). **Open** 10am-12.30pm, 1.30-6pm Mon-Sat; 10am-12.30pm Sun. **Admission** free.

Musée des Beaux-Arts

113 bd du Maréchal Leclerc (04.94.36.81.01). **Open** 1-6.30pm Tue-Sun. **Admission** free.

Musée de la Marine

pl Monsenergue (04.94.02.02.01/www.musee-marine.fr). **Open** *Apr-15 Sept* 10am-6.30pm daily. *16 Sept-Mar* 10am-noon, 2-6pm Mon, Wed-Sun. **Admission** €4.60; free under-18s. Closed mid Dec to Jan. **No credit cards.**

Musée Mémorial du Débarquement

Sommet du Mont Faron (04.94.88.08.09). **Open** 9.45-11.45am, 1.45-4.30pm Tue-Sun (till 5.30pm daily July-Sept). **Admission** €3.80; €1.55 8-16s; free under-8s. **No credit cards.**

Musée de la Mine de Cap Garonne

chemin du Bauo Rouge, Le Pradet (04.94.08.32.46/ www.mine-capgaronne.fr). **Open** 2-5pm Wed, Sat, Sun (daily July, Aug). **Admission** €6.20; €3.80 6-18s; free under-5s. **No credit cards.**

Musée Naval du Fort Balaguier

924 corniche Bonaparte, La Seyne-sur-Mer (04.94.94.84.72). **Open** 10am-noon, 2-6pm Tue-Sun (3-7pm mid-June to mid-Sept). Closed Jan, Feb. **Admission** €2; 5-12s €1; free under-5s. **No credit cards.**

Musée du Vieux Toulon

69 cours Lafayette (04.94.62.11.07). **Open** 2-5.45pm Mon-Sat. **Admission** free.

Opéra de Toulon

pl Victor Hugo (04.94.92.70.78). **Box office** 10am-12.30pm, 2.30-5pm Tue-Sat. Closed July, Aug. **Tickets** €15-€51. **Credit** V.

Villa Tamaris Pacha

av de la Grande Maison, La-Seyne-sur-Mer (04.94.06.84.00). **Open** *during exhibitions* 2-6.30pm Tue-Sun. **Admission** free.

Zoo du Mont-Faron

Mont Faron (04.94.88.07.89). **Open** 2-5.30pm daily. Closed rainy days. **Admission** €7; €5 4-10s; free under-4s. **No credit cards.**

'They want you! They want you! They want you as a new recruit!'

Where to eat & drink

Restaurants along the port specialise in seafood, including mussels raised in the bay. **Restaurant Le Mayol** (462 av de la République, 04.94.41.39.36, closed dinner Sun Sept-June, menu €24.50-€38) is a classic Mediterranean choice, named after opera singer Félix Mayol, who donated the land for Stade Mayol and was one of Toulon's first out-of-the-closet gays. At No.224, the yellow deckchairs of the swanky **Le Grand Café de la Rade** (04.94.24.87.02) are perfect for an evening apéritif as the sun drips rose-coloured into the sea. At **Au Sourd** (10 rue Molière, 04.94.92.28.52, closed Mon & Sun, menu €23) catch fresh fish from Hyères and La Ciotat. More formal **La Chamade** (25 rue de la Comédie, 04.94.92.28.58, closed Sun; menus €22) is cheery with a dash of exoticism, while **Le Cellier** (52 rue Jean-Jaurès, 04.94.92.64.35, closed Sat lunch & Sun; menus €25) is perfect for season-fresh Toulon specialities. Couscous is pure joy at **Sidi Bou Saïd** (43bis rue Jean Jaurès, 04.94.91.21.23, closed Mon lunch & Sun, average €20), a slightly wild hangout of Toulon's North African community. In Le Pradet, gourmet Provençal cuisine is served in the gardens of **La Chanterelle** (port des Oursinières, 04.94.08.52.60, closed Mon, Sept-Easter, all Jan-Feb, menus €35-€45).

For drinks and billiards, the **113 Café** (113 av Infanterie de Marine, 04.94.03.42.41, restaurant closed lunch Sun, menus €8-€25) is a bar-restaurant in a warehouse near the ferry port, with billiards, live jazz and salsa, and DJs on Fri & Sat nights. In Le Mourillon, studenty **Bar à Thym** (32 bd Dr Cuneo, 04.94.41.90.11) is a great spot for after-beach beers and has tapas and live music. **Le Navigateur** (128 av de la République, 04.94.92.34.65) is a glitzy DJ bar where DJ Manix heats up the pre-club set.

Where to stay

Toulon's long-shabby town-centre hotels show signs of improvement. Newly renovated and upgraded **Hôtel Little Palace** (6 rue Berthelot, 04.94.92.26.62, double €45-€50) has sparkling rooms and a great old town location; it belongs to the same people as the **Hôtel les 3 Dauphins** (9 pl des 3 Dauphins, 04.94.92.65.79, double €30-€40), ask for a room with WC. Facing the gardens of the Hôtel des Arts, **New Hôtel Amirauté** (4 rue Adolphe Guiol, 04.94.22.19.67, www.new-hotel.com, double €83) is a surprisingly plush air-conditioned hotel in a 1930s building. Under the same ownership, the 60s **New Hôtel La Tour Blanche** (bd Amiral Vence, 04.94.24.41.57, double €84-€108, menus €19.50-€28) is built on stilts on the hill next to the Mont Faron cable car, with futuristic modular furniture and a cliffside pool and restaurant. Ask for one of the renovated rooms with a view.

Resources

Hospital
Hôpital Font Pré, 1208 av Colonel Picot (04.94.61.61.61).

Internet
Cybercafé Puget, pl Puget (04.94.93.05.54). **Open** 8am-8pm daily.

Police
1 rue Commissaire Morandin (04.98.03.53.00).

Post office
16 rue Jean Bartolini (04.94.16.60.20).

Tourist information
Office de Tourisme, pl Raimu, 83000 Toulon (04.94.18.53.00/www.toulontourisme.com). **Open** *June-Sept* 9am-6pm Mon-Sat; 10am-noon Sun. *Oct-May* 9.30am-5.30pm Mon-Sat; 10am-noon Sun.

The Western Côte

West of Toulon lie a string of family beach resorts, secluded hill villages and the terraced vineyards of the Bandol appellation that produce some of the south's finest wines.

Bandol & La Cadière d'Azur

Bandol is a curate's egg of a town. Its old port is today a massive grey parking lot but the old town that fronts the quays is lined with palm trees, cafés and designer swimgear, and the *ruelles* around the 18th-century **Eglise St-François-de-Sales** buzz with shops and restaurants. Westwards towards the Bay of Renecros are elegant *belle époque* homes and terraced vineyards. On the first Sunday in December, the vintners bring kegs of their three-month-old baby wines to the port for a public tasting, before putting them to bed in wooden casks for 18 months.

Two kilometres out to sea, the tiny **Ile de Bendor**, bought by pastis magnate Paul Ricard in the 1950s, has been heavily cemented with apartments, but its main attraction is the **Exposition Universelle des Vins et Spiritueux** (04.94.29.44.34, open July & Aug,

Fishing boats bob by the shore at **Sanary-sur-Mer**.

closed Wed & Sat mornings), a collection of 8,000 bottles of alcoholic spirits but, sadly, no tastings. Paul Ricard ferries sail hourly from the Embarcadéro in Bandol port (06.11.05.91.52).

Inland from Bandol lie the pretty medieval hilltop villages of **La Cadière-d'Azur** and **Le Castellet**, a fortified village once owned by King René of Provence, with ramparts, a stern 15th-century château and a sprinkling of artsy shops. Outside the village, Formula One drivers test the latest racecars, oblivious to the region's alcholic produce, at the Circuit Paul Ricard.

The N8 continues east via the grey stone village of **Ste-Anne-d'Evenos** and winds gently south along the river Reppe through the **Gorges d'Ollioules**, where steep cliffs are riddled with caves that once hid Gespard, bandit-hero of local folklore. **Ollioules** is set amid terraced hills where locals tend olives, vines, citrus fruits and, most importantly, flowers, which end up in the town's wholesale cut flower market. Medieval streets climb from the massive 11th-century Romanesque church (open 9am-noon daily) on the main square up to a ruined 13th-century château. In the eastern pine forests, the **CNCDC Chateauvallon** was known for its summer dance festival until a run-in with Toulon's right-wing politicos in the mid-90s. A new regime now presents a varied multicultural programme of theatre, dance and music in its stunning open-air amphitheatre (June-Aug) or on its indoor stage.

CNCDC Chateauvallon

794 chemin du Chateauvallon, Ollioules (04.94.22.74.00). **Box office** 2-7pm Mon; 10am-7pm Tue-Sat. **Tickets** €20; €12 students. **Credit** MC, V.

Where to stay, eat & drink

In Bandol, escape holiday crowds on the private beach of the **Golf Hôtel**, once the casino (plage Renécros, bd Lumière, 04.94.29.45.83, www.golfhotel.fr, closed 7-20 Dec & 4 Jan-1 Feb, double €54-€100). Near the port, **Hôtel L'Oasis** (15 rue des Ecoles, 04.94.29.41.69, www.oasisbandol.com, closed Dec, double €48-€64) is a former parsonage. White linen tablecloths flap in the sea breeze at **Auberge du Port** (7 allée Jean Moulin, 04.94.29.42.63, menus €32-€43) a lively brasserie with a chic feel. In La Cadière, **Le Bérard** (av Gabriel Péri, 04.94.90.11.43, www.hotel-berard.com, closed Jan, double €99-€249, restaurant closed lunch Mon & Sat, menus €42-€55) has rooms in an old convent and a restaurant that serves snazzy Provençal fare. In Ste-Anne-d'Evenos, the Marquise Dutheil de La Rochère offers *chambres d'hôtes* at the **Château-Ste-Anne** vineyard (04.94.90.35.40, double €98). There's a

pool under the olive trees. **Hôtel du Castellet** (3001 rte des Hauts du Camp, Le Beausset, 04.94.98.38.88, www.hotelducastellet.com, double €280-€550, restaurant closed lunch Mon, menus €40-€80) at the Circuit Paul Ricard is a luxury pit-stop for racing teams and fans, where you can park your private jet at the adjoining aerodrome. Outside Ollioules, **La Table du Vigneron** (724 chemin de la Tourelle, 04.94.88.36.19, www.latableduvigneron. com, closed Mon, dinner Sun & Feb, menu €39) does good seasonal cooking, plus tastings of its Domaine de Terrebrune wines.

Resources

Bandol market is on the port on Tuesday morning, with small art markets nightly in summer. Ollioules market is on Thursday morning, with a farmers' market on Saturday.

Internet

Boss Cyber Café, 9 rue des Ecoles, Bandol (04.94.29.03.03). **Open** 9am-noon, 3-6.30pm Mon-Sat.

Tourist information

Bandol *Maison du Tourisme, allée Vivien, 83150 Bandol (04.94.29.41.35/www.bandol.fr).* **Open** July-Aug 9am-7pm daily. Sept-June 9am-noon, 2-6pm Mon-Fri; 9am-noon Sat.
Ollioules *Office de Tourisme, 116 av Philippe de Hautecloque, 83190 Ollioules (04.94.63.11.74/www.ollioules.com).* **Open** July, Aug 9am-12.30pm, 3-7pm Mon-Sat. Sept-June 9am-noon, 2:30-6pm Mon-Fri; 9am-noon Sat.

Sanary-sur-Mer to Six-Fours

Colourful boats bob by the quayside and fishermen still sew sardine nets along the palm-lined port of **Sanary-sur-Mer**. On hot mornings, market vendors hawk their wares in a frenzy that competes with the seagulls. No wonder that in the 1930s, Sanary became the refuge of Thomas Mann, Lion Feuchtwanger, Stephan Zweig and other German intellectuals escaping the Nazi regime. Aldous Huxley also lived here and a young Sybille Bedford records the period in *Jigsaw*. At the western end of the port, in a 13th-century tower, the **Musée Frédéric Dumas** houses ancient diving equipment and wine amphorae – Frédéric being one of Cousteau's original 'Mousque-mers'.

On the wind-battered Sicie peninsula, **Six-Fours-les-Plages** is a string of modern beach bars and restaurants. When the mistral is blowing, angry waves make 'Brutal Beach',

▶ For more on touring the Bandol wine châteaux, *see p27.*

The Var

as it has been nicknamed, a surfer's paradise. On a hill to the north, the **Collégiale-St-Pierre**, spanning the Romanesque and Gothic periods, is all that remains of the old village of Six-Fours. About 3km further north, **Chapelle Notre-Dame-de-Pepiole** (open 3-6pm daily) is one of France's oldest Christian churches. Dating back to the sixth century, it has three unusual naves.

The modern beach resort of **Le Brusc** is on the site of the port of Tauroentium, founded by the Phocean Greeks from Marseille; today most visitors stay only long enough to get a ferry to the **Iles des Embiez** (Paul Ricard Ferries 04.94.10.65.21), former salt-panning islands bought by Paul Ricard in 1958. The main island houses the **Institut Océanographique Paul Ricard**, a research centre into Mediterranean pollution, and offers miles of footpaths and cycle tracks. Bikes can be hired on the quay.

Collégiale-St-Pierre

montée du Fort Militaire, Six-Fours-les-Plages (04.94.34.24.75). **Open** *June-Sept* 10am-noon, 3-7pm Mon, Wed-Sun. *Oct-May* 10am-noon, 2-6pm Mon, Wed-Sun. **Admission** free.

Musée Frédéric-Dumas

pl de la Tour, Sanary-sur-Mer (04.94.74.80.23). **Open** *July-Aug* 10am-noon, 3-7pm daily. *Sept-June* 10am-noon, 3-7pm Sat, Sun. **Admission** free.

Where to eat, drink & stay

On the port in Sanary, the **Hôtel-Restaurant de la Tour** (24 quai Général de Gaulle, 04.94.74.10.10, double €72-€94, restaurant closed Tue, Wed & Dec, menus €20-€44) serves gourmet seafood and has pleasantly ageing rooms. **Restaurant L'enK** (13 rue Louis Blanc, 04.94.74.66.57, www.monmenu.com/83/l-en-cas, closed dinner Mon Sept-June, menu €25) serves regional produce with an exotic flair. Sanary also has a thriving bar scene. Start at tiny **Café Mac'Sym's** (10 quai de Gaulle, 04.94.74.45.34) before clubbing at **Mai-Tai** (1370 rte de Bandol, 04.94.74.23.92).

In Six-Fours-les-Plages, smart **Le Dauphin** (36 sq des Bains, Plage de Bonnegrace, 04.94.07.61.58, www.restaurant-ledauphin.com, closed Mon & dinner Sun Sept-June, menus €25-€45) has recently opened the more casual **Le Bistro Du Dauphin** (menus €11-€16). In Le Brusc, **Restaurant Le St-Pierre** (47 rue de la Citadelle, 04.94.34.02.52, closed lunch Mon in July & Aug, dinner Sun & all Mon Sept-June, all Jan; menus €18-€34.50) serves grilled fish and excellent *bouillabaisse* (reserve). **Jardin de la Ferme** (688 chemin des Faisses, 04.94.34.01.07) in an olive grove on Cap Sicié, 400m from the sea, offers rooms (€53-€58), cabins (€350-€595/wk) and tent pitches (€13 for two).

Resources

Sanary has a daily produce market and a flea market last Saturday of the month. There are markets in Six-Fours on Saturday morning and Le Brusc on Thursday morning.

Internet

Cyber Espace @ Fenyx, 8 rue Lauzet Ainé, Sanary-sur-Mer (04.94.88.10.78). **Open** *Jan-Dec* 3-7pm Tue; 10.30am-7pm Wed-Sun. *July, Aug* 11am-1am daily.

Tourist information

Sanary *Maison du Tourisme, Les Jardins de la Ville, 83110 Sanary-sur-Mer (04.94.74.01.04, www.sanarysurmer.com).* **Open** *July, Aug* 9am-7pm Mon-Sat; 9am-noon Sun. *Sept-June* 9am-noon, 2-5.30pm Mon-Sat.
Six-Fours *Office du Tourisme, promenade Charles de Gaulle, 83140 Six-Fours-les-Plages (04.94.07.02.21/www.six-fours-les-plages.com).* **Open** *Apr-June, Sept* 9am-noon, 2-6.30pm Mon-Sat. *July-Aug* 9am-7pm Mon-Sat; 10am-1pm Sun. *Oct-Mar* 8.30am-noon, 1.30-5.30pm Mon-Fri; 9am-noon, 1.30-5.30pm Sat.

Getting there & around

By air

Toulon-Hyères airport is 35km away in Hyères.

By car

The A50 from Marseille in the west and the A57 from the east pour direct into the centre of Toulon. After decades of work, a cross-city tunnel linking the two opened in 2003 – but only in one direction. Leave the A50 at exit 12 for Bandol, 13 to Six-Fours, Sanary-sur-Mer and Ollioules, 14 for Chateauvallon. The coastal D559 goes between Marseille and Toulon via Bandol and Sanary.

By train

Toulon is on the main TGV line from Paris and is served by local trains from Marseille and Nice. Local trains between Marseille and Toulon stop at Bandol and Sanary-Ollioules.

By bus

Cartreize (04.42.08.41.05) runs 6 buses a day between Marseille and Bandol. **Littoral Cars** (04.94.74.01.35) runs buses between Bandol and Sanary, Le Brusc, Six-Fours, La Seyne and Toulon. **RMTT** (04.94.03.87.03, www.reseaumistral.com) runs buses from Toulon to Ollioules, La Seyne and Sanary. **Sodétrav** (04.94.12.55.12) runs buses between Toulon and Hyères. **RMTT** (04.94.03.87.03, www.reseaumistral.com) runs an extensive network of local buses in Toulon (take Nos.3, 13 or 23 for the beaches at Mourillon and No.40 to the cable-car).

By boat

Boat services (www.reseaumistral.com) run from Toulon port to La Seyne, Les Sablettes, Tamaris and St-Mandrier. Toulon is also a ferry port to Corsica (www.corsicaferries.com).

Hyères to Les Maures

Explore exotic gardens, a village named after its mimosa trees and an island pungent with eucalyptus, or simply laze on superlative sandy beaches.

The coast from Hyères to Cavalaire boasts some of the best sandy beaches in France. Inland, the wild Maures mountains offer respite from the summer crowds and heat but were decimated by the forest fires of 2003 (see p18).

Hyères & Giens

Palmy Hyères led the seaside brigade in the 19th century, when its mild climate was recommended for the consumptive. It was particularly favoured by the British: Queen Victoria paid a visit in 1892. But when the fashionable season changed from winter to summer, Hyères, perched up on a hill 5km from the sea, was left high and dry. Today the grand hotels have all gone, holidaymakers remain firmly on the seaside strip and the busy, multiracial town lives by salt, cut flowers and date-palm rearing as much as tourism.

Hyères' medieval *vieille ville* is reached at the end of avenue Gambetta, the main drag leading up from the coast, or through the fortified Porte Massillon. From there rue Massillon, busy with food shops, leads to café-filled place Massillon, where the much-restored, barrel-vaulted **Tour St-Blaise**, now used for exhibitions, is all that remains of a Templar monastery. Climb the steps from the square and take steep rue Ste-Catherine to the **Collégiale St-Paul**, with its medieval belltower and Renaissance doorway; the front room is crowded with naive *ex-voto* paintings. On place de la République, the 13th-century **Eglise St-Louis** (open 8am-7pm daily) was once a Franciscan monastery where Louis IX prayed in 1254 on his return from the Crusades.

Climb up above the church for Hyères' most compelling sight, the **Villa Noailles**, a masterpiece of Modernist architecture, all horizontal lines and Cubist stained glass, designed in 1924 by Robert Mallet-Stevens for avant-garde aristos Charles and Marie-Laure de Noailles. In its day, it was the scene of trysts and parties frequented by A-list bohemians including Picasso, Stravinsky, Buñuel and Man Ray, who shot part of his film *Les Mystères du Château de Dé* here. The house was restored by the municipality in the 1990s and is now used for exhibitions. Continue up the montée de Noailles to the ruins of the 11th- to 13th-century castle of the Lords of Fos, surrounded by the

Parc St-Bernard and the equally lush **Parc Ste-Claire** (both open 8am-7pm summer, 8am-5pm winter), around the 19th-century castle once lived in by Edith Wharton.

The charms of the modern town are now distinctly faded and marred by an appalling one-way system, though near the town hall on avenue Joseph Clotis, fine *belle époque* houses have become arty restaurants and tearooms, and the **Casino des Palmiers** still supplies a touch of glamour. In place Lefebvre, the **Musée Municipal** contains archaeological finds, furniture and local paintings. On avenue Ambroise Thomas, the **Jardins Olbius Riquier** (open 7.30am-dusk daily) has subtropical gardens, hothouse and mini-zoo around a pseudo-Moorish villa. Sticking up on the Costebelle hill is the pierced concrete tower of **Eglise Notre-Dame de la Consolation**, which replaced an ancient church bombed in World War II.

Beach territory below the town runs either side of a long, narrow isthmus. To the east, the Plage d'Hyères is a long, over-charged stretch of sand running from the busy marina along the Rade d'Hyères bay. In the Almanarre district to the west, the **Site Archéologique d'Olbia** bears fragmentary traces of the Greek trading post of Olbia, along with Roman homes and baths and part of a medieval abbey. The 4km-long **Almanarre beach** hosts heats of the world windsurfing championships. Between here and La Capte stretch the disused Etang des Pesquiers salt pans, liable to flooding in winter.

The bulge at the end of the isthmus is pretty though built-up **Giens** peninsula, with its namesake hilltop village. Place Belvédère affords fantastic views and hosts a market on Tuesday morning. Boats leave for the islands from **La Tour Fondue**, a squat 17th-century fortress built by Cardinal Richelieu.

Casino des Palmiers

1 av Ambroise Thomas, Hyères (04.94.12.80.80). **Open** *slot machines* 10am-4am daily; *gaming rooms* 8.30pm-4am daily. **Admission** (over-18s only) slot machines free; gaming rooms €10 (bring ID). **Credit** AmEx, DC, MC, V.

Collégiale St-Paul

pl St-Paul, Hyères (no phone). **Open** *Apr-Oct* 3-6pm Mon; 10am-noon, 3-6.30pm Wed-Sat; 10am-12.30pm Sun. *Nov-Mar* 3-6pm Mon, Wed-Sun. **Admission** free.

Musée Municipal

Cité Administratif, pl Théodore Lefebvre, Hyères (04.94.00.78.42). **Open** 10am-noon, 2.30-5.30pm Wed-Sun. **Admission** free.

Site Archéologique d'Olbia

quartier de l'Almanarre, Hyères (04.94.57.98.28/ www.monum.fr). **Open** Apr-Sept 9.30am-12.30pm, 3-7pm daily. Closed Oct-Mar. **Admission** €4.60; €3.10 students; free under-18s. **No credit cards.**

Villa Noailles

montée de Noailles, Hyères (04.94.12.70.63). **Open** mid-June to mid-Sept 10am-noon, 4-7.30pm Wed-Sun. mid-Sept to mid-June during exhibitions only 10am-noon, 2-5.30pm. **Admission** free.

Where to stay & eat

Hyères lacks the stylish accommodation of its elegant past. **Hôtel de Portalet** (4 rue de Limans, 04 94 65 39 40, double €36-€45), in the old town, is simple but clean. Overlooking La Gavine port, **La Potinière** (27 av de la Méditerranée, 04.94.00.51.60, closed mid-Jan to mid-Feb, double €50-€85) has large rooms and a private beach. La Capte is dotted with campsites and mostly downmarket hotels. Best choice is the **Hôtel Ibis Thalassa** (allée de la Mer, La Capte, 04.94.58.00.94, www.thalassa.com, closed 3wks in Jan, double €59.50-€125), a modern building with gardens, a restaurant, direct access to the spa and a private beach.

Deep in the *vieille ville*, **Bistrot de Marius** (1 pl Massillon, 04.94.35.88.38, closed lunch Tue & Wed, and mid-Nov to mid-Dec, mid-Jan to mid-Feb, menus €15-€30) serves authentic Provençal cuisine including *bouillabaisse*, or for a light meal try **L'Eau à la Bouche** (2 pl Massillon, 04.94.35.33.85). In the modern town, **Les Jardins de Bacchus** (32 av Gambetta, 04.94.65.77.63, www.les-jardins-de-bacchus.com, closed Mon, lunch Sat, dinner Sun, 2wks in Jan & June, menus €33-€49) does good contemporary Provençal fare. **Art et Tea** (21 av Joseph Clotis, 04.94.65.09.34) is a tea room-cum-gallery in a lush garden setting. On Plage de l'Almanarre, try the **Zone Bleue** (3 rte de Sel, 04.94.57.68.40, average €15) for a drink or fresh fish in the tangy marine air.

In Giens, the 1950s **Provençal** (pl St-Pierre, 04.98.04.54.54, www.provencalhotel.com, closed Nov-Mar, double €60-€107) has a pool and terraced gardens that descend right to the sea. The **Tire Bouchon** (1 pl St-Pierre, 04.94.58.24.61, closed all Tue & Wed, 2wks in Oct, mid-Dec to mid-Jan, menus €23-€29) does an excellent octopus *fricassée*. In the tiny cove of Port du Niel, **L'Eau Salée** (04.94.58.92.33, closed all Sun & Mon and Jan, menus €25-€34) serves fish (and clients) straight off the boat.

Resources

Internet

Maison de l'Internet, rue Soldat Bellon (04.94.65.92.82). **Open** 9am-12.30pm, 2-5pm Mon-Fri.

Tourist information

Office de Tourisme, 3 av Ambroise Thomas, 83400 Hyères (04.94.01.84.50/www.ot-hyeres.fr). **Open** July-Aug 8am-8pm daily. Sept-June 9am-6pm Mon-Fri; 10am-4pm Sat.

Iles de Hyères: Porquerolles, Port-Cros, Ile de Levant

Robert Louis Stevenson supposedly found inspiration for *Treasure Island* on the Ile de **Porquerolles**, the largest of the three islands strung across the entrance to Hyères bay. Colonised in the fifth century by the monks of Lérins (*see p232*), the islands were seized by the Saracens in 1160. The latter were turfed out by François 1er, who fortified Porquerolles, with the Fort du Petit-Langoustier and the Fort Ste-Agathe, which looms over the yacht marina. Up the hill from the port, Porquerolles village was built as a retirement colony for Napoleonic officers and still resembles a colonial outpost, centred on place d'Armes, with its pungent eucalyptus trees. Here there are plenty of cafés as well as stalls for picnic supplies. For 60 years from 1911, the village was the private property of Belgian engineer Joseph Fournier, who introduced the exotic flora. Full of well-dressed French *BCBGs* (French sloanes) cycling *en famille*, Porquerolles still feels privileged today. There are numerous bike hire outlets in both port and village. You don't need two wheels to get to the white sand and lush backdrop of the Plage d'Argent (west) or Plage de la Courtade (east), each an easy 10-15 minute walk from the village through pine woods. Forest tracks lead to the more mountainous southern half of the island and the lighthouse of the Cap d'Arme; note that these may be closed during high winds in summer due to fire risk.

The hilly, lush **Ile de Port-Cros** is a nature reserve with no cars, no smoking (!) and nature paths that extend under the sea for swimmers and divers to look at marine flora.

Eighty per cent of the **Ile du Levant** is still military property, though no longer a shooting range. The remaining area, Héliopolis is a nudist colony where participating visitors, as opposed to voyeurs, are welcome.

Where to stay & eat

On Porquerolles, **Le Mas du Langoustier** (04.94.58.30.09, closed Nov-Apr, double €180-

€281 incl. dinner), 3km west of the port, has luxurious rooms, beautiful gardens, fabulous fish cooking and a snooty reputation. Guests are met at the ferries by electric buggy. Simpler **Les Glycines** (22 pl d'Armes, 04.94.58.30.36, double €109-€269, menus €24.90) has lovely rooms in Provençal hues. Bar-restaurant **L'Oustaou** (pl d'Armes, 04.94.58.30.13, double €76-€130, average €23) serves pasta or *plats du jour* like squid cooked in its ink and also has six rooms, some with sea view. On Port-Cros, **Le Manoir** (04.94.05.90.52, closed Oct-Apr, double €270-€390 incl dinner, menus €40-€45) is the only hotel; its restaurant serves Provençal classics.

Ferry services

There are frequent ferries in July and August; more limited services the rest of the year. TLV (04.94.58.21.81, www.tlv-tvm.com) runs ferries from La Tour Fondue in Giens to Porquerolles (takes 20 mins, €14.30 return, €13 4-10s, free under-4s) and from Hyères to Port-Cros and Le Levant (takes 60-90 mins, €19-€22 return, free under-4s). **Vedettes Iles d'Or** (04.94.71.01.02, www.vedettesilesdor.fr) runs boats from Le Lavandou to Port-Cros and Levant (takes 35-60 mins, €21 return; €16.80 4-12s, free under-4s). There are also daily services to Porquerolles and Port-Cros from Cavalaire and to Porquerolles from Toulon in summer.

Bormes-les-Mimosas

Set above the coast in the hills, the old village of **Bormes-les-Mimosas** is a picturesque clutter of colour-washed houses where sun terraces point to contemporary preoccupations but covered passages (*cuberts*) and vaulted interiors betray their medieval origins. The floral handle was added to the name in 1968, to emphasise the point that Bormes had the highest density of these scented, yellow, puffball-bearing trees on the Riviera. Mimosa blooms January to March; the rest of the year, beautifully planted terraces drip with creepers and bougainvillea. On the edge of the old village, next to the Wednesday market-place, the **Chapelle St-François** was built in 1560 in thanks to St François de Paule, who delivered the village from the Plague in 1481. Place Gambetta, with its cafés and restaurants, leads into the main street rue Carnot from where you can wander down streets like ruelle du Moulin, venelle des Amoureux and the 83 steps of rue Rompi Cuou, or up to the remains of the medieval castle of the Lords of Fos (closed to the public). The 18th-century **Eglise St-Trophime** contains some curious polychrome wood saints' reliquaries as well as *trompe l'oeil* frescoes round the choir. Further down the hill, the **Musée d'Art et d'Histoire** has some Rodin sketches plus local paintings and history. Bormes' beach suburb of

The castle ruins in **Hyères**. See p181.

The Var

La Favière is a modern but inoffensive low-rise development with marina, diving club, plenty of shops for swimgear and picnic fare, and a long, family-oriented sandy public beach.

The Sentier du Littoral coast path (waymarked in yellow) winds round the peninsula. Apart from the small hamlet of Cabasson and the heavily guarded 16th-century Fort de Brégançon (the French president's official summer retreat), **Cap Bénat**, which juts out south-west of Bormes, is one of the least built-up stretches of coast in the Midi. Here there's no urban sprawl, nor even any luxury villas, just the **Château de Brégançon**, source of a robust Côtes de Provence wine (*see p29*), woods, vineyards and a number of unspoiled beaches (you pay for the car park, but entrance is free). West of Brégançon, the **Plage de l'Estagnol** (parking €7-€8 Apr-Oct) is a lovely sandy strip shaded by pine woods, with shallow water, a café and good fish restaurant (*see p185*).

Musée d'Art et d'Histoire de Bormes
103 rue Carnot (04.94.71.56.60). **Open** 10am-noon, 2.30-5pm Tue-Sat; 10am-noon Sun. **Admission** free.

Where to stay & eat

Bormes Village offers the best gastronomic choices in the area. Stylish **Restaurant La Tonnelle** (23 pl Gambetta, 04.94.71.34.84, closed Wed & Thur Sept-Apr, all Wed & lunch Thur May & June, all lunch July-Aug, and mid-Nov to end Dec, menus €25-€40) is a true discovery thanks to the inventive cooking of chef Gilles Renard. **Hôtel-Restaurant La Bellevue** (14 pl Gambetta, 04.94.71.15.15, closed mid-Nov to mid-Jan, double €39-€50, menus €14-€21) offers a *belle* view and lots of boho allure, with breakfast on the terrace. Its simple café-restaurant serves mussels, salads, Provençal specialities and ice cream. Also on the square, venerable **Café Le Progrès** (04.94.71.15.36) serves up salads at lunch and live music and street theatre on summer evenings. Atmospheric **Lou Portaou** (rue Cubert des Poètes, 04.94.64.86.37, closed Tue, lunch June-Sept, all mid-Nov to mid-Dec, menus €38) in a medieval tower has a short but original choice of Provençal dishes, while simpler **Lou Poulid Cantoun** (6 pl du Lou Poulid Cantoun, 04.94.71.15.59, closed Mon, Oct-May, menus €30-€33) has tables around the fountain of a tiny paved square. **L'Escoundudo** (2 ruelle du Moulin, 04.94.71.15.53, closed Mon, Tue & all Mar, menus €35-€78) offers trad southern fare. Near the sea, **Hôtel de la Plage** (rond-point de la Bienvenue, La Favière, 04.94.71.02.74, closed Oct-Mar, double €100-€124 incl dinner) has been run by the same matronly management since the 1960s (average age of staff about 70). Rooms are spotless with balconies or terraces. In Cabasson **Les Palmiers** (240 chemin du Petit

Invest in a sunlounger for lazy days at **Cavalaire-sur-Mer**.

Fort, 04.94.64.81.94, www.hotel-palmiers.com, closed mid-Nov to mid-Feb, doubles €80-€210, half-pension obligatory July-Sept, menus €28-€45) is resolutely provincial with steps to the beach and a reliable restaurant. At **Plage de l'Estagnol**, the animated restaurant (04.94.64.71.11, closed Oct-Mar, average €40) serves superb fish and langoustines grilled on a wood fire and big vats of *bouillabaisse*. Reserve.

Resources

Bormes market is Wednesday morning. La Favière has a market on Saturday morning and Monday evening in July and August.

Tourist information

Office de Tourisme, 1 pl Gambetta, 83230 Bormes-les-Mimosas (04.94.01.38.38/www.bormesles mimosas.com). **Open** *Apr-Sept* 9am-12.30pm, 2.30-6.30pm daily. *Oct-Mar* 9am-12.30pm, 2-6pm Mon-Sat. **Branches**: La Favière, bd du Front de Mer (04.94.64.82.57); Maison de Bormes, 2273 av Lou Mistraou, Pin de Bormes (04.94.00.43.43).

Le Lavandou to Cavalaire

Le Lavandou hugs the coast east of Bormes. A concretey promenade and a couple of tower blocks hide a pretty old town, behind what was once a major fishing port, now a pleasure marina. Its glitzy seafront is animated at night. By day, the main beach gets very crowded, though the quieter, more steeply shelving Plage St-Clair further east in a bay surrounded by mountains is more attractive for bathing. From here to Cavalaire-sur-Mer, the **Corniche des Maures** follows some of the coast's most unspoiled scenery, the view uphill from silver-sand beaches unimpeded by development. Cap Nègre and the Plage de Pramousquier were key points of the 1944 Allied landings.

The village of Le Rayol-Canadel is home to the fabulous **Domaine du Rayol** gardens, created in 1910 by Paris banker Alfred Courmes, who packed the grounds with exotic plants before losing all his money in the crash of 1929. Since 1989, gardening wizard Gilles Clément has added New Zealand and Asiatic gardens and a 'Garden in Motion'. Gullies, bowers and secret paths are dotted about this jungle of green and dramatic vistas and seaside drops. Buy the guided-walk leaflet which leads you on a treasure hunt for bottlebrushes, blackboys and other unusual species. Outdoor concerts are held in July and August. Above Le Rayol-Canadel, spectacular sea views can be had from the Col du Canadel pass, which crosses over into the heart of the Maures. The idyll comes to a halt at **Cavalaire-sur-Mer**, a built-up sprawl with a long unglamorous beach.

Domaine du Rayol

av des Belges, Le Rayol-Canadel (04.98.04.44.00/ www.domainedurayol.org). **Open** *Apr-Sept* 9.30am-12.30pm, 2-6.30pm daily. *Sept-June* 9.30am-12.30pm, 2.30-5.30pm daily. Closed mid-Nov to Jan. **Admission** €6.50; €3.50 6-18s; free under-6s. **Credit** MC, V.

Where to stay & eat

In Le Lavandou, Hispano-Moresque **Auberge de la Calanque** (62 av du Général de Gaulle, 04.94.71.05.96, closed Nov-Easter, double €92-€183, restaurant closed Wed lunch & Thur, menu €36) has a 1930s hacienda-style interior, a pool and garden. By the Vieux-Port, simpler **Hôtel Le Rabelais** (2 rue Rabelais, 04.94.71.00.56, www.le-rabelais.fr, closed mid-Nov to mid-Jan, €50-€85) has recently redecorated rooms, some with a balcony. Pick of the fish restaurants overlooking the port is **Restaurant du Vieux-Port** (quai Gabriel Péri, 04.94.71.00.21, closed Tue & Wed and mid-Nov to Feb, menus €20-€34). One street back from the seafront, **Auberge Provençale** (11 rue Patron Ravello, 04.94.71.00.44, closed 2wks Nov & 2wks Jan, double €39-€62, restaurant closed Mon, menus €23-€25) serves carefully prepared southern dishes, both land and sea, and has some simple, spacious rooms. Seafront eateries in St Clair tend more towards pizza, mussels and atmosphere than great cuisine. An upmarket exception is **Les Tamaris** (chez Raymond, Plage de St-Clair, 04.94.71.07.22, closed Nov to mid-Feb except 1 wk at Christmas, and Tue in Oct, Mar, Apr, average €40) which has excellent fish cooking, including *bourride*. Luxurious **Hôtel Les Roches** (1 av des Trois Dauphins, Aiguebelle Plage, 04.94.71.05.07/ www.hotellesroches.com, closed Jan-Mar, double €160-€720, menus €50-€88) plunges down the cliff to the sea, and has chic bar, antiques-furnished rooms and half-seawater pool.

In Le Rayol-Canadel, **Le Maurin des Maures** (bd de Touring Club, 04.94.05.60.11, closed dinner mid-Nov to mid-Dec, menus €11-€26) is always packed, as much for the fantastic atmosphere as local youngsters pile in for *babyfoot*, as for the fresh fish and Provençal faves. Be sure to reserve. Overlooking the beach below the Domaine de Rayol, lovely **Hôtel Le Bailli de Suffren** (av des Américains, 04.98.04.47.00, www.lebaillidesuffren.com, closed mid-Oct to Easter, double €154-€323) is a curved 1960s building, renovated in calm, modern Provençal-chic with bar, restaurant, private beach and hire boats.

Resources

Le Lavandou has a huge market on Thursday morning; Cavalaire is Wednesday morning.

Internet

La Chaloupe, quai Baptistin Pins, Le Lavandou (04.94.71.66.36). **Open** *summer* 7am-11pm daily. *winter* 9am-9pm daily.

Tourist information

Cavalaire *Office de Tourisme, Maison de la Mer, 83240 Cavalaire-sur-Mer (04.94.01.92.10/ www.golfe-info.com/cavalaire).* **Open** *June-Sept* 9am-7pm daily. *Oct-May* 9am-12.30pm, 2-6pm Mon-Fri; 9am-12.30pm Sat.
Le Lavandou *Office de Tourisme, quai Gabriel Péri, 83980 Le Lavandou (04.94.00.40.50/ www.lelavandou.com).* **Open** *Apr-Sept* 9am-12.30pm, 3-7pm daily. *Oct-Mar* 9am-12.30pm, 3-6pm Mon-Sat.

The Massif des Maures

Taking the D41 out of Bormes to Collobrières, you are at once in a surprisingly wild mountain area with a hair-raisingly winding road that zigzags up to the Col du Babaou. The heart of the Massif, dotted with remote chapels and Neolithic menhirs, can only be reached on foot. It is crossed east-west by the GR9 and GR51 footpaths and north-south by the GR90. For the less ambitious, two short waymarked discovery footpaths leave from near the Office de Tourisme in Collobrières. The ONF organises themed guided walks; details from tourist offices.

Surrounded by massive chestnut trees and the cork oak trees from which cork is hewn, **Collobrières** is France's *marron glacé* capital – and celebrates the chestnut in a festival each October. Around 1850, it was an important logging centre, and 19th-century wood barons' houses contrast with higgledy-piggledy medieval streets. 12km east, off the D14 to Cogolin, the isolated **Chartreuse de La Verne** looms like a fortress halfway up a remote hillside. Founded by a group of Carthusian monks in 1170, it was burned on several occasions in the Wars of Religion and rebuilt each time in a mix of brown-grey schist and local dark-green serpentine facing around doorways and vaults. After the Revolution the monks fled to Nice from the Plage St-Clair. Restoration began in the 1970s and since 1983 the monastery has been occupied by a community of nuns.

Further east, picture-perfect *village perché* **Grimaud** was a Saracen stronghold before falling to the Templars. Nowadays, the quaint-shops brigade is firmly in command. Up top are the ruins of an 11th-century castle.

Reached through the cork woods north of here, **La Garde-Freinet** is a lively stopping-off point where the main street, rue St-Jacques, and place Vieille abound with bistros, *brocantes* and designer gifts, and a superb old-fashioned *quincaillerie* (hardware store). Beyond the solid 15th- to 18th-century church, rue de la Planète is

the start of an energetic climb to the ruins of the abandoned original village, inhabited until the 15th century, allegedly built on the foundations of a Saracen stronghold. The **Conservatoire du Patrimoine** in the same building as the tourist office has a display about the fortress and exhibitions on local heritage and pastimes. Further west on the northern side of the Massif, near Gonfaron, the **Village des Tortues** is a conservation centre for Hermann's tortoise, found only in the Maures and in Corsica.

A busy crossroads between the Maures and St-Tropez, **Cogolin** wins no prizes for beauty, but it does qualify as a real town with an economy based around the manufacture of corks, briar pipes, bamboo furniture and carpet-making (the latter introduced by Armenian immigrants in the 1920s). The 11th-century church of St-Sauveur (open 8am-7pm daily) has a lovely 16th-century altarpiece by Hurlupin.

Chartreuse de La Verne

off D214 (04.94.43.45.41). **Open** *Apr-Sept* 11am-6pm Mon, Wed-Sun. *Oct-Mar* 11am-5pm Mon, Wed-Sun. Closed Jan. **Admission** €5; €3 10-16s; free under-10s. **No credit cards.**

Conservatoire du Patrimoine et des Traditions du Freinet

1 pl Neuve, La Garde-Freinet (04.94.43.08.57). **Open** 10am-12.30pm, 3-6pm Tue-Sat. **Admission** €1.50; free under-12s. **No credit cards.**

Village des Tortues

rte des Mayons, Gonfaron (04.94.78.26.41/ www.tortues.com). **Open** *Mar-Nov* 9am-7pm daily. **Admission** €8; €5 3-16s; free under-3s. **Credit** V.

Where to stay & eat

In Collobrières, **Hôtel-Restaurant Notre-Dame** (15 av de la Libération, 04.94.48.07.13, closed Dec-15 Feb, double €31, restaurant closed Tue, menus €16-€23) is a simple Logis de France overhanging a stream. For a truly rustic experience, sample the **Ferme de Peigros** (Col de Babaou, 04.94.48.03.83, closed dinner Sept-June, menu €20) down a track by the Col du Babaou pass, which produces its own goat's cheese. In La Garde-Freinet, **La Claire Fontaine** (pl Vieille, 04.94.43.63.76, double €45) is a busy café and ice cream shop in a lofty building on the main square. Bedrooms are simple but clean, none have en suite facilities, but some have a shower. Restaurants include **La Colombe Joyeuse** (12 pl Vieille, 04.94.43.65.24, closed Tue except July & Aug, all 15 Nov-15 Dec & 3-31 Jan, menus €15-€26), which despite the name (happy dove) specialises in pigeon.

On the D558 out of Grimaud, **Les Santons** (D558, 04.94.43.21.02, closed Nov-Mar, menu €33-€42) is a little stiff but dishes such as

Bougainvillea-draped **Bormes-les-Mimosas**. *See p183.*

chicken with a ginger and citrus sauce are excellent. In Cogolin, **La Maison du Monde** (63 rue Carnot, 04.94.54.77.54, closed late Jan to mid-Feb, double €70-€150) has 12 stylish rooms, pool and garden; rooms near the road can be noisy. New **La Petite Maison** (34 bd Delattre de Tassigny, 04.94.54.58.49, closed Sun, €16-€30) is a pretty restaurant serving warming soups and excellent fish.

Resources

Morning markets are Sunday at Collobrières, Wednesday & Saturday at Cogolin (plus Mon & Fri in summer), Wednesday and Sunday in La Garde-Freinet, Thursday at Grimaud.

Tourist information

Cogolin *Office de Tourisme, pl de la République, 83310 Cogolin (04.94.55.01.10/www.cogolin-provence.com).* **Open** *July, Aug* 9am-1pm, 2-7pm Mon-Sat; 10am-1pm Sun. *Sept-June* 9am-12.30pm, 2-6.30pm Mon-Fri; 9.30am-12.30pm Sat.
Collobrières *Office de Tourisme, bd Caminat, 83610 Collobrières (04.94.48.08.00/www.collotour. com).* **Open** *July, Aug* 10am-12.30pm, 3-6.30pm Mon-Sat. *Sept-June* 10am-noon, 2-6pm Tue-Sat.
La Garde-Freinet *Office de Tourisme, 1 pl Neuve, 83680 La Garde-Freinet (04.94.43.67.41/www. lagardefreinet-tourisme.com).* **Open** 10am-12.30pm, 2.30-5.30pm Mon-Sat (3-6.30pm July, Aug).

Grimaud *Office de Tourisme, 1 bd des Aliziers, 83310 Grimaud (04.94.55.43.83/www.grimaud-provence.com).* **Open** 9am-12.30pm, 2.30-5.30pm Mon-Sat (3-7pm July, Aug).

Getting there & around

By air

Toulon/Hyères airport (04.94.00.83.83) is near to Hyères port.

By car

The A570 runs into Hyères before merging with the N98 coast road, which continues to Bormes and then cuts along the south of the Massif des Maures. The D559 at Bormes follows the coast to Le Lavandou and Cavalaire-sur-Mer.

By train

Nearest mainline stations are Toulon, Draguignan-Les Arcs and St-Raphaël. Hyères is on a branch line served by several trains a day from Toulon.

By bus

Sodétrav (04.94.12.55.12) operates bus services between Toulon and Hyères and from Hyères to St-Tropez, stopping at Bormes, Le Lavandou, Le Rayol-Canadol and Cavalaire-sur-Mer; there are few buses on Sunday. From June-Aug, a bus connects Bormes Village and beaches at La Favière and Le Lavandou. **Phocéens Cars** (04.93.85.66.61) runs 2 buses a day (Mon-Sat) between Nice airport and Hyères.

The Var

St-Tropez

The fishing village where God created woman lives on as an essential port of call for the yachting set and an over-the-top spectacle for the rest.

Sleep-starved locals have successfully petitioned for St-Tropez's clubs to close at 5am, the traffic problem gets worse each year and there is talk of installing video surveillance cameras in the village centre. It's a far cry from Bardot and bohemia, and even further from St-Trop's humble beginnings. But the St-Tropez show still goes on; if you can do it on a yacht, then so much the better.

St-Tropez

Given the hedonistic reputation of St-Tropez, it's fitting that the arch-hedonist Nero should have put the place on the map. In the first century AD, the emperor had a Christian centurion by the name of Torpes beheaded in Pisa. Torpes' headless trunk was loaded aboard a boat and set adrift with a rooster and a dog. When the boat washed up on the beach that is now named after the hapless centurion, the starving dog hadn't taken so much as a nibble of the corpse, a sure sign of sainthood.

In the Middle Ages, the small fishing community at St-Tropez was harried by Saracens until the 15th century, when tough Genoese settlers were imported to show the pirates who was who. The place was still a tiny backwater in 1880 when Guy de Maupassant sailed his boat in to give the locals their first taste of bohemian eccentricity. A decade later, post-Impressionist painter Paul Signac, driven into port by a storm, liked the place so much that he bought a house, La Hune (on what is now avenue Paul Signac), inviting his friends – including Matisse, Derain, Vlaminck, Marquet and Dufy – and converting their palettes from dark northern tones to brilliant St-Tropez hues. Colette lived here, too: her only complaint about the place was that in order to concentrate on writing, she had to turn her back on the attention-monopolising view.

Another wave of personalities washed up in 1956 after Roger Vadim, his young protégée Brigitte Bardot and a film crew descended on the town to make *Et Dieu créa la femme* (And God Created Woman). It was no time before St-Tropez became the world's most famous playboy playground. The millionaires and superstars are still there, but not all come out to play in the high season madness, remaining

bolt-holed in their luxury seaview abodes. And when they do venture out, they are often whisked to an ultra-discreet HIP (Highly Important Person) room. Bardot herself, who alternates between her house up in the hills and her seafront home-cum-animal-rights-HQ at La Madrague, is unlikely to be spotted swinging a baguette at the market these days. An ever-loyal flock of fans make do instead with a boat tour of the headland's A-List abodes (MMG leaves from Vieux Port, 04.94.96.51.00).

St-Tropez is at its most bacchanalian from May to August. Just after 'le jet set' has moved on to its next season fixture, the village is quietly bustling and more family-orientated – in winter it is pretty much deserted. Partying is not St-Tropez's only draw: Les Voiles de St-Tropez (end Sept-beg Oct) is a yacht fest that attracts large crowds, as does Les Bravades, a procession paying homage to saintly Torpes, for which villagers don full costume (17 May).

Sightseeing

St-Tropez is built on a slope, with all the action sliding inexorably towards the Vieux Port. Here the richer-than-thou crowd wine and dine smugly on their gin palaces, in full view of the café terraces, where even the most sanguine holidaymaker is trapped as a gawping spectator. The port was badly bombed in World War II and reconstructed pretty much as it was, with multi-coloured houses that line the quays.

East of the Vieux Port, the **Château de Suffren**, where the occasional art show is staged, dates back to 980. Back from the quai Jean Jaurès, heading towards the Port des Pêcheurs (yes, even in glitzy St-Tropez there are real, working fishermen), the place aux Herbes and rue de la Ponche are quieter, less-sanitised, more lived-in areas of town. The former is home to a small, but nevertheless lively and smelly, daily fish market. The steep rue de la Citadelle leads to a swarm of tourist-trap restaurants and the impressively walled 17th-century citadel perched at the top of the village. It contains the fairly bland **Musée Naval**, and allows access to ramparts with a fantastic view over town and

The parish church of **St-Tropez**, the **Vieux Port** and one of its not-so-exclusive beaches.

coast. The seaside Cimetière Marin, just below the citadel on chemin des Graniers, is where film director Roger Vadim is buried.

West of the Vieux Port, the moorings in the Nouveau Port are less coveted, overshadowed by the proximity of the heaving municipal car park, shabby boutiques and the noisy hordes piling in and out of the clubs. Situated between the old and new port areas is the **Musée de l'Annonciade**, a superb and under-visited collection of early 20th-century art housed in a 16th-century chapel. Pointillists, Fauves, Nabis, Expressionists and Cubists are all represented; including a lovely Vuillard interior and Fauve canvases by Derain, Braque and Vlaminck.

Behind the Vieux Port, St-Tropez's *pétanque*-playing fraternity hangs out on plane-tree-lined place des Lices. It's also home to a market on Tuesday and Saturday. Fruit, vegetables, charcuterie, honey and wine fill the stalls but traders are really there to catch up on the local gossip and see friends. On the hill, 1km south out of town, the pretty Chapelle Ste-Anne (closed to the public) commands spectacular views over the bay, and hosts flash weddings.

Musée de l'Annonciade
pl Gramont (04.94.97.04.01). **Open** *June-Oct* 10am-1pm, 4-10pm daily. *Dec-May* 10am-noon, 2-6pm Mon, Wed-Sun. Closed Nov. **Admission** €5.50; €3.50 12-25s, students; free under-12s. **Credit** AmEx, MC, V.

Musée Naval
Mont de la Citadelle (04.94.97.59.43). **Open** *Sept* 10am-12.30pm, 1.30-6.30pm daily. *Oct-Apr* 10am-12.30pm, 1.30-5.30pm daily. **Admission** €4; €2.50 8-25s, students; free under-8s. **No credit cards**.

Activities

Boat hire
Boats ranging from a dinky 6m-long Corail 216 (€350 /day) to a 25m-long AZ 83 Circus (€6,000/day with crew) are for hire from **France Yachting Locations** (83310 Port Cogolin, Golfe de St-Tropez, 04.94.56.56.69). **MSC Yachting Ltd** (rue Portalet, 04.94.97.73.86) can set you up in style with the classic mahogany Riva (€600 for three hours).

Restaurants

Spoon Byblos
av du Maréchal Foch (04.94.56.68.20/www.spoon.tm.fr). **Open** *mid-Apr to mid-Oct* 8pm-12.30am daily. **Average** €95. **Credit** AmEx, DC, MC, V.
Alain Ducasse's modish Spoon concept and the St-Trop crowd rub along nicely at this spruce dining room and its teak-tabled terrace, lit by hurricane lamps in summer. The signature mix'n'match Spoon formula saturates tastes of the Riviera, Catalonia, Andalucia and Morocco. Fabulous starters include steamed lobster dim sum; desserts are also superb.

Fashionistas head for **rue Allard**. *See p193*.

Le Café
5 pl des Lices (04.94.97.44.69). **Open** daily; hours vary. **Menus** €26-€35. **Credit** AmEx, MC, V.
The terrace doubles as a stadium for watching the endless *boules* matches fought out on place des Lices. The blackboard menu offers perky fish numbers and the desserts are spot-hitters. The restaurant at the rear is a summer hideout for celebs.

Le Frégate
52 rue Allard (04.94.97.07.08). **Open** noon-2pm, 7-11pm daily. Closed mid-Jan to Feb. **Menus** €17-€24. **Credit** MC, V.
This unassuming restaurant, which seats just 25, serves unpretentious Provençal cuisine, including fish soups and grills, plus a *grand aïoli* every Friday.

Leï Mouscardins
Tour du Portalet (04.94.97.29.00). **Open** *July, Aug* 7-11pm daily. *Sept-June* noon-2pm, 7-10pm Mon, Thur-Sun. Closed mid-Jan to mid-Feb. **Menus** €60. **Credit** AmEx, DC, MC, V.
Laurent Tarridec's quayside restaurant is the most respected table in town. The seasonal menu may include baby squid and veg in a balsamic vinegar and squid-ink dressing and stuffed scorpion fish.

La Table du Marché
38 rue Georges Clemenceau (04.94.97.85.20). **Open** 8am-midnight daily. **Menus** €18-€30. **Credit** AmEx, MC, V.

Celebrity chef Christophe Leroy's bistro/deli is a rather casual reflection of his talent, but nevertheless offers good wines and fresh marine treats if you avoid the daily *formule* and go *à la carte*. Upstairs is a cosy wicker-and-wood sushi bar (8pm-midnight).

Bars & cafés

Bar du Port
7 quai Suffren (04.94.97.00.54). **Open** *July, Aug* 7am-3am daily. *Sept-June* 7am-11pm daily. **No credit cards**.
A buzzing crowd congregates for pre-club warm-ups serviced by a long bar, long drinks and live DJs. The ideal place to sip Piscine cocktails (Champagne and ice); prices are steep but not vertical.

Café de Paris
15 quai Suffren (04.94.97.00.56). **Open** *Apr-Oct* 7am-3am daily. *Nov-Mar* 7am-1am daily. **Credit** V.
The terrace is beginning to look tatty, but inside, this Philippe Starck-designed sushi bar (average €40) exudes mysterious chic with backlit white drapes, chandeliers and red velvet banquettes. The live DJing is lounge for grown-ups.

Café Le Senequier
quai Jean Jaurès (04.94.97.00.90). **Open** *July, Aug* 8am-3am daily. *mid-Sept to June* 8am-6.30pm daily. Closed mid-Nov to mid-Dec. **No credit cards**.
The scarlet director's chairs on the legendary terrace remain a thoroughly entertaining must for apéritifs, people-watching and yacht-gazing at sunset.

Chez Fuchs
7 rue des Commerçants (04.94.97.01.25). **Open** *June-Sept* 7am-2am Mon, Wed-Sun. *Oct-May* 7am-11pm Mon, Wed-Sun. Lunch all year, dinner only June-Sept. Closed mid-Jan to end Feb. **Credit** MC, V.
This tiny *bar-tabac* specialising in cigars doubles as a moderately priced bistro, with tasty beef *daube*, stuffed vegetables and a friendly atmosphere.

Le Gorille
1 quai Suffren (04.94.97.03.93). **Open** *July, Aug* 24hrs daily. *Sept-June* 6am-8pm daily. Closed Jan. **No credit cards**.
A corner caff, Le Gorille is open 24 hours a day in summer, when its menu is honed down to burgers or steak served with the house *frites*.

Nightlife

Les Caves du Roi
Hôtel Byblos, av Paul-Signac (04.94.97.16.02). **Open** *Easter-May, Sept to mid-Oct* 11pm-5am Fri, Sat. *June-Sept* 11pm-5am daily. Closed mid-Oct to Easter. **Admission** free. **Credit** AmEx, DC, MC, V.
The basement club at Hôtel Byblos is a Champagne drain where millionaires schmooze and their progeny misbehave. Music is serotonin-soaked house and hip-hop. Getting in is never easy so arrive early or reserve a table and order a bottle.

On the beaches

Going to the beach in St-Tropez is about showing off as much flesh and cash as possible – there's even a local helpline (listed on posters near the beach) for jewellery lost at sea. The most accessible beaches from town are the built-up **Bouillabaisse** to the west (try the excellent Bouillabaisse restaurant, 04.94.97.54.00, closed mid-Nov to May, average 34), the unpretentious **Les Graniers** in Baie des Canebiers past the Citadel (follow the yellow marks of the *sentier littoral* from the Chemin des Graniers), and the horribly crowded **Les Salins** (a 5km drive or 1.2km hike round the headland). But it is the **Baie de Pampelonne** that made St-Trop's reputation, a 5km stretch of white sand that is technically in Ramatuelle (*see p193*).

Pampelonne's bohemian beach shacks of yore have aged into rather more exclusive institutions, with the legendary clubs **Tahiti** (04.94.97.18.02), **Club 55** (04.94.55.55.55) and **La Voile Rouge** (04.94.79.84.34) still attracting a healthy share of celebrities. Shaded four-poster beds, white loungers and a pool party atmosphere have made the new **Nikki Beach** (04.94.79.82.04) a wannabe heaven. **Chez Camille** (Plage de Bonne Terrasse, 04.98.12.68.98, closed Oct-Easter) is great for a generous, fresh fish dinner on the beach. More family, low-key beach clubs/restaurants include **Key West** (04.94.79.86.58).

An area map from the Office de Tourisme has a detailed plan of the beaches and their clubs. Pampelonne beach outings require a scooter, car or bike – in that order of preference. For rentals try the friendly and reasonably priced **Holiday Bikes** (av du Général de Gaulle, 04.94.97.09.39, www.holiday-bikes.com).

The Var

Octave Café

pl de la Garonne (04.94.97.22.56). **Open** *Mar-Oct* 10pm-5am daily. *Nov-Dec* 6pm-1am Tue-Sat. Closed Jan-Feb. **Admission** €11-€14 (incl 1st drink). **Credit** AmEx, MC, V.

A stylish piano bar with soft, loungey music, squishy cushioned chairs, low black tables and a chic clientèle. Liza Minnelli and the inimitable Johnny Hallyday have been known to pop in and croon a few tunes just for fun.

Le Papagayo

résidences du Nouveau Port (04.94.97.07.56). **Open** *Apr-June, Sept to mid-Oct* 11.30pm-5am Fri, Sat. *July, Aug* 11.30pm-5am daily. Closed mid-Oct-Mar. **Admission** free. **Credit** AmEx, MC, V.

St-Trop's best sound system pumps out bona fide club beats in this dark, den-of-misdemeanours setting. El Bodega du Papagayo (04.94.97.76.70) restaurant is a favourite early-evening rendezvous with a playful, clubby vibe.

Le VIP Room

résidences du Nouveau Port (04.94.97.14.70). **Open** 7pm-5am daily. *Oct-May* 7pm-5am Fri, Sat. **Admission** free. **Credit** AmEx, MC, V.

The southern outpost of Jean Roch's Champs-Elysées club is where the gilded youths who slip between Paris and St-Tropez spend their pocket money – or, to really impress, eat it for show. Music is boppy and feel-good. The mezzanine houses fashionable restaurant Madrague (menu €29).

How to do St-Tropez

St-Tropez, more than most of the world's storied fleshpots, is a place with a strong underlying communal schedule, and if you're aware of the basic boilerplate, you'll have much more fun. Rule number one – with the exception of the very popular Provençal market on Tuesday and Saturday mornings in place des Lices – never, ever be early for anything. This includes, more likely than not, checking in to your hotel, since in season the traffic is heavy coming on to the presqu'ile of St-Trop (do pronounce the p, and do get the *double entendre*; in French *trop* means 'too much').

Day one: after checking in early evening at your hotel (**Villa Marie** in Ramatuelle is the current hot address), stroll along the waterfront in town to see who's about and let everyone know that you're on deck. Now head for dinner at **Leï Mouscardins** (for seriously good food, but book well in advance), **Les Moulins de Ramatuelle** (decent food by star chef Christophe Leroy and a glittery crowd) or **Spoon Byblos** (Ducasse's concept eat). Skip dessert and return to town for coffee on a terrace, maybe at **Le Senequier**. Now, at around 1.30am, head for **Les Caves du Roi** to find out if there are any parties in the offing.

Day two: have coffee and a croissant at Senequier around 11am. Read the papers, people-watch, do some light shopping and then head to the beach around 1pm. Which beach? Well, this is crucial, since your choice of beach club defines you. The hottest beach club is the new St-Tropez branch (the original is in Miami) of **Nikki Beach**, while the **Voile Rouge** pulls an equally frisky but slightly older crowd, and **Club 55** is funky but chic and tame enough for you to bring your children without giving them an inadvertent anatomy

lesson. The French establishment and old St-Trop hands remain loyal to **Tahiti Beach**. After a long lunch with lots of rosé, lounge on the beach until about 6pm. Then it's back to hotel for a shower and a nap, or a shower and change before shopping. Be sure not to wear the same clothes to dinner that you wore while shopping. Dinner tonight is casual, so have an apéritif at the **Le Café** and then go for sushi or pizza, followed by an after-dinner drink at the **Hôtel Sube** or **Cohiba Café** (23 rue du Portail Neuf, 04.94.97.26.20) after which it's time for a party at **Papagayo**.

Day three: ad lib to fade.

Shopping

Designer boutiques are popping up wherever there is space in St-Tropez, but rues Allard and Gambetta are the main fashion runways. The trademark at family-run **Atelier Rondini** (16 rue Georges Clemenceau, 04.94.97.19.55, closed Mon, Sun in winter, and Oct-Nov) is 'sandales tropéziennes'– strappy handmade Spartacus sandals also available in funky updates; Charlotte Gainsbourg is a fan. **La Tarte Tropézienne** (36 rue Georges Clemenceau, 04.94.97.71.42, closed Thur) is the place to discover *la tropézienne*, a light sponge cake filled with custard cream. **La Cave de St-Tropez** (av Augustin Grangeon, 04.94.97.01.60, closed Sun) sells wines from the local co-op. There's a handy oyster stall outside on Saturdays.

Where to stay

If you're planning to stay in St-Tropez in high season, book months ahead.

Château de la Messardière

rte de Tahiti (04.94.56.76.00/www.messardiere.com). Closed Oct-Mar. **Double** €200-€620. **Credit** AmEx, DC, MC, V.

Perched on a hilltop of parasol pines, this 19th-century castle, complete with turrets and canopy beds, once belonged to an aristocratic family whose spirit lives on in the tarot-inspired art around the lobby.

Hôtel Le Baron

23 rue de l'Aïoli (04.94.97.06.57/www.hotel-le-baron.com). **Double** €46-€100. **Credit** MC, V.

This quiet hotel overlooks the citadel. The ten Provençal-style bedrooms are clean and simple but not without character. A pleasant terrace restaurant serves Italian food.

Hôtel Byblos

av Paul Signac (04.94.56.68.00/www.byblos.com). Closed mid-Oct to Easter. **Double** €360-€690. **Credit** AmEx, DC, MC, V.

The perennially trendy Byblos has 52 rooms and 45 suites spread over twee chalets amid fountain-filled gardens, right in the middle of town. New poolside restaurant Le Bayader is accomplished; Spoon is even better (*see p190*).

Hôtel Lou Cagnard

18 av Paul Roussel (04.94.97.04.24). Closed Nov, Dec. **Double** €44-€100. **Credit** MC, V.

Not far from the glamour, but totally unaffected by it is this decent budget option, which has a leafy garden for al fresco breakfasting. All rooms are clean and comfy; the first-floor gets very hot in summer.

Hôtel La Maison Blanche

pl des Lices (04.94.97.52.66/www.hotellamaison blanche.com). Closed Feb. **Double** €168-€748. **Credit** AmEx, DC, MC, V.

The stylish facelift by minimalist designer Fabienne Villacrèces is aging well at this exclusive yet villagey hotel. In the evening laze on wicker loungers on the terrace in arm's reach of the Champagne bar.

Les Palmiers

24-26 bd Vasserot (04.94.97.01.61/www.hotel-les-palmiers.com). **Double** €63-€191. **Credit** MC, V.

A verdant path leads to reception and in season the branches are loaded with limes, mandarins and grapefruits. Rooms are basic but pleasant and there are plans for full air-conditioning by summer 2004. Rooms giving on to the courtyard each have a patio.

Le Pré de la Mer

rte des Salins (04.94.97.12.23/www.lepredelamer.com). Closed Oct-Easter. **Double** €86-€139. **Credit** AmEx, V.

Here are three conventional bedrooms and eight self-contained studio apartments in a pretty Provençal setting slightly outside town.

Résidence de la Pinède

plage de la Bouillabaisse (04.94.55.91.00/ www.residencepinede.com). Closed Oct to Easter. **Double** €235-€805. **Credit** AmEx, DC, MC, V.

Only a stone's throw from the mad summer hordes, this tranquil oasis of luxury has its own beach, a spillover pool, an unbeatable view of the bay and fine cooking (menus €75-€104).

Le Sube

15 quai Suffren (04.94.97.30.04). Closed 3 wks Jan. **Double** €150-€250. **Credit** AmEx, DC, MC, V.

Plum in the centre of the old port, the woody Sube is a favourite with yachting enthusiasts. A fire burns in winter in the Chesterfield-filled bar and regulars vie for seats on its minuscule balcony.

Resources

Tourist information

Office de Tourisme, quai Jean Jaurès, 06390 St-Tropez (04.94.97.45.21/www.ot-saint-tropez.com). **Open** *Apr-June, Sept, Oct* 9am-12.30pm, 2-7pm daily. *July, Aug* 9.30am-8pm daily. *Nov* 9.30am-noon, 2-6pm Mon-Sat, 2-6pm Sun. *Dec-Mar* 9.30am-noon, 2-6pm daily.

St-Tropez peninsula

When the truly chic or truly rich talk about summering in St-Trop, often as not they actually mean hiding out in Garbo-esque seclusion in the hills above the town, well away from the wannabes who frequent the old port. Here, amid parasol pines and Côtes de Provence vineyards with views down to pristine blue coves, the hill villages of Ramatuelle and Gassin retain a sense of exclusivity.

Ramatuelle began as a Saracen stronghold; it was razed in 1592 during the Wars of Religion, then rebuilt in 1620, as many inscriptions above doors testify. It still has a fortified feel as tightly knit houses climb snail-like up around the hill; a gateway next to the church leads through to the partly pedestrianised old town. Popular for an evening meal away from the St-Trop hoi polloi, it has respected jazz and theatre festivals in summer. Smaller **Gassin**, where Mick and Bianca Jagger honeymooned in the 70s, sits at the end of some frightening hairpin bends, and is a delightful place to stroll when it's too hot to breathe down on the coast.

Slightly back from the coast, **La Croix-Valmer** is a residential town with fine views across cliffs dotted with the holiday villas of discreetly well-heeled French families. Though the *croix* (cross) in its name refers to an airborne one allegedly seen around here by the co-Emperor Constantine, the town was only built in 1934. From here, there is easy access to the stunning coastal conservation area on the Cap Lardier and the lovely Plage de Gigaro.

Where to stay & eat

Below Ramatuelle, **Les Moulins** (rte des Plages, 04.94.97.17.22, www.christophe-leroy.com, closed mid-Nov to Feb, double €195-€289, menus €34-€88) has five pretty rooms done up in cottage chic and a trellis-shaded restaurant. The Provençal cooking can falter slightly, but vegetables come from the kitchen garden and the dessert and cheese courses are not to be missed. Christophe Leroy has introduced summer night buffets in the garden, with music, sushi and showing off. Set in cypress-dotted gardens, **La Villa Marie** (rte des Plages, Chemin Val Rian, Ramatuelle, 04.94.97.40.22, www.c-h-m.com, closed mid-Dec to Jan, double €190-€610), latest creation from the couple behind the super-chic Fermes de Marie in Megève, has 42 rooms with a Provençal Renaissance look, an open-air bar, landscaped pool and a spa. Suites have distant sea views.

In Ramatuelle, café-tabac-newsagent **Café de l'Ormeau** (pl de l'Ormeau, 04.94.79.20.20, closed Wed and mid-Jan to mid-Feb) is pure central casting, with creeper-covered terrace and long wooden bar. At **La Forge** (rue Victor Léon, 04.94.79.25.56, closed Nov to mid-Mar, menu €29) chef Pierre Fazio and his wife serve up good Provençal cuisine to a dressy crowd in a cleverly converted smithy. A little further down the street, friendly **La Farigoulette** (rue Victor Léon, 04.94.79.20.49, closed Oct-Apr, average €30) offers a richly bayleaf-infused daube, gigot, *anchoïade* or pasta, on the street or garden terraces or in the beamed stone interior. Perched just beneath the town, **Terrasse-Hostellerie Le Baou** (av Gustave Etienne, 04.98.12.94.20, closed mid-Oct to mid-May, double €185-€390, menus €37-€60), has

spectacular views across the peninsula, pleasant rooms, a pool and a serious restaurant. In Gassin, **Le Micocoulier** (pl des Barrys, 04.94.56.14.01, closed Mon & mid-Oct to Apr, menus €27-€40) serves Provençal food with an Italian twist.

South-east of the Croix-Valmer, the 19th-century **Château de Valmer** (rte de Gigaro, 04.94.79.60.10, www.chateau-valmer.com, closed Nov-Apr, double €185-€360) has a pool amid vines, palms and fruit trees, soothing salons and Laura Ashley or Pierre Frey fabrics. Under the same ownership, comfortable **La Pinède Plage** (plage de Gigaro, 04.94.55.16.16, www.pinede-plage.com, double €185-€355, menu €48) has a restaurant and pool overlooking *la grande bleue*. The two share La Pinède's beach which has windsurfing, kayaks and pedalos.

Resources

Tourist information

La Croix-Valmer *Office de Tourisme, Esplanade de la Gare, 83400 La Croix-Valmer (04.94.55.12.12).* **Open** *mid-June to Sept* 9.30am-12.30pm, 2.30-7pm Mon-Sat; 9.15am-1.30pm Sun. *Oct to mid-June* 9am-noon, 2-6pm Mon-Fri; 9.15am-noon Sat; 2.30-6.30pm Sun.
Ramatuelle *Office de Tourisme, pl de l'Ormeau, 83350 Ramatuelle (04.98.12.64.00/www.nova.fr/ ramatuelle).* **Open** *Apr to mid-Oct* 8.30am-12.30pm, 2.30-6.30pm Mon-Sat. *mid-Oct to Mar* 8.30am-12.30pm, 3-6pm Mon-Fri.

Port Grimaud & Ste-Maxime

Hugging the curve in the bay east of St-Tropez, **Port Grimaud** was designed in the late 1960s by architect François Spoerry to look like a miniature slice of the Venice lagoon. Kitschily pretty, this is real estate for the seriously rich, but the owners let visitors wander along the brasserie-lined canals to admire the yachts parked at the bottoms of gardens.

Ste-Maxime has lost the allure it exuded in 1930s posters, and is a relatively inexpensive place to stay next to St-Tropez – though the bad news is that traffic jams can make the latter nigh impossible to reach (a smarter move is to take the boat service, approx every 30 mins, closed 3wks Jan). The esplanade is crowded with family restaurants facing the port. Ste-Maxime's only sight as such is the stone **Tour Carrée**. Built in 1520 against pirates, it served as barn, courtroom and town hall before being turned into a folklore museum.

▶ For a tour of Côtes de Provence's acclaimed vineyards, see p27.

The Var

Port Grimaud, built on reclaimed land to imitate the Venice lagoon.

Tour Carrée

pl de l'Eglise, Ste-Maxime (04.94.96.70.30). **Open**
3-6pm Mon; 10am-noon, 3-6pm Wed-Sun (till 7pm July,
Aug). **Admission** €2.30, €0.60 5-15s. **No credit cards.**

Where to stay, eat & drink

In Port Grimaud, the luxurious **Giraglia** (pl du
14 Juin, 04.94.56.31.33, www.hotelgiraglia.com,
closed Oct-May, double €225-€435) has a pool
and garden perfect for boat watching. Next to
the Golf Club de Beauvallon (packages available),
Hôtel de Beauvallon (Baie de St-Tropez,
04.94.55.78.88, www.lebeauvallon.com, closed
mid-Oct to Apr, double €275-€540, restaurant
closed lunch, average €70, beach restaurant
€35) sits amid manicured lawns. A tunnel
under the road leads to a private beach, pool,
restaurant – and shuttle boats into St-Trop.

The seafront at Ste-Maxime is lined with
restaurants, brasseries and ice cream parlours.
La Marine (6 rue Fernard Bessy, 04.94.96.53.93,
closed Nov-Feb, menus €23-€60) serves reliable
seafood, **La Maison Bleue** (48 rue Bert,
04.94.96.71.69, closed Tue and Nov-end Dec,
Jan-Feb, menus €16-€22) serves pasta and fish
al fresco. **La Réserve** (8 pl Victor Hugo,
04.94.96.18.32, menus €12.30-€25) serves
inexpensive bistro classics. The **Mas des
Oliviers** (quartier de la Croisette,
04.94.96.13.31, closed Dec-Jan, double €47-
€134), 1km west of the centre, has 20 rooms,
plus a pool and tennis courts.

Resources

Tourist information

Port Grimaud *Office de Tourisme, 1 bd Aliziers,
83310 Port Grimaud (04.94.56.02.01).* **Open** *June-Sept*
9am-12.30pm, 2.30-5.30pm Mon-Sat (3-7pm July, Aug).
Ste-Maxime *Office de Tourisme, pr Simon Lorière,
83120 Ste-Maxime (04.94.55.75.55).* **Open** *June,
Sept* 9am-12.30pm, 2-7pm Mon-Sat. *July-Aug* 9am-
8pm Mon-Sat. *Oct-May* 9am-noon, 2-6pm Mon-Sat.

Getting there & around

By air

Private jets land on the Le Môle airstrip, 35km away
in the Massif des Maures. There is no train station.

By car

Sweat it out on the N98 coast road. There are plans
for an expressway in 2005. Ramatuelle is on the D61
south of St-Tropez; for Gassin take one of the
signposted roads off the D61 or D559. Ste-Maxime is
on the D98 coast road or by A8 exit 36 and D25.

By bus

Sodetrav (04.94.12.55.12) runs daily buses between
St-Tropez and Toulon via Hyères. There is one
morning service a day between St-Tropez, Ramatuelle
and Gassin in July & Aug and on Tue, Wed, Fri & Sat
in Sept & June, and daily services between St-Tropez
and St-Raphaël, via Grimaud, Cogolin and Ste-Maxime.

By boat

Les Bateaux Verts (04.94.49.29.39) runs hourly boat
services from Ste-Maxime to St-Tropez Apr to Oct.

St-Raphaël & the Estérel

Family resort St-Raphaël is the departure point for the breathtaking cliffs of the Corniche de l'Estérel and the stunning Roman remains of Fréjus.

Though a fashionable hotspot in the 1880s, when its grand hotels were built, St-Raphaël is now a friendly, family resort – affordable and unthreatening, with its sheltered beach and double marina. To the north, the small town of Fréjus contains some of the most stunning Roman remains in the area, while to the east the red volcanic rocks of the Massif de l'Estérel loom over the deep blue sea, providing the most striking colour contrasts on the Côte d'Azur.

St-Raphaël

It was wealthy Romans, coming down from Fréjus to take the sea air, who established the Gallo-Roman resort of St-Raphaël (on the site now occupied by the casino). The town might have fallen into obscurity, had not Napoléon landed here in 1799 after his defeat by the British in Egypt. His arrival is commemorated by a pyramid on avenue Commandant Guilbaud. But it was Alphonse Karr (1808-90), a journalist opposed to Napoléon III and exiled in Nice, who was the resort's greatest PR-man. Writing to a friend in 1864, he said 'Leave Paris and plant your stick in my garden: next morning, when you wake, you will see it has grown roses.' Writers, artists and composers heeded his invitation: Dumas, Maupassant and Berlioz all found inspiration here.

Following their lead, Félix Martin, local mayor and civil engineer, transformed the village into a smart getaway. Further illustrious guests began to mark their stay with works of art: Gounod composed *Romeo and Juliet* here in 1869, Scott Fitzgerald wrote *Tender is the Night*, while Félix Ziem painted some of his works.

Following the 1920s craze for diving (Zelda used to do it drunk, from the cliffs of the Fitzgeralds' nearby hideaway), and hosts of submerged antiquities all along the Estérel, St-Raphaël gave birth to France's first sub-aqua club. There is now a plethora of diving clubs.

All that said and done, you may feel that today's St-Raph lacks atmosphere. The medieval and *belle époque* centre was largely destroyed by wartime bombing, leaving just a few wiggly old streets around the covered market on place de la République and the church of St-Pierre-des-Templiers (currently closed for renovation). Built in the 12th century, this ancient church doubled as a fortress at times of attack by pirates. It is home to a gilded wooden bust of St Peter that is still carried by fishermen in a torch-lit procession to the Vieux Port on the first Sunday in August.

Next door, beside the remains of the Roman aqueduct, the **Musée Archéologique** contains artefacts from the harbour, plus a display on underwater archaeology.

If you are willing to dodge the rollerbladers, promenade René Coty offers a worthwhile view of the sea and the twin rocks known as the Land Lion and the Sea Lion. The promenade, opened by Félix Martin in 1882, marked the beginning of St-Raphaël's touristic heyday. Other remnants of the era are seen in the Casino, the neo-Byzantine church of **Notre-Dame-de-la-Victoire-de-Lépante**, the Hôtel Excelsior, built by the same architect, Pierre Aublé, and the 1914 Résidence Le Méditerranée.

Musée Archéologique

pl de la Vieille Eglise (04.94.19.25.75). **Open** *June-Sept* 10am-noon, 3-6.30pm Tue-Sat. *Oct-May* 10am-noon, 2-5.30pm Tue-Sat. **Admission** (incl St-Pierre-des-Templiers) €1.50; €0.70 10-18s; free under-10s. **No credit cards**.

Activities

Diving

There are several diving schools on the Estérel, including **Aventure sous-marine** (56, rue de la Garonne, 04.94.19.33.70, www.plongee83.com).

Where to stay & eat

The family-run **Excelsior** (193 bd Félix Martin, 04.94.95.02.42, www.excelsior-hotel.com, double €115-€160) is a *belle époque* hotel on the sea front with 40 rooms and an English pub. **Le Méditerranée** (1 av Paul Doumer, 04.94.82.10.99, www.lemediterranee.fr) has airy apartments (double €287-€511/wk) and friendly staff. **La Thimothée** (375 bd

The **Cité Episcopale** in Fréjus.

Christian Lafon, 04.94.40.49.49, double €35-
€75), to the east of the town provides good-
value accommodation in a residential area.
It has a pool and 12 rooms, two with a view
of the sea. In the centre of town, **Le Jardin
des Arènes** (31 av du Général Leclerc,
04.94.95.06.34, double €21-€49) is a charming
place with stained-glass windows in the
stairwell, a garden and extremely helpful staff.
The **Hôtel San Pedro** (890 av du Colonel
Brooke, 04.94.19.90.20, www.hotelsanpedro.fr,
double €118-€160, menus €18-€50) has a good
Provençal-style restaurant. Gastronomes make
a bee-line for **L'Arbousier** (6 av de Valescure,
04.94.95.25.00, closed Mon, lunch Tue, dinner
Sun, end Dec to mid-Jan, menus €26-€55),
where Philippe Troncy is one of St-Raphaël's
most innovative chefs.

Resources

There is a daily market in St-Raphaël.

Tourist information

*Office de Tourisme, 210 rue Waldeck Rousseau,
83702 St-Raphaël (04.94.19.52.52/www.saint-
raphael.com).* **Open** *July-Aug* 9am-7pm daily.
Sept-June 9am-12.30pm, 2-6.30pm Mon-Sat.

Fréjus & Roquebrune-sur-Argens

While **Fréjus Plage** with its bars and
amusements feels like a continuation of St-
Raphaël, the Roman town up above has a great
deal of charm and historical interest once you
have battled with the infernal traffic system
connecting it with St-Raphaël. Its Roman ruins
include the most extensive naval base of the
Roman world, alongside that of Ostia in Italy.
Fréjus was founded – as Forum Julii – by Julius
Caesar in 49BC and became a naval post for
Augustus' swift-sailing galleys, which defeated
Antony and Cleopatra at Actium in 31BC. The
harbour was guarded by two large towers; one,
the **Lanterne d'Auguste**, still rises high on
the site of the old port. But the town is not just a
living museum – with its ochre and apricot-
painted houses and squares dripping with
hanging baskets, it's a pleasant place to while
away an afternoon on a café terrace. Families
with children might also want to visit the 50-
acre safari-park-style **Parc Zoölogique** (zone
du Capitou, just off the A8, 04.98.11.37.37,
www.zoo-frejus.com) or burn off some energy
at the **Aquatica** water park (RN 98,
04.94.51.82.51, www.parc-aquatica.com).

It takes the best part of a day to see Fréjus'
scattered Roman remains. Most impressive is
the **Amphithéâtre**, which can still seat 10,000
and is used for bullfights and plays. Near the
railway station, the half-moon-shaped Porte des
Gaules was part of the Roman ramparts. On the
other side of the station around the port, the
Butte St-Antoine mound formed a western
citadel and has a tower which was probably a
lighthouse. The Platforme, its counterpart on
the east, served as military headquarters.
Inland, stretches of the Roman aqueduct are
visible from avenue du XVe Corps d'Armée.
Further north, the **Théâtre Romain** has had
modern seats installed for summer concerts.

Facing on to place Formigé, the Cathédrale
St-Léonce is at the heart of the unusual fortified
Cité Episcopale (cathedral close), which
contains a fascinating 15th-century bestiary
painted on the ceiling of its two-tier, 13th-
century cloisters. The carved cathedral doors
show Mary and Saints Peter and Paul amid
scenes of Saracen butchery. Opposite is the
fifth-century octagonal baptistry where
excavations have uncovered the original white
marble pavement and the pool. Upstairs, the
Musée Archéologique has some outstanding
Gallo-Roman antiquities recovered from the
Fréjus excavations. Emphasising that Fréjus is
also a Provençal town, the **Musée d'Histoire
Locale et des Traditions** concentrates on

The Var

artisanal traditions and events such as the *bravade* bull run and grape harvest.

One km north-east of Fréjus, the **Villa Aurélienne** (rte de Cannes, 04.94.53.11.30), a Palladian house in 22 hectares of gardens, hosts occasional photographic exhibitions. Further north, two surprising constructions evoke France's colonial past. On the N7, the **Pagode bouddhique Hông Hiên** (Buddhist pagoda) was built by Vietnamese soldiers who fought in France in 1917, and has an exotic garden with a collection of sacred animals and guardian spirits. Nearby, a war memorial rises above the graves of over 24,000 soldiers and civilians who died in Indochina. Jutting out amid pine woods stands the **Mosquée de Missiri**, a replica of the celebrated Missiri de Djenné mosque in Mali, built for Sudanese troops in the 1920s.

At La Tour de Mare, 5km north of Fréjus on the interior road to Cannes, the RN7, is another curiosity, this time of more interest to art fans. Deep in the forest, where it holds a mystical appeal, uniting nature and arcane symbolism, the **Chapelle Notre-Dame-de-Jérusalem** was designed by Jean Cocteau in 1961 as part of a proposed artist's colony that never took off. The octagonal chapel, built around an atrium (now glassed in), incorporates the mythology of the First Crusade in its stained glass, floor tiles and frescoes. In the painting of the apostles above the main door can be recognised Cocteau's lover actor Jean Marais, Coco Chanel and poet Max Jacob.

North-west of Fréjus, **Roquebrune-sur-Argens** is perched on a rocky peak at the foot of the Rocher de Roquebrune. Originally a stronghold, the *castrum*, located near the church, was once surrounded by a curtain wall destroyed in the Wars of Religion in 1592. Traces of the wall are visible in boulevard de la Liberté.

The first left fork on the D7 north of town leads to the red sandstone **Rocher de Roquebrune**. At the summit stand three crosses by sculptor Bernar Veanet, in memory of crucifixions painted by Giotto, Grunewald and El Greco, using the summit to symbolise Golgotha. Take the trail marked with yellow paint and expect breathtaking views.

Amphithéâtre Romain

rue Henri Vadon (04.94.51.34.31). **Open** *Apr-Oct* 10am-1pm, 2.30-6.30pm Mon, Wed-Sat; 8am-7pm Sun. *Nov-Mar* 10am-noon, 1-5.30pm Mon-Fri; 9.30am-12.30pm, 1.30-5.30pm Sat; 8am-5pm Sun. **Admission** free.

Chapelle Notre-Dame-de-Jérusalem

av Nicolaï, La Tour de Mare (04.94.53.27.06).
Open *Apr-Oct* 2.30-6.30pm Mon, Wed-Fri; 10am-1pm, 2-6.30pm Sat. *Nov-Mar* 1.30-5.30pm Mon, Wed-Fri; 9.30am-12.30pm, 1.30-5.30pm Sat. **Admission** free.

Fréjus' stunning 10,000-capacity **Amphithéâtre Romain** is used for bullfights and concerts.

Cité Episcopale

58 rue de Fleury (04.94.51.26.30). **Open** *June-Sept*
9am-6.30pm daily. *Oct-May* 9am-noon, 2-5pm Tue-
Sun. **Admission** €4.60; €3.10 18-25s; free under-18s.
No credit cards.

Musée Archéologique

pl Calvini (04.94.52.15.78). **Open** closed until June
2004 for renovation. *Apr-Oct* 10am-1pm, 2.30-6.30pm
Mon, Wed-Sat. *Nov-Mar* 10am-noon, 1.30-5.30pm
Mon-Fri; 9.30am-12.30pm, 1.30-5.30pm Sat.
Admission free.

Musée d'Histoire Locale et des Traditions

153 rue Jean Jaurès (04.94.51.64.01). **Open** *Apr-June,
Sept-Oct* 2.30-6.30pm Mon, Wed-Fri; 10am-1pm, 2.30-
6.30pm Sat. *July, Aug* 10am-1pm, 2.30-6.30pm Mon,
Wed-Sat. *Nov-Mar* 1.30-5.30pm Mon, Wed-Fri;
9.30am-12.30pm, 1.30-5.30pm Sat. **Admission** free.

Pagode Bouddhique Hông Hiên

13 rue Henri Giraud (04.94.53.25.29). **Open** 9am-
noon, 2-7pm daily. **Admission** €1.50.

Théâtre Romain

rue du Théâtre Romain (04.94.53.58.75). **Open**
Apr-Oct 10am-1pm, 2.30-6.30pm Mon, Wed-Sat; 8am-
7pm Sun. *Nov-Mar* 10am-noon, 1.30-5.30pm Mon-Fri;
8am-5pm Sun. **Admission** free.

Where to stay & eat

The **Aréna** (145 rue Général de Gaulle,
04.94.17.09.40, www.arena-hotel.com, closed
mid-Dec to mid-Jan, double €80-€145,
restaurant closed lunch Mon & Sat, menus €35-
€55) in the old town offers a warm welcome,
garden and pool, while its restaurant serves the
best Provençal cuisine in town. The **Bellevue**
(pl Paul Vernet, 04.94.17.21.58, double €40) is
cheaper with smallish rooms but good views.
Down on the beach, the modern **Sable et
Soleil** (158 rue Paul Arène, 04.94.51.08.70,
closed mid-Nov to mid-Dec, double €39-€56)
is bright and friendly.

La **Cave Romaine** (114 rue Camelin,
04.94.51.52.03, open dinner only, closed Tue,
average €30) serves Italian pasta and pizzas, and
grilled meat and fish. Hidden down a backstreet,
tiny **Les Potiers** (135 rue des Potiers,
04.94.51.33.74, closed Tue, lunch Wed, and 1wk
Jan & Feb, menus €21-€28) offers the personal
touch of chef Richard François and his wife. Foie
gras, the most tender lamb and beef and subtle
desserts await food lovers and the set menu is
superb value. The **Bar du Marché** (5 pl de la
Liberté, 04.94.51.29.09) offers a filling *plat du jour*
for €7. In Roquebrune-sur-Argens try
Le Gaspacho (21 av Général de Gaulle,
04.94.45.49.59, closed Wed, menus €11-€18.50).
Food is traditional French and the chocolate
mousse worth every guilty calorie.

Resources

Market days are Wednesday, Saturday and
Sunday in Fréjus and Tuesday and Friday in
Roquebrune-sur-Argens.

Tourist information

Fréjus *Office de Tourisme, 325 rue Jean Jaurès,
83600 Fréjus (04.94.51.83.83/www.ville-frejus.fr).*
Open *Apr-Aug* 9am-12.30pm, 2-7pm daily. *Sept-Mar*
9am-noon, 2-6pm Mon-Sat.
Roquebrune *Office de Tourisme, rue Jean Aicard,
83520 Roquebrune-sur-Argens (04.94.45.72.70/
www.ville-roquebrune-argens.fr).* **Open** *Apr-Sept*
9am-noon, 2-6pm Mon-Sat; 9am-noon Sun. *Oct-Mar*
9am-noon, 2-6pm Mon-Fri.

The Corniche de l'Estérel

RN 98, more glamorously known as the
Corniche de l'Estérel, was opened 100 years ago
by the Touring Club de France. If the hairpin
turns on the clifftop road don't steal your breath
away, the coastal views certainly will.

Just west of St-Raphaël at **Boulouris** there
are some pleasant beaches, but drive on to the
Pointe du Dramont, 10km east. In 1897
Auguste Lutaud bought tiny **Ile d'Or** just off
the point. After building a four-storey mock-
medieval tower he proclaimed himself King
Auguste I of the Ile d'Or and threw some of the
wildest parties on the Côte. The **Plage du
Dramont** is famous for being the bit of sand
where the 36th division of the US Army landed
on 15 August 1944. For a great view, take the
signposted, one-hour walk up to the
Sémaphore du Dramont. Another path
descends to the port of **Agay**, a family resort
with a sandy beach shadowed by the slopes of
the Rastel d'Agay. Daredevil author of *Le Petit
Prince,* Antoine de St-Exupéry, crashed his
plane just around the bay in World War II.

The beach of **Anthéor** is dominated by the
Plateau d'Anthéor, from where a path leads up
to the Rocher de St-Barthélémy. Climbing to the
Cap Roux peak takes about two hours return.
Further along the coast road is the **Pointe de
l'Observatoire**, offering views over the crags.
Steep paved paths descend through vegetation to
secluded coves. It's blissful, but swimming can be
dangerous when the tide is high.

Le Trayas has a pleasant, modest beach.
The bay of La Figueirette, reached from the
harbour of **Miramar**, was a tuna-fishing centre
in the 17th century and has ruins of a lookout
tower. As you approach Miramar be prepared
for a double-take when you see, perched high on
the cliffs, Pierre Cardin's James Bond-villain-
shag-pad Le Palais Bulles, which is opened for
a jazz and theatre festival in July and early August.
The coast road then leads into La **Galère** and

The Var

Théoule-sur-Mer, a friendly seaside town with some great fish restaurants. From here you can follow walking and mountain biking trails up to the church of Notre-Dame d'Afrique, a place of pilgrimage for *pieds-noirs* (*see pp15-18*).

The chief curiosity at **La Napoule** is the **Fondation Henry Clews**, a pseudo-medieval folly conjured out of the ruins of a Saracen castle in 1917 by Henry Clews, a failed Wall Street banker-turned-sculptor. Today it hosts artists' residencies and workshops. Though L'Oasis restaurant draws gastronomes, the town is something of a sub-Cannes, filled with yachting boors and retirement homes. You'll wish you had stayed on the Estérel.

Fondation Henry Clews

Château de la Napoule, av Henry Clews (04.93.49.95.05/www.lnaf.org). **Open** *Mar-June, Sept, Oct* 2.30-5.30pm Mon, Wed-Sun. *July-Aug* 2.30-6.30pm Mon, Wed-Sun. Closed Nov-Feb. **Admission** €4.60; €3.05 3-18s; free under-3s. **Credit** MC, V.

Where to stay & eat

Overlooking the Ile d'Or, the isolated **Sol et Mar** (rte Corniche d'Or, 04.94.95.25.60, closed mid-Oct to early Feb, double €64-€137, menus €28-€35) has large rooms, saltwater pool and Provençal restaurant. In Agay, the **Hôtel L'Estérella** (197 bd de la Plage, 04.94.82.00.58, closed Nov-Jan, double €59-€88; restaurant closed Mon from Oct to June, menu €23) is a quiet option on the beach with smallish rooms. **Hôtel Restaurant Le Lido** (bd de la Plage, 04.94.82.01.59, closed end Oct-Feb, double €83-€95, average €20) has a private beach, friendly service and a fish restaurant.

The enchanting **Relais des Calanques** (rte des Escales, 04.94.44.14.06, double €70-€110, restaurant closed Tue and Oct-Mar, *plat du jour* €15) near Le Trayas has cliff-top gardens filled with bric-a-brac, a pool, diving creek and restaurant. **Le Trayas** Youth Hostel (9 av de la Véronèse, 04.93.75.40.23, www.fuaj.org, closed Jan to mid-Feb, rates €11.50 per person) is 2km up the hill with rooms for four to eight. Down in the marina at Port Miramar is a very good fish restaurant with lively bar, **La Marine** (04.93.75.49.30, Apr-Sept daily, menus €25-€50). More expensive, but worth it for the mod-Med cuisine, is the **Etoile des Mers** at the **Miramar Beach Hôtel** (47 av de Miramar, 04.93.75.05.05, www.mbhriviera.com, double €130-€400, restaurant closed lunch Mon-Fri in July, Aug, menus €37-€69). A little further on, **La Tour de l'Esquillon** (Miramar, Théoule, 04.93.75.41.51, double €120-€160, menu €34), a 20s hotel, recalls the era of Scott and Zelda.

Théoule has plenty of tasty eating options, including fish restaurant **Le Marco Polo**

(av de Lérins, 04.93.49.96.59, menus €27, closed Mon) with its feet in the sea. In Mandelieu-la-Napoule, the **Ermitage du Riou** (av Henry Clews, 04.93.49.95.56, www.ermitage-du-riou.fr, closed Jan, double €126-€301, menus €39-€85) is a smart hotel with a private beach, pool and good restaurant. At **L'Oasis** (rue Jean-Honoré Carle, 04.93.49.95.52, www.oasis-raimbault.com, closed Mon & dinner Sun from mid-Oct to Jan and 2 wks in Feb, menus €58-€115), you can splash out on Stéphane Raimbault's fine classical cooking and sumptuous desserts.

Resources

Market is Wednesday at Agay, Friday at Théoule-sur-Mer, Thursday at Mandelieu, Thursday & Saturday at La Napoule.

Tourist information

Agay *Office de Tourisme, pl Giannetti, 83530 Agay (04.94.82.01.85/www.esd-fr.com/agay).* **Open** *Apr to mid-June* 9am-noon, 2-6pm Mon-Sat. *mid-June to Sept* 9am-8pm Mon-Sat. *Oct-Mar* 9am-noon, 2-5pm Mon-Fri.
Mandelieu *Office de Tourisme, av Henry Clews, 06210 Mandelieu-la-Napoule (04.93.49.95.31/ www.ot-mandelieu.fr).* **Open** *July, Aug* 10am-12.30pm, 2-7pm daily. *Sept-June* 10am-12.30pm, 2-6pm Mon-Fri.
Théoule *Office de Tourisme, 1 Corniche d'Or, 06590 Théoule-sur-Mer (04.93.49.28.28/ www.theoule-sur-mer.org).* **Open** *May-Sept* 9am-7pm Mon-Sat; 10am-1pm Sun. *Oct-Mar* 9am-noon, 2-6.30pm Mon-Sat.

Getting there & around

By car

Leave the A8 at exit 37 or 38 for both St-Raphaël and Fréjus; St Raphaël is also on the N98 coast road. The D2098 follows the coast. For Mandelieu-la-Napoule, leave the A8 at exit 40.

By train

St-Raphaël is on the main coastal line with **TGV** links from Paris, Nice and Marseille. Frequent trains from Nice and Marseille also stop at Fréjus and Mandelieu. Local trains on the St-Raphaël-Cannes line stop at Agay and Théoule-sur-Mer.

By bus

Cars Phocéens (04.93.85.61.81) runs a daily service from Nice to St-Raphaël and from Marseille to Fréjus (12.45pm, Mon-Sat). From Hyères airport there are 4 buses a day to Hyères bus station, from where you can catch a connection (8 daily) to St-Raphaël. **Estérel Bus** (04.94.52.00.50) runs between St-Raphaël and Draguignan, via Fréjus and Roquebrune (12 services daily Mon-Sat; 5 on Sun). Between Mandelieu and Cannes, **Bus Azur** (04.92.99.20.05) runs 9 buses daily. Estérel Bus runs between St-Raphaël and Agay (15 daily Mon-Sat; 10 on Sun) and frequently from Le Trayas to Cannes, via Miramar and Théoule-sur-Mer.

Brignoles & the Sainte-Baume

Organic food, holy caves, canoeing and walking make the verdant western part of the Var a healthy, outdoor paradise.

Brignoles & the Green Var

Set amid green hills, **Brignoles** looks sweet, but it is the busy commercial centre of the western villages, spewing a steady stream of traffic along the RN7. Once famous for its 'sugar plums' (now mysteriously extinct) that were sent for 1,000 years to the royal courts of Europe, it later became prosperous through bauxite mining. The old town around place Carami bustles with café life. The tourist office, itself in a fine 17th-century building, can provide a walking-tour map (Découvrir Brignoles) around its fine houses, towers and thick 13th-century ramparts. Stroll up the covered stairway of rue du Grand Escalier past Eglise St-Sauveur to the Palace of the Counts of Provence, built in 1264 as a summer residence.

Fountains have mushroomed at **Barjols**.

It is now the **Musée du Pays Brignolais**, which has a collection of Provençal curiosities, an ancient sarcophagus, a reconstruction of a bauxite mine and a tiny plum tree (la pistoline prune) planted in the courtyard in an attempt to revive the Brignoles delicacy. There's a packed flea market on the promenade along the Carami river every second Sunday of the month.

Brignoles is also a springboard to the outdoor life of La Provence Verte – or the Green Var – a name inspired by the rich underground water sources that protect the region against drought. Take the D554 north from Brignoles, then the D45 at Châteauvert for the **Vallon Sourn**, the steep upper valley of the Argens river, which is a favourite area for rock-climbing, kayaking and biking. **Correns**, capital of the Argens, is the number-one organic village of France with 95 per cent of its wines and farm-produce grown organically. **Domaine des Aspras**, owned by the mayor of Correns (04.94.59.59.70, closed Mon, Sun), offers winetasting in idyllic vineyards just south of town.

Barjols, 22km north of Brignoles, lies in a valley fed by fresh-water springs. Fifteen wash basins and 32 mossy fountains have earned it the hopeful nickname of 'the Tivoli of Provence'. In Réal, the old part of town north of the Romanesque-Gothic **Eglise Notre-Dame des Epines** built in 1014, former tanneries along streams now house galleries and artists' studios. Pretty terraces and café tables squeeze into the crooked streets, and on place de la Mairie the largest plane tree in Provence (12m circumference) has lifted up the cobblestones. Townspeople celebrate every mid-January for the decidedly pagan weekend of Fête de St-Marcel, when the saint's statue is paraded through town with a garlanded ox that is later sacrificed, roasted and eaten, after a drink of water at the Fontaine du Boeuf. Atop a hill in rolling countryside east of Barjols is the village of **Pontevès**, whose ruined château and scenic vista make a good picnic spot.

On the southern outskirts of Brignoles by D405, the tiny village of **La Celle** once attracted those seeking religious solace at the

12th-century **Abbaye Royale**. Today's visitors might have more venal aims, as the abbey is now partially a luxury hôtel/restaurant under the sway of super-chef Alain Ducasse.

Tiny **La Roquebrussanne**, 15km south, is reached through woods beneath the odd-shaped rock formations of La Loube. The village sits squat on a plain of Coteaux Varois vineyards and serves as the central wine pressing co-operative for the region. The D64 leads east of here past two lakes (a couple of spooky holes in the earth with no visible water source) to the British-owned **Château des Chaberts** (04.94.04.92.05) vineyard, a reliable wine producer of rosés and reds, which offers tastings. South of La Roquebrussanne, the D5 winds through vineyards (try Domaine des Laou and Domaine la Rose des Vents) to the sleepy village of **Méounes-les-Montrieux**, a refreshing stop with its streams, meandering streets and shady fountain and cafés under the plane trees of place de l'Eglise.

Abbaye Royale de la Celle

La Celle (04.94.59.19.05). **Open** *from June 2004* 9am-noon, 2-5pm Mon-Sat; 10am-noon, 2-5.30pm Sun. **Admission** call for details.

Musée du Pays Brignolais

pl des Comtes de Provence, Brignoles (04.94.69.45.18). **Open** 10am-noon, 3-5pm Wed-Sat; 9am-noon, 3-5pm Sun. **Admission** €4; €2 12-16s, students; free under-12s. **No credit cards**.

Activities

Canoeing & kayaking

For canoe trips on the river Argens call **Provence Canoë** (D562 east of Carcès, 04.94.29.52.48, June-Aug daily, Apr, May, Sept-Nov by appointment, €13-€25).

Where to stay & eat

In Brignoles, **Hôtel de Provence** (pl du Palais de Justice, 04.94.69.01.18, closed 2wks Nov, Dec, 2wks Feb, double €40, menus €12.50-€30) is the only hotel in the old town, and convenient if you like cigarette smoke and the roar of passing scooters. Nearby, **Café le Central** (pl Carami, 04.94.69.11.10, closed Mon, Sun) serves a good lunchtime *plat du jour* (€7.80). Artsy *maison d'hôtes* **La Cordeline** (14 rue des Cordeliers, 04.94.59.18.66, www.lacordeline.com, double €62-€95, dinner Wed & Sat only, menu €25) offers five rooms in a 17th-century residence and serves intimate family dinners and sugary plum jam *à la brignolaise* at breakfast.

Checking into a posh room at Alain Ducasse's **Hostellerie de l'Abbaye de la Celle** (pl du Général de Gaulle, La Celle, 04.98.05.14.14, www.abbaye-celle.com, double €220-€285, closed 2wks Jan-Feb, restaurant closed Tue & Wed, menus €40-€74) is the only way to go after candlelit dinner in the adjoining Gothic convent. 5km east of Brignoles, **Golf Club Barbaroux** (D79, rte de Cabasse,

Basilique Ste-Marie-Madeleine: splendid Gothic shroud for the Magdalene's tomb. *See p204*.

04.94.69.63.63, www.barbaroux. com, double
€92-€112, menus €26, closed Sun, Mon dinner)
is a hotel-restaurant on an 18-hole golf course
(fees €53). In La Roquebrussanne, **Hôtel-Resto
de la Loube** (04.94.86.81.36, closed 2wks Dec-
Jan, double €69, restaurant closed dinner Mon
& Tue, menus €24-€34) has become a trendy
international hang-out; it's changing hands in
2004, so prices may change. At Méounes, **La
Source** (04.94.48.99.83, www.les-sourciers.com,
double €40, restaurant closed Tue & Wed,
lunch menus €19 €28, dinner average €40) has
four sweet rooms and a stark white restaurant,
where the chef works magic on rainbow trout
and crayfish from its own springs.

In outdoorsy Correns, you can live in the
woods, in elegant privacy at **La Terrasse**
(04.94.59.57.15, www.terrasse-provence.com,
double €90, closed Nov-Feb), which has air-
conditioned duplexes and a pool. For hardier
sports lovers, camp at the **Camping
Municipal le Grand Jardin** (Mairie de
Correns 04.94.37.21.95, tent €3, adults €2.50).
The Bruno Clément (think expensive truffle
lunches) extravaganza is the **Auberge du
Parc** (04.94.59.53.52, www.aubergeduparc.fr, pl
Général de Gaulle, double €109-€139,
restaurant closed Thur dinner, Sun lunch Nov-
Mar, & Tue Apr-Oct, menu €42) with its baby
blue cupid murals and a fumoir. On summer
evenings, locals flock to the open-air **La Cigale
Provençal** in the Vallon Sourn (06.81.30.52.91,
2km north of Correns towards Châteauvert,
open May-Sept, closed lunch except Sat & Sun).

In Pontevès, **Domaine-de-St-Ferréol** (1km
west of Pontevès on D560, 04.94.77.10.42, closed
Nov-Feb, double €50-€60) offers upmarket
chambres d'hôtes in an 18th-century farm that
bottles its own wine and has a superb pool.

Resources

Market in Brignoles and Barjols is Saturday.

Internet

*L'Ourson Surfeur, 9 rue du Dr Barbaroux, Brignoles
(04.94.69.02.22/www.oursonsurfeur.free.f).*
Open 10am-9pm Tue-Sat; 11am-9pm Sun.

Tourist information

Barjols *Office de Tourisme, bd Grisolle, 83670
Barjols (04.94.77.20.01, www.ville-barjols.fr).*
Open 9am-noon, 3-6pm Mon-Sat.
Brignoles *Syndicat d'Initiative, Hôtel de Clavier,
rue des Palais, 83170 Brignoles (04.94.69.27.51/
www.ville-brignoles.fr).* **Open** 10am-12.30pm,
2-5.30pm Mon-Fri.
La Provence Verte Maison du Tourisme
*carrefour de l'Europe, 83170 Brignoles
(04.94.72.04.21/www.la-provence-verte.org).*
Open *June-Sept* 9am-12.30pm, 2-7.30pm daily.
Oct-May 9am-12.30pm, 2-6.30pm Mon-Sat.

St-Maximin-la-Ste-Baume & the Sainte-Baume Massif

In the farming country between Brignoles and
Aix, the **Basilique Ste-Marie-Madeleine** at
St-Maximin-la-Ste-Baume soars above miles of
vineyards: once a divine beacon to caravans of
pilgrims, today an excellent marker for anyone
travelling the A8 motorway. The basilica is the
finest Gothic edifice in Provence – and one of
the few outposts of this style in the largely
Romanesque South – and pilgrimage site for the
tomb of Mary Magdalene, buried here by her
friend Maximin with whom she is said to have
landed in France from Palestine at Stes-Maries-
de la Mer (*see p74*). It was founded in 1295 by
Charles II d'Anjou, King of Sicily and Count of
Provence, who hoped to improve his standing
by building a resplendent shrine for Mary's
relics, above the fourth-century crypt where her
sarcophagus had been found in 1280. The
interior of the basilica contains much
fascinating decoration by Dominican monks,
such as the 94 choir stalls carved in walnut by
Brother Vincent Funel. The altarpiece of the
Passion by Antoine Ronzen was painted in
1520. Over the altar is a gilded plaster sunburst
of cherubs and saints (1678-82) by Lieutaud.
The monumental 18th-century organ was saved
from destruction during the Revolution by
Lucien Bonaparte, Napoléon's youngest brother,
who used it for performances of *La Marseillaise*.

Adjoining the basilica is the **Couvent
Royal**, a royal foundation begun at the same
time as the church, now a lovely hotel (*see
p204*). You can visit the chapel, the refectory
and the Gothic cloister. Just south of the
basilica, rue Colbert runs through the 13th-
century medieval quarter and along the sombre
arcades of the Jewish district established in
1303 in this passionately Catholic town.
Street life revolves around place Malherbe,
where the Wednesday market creates a turmoil
of shoppers and traffic, and **Café La
Renaissance** (04.94.78.00.27) tries to keep up
with the demand for *pastis* at its terrace tables.

Stretching southwest of St-Maximin are the
forested limestone hills of the Massif-de-la-Ste-
Baume. **Nans-les-Pins** is a hiking centre on
the GR9 to Signes and the Chemin des Rois
royal pilgrimage route leading from St-Maximin
through sacred forests to the Grotte Ste-Marie-
Madeleine, where Mary Magdalene lived out the
last 33 years of her life in solitary penitence
until, too frail to walk, she was carried by
angels to her old friend Maximin in St-Maximin
(then known as Villalata). Each Good Friday, a
procession led by Dominican monks climbs the

The Var

mountain for mass inside the cave; otherwise contact the tourist office in Plan d'Aups for guided visits. The cave is hidden in the cliffs at 950m, and can be reached by climbing a 1km footpath from the Hôtellerie de la Baume (*see below*). Across the road from the Hôtellerie, the **Ecomusée de la Ste-Baume** displays ancient crafts, especially wool dyeing and weaving. The forest was also long associated with fertility rites – the GR9 footpath follows an ancient muletrack past the huge oval Cave of Eggs, where medieval mothers came to 'find' (conceive) their children. **Plan d'Aups**, a village on a barren mountain plateau has a Friday market with good farmhouse goat cheeses and jams. Monks from the 11th-century church shop in billowing white robes along with more mundane locals. At the eastern end of the massif, the village of **Mazaugues** for centuries sent ice (to preserve fresh fish) to Toulon and Marseille from its numerous ice factories. Ice production is explained in the **Musée de la Glace**, which has ice tools and a reconstructed *glacière*. It also runs an ice fair in February and organises visits to the restored Glacière de Pivaut, an impressive 19th-century stone igloo, a short walk from the village, where the ice collected from adjacent freezing basins and cut into blocks was stored.

Basilique Ste-Marie-Madeleine

pl de Prêcheurs, St-Maximin (04.42.38.01.78). **Open** 7.30am-11.30am, 3-5.30pm Mon-Sat; *mass* 9am Mon-Sat; 8am, 11am Sun. **Admission** free.

Ecomusée de la Ste-Baume

Plan d'Aups (04.42.62.56.46). **Open** ring for details. **Admission** €3; under-14s free. **No credit cards.**

Musée de la Glace

Hameau du Château, Mazaugues (04.94.86.39.24/ www.museeglace.fr.st). **Open** *June-Sept* 9am-noon, 2-6pm Tue-Sun. *Oct-May* 9am-noon, 2-5pm Sun. **Admission** €2.30; free under 6s. *museum plus glacière* €4; free under 6s. **No credit cards.**

Where to stay & eat

Hôtellerie du Couvent Royal (pl Jean Salusse, 04.94.86.55.66, www.hotelfp-saintmaximin.com, double €75-€100) is the only place worth staying in St-Maximin. Cells inhabited by monks from 1316 to 1957 have been converted with a sense of monastic calm. The vaulted capitular room is now a restaurant run by the **Maison des Vins du Var** (04.94.78.09.50, closed Mon & dinner Sun, average €44), which also does tastings.

Beween Nans-les-Pins and Plan d'Aups, the **Hôtellerie de la Baume** (D95, 04.42.04.54.84, dormitory €9, double €22, meals €12 by reservation), a Benedictine convent, still offers accommodation for pilgrims. At Nans-les-Pins, the **Hôtel Domaine de Châteauneuf** (rte N560, 04.94.78.90.06, www.domaine-de-chateauneuf.com, closed Nov-Mar, double €130-€626, restaurant closed lunch Mon-Fri, menus €50-€70) sits in the middle of the 18-hole Golf Club La Ste-Baume. It was once a stopping point for Crusaders heading to the Holy Land, the present building later hosted Napoléon's family; guests get preferential greens fees (€50/day), it also has a pool and tennis courts. Across the N560, the elegant **Château de Nans** (04.94.78.92.06, www.chateau-de-nans.fr, closed 1wk Nov, mid-Feb to mid-Mar, double €122, restaurant closed Mon & Tue, menus €38-€52) dishes up divine delicacies, such as wild rabbit and venison with juniper berries. Classy hikers can throw down their backpacks at the 18th-century **La Vieille Bastide** (300 chemin du plan de Chebron, 04.94.90.81.45, closed Jan-Mar, double €70-€95), a lovely *chambres d'hôtes* just west of Signes; book for the Provençal dinner (€27).

Resources

Market day is Wednesday in St-Maximin, Sunday in Nans-les-Pins.

Internet

SMI St-Maximin Informatique, 9 rue de la République, St-Maximin (04.98.05.92.70). **Open** 9am-noon, 3-6.30pm Tue-Sat.

Tourist information

Nans-les-Pins *Office de Tourisme, 2 cours Général de Gaulle, 83860 Nans-les-Pins (04.94.78.95.91, http://membres.lycos.fr/nanslespins).* **Open** *July, Aug* 9am-noon, 3-6pm Mon-Sat, 9am-noon Sun. *Sept-June* 9am-noon, 2-5pm Mon-Sat, 9am-noon Sun.
Plan d'Aups *Office de Tourisme, pl de la Mairie, 83640 Plan d'Aups Ste-Baume (04.42.62.57.57).* **Open** 10am-noon, 2.30-5pm Mon-Fri, 9am-noon Sat, Sun.
St-Maximin *Office de Tourisme, Hôtel de Ville, 83470 St-Maximin-la-Ste-Baume (04.94.59.84.59).* **Open** *June-Sept* 9am-12.30pm, 2-6pm daily. *Oct-May* 9am-12.30pm, 2-5.30pm daily.

Getting there & around

By car

Leave the A8 at exit 34 for St-Maximin, exit 35 for Brignoles, both are also on the N7.

By bus

Autocars Blanc (04.94.69.08.28), based in Brignoles, runs 6 buses daily between Brignoles and St-Maximin and St-Maximin and Aix, daily services between Brignoles and Barjols; around 2 buses a day towards Les Arcs stop at Correns.
Phocéen Voyages (04.93.85.66.61) runs buses twice daily from Nice, and once a day from Marseille to both Brignoles and St-Maximin.

Draguignan & the Central Var

There be dragons here: the inland Var's pock-marked gorges and wild woodlands hold plenty of surprises.

Rolling out from the busy hub of Draguignan, the interior of the Var département is a land of Côtes de Provence vineyards, truffle woods and perched villages with wrought-iron belfries. The Var has been discovered by the British but many villages remain pleasantly untrafficked.

Draguignan & the Gorges de Châteaudouble

With its military barracks (the town hosts the French army artillery school) and broad boulevards laid out in the 19th-century by Baron Haussmann in a dress rehearsal for his reworking of Paris, **Draguignan** doesn't conform to all those *pétanque*, lavender and village-fountain clichés. But once past all the shopping malls, discount stores and fast food joints on the outskirts, the town centre is a surprisingly pleasant place to while away a couple of hours. During the day at least, Draguignan (whose name derived from the dragon-slaying exploits of fifth-century St Hermentine) tries to emulate its prestigious past, when from 1797 to 1974 it was capital of the Var. To appreciate the town's real charm, take the pedestrianised Montée de l'Horloge to look at the 17th-century bell tower, and carry on to place du Marché, lined with elegantly dilapidated townhouses, adorned with blue shutters and hanging plants. If you can face the crowds in the summer heat, come on market days (all day Wednesday and Saturday morning) when the square and surrounding alleys are perfumed with the scents of roasting chickens, thyme, goats' cheese and pastis. There are two worthwhile museums in the old town. First is the **Musée Municipal**, housed in the summer palace of the Bishop of Fréjus. Besides a patchy collection of antiques and archaeology it has some fine sculptures and paintings, including *Rêve au coin du feu*, a marble sculpture by Camille Claudel from 1903, and *L'Enfant au béguin* by Renoir, dating from when the artist lived in Cagnes-sur-Mer. Look out, too, for the painting *St-Pierre de Rome* by 17th-century Italian master Panini. The second

museum is the **Musée des Traditions Provençales**, which recreates traditional life through displays of agricultural tools, furnishings, glass and tiles, plus a collection of *santons*. American visitors might be interested by the US war cemetery on the boulevard John Kennedy; 861 soldiers who participated in the 1944 landings are buried here and a wall commemorates 3,000 men who disappeared.

As for the dragon, apparently it hung out in the **Gorges de Châteaudouble** north of town, reached via the scenic D955. First stop on this road is the Pierre de la Fée (fairy stone), a giant dolmen dating from 2400 BC. Further along, a dirt road on the right takes you through the beautiful vineyard of the **Domaine du Dragon** (04.98.10.23.00), once the 12th-century fortified Castrum de Dragone of the Draguignan family, where archeologists have recently discovered a medieval chapel on first-century foundations. The D955 winds along the gorge floor passing **Rebouillon**, a hamlet built like a horseshoe around a central meadow on the banks of the Nartuby. From the gorge road, Châteaudouble (also reached direct by D45) suddenly appears high on spectacular cliffs, as the scenery changes dramatically to a far more Alpine landscape with jagged rock formations. Châteaudouble was originally called the Devil's Gap. In winter the village is full of huntsmen, buying arms for tracking wild boar.

West of Draguignan is a flatter landscape, ripe with vineyards and fruit trees. The D557 heads into the fortified village of **Flayosc**. Life revolves around the little place de la République with its timeworn fountain; unlike the majority of other fountains in the area, though, the water is not suitable for drinking. Fruit, vegetable and wine producers set up their stalls here on Monday mornings. This is also a good time to pick up some ultra-fresh pasta and homemade pesto from **Les Pâtes Flayoscaises** at 23 boulevard Jean Moulin, a small street (despite its name) that runs into the square. Shopping done, everyone relaxes on the terrace of the **Café du Commerce**. The 12th-century church, with the wrought-iron belfry characteristic of these parts, is also worth a visit at the east end of the village. In a bucolic hamlet just north of Flayosc, the 13th-century **Moulin du Flayosquet** (04.94.70.41.45, open Tue-Sat) is the oldest operating olive mill in the Var. Fifth-generation owner Max Doleatto offers guided visits and tastings of olive oil.

Musée Municipal

9 rue de la République, Draguignan (04.98.10.26.85). **Open** 9am-noon, 2-6pm Mon-Sat. **Admission** free.

Musée des Traditions Provençales

15 rue Roumanille, Draguignan (04.94.47.05.72). **Open** 9am-noon, 2-6pm Tue-Sat; 2-6pm Sun. **Admission** €3.50; €1.50 6-18s; free under-6s. **No credit cards**.

Where to stay & eat

The surrounding countryside is so seductive it generally makes more sense to stay in a *chambres d'hôtes* with a garden than in one of Draguignan's hotels. Then again, for those who like to be where the action is, there's the **Victoria Hôtel** (54 av Carnot, 04.94.47.24.12, double €69-€130). **Les Milles Colonnes** (2 pl aux Herbes, 04.94.68.52.58, closed Sun and last 2wks Aug, dinner served June to July, otherwise lunch only, menu €17) is a lively brasserie in the old town serving up fresh market dishes. Specialities include *petits farcis niçois, rougets à la tapenade* and apple crumble. 2km outside Draguignan is the 12-room **Les Oliviers** (rte de Flayosc, 04.94.68.25.74, double €48-€54).

In Châteaudouble, the view's the thing at the **Restaurant de la Tour** (pl Beausoleil, 04.94.70.93.08, closed Wed and Christmas to New Year, menus €18.50-€26) but the food comes a close second – do try the excellent game dishes and the truffle omelette if you're around between November and February. **Château** (04.94.70.90.05, closed Mon-Wed in Oct-Mar, menus €30-€43) offers a modern take on Provençal cuisine, along with homemade foie gras, plus views over the Nartuby gorge. In Flayosc, **L'Oustaou** (5 pl Brémond, 04.94.70.42.69, closed dinner Tue & Sun and all Wed, menus €21-€44) is a well-regarded regional restaurant with a terrace. Specialities include *daube provençale* and *pieds et paquets marseillais*. Opened quite recently by Dutch chef Elisabeth Abbink, **La Salle à Manger** (9 pl de la République, 04.94.84.66.04, menus €30) uses only the freshest produce and changes its menu weekly, so dishes such as brochette of Landes foie gras with apricots, grilled pepper soup, *brandade de loup*, rabbit stew, rack of lamb, and even ostrich (from a farm near Ste-Maxime) are eminently tasty.

Resources

Market is all Wednesday and Sunday morning in Draguignan, Monday morning in Flayosc, Tuesday in Lorgues and Friday Châteaudouble.

Hospital

Hopital de Draguignan, rte de Montfarrat, Draguignan (04.94.60.50.00).

Internet

L'Endroit, 212 rue Jean Aicard, Draguignan (04.94.68.90.39). **Open** 10am-1pm, 3-8pm Mon-Wed, Fri; 10am-1pm, 3-7pm Thur, Sat.

Police

Commissariat, 1 allée Azémar, Draguignan (04.94.60.62.60).

Post office

rue St-Jaume, Draguignan (04.94.50.57.35).

Tourist information

Châteaudouble *Office de Tourisme Hôtel de Ville, pl de la Fontaine, 83300 Châteaudouble (04.98.10.51.35).* **Open** 9-11.30am Mon-Fri. **Draguignan** *Office de Tourisme, 2 av Lazare Carnot, 83300 Draguignan (04.98.10.51.05/www.ot-draguignan.fr).* **Open** 9am-6pm Mon-Sat. **Flayosc** *Office de Tourisme, pl Pied-Barri, 83780 Flayosc (04.94.70.41.31/www.ville-flayosc.fr).* **Open** *July-Aug* 9am-noon, 3-6pm Mon-Sat; 10am-noon Sun. *Sept-June* 9am-noon, 3-6pm Mon-Sat.

Salernes, Aups & Tourtour

Salernes was made for market days, thanks to its large central square, cours Théodore Bouge, shaded by centuries-old plane trees. This is a far more civilised spot than it was 7,000 years ago, when its citizens were cannibals (just check the proud plaque at the entrance to the Intermarché supermarket on the eastern edge of town, but don't let this dissuade you from opting for the succulent, herb-fed Sisteron lamb available here). On Wednesday and Sunday market mornings, parking places and café seats are rare finds, especially at the bustling **Café de la Bresque**. When not crammed with stalls selling fresh produce and pottery, the town is surprisingly quiet, even at the height of summer. This is the moment to explore its pretty backstreets and squares, especially the handsome place de la Révolution which has a superb Roman fountain dribbling spring water. Down by the river Bresque, which flows along the southern side of the town, La Muie is an exceptionally pretty bathing site, with crystal-clear water and sandy banks.

Thanks to local clay, water and abundant wood from nearby forests to fuel its kilns, Salernes has been renowned for centuries for the manufacture of the hexagonal terracotta

Draguignon still remembers its monster infested past.

tiles, known as *tommettes,* that cover the floor of traditional Provençal homes. Today, there are 16 tile workshops, mostly on the western outskirst of town. Check out **Sismondini** (rte de Sillans, 04.94.04.63.06, closed Sun) and **Jacques Brest Céramiques** (quartier des Arnauds, 04.94.70.60.65, closed Sun) for traditional tiles, **Carrelages Pierre Boutal** (rte de Draguignan, 04.94.70.62.12, closed Sun) for painted designs, and **Alain Vagh** (rte d'Entrecasteaux, 04.94.70.61.85) for colourful glazes and wacky creations from a pink-tiled Harley Davidson to a tiled grand piano.

A short drive north on the D31 brings you to the tightly knit town of **Aups**, truffle capital of the Var. Every Thursday at 10am from late November to late February there is a high-stakes truffle auction in the main square, where the precious commodity – all the more valuable as it is exempt from taxes – is sold out of car boots. The 2003 harvest was very meagre: bad news for the luxury restaurant trade, as the Chênes Verts (*see p208*) near Tourtour, Fontaine d'Ampus (*see p208*) and Chez Bruno (*see p211*) in Lorgues all specialise in the black fungus.

Aups life revolves around the cafés on tiny place Girard which leads into rue Maréchal Foch, filled with boutiques hawking Provençal artefacts and the antique shop Le Déniche,

which sells beautiful old Provençal linen. A little further up on avenue Albert 1er, don't miss the **Musée Simon Segal**, housed in a former Ursuline convent, and containing the work of Russian-born artist Simon Segal and other lesser-known but impressive artists of the Ecole de Paris.

The 7km drive along the D557 from Aups to Villecroze offers breathtaking views of the Var's wooded landscape as far as the Maures mountain range. Just before the entrance to the town, lies the adorable 12th-century chapel of St-Victor, muffled by centuries-old cypresses and olive trees. The chapel is cared for by the **Académie Musicale de Villecroze** (9 rue Roger Maurice, 04.94.85.91.00, www.academie-villecroze.com) whose pupils perform here in summer (8.30pm Fri, Apr-Oct). **Villecroze** (meaning hollow town) is set against a cliff face riddled with caves known as the **Grottes Troglodytes** (reserve at tourist office for visits May-Sept), which a local lord turned into dwellings in the 16th century. Until a few years ago a waterfall cascaded year-round down the cliff into a crystal-clear stream in the picturesque garden beneath. Lately, however, drought conditions have encouraged home owners to divert the water for their gardens, and it now runs dry from June to autumn.

The perched medieval village of **Tourtour** is situated just above Villecroze, reached by a twisting switchback road that gives credence to its title 'the village in the sky'. St Trinian's illustrator Ronald Searle had the good taste to settle here in the mid-70s and hasn't moved his drawing board since. Luckily, it is too small to house many souvenir shops, while **Florence** (pl des Ormeaux, 04.94.70.56.90), the only clothes boutique, is as sophisticated as a Paris equivalent. The boules pitch below the town hall has a 180° view over the region and is particularly picturesque on Wednesday and Saturday market days. Further up, the 11th-century church dominates the valley. The village also has a still-operative 17th-century olive press, a *lavoir* and the medieval Tour Grimaldi watchtower.

Take the quiet D51 out of Tourtour to reach the sleepy hamlet of **Ampus**, which harbours an 11th-century Romanesque church and the pretty chapel Notre-Dame-de-Spéluque, which has a beautifully sculpted altar.

Musée Simon Segal

av Albert 1er, Aups (04.94.70.01.95). **Open** *15 June-15 Sept* 10am-noon, 4-7pm daily. **Admission** €2.30; €1.50 10-18s; free under 10s. **No credit cards.**

Aups: quiet except at truffle time. *See p207.*

Where to stay & eat

Aups comes alive in January for the Fête des Truffes, which starts on the third Thursday of November. Catherine at **Le Yucca** (3 rue Foch, 04.94.70.12.11, closed dinner Mon & all Tue and Nov, menus €13.50-€23) prepares *brouillade* (scrambled eggs) with truffles and the rest of the year serves divine ravioli; jazz and Latin musicians play here in summer. **Les Gourmets** (5 rue Voltaire, 04.94.70.14.97, menus €17-€29) is a discreet restaurant on the road to Tourtour serving consistently good seasonal cuisine, whether pheasant or foie gras in winter or snails and morels in spring. Best by far of the cafés and restaurants in Tourtour's main square is **Farigoulette** (pl des Ormeaux, 04.94.70.57.37, menu €21), where the olive oil is divinely perfumed, the *daube provençale* one of the best in the region and the service relaxed and welcoming. Just outside Tourtour, **Le Mas l'Acacia** (rte d'Aups, 04.94.70.53.84, double €54) is a *chambres d'hôtes* with spectacular views and a small pool. **La Bastide de Tourtour** (04.98.10.54.20, double €130-€241, restaurant dinner only except July & Aug, menus €24-€49) invariably has an array of Bentleys and Jaguars in its carpark. However, despite its spectacular views and large park, this château hotel has never managed to shake off its charmless atmosphere and, surprisingly, given the prices, its rooms are not air-conditioned. On a hill below Tourtour, the **Mas des Collines** (camp Fournier, 04.94.70.59.30, double €80-€136) has magnificent views from the balconies of its rather charmless rooms, and a swimming pool. 2km out towards Villecroze, **Les Chênes Verts** (04.94.70.55.06, closed June, double €92, restaurant closed Tue & Wed, menu €43) is a gourmet restaurant where chef Paul Bagade does great things with truffles (when available); it also has three charming bedrooms.

Hidden in the country 3km from Villecroze, **Hôtel au Bien-Etre** (04.94.70.67.57, closed Nov & Feb, double €45-€62, restaurant closed lunch Mon-Wed, menus €22-€36) has motel-style rooms with little terraces (neighbours can be a little too close for comfort) in a small garden, but locals come for the sophisticated cuisine of owner-chef Michel Audier.

Gourmets should not miss the **Fontaine d'Ampus** (04.94.70.98.08, closed Mon, Tue and Feb & Oct, menu €34) in Ampus. Owner-chef Marc Haye changes his four-course menu weekly and claims never to repeat himself. He is particularly clever at combining herbs and local produce to create flavours tastebuds have rarely encountered. If only the service wasn't so bossy, it would be a real treat.

High-rise living at **Villecroze**. *See p207.*

Resources

Weekly markets are on Wednesday and Sunday in Salernes, Wednesday and Saturday in Aups and Tourtour.

Tourist information

Ampus *Office de Tourisme, Hôtel de Ville, 83111 Ampus (04.94.70.97.11/www.mairie-ampus.fr).* **Open** 9.30am 12.30pm Mon Fri.
Aups *Office de Tourisme, pl Mistral, 83630 Aups (04.94.84.00.69).* **Open** *July, Aug* 9am-7pm Mon-Sat; 9am-noon Sun. *Sept-June* 9am-noon, 2-5.30pm Mon-Sat.
Salernes *Office de Tourisme, pl Gabriel Péri, 83690 Salernes (04.94.70.69.02).* **Open** *July, Aug* 9am-7pm Mon-Sat. *Sept-June* 9.30am-12.30pm, 3-6.45pm Mon-Sat.
Villecroze *Office de Tourisme, rue Ambroise Croizat, 83690 Villecroze (04.94.67.50.00).* **Open** times vary, generally *June-Sept* 8.30am-12.30pm, 1.30-6.30pm daily. *Oct-May* 9am-noon, 1.30-4.30pm Mon-Fri; 2-5pm Sat, Sun.

Cotignac & around

Framed by an 80m-high and 400m-wide rock face pierced with caves and topped with the ruins of a 15th-century castle, lively **Cotignac** has long seduced the British who buzz around its estate agents. The village takes its name from *coing* (quince), as for centuries the community has made jelly from the fruit. Locals and would-be locals lounge on café terraces under the huge old plane trees that line the cours Gambetta. The liveliest and most picturesque time to come is on flea-market days (call 04.94.76.85.91 for dates) when the town becomes one big bric-à-brac emporium. To witness Provençal Romanesque architecture in its purest form it's worth visiting the 12th-century **Eglise St-Pierre** in the town centre; though it is **Notre-Dame-des-Grâces** at the southern entrance that holds a special place in French history. A Paris monk dreamed that the only way Louis XIII could have children was for Anne of Austria to carry out three novenas, including one at Cotignac. Lo and behold, Louis XIV was born after the Queen left the town. To be on the safe side, Louis XIV paid his respects here in 1660 en route to marry the infanta Marie-Thérèse in St-Jean-de-Luz. The medieval rue Clastre has the oldest houses, while the place de la Mairie has an exquisite belfry dating from 1496. On and around the Grande Rue there are elegant 16th- and 17th-century townhouses, while place de la Liberté boasts the prettiest of Cotignac's 18 fountains. The magnificent waterfall La Trompine that cascades down the cliff from the river Cassole provides hydroelectric power. Just outside Cotignac, the Théâtre de Gassière, an outdoor amphitheatre, is used for outdoor concerts in July and August.

About 3km outside Cotignac on the D13 lies the impressive **Monastère St-Joseph-du-Bressillon**, whose cloister and dormitories have been lovingly restored by its 16 resident Benedictine nuns. To hear the Gregorian chants and mass in Latin is a rare, moving experience (mass 11am, vespers 5pm daily).

Continue north on the D13 to **Fox-Amphoux**, first a Roman encampment, later a staging post of the Knights Templar. Locals still pronounce it 'foks-amfooks' in true Provençal style, though there are precious few locals left the village, which has been turned into a northern European vision of what a Provençal village should look like. In ruins only 20 years ago, it is now a soulless place full of over-restored second homes. Still, the 12th-century Romanesque church is intact on place de l'Eglise.

Between Fox-Amphoux and Salernes, **Sillans-la-Cascade** is a refreshingly unrestored village with a sunny square and two restaurants facing the river Bresque. In front of the old chapel, a painted wooden sign indicates a 30-minute hike to *la cascade* itself, a waterfall that crashes down into a refreshingly cool pool.

East of Cotignac on the D50, the delightful village of **Entrecasteaux**, is dominated by the magnificent 17th-century **Château**

d'Entrecasteaux. Narrowly saved from destruction during the Revolution, it was in ruins when Scottish painter Ian McGarvie-Munn – whose chequered life included a stint as commander of the Guatemalan navy – purchased it and began repairs in the 1970s. Although very long, the structure is only one room deep but it has a surrounding formal garden designed by André Le Nôtre.

Château d'Entrecasteaux

Entrecasteaux (04.94.04.43.95). **Open** *guided tours Apr-June* 4pm Mon-Fri, Sun. *July-Sept* 11am, 4pm, 5pm Mon-Fri, Sun. Closed Oct-Mar. **Admission** €7; €3.50 12-16s; free under-12s. **No credit cards.**

Where to stay & eat

On a quiet street in Cotignac, **Maison Gonzagues** (9 rue Léon Gérard, 04.94.72.85.40, double €107-€115) offers five handsome rooms in an 18th-century townhouse furnished with antiques. The **Modern Bar** (12 cours Gambetta, 04.94.04.65.92, closed Mon) is the best place for a drink on the town's main drag. At No.27, **La Table de la Fontaine** (04.94.04.79.13, closed Mon & dinner Sun Nov-Apr, menus €20-€26) is good for a terrace lunch, especially on market day. Olives grow all around **La Radassière**, 1km east of Cotignac (rte d'Entrecasteaux, 04.94.04.63.33, closed Jan, double €70), a friendly B&B where Maryse Artaud serves local quince jelly for breakfast; there is a nice garden and pool.

In Fox-Amphoux take a room with a view at the 11th-century **Auberge du Vieux Fox** (pl de l'Eglise, 04.94.80.71.69, closed mid-Nov to mid-Dec, double €63-€95). For an antidote to this prettiness, phone ahead to book a table for lunch at **Chez Jean** (04.94.80.70.76, closed dinner and 2wks Nov, menu €10) at the La Bréguière roundabout north of the village. Under the vigilant gaze of a stuffed owl and boar, Jean and Chantal Serre serve abundant, wholesome fare, with wine charged according to how much you drink. In Sillans-la-Cascade, **Hôtel-Restaurant Les Pins** (04.94.04.63.26, double €39, menus €14-€32) offers pleasant rooms and meals in a rustic dining room. Try fish stew with *pistou* in summer, game in winter.

Resources

Market day is Tuesday in Cotignac, Friday in Entrecasteaux.

Tourist information

Cotignac *Office de Tourisme, 2 rue Bonaventure, 83570 Cotignac (04.94.04.61.87).* **Open** *summer* 10am-noon, 3-6pm Tue-Sat. *winter* 10am-noon, 3-6pm Tue-Fri; 10am-noon Sat.

Entrecasteaux *Office de Tourisme, cours Gabriel Péri, 83570 Entrecasteaux (04.98.05.22.05).* **Open** 10am-noon, 2-5pm Tue-Sat.
Sillans *Office de Tourisme, Le Château, 83690 Sillans-la-Cascade (04.94.04.78.05).* **Open** *May, June, Sept-Dec* 9am-noon, 4-6pm Wed-Sat. *July-Aug* 9am-noon, 3-7pm Wed-Sat. Closed Jan-Apr.

The Argens Valley & Abbaye du Thoronet

South of Draguignan, Côtes-de-Provence vineyards line the gentle slopes either side of the Argens river. The most popular sport here is the estate crawl – something best done by bicycle, with a solemn promise that you'll come back later with the car to pick up the 15 cases of rosé. Most French think of **Le Muy** as the motorway exit for St-Tropez. But this small, flat, militantly working-class town has been caught in the crossfire of history a couple of times: once when the locals failed to assassinate Holy Roman Emperor Charles V and again when Le Muy was the parachute bridgehead for Operation Dragon, the August 1944 Allied liberation of Provence. The **Musée de la Libération**, where memorabilia includes jeeps, parachutes and documents, complements a visit to the American War Cemetery in Draguignan.

Between Le Muy and Les Arcs lie the vineyards and chapel of the **Château Ste-Roseline**. Saintly noble lass Roseline de Villeneuve (1263-1329) used to feed starving peasants during Saracen invasions; after her death, her corpse refused to decompose and has since reclined in a glass casket in the chapel. The mainly Baroque chapel has some unexpected music stands by Diego Giacometti, brother of Alberto, and a mosaic by Chagall.

Les Arcs itself has a pretty cream-coloured medieval centre that twists up steeply to the keep of the 11th-century Villeneuve castle. The **Maison des Vins** on the N7 south of town is an excellent one-stop shop for those who don't have the time or patience to tour the vineyards; though it also has maps and brochures for those who do. Just outside Taradeau, the **Château St-Martin** gives a *son et lumière* show (in French or English) in the 15th-century cellar, portraying the history of Provençal wines.

The D48 north to Lorgues crosses the Argens river, passing the imposing **Château d'Astros** (04.94.99.73.00), which featured in Yves Robert's film of Pagnol's *Le Château de ma mère*. **Lorgues** has a pleasant main street lined with peeling plane trees, fountains and cafés, an old town full of medieval houses and foodie destination Chez Bruno (*see p211*). Park by the 18th-century **Collégiale St-Martin** and look in at the multi-coloured marble altar.

The Var

Nestling in the Darboussière forest, the **Abbaye du Thoronet** is a silent and imposing place, whose sparse, geometric lines, pure and stripped of ornament, reflect the austere lifestyle of the back-to-basics Cistercian order. Man-made reinforcements are shunned: the blocks of warm pinkish stone are glued together by gravity alone. The first of the three great Cistercian foundations of Provence (with Silvacane and Sénanque), Thoronet stays faithful to the Romanesque, though by 1160, when work began, northern France was already under the sway of Gothic. The cloister, built on different levels to accommodate the slope of the ground, has a charming fountain house. This extraordinary haven is, however, under threat. Every day lorries loaded with bauxite from nearby mines shudder past, putting enormous pressure on the building. Sadly, experts are now advocating that concrete columns be used to reinforce the site.

Abbaye du Thoronet

(04.94.60.43.90). **Open** *Apr-Sept* 10am-6.30pm daily. *Oct-Mar* 10am-1pm, 2-5pm daily. Closed for visits during Sun mass (noon-2pm). **Admission** €6.10; free under-18s. **Credit** V.

Chapelle & Château Ste-Roseline

D91 4km E of Les Arcs (04.94.99.50.30/tours 04.94.47.56.10/www.sainte-roseline.com). **Open**

Abbaye de Thoronet: Cistercian chef d'oeuvre.

chapel May-Sept 2-6pm Tue-Sun. *Oct-Apr* 2-5pm Tue-Sun. *wine tasting* 9am-noon, 2-6.30pm Mon-Fri; 10am-noon, 2-6pm Sat, Sun. **Admission** *chapel* free; *guided tours* €11.50 (incl wine); €3 under-16s. **No credit cards.**

Château St-Martin

rte des Arcs (04.94.99.76.76). **Open** *Apr to mid-Oct* 9am-6pm daily. *mid-Oct to Mar* 9am-1pm, 3-7pm Mon-Sat. **Admission** free; *son et lumière* €3.80; *tastings* €3.50-€8.50. **Credit** AmEx, MC, V.

Maison des Vins Côtes de Provence

Les Arcs (04.94.99.50.20/www.caveaucp.fr). **Open** *June-Sept* 10am-1pm, 1.30-7pm daily. *Oct-May* 10am-1pm, 1.30-6pm daily.

Musée de la Libération

Tour Charles-Quint, Le Muy (info Office du Tourisme 04.94.45.12.79). **Open** *Apr-June, Sept* 10am-noon Sun. *July, Aug* 10am-noon Thur, Sun. *Oct-Mar* by appointment. **Admission** free.

Where to stay & eat

In Les Arcs, book well ahead for **Le Logis du Guetteur** (04.94.99.51.10, www.logisduguetteur. com, closed mid-Jan to mid-Mar, double €118, menus €32-€82), which occupies part of the Villeneuve château; it has 13 charming rooms and dining in vaulted rooms. The jovial Boeuf brothers have the gourmet scene in Vidauban sewn up: Alain runs hearty **La Concorde** on the main square (pl de la Mairie, 04.94.73.01.19, closed dinner Tue Sept-June, all Wed, 2wks Nov & 2wks Feb, menus €28-€55), while brother Christian recently opened the more designer **Bastide des Magnans** (D48, rte de La Garde-Freinet, 04.94.99.43.91, closed all Mon, dinner Sun, and dinner Wed Oct-June, menus €25.50-€35); both offer solid but elegant *cuisine de terroir*. In Lorgues, the jet set flock to truffle king Bruno Clément at **Chez Bruno** (rue des Arcs, Campagne Mariette, 04.94.85.93.93, www.restaurantbruno.com, closed Mon, menus €54-€110) where the black fungus gets into everything from lobster to ice cream.

Resources

Market is on Thursday and Sunday morning at Le Muy; Tuesday at Lorgues.

Tourist information

Les Arcs *Office de Tourisme, pl Général de Gaulle, 83460 Les Arcs (04.94.73.37.30).* **Open** *July, Aug* 9am-noon, 2-6pm Mon-Fri; 9am-noon Sat; 10am-noon Sun. *Sept-June* 9am-noon, 1.30-5pm Mon-Fri; 9am-noon Sat.
Le Muy *Office du Tourisme, 6 rte de la Bourgade, 83490 Le Muy (04.94.45.12.79/www.lemuy-tourisme.com).* **Open** *July, Aug* 9.30am-noon, 4-7pm

Mon-Sat; 10am-noon Sun. *Sept-June* 9.30am-noon, 3-6pm Mon-Fri; 9.30am-noon Sat, Sun.

Lorgues *Office de Tourisme, pl d'Entrechaux, 83510 Lorgues (04.94.73.92.37).* **Open** 9am-noon, 3-6pm Mon-Sat; 10am-noon-Sun.

Bargemon & Bargème

Highway D25 slices through the countryside towards Alpine Bargème, impressing motorists with its riotous display of olive groves, vineyards and lavender in the south – as well as forests devastated by the 2003 summer fires –

At home with the Beckhams

With St-Tropez as its highest-profile resort, the Var and celebrity are joined at the hip. But until the Beckhams bought a château in hitherto low-key Bargemon, the inland Var was the preserve of a higher-drawer of British emigré: a Nigella set of virgin olive oil, herbes de Provence and trips to the chicest *brocantes*. The British press made much of the arrival of Posh and Becks and fears that it would drag the region into the media melting pot of the glitzy Riviera. Peter Mayle and his Provençal reverie was bad enough, now *Hello* magazine was to focus on this elegant retreat. Disgusted of Draguignan was spitting at the horrors about to be foisted on the area. It was not so much the arrival of the media pack – they soon went – as the nightmare of sharing a départemental address with a footballer and his Spice Wife. The outcry echoed the stropp of the original totty Brigitte Bardot, who deserted St-Tropez in disgust at the hoi polloi invasion. The departure of the Beckhams for Spain has diverted attention from their French idyll, but more recently the Var's most famous international film star resident, Johnny Depp, received the accolade of world's sexiest male. Half a century after the world was wowed by the Bardot curves, it was admiring the male form in the same way. And God Created Depp, who owns a villa in Bormes-les-Mimosas with his Gallic Lolita, Vanessa Paradis, and their two children. While the Home-Counties-from-Home folks fret about the Becks, Monsieur Depp is more relaxed. 'Yeah, I'd give him them a cup of sugar if he came round,' says Depp, should fellow Adonis David come a-calling.

before reaching the red-faced Gorge of Pennafort. Just to the north, **Callas** is a tidy village, where hand-hewn stone houses cluster around a Romanesque church and a once-splendid castle, and spectacular views radiate south to the Maures and Estérel massifs.

Cross the Boussague Pass directly to Bargemon or detour through woody ravines past **Claviers**, a quaint village of leftist politics, where a fiercely patriotic church clock towers over the main square. It is one of the few remaining from the Revolution, still ticking and emblazoned 'Fraternité, Liberté, Egalité'.

Enchantingly leafy **Bargemon** was the last link in a chain of six perched Roman fortified settlements stretching east to Fayence and Montauroux, built to ward off northern invaders. Today, northern Europeans – much cherished for the cash-flow tourism that long ago replaced local shoe workshops – do up the residences and stroll along the still-impressive ramparts. The **Chapelle Notre-Dame de Montaigu** (ask the priest next door for the key) in the village centre has a giant golden altar and a miraculous statue of the Virgin, which is brought out once a year on Easter Monday. In the 14th-century **Eglise St-Etienne**, built just outside the town wall next to a so-called 'Roman' (in fact 12th-century) gate, is a fascinating collection of votive letters.

North of Bargemon, there's a distinct change of climate and vegetation as the D25 loops ever upwards in hairpin bends to the Col de Bel Homme. The road flattens out across the military training grounds of Camp Canjuers, where signs tell cars to yield to tanks and a couple of deserted villages have been left behind for war-games. Perched at 1,097m on limestone cliffs, windswept **Bargème** is the highest village in the Var, with a population of just 15. The Amis du Vieux Bargème in the town hall run guided tours (July, Aug 2.30-5.30pm) to the fortified gateways, the 12th-century church and the Pontevès family château, which was destroyed during the Wars of Religion. Bargème is still unspoiled (0 tourist shops, 0 restaurants) with only spectacular beauty and the nearby GR49 footpath as assets.

Where to stay & eat

In Callas, shady place Clemenceau offers a cool rest in the spray of the old fountain, at the café tables of the **Hôtel de France** (04.94.76.61.02, double €34) or **Le St-Eloi** (04.94.76.78.06). With 12 rooms and four suites, the **Hostellerie Les Gorges de Pennafort** (D25 7km S of Callas, 04.94.76.66.51, www.hostellerie-pennafort.com, double €150-€175, closed mid-Jan to mid-Mar, menus €39-€110, restaurant

Trainee truffle hunters abound around **Aups**. *See p206.*

closed Mon & lunch Wed, plus Sun dinner Oct-May) cultivates manicured flower beds in a rocky gorge far from it all. Host Phillippe da Silva cooks excellent regional dishes in classic cordon bleu mode and succulent desserts. Hikers coming through the gorges might try **Camping Les Blimouses** (D225, Callas, 04.94.47.83.41, two people €12, closed mid-Nov to mid-Mar). In Claviers, **Auberge le Provençal** (2 pl du 8 Mai 1945, 04.94.47.80.62, closed Mon and Jan, menus €10-€15) is good for a cheap meal with lots of salads and fish. By the *lavoir* in Bargemon, **Auberge L'Oustaloun** (2 av Pasteur, 04.94.76.60.36, www.oustaloun.fr, double €60-€70, closed Nov, restaurant closed all Mon, lunch Tue, dinner Sun, menus €20-€38) is a classic Provençal inn with good home cooking (lamb, trout, game) and a shady terrace. A young couple serve tasty regional fare at **Restaurant La Taverne** (pl Chauvier, 04.94.47.89.82, menus €21-€29), which has terrace tables by a fountain. In tiny Bargème, Annie Noël provides five *chambres d'hôtes* and good regional fare at **Les Roses Trémières** (04.94.84.20.86, closed Nov-Mar, double €54, menu €17) in a renovated village house. Just off the GR49, **La Ferme Rebuffel** (La Roque Esclapon, 04.94.76.80.75, double €50, menu €19 reservation necessary) has spacious new duplex rooms on a working farm with sheep, potato fields and ponds of ducks and geese. Meals served in a dining room, which until 2000 housed the milking goats, abound in farm produce.

Resources

Morning markets are on Thursday in Bargemon, Saturday and Tuesday in Callas.

Tourist information

Bargème *Mairie, 83840 Bargème (04.94.50.23.00).* **Open** *July-Aug* 11am-6pm daily. *Sept-June* 11am-5pm Mon, Tue, Thur, Fri.
Bargemon *Office de Tourisme, av Pasteur, 83830 Bargemon (04.94.47.81.73/www.ot-bargemon.fr).* **Open** *summer* 9am-noon, 1-7pm Mon-Fri; 9am-1pm, 3-6pm Sat. *winter* 9am-12.30pm, 1-4.30pm Mon-Fri; 9am-12.30pm Sat.
Callas *Syndicat d'Initiative, pl du 18 Juin 1940, 83830 Callas (04.94.39.06.77).* **Open** *July, Aug* 9am-noon, 2.30-6pm Mon-Sat. *Sept-June* 9.30am-noon Tue, Thur, Sat.

Fayence to Montauroux

Pottery and antiques are big at **Fayence** and on Saturday market mornings, locals both native and international pour into the **Bistrot Fayençais** (04.94.76.24.38) on place de la Mairie for a drink. The **Four du Mitan**, an old bakery, has a tableau vivant breadmaking display. On place St-Jean-Baptiste, with its glorious mountain vista, the 18th-century **Eglise Notre-Dame** has a marble altarpiece by Provençal mason Dominique Fossatti.

West of Fayence, the D19 passes the Romanesque **Chapelle Notre-Dame de l'Ormeau**, with a fine 16th-century altarpiece

(visits 11am Thur by Seillans tourist office €2).
Cream-coloured fortified **Seillans** appears to be
cut out of the forest like a Cubist sculpture.
Three Roman gates lead into town, where
cobbled streets ascend to a château and tower.
The name Seillans is derived from the
Provençal *seilhanso* – the vat of boiling oil that
villagers dumped on the heads of Saracen
attackers. Today's less martial inhabitants
concentrate their energies on honey and
perfume. Max Ernst lived in the village at the
end of his life and 71 of his lithographs can be
seen in a room above the convent (rue des
Remparts, 04.94.50.45.54, open July-Aug 10am-
noon, 3-7pm, Sept-June 2-3.30pm, €2).

East of Fayence, **Tourrettes** is named after
the two square towers of its château, another
home of the powerful Villeneuve family. East of
here, tiny pedestrian **Callian** spirals up to an
impressive feudal château. In summer cool your
feet in the fountain on place Bourguignon,
which is fed by the same Roman aqueduct that
once supplied Fréjus. The main square in
nearby **Montauroux** opens on to a spectacular
panorama. Montauroux has taken to selling
itself as 'the village of Christian Dior'. The Dior
family once owned the 12th-century **Chapelle
St-Barthélémy** (open June-Sept 10am-noon
Wed, 2-5pm Sat) above the village, bequeathing
it to the community when the couturier died.

For lake swimming, make like the rest of the
locals and head to the beautiful **Lac de St-
Cassien**, a nature reserve 6km south-east of
Montauroux, with its protected waterline, clean
water and small beaches with kid-friendly cafés.

Where to eat & stay

The spectacular **Moulin de Camandoule**
(chemin Notre-Dame-des-Cyprès, 04.94.76.00.84,
www.camandoule.com, double €70-€110,
restaurant closed dinner Wed & all Sun Apr-
Sept, Wed & Thur Oct-Mar, menu €35-€55)
is the best address around Fayence. Its 11
Provençal-styled rooms and the restaurant
where British hostess Shirley Rilla serves
classic French cuisine with Mediterranean
flavours are a treat. In Fayence, **Hôtel La
Sousto** (4 pl du Paty, 04.94.76.02.16, double
€44-€46) provides a cheerful taste of village life.
2.5km out, **Restaurant Le Castellaras** (rte
de Seillans, 04.94.76.13.80, closed Mon & Tue
and 1wk June/July, 2wks Mar, 2wks Nov,
menus €40-€55) is the area's gourmet pull. *Père
et fille*, Alain and Hermance Carro offer creative,
market dishes (rolls of foie gras and elderberry)
in a lovely garden filled with sculpture, roses,
red-pepper bushes and a swimming pool. 3km
east of Montauroux, chef Eric Maio serves
Mediterranean fare and truffles at the **Auberge**

des Fontaines d'Aragon (D37, 04.94.47.71.65,
www.fontaines-daragon.com, closed Mon, Tue
and Jan, menus €37-€110). 2004 sees the
opening of **Four Seasons Resort Provence**
(Domaine des Terre Blanche, Tourrettes,
04.94.39.90.00, www.fourseasons.com, double
€600-€1,500), a luxury enclave with villas, spa,
gym, golf course and tennis courts.

Resources

Morning markets are Tuesday, Thursday and
Saturday in Fayence, Tuesday in Montauroux.

Tourist information

Fayence *Office de Tourisme, pl Léon Roux, 83440
Fayence (04.94.76.20.08/www.paysdefayence.com).*
Open *15 June-15 Sept 9am-noon, 3-7pm Mon-Sat;
9.30am-noon Sun. 16 Sept-14 June 9am-noon, 2-6pm
Mon-Sat.*
Montauroux *Office de Tourisme, pl du Clos, 83440
Montauroux (04.94.47.75.90/http://tourisme.
montauroux.com).* **Open** *9am-noon, 2-6pm Mon-Fri;
9am-noon Sat (and 2-6pm Sat Easter-Oct).*
Seillans *Office de Tourisme, pl du Valat, 83440
Seillans (04.94.76.85.91/www.seillans-var.com).*
Open *Jan, Feb 9.30am-12.30pm, 2.30-6pm Tue-Sat.
Mar-Dec 9.30am-12.30pm, 2.30-6.30pm Mon-Sat (and
10am-1pm, 3-6pm Sun July, Aug).*

Getting there & around

By car

The A8 runs along the Argens valley. Take exit 36
(Le Muy) and then N555 for Draguignan; same exit
and N7 for Les Arcs and Lorgues. Salernes is W of
Draguignan on the D557 and D560. Cotignac is SW of
Salernes on the D22. Bargemon is 25km NE of
Draguignan on the D562, D225 and D25. Fayence lies
off the D562 between Draguignan and Grasse.

By train or bus

The station at Les Arcs-Draguignan is on the main
Paris-Nice line served by TGVs and slower trains
between Nice and Marseille. **Les Rapides Varois**
(04.94.50.21.50) runs hourly buses to Draguignan
(fewer on Sun) from Les Arcs station timed to
connect with trains, 2 to 5 buses a day (Mon-Sat)
between Draguignan and Aups via Tourtour and
Ampus, and buses from Les Arcs station to Lorgues
and Le Thoronet (Mon-Sat, none Wed in school
holidays). **Cars Blanc** (04.94.69.08.28) runs 2 buses
a day between Draguignan and Marseille via
Brignoles and Aix-en-Provence, and buses between
Brignoles and Aups, Sillans, Villecroze, Salernes,
Entrecasteaux, Cotignac and Lorgues. **Estérel Cars**
(04.94.52.00.50) runs buses from Draguignan to St-
Raphaël via Le Muy. **Transvar** (04.94.28.93.28) runs
roughly 5 buses a day (3 on Sun) between
Draguignan and Toulon via Les Arcs and Vidauban.
Gagnard (04.94.76.02.29) runs 2 to 3 buses a day
Mon-Sat between Draguignan and Grasse, via Callas,
Claviers, Bargemon & Seillans, Fayence, Callian and
Montauroux. It also runs about 4 buses daily
between Fayence and St-Raphaël.

Gorges du Verdon

It's dizzying work, but the fantastic jagged cliffs and an epic forested wilderness make the Midi's very own Grand Canyon worth the effort.

For countless centuries the emerald-green torrent of the Verdon river has chiselled away the limestone plateau of France's own Grand Canyon, carving out steep white cliffs that trail down to sloping, moss-covered rocks. Fantastic jagged bluffs nestled in an epic forested wilderness present a world of genuinely awe-inspiring beauty. The dizzying chasm ranges between 215m and 1,650m wide in the eastern Upper Gorge and narrows claustrophobically in the lower section to between six and 108m wide. The Grand Canyon proper runs for 21km from south of Rougon to the reservoir at the Lac de Ste-Croix.

Few people, save locals, even knew about the existence of this natural wonder until its depths were fully explored by potholer Edouard Martel in 1905. Even then, some avid Parisian nature-lover suggested the best thing to do with such a large, unproductive gash would be to wall it up and make a dam. In the event, dams were built downstream at the Lac de Ste-Croix and below the Basses Gorges. The whole spectacular, sparsely populated but much-visited area was made into a Parc Naturel Régional in 1977.

The Grand Canyon

Perilous roads perched on either side of the canyon offer up a dramatic 130km circuit, fraught with hairpin bends requiring a fair share of white-knuckled driving courage. During peak summer months, traffic jams and tempers rise as cars inch along in a sweltering crawl that would normally take three hours but takes five in July and August, thanks to frequent stops along impossibly narrow roads for picture-perfect photo opportunities. The best times to go are in April, May, September or October, but even if it is hot, it is congested and it is summer, the experience is well worth it.

The route is best tackled from **Castellane** (take the Grasse exit from the A8 and follow the N85), a small town situated on the Route Napoléon (*see p293*). Castellane nestles beneath a massive rocky outcrop topped by the **Notre-Dame-du-Roc** chapel. The ascent is a difficult 20-minute walk from the centre but once there, wander into the interesting 18th-century shrine boasting a large statue of the Virgin covered in *ex-votos*. The village itself is a tightly packed

Towering **Moustiers-Ste-Marie**. *See p216.*

maze of streets, and home to at least to half a dozen companies proposing canyoning and rafting trips. Napoléon stopped off for a bite in March 1815 at what is now the **Conservatoire des Arts et Traditions Populaires**. Also worth a peek is the **Musée Sirènes et Fossiles**, which has an impressive collection detailing the history of mythological mermaids combined with fossils of sirenians, marine mammals dating from the era when the sea still covered the region four million years ago. Just ten minutes north from Castellane, walk into the **Vallée des Sirènes Fossiles** to see where the first of these fossils were discovered.

12km out of Castellane, the D952 Gorges road splits in two. Turn left along the D955 to the small town of **Trigance**. Today, it is really no more than a jumble of artists' studios barely worth noting except for the beautiful **Château de Trigance**. Faithfully rebuilt and restored in

The Var

Le Pont d'Artuby, perfect for bungee-jumpers.

the loving hands of Jean-Claude Thomas, it is now a romantic getaway hotel-restaurant (*see p217*). From here, take the narrow D90 for access to the **Corniche Sublime** (D71) road, an engineering feat completed only in 1947. It's comprised of a series of death-defying twists and turns with edges that plunge a sheer 800m to the bright ribbon of the river below along the canyon's southern flank. But don't be too concerned: for the most part, drivers are considerate and there are plenty of scenic shots and spectacular look-out points along the way.

To reach the beginning of the Corniche Sublime you need to drive over the **Pont d'Artuby**, Europe's highest bridge, suspended 650m above the Artuby torrent. If a simple crossing does not set your pulse racing, tourist offices in the area will direct you to sports clubs that organise bungee-jumping over the edge. The first glimpse of the canyon is from the **Balcon de la Mescla** lookout further along the Corniche Sublime. Twisty and gut-clenchingly narrow, it winds above the gorge towards the splendidly perched town of **Aiguines**, which has the western entrance to the canyon to one side and the **Lac Ste-Croix** to the other. The fairytale castle – a faux-Renaissance pile with multicoloured towers – is not open to the public. Aiguines was once famed for wood-turning, especially boules-making (using boxwood gathered by intrepid

climbers from trees at the base of the gorge). The high fluorine content of the water makes for an unnatural vibrant green; it also makes it undrinkable. The lake is, however, a lovely place to splash about on a pedalo or swim, unless the level is low, when it becomes muddy.

The northern and southern roads meet in **Moustiers-Ste-Marie**. Built around its Romanesque church on the edge of a precipice, Moustiers enjoys a Mediterranean climate despite its altitude. On a rock high above town is the medieval **Notre-Dame-de-Beauvoir** chapel. Suspended from a chain between two rocks above the chapel is a star said to have been hung there by a knight, relieved at having returned from the Crusades unscathed. Moustiers was renowned in the 17th and 18th centuries for its faïence. After 200 years of production it was dethroned by the fashion for porcelain and English bone china, and the last oven went cold in 1874. Recently, attempts have been made to resuscitate the craft, and there are now 19 workshops in operation, the output of which is given a very hard sell in the town's all-too-numerous crafts and souvenir shops. The small but excellent **Musée de la Faïence** chronicles this struggle with delicate porcelains dating back to the end of the 17th century.

Further east along the D952, the tiny village of **La Palud-sur-Verdon** is thronged with hikers and climbers sporting baggy shorts and Birkenstock sandals. There is plenty of accommodation, and the friendly grocery store sells flashlights and cooking propane. Just before La Palud, the D23 branches off to the left, offering an airy circular route that climbs more than 500m before plunging halfway down the side of the canyon to the **Chalet de la Maline**, departure point for the Sentier Martel, a six- to nine-hour walk along the valley floor (*see p218*). Just past La Palud, direction Castellane, enjoy the aptly named **Point Sublime** viewpoint.

Conservatoire des Arts et Traditions Populaires

34 rue Nationale, Castellane (04.92.83.71.80). **Open** *mid-May to June, Oct* 9am-noon, 2-6pm Tue-Sat. *July-Sept* 10am-1pm, 2.30-6.30pm Tue-Sun. Closed Nov-Apr. **Admission** €2; €1 7-18s; free under-7s. **No credit cards.**

Musée de la Faïence

pl du Tricentenaire, Moustiers (04.92.74.61.64/ www.mairie.wanadoo/moustiers). **Open** *Apr-Oct* 10am-noon, 2-6pm Wed-Mon (until 7pm July, Aug). *Nov-Mar* 2-5pm Sat, Sun. **Admission** €2; free under-16s. **No credit cards.**

Musée Sirènes et Fossiles

pl Marcel Sauvaire, Castellane (04.92.83.19.23/ www.resgeol04.org). **Open** *May-June, Sept* 10am-noon, 2-5pm Mon-Fri. *July, Aug* 10am-12.30, 2-6.30pm daily. Closed Oct-May. **Admission** €3.85, €2.75 7-15s; free under 7s. **No credit cards.**

Activities

Watersports

Head down to the lakeshore beach in Les Salles-sur-Verdon, below Aiguines, where **Verdon Loisirs** 04.92.77.70.20) and **Le Petit Port** (04.92.77.77.23) rent electric boats (€25/hr), pedalos (€12/hr) and kayaks (€5/hr) on Lac de Ste-Croix. For the more adventurous, numerous outlets in Castellane organise canyoning and rafting trips. **Verdon Passion** (rue Frédéric Mistral, 04.92.74.69.77, www.verdon-passion.com) in Moustiers organises cliff parachuting and climbing as well as canyoning.

Where to stay & eat

Castellane abounds with mid-range hotels, gîtes, campsites and B&Bs. The **Hôtel du Commerce** (pl Marcel Sauvaire, 04.92.83.61.00, www.hotel-fradet.com, closed Nov-Feb, double €59-€65, restaurant closed Tue & lunch Wed, menus €21-€31) has an excellent restaurant run by a pupil of Alain Ducasse. The **Canyons du Verdon** (bd St-Michel, rte de Digne, 04.92.83.76.47, www.studi-hotel.com, closed Nov to mid-Mar, double €43-€63) rents rooms and studio apartments for up to four people, and has a pool. In the pedestrianised old town, **La Main à la Pâte** (rue de la Fontaine,

04.92.83.61.16, closed Tue, Wed and 15 Dec-15 Feb, average €20) is a friendly, beamed bistro serving pizzas and fabulous salads.

Rooms at the **Auberge du Teillon** in the nearby hamlet of Garde (rte Napoléon, 04.92.83.60.88, closed mid-Nov to mid-Mar, double €49) are pretty straightforward but the restaurant is excellent so book well ahead (closed Mon Sept-June, dinner Sun Oct-Apr, menus €18-€40). The grandest option is the medieval **Château de Trigance** (04.94.76.91.18, www.chateau-de-trigance.fr, closed Nov-Mar, double €110-€160, menus €35-€70), dominating the delightful hilltop village of the same name, with its baronial halls, four-poster beds and a vaulted restaurant.

In Aiguines, the **Auberge Altitude 823** (04.98.10.22.17, closed Nov-Mar, double €96-€104 including dinner) is a good budget option. In the town centre, **Hôtel Vieux Château** (pl de Fontaine, 04.94.70.22.95, closed Oct-Mar, double €75-€102 with half-board) is more upmarket, and has cosy rooms and a restaurant. The **Grand-Hôtel-Bain** in Comps-sur-Artuby (rue Praguillon, 04.94.76.90.06, www.grand-hotel-bain.fr, closed mid Nov to late Dec, double €47-€57) has been run by the same family for eight generations and has plain, old-fashioned rooms and homely traditional fare.

In Moustiers, **La Bonne Auberge** (04.92.74.66.18, closed Nov-Mar, double €56-€80) has cheerful decor and friendly owners, and **Le Relais** (pl du Couvert, 04.92.74.66.10, www.lerelais-moustiers.com, closed mid-Nov to Feb, double €59-€75) is very comfortable. Outside town, **La Ferme Rose** (04.92.74.69.47, www.lafermerose.free.fr, closed mid-Nov to mid-Mar, except Christmas, double €65-€135) favours soft whites and wood-beamed ceilings and **La Bastide des Oliviers** (04.92.74.61.10, www.la-bastide-des-oliviers.com, double €98-€140) is a hospitable escape. **Les Santons** restaurant (pl de l'Eglise, 04.92.74.66.48, closed dinner Mon, all Tue and mid-Nov to Jan, average €70) is pricey but well worth a visit (booking advised). For a gourmet experience, head for super-chef Alain Ducasse's **La Bastide de Moustiers** (chemin de Quinson, 04.92.70.47.47, www.bastide-moustiers.com, closed Dec-Mar, double €155-€310, menu €57), which also has 11 delightful rooms.

At La Palud-sur-Verdon, **Le Provence** hotel (rte de la Maline, 04.92.77.38.88, closed Nov-Mar, double €42-€54, average €22) has stunning views, a terrace, and a restaurant.

Resources

Market is Friday in Aiguines, Wednesday and Saturday in Castellane, Friday in Moustiers.

Tourist information

Aiguines *Office de Tourisme, av des Tilleuls, 83630 Aiguines (04.94.70.21.64/www.aiguines.com).* **Open** *July-Aug* 9am-12.30pm, 3-6pm Mon-Sat. *Sept-June* 9am-noon, 1.30-5pm Mon-Fri.

Castellane *Office de Tourisme, rue Nationale, 04120 Castellane (04.92.83.61.14/ www.castellane.org).* **Open** *July, Aug* 9am-12.30pm, 1.30-7pm Mon-Sat, 10am-1pm Sun. *Sept-June* 9am-noon, 2-6pm Mon-Fri.

Moustiers-Ste-Marie *Office de Tourisme, Hôtel Dieu, 04360 Moustiers-Ste-Marie (04.92.74.67.84/www.ville-moustiers-sainte-marie.fr).* **Open** *Mar-June* 9.30am-12.30pm, 2-6pm daily. *July-Aug* 9.30am-7pm daily. *Sept-Feb* 2-6pm daily.

Riez & the Basses Gorges du Verdon

West of the Lac de Ste-Croix the cliffs are only half as sheer as in the Grand Canyon and the area is devoted more to agriculture than to untamed wilderness. Lavender is the main crop on the Plateau de Valensole between the Basses Gorges from the town of Riez; it colours and perfumes the whole area in summer.

Sleepy **Riez** is a pretty, unspoiled little place whose impressive main street suggests it has seen better days. Four seven-metre-high columns in a field on the western outskirts bear

Gorge(ous) walks

For all walks, check with the tourist offices at Castellane or Moustiers-Ste-Marie, which sell an in-depth walkers guidebook and/or can arrange for professional guides. For climate/safety information, call the Parc Naturel Régional du Verdon (04.92.74.68.00, www.parcduverdon.fr).

Walk 1: The Sentier Martel

Length 14km.
Time six to nine hours (including breaks).
Difficulty Very strenuous. Do not do it alone. Wear stout boots and bring lots of water, a map, a sweater and a flashlight. Bring two cars, one to park at the end point to save a long walk back. It's best to start from the Chalet de La Maline, striking out from the parking lot along the signposted GR4, tackling the long descent and then working your way back up through the Samson Couloir to the Point Sublime car park.

Shortly after leaving the Chalet, the steep, narrow trail becomes difficult, with a rock wall on one side and sheer nothingness on the other. To complicate matters, some parts are covered in loose rubble and slippery moss-covered limestone. Take a deep breath, calm your racing heart and continue along the trail, it widens up again about ten minutes later. The path is very well-marked with two painted

lines (one white and one red) splashed on the cliffside, on thick tree trunks or on rocks. After about three hours of breathtaking views and some long downhill stretches, you will come to a cliff with an iron ladder that you must clamber down to continue the hike. It's not a completely sheer drop, although difficult for the faint of heart. The ladder is broken up into five stages, with much-needed places to rest along the way: there are around 240 rungs. Once at the bottom, the trail becomes a bit slippery with loose rocks and shale, snaking down to the riverbed and the Plage des Baumes Frères – which is not a beach at all but a flat area with lots of pebbles. Do not swim here. Because the Verdon is controlled by two dams, the water levels can rise unexpectedly. Throughout this part of the trail you'll often be confronted by disturbing signs of a stick figure running for its life before a tidal wave. This is to warn you to keep to the path or, if you choose to wade in at your own risk, have a well-planned escape route. Check with the EDF electricity board, which controls the gates (recorded information 04.92.83.62.68).

The trail itself stays at all times above the water danger-line. It is a flat-ish tree-covered path for about a half hour before leading back upwards along another series of vertiginous cliffs. Think drops of 200m. Continue to

witness to the town's Roman past. On the opposite bank of the river stands a rare early Christian monument: a sixth-century Merovingian baptistry with more plundered Roman columns. Inside, the **Musée Lapidaire de Riez** has an interesting collection of Gallo-Roman artefacts. Ramparts surround the old town, which is dominated by a 16th-century clock tower. The western gate, the Porte Saint-Sols, opens on to the Grande Rue where flamboyant Renaissance constructions include the Hôtel de Mazan at No.12, which has a beautiful 16th-century staircase. The market, on Wednesday and Saturday, is a good place for local truffles, honey, lavender and faïence.

Follow the D952 southwest along the Colostre river to reach the **Château d'Allemagne-en-Provence**, a part-13th-century, part-Renaissance splendour renowned for its fine, moulded-plasterwork chimneypieces; guided visits are a delight for history buffs. It also has five rooms (double €80-€140) or can be rented by the week (€800-€1,600).

The best approach to the Basses Gorges themselves is from **Quinson**, 21km south-west of Riez. This tiny village is the site of the ambitious **Musée de Préhistoire** opened in 2001, which lies in a partially buried, elliptical building designed by Lord Norman Foster. A million years of prehistory is presented using

follow the red-and-white trail markers upwards until you reach an open plain filled with the wonderful scents of any and all possible wild plants: raspberry bushes, ceps and mint. Moving constantly upwards, you will soon find a series of tunnels; put on your sweater and pull out your flashlight. The first is interesting for the iron rails left over from the era when the tunnels were being dug out; the second is unremarkable; the last and longest has 'windows' that let you see out over the spectacular Verdon and cliffs reflecting sunlight. From here keep on walking, control your vertigo as you tiptoe across a footbridge suspended over the Baou. Finish the hike by scrambling up to the Point Sublime car park and sink tiredly into your car. The relatively quick drive back to the Chalet de la Maline to pick up the second car will give you plenty of time left over to have a well-earned victory drink at the bar.

Walk 2: The Samson Couloir
Length 2km.
Time two hours (including pauses).
Difficulty Moderate: rainfall can make parts slippery.
This lovely, shorter walk through the Samson Couloir begins from the parking lot of the Point Sublime lookout. The entrance of the trail is well-marked and leads immediately to

a cul-de-sac with picnic tables and public toilets. After having a quick look at the Gorges from the Cauvin viewpoint, follow the GR49 trail indicated by a sign with a large painted green lizard. The first stretch is steep and rather rocky – wear good shoes and be prepared to slide a bit. At the bottom the trail follows the riverbed to the remarkable 17th-century Tusset bridge, which bears a resemblance to the Pont d'Avignon and is a good photo opportunity. After the bridge, follow the GR49 sign: the path twists and turns upwards in a difficult climb to a clearing. Stop, breathe the pine-scented air and take a break. After the clearing, the path is flatter. Don't miss the Rocher de la Renardière: a mysterious rock with a hole through it.

Shortly after, a splash of red paint on a tree means that the trail splits in two: one continues up along the GR49, the other downwards to another viewpoint. Take the left (down) path, cross the stream and continue until you reach a large field. On the far side is a clifftop lookout called the Rancoumas viewpoint. Black paint on the rocks shows the best places to stand for the most beautiful views: the cliffs of the l'Escales, over the Martel trail and to the village of Rougon. You will need to backtrack to return to the parking lot – but the glorious scenery is worth a second look.

clever reconstructions, including a mock-up cave complete with paintings, dioramas of Stone Age life and archaeological finds.

The twisty but scenic D82 winds southwest over the mountain to **Esparron-de-Verdon**, dominated by its fortified château (*see below*), beside a lake popular for sailing, windsurfing and pedalos. The ancient spa town of **Gréoux-les-Bains** offers a large choice of hotels, an old town crowded around a severe Templar castle, and the **Thermes de Gréoux-les-Bains**, a troglodyte spa (so as not to lose the therapeutic qualities of the calcium-, sodium-, suphate- and magnesium-rich water through exposure to daylight). After a therapeutic massage, wander to the edge of town to see the **Crèche de Haute-Provence**, a doll-scale village constructed of natural materials evoking the harsh beauty of windswept mountain life.

Château d'Allemagne-en-Provence

(04.92.77.46.78/www.chateauxandcountry.com/ chateaux/allemagneenprovence). **Open** by reservation July to mid-Sept Wed-Sun. *Apr-June, mid-Sept to Oct* Sat, Sun. **Admission** €5. **No credit cards.**

Crèche de Haute-Provence

36 av des Alpes (rte de Vinon), Gréoux-les-Bains (04.92.77.61.08). **Open** 9am-noon, 2-7pm Tue-Sun. Closed Jan, Feb. **Admission** €4; €2.50 7-12s; free under-7s. **No credit cards.**

Musée Lapidaire de Riez

Riez Baptistery. **Open** *mid-June to mid-Sept* 3-7pm Tue, Fri, Sat or by appointment via tourist office (04.92.77.99.09). **Admission** €2. **No credit cards.**

Musée de Préhistoire des Gorges du Verdon

rte de Montmeyan, Quinson (04.92.74.09.59/ www.museeprehistoire.com). **Open** *Feb-June, Sept to mid-Dec* 10am-6pm Mon, Wed-Sun. *July, Aug* 10am-8pm daily. **Admission** €7; €5 6-18s; free under-6s. **Credit** MC, V.

Thermes de Gréoux-les-Bains

av des Thermes, Gréoux-les-Bains (04.92.70.40.01). **Open** *Mar to mid-Dec* 6am-6pm daily. Closed mid-Dec to Feb. **Admission** *1 day* €43; *6 days* €228. **Credit** AmEx, DC, MC, V.

Where to stay & eat

In Riez itself there's not much choice. The **Carina** hotel (Quartier St-Jean, 04.92.77.85.43, closed Nov-Mar, double €47-€55) has basic rooms and is prettier when looking out. Just outside of town, on the D6 towards Valensole, the more impressive **Château de Pontfrac** (04.92.77.78.77, www.chateaudepontfrac.com, double €46-€69) has a beautiful setting and serves simple, hearty meals (menus €22-€25). Quinson's bars are strong on hunting dogs and

low on gourmet facilities, but the museum happily has a café. At Esparron get a feel for the aristocratic lifestyle at the *chambres d'hôtes* in the **Château d'Esparron** (Esparron de Verdon, 04.92.77.12.05, www.esparron.com, closed mid-Nov to mid-Apr, double €130-€220), still in the hands of the Castellane family who built it in the 12th century. Although it has something of a geriatric feel as curists come to take the waters, Gréoux-les-Bains offers plenty of hotels and restaurants. Try **Villa La Castellane** (av des Thermes, 04.92.78.00.31, closed mid-Dec to Mar, double €49-€69), a former hunting lodge in an attractive garden, or the **Villa Borghèse** (av des Thermes, 04.92.78.00.91, www.villa-borghese.com, closed mid-Nov to mid-Mar, double €74-€218), which has a lovely garden and a small spa.

Resources

Market is Thursday in Gréoux-les-Bains, Wednesday and Saturday in Riez.

Tourist information

Gréoux *Office de Tourisme, 5 av des Maronniers, 04800 Gréoux-les-Bains (04.92.78.01.08/www. greoux-les-bains.com).* **Open** *Apr-June, Sept-Oct* 9am-noon, 2-6pm Mon-Sat; 9am-noon Sun. *July, Aug* 9am-12.30pm, 2-6.30pm Mon-Sat; 9am-noon, 2-6pm Sun. *Nov-Mar* 9am-noon, 2-6pm Mon-Fri; 9am-noon, 2-5pm Sat. **Riez** *Office de Tourisme, 4 allée Louis Gardiol, 04500 Riez (04.92.77.99.09/www.ville-riez.fr).* **Open** *mid-June to mid-Sept* 9am-1pm, 3-7pm Mon-Sat (plus 9am-noon Sun July, Aug). *mid-Sept to mid-June* 8.30am-12.30pm, 1.30-5.30pm Mon-Sat.

Getting there & around

By car

For the Grand Canyon, leave the A8 at exit 42 and take the N85 to Castellane via Grasse, or exit 36 for Draguignan and then D955. For Quinson, leave the A8 at exit 34 at St-Maximin and take the D560/D13. From Aix-en-Provence, take the A51 or D952 to Gréoux-les-Bains; the latter continues to Moustiers.

By bus

Public transport is very limited. **Sumian Cars** (04.42.67.60.34) runs buses from Marseille to Castellane via Aix, La Palud and Moustiers (July to mid-Sept, 1 daily Mon, Wed, Sat; mid-Sept to July Sat only), and from Marseille to Gréoux-les-Bains via Aix (1 daily, Mon-Sat). **VFD** (04.93.85.24.56) runs a daily service between Nice and Grenoble via Grasse and Castellane. **Guichard** (04.92.83.64.47) runs buses around the canyon (Apr-June Sat, Sun only; July, Aug daily) linking Castellane with Point Sublime, La Palud and La Maline, and can also organise custom-made tours or airport pick-up. Otherwise the best option for the carless might be a day trip; try **Santa Azur** in Nice (04.97.03.60.00) who operate day trips to the Gorges du Verdon every Sun, Apr-Oct.

The Riviera & Southern Alps

Features

Maps

Introduction

The Niçois don't just stuff sardines, they pack you in like them on their beaches; but head inland and you can find art, olives – and wolves.

The Alpes-Maritimes *département* sums up all that is best and worst about the South of France: a stunning natural coastline covered in some of the most banal concrete architecture of the postwar period; the glamour circuit of **Cannes**, **Monte-Carlo** and **St-Jean-Cap-Ferrat**, watersports and yachts, and pebbly, packed public beaches; a sub-tropical climate that sustains citrus fruits, fabulous gardens and **Menton**'s wintering pensioners; memories of Picasso, Matisse and Renoir, and countless drab daubers, while the money that pours into expat residences and film festivals sustains the haute-cuisine extravaganzas of **Mougins**.

But to concentrate just on the Riviera coastal strip would be a mistake. Just back from the sea, you find ancient olive groves and picture-perfect villages like **Haut de Cagnes**, **Coaraze**, **Peillon** and **Castellar**. Further inland are art-packed **Vence** and **St-Paul-de-Vence**, the stalactite-hung **Grottes de St-Cézaire**, the dramatic **Gorges du Loup** and the rare Alpine wildlife and wolves of the **Parc National du Mercantour**.

The eastern half of the *département* is still marked by its Italianate past (some places changed nationalities on numerous occasions), visible in the Genoese *palazzos* of **Vieux Nice**, frescoed trompe l'oeil facades of **Villefranche-sur-Mer** and the Baroque churches of **Sospel** and the upper valleys, as well as in culinary specialities such as gnocchi and ravioli.

Today, **Nice** itself is sophisticated and cosmopolitan, a vibrant commercial and congress centre with lively bars, *belle époque* villas and first-rate museums devoted to Chagall and Matisse, while **Monaco** provides an autocratic, princely anomaly in the midst of fiercely Republican France, with all the requisite state trappings (and more) on a miniature scale.

Don't miss The Riviera & Southern Alps

La Bastide St-Antoine
Sun-spun creative cuisine by Jacques Chibois in an olive grove near Grasse. *See p288.*

Château Chèvre d'Or, Eze
Extravagant views and luxury. *See p273.*

La Croisette, Cannes
Your chance to stand two feet away from the stars as they walk up *les marches*. *See p225.*

Hi Hôtel, Nice
Conceptual bedrooms, your own pet fish and a violet-flavoured cocktail. *See p262.*

Hôtel Martinez, Cannes
Newly renovated art deco delight. *See p231.*

Iles de Lérins
A fragrant and peaceful haven on monastic isles just 15mins from Cannes. *See p232.*

Matisse
Virtuoso of colour and line at the Musée Matisse, Nice (*see p253*) and Chapelle du Rosaire, Vence (*see 297*).

New Open Air Cinema, Monaco
Outdoor flicks on balmy summer evenings on *le rocher*. *See p225.*

Palais Lascaris
Nice's Genoan past in a frescoed palace. *See p250.*

Plage La Salis
Antibes' prettiest beach, between town and Cap. Sandy, clean and noisy. *See p236.*

Saut du Loup
Dramatic water shoot. *See p291.*

Skiing
Yes, there's snow as well as sun. Head into the Alps. *See p305.*

Vallée des Merveilles
Bronze Age scratchings and arcane messages from early shepherds. *See p300.*

Villa Arson
Cutting edge art exhibitions to fire up debate in Nice. *See p253.*

Cannes

Though the most famous film festival in the world keeps Cannes in tinsel year-round, there are surprisingly low-key escapes not far away.

The grande dame of Cannes' festival season – the annual Film Festival – jealously guards its status as the city's top headliner. And no wonder. Because of it, Cannes receives more media coverage than any French city outside Paris. Palme d'Or contenders, pouty hangers-on and temperamental superstars skip from one gloriously excessive minute to another, gossiped about around the world in the next day's papers. But Cannes isn't just about two weeks in May. It's endlessly fascinating: festival frenzies, bathing beauties, glittery decadence and that inevitable one step too far, conveniently located in a spectacular one-stop shop on the turquoise Mediterranean.

Cannes already attracted the high fashion crowd long before the festival circuit began. In 1834, the British Lord Chancellor Lord Brougham settled in the fishing village of Cannes after an outbreak of cholera made it impossible to continue on to Nice. He built a palatial house, invited all his friends, and for the next 34 years spent the summers here. It wasn't long before the provincial village

turned cosmopolitan as English aristocracy invaded *en masse*, and art and literature celebs were quick to follow suit.

Cannes' first real glimpse at renown came in 1939 when it was selected to host an International Festival of Cinema. World War II disrupted the preparations, so the first festival actually took place in 1946 at the old Palais des Festivals (where the Noga Hilton now stands). Local legend has it that the architects forgot to put a window in the projection booth – only after several embarrassed minutes of hammering and chiselling was a glamorous audience able to enjoy its first festival movie.

No slouch when it comes to capitalising on a good thing, the city has since launched itself as the European media festival hub. The new **Palais des Festivals** (affectionately called the 'bunker' by local residents) now swarms at various times of the year with advertisers (MIPCOM), music-makers (MIDEM), TV producers (MIP-TV) and a range of other conference-goers who keep the glamour contingent high and the hotels full.

Roughing it on the beach.

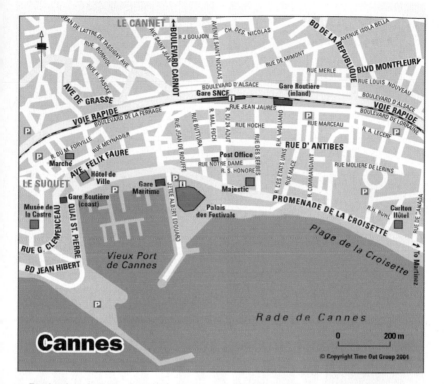

Cannes

0   200 m

© Copyright Time Out Group 2001

Beach culture in Cannes is upmarket too. In the summer every available inch of sand is covered by bronzing, often topless, bodies. (If you prefer to leave your entire bikini at the hotel, there is a straight and gay nude beach, La Batterie, on the N7 towards Antibes.) Public beaches are mostly along boulevard du Midi, although you can find some along La Croisette. The key is if there is a row of beach chairs don't sit – unless you want to pay €15-€25 per day to swim in the same water as everyone else.

Cocktail hour is another important Cannoise ritual. The two main seafront drags, boulevard du Midi and La Croisette, are a late-afternoon must. Along La Croisette are the Palais des Festivals, with its film star handprints in the pavement, the trinity of palace hotels (the Majestic, the Martinez and the Carlton) and **La Malmaison**, a 19th-century villa used for art and photography exhibitions and the Film Festival's Quinzaine des Réalisateurs. Stroll down to the Pointe de la Croisette to take in a view across the bay of La Napoule.

To the west is the port. Perched on the hill above is the old town, **Le Suquet**, which is

pedestrian only, jammed with restaurants, and has one of the best food markets in the Midi. The **Musée de la Castre** occupies what's left of the 12th-century fortifications and has breathtaking views, as well as an eclectic collection ranging from a painting by Pasteur to ancient musical instruments. Easily overlooked amid the shops around rue Meynadier is **Le Musée de l'Enfance**, where passionate collector Mme Nicod gives a dolls' version of 19th-century French history.

West of the centre, **Cannes-La Bocca** is a less-expensive residential area, with a pleasant stretch of public beach and cheaper stores and restaurants on avenue Francis Tonner. On the other side of Cannes is the **Quartier de la Californie** which has the Chapelle Bellini (allée de la Villa-Florentina) designed in elaborate baroque style, as well as **l'Eglise orthodoxe St-Michel Archange** (30 bd Alexandre III), whose choral group is renowned for its interpretations of Russian liturgy. The hilltop suburb of **Le Cannet** has been popular with many artists, from Renoir and Bonnard to the playwright Victorien Sardou. The chemin des

Collines is a lovely drive, winding through the hills above Cannes. On avenue Victoria sits the Oriental-style Villa Yakimour (private) given to Yvette Labrousse by her husband, the Aga Khan. Le Cannet is also home to **La Palestre** (730 av Georges Pompidou, 04.93.46.48.88), a large sports complex and concert venue.

La Malmaison

47 La Croisette (04.97.06.44.90). **Open** *Apr-June* 10.30am-1pm, 2.30-6.30pm Tue-Sun. *July-15 Sept* 11am-8pm Tue-Thur, Sat, Sun; 11am-10pm Fri. *15 Sept-Mar* 11am-8pm Tue-Sun. **Admission** €3; €2 students; free under-18s. **No credit cards**.

Musée de la Castre

Château de la Castre, pl de la Castre (04.93.38.55.26). **Open** *Apr-June* 10am-noon, 2-6pm Tue-Sun. *July-Sept* 10am-noon, 3-7pm Tue-Sun. *Oct-Mar* 10am-noon, 2-5pm Tue-Sun. **Admission** €3; €2 18-25s; free under-18s, all 1st Sun of month. **No credit cards**.

Le Musée de l'Enfance

2 rue Venizelos (04.93.68.29.28). **Open** 2-6pm Tue-Sat (daily in school holidays); at other times by appointment. **Admission** €6; €4 13-18s; €3 under-13s. **No credit cards**.

Palais des Festivals

1 La Croisette (04.93.39.01.01/www.cannes.com). **Admission** varies. **Credit** AmEx, MC, V.

Activities

Watersports

Check out **Cannes Jeunesse Nautisme** (Port du Mourre Rouge, 04.92.18.88.88), **Ski Nautique/ Motonautisme** (04.93.38.64.85) or **Centre Nautique Municipal** (9 rue Esprit Violet, 04.93.47.40.55), which organise sailing, water-skiing, surfing and diving.

Restaurants

Astoux et Brun

27 rue Félix Faure (04.93.39.21.87). **Open** noon-3pm, 7-11.30pm daily. **Average** €40. **Credit** AmEx, MC, V.

This beacon for seafood lovers is the best place in Cannes for sparkling fresh *fruits de mer*. Never mind the cramped tables and unimaginative decor, what you're here for is oysters shucked to order, specials like fish casserole or the ultimate seafood platter.

La Brouette de Grandmère

9bis rue d'Oran (04.93.39.12.10). **Open** 7.30-11pm Mon-Sat. **Menu** €33. **Credit** AmEx, MC, V.

Like an unexpectedly good, inexpensive stage show, tiny 'grandmother's wheelbarrow' delivers value for money. Inside is reminiscent of a film set – frilly curtains, fireplace and film posters. Outside, waiters magically fit extra tables on to an already jammed pavement, while passing street performers warm up the crowd. The *carte* includes everything from basic good food to Champagne.

Coté Jardin

12 av St-Louis (04.93.38.60.28/www.restaurant-cotejardin.com). **Open** 12.30-2pm, 7.30-10pm Tue-Sat. Closed 1st 2wks Jan. **Menus** €20-€27 (lunch); €35-€45 (dinner). **Credit** AmEx, MC, V.

Tucked in on a narrow street, this charming spot offers some of Cannes' most notable cuisine. In summer, ask for a table on the garden terrace and dig into items like goat cheese and avocado gratin drizzled with lavender honey. Book in advance.

Le Farfalla

1 La Croisette (04.93.68.93.00). **Open** 11am-2am daily (food till 1am). **Average** €38. **Lunch menu** €15. **Credit** AmEx, MC, V.

Farfalla's burnished wood milk-bar decor acts as a magnet for bright young things. The terrace is for grade-A star-ogling; alternatively, seek refuge in a booth on the mezzanine. There's a full brasserie-style menu, or lighter salads and snacks.

La Liberia

17 rue du Commandant-André (04.92.99.00.19) **Open** noon-2.30pm, 7-10.30 pm daily. **Average** €15-€30. **Credit** AmEx, DC, MC, V.

This classic Italian trattoria serves excellent salads and pasta to appreciative locals and tourists alike.

Mantel

22 rue St-Antoine, Le Suquet (04.93.39.13.10). **Open** noon-2.30pm, 7-11pm Mon, Tue, Fri Sun; 7-11pm Wed, Thur. **Menus** €23-€54. **Credit** MC, V.

Young chef Noël Mantel and friendly *maitre d'* Demetrio Argibay, both from Les Muscadins in Mougins, set up shop in Le Suquet two years ago. The fixed-price menus are excellent, the *à la carte* better, and the eclectic clientele is very faithful.

La Mère Besson

13 rue des Frères Pradignac (04.93.39.59.24). **Open** 7-10.30pm Mon-Sat. **Menus** €27-€32. **Credit** AmEx, DC, MC, V.

This relaxed, family-run favourite has charmed the likes of Sophia Loren and Gina Lollobrigida. Enjoy Provençal cuisine with twist: scorpion fish baked with mussels, mushrooms and tomato, or duck breast in a creamed peppercorn sauce.

La Pizza

3 quai St-Pierre (04.93.39.22.56). **Open** noon-1.30am daily. **Average** €20. **Credit** AmEx, MC, V.

A veritable institution in Cannes, this hot spot never accepts reservations. Although it is constantly busy, you'll never wait more than half an hour – and the wood-fired pizza is the best in town.

Le Restaurant Arménien

82 La Croisette (04.93.94.00.58/www.lerestaurant armenien.com). **Open** 7-10.30pm Tue-Sat (daily July & Aug); noon-2.30pm, 7-10.30pm Sun. Closed 1wk in Dec. **Menu** €40. **Credit** DC, MC, V.

At this unusual and exotic restaurant at the Port Canto end of La Croisette, succulent mezze include ravioli with mint, stuffed mussels and barley pasta with pistachios. Vegetarians are in heaven here.

Villa de Lys

Hôtel Majestic, 10 La Croisette (04.92.98.77.41).
Open 7.30-10pm Tue-Sat. Closed mid-Nov to late
Dec. **Menus** €75-€190. **Credit** AmEx, DC, MC, V.
With theatrical decor by Jaques Garcia, a movable
roof and a Croisette-side terrace, this swanky restaurant
lives up to its reputation. Wonder-chef Bruno
Oger continues to astonish with mouth-watering
dishes such as lamb roast in *tapenade*, or caviar with
green beans and a langoustine cappuccino.

Bars, cafés & nightlife

Bar 4U

6 rue Frères Padignac (04.93.39.71.21). **Open** 6pm-
2.30am daily. **Credit** MC, V.
With its sleek geometric shapes, large circular bar
and dim lighting, this popular new spot attracts
crowds for the pre-club drink.

Le 72 Croisette

72 La Croisette (04.93.94.18.30). **Open** *May-Oct*
7am-4am daily. *Nov-Apr* 7am-9pm daily. **Credit**
AmEx, MC, V.
Of all the Croisette bars this remains the most feistily
French. Battle through hordes of locals for a
ringside seat to watch the rich and famous enter the
Martinez next door. Food is served at lunch only.

Alcharc Spécialités Libanaises

20 rue Rouaze (04.93.94.01.76/www.alcharq.com).
Average €10-€15. **Open** 11am-10pm Tue-Sun.
Credit MC, V.
A local favourite tucked behind the Martinez, this
busy deli has absolutely the best falafel, humous,
grilled aubergine and pita-wrapped chicken in town.

Le Bâoli

Port Pierre Canto (04.93.43.03.43/www.lebaoli.com).
Open 8.30pm-2.30am daily. Closed mid-Nov to mid-
Apr. **Admission** varies. **Credit** AmEx, MC, V.
This super-stylish lounge is the biggest player in the
Cannes nightlife scene. Leonardo DiCaprio, Martin
Scorsese and Tim Robbins have all stopped by, and
Ivana Trump organised a VIP party or two here.
Even outside festival time, it is usually packed.

Café Roma

1 sq Mérimée (04.93.38.05.04). **Open** 7.30am-2.30am
daily (until 4am in July & Aug). **Credit** AmEx, MC, V.
Put on your sunglasses and join the trendies on the
terrace of this well-placed café to watch the comings
and goings of the town: rich, famous, or not. The
espressos are strong and the pasta (menus €20-€25)
is surprisingly good.

Caliente

84 La Croisette (04.93.94.49.59). **Open** 10pm-dawn
daily. **Credit** AmEx, MC, V.
Open year-round and packed nightly with salsa-
dancing-Corona-drinking regulars, this posey Latino
bar (pumped muscles and silicone busts are prevalent)
has Brazilian groups that play regularly and
DJs playing salsa and R'n'B.

Cannelle

Gray d'Albion, 32 rue des Serbes (04.93.38.72.79).
Open 9.30am-6.30pm Mon-Sat. **Average** €20-€25.
Credit AmEx, MC, V.
At this café-cum-grocer you can enjoy quiches and
salads, or be extravagant and savour raviolis stuffed
with chicken in a mushroom and foie gras sauce.
The few tables inside are nestled among hard-to-
resist gastronomic products, fine wines and caviar.

Le Cat Corner

22 rue Macé (04.93.39.31.31). **Open** 10.30pm-5am
daily. **Admission** €15 (incl. 1 drink). **Credit** AmEx,
MC, V.
The Ferrandini brothers run two of the hottest spots
in town – Le Farfalla (*see p227*) and this popular
twenty-somethings, late-night dance club. Guest
DJs, drinks specials and a selective, up-town mix
ensures a loyal crowd that throbs till dawn.

Le Lady Bird

115 av de Lerins (04.93.43.20.63). **Open** 11pm-5am,
Fri, Sat. **Admission** €15 (incl. 1 drink). **Credit**
AmEx, MC, V.
The former Whisky-à-Go-Go attracts pretty young
things. The main room is two stories high and maze-
like: no matter, guests, carefully selected at the door,
cheerfully elbow their way to the dancefloor.

Le Loft

13 rue du Dr Monod (06.21.02.37.49). **Open**
10.30pm-2.30am daily. **Admission** varies. **Credit**
AmEx, MC , V.
This upmarket dance bar attracts the young, well-
dressed and beautiful. Start the night downstairs, at
Tantra, its sleek bar-restaurant (7.30pm-2.30am)
over a cocktail and Thai food or sushi (average €40).

Morrison's Irish Pub

10 rue Teisseire (04.92.98.16.17/www.morrisonpub.com).
Open 5pm-2.30am daily. **Credit** AmEx, MC, V.
An excellent Irish pub with live music every
Wednesday and Thursday at 10pm and big-screen
TV tuned to English and Irish news and football.
The Quays (04.92.98.16.17) is a port-side offshoot.

Volupté

41 rue Hoche (04.93.38.20.41). **Open** 9am-7pm Mon-
Sat; noon-7pm Sun. **Credit** DC, MC, V.
Serving tea from around the world, delicious cakes
and homemade crumbles, this gourmet tea-room has
brews with exotic names like Sailor from Hamburg
and Poet's Garden. There's a shop at No.32.

Shopping

La Croisette, rue d'Antibes and the streets that
link the two are the luxury shopper's paradise.
Chopard (9 La Croisette, 04.92.98.07.07, closed
Sun) will be happy to help you choose between

If you can't afford a grand hotel to impress
the missus, build a sandcastle instead.

platinum or solid gold for that new trinket. Then skip over to **Jacques Loup** (3 rue du Dr Monod, 04.92.98.62.00, closed Mon & Sun) for the perfect shoe, making sure you stop off at **55 La Croisette** (55 La Croisette, closed Sun am) for avant-garde designs by the likes of McCartney, McQueen and Miyake. For typical Provençal articles, make for rue Meynadier which runs parallel to the port. The winding streets of Le Suquet are also a good bet for

souvenirs and trinkets. In **allée de la Liberté**, a Saturday market offers regional crafts. **Forville produce market** on rue Forville behind the old port is a magnificent covered market (Tue-Sun mornings) that turns into a *brocante* on Mondays. **Cannolive** (16, 20 rue Venizelos, 04.93.39.08.19, closed Mon morning & all Sun) is the place for regional goodies: olive oil, lemon and raspberry honey, rosewater. **La Ferme Savoyard-Ceneri** (22 rue Neynadier,

How to crash Cannes Film Festival

The world's biggest film festival attracts hordes of people desperate to get in to screenings and behind the velvet rope – or, as is more often the case, the crash barrier. The celebrity hunger that Cannes feeds cuts both ways, forcing the festival to adapt to the needs of the outside world and, specifically, big business sponsors. The mass marketeers have come to Cannes and this opens up avenues for the ordinary Joe and Josephine consumer of perfumes, cars and mobile phones. At the same time, the Festival increasingly recognises the public as essential extras in this rarefied red-carpet world. The Cannes website (www.cannes.fr) announces the programme of free open-air beach screenings and other events for non-accredited visitors. If you are interested in joining in the mob action for the arrival of a Hollywood name, approach one of the camera-wielding anoraks to find out arrival times – they will have the full schedule. In 2003 Arnold Schwarzenegger descended on the Carlton

to promote *Terminator 3* and waved in gubernatorial style at the cheering crowds. The top three hotels, the Carlton, Majestic and Martinez, are always thronged with autograph hunters. Gladhanding the crowds is not unheard of, even by the A-list, though for the most part it is French celebrities who raise hysterical cries from the (mainly French) onlookers, and blank faces from everyone else.

Getting in to screenings is by no means impossible, but does require a large measure of either patience or luck. The long route is to join the queues for the batch of public tickets

early in the morning at the Palais des Festivals. But there are other avenues worth exploring. An allocation is made to the townsfolk and it is quite possible that the *boulanger* may have a spare ticket. Otherwise, should your self-respect levels permit, just ask total strangers before the screenings as, no matter how grand they might be, it's always possible that they have been stood up in the crazy whirl that is Cannes. Remember, if you manage to bag a ticket for the major evening gala, evening dress is de rigueur. The increased lack of respect for the dress code by the big names means that door staff impose an even greater strictness on the paying crowds.

Since the legendary *Trainspotting* party at the Palm Beach in 1996, Cannes has become a magnet for the party crowd who jostle with the film folk to groove the night away. Paris clubs Man Ray and VIP decamp to the Riviera resort for the festival. Promotional parties are held nightly, from the latest vodka mixer to the annual lovelies' parade vaunting the merits of Hawaiian Tropic suntan lotion. Should you wish to party, strap on a smile and hip threads and head for Croisette haunts, such as the Petit Majestic behind the Grand Hôtel, to plug into the evening circuit. Londoners might be advised to hook into the Soho House membership list. Greek-Street-on-Sea is found in a variety of locations, from swank yacht to Gatsbyesque villa. Who knows, you could be quaffing Champagne in the company of boy band Blue and Hanif Kureshi, just two of the names on the guest list at the 2003 bash. Give in to the glamour and the glamour will give in to you.

04.93.39.63.68, closed Mon, Sun) has cheeses and gourmet delights. For hand-made chocolates, head to **Schies** (125 rue d'Antibes, 04.93.39.01.03, Mon morning & all Sun), while **Vilfeu Père et Fils** (19 rue des Etats Unis, 04.93.39.26.87, closed mid-Oct to Mar) has the best ice creams in Cannes. A branch of **Fnac**, selling CDs, books, and electrical goods, is at 83 rue d'Antibes (04.97.06.29.29, closed Sun). **Cannes English Book Shop** is at 11 rue Bivouac-Napoléon, 04.93.99.40.08, closed Sun).

Where to stay

Palace hotels

Hôtel Carlton

58 La Croisette (04.93.06.40.06/www.cannes.interconti. com). **Double** €280-€905. **Credit** AmEx, DC, MC, V.
Top stars of today may have shipped camp to the super swank Hôtel du Cap Eden-Roc (*see p238*), but this listed monument remains the first choice for festival purists. Legend has it that architect Charles Dalmas modelled its two *coupoles* on the breasts of gypsy courtesan la Belle Otéro. Rumours of an ambitious programme for a new 100-room wing, spa and convention centre are in the air.

Hôtel Martinez

73 La Croisette (04.92.98.73.00/www.hotel-martinez.com). **Double** €250-€790. **Credit** AmEx, DC, MC, V.
Reopened in 2003 after an ambitious renovation, the art deco Martinez, owned by the bubbly Taittinger family, is finally coming into its own. Panoramic views off the large teak terraces of the junior suites are spectacular, as is the set-up inside, inspired by the great French designers of the 1930s and 40s. Relax at the new Givenchy Spa before a decadent evening at the Palme d'Or restaurant.

Majestic Barrière

10 La Croisette (04.92.98.77.00/www.lucienbarriere. com). Closed mid-Nov to Dec. **Double** €190-€840. **Credit** AmEx, DC, MC, V.
During the film, music or advertising festivals the Majestic throbs as industry folk loudly renew acquaintances. In 1999 a 41-room wing decorated by Jacques Garcia was added. The Villa des Lys offers one of Cannes' best dining experiences (*see p228*); there's also a fumoir, Fouquet's offshoot, and the mythical Majestic bar with Cecil B DeMille decor.

Budget & moderate hotels

Adriana

12 rue des Belges (04.92.98.44.48/www.adriana-cannes.com). **Rates** €335-€600 2-person studio per wk. **Credit** AmEx, MC, V.
This beautiful 19th-century manor house near the Croisette has self-catering studios and apartments decorated with an intimate, atmospheric touch.

Le Cavendish Boutique-Hotel

11 bd Carnot (04.97.06.26.00/www.cavendish-cannes.com). Closed 15 Dec-15 Jan. **Double** €285-€1,350. **Credit** AmEx, DC, MC, V.
The former residence of Lord Henry Cavendish suits those who have become blasé about Cannes' grand hotels. Christophe Tollemar's interior evokes a toned-down 19th-century opulence. The soundproofed, air-conditioned rooms have elegant touches like lavender-scented sheets. Breakfast is lavish.

Hôtel Canberra

120 rue d'Antibes (04.97.06.95.00/www.hotels ocre azur.com) **Double** €90-€199. **Credit** AmEx, DC, MC, V.
Renovated in 2002, this neo-classical hotel has made modern use of rich reds, soft creams and black lacquer. Rooms are comfortable, most with a terrace or balcony; breakfast outside is a lovely moment of tranquillity, and there is a private beach.

Hôtel Embassy

6 rue de Bône (04.97.06.99.00/www.embassy-cannes.com). **Double** €119-€180. **Credit** AmEx, MC, V.
With a garden and a roof-top swimming pool right in the centre of Cannes, this quiet, air-conditioned hotel is good value. Rooms tend to matching floral and are clean and fresh.

Hôtel Festival

3 rue Molière (04.97.06.64.40/www.hotel-festival.com). **Double** €83-€125. **Credit** AmEx, DC, MC, V.
Right in the centre of Cannes, this small, friendly hotel sports marble baths and modern pastel decor. Some rooms overlook neighbouring orange trees and palms. Reserve for the sauna and whirlpool.

Hôtel Molière

5 rue Molière (04.93.38.16.16/www.hotel-moliere.com). **Double** €93-€130. **Credit** AmEx, MC, V.
With rooms in pale Provençal colours, pretty tiled bathrooms and intimate gardens, this friendly hotel is a favourite among journalists and film critics during the Festival.

Hôtel Le Mondial

77 rue d'Antibes (04.93.68.70.00/www.hotelmondial. activehotels.com). **Double** €66-€170. **Credit** AmEx, DC, MC, V.
Only a short walk from La Croisette, this 1930s art deco edifice dominates the area and looks southwards to the sea. Rooms are soundproofed and straightforward. Many have tiny balconies.

Hôtel Splendid

4-6 rue Félix Faure (04.97.06.22.22/www.splendid-hotel-cannes.fr). **Double** €103-€246. **Credit** AmEx, DC, MC, V.
The original Cannes palace stands wedding-cake proud with flags fluttering, across from the festival HQ. Its picture-postcard charms lure a loyal clientele and its Palm Square restaurant is quietly gaining a reputation for its mix of Thai, French and Italian cuisine (menus €50-€75, closed Wednesdays).

Resources

Hospital

Centre Hospitalier de Cannes (04.93.69.70.00/
www.hopital-cannes.fr).

Internet

Webcenter, 26 rue Hoche (04.93.68.72.37). **Open**
10am-10pm Mon-Sat; noon-10pm Sun.

Police

Commissariat, 1 av de Grasse (04.93.06.22.22).

Post office

22 rue Bivouac Napoléon (04.93.06.26.50).

Tourist information

*Office de Tourisme, Palais des Festivals, 1 La
Croisette (04.93.39.24.53/www.cannes.fr).* **Open**
9am-7pm daily (until 8pm in July & Aug).
Branch: *Gare SNCF, rue Jean-Jaurès
(04.93.99.19.77).* **Open** 9am-7pm Mon-Sat.

Iles de Lérins

When you've had enough of glamour queens
and dyed-to-match poodles, head off to the
tranquil Iles de Lérins, only a 15-minute boat
ride from the old port of Cannes. Known to the
ancients as Lero and Lerina, the islands were
renamed **St-Honorat** and **Ste-Marguerite**
after the siblings who founded monastic
communities here in the fourth century. By the
seventh century Lérins was one of Europe's key
monastic institutions. Today, it's a beautiful
religious backwater where a handful of
Cistercian monks make and sell a liqueur called
Lerina. Visitors can wander through forests of
pine and eucalyptus and swim discreetly off the
rocky outcrops. The little that remains on St-
Honorat of the earlier monastery buildings was
incorporated into the current Abbaye de Lérins
in the 19th century. The **Monastère Fortifié**
was built by the monks in 1073 to protect
themselves from the Saracens.

Ste-Marguerite is more touristy. The **Musée
de la Mer** in the Fort Ste-Marguerite is visited
not so much for its collection of underwater
archaeology as for its reputation as the prison
of the Man in the Iron Mask. Made famous by
novelist Alexandre Dumas, the Man may have
been Louis XIV's twin brother. Many hapless
Huguenots were confined here during Louis'
religious crackdown. The port is awash with
overpriced fish restaurants, but the sea around
the islands is cleaner than on the mainland.

Monastère Fortifié

St-Honorat (04.92.99.54.00). **Open** *mid-June to
mid-Sept* 10.30am-4pm daily. *mid-Sept to mid-June*
10.30am-12.30pm, 2.30-4pm daily. Closed during Sun
mass. **Admission** free (€2 in July-Aug).

Musée de la Mer

Fort Ste-Marguerite (04.93.43.18.17). **Open** *Apr-
Sept* 10.30am-1.15pm, 2.15-5.45pm daily. *Oct-Mar*
10.30am-1.15pm, 2.15-4.45 pm Tue-Sun. Closed 3wks
in Jan. **Admission** €3; €2 for under 25s; free under-
18s. **No credit cards**.

Getting to the islands

Planaria (04.92.98.71.38, St Honorat €9 return,
Ste Marguerite €10 return) and **Horizon/
Caraïbes** (04.92.98.71.36) run daily boats from
the old port 8am-4.30pm. **Compagnie Estérel
Chantelclair** (04.93.39.11.82) runs daily
crossings (€10 return, 7.30am-5pm) to Ste-
Marguerite from promenade La Pantiero.
Vintage boats equipped with all the necessary
comforts and skipper can be hired at **Chantier
Naval des îles** (04.92.18.84.84) in Port Canto.

Mougins

Sophisticated and yet still charmingly rural,
Mougins offers an escape from the crush of
Cannes. The old village is an extraordinary
hilltop site carpeted in flowers and bushes with
narrow lanes and restored houses built on the
line of the old medieval ramparts.

In the interwar period, Mougins was
discovered by the Surrealists, among them
Cocteau, Picabia (who built the fanciful Château
de Mai) and Picasso, who came to Mougins in
the company of Dora Maar and Man Ray. Local
lore has it that cash-strapped Picasso covered
his room and the outside walls with art to pay
for his board; the enraged owner made the still
obscure artist whitewash over them the next
day. Undaunted, he settled here in 1961 with his
wife Jaqueline, and spent much of his time in
the area until his death in 1973 – their house,
L'Antre du Minotaur (the Minotaur's Lair), can
be seen just opposite the strikingly beautiful
chapel of Notre-Dame-de-Vie (1.5km southeast
of Mougins, closed except for Mass, 9am Sun).

Today Mougins bristles with galleries and
painters and offers second homes for the better
sort of resident, recognisable by all the closed-
circuit cameras peeping out from behind the
bougainvillea. The worst sort of residents are
welcome, too, as long as they are discreet:
Haitian dictator Baby Doc Duvalier used to
have a pied-à-terre here.

The **Musée Maurice Gottlob** is upstairs in
the town hall. It explores the history of Mougins
using period literature. **Le Lavoir**, once the
village laundry, now showcases local artists.
Next to the 12th-century Porte Sarassin, the
Musée de la Photographie includes old
cameras, a series of photos of Picasso by André
Villers, and photos by Doisneau and Lartigue.

Mougins.

South-east of Mougins on the A8 is the **Musée de l'Automobiliste**. Adrien Maeght, son of Aimé and Marguerite Maeght (*see p297*), set up this state-of-the-art glass and concrete tribute to racing cars and motorbikes.

Le Lavoir
av Charles Mallet (04.92.92.50.42). **Open** *Mar-Oct* 10am-7pm daily. **Admission** free.

Musée de l'Automobiliste
772 chemin de Font-de-Currault, access Aire de Bréguières on A8 (04.93.69.27.80/www.musauto.fr.st). **Open** *Apr-Sept* 10am-7pm daily. *Oct-Mar* 10am-1pm, 2-6pm daily. Closed mid-Nov to mid-Dec. **Admission** €7; €4 12-18s; free under-12s. **Credit** AmEx, MC, V.

Musée Maurice Gottlob
2 pl Commandant Lamy (04.92.92.50.42/ www.culture-villedemougins.com). **Open** 9am-5pm Mon-Fri. Closed Nov. **Admission** free.

Musée de la Photographie
67 rue de l'Eglise (04.93.75.85.67). **Open** *July-Sept* 10am-8pm daily. *Oct-June* 10am-noon, 2-6pm Wed-Sat; 2-6pm Sun. Closed Nov. **Admission** €2. **No credit cards.**

Where to stay & eat

Mougins may be small, but it packs a gastronomic punch. Culinary event of 2004 is the arrival of brilliant young chef Alain Lorca, from the Negresco in Nice, at Roger Vergé's **Le Moulin de Mougins** (av Notre-Dame-de-Vie, www.moulin-mougins.com, 04.93.75.78.24, closed Mon and 10 Dec-10 Jan, double €140-€190, menus €48-€150). It has three rooms and four suites (€300-€330). Another new heavyweight on the scene is chef Serge Gouloumes at **Le Candille** (Hôtel Le Mas Candille, bd Clement-Rebuffel, 04.92.28.43.43, www.lemascandille.com, closed lunch in July & Aug, double €304-€495, menus €38-€85), who opened here after graceful stints at Ma Maison in Beverly Hills and the Miramar Beach in Théoules-sur-Mer. His creations are mouth-watering: sea bass in a rosemary clay crust or tempura of langoustines with soya caramel and basil. Rooms are sublimely luxurious, as are the manicured grounds and the Shiseido spa. **Les Muscadins** (18 bd Courteline, 04.92.28.43.43, closed Nov-Apr, double €160-€375), where Picasso fell in love with Mougins in 1936, is also now a part of the Le Mas Candille empire; take advantage of authentic, charming rooms and indulge in the gourmet sweets downstairs in the new Café Candille. At **Le Feu Follet** (pl du Commandant Lamy, 04.93.90.15.78, www.feu-follet.fr, closed Mon, dinner Sun, mid Dec-mid Jan, menus €22-€42) Jean-Paul Battaglia creates spectacular dishes like Salade-Feu Follet with smoked salmon and foie gras. Young chef Arnaud Care, who trained with the Jacques Chibois at the Bastide St-Antoine in Grasse, has gone out on his own at the **Brasserie de la Mediterranée** (pl du Commandant Lamy, 04.93.90.03.47, menus €23-€45). Try the tomato and melon gazpacho or lobster with truffles. **La Terrasse à Mougins** (31 bd Courteline, 04.92.28.36.20, www.la-terrasse-a-mougins.com, closed Jan to mid-Feb, double €107-€190, menus €25-€59) is a super-chic hotel/restaurant with panoramic views.

Resources

Tourist information
Office de Tourisme, 15 av Jean-Charles Mallet, 06250 Mougins (04.93.75.87.67/www.mougins-coteazur.org). **Open** *June-Sept* 10am-8pm daily. *Oct-May* 2.30-5.30pm Mon; 10am-5.30pm Tue-Sat.

Vallauris & Golfe-Juan

Vallauris is now an important French centre for ceramics but it would have had little to offer were it not for Picasso. Georges and Suzanne Ramié, who owned the Madoura pottery workshop, introduced the painter to the joys of clay and he single-handedly rekindled the town's dying ceramics industry – a mixed blessing, in view of some of the crimes committed in the name of *céramique artistique* along avenue Georges Clemenceau. Today,

The Riviera & Southern Alps

Vallauris seems to be split in two: busy tourist shops selling too much of the same pottery, and the deserted old town, famous more for its Roman-style street grid than for its beauty. But don't despair, there are a few serious workshops lurking behind the hordes of souvenir-driven merchants. **Galerie Madoura** (rue Suzanne Georges Ramié, 04.93.64.66.39, closed Sat, Sun and Nov), now run by the son of the original owners, still has the rights to reproducing Picasso's designs in signed, limited editions. Prices start at around €1,200.

By 1949 Picasso's passion for clay was waning; perhaps worried that such a prestigious resident was about to desert them, the good people of Vallauris gave him *carte blanche* to decorate the tiny, medieval chapel in the courtyard of the village castle – now the **Musée National Picasso**. The speed-painted essay on the theme of war and peace is breathtaking in its visual power. The ticket also gives admission to the **Musée Magnelli/ Musée de la Céramique** on the second floor of the castle, with more Picasso ceramics. The bronze statue of a man and sheep in place de la Libération is also a Picasso creation, presented to his adopted town in 1949 on the condition that children be allowed to climb all over it.

Vallauris' seaward extension, Golfe-Juan, has a fine kilometre-long sandy beach, sheltered from the worst of the Mistral. This is where Napoléon landed on 1 March 1815, at the beginning of the Hundred Days (*see p293*).

Musée National Picasso, Musée Magnelli, Musée de la Céramique

Château de Vallauris, pl de la Libération (04.93.64.16.05). **Open** *mid-June to mid-Sept* 10am-12.15pm, 2-6pm Mon, Wed-Sun. *mid-Sept to mid-June* 10am-12.15pm, 2-5pm Mon, Wed-Sun. **Admission** €3; €1.60 students; free under-16s. **No credit cards**.

Where to stay, eat & drink

In Vallauris, **Le Manuscrit** (224 chemin Lintiur, 04.93.64.56.56, closed Mon, dinner Sun, and Tue in low season, and mid-Nov to mid-Dec, mid-Jan to mid-Feb) has a beautiful terrace and nicely balanced menus (€22-€30): try the mouth-watering snails with garlic cream. Old-fashioned style is the hallmark of **La Gousse d'Ail** (11 rte de Grasse, 04.93.64.10.71, closed dinner Tue & Sun, all Mon, all Nov, 2wks in June), just behind the church (menus €15-€33). It's the *bouillabaisse* that's the draw at elegant **Bijou Plage** (bd du Littoral, 04.93.61.39.07, closed Tue dinner & Wed, menus €18.50-€45).

Good hotels are limited in Vallauris. Try **Auberge Siou Aou Miou** (105 chemin des Fumades, 04.93.64.39.89, double €54) with old

manor-house charm. It's better to stay down at Golfe-Juan, where the selection includes the upmarket **Résidence Hotelière Open** (av Georges Pompidou, 04.93.63.33.00, www.resorts-open.com, double €75-€135) and the charming **Mas Samarcande** *chambres d'hôtes* (138 Grand bd de Super Cannes, 04.93.63.97.73, www.stpaulweb.com/samarcande, double €110-€125) where Mr and Mme Diot lay on all home comforts. Basic comfort and a pool can be found at **Hôtel Beau Soleil** (impasse Beau Soleil, 04.93.63.63.63, www.hotel-beau-soleil.com, double €85-€140). In Golfe-Juan: **L'Abri Côterie** (port Camille Rayon, 04.93.63.06.13, closed Dec, menus €15-€23) offers a good lunch menu and doubles as a piano bar in summer. A must for seafood is **Nounou** (av des Frères Roustan, plages des Soleil, 04.93.63.71.73, closed Sun night, Mon and Nov) with great decor. **Restaurant Tetou** (bd des Frères Roustan, plages des Soleil, 04.93.63.71.16, closed Wed and Nov to mid-Mar, menus €30-€43) is a beautiful New York-style restaurant.

Tourist information

The market is daily (except Mon) at place de l'Homme au Mouton in Vallauris. In Golfe-Juan, there's a food market Friday mornings in Parking Aimé Berger, and a night-time craft market Fri-Sun June-Sept on Promenade des Ports.

Vallauris Office de Tourisme

sq du 8 Mai 1945, 06220 Vallauris (04.93.63.82.58/ *www.vallauris-golfe-juan.com*). **Open** *July-Aug* 9am-7pm daily. *Sept-June* 9am-noon, 2-6pm Mon-Sat.

Getting there & around

By car
For Cannes, leave the A8 at exit 41 or 42, or take the N7 direction Cannes. Mougins is 3.5km north of Cannes on N85. For Vallauris, leave the A8 at exit Antibes and follow signs to Vallauris on the D435. The N7/N98 coast road runs through Golfe-Juan.

By train
Cannes is served by the TGV from Paris (5hrs 10 mins). There are regular trains along the coast to Juan-les-Pins, Antibes and Nice.

By bus
Cannes' main bus station by the port serves coastal destinations: **RCA** (04.93.39.11.39, www.rca.tm.fr) goes to Nice via the villages along the coast and to Nice airport (every 30mins, Mon-Sat). From the SNCF station RCA goes to Grasse (every 30mins Mon-Sat, hourly Sun) via Mougins. **Phocéen cars** (04.93.85.66.61) runs three services a day (Mon-Sat) to Marseille airport and one to Avignon via Aix-en-Provence. From Vallauris bus station, **STGA** (04.93.64.18.37) has frequent buses to Golfe-Juan SNCF station and to Cannes.

Antibes to Cagnes

Take a walk on the wild side between Antibes and Juan-les-Pins, then head uphill to the heights of medieval Cagnes.

Antibes and its beachside satellite Juan-les-Pins attracts the rich and famous all year round. The seaward extensions of the next towns east, Villeneuve-Loubet and Cagnes-sur-Mer, are more downmarket, but both have magnificent medieval citadels high above the coastal strip.

Antibes & Juan-les-Pins

The Greeks set up their trading post of Antipolis in the fifth century BC. Ligurian tribes fought hard to get their hands on the town over the following centuries, forcing Antibes' residents to turn to Rome for protection in 154BC. But the fall of Rome left Antibes prey to attacks from every passing marauder, from Barbarians to Vandals, Visigoths, Burgundians, Ostrogoths and Franks. In the tenth century, Antibes fell into the hands of the Lords of Grasse before passing to the bishops of Antibes and, at the end of the 14th century, to the Grimaldis of Monaco. It remained theirs until 1608, when Henri IV of France purchased Antibes, turning it into his front-line defence against the Savoy kingdom across the bay in Nice.

To host the initial trickle of Europe's titled and wealthy who came seeking winter sunshine, a local entrepreneur had opened the Grand Hôtel du Cap in 1870. But it was Coco Chanel and US tycoon Frank Jay Gould who turned Antibes and Juan-les-Pins into a year-round playground, and artists, writers and alcohol-fuelled socialites, such as F Scott and Zelda Fitzgerald, hightailed it down to what was the Riviera's first chic society resort.

These days yachties and zillionaires mix with artists and easyJetsetters to create a genuinely cosmopolitan atmosphere. While Juan-les-Pins is unashamedly touristy and near dead in the winter, Antibes buzzes with markets, culture and café society year round. The lived-in feel of Antibes' atmospheric alleys is a far cry from the brash streets of Juan-les-Pins, although both throng with crowds in the summer heat.

The conurbation of Antibes Juan-les-Pins is a mainly unappealing mass wedged between the sea and the A8 motorway. The old districts are best approached from **Fort Carré**, which stands on the point separating the St-Roch inlet from Baie des Anges. The original fort was constructed in the 16th century to counter the Savoy threat to the east; in the 17th century, Louis XIV's military architect Vauban gave it its eight-pointed star shape. Just to the south of the fort, Port Vauban is Europe's largest yacht marina, harbouring some of Europe's largest pleasure craft and plenty of glitzy boutiques, where you can hire – sorry, charter – your own craft and join the yachterati. In early June the Voiles d'Antibes fills the bay with splendid sailing vessels and motor yachts for five days.

Hidden behind the sheltered ancient walls of the quay is Plage de la Gravette, a free sandy beach with gently shelving waters, in the heart of town. South of the marina, at the other end of the ramparts, is the **Musée d'Histoire et d'Archéologie**, containing reminders of the town's multi-faceted past, including Greek and Etruscan amphorae. Also squeezed within the ramparts is the **Eglise Notre-Dame de l'Immaculée Conception** (04.93.34.06.29, open 8am-noon, 3-6.30pm daily), Antibes' former cathedral, built on the site of a Roman temple to Diana, a rich concoction of marble virgins, Baroque stylings and deep ochres, lapis blues and blood-red walls.

The **Château Grimaldi** next door still follows the plan of the earlier Roman fort, despite rebuilding in the 16th century by the Grimaldis. In 1946, when Picasso (who had first painted beach life at Juan-les-Pins in 1920) rented a cold, damp room on the second floor, it belonged to a certain Romuald Dor, and already contained a small archaeological collection. Dor had ulterior motives in his offer of such prime Riviera studio space; the works Picasso left behind in lieu of rent enabled him to upgrade his lacklustre collection and re-baptise it the **Musée Picasso**. This was a fertile period for the balding Spaniard. As artists' materials were almost impossible to get hold of in 1946, Picasso used ships' paint slapped on to some odd-looking bits of wood, and discovered the joys of pottery (*see p233* Vallauris). Picasso's treasures here are disappointingly limited, occupying only one floor of the collection, though the Germaine Richier sculptures and Nicolas de Staël paintings help compensate.

Just inland from the castle, the Cours Masséna, the Greek town's main drag, plays host to one of the region's liveliest and best-supplied produce markets, the Marché

Provençal (every morning, except Mon in winter). **Balade en Provence** (25bis cours Masséna, 04.93.34.93.00) sells 50 sorts of olive oil, pistou, honey, hams and absinthe (with a bar where you can try out the absinthe). This area of the old town is a hive of Anglo-Frenchness and home to **Heidi's English Bookshop** (24 rue Aubernon, 04.93.34.74.11, open daily 10am-7pm) and the **Antibéa Theatre** (15 pl Clemenceau, 04.93.34.24.30), which stages plays in English by the Red Pear Company. Just beyond the theatre, in place Nationale, comic artist Raymond Peynet's **Musée Peynet** is dedicated to cartoon art.

Heading south out of Antibes, the scenery changes dramatically from built-up citadel to leafy lap of luxury. The Cap d'Antibes peninsula is a playground for the very wealthy although most of the houses are of the classic, understated variety; definitely not the glitzy Footballer's Wives type. To appreciate the prosperity to the full, rent a bike from one of the many outlets along boulevard Wilson and take in the views as you wend your way up to **Parc Thuret**, a botanical testing site established in 1856 with the aim of introducing more varied flora to the Riviera – 200 new species are introduced each year and their acclimatisation carefully studied. If cycling sounds like too much exertion, take advantage of the Cap's long stretches of public beach, Plage de la Salis and Plage de la Garoupe. Both can be walked to from Antibes or Juan-les-Pins (*see p242*).

Between the two, and a fair hike uphill, the **Sanctuaire de la Garoupe** has a great collection of unlikely ex-votos. At the southern tip of the peninsula, the **Musée Naval et Napoléonien** has model ships and charts and mementos of the great man, who parked his mother in Antibes on one occasion. Next to the museum is another historical landmark where most people would opt to park themselves, rather than their mothers: the Hôtel du Cap.

To the west of the peninsula, Juan-les-Pins has no pretensions to history: a sandy, forested, deserted bay until the 1920s, it was conceived as, and still is, a magnet for Riviera hedonists. The centre is a seething mass of boutiques and restaurants and if it seems frantic during the day, then you should see it on a summer's night: Juan-les-Pins isn't in the habit of wasting good partying time on sleep. The beautiful beach has public and private sections; on the latter, a patch of sand with deckchair will set you back around €10 a day.

East of Antibes (4km by N7) is **Marineland** marine theme park, the most visited (paid-for) attraction in the South of France. Launched in 1970, it is a must for any child visiting the Côte d'Azur and contains five parks, the best of

which, Marineland itself, offers the sort of view of marine life you can only otherwise get in a cage at sea. Through the glass-surround whale tank, you can watch killer whales interact with their trainer in a relationship that strikes one as more like friends than master and subject; three out of the nine whales in the world born in captivity were born here. The dolphins occupy one of the biggest dolphin pools in Europe. There's a walk-through, underwater shark tunnel and a ray touch-pool. Then there are the other four parks. The Little Provençal Farm, best for under-5s, has domestic animals, pony rides, an enchanted river boat ride and bouncy inflatables. Jungle of Butterflies harbours butterflies, iguanas, parrots, snakes and bats. Aqua-Splash (mid-June to mid-Sept, 10am-7pm) features seawater wave pools, a lazy river, giant toboggans and a toddlers' pool. Adventure Golf boasts three tricky mini-golf courses.

A Richier beauty at **Musée Picasso**. *See p235.*

Fort Carré

rte du Bord de Mer, N98 (06.14.89.17.45). **Open** *mid-June to mid-Sept* 10am-6pm Tue-Sun. *mid-Sept to mid-June* 10am-4pm Tue-Sun. **Admission** €3; €1.50 students; free under-18s. **No credit cards.**

Marineland

306 av Mozart (04.93.33.49.49/www.marineland.fr) **Open** *Apr-June, Sept* 10am-8pm daily. *July-Aug* 10am-10.30pm daily. *Oct-Mar* 10am-6pm daily. Closed 5-30 Jan. **Admission** €28; €21 3-12s; free under-3s; two/three park combination €30-€35; €23-€25 3-12s, free under-3s. **Credit** V.

Musée d'Histoire et d'Archéologie

Bastion St-André, 3 av Mezière (04.92.90.54.37). **Open** *June-Sept* 10am-6pm Tue-Sun (until 8pm Wed, Fri July & Aug). *Oct-May* 10am-noon, 2-6pm Tue-Sun. **Admission** €3; free under-18s. **Credit** MC, V.

Musée Naval et Napoléonien

bd Kennedy (04.93.61.45.32). **Open** *June-Sept* 10am-6pm Tue-Sat. *Oct-May* 10am-4.30pm Tue-Sat. **Admission** €3; free under-18s. **No credit cards.**

Musée Peynet et du Dessin Humoristique

chemin Raymond, pl Nationale (04.92.90.54.30). **Open** *June-Sept* 10am-6pm Tue-Sun (until 8pm Wed, Fri July & Aug). *Oct-May* 10am-noon, 2-6pm Tue-Sun. **Admission** €3; free under-18s. **No credit cards.**

Musée Picasso

Château Grimaldi, pl Mariejol, Antibes (04.92.90.54.20). **Open** *June-Sept* 10am-6pm Tue-Sun. *Oct-May* 10am-noon, 2-6pm Tue-Sun. **Admission** €5; free under-15s. **Credit** V.

Parc Thuret

62 bd du Cap, Cap d'Antibes (04.93.67.88.00). **Open** *summer* 8am-6pm Mon-Fri. *winter* 8.30am-5.30pm Mon-Fri. **Admission** free.

Activities

Watersports & yacht hire

If playing at sardines on the strand is not your thing, there are watersports galore; it was in Juan-les-Pins, they say, that water-skiing was invented in the 1930s at the beach of the glamorous Hôtel Belles Rives, which still has its own water-skiing club. The **Ecole de Ski Nautique** (plage Bretagne, 06.13.61.51.17) is another water-skiing specialist. For diving, **Golfe Plongée Club** (port de Golfe-Juan, 06.09.55.73.36) offers beginners' courses, while **Côté Plongée** (bd Maréchal Juan, 06.72.74.34.94, www.coteplongee.com) by the Musée Naval on Cap d'Antibes runs children's courses and exploratory and night dives. On the Antibes side of the Cap, the **Club Nautique** (plage de la Salis, 04.93.67.22.50, www.club-nautique-antibes.com) is a professional set-up with dinghies and catamarans to hire or learn on. If a cruise is your idea of nirvana, **Yachtbrokers International** (21 rue Aubernon, 04.93.34.04.75, www.yachtbrokers-int.com, closed Sun) can provide a six-berth, 29-knot motoryacht with two crew from €1,500 a day, plus

fuel, port fees, food and drink. A week on a yacht sleeping 20-22 with palatial staterooms, studies, dining rooms and a one-to-one guest to crew ratio, will set you back considerably more.

Where to eat

Antibes' cosmopolitan old town is best for cafés and bistros rather than swanky restaurants. For an atmospheric coffee try the age-old **Pimm's** (3 rue de la République, 04.93.34.04.88), which still has a few writers and lovers hiding in the woodwork, or head to the place Nationale, cours Masséna or boulevard d'Auguillon café strips. **L'Oursin** (16 rue République, 04.93.34.13.46, closed Sun & Mon dinners, & 2wks in Feb & Nov, menu €17) is something of an oyster specialist; snails, scallops and a daily dip of *aïoli* are also available. **La Marmite** (20 rue James Close, 04.93.34.56.79, closed Mon and mid-Nov to mid-Dec, menus €12-€25) is a similar establishment around the corner with fresh seafood cooked to order, including Provençal prawns and swordfish steaks. Classy **Oscar's** (8 rue du Dr Rostan, 04.93.34.90.14, www.oscars-antibes.com, closed Mon, Sun, 1-15 Aug and 20 Dec-5 Jan, menus €23.50-€49) has an all-white Italian-style interior. Its most expensive set menu is a five-course affair featuring lobster, caviar and truffles. As far as foreign fare is concerned, **L'Ancre de Chine** (26 bd d'Aiguillon, 04.93.34.27.70, closed lunch Sat, menus €28-€31) is justifiably busy, as it's the best Chinese in town, while **L'Eléphant Bleu** (28 bd d'Aiguillon, 04.93.34.28.80, menus €19-€30) next door, serves up excellent Thai.

Stylish foodies make straight for Cap d'Antibes and its luxury hotel restaurants. Alternatively try a knockout *bouillabaisse* or platter of langoustines at the venerable **Bacon** (bd de Bacon, 04.93.61.50.02, www.restaurantde bacon.com, closed Nov-Jan and Mon & Tue lunch, menus €45-€75). Overlooking the Baie des Anges, the almost all-white dining room has a tented ceiling that is rolled back in summer.

At Juan-les-Pins there are plenty of beach establishments. The family-friendly **Plage Epi Beach** (bd Guillemont, 04.93.67.27.84) specialises in salads and simple grilled fish such as sardines. Lively **La Bodega** (av du Dr Dautheville, 04.93.61.07.52, menu €20) stays open until all hours in summer to feed revellers from local nightlife haunts. **Bijou Plage** (bd du Littoral, 04.93.61.39.07, menus €19-€45) serves reliable seafood on the seafront. For a touch of crustacean class try the **Festival de la Mer** (146 bd Wilson, 04.93.61.04.62, average €40) with buckets of oysters, scallops and snails. The highly regarded **Perroquet** (av Georges Gallice, 04.93.61.02.20, closed lunch July & Aug, all Nov & Dec, menus €25-€30) is possibly Juan-les-Pins finest with the emphasis on traditional French cuisine. Elegant **La Terrasse** (Hôtel Juana, La Pinède, av Gallice, 04.93.61.08.70, menus €92-€120) attracts a clientele more likely to spend the day in white linen than in bathing suits. It was here that Alain Ducasse won the second star that propelled him to fame; chef Christian Morisset continues the tradition of wonderful food.

Bars & nightlife

Juan-les-Pins' annual jazz festival earns the most international attention but, as a more affordable club scene than St-Tropez or Monaco, Juan attracts the young end of the market, creating some of the liveliest nightlife on the Côte. Without doubt, the best club is **Le Village** (1 bd de la Pinède, Juan-les-Pins, 04.92.93.90.00, open Fri & Sat only, except daily July & Aug, admission €16), rumoured to be the favourite haunt of Noel Gallagher. DJs play a mix of pop and house and the club oozes atmosphere, enhanced by the pumped-up, topless barmen in bow-ties who dance and mingle with the fashionable, mixed (straight/gay) crowd. The vast monastic interior is très cool, although the hefty drinks prices could easily blow a hole in one's pocket. Nearby, Juan icon **Whisky à Go Go** (5 av Jacques Léonetti, La Pinède, 04.93.61.26.40, open Fri & Sat only, except daily mid-June to mid-Sept, closed Nov-Mar, admission €16) is showing its age with a kitsch 70s disco feel. Just metres away, the **Crystal** (av Georges Gallice, 04.93.61.02.51) is a classic early-20th-century open-air cocktail bar. The suavest hangout in town for drinks is the **Hôtel St-Charles Lounge** (4 rue St Charles, Juan-les-Pins, 06.17.71.08.50, hotel closed Jan & Feb, double €50-€60, bar open daily until midnight), where DJs attempt to raise cocktail drinkers from their stylish seats. A superb club and casino on the seafront east of Antibes is **La Siesta** (rte du Bord de Mer, 04.93.33.31.31, admission €20), where in summer you can dance to pop and house in the open air and people-watch on terrace loungers. It's less special in winter, when dancing moves indoors to a small piano bar. **Xtrême Café** (6 rue Aubernon, 04.93.34.03.90) is a fashionable bar for cocktails, apéritifs and nibbles, open till 2am in summer. The **Hop Store** around the corner (38 bd Aguillon, 04.93.34.15.33) is a buzzing Irish bar with a domed brick roof and outside terrace. Between these two, yacht crew favourite the **Café de la Porte du Port** (32 rue Aubernon, 04.93.34.68.94), by the arches that lead to the marina, is as raucous as it gets in the classy confines of Antibes.

Where to stay

Of all the hotels on the French Riviera, the **Hôtel du Cap Eden-Roc** (bd Kennedy, Cap d'Antibes, 04.93.61.39.01, www.edenroc-hotel.fr, closed mid Oct-mid Apr, double €420-€1,200) is probably the most exclusive, and certainly the most expensive. The gleaming white building nestles back from the coast in 25 acres of woodland. It was here that the cult of the suntan was born, when a poor winter season persuaded Antoine Sella to keep his doors open through the summer of 1923. American society hosts Gerald and Sara Murphy (immortalised as Dick and Nicole Diver in F Scott Fitzgerald's *Tender is the Night*) came down from Paris and told all their friends. The hotel is pretentious enough not to accept credit cards, and can be annoyingly overrun by celebrities and their bodyguards. Smartly dressed non-residents can use the bar and swimming pool, but expect a hefty fee if you so much as glance at a towel or sun-lounger. A comparatively cheap alternative nearby is the **Hôtel Beau Site** (141 bd Kennedy, 04.93.61.53.43, www.hotelbeausite.net, closed Nov-Feb, double €60-€120), offering clean, simple accommodation and a pool.

In a central, peaceful location by Antibes' main square, former coaching inn **Le Relais du Postillon** (8 rue Championnet, Antibes, 04.93.34.20.77, www.relais-postillon.com, double €44-€82, restaurant closed lunch and 2wks Jan, 2wks Nov, average €30) has cheery rooms overlooking the park or courtyard. Its highly regarded restaurant uses fine ingredients to create melt-in-the-mouth risottos, salads and grills. Nearby, the **Modern Hôtel** (1 rue Fourmilière, 04.92.90.59.05, closed Dec to mid-Jan, double €58-€85) has comfortable rooms with a slight 1980s air in the dead centre of town. Somewhat cosier is the **Hôtel le Ponteil** (11 impasse Jean Mensier, 04.93.34.67.92, closed mid-Nov to Dec, double €46-€82) with its leafy exterior. For thalassotherapy spa treatments, including diet and anti-stress cures, the huge modern **Thalazur** (770 chemin des Moyennes Bréguières, Antibes, 04.92.91.82.00, www.thalazur.fr, double €110-€186) uses water pumped up from the sea. **Hôtel Juan Beach** (5 rue de l'Oratoire, Juan-les-Pins, 04.93.61.02.89, closed Oct-Mar, double €75-€130) is a five-minute walk from the nightlife action. The **Hôtel Castel Mistral** (43 rue Bricka, Juan-les-Pins, 04.93.61.21.04, closed Oct-Mar, rates €64-€94) is a charmingly dilapidated place, handy for the beach, with a pretty terrace out the front. To do Juan in style stay at the **Hôtel Juana**

Luxury comes only in the very best taste in **Antibes** and **Juan-les-Pins**.

(La Pinède-av Gallice, Juan-les-Pins, 04.93.61.08.70, www.hotel-juana.com, double €235-€555), a refined art deco jewel with a lovely pool and sitting area, two minutes from the sea. In a similar vein is the classic **Hôtel Belles-Rives** (33 bd Edouard Baudoin, 04.93.61.02.79, www.bellesrives.com, double €140-€660). Indulge in the luxurious bars, lounges and private beach. For inexpensive charm, antiques and a sunny terrace make **La Marjolaine** (15 av Dr Fabre, 04.93.61.064.60, closed Nov to mid-Dec, double €51€-66), 100m from Juan-les-Pins station, a truly delightful find.

Resources

Internet

Art-116, 116 bd Wilson, Juan-les-Pins (04.92.93.14.13/ www.art-116.com). **Open** 9am-11pm daily.

Tourist Information

Antibes *Office de Tourisme, 11 pl de Gaulle, 06160 Antibes (04.92.90.53.00/www.antibes-juanlespins.com).* **Open** *July, Aug* 9am-7pm daily. *Sept-June* 9am-12.30pm, 1.30-6pm Mon-Fri; 9am-noon, 2-6pm Sat.
Juan-les-Pins *Office de Tourisme, 51 bd Guillaumont, 06160 Juan-les-Pins (04.92.90.53.05/www.antibes-juanlespins.com).* **Open** *July, Aug* 9am-7pm daily. *Sept-June* 9am-noon, 2-6pm Mon-Fri; 9am-noon Sat.

Biot

Once, long ago, a clever PR company was sent into the hinterland of the Côte d'Azur to give its villages instant brand recognition. That, at least, is how it sometimes appears. Grasse is perfume, St-Paul-de-Vence is art, Vallauris is pottery and Picasso, and Biot (pronounced Bee-ot) is glass and Fernand Léger. But it was not always so. In fact, until as late as the 1950s, the name of this picturesque village was more linked to pottery. One of Léger's protégés set up a ceramic workshop in Biot dedicated to reproducing the master's designs, and Léger spent his last few years here.

Fifteen days before he died, in 1956, the artist acquired a piece of land in Biot, intending to build a house. His widow, Nadia, used the site to build a fitting tribute to her husband, the **Musée National Fernand Léger**. The low-slung building is set back from the road in undulating sculpture gardens. It traces the work of this restless, politically committed artist from his first Impressionist stirrings in 1905, through the boldly coloured 'machine art' of the 20s and 30s to his later murals, stained glass, ceramics and tapestries. It is closed for renovation until early 2005, but some paintings are on show at Fondation Maeght (*see p298*).

Glass came to Biot only at the end of the 50s, when the **Verrerie de Biot** fired up its furnaces.

Biot's pretty and ancient village church.

Half working factory and half gallery, the Verrerie is just off the main D4 road, below the town walls. One can watch the unique Biot 'bubble glassware' (*verre bullé*) being blown, and there are plenty of chances to buy both here and in the village, where rue St-Sébastien is lined with glass workshops. Across the road, the **Galerie Internationale du Verre** (04.93.65.03.00) is also worth a visit, with its collection of highly sculptural glass by US and European artists. At No.9 the **Musée d'Histoire et de la Céramique Biotoises** has a patchy but charming collection of local costumes and artefacts. Past the boutiques and bars is the pretty place des Arcades, surrounded by Italianate loggias – a home-from-home touch brought by Genoese settlers who moved in to repopulate Biot after the Black Death. The pretty village church has two good altarpieces by Louis Bréa and Giovanni Canavesio. Classical concerts are held in the square on summer evenings. Today's Biot is a vivid mix of galleries, cafés and beautiful little lanes. The tourist information office has a well-researched historical walking tour leaflet.

On the way out of Biot, miniaturist fans can pick up tips and buy plants at the **Bonsai Arboretum**, a collection of over 1,000 bonsai in a 2,000m² Japanese garden, worked on for two generations by the Okonek family.

Bonsai Arboretum

229 chemin du Val de Pôme (04.93.65.63.99).
Open 10am-noon, 2-6pm Mon, Wed-Sun.
Admission €4; €2 students, 6-18s; free under-6s.
No credit cards.

Musée d'Histoire et de la Céramique Biotoises

9 rue St-Sébastien (04.93.65.54.54). **Open** *July-Sept*
10am-6pm. *Oct-June* 2-6pm. Closed Mon & Tue.
Admission €2; €1 students; free under-16s.
No credit cards.

Musée National Fernand Léger

chemin du Val de Pôme (04.92.91.50.30). Closed for
renovation until early 2005.

La Verrerie de Biot

chemin des Combes (04.93.65.03.00/
www.verreriebiot.com). **Open** *July, Aug* 9.30am-8pm
Mon-Sat; 9.30am-1pm, 3-8pm Sun. *Sept-June* 9.30am-
7pm Mon-Sat; 9.30am-1pm, 2.30-7pm Sun.
Admission free.

Where to stay & eat

The charming **Hôtel des Arcades** (16 pl des
Arcades, 04.93.65.01.04, double €50-€90, menus
€28-€30) is a 15th-century mansion that mixes
ancient (huge fireplaces, four-poster beds) and
modern. The owner is a collector, and the
gallery/restaurant – a good, reasonably priced
alternative to the town's more serious eating
options – displays works by artists including
Vasarely, Léger and Folon. Benoît Paudrat is
chef at **Le Jarrier** (30 passage Bourgade,
04.93.65.11.68, closed Mon & lunch Sat, menus
€29-€36), a relaxed restaurant in a converted jar
factory at the end of a laundry-festooned
passageway, serving Mediterranean dishes
laced with truffles, nuts and fruit. Midway
down the central thoroughfare, rue St-
Sébastien, **Le Piccolo** (04.93.65.16.91, menu
€23) dishes up grand plates of seafood and
local meat on solid wooden tables. More down
to earth is the traditional, lively hangout
l'Auberge du Coin (04.93.65.10.72, closed
Wed, average €15) on the same street. Huge
salads and grilled meats are eaten with local
wine and a healthy selection of beers. Tucked
away in what was a 16th-century potter's
workshop near the foot of the old town, stylish
Les Teraillers (11 rue du Chemin Neuf,
(04.93.65.01.59, closed Wed, Thur & Nov,
menus €31-€64) has a delightful atmosphere
and a host of Provençal dishes. Out-of-town
elegance can be found at the **Domaine du
Jas** (625 rte de la Mer, 04.93.65.50.50,
www.domaindujas.com, double €140-€235), a
2km drive towards the sea. It has a mosaic-
bottomed swimming pool set in palm trees and
several homely reception rooms.

Resources

Market days are Tuesday and Friday mornings.

Tourist information

*Office du Tourisme, 46 rue St-Sébastien, 06410 Biot
(04.93.65.78.00/www.biot-coteazur.com).* **Open** *July-
Aug* 10am-7pm Mon-Fri; 2.30-7pm Sat, Sun. *Sept-
June* 9am-noon, 2-6pm Mon-Fri; 2-6pm Sat, Sun.

Villeneuve-Loubet & Cagnes

Zip through the beachside resorts between
Antibes and Nice and you will be missing out.
The interest lies just a few kilometres inland, in
the medieval centres of Villeneuve-Loubet and
Haut-de-Cagnes, where vine-covered houses and
traditional restaurants meet fine views and a
noticeable lack of tourists.

The graceful lanes of **Villeneuve-Loubet**
hide more than their fair share of galleries, cafés
and attractive squares. So peaceful is it that it
becomes a stopping off point for several
holidaying rock and film stars who seek to hide
from the silly season paparazzi on the coast.
The **Musée de l'Art Culinaire** celebrates one
of Villeneuve's most famous sons, Auguste
Escoffier, who was taken under the wing of
Britain's King Edward VII after transforming
cooking from a trade to an art. Escoffier later
became head chef of the Savoy in London. A
photograph of opera star Nellie Melba – after
whom the peachy sundae was named – just
about sums up the modest charms of this
collection, whose highlights are the menus and
cuttings elaborating tales of Escoffier's life as
chef to political leaders and kings. Just above
the tourist office at the foot of the old town is
the **Musée d'Histoire et d'Art**. Military
objects gleaned from the French Army share
the small display space with a handful of
portraits and a revolving art exhibition.

Three kilometres away is **Villeneuve-Loubet
Plage**. This purpose-built resort stretches
around the **Marina Baie des Anges**, a huge
apartment complex built 1969-70, shaped like a
giant wave, which can be seen for miles around;
weekly visits are organised by the tourist office
(10am Thur, book one day ahead). The seafront
is home to an assortment of seafood and pizza
restaurants, watersports activities and a long
pebbly beach packed out with happy families.

Cagnes, a few kilometres down the coast
towards Nice, is in fact three separate entities:
unalluring Cros-de-Cagnes on the seafront,
misleadingly named Cagnes-sur-Mer, which is
in fact inland, and medieval Haut-de-Cagnes,
perched on high and home to the UNESCO-
sponsored Festival International de la Peinture
(International Painting Festival) each summer.

Cros-de-Cagnes was once a fishing village but today offers little more than a crowded pebbly beach, watersports hire and a string of restaurants and hotels along the beachfront. On the other side of the busy A8 lies Cagnes-sur-Mer, best known for Auguste Renoir's estate, **Les Collettes**. The artist had the house built in 1908 after his doctor prescribed a drier, warmer seaside climate for his rheumatoid arthritis. Although Renoir painted his late, almost garish *Grandes Baigneuses* here, he complained that the sun was too dazzling and concentrated in his last years on sculpture, working right up until his death in 1919, and battling against the growing paralysis in his hands. The house is preserved pretty much as he left it, and his olive-tree-filled garden is worth visiting, particularly on the evening in summer when professional storytellers visit. There's also a collection of paintings of the artist by his friends, as well as a few of the works he created here. The town also has a wonderful food and clothes market on rue du Marché. On the slip road between the A8 and Cagnes-sur-Mer lies the **Atelier des Parfums**

perfume factory. Guides take you through a history of perfume, give you a free guided tour of the factory and let you sample one of scores of different scents. More exhilarating is the **Hippodrome Côte d'Azur** on the coast. In summer, racing is of the Ben Hur chariot style (known as 'le Trot'). Facilities are top class with grandstands, bars and betting booths. The Cannes to Nice coastal train stops here most evenings during the summer racing season.

High on the hill within walking distance of Cagnes-sur-Mer is **Haut-de-Cagnes**, a hidden gem, as large as nearby Biot and St-Paul-de-Vence, yet wonderfully unspoilt and calm. It's a favourite spot for contemporary artists of all persuasions, drawn by an annual arts festival but by the Musée Mediterranéen d'Art Moderne and the Donation Suzy Solidor (a collection of 40 portraits by Cocteau, Dufy and Lempicka), both of which are housed the dramatic **Château-Musée Grimaldi**, part-Renaissance residence, part 14th-century fortress. In the centre of town the Eglise St-Pierre has fine stained glass and a marble font. To the east is the stunning Chapelle Notre-Dame de Protection

Coastal walk Cap d'Antibes

Length 8km from the centre of Juan-les-Pins to the centre of Antibes.
Time Three and a half hours (including half-hour picnic stop).
Difficulty Moderate. A lot of the walking is by road, while the rocky coastal sections are well marked.

Of the many surprisingly wild peninsulas on the Côte d'Azur, the Cap d'Antibes carries the largest sense of history and grandeur. This rocky outcrop is where books have been set (F Scott Fitzgerald's *Tender is the Night*), empires discarded (Edward VII gave up his crown to join a waiting Wallis Simpson here) and millions spent on home improvements. It is also the most accessible of the Riviera Caps, letting hikers rub shoulders with the security gates of regal, royal or just plain rich residents. A free map from the tourist office in Antibes or Juan-les-Pins is all you need for three hours or so of sublime walking.

Parking spaces are hard to find at the end of the Cap in summer, so many people begin at the Pinède in Juan-les-Pins, where the Jazz à Juan festival greats have stamped their hands in cement along the pavement. Dodge the *boules* players and head towards the sea to pick up the coastal trail by the Pirate restaurant or the splendid Hôtel Belles-Rives. Two marinas and two secluded sandy coves make up the next 500m, the latter stretches of beach being something of a secret for Juan-les-Pins' sun-worshipping residents. The coast road boulevard Maréchal Juin leads on from here. Follow the Porsches of the local residents and the Volvos of holidaymakers for another 1km past more pretty beaches and boats until heading inland on boulevard John F Kennedy, by the Musée Napoléonien.

Those who brought a picnic can afford to ignore the entrance to the Hôtel du Cap-Eden where statues and a host of wonderful arches are backdropped by a batch of warm-coloured frescoes. Further down the coast just before Nice airport, the faceless suburb of St-Laurent-du-Var has just one saving grace: discount shopping. Follow the signs for the Cap3000 shopping complex for thousands of square metres of sports, shoe and clothes superstores.

Atelier des Parfums

43 chemin des Presses, Cagnes-sur-Mer (04.93.22.69.01/www.atelier des-parfums.com). **Open** 9.30am-noon, 2-6.30pm Mon-Sat. **Admission** free.

Château-Musée Grimaldi

pl Grimaldi, Haut-de-Cagnes (04.92.02.47.30). **Open** *May-Sept* 10am-noon, 2-6pm Mon, Wed-Sun. *Oct-Apr* 10am-noon, 2-5pm Mon, Wed-Sun. Closed 1st 3 wks Nov. **Admission** €3 (€4.50 with Musée Renoir); students €1.50; free under-18s. **No credit cards**.

Hippodrome Côte d'Azur

Cagnes-sur-Mer (04.93.22.51.00). **Open** *mid-Dec to mid-Mar* steeplechasing. *July, Aug* trotting *nocturnes* Mon, Wed, Fri. **Admission** €4.50; free under-16s. Free guided visits in the morning.

Musée de l'Art Culinaire

3 rue Escoffier, Villeneuve-Loubet (04.93.20.80.51/ www.fondation-escoffier.org). **Open** 2-6pm Mon-Fri,-Sun. Closed Nov. **Admission** €5; €2.50 11-16s; free under-11s. **No credit cards**.

Musée d'Histoire et d'Art

pl de l'Hôtel de Ville, Villeneuve-Loubet (04.93.02.60.38). **Open** 9am-noon, 2-6pm Mon-Fri; 9am-12.30pm Sat. **Admission** free.

Musée Renoir, Les Collettes

chemin des Collettes, Cagnes-sur-Mer (04.93.20.61.07). **Open** *May-Sept* 10am-noon, 2-6pm Wed-Mon. *Oct-Apr* 10am-noon, 2-5pm Wed-Mon. Closed last 2wks Nov. **Admission** €3 (€4.50 with Château-Musée Grimaldi); free under-18s. **No credit cards**.

Where to stay, eat & drink

The area's most luxurious accommodation option is **Le Cagnard** (rue Sous-Barri, 04.93.20.73.22, www.le-cagnard.com, double €170-€280, restaurant closed lunch Mon-Wed & Nov to mid-Dec, menus €60-€81) in Haut-de-Cagnes. Its many modern comforts have failed

Roc and turn right down the poorly marked chemin Eilenroc, the only path that leads to the wild section of the coastal route. Either head straight on to Villa Eilenroc, designed by Paris opera house architect Charles Garnier (04.93.67.74.33, open Wed except July & Aug), or take a left down chemin des Douaniers to where the action really starts.

The rocky Sentier Piéton begins as you pass through a wide hole in the wall. At times the path runs scarily close to the crashing waves – a sign warns walkers not to set off in bad weather or at twilight lest someone get swept out to sea (which seems to be a yearly occurrence). For the best part, however, the way is well maintained with handrails and signs telling you how far to go. Nicest of all are the purpose-built picnic spots where you can lay out your feast on the shores of the Med. These are great places to snorkel and fish too. Frequently the path weaves in and out of one of the Cap's private gardens via a perfectly manicured walkway. More often you're left wanting as you walk by

a tiny garden gate by the sea in full knowledge that the owners count this beautiful piece of the world as their own back garden. After another half hour of herb-scented bends, each revealing a new panorama, you come to the bay of La Garoupe with its sandy beach. There are several bars and restaurants although the serious walker will carry on the extra mile to Port de la Salis at Antibes.

A more interesting stroll from La Garoupe beach is to head up the winding chemin de la Garoupe and on to boulevard du Cap; then follow the signs to the Garoupe chapel and lighthouse on the highest point of the peninsula. The tiny church is bedded in with scores of aged olive trees, cobbled terraces, stone benches and immense 360° view. Outside the church a 100-year-old orientation table points out every spot of land visible from St-Tropez to San Remo including Biot, the Iles de Lérins and the glitz of Monte Carlo. Several tiny paths lead down to the eastern side of the Cap from here, or you can follow the road back down to Juan-les-Pins on the west.

to disturb the 12th-century magic of the building, which offers spectacular views. Try roast pigeon, duck or lamb under the coat-of-arms-studded ceiling of the restaurant. Sheer luxury can be found at the **Villa Estelle** at the foot of the old town (5 montée de la Bourgade, Haut-de-Cagnes, 04.92.02.89.83, www.villa-estelle.com, double €145-€185), a medieval coaching inn with a sumptuous terrace. The modern, almost cool, **Grimaldi** (6 pl du Château, Haut-de-Cagnes, 04.93.20.60.24, www.hotelgrimaldi.com, closed Feb, double €90-€120, restaurant closed Tue, menus €28-€40) overlooks the delightful main square and offers the finest meats, cheeses and fish.

In Cros-de-Cagnes, **Hôtel Beaurivage** (39 bd de la Plage, 04.93.20.16.09, www.beaurivage.org, closed Dec to mid-Jan, double €62-€75) has rooms with balcony and sea view. For those who want to sample the effects of the local waters, **Biovimer Spa** (Marina Baie des Anges, 04.93.22.71.71, www.biovimer.fr), tucked into the Marina Baie des Anges in Villeneuve-Loubet Plage, is a modern spa with rooms and apartments. Weekend thalassotherapy packages start at €324; one-day use of heated outdoor seawater pool, indoor pool, sauna, jacuzzi, hammam and gym starts at €53.

Haut-de-Cagnes' fine range of restaurants is centred on the montée de la Bourgade leading uphill and the place du Château at the top. **Fleur de Sel** near the summit (85 montée de la Bourgade, 04.93.20.33.33, closed Wed & lunch Thur, and Jan, menus €21-€52) serves classic *soupe au pistou* and imaginative seafood. **Cour et Jardin**, with its cosy vaulted cellar (102 montée de la Bourgade, 04.93.20.72.27, closed Tue and two weeks in Jan, menus €19-€29) is innovative, too, with its gazpachos, fish carpaccios and traditional *farcis niçois*. Nearby rue Hippolyte Guis, yet another street saturated with hanging baskets, features **Le Clap** (04.93.73.92.80, menus €14-€29), a grill specialist using ingredients from around France from scallops to snails. In the main square **Le Sain' Elena** (1 pl Grimaldi, 04.93.73.91.49, menu €14) does cracking salads and offers some of the best daily specials in town.

Good seafood can be found at the port in Cros-de-Cagnes at **La Réserve** aka **Lou Lou** (91 bd de la Plage, 04.93.31.00.17, July & Aug closed lunch daily & Sun; Sept-June closed Sat lunch & Sun, menu €36), a chic, snooty but justifiably acclaimed restaurant. Crustaceans stud the menu, from prawns in ginger to lobster à l'armoricaine. **La Caravelle**, near the Hôtel Beaurivage (42 bd de la Plage, 04.93.20.10.09, menus €13-€25), is a more down to earth *moules-frites* specialist. In Cagnes-sur-Mer, **Brasserie des Halles** (8 rue Raimond

Giacosa, 04.92.02.77.29, closed Mon, dinner Sun, menus €12-€20) next to the market does hearty food such as *faux-filet* with sautéed potatoes.

In Villeneuve-Loubet **La Vieille Auberge** (13 rue des Mesures, 04.93.73.90.92, closed Wed, lunch Sat & dinner Sun and all lunches July & Aug, average €30) serves hearty dishes in traditional surroundings, while **L'Olivier** (pl de Verdun, 04.93.73.69.87, closed lunch Tue & all Wed, menus from €13) is the place to come for succulent Provençal lamb.

Resources

Cagnes-sur-Mer has a market every day but Monday; Villeneuve-Loubet on Tuesday and Friday mornings.

Tourist information

Cagnes-sur-Mer *Office de Tourisme, 6 bd Maréchal Juin, 06800 Cagnes-sur-Mer (04.93.20.61.64/www.cagnes.com). Open June-Sept* 9am-7pm daily. *Oct-May* 9am-noon, 2-6pm Mon-Sat.
Villeneuve-Loubet *Office de Tourisme, rue de l'Hôtel de Ville, 06270 Villeneuve-Loubet (04.93.20.16.49). Open July-Aug* 9am-7pm Mon-Sat; 10am-1pm Sun. *Sept-June* 9am-noon, 2-6pm Mon-Fri; 9.30am-12.30pm Sat.
Villeneuve-Loubet Plage *Office de Tourisme, 16 av de la Mer, 06270 Villeneuve-Loubet (04.92.02.66.16/www.ot-villeneuveloubet.org). Open July-Aug* 9am-7pm daily. *Sept-June* 9am-noon, 2-6pm Mon-Fri; 9am-noon, 2.30-5.30 Sat.

Getting there & around

By car

For Antibes Juan-les-Pins, leave the A8 at exit 44, or drive along the prettier N98 coast road. Juan-les-Pins is west of Cap d'Antibes, Villeneuve-Loubet and Cagnes are east of Antibes. In summer, avoid the N7 Antibes to Nice at the Biot junction, which becomes one long car park, especially when Marineland is emptying out. For Biot, take the N7 and then D4 Biot-Valbonne road, 3km after Antibes.

By train

Antibes is on the main south coast route, served by high-speed TGVs from Paris and more frequent local trains, which also stop at Juan-les-Pins, Biot, Cagnes-sur-Mer, Cros-de-Cagnes and Villeneuve-Loubet-Plage. Shuttle buses connect Cagnes-sur-Mer and Haut-de-Cagnes and Villeneuve-Loubet-Plage and the old town.

By bus

RCA (Rapides Côte d'Azur 04.93.39.11.39) bus No.200 between Cannes and Nice runs every 20 minutes Mon-Sat, 30 mins Sun, stopping at Antibes, Juan-les-Pins, Biot, Villeneuve and Cagnes. Shuttle bus 10A runs hourly between Antibes station and Biot. More information at Antibes bus station (04.93.34.37.60). Regular **TAM** (04.93.85.61.81) buses run between Cagnes and Nice, also serving Biot, Antibes, Cannes, Vence and St-Paul.

Nice

Some think vice is rather Nice, but the 'queen of the Riviera' has kicked back with a cultural renaissance that befits its location and history.

The fifth largest city in France, Nice is often in the public eye: either glorified for its seaside palaces or maligned for its high crime rate. Yet the charm of its setting and its wonderful climate make it a consistent number one tourist destination. Visitors find an intriguing balance between old-world decadence and urban energy. Aristocrats have been replaced by backpackers, but cosmopolitan sophisticates crowd the pavement cafés, and a revitalised jazz festival and inspiring art exhibitions make Nice a rising cultural force. There's a healthy dose of the young and hip, too, thanks to its universities and a plethora of bars and boutiques. The beaches are rocky, but the hypnotic blue of the Baie des Anges is worth every careful step.

HISTORY
Prehistoric man set up camp some 400,000 years ago at the site known as Terra Amata at the foot of Mont Boron, not far from where Sir

Elton John's hilltop mansion now sprawls. In the fourth century BC, Phocaean Greeks from Marseille sailed into the harbour and founded a trading post around another prominent hill (now the Colline du Château) and named it Nikaïa. Then the Romans arrived in 100BC and built an entire, no-expense-spared city on a third hill that they called Cemenelum (today's Cimiez). Cimiez's prime location made it an obvious target in the Dark Ages for invading Saracens and Barbarians, who left it in ruins, but by the 14th century the once-Greek part of the city, including the port, was thriving again.

In 1382, Jeanne, Queen of Sicily and Countess of Provence, was smothered to death on the order of her cousin Charles of Durazzo, Prince of Naples. Both he and another cousin, Louis of Anjou, staked their claims on the rich area. After sizing up the local balance of power, the wily Niçois decided to shun them both, opting instead to ally themselves with the Counts of

Sweep by in style on the palmy **Promenade des Anglais**.

Savoy. Apart from brief control 1792-1814 by Revolutionary forces, Nice belonged to the House of Savoy until 1860. Italian art, food and culture became an intrinsic part of the region.

An envious France tried several times to get Nice back; Napoléon III finally succeeded by signing the Treaty of Turin in 1860 with the King of Sardinia. The treaty was ratified later in a plebiscite (the result of some 25,700 pro-French to 260 anti-French votes had a strong smell of election-rigging about it).

Over a century before that, however, Nice had been discovered by British travellers seeking winter warmth. They raised a subscription in 1822 for the building of the seafront esplanade still called the promenade

des Anglais. By the time Queen Victoria visited in the 1890s, the Cimiez district was the place to stay. The queen pitched camp at the Régina Palace hotel, as did Henri Matisse in the 1940s.

In the early 1960s, Nice became a cutting-edge artistic centre, thanks to the impetus of the New Realists Yves Klein and Arman. Other artists flourished under the movement; work by Venet, César and Ben can still be seen at the Musée d'Art Moderne et d'Art Contemporain and in various public places around the city. But 20th-century Nice was not just about wholesome creative energy. Nice was (and still is) infamous for high crime levels and the financial shenanigans of its late, long-time mayor, Jacques Médecin. This seedy, corrupt

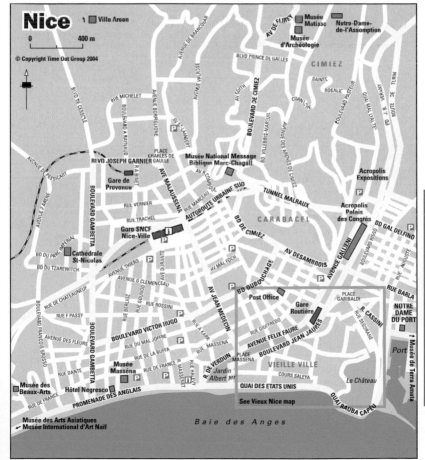

The Riviera & Southern Alps

reputation has lasted into the 21st century with an ongoing investigation of the city's legal favours and a vice scene fuelled by Eastern European prostitution rings. Today, after dark, certain neighbourhoods and whole blocks of the Promenade still have a thriving unsavoury element, much to the dismay of city officials.

Sightseeing

Vieux Nice & Colline du Château

With its ancient, pastel-coloured buildings and narrow alleys filled with countless shops, galleries and bistros, the Old Town is certainly the most colourful quarter of Nice. Though it was once shunned as crime-plagued and poverty-stricken, urban renewal has encouraged young trendies to take up residence and dodgier streets have received much-needed facelifts. The heart of the *vieille ville* lies just back from the seafront, along **cours Saleya**, where cut flowers perfume the air and stalls piled high with lush fruit and vegetables operate from dawn to lunch, Tuesday to Sunday. Niçois institution Chez Thérèse cheerfully touts chickpea *socca* from a stand every morning (see *p259*). On Monday there are antiques, junk and second-hand clothes. Shoppers and onlookers crowd bars and

eateries, or seek the tranquility and shade of the **Chapelle de la Miséricorde**, a superb Baroque structure decorated with frescoes, gilt and a Bréa altarpiece. Also of note is the tall, washed yellow building at the end of cours Saleya where Henri Matisse lived from 1921 to 1938. On neighbouring place du Palais de Justice there's a book and print market on Saturday. Towards the seafront, the **Opéra de Nice** is grandly *belle époque*. Nearby, on the quai des Etats-Unis, the **Galerie des Ponchettes** and **Galerie de la Marine** exhibit contemporary art in an old fish market.

The main square, place Rosetti, is home to two places of pilgrimage: the **Cathédrale de Ste-Réparate**, loving tribute to Nice's patron saint and remarkable for its glazed-tile roof, and the **Fenocchio** ice-cream parlour. The nearby Baroque **Chapelle de l'Annonciation** is known locally as the Chapelle Ste-Rita, out of respect for an Italian saint still venerated in Nice as a miracle curist for terminal diseases. A few blocks north-east, through bustling streets of little shops, is the stunning **Palais Lascaris**, a treasure-trove of Flemish tapestries and 17th-century furniture. Further up, rue Droite goes into rue St-François, busy with food shops, tourist trinkets, third-rate art and some curious ecological clothing. Place St-François is the site of the fish market (daily,

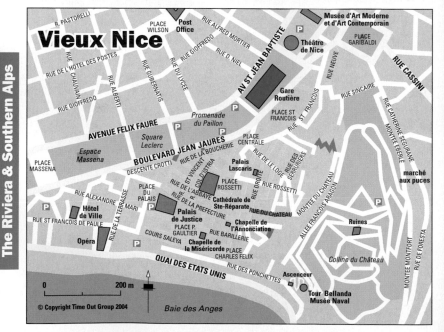

Hip-hoppin' in **Vieux Nice**'s place Charles Félix.

except Tuesday), plus the city's 17th century former town hall and the campanile from a former Franciscan monastery (entrance rue de la Tour). Bordering the old town to the north is the elegantly arcaded, though traffic-infested, **place Garibaldi**. It was laid out in 1750-80 and later named after the Italian unification hero, who was born in the Vieux Port in 1807.

Rising up to the east of Vieux Nice is the **Colline du Château**, a grassy park with an impressive waterfall but no château: it was destroyed in the 18th century. If you don't fancy the long slog up (steps rise from rue du Château or rue Ste-Claire), there's a lift (open 8am-6pm daily) next to the 19th-century Tour Bellanda.

Continuing round the quai or via place Garibaldi, you arrive at the attractive **Vieux Port**, which is lined with tall, multi-coloured houses, the neo-classical church of **Notre-Dame-du-Port** and plenty of simple cafés where you can snack on a *pan-bagnat* and watch the ferries to Corsica. The port's possible extension has been the subject of heated debate for the past few years. The significant drop in tourist dollars after September 11 and the Iraq war has led to an indefinite postponement of the project, but that doesn't stop feisty local discussions over an afternoon glass of *pastis*.

East of the Colline du Château, the **Parc Forestier le Mont Boron** is an idyllic spot for a picnic, with winding paths through acres of pines and breathtaking views down to the coast. Between the two hills, in an area dotted with 19th-century villas, the **Musée Terra Amata** documents the area's earliest settlement.

Cathédrale de Ste-Réparate

pl Rossetti (04.93.62.34.40). **Open** 8am-noon, 2-6pm daily. **Admission** free.
Located on Vieux Nice's most charming square, this 17th-century church, replete with stucco, marble and a colourfully tiled dome, is named after a 15-year-old virgin martyred in the Holy Land, who was towed here in a flowery boat by angels (landing, naturally, in what is now the Baie des Anges) in the fourth century. The church is an atmospheric venue for Baroque music concerts and other musical events.

Chapelle de l'Annonciation

1 rue de la Poissonnerie (04.93.62.13.62). **Open** 7.30-noon, 2.30-6.30pm daily. **Admission** free.
Join a steady trickle of locals in this lovely little gilded Baroque gem and light a candle for St Rita – the patron saint of the terminally ill – to whom the chapel is dedicated.

Galerie de la Marine & Galerie des Ponchettes

59 and 77 quai des Etats Unis (04.93.62.37.11/ 04.93.62.31.24). Bus 1, 2, 14. **Open** 10am-6pm Tue-Sat. **Admission** free.
The ancient fish hall was transformed into two municipal art galleries in 1967. Temporary exhibitions often feature up-and-coming local artists.

Musée Terra Amata

25 bd Carnot (04.93.55.59.93). **Open** 10am-6pm Tue-Sun. **Admission** €4; €2.50 students; free under 18s, all 1st & 3rd Sun of month. **No credit cards**.
Find out what life was like on the Riviera 400,000 years ago. The highlights of this museum, built on an excavation site, include a reconstituted prehistoric cave, a human footprint in limestone, traces of fire and records of ancient elephant hunters.

Palais Lascaris

15 rue Droite (04.93.62.05.54). **Open** 10am-6pm Wed-Mon. **Admission** free.
Ornate Baroque furniture, 17th-century paintings and Flemish tapestries are displayed in a wonderful miniature Genoese-style palace with frescoed ceilings of mythological scenes. 17th-century faïence from the Musée Masséna is on display on the first floor until the latter reopens (*see p253*).

The New Town

Westward, the new town of Nice takes on a completely different look. Laid out in the 18th and 19th centuries with inviting gardens, broad city blocks and stucco apartments, it is divided from the old town by the river Paillon – though you'd never know it as the river is covered over for most of its length by the pink facades of place Masséna and the Jardins Albert 1er. Smart shops congregate near here on rues de Paradis, de Suède and Alphonse Karr, while the pedestrianised eastern end of rue de France is lively with restaurants and pizzerias.

Among the 20th-century buildings north of place Masséna is the striking **Musée d'Art Moderne et d'Art Contemporain (MAMAC)** with art from 1960 onward, including the Ecole de Nice (Arman, César, Klein). Also here is the **Théâtre de Nice**, which has injected new life into the Niçois performing arts scene.

On the seafront west of the river mouth, the **promenade des Anglais** is 19th-century Nice's most famous landmark. A daily parade of rollerbladers, joggers and strolling sun-worshippers drift along its pavement. Getting safely across what's now the last gasp of the N98 through constant and manic traffic can be a challenge, but look back once you reach the curb: the grandiose *belle époque* and art deco palaces that line the Promenade – such as the **Hôtel Negresco** and **Musée Masséna** – are a joy. Shortly before the Musée Masséna, the **Palais de la Méditerranée**, an art deco jewel built by American millionaire Frank Jay Gould in 1929, was shamefully gutted in the 1990s, preserving only the facade, but has been reborn as a luxury hotel and casino (*see p262*).

A few blocks back from the Promenade des Anglais, broad boulevard Victor Hugo is lined with *belle époque* villas. Further west, the

Musée des Beaux-Arts has a small but noteworthy collection, including the plaster study for Rodin's *Le Baiser*. A kilometre further on is the **Musée International d'Art Naïf Anatole Jakovsky**, while just before the airport, the **Musée des Arts Asiatiques** nestles among the botanical species and giant hothouse of the **Parc Floral Phoenix.**

Aside from the view, the beach itself, though long, is not particularly spectacular: pebbly, and not sparklingly clean. While some stretches are open to anyone and have attractions ranging from parascending to kids' sandpits, other parts of it are carved up by private beach concessions. One of the nicest is **Castel Plage**, down below the *vieille ville*.

Slicing north-west through the new town from place Masséna, **avenue Jean Médicin** is Nice's prime shopping street. At its northern end is the main train station, to the west of which, across boulevard Gambetta, stands the Russian Orthodox **Cathédrale St-Nicolas**, Nice's most-visited attraction. Further north, **Villa Arson** puts on adventurous contemporary art in a lovely garden setting.

Cathédrale St-Nicolas (Eglise Russe)

av Nicolas II (04.93.96.88.02). **Open** *June-Sept* 9am-noon, 2.30-6pm daily. *Oct-May* 9.30am-noon, 2.30-5pm daily. **Admission** €2.50; free under-12s. **No credit cards**.
If you visit only one church, go and see this beautiful pink and grey marble, brick and tile oddity with its five brilliantly coloured onion-domed cupolas. Built 1903-12, it is filled with intricate carving, icons and frescoes, and a marvellous *iconostasis*. In the garden behind the cathedral, a small chapel remembers Grand Duc Nicolas Alexandrovitch, son of Tsar Alexander II, who died here in 1865 at the age of 21.

Musée des Arts Asiatiques

405 promenade des Anglais (04.92.29.37.00/ www.arts-asiatiques.com). Bus 9, 10, 23. **Open** *May to mid-Oct* 10am-6pm Mon, Wed-Sun. *mid-Oct to Apr* 10am-5pm Mon, Wed-Sun. **Admission** €6; €4 14-18s, students; free under-14s. **Credit** V.
This impressive minimalist glass and metal structure designed by Kenzo Tange boasts a small but stunning collection of rare pieces that range from a 12th-century Japanese Buddha to the latest in Asian hi-tech design. Don't miss the tea pavilion under the gingko trees (€10, reserve on 04.92.29.37.02).

Musée d'Art Moderne et d'Art Contemporain (MAMAC)

promenade des Arts (04.93.62.61.62/www.mamac-nice.org). **Open** 10am-6pm Tue-Sun. **Admission** €4; €2.50 students; free under 18s, all 1st & 3rd Sun of month. **No credit cards**.

19th-century buildings and 21st-century wheels in the **New Town**.

This sprawling, multi-level marble home of European and American art from the 1960s onwards stages first-rate shows. In addition to a new room for the Nice school (Arman, César, Klein and Sosno), the museum's most recent pride and joy is Nikki de Saint Phalle's exceptional donation of 170 works.

Musée des Beaux-Arts

33 av des Baumettes (04.92.15.28.28/
www.museebeauxarts-nice.org). **Open** 10am-6pm Tue-Sun. **Admission** €4; €2.50 students; free under 18s, all 1st & 3rd Sun of month. **No credit cards.**
Built for a Ukranian prince in 1878, this Genoese-inspired villa houses a fine collection of 15th- to early-20th-century art. Highlights include works by Niçois pastel artist and pioneering lithographer Jules Cheret, *Le Tango* by Van Dongen, and canvases by Bonnard, Sisley, Dufy, Signac and Kisling.

Musée International d'Art Naïf Anatole Jakovsky

Château Ste-Hélène, av Val-Marie (04.93.71.78.33).
Bus 9, 10, 12. **Open** 10am-6pm Mon, Wed-Sun. **Admission** €4; €2.50 students; free under 18s, all 1st & 3rd Sun of month. **No credit cards.**
Once the home of perfume creator René Coty, this lovely pink villa now houses a private collection that traces the history of naive art from the 18th century to the present, including Bombois, Séraphine, Rimbert and Grandma Moses.

Musée Masséna

65 rue de France (04.93.88.11.34). **Closed for renovation.** **Admission** ring for details.
Closed until at least 2006, the Masséna's Empire salons contain Nice primitive painters, armour and Napoléon's coronation robe and death mask.

Villa Arson

20 av Stephen Liegeard (04.92.07.73.73/www.villa-arson.org). *Bus 4, 7, 10, 18.* **Open** *June-Sept* 2-7pm Mon, Wed-Sun. *Oct-May* 2-6pm Mon, Wed-Sun. **Admission** free.
The cutting edge of adventurous, young, avant-garde art, with a related art school. Listen to heated discussions about art and philosophy in the small café (open Mon-Thur 8.30am-5pm; Fri 8.30am-3pm).

Cimiez

Cimiez, once the powerful Roman settlement Cemenelum, to the north of the city centre, is Nice's most luxurious suburb: an affluent hillside swathed in large villas, Roman ruins and sweeping *belle époque* apartments. To visit you need to combine foot and bus fare (No.15 from pl Masséna, No. 17 from av Jean Médecin) or arm yourself with a car, patience and a map.

Just off the lower reaches of boulevard de Cimiez is the **Musée National Message Biblique Marc-Chagall**, showing large-scale Biblical works. Further up, sweeping round the corner of boulevard de Cimiez and avenue

Régina, you can't miss the eye-stopping facade of the **Excelsior Régina Palace**. Designed by Biasini, the hotel where Queen Victoria stayed from 1897 to 1899 is now a smart apartment building. Matisse lived here from 1938 to 1943. At the top of the hill, the fabulous **Musée Matisse** stands in the centre of an olive-tree-dotted park behind the ruins of the Roman amphitheatre and the **Musée d'Archéologie**. The nearby church of **Notre-Dame-de-l'Assomption** and its 16th-century Franciscan monastery are flanked by a glorious rose-perfumed garden and a cemetery where Matisse and Dufy are buried. Lower down on rue Grammont, take a look at Nice's most unusual church, **Eglise Ste-Jeanne d'Arc**, a radical 1930s reinforced-concrete structure nicknamed 'the egg', designed by Jacques Droz.

Eglise Notre-Dame-de-l'Assomption (Musée Franciscain)

pl du Monastère (04.93.81.00.04). *Bus 15, 17.* **Open** *church* 9am-6pm daily; *museum* 10am-noon, 3-6pm Mon-Sat. **Admission** free.
At the edge of the gardens of Cimiez, this church is a heavy-handed 19th-century reworking of a 16th-century building. Inside, three Louis Bréa altarpieces survive. The adjoining 16th-century monastery includes a couple of pretty cloisters – one with some strange, perhaps alchemical murals – as well as the Musée Franciscain where the uncomfortable ends of Franciscan martyrs are documented.

Musée d'Archéologie

160 av des Arènes (04.93.81.59.57). *Bus 15, 17, 20, 22, 25.* **Open** 10am-6pm Mon, Wed-Sun. **Admission** €4; €2.50 students; free under-18s. **Credit** AmEx, DC, MC, V (shop only).
The smart archaeological museum charts Nice's history from 1100BC up to the Middle Ages through an impressive display of ceramics, sculpture, coins, jewellery and tools. Outside are the first- to fourth-century ruins on the ancient site of Cemenelum, with vestiges of the Roman public baths, paved streets and a 4,000-seat stone amphitheatre – now a concert venue during the Nice Jazz Festival.

Musée Matisse

164 av des Arènes (04.93.81.08.08). *Bus 17, 20.* **Open** 10am-6pm Mon, Wed-Sun. **Admission** €4; €2.50 students; free under-18s. **Credit** MC, V.
This 17th-century villa with a modern extension houses a fascinating collection, tracing Matisse's development, from his dark, brooding early works through to his colourful paper cut-outs. One room holds sketches for the Chapelle du Rosaire (*see p297*).

Musée National Message Biblique Marc Chagall

av du Dr Menard (04.93.53.87.20/www.ac-nice.fr/chagall/chagall.htm). *Bus 17, 20.* **Open** 10am-5pm Mon, Wed-Sun. **Admission** €6.70; €5.20 students; free under-18s. **Credit** MC, V.

This is long-time Riviera resident Chagall at his best, a purpose-built space with a stunning selection of large paintings on Old Testament themes, notably the Song of Songs. Chagall provided stained glass, mosaics and sketches for the gallery, which holds frequent temporary shows and small acoustic concerts in the lovely amphitheatre (8.30pm Thur, tickets from Fnac or one hour before show, €8).

Arts & entertainment

For music and theatre listings, buy the weekly French-language *Semaine des Spectacles* available from newsagents, or pick up *Le Pitchoun*, a free French-language guide to clubs, restaurants and leisure activities.

Acropolis
1 esplanade Kennedy (04.93.92.83.00).
A modern mega-structure that hosts special events, conventions, concerts, ballet and opera.

Casino Ruhl
1 promenade des Anglais (04.97.03.12.33). **Open** 10am-5am daily. **Admission** (over-18s only) *slot machines* free; *gaming rooms* €13 (bring ID). **Credit** AmEx, MC, V.
A modern expanse of gaming rooms offers French and English roulette, blackjack, punto banco, craps and clanging slot machines.

Cinémathèque de Nice
3 esplanade Kennedy (04.92.04.06.66/ www.cinematheque-nice.com). **Films** 2.30pm, 5pm, 8pm Tue-Sat (+ 10pm Fri, Sat); 3pm Sun. **Tickets** €3; €6 three-film pass. **No credit cards.**
An international selection of classics and quality recent films are screened in their original language.

Galerie Soardi
8 rue Desiré Niel (04.93.62.32.03/www.soardi.com). **Open** 9am-7pm Mon-Sat. **Admission** free. **Credit** AmEx, DC, MC, V.
In the former atelier of Henri Matisse is a private gallery presenting innovative shows of young artists and the Ecole de Nice. It also sells lithographs, frames and arty gifts and offers cultural excursions.

Opéra de Nice
4 rue St-François-de-Paule (04.92.17.40.40/ www.ville-nice.fr). **Box office** 9am-6pm Mon-Sat. **Tickets** €8-€80. **Credit** MC, V.
The small 19th-century gem of an opera house is done out in sumptuous red velvet with crystal chandeliers and lashings of gold. It attracts top-notch visiting artists for symphonies, ballet and opera.

Palais Nikaïa
163 rte de Grenoble (04.92.29.31.29/ 08.20.02.04.06/www.nikaia.fr). **Box office** 1-6pm Mon-Fri. **Tickets** vary. **Credit** V.
This massive state-of-the-art modular concert hall-cum-stadium hosts crowd-pleasing rock and classical stars, plus sporting events.

Notre-Dame-de-l'Assomption. *See p253.*

Palais des Sports Jean Bouin
esplanade de Lattre de Tassigny (04.93.80.80.80). **Open** hours vary Mon-Sat. **Admission** *pool* €3.50-€4.30; *ice rink* €3.15-€4.30. **No credit cards.**
The vast municipal sports complex has a well-kept indoor Olympic-sized pool and covered ice rink.

Théâtre de Nice
promenade des Arts (04.93.13.90.90). **Box office** 2-7pm Tue-Sat. **Tickets** *grande salle* €10-€30; *petite salle* €20. **Credit** AmEx, DC, MC, V.
One of the most important theatres in the south of France is now directed by Daniel Bunoin, staging high-profile productions of French and foreign classics and varied contemporary drama.

Théâtre de la Photographie et de l'Image
27 bd de Dubouchage (04.97.13.42.21). **Open** 10am-6pm Tue-Sun. **Admission** free.
A restored vintage theatre now provides a vast space for big-name photography shows, plus lectures, an Internet archive and a convivial coffee bar.

Restaurants

Le 22 Septembre
3 rue Centrale (04.93.80.87.90/ www.le22septembre.com). **Open** 7-11pm Tue-Sat. **Menus** €12-€15. **Credit** MC, V.
This budget eatery in Vieux Nice is a magnet for

stylish students and savvy young couples. Food is hearty and good – try the beef stroganoff, sea bass with basil butter or the fried camembert.

L'Allegro

6 pl Guynemar (04.93.56.62.06). **Open** noon-1.45pm, 8-10pm Mon-Fri; 8-10pm Sat. **Menus** €19-€31. **Credit** MC, V.

In a Venetian setting under the watchful eye of characters from the Commedia dell'Arte, savour exquisite home-made ravioli, risotto and fresh pasta cooked up right in front of eager customers. Book.

L'Auberge de Théo

52 av Cap de Croix (04.93.81.26.19/www.auberge-de-theo.com). **Open** noon-2pm, 7-10.30pm Tue-Sat; noon-2pm Sun. Closed 20 Aug-10 Sept. **Menus** €19-€29.50. **Credit** V.

Near the Chagall and Matisse museums, this trattoria with an open-air patio is a perfect place for Italian specialities, including cep pasta and *tagliata*.

La Baie d'Amalfi

9 rue Gustave Deloye (04.93.80.01.21). **Open** noon-2pm, 7-11pm daily. **Menus** €18-€30. **Credit** MC, V.

Pizza, pasta and fish enthusiasts are in heaven in this bustling old-style mansion. Try the risotto with courgette flowers and scampi, or the gnocchi.

Bistrot du Port

28 quai de Lunel (04.93.55.21.70). **Open** noon-2.15pm, 7.40-10.30pm Mon, Thur-Sun; noon-2.15pm Tue. **Menus** €23-€30. **Credit** DC, MC, V.

At this big yellow brasserie on the old port, excellent specialities include warm lobster salad with olive *tapenade* and Grand Marnier soufflé. Friendly service and top-notch, affordable wines.

Brasserie Flo

4 rue Sacha Guitry (04.93.13.38.38). **Open** noon-3pm, 7pm-midnight daily. **Menus** €20.90-€29.90. **Credit** AmEx, DC, MC, V.

This is a dining experience not to be missed. Set in an old theatre, the kitchen is where the stage used to be, with the best seats on the upper balcony. Food is uncomplicated Provençal and good – the Faim de Nuit menu is perfect late at night. Book.

Le Chantecler

Hôtel Negresco, 37 promenade des Anglais (04.93.16.64.00). **Open** 12.30-2pm, 8-10pm daily. **Menus** €90-€130. **Credit** AmEx, DC, MC, V.

Nice's grandest restaurant has sumptuous food, excellent service and a very good wine list. Chef Michel del Burgo, previously at Taillevent and Le Bristol in Paris, took over the reins in January 2004.

Chez René Socca

2 rue Miralheti (04.93.92.05.73). **Open** 9am-11pm Tue-Sun. Closed Nov. **Average** €10. **Credit** MC,V.

Rustic tables spill out into the street of this Old Town landmark, the oldest and most popular address for *socca*. Stern waiters slam down your drinks and you have to fetch the steaming Niçois specialities yourself – but don't worry, you're here for the food.

Nice v Monaco: coastal rivalry

While both trot out in black and red football strips, the teams of AS Monaco (www.asm-foot.mc) and OGC Nice (www.ogcnice.fr) are separated by far more than 15km of coast. Monaco, currently trained by World Cup-winning captain Didier Deschamps, have won seven French league titles and lifted the Coupe de France five times. Nice, on the other hand, have yo-yoed between the top two divisions for the past 50 years with their most recent premier league title coming in 1956.

Many expected newly promoted Nice to be the whipping boys of the 2002/03 season. Instead, they confounded critics by taking an early lead in the league. As flags waved from windows around Nice, the squad carried on winning and midway through the season looked, as far as ecstatic locals were concerned, to be 'going all the way'. Sadly the team's inexperience put them on a losing streak but they still gained a respectable tenth league placing. Many have high hopes for the squad's centenary season in 2004.

French football has never entertained the

commercial sideshow, and thus the crowd sizes, common in England, Spain and Italy. Monaco's Stade Louis II and Nice's Stade du Ray (2km north of Nice-Ville rail station) only have capacities of around 18,000 each. Games, at around 10 per ticket, lack prima donna hype and have a focus on both team skill and homegrown passion. Despite being a sunny pasture for ageing players a decade ago (Glenn Hoddle, Tony Cascarino), Monaco is now a net exporter of talent (Fabien Barthez, Thierry Henry), giving visitors the chance to see a future great.

Winter warmer

Stuff Pancake Day. Nice residents in the Middle Ages celebrated the start of Lent with a giant street party. Better still, the revellers all wore masks, making it a day of anonymous fun-poking and merriment. Sadly, it all looked a bit washed out two centuries ago as posh partygoers detracted from the main event by holding private masked balls. Worse still, carousing stopped altogether when wily Corsican Napoléon was in charge.

In 1873, local lad Andriot Saëtone seized the initiative and created an official Carnaval committee to promote and expand the yearly event. In keeping with the anonymous mischief of early years, many revellers donned huge 'big heads' made from paper and proceeded to fling, over the next 100 years, eggs, flour, sugared seeds and pasta at each other.

1873 also saw the start of the 'His Majesty' theme tradition, recently exploited as the King of Cinema (1995), King of the 20th Century (2001) and the King of Clownery (2004). The current programme revolves around 'big head' processions through the streets armed with flowers by day and illuminations by night. www.nicecarnaval.com. Tickets cost €10 standing or €20 seated.

La Cigale
7 av de Suède (04.93.88.60.20). **Open** 10am-midnight daily. **Menus** €20-€35. **Credit** AmEx, MC, V.
Perfect for an affordable lunch on designer boutique row. Try the yummy chicken doner kebab and the scrumptious honey-soaked pastries. Liveliest on weekend nights when a belly-dancer performs.

Delhi Belhi
22 rue de la Barillerie (04.93.92.51.87). **Open** 8pm-22.30am Mon-Sat. **Average** €40. **Credit** MC, V.
Delhi Belhi's softly lit, sweet-smelling dining room offers the best Indian food on the Côte d'Azur. Mainly Pakistani cooks dish up a fabulous chicken *lal masal wali* (with red peppers, almonds and ginger cream). Vegetarians settle in to the vegetarian *thali* or red lentils with tomato and coriander.

Don Camillo
5 rue des Ponchettes (04.93.85.67.95). **Open** 7.30-11pm Mon; noon-2.30pm, 7.30-11pm Tue-Sat. **Menus** €32-€56. **Credit** AmEx, MC, V.
Don't be misled by the rather staid decor – this restaurant has long been a magnet for creative cuisine. Lately, chef Stéphane Viano has been getting top marks for his artful Mediterranean style.

L'Estrilha
11-13 rue de l Abbaye (04.93.62.62.00). **Open** 7-11pm Mon-Sat. **Average** €23. **Credit** MC, V.
The speciality of this Old Town restaurant is the delicious 'amphore': a copious mixed fish, tomato, white wine and basil stew baked in a clay pot and served steaming at the table.

Fleur de Jade
8 rue d'Italie (04.93.88.34.01). **Open** noon-2pm, 7-10pm daily. **Menus** €14-€29. **Credit** MC, V.
The hum of a brimming fish tank accompanies clients through their foray into wonderfully prepared Vietnamese dishes: noodle soup, lacquered duck, and fresh fruit flamed with rice wine.

Le Frog
3 rue Milton Robbins (04.93.85.85.65). **Open** 8pm-midnight Mon-Sat. **Average** €30. **Credit** AmEx, MC, V.
With T-bone steak and cheesecake, this Tex Mex bistro is little slice of North America in the heart of Vieux Nice – even most of the wines are from the New World. Live music every night after 9pm.

Le Grand Balcon
10 rue St-François-de-Paule (04.93.62.60.74). **Open** noon-2pm, 7.30-11pm Mon-Fri; 7.30-11pm Sat, Sun. **Menus** €32-€45. **Credit** AmEx, MC, V.
Fashionable Parisian decorator Jacques Garcia has created the mood of a comfortable English library. Chef Marc Hamel, previously at La Petite Maison, offers a tropical menu that favours fish, but do try the chicken breast with basil and coconut or the balsamic duck breast, which are truly excellent.

Le Grand Café de Turin
5 pl Garibaldi (04.93.62.29.52). **Open** 8am-10pm

Ride a cock horse at **Le Chantecler**. *See p255.*

Mon, Tue, Thur-Sun. **Average** €25. **Credit** AmEx, DC, MC, V.
With some of the best shellfish in town, this classic Niçois brasserie is on a perfect people-watching corner. It opened in 1910 and has been jammed ever since with oyster-slurping locals. Service can be testy but the atmosphere is the real thing.

Indyana
11 rue Gustave Deloye (04.93.80.67.69). **Open** 7pm-midnight Mon, Sun; noon-2pm, 7pm-midnight Tue-Sat. **Average** €50. **Credit** AmEx, DC, MC, V.
This swanky dining spot serves a Franco-Japanese fusion cuisine that matches the ethno-loft decor. Regulars are an intriguing mix of fashionistas, artsy intellectuals and stiff business-suit types.

Karr
10 rue Alphonse Karr (04.93.82.18.31). **Open** noon-2.30pm, 7.30-11.30pm Mon-Sat (bar 8am-12.30am). **Menus** €18-€40. **Credit** AmEx, MC, V.
Although renowned chef Philippe Soublet has left, this contemporary eatery continues to dish up a creative, cosmopolitan menu that goes beyond Provençal. Live jazz (Thur, Fri) adds an intimate note.

Kei's Passion
22ter rue de France (04.93.82.26.06). **Open** 7.30-10pm Mon, Wed; noon-2pm, 7.30pm-10pm Tue, Thur-Sat. **Menus** €18-€65. **Credit** V.
The hot new word-of-mouth address where Japan-ese chef Keisuko Matsushima (ex-Pourcel Brothers, ex-Regis Marcon) has been wowing the locals with creations like cold asparagus soup with sea-urchin cream and roast lobster in a curried vinaigrette.

La Merenda
4 rue de la Terrasse (no phone). **Open** lunch and dinner Mon-Fri. Closed 3wks Aug. **Menus** €25-€30. **No credit cards.**
Dominique Le Stanc shed his perch at the Negresco for this rustic place near Cours Saleya. He serves a repertoire of Niçois classics, such as stuffed sardines and *stockfissa*. It's noisy, but the food is delicious.

La Mousson
167 promenade des Flots Bleus, St-Laurent-du-Var (04.93.31.13.30). **Open** 6.30-10.30pm Mon, Sun; noon-2.30pm, 6.30-10.30pm Thur-Sat. **Lunch menu** €19. **Average** €36. **Credit** AmEx, MC, V.
Truly exquisite Thai cuisine, a stone's throw from the airport at the seaside port of St-Laurent-du-Var. Highlights include the spicy beef sautéed with Thai basil and caramelised mango with sticky rice.

Le Parcours
1 pl Marcel Eusebi, Falicon (04.93.84.94.57). **Open** 8-9.30pm Tue; 12.30-2.30pm, 8-9.30pm Wed-Sat; 12.30-2.30pm Sun. **Menus** €30-€45. **Credit** MC, V.
Jean-Marc Delacourt left the prestigious Château Chèvre d'Or in Eze to open up this cosy restaurant in the hills above Nice. Strategically placed plasma screens amid the Zen decor reveal what's happening in the kitchen. Menus are gorgeous, changing every three days, and reasonably priced. Book.

La Part des Anges
17 rue Gubernatis (04.93.62.69.80). **Open** noon-8pm Mon-Thur; noon-2pm, 7-10pm Fri, Sat. **Average** €25. **Credit** AmEx, DC, MC, V.
The captivating aroma as you walk past this intimate wine cellar and bistro draws you inside, where owner and sommelier Olivier Labarde offers expert advice on his superb selection of local and rare vintages, as well as delicious French regional cooking.

La Petite Maison
11 rue St-François-de-Paule (04.93.85.71.53). **Open** noon-2pm, 7.30-10pm Mon-Sat. **Average** €45. **Credit** AmEx, MC, V.
This venerable restaurant draws colourful locals at noon, top models and cinema stars by night. Start with the Niçois hors d'oeuvres (*pissaladière*, stuffed vegetables, etc) and then have sea bass cooked in a salt crust and the fabulous house ice cream.

Restaurant du Gésu
1 pl du Gésu (04.93.62.26.46). **Open** noon-1.45pm, 7.30-10.30pm Mon-Sat. **Average** €18. **No credit cards.**
With this Old Town atmosphere, the patio here is jammed with locals and tourists alike. Service is excellent and customers are happy to bandy jokes while savouring Niçois cooking in all its splendour. The *pissaladière* and stuffed veggies (*farcis*) are scrumptious and desserts well worth the wait.

La Table Alziari

4 rue François Zanin (04.93.80.34.03). **Open** noon-2pm, 7.30-10pm Tue-Sat. Closed 2wks Aug, 2wks Dec. **Average** €25. **Credit** MC, V.

From the family that sells the best local olive oil in town, this low-key but authentic Nissart bistro offers home-style cooking with the freshest ingredients.

Terres des Truffes

11 rue St-François-de-Paule (04.93.62.07.68). **Open** noon-2pm, 8-10pm Mon-Sat. **Menus** €30-€35. **Credit** AmEx, MC, V.

Truffles meet fast food in this stylish wood-panelled bistro-cum-deli, created by celeb chef Bruno Clément. Truffles with everything range from sand-wiches and delectable truffle-studded warm brie to caramelised truffle ice-cream.

Le Tire Bouchon

19 rue de la Préfecture (04.93.92.63.64). **Open** 7-10.30pm daily. **Menus** €25-€35. **Credit** AmEx, MC, V.

This Lyonnais bistro in the Old Town has a relaxed lounge atmosphere. The ever-changing blackboard menu includes delicious dishes like scallop casserole and duck confit with ginger and honey.

L'Univers de Christian Plumail

54 bd Jean Jaurès (04.93.62.32.22). **Open** noon-2pm, 7.30-10pm Mon-Fri; 7.30-10pm Sat. **Menus** €18-€65. **Credit** AmEx, MC, V.

Renowned Niçois chef Christian Plumail has trans-formed a former brasserie into an unpretentious haven for simple yet refined Mediterranean cuisine at surprisingly affordable prices.

La Zucca Magica

4bis quai Papacino (04.93.56.25.27). **Open** noon-2.45pm, 7-10.30pm Tue-Sat. **Menus** €17 (lunch); €27 (dinner). **No credit cards.**

Marco Folicardi, once Rome's best vegetarian chef, serves a remarkable daily-changing, no-choice menu (wine included) in a grotto-like tavern by the old port.

Bars & cafés

Le Bar des Oiseaux

5 rue St-Vincent (04.93.80.27.33). **Open** 7-11pm Tue-Sun. Closed Aug. **Credit** MC, V.

There is lots of local atmosphere at this popular restaurant, bar and theatre. Live bands and live birds, too (in cages, most of the time) and uproarious comic sketches written by proprietor Noëlle Perna.

Café Borghèse

9 rue Fodéré (04.92.04.83.83). **Open** 9am-10.30pm Mon-Fri; 11am-2pm, 7-10pm Sat. **Credit** MC, V.

Located behind the church of the Vieux Port, this is the place for cappuccino, apéritifs, antipasti platters and copious portions of gnocchi and ravioli.

Chez Pipo

13 rue Bavastro (04.93.55.88.82). **Open** 5.30-10pm Tue-Sun (daily July & Aug). Closed Nov. **No credit cards.**

This lively port-side spot has a huge wood-burning oven and long tables where old-timers gossip in Niçois dialect. The perfect place for an early evening snack on *socca* and a glass of local rosé.

There's a list of flavours as long as your nose at **Fenocchio**'s ice-cream parlour.

The Riviera & Southern Alps

Fenocchio
2 pl Rossetti (04.93.80.72.52). **Open** 10am-11.30pm
Tue-Sun. Closed Dec-Jan. Credit MC, V.
Settle in at a table by the fountain on the cathedral
square and choose from a superb range of home-
made ice cream and sorbets, including what is surely the world's best peach ice cream.

La Havane
32 rue de France (04.93.16.36.16). **Open** 4pm-
2.30am Mon, Sun; 11am-2.30pm, 4pm-2.30am Tue-
Sat. **Credit** AmEx, MC, V.
No one can resist dancing in this restaurant/bar
(restaurant closed Mon), where a hot Cuban group
plays nightly. Great place for cocktails

Nocy-Bé
4-6 rue Jules Gilly (04.93.85.52.25). **Open** 4pm-
midnight Wed-Sun. **Credit** MC, V.
At this cosy Moroccan boutique, doubling as a tea
room, you can shop till you drop… on to a comfortable cushion, for invigorating mint tea and pastries.

Oliviera
8 bis rue du Collet (04.93.13.06.45). **Open** *May-Oct*
10am-10pm Mon-Sat; 10am-6pm Sun. *Nov-Apr* 10am-
8pm Mon-Sat; 10am-3pm Sun. **No credit cards.**
This friendly Old Town olive oil shop/café is the perfect spot for a quality salad or pasta dish (€8-€15).

O'Neill's Irish Pub
40 rue Droite (04.93.80.06.75). **Open** 5pm-2am
nightly. **Credit** MC, V.
All the friendly Irish fixings: burnished wood, cheerful staff, excellent beer on tap and busy happy hour.

Pâtisserie Cappa
7-9 pl Garibaldi (04.93.62.30.83). **Open** 7.30am-
7.30pm Tue-Sun. Closed Sept. **Credit** MC, V.
Venture under the arches for heavenly pastries,
mousse cakes and *tourte de blettes* to take away or
consume in the miniature tea room.

Clubs & music venues

For concerts see also *p255*, **Palais Nikaïa.**

Le Barrio
73 quai des Etats Unis (04.93.92.94.04). **Open** 8pm-
2.30am daily. **Admission** free. **Credit** V.
Nightly salsa lessons (€8-€12) for Latino fans; newcomers crowd in to watch, sipping tropical cocktails
for courage while regulars take up the beat.

Blue Boy Enterprise
*9 rue Jean-Baptiste Spinetta (04.93.44.68.24/
www.blueboy.fr)*. **Open** 11pm-dawn daily.
Admission free (Sat €8). **Credit** DC, MC, V.
The best-known gay disco in town. Young boys
prance and dance, Riviera queens cosy up or bitch
and the rest hit the booze and the dance floor.

Le Blue Whales
1 rue Mascoïnat (04.93.62.90.94). **Open** 5.30pm-
4.30am daily. **Admission** free. **Credit** V.

Nice snacks

A Niçois is easy to spot in a crowd of bronzed
southerners – he's the one who is always
eating. Snacking is an essential part of the
lifestyle here, from early-morning *socca* to
pissaladière with late-night beer. A guide to
local street food follows, but as you'll see
versions in nearly every boulangerie and
café it's worth munching your way around
to find your own favourites.

Socca, perhaps even more than
pissaladière, symbolises Niçois street
food. This thin pancake made with
chickpea flour, garlic and plenty of olive oil,
and traditionally cooked on a flat copper
pan in a wood-fired oven, tastes best as
you soak up the atmosphere of the vividly
coloured Cours Saleya market, where Chez
Thérèse's outdoor stand with a few tables
has become an institution. At its worst
socca can be greasy and pasty, but Lou
Pilha Leva (10 rue du Collet), in Vieux Nice,
has a thin, not-too-oily version, perfect with
a chilled glass of rosé.

Pissaladière is more of a pizza than
a salad, but without any tomatoes or
cheese. The thin, olive-oil-flavoured crust
is topped with anchovy paste, then lightly
caramelised onions, a few Niçois olives
and anchovy fillets. The result is crunchy,
sweet and salty – you'll find a good version
at the Restaurant du Gésu (*see p257*) and
in many boulangeries, but don't allow them
to zap the life out of it in the microwave.

Petits farcis are little stuffed vegetables,
usually *courgettes niçoises* (which are
small, round and pale green), aubergines,
bell peppers and onions. Filled with veal,
ham and vegetables or occasionally *daube*
(a richly flavoured stew which is also used
as a ravioli filling) and then baked for at
least an hour, they are popular finger food.

A good *pan bagnat* is a glorious thing –
layer upon layer of salad and crunchy
vegetables, tuna and egg, all packed
inside a giant round bun dripping with olive
oil. Many boulangeries do them well,
perfect for a picnic on the beach.

Perhaps the oddest Niçois snack is the
tourte de blettes, made with Swiss chard,
rum-soaked raisins and sugar. Is it a
starter, main course or dessert? No one
seems to know or care, and the Niçois eat
it at any time of day but especially in the
morning. Now that's what we call *liberté*.

have a Nice time

Stay in the charming boutique hotel that is the Hotel Massena and enjoy a stay exceeding all your expectations. Superbly situated in the heart of Nice, you will be only minutes walk away from all the main distractions; the Old Town, the beach and some fabulous shopping. Inside the hotel you will discover an intimate atmosphere, complimented by an attentive personnel and the classic Provencal character that runs through from the delicate frescoes in the hall to the cosy and luxurious bedrooms.

A relaxed, thirtysomething crowd frequents this better-than-most pub where you can shoot pool and dance to a DJ or live music from jazz funk to salsa.

La Casa del Sol
69 quai des Etats Unis (04.93.62.87.28). **Open** *mid-May to Sept* 6.30pm-2.30am daily. *Oct to mid-May* 7pm-2.30am Tue-Sat (Fri, Sat in Jan). **Credit** MC, V.
This before- and after-hours tapas bar has a lively atmosphere and a Spanish-Latino beat (DJs Thur-Sat). Dress cool, clean and casual to get past the door.

Dizzy Club
26 quai Lunel (04.93.26.54.79). **Open** 11.30pm-5am Wed-Sun. **Admission** €9-€12. **Credit** MC, V.
One of the few clubs where you can actually have a conversation at the bar. Sleek decor, piano-bar, a dance floor with live bands, working out from jazz to electro, and DJs draw pretty people from 25 to 50.

Le Ghost House
3 rue Barillerie (04.93.92.93.37). **Open** 8pm-2.30am daily. **Admission** free. **Credit** DC, MC, V.
Trip-hop, drum 'n' bass and house fans flock to this tiny club in Vieux Nice, which leads the way on the Nice electronic scene. DJs Wednesday to Saturday.

Le Grand Escurial
29 rue Alphonse Karr (04.93.82.37.66). **Open** 8pm-5am Fri, Sat. **Admission** €16. **Credit** MC, V.
A cavernous disco (full in the summer) with a surprisingly cosy restaurant/lounge on the mezzanine.

Le Klub
6 rue Halévy (04.93.16.27.56). **Open** 11pm-5am daily (closed Mon in winter). **Admission** free (Sat €9). **Credit** MC, V.
Super-minimalist with wrought iron and woodwork downstairs and a cosy salon upstairs, the ultra-sleek gay Klub plays the latest in house music and techno.

La Suite du Comptoir
2 rue Bréa (04.93.92.92.91). **Open** 11pm-2.30am Tue-Sat. **Admission** €13. **Credit** AmEx.
Sexy, stylish and pretty young things throng to this predominantly gay club to dance to house and R&B amid splendid baroque deco. Reserve.

Wayne's
15 rue de la Préfecture (04.93.13.46.99/www.waynes.fr). **Open** noon-1am Mon-Thur, Sun; noon-1.30am Fri, Sat. **Admission** free. **Credit** AmEx, MC, V.
This live-music Mecca for Anglophones in Vieux Nice attracts young party-goers with British up-and-comers like Breathe and Sugar Monkey. Fun theme nights and karaoke on Sundays bring added spice.

Shopping

The split-level Etoile mall, department store Galeries Lafayette, book and record emporium Fnac and countless clothing chains line avenue Jean Médecin. Luxury labels congregate on rue Paradis (Chanel, Emporio Armani, Kenzo, Sonia Rykiel), avenue de Suède (Yves Saint-Laurent, Rolex, Louis Vuitton) and avenue de Verdun (Cartier, Hermès). Food and funky speciality emporia clutter the narrow Old Town streets, while the Cours Saleya market (mornings, except Mondays) is a foodie must.

Alziari
14 rue St-François-de-Paule (04.93.85.76.92). **Open** 8.15am-12.30pm, 2.15-7pm Tue-Sat. **Credit** MC, V.
Since 1879, the Alziari family has been producing a superb nutty olive oil, sold in yellow and blue tin drums. There is a selection of other natural products.

L'Atelier des Jouets
1 pl de l'Ancien Sénat (04.93.13.09.60). **Open** 10.30am-7pm Mon, Tue-Sun; 2-7pm Wed. **Credit** AmEx, DC, MC, V.
A charming old-fashioned toy shop on a pretty square in the Old Town, packed with everything from soft toys, puzzles and puppets to stocking fillers.

Au Brin de Soleil
1 rue de la Boucherie (04.93.62.89.00). **Open** daily 9.30am-7pm. **Credit** AmEx, DC, MC, V.
A haven of Provençal decor: hand-painted faïence, bed covers, kitchenware, candles and soaps.

Boutique 3
3 rue do Longchamp (04.93.88.35.00). **Open** 1-6.30pm Tue-Sat. **Credit** MC, V.
Check out designer Jacqueline Morabito's creamy linen tablecloths, flowing white shirts, shawls, ceramic dishes, and a range of gourmet goodies.

La Chapellerie
36 cours Saleya (04.93.62.52.64). **Open** daily 9.30am-1pm, 2-6.30pm. **Credit** V, MC.
Check out every imaginable sort of hat, from the basic beret to frilly things with serious plumage.

Façonnable
7, 9, 10 rue Paradis (04.93.87.88.80). **Open** 10am-7pm Mon-Sat. **Credit** AmEx, DC, MC, V.
The menswear label that began in this shop now has stores in every major city, selling elegantly preppy sportswear, suits and ties. Womenswear at No.10.

Fayences de Moustiers
18 rue du Marché (04.93.13.06.03). **Open** 9.45am-7pm Mon-Sat. **Credit** AmEx, MC, V.
The only shop in Nice with delicately hand-painted porcelain from Moustiers; everything from cream jugs to fruit bowls. Pricey, but the real thing.

Le Frigo
3 rue Benoît Bunico (04.93.13.48.10). **Open** 10am-1.30pm, 3-7pm Mon-Sat. **Credit** MC, V.
Trendy vintage store, where gems include original Levis, plaid bell-bottoms and wicked leather jackets.

Matarosso Bookstore/Gallery
2 rue Longchamp (04.93.87.74.55). **Open** 10am-12.30pm, 4-7.30pm Tue-Sat. **Credit** MC, V.

The Riviera & Southern Alps

This pioneer Niçois gallery also stocks contemporary art books, original editions and engravings.

Movida
2 rue Longchamp (04.93.88.90.80). **Open** 10am-1pm, 2-7pm Mon-Sat. **Credit** AmEx, MC. V.
Haute-couture of the new generation includes leather, fur, eyewear and fashion by Dolce e Gabbana, Sonya Rykiel and Thierry Mugler.

Star Dog & Cat
40 rue de France (04.93.82.93.71). **Open** 9.30am-noon, 2.30-7pm Mon-Sat. **Credit** AmEx, DC, MC, V.
Buy a souvenir for your dog or cat at this temple for pampered pets. Treasures include diamanté dog collars, Burberry check coats and bejewelled bowls.

Village Ségurane
main entrance on rue Ségurane (no phone). **Open** 10am-noon, 3-6.30pm Mon-Sat. **Credit** AmEx, MC, V.
When Elton John went on a decorating spree for his villa in Mont Boron, this is where he shopped: a two-storey village of antiques shops, stacked together.

Where to stay

Luxury

Château des Ollières
39 av des Baumettes (04.92.15.77.99/ www.chateaudesollieres.com). **Double** €165-€503. **Credit** AmEx, MC, V.
The Mauresque palace of Prince Lobanov-Rostowsky was transformed in 1990 into a luxurious inn. The nine rooms have authentic period touches and marble bathrooms. The garden restaurant turns into a candlelit paradise at night.

Hôtel La Pérouse
11 quai Rauba-Capeau (04.93.62.34.63/ www.hroy.com/la-perouse). **Double** €171-€395. **Credit** AmEx, MC, V.
This secret treasure cut into the cliff of the château hill has breathtaking views over the Baie des Anges. Just steps away from Vieux Nice, yet an oasis of tranquility – the sundeck, sauna, and lovely pool simply add to the sense of luxury.

Hôtel Negresco
36 promenade des Anglais (04.93.16.64.00/ www.hotel-negresco-nice.com). **Double** €213-€460. **Suite** €556-€1,410. **Credit** AmEx, DC, MC, V.
You can't miss this pink and white wedding cake, built by Edouard Niermans, 'the Offenbach of architecture'. Initially considered a folly, the Negresco eventually drew everyone, from crowned heads to stars. Sumptuous bedrooms range from Oriental to Napoléon III pomp, though the bathtubs are oddly Las Vegas. No pool but there is a private beach.

Hôtel Palais Maeterlinck
30 bd Maurice Maeterlinck (04.92.00.72.00/ www.palais-maeterlinck.com). Closed mid-Jan to mid-Mar. **Double** €245-€500. **Credit** AmEx, DC, MC, V.
Once a villa belonging to Belgian writer Count Maurice Maeterlinck, this sprawling 'neo-classic style' palace on the Basse Corniche is now a hotel boasting luxurious rooms, an excellent restaurant and lovely outdoor pool. The atmosphere is somewhat stiff and formal, but the views are superb.

Hôtel West End
31 promenade des Anglais (04.92.14.44.00/ www.hotel-westend.com). **Double** €214-€628. **Credit** AmEx, DC, MC, V.
Built in 1842, the West End was the first grand hotel on the Baie des Anges. There are lovely salons and a listed bar downstairs, but the repro Gainsboroughs and Fragonards in the corridors are a crime.

Palais de la Méditerranée
15 promenade des Anglais (04.92.14.77.00/ www.concorde-hotels.com). **Double** €280-€550. **Credit** AmEx, DC, MC, V.
This new luxury hotel opened in January 2004, keeping only the facade of the fabulous art deco Palais de la Med. Most rooms have fantastic sea views but a heads-on-beds policy means they squashed in too many floors (ie low ceilings). Lots of security features include its own fireman. There's a pool and a restaurant headed by talented chef Bruno Sohn.

Moderate & inexpensive

Hi Hôtel
3 av des Fleurs (04.97.07.26.26/www.hi-hotel.net). **Double** €175-€385. **Credit** AmEx, DC, MC, V.
The radically experimental new hotel by designer Matali Crasset encourages you to try out different ways of living. One room puts both bed and transparent glass shower on a wooden pontoon island, another allows you to watch DVDs on a screen that divides bed from bath. Bathrobes are by Ron Orb, the hotel soundtrack mixed by hip label F.Com. There's a rooftop terrace, though the minuscule pool is barely large enough to dip a toe. The bar is open to non-residents, with DJ soirées often on Saturday.

Hôtel Albert 1er
4 av des Phocéens (04.93.85.74.01/www.hotel-albert-1er.fr). **Double** €75-€160. **Credit** AmEx, MC, V.
Just steps from the flower market, this charming hotel offers a friendly welcome with oak bedsteads, sleek whites and cornflower blues and views out to the sea or over the gardens.

Hôtel Atlantic
12 bd Victor Hugo (04.97.03.89.89). **Double** €84-€200. **Credit** AmEx, MC, V.
Beyond the sumptuous *belle époque* stained-glass lobby – used by François Truffaut as a location in his film *Day for Night* – the modern, renovated rooms are spacious and comfortable.

Hôtel Beau Rivage
24 rue St-François-de-Paule (04.92.47.82.82). **Double** €140-€400. **Credit** AmEx, DC, MC, V.

Russian Riviera

'Princes! Princes everywhere!' exclaimed Guy de Maupassant about the Riviera in 1888. And with good reason. The impressive pre-revolutionary courts of Empress Féodorovna and Tsar Nicholas II, dubbed '*les excentriques*' by the Niçois for their exotic lifestyles, had literally invaded the Riviera in the latter half of the 19th century, when princes, aristocrats, high court and rich business magnates travelled the St-Petersburg-Vienna-Cannes railway with astonishing regularity, snapping up sprawling villas and spending money with reckless abandon. Like the English, they came for the warm climate, the great food and spectacular scenery; they also came for political reasons.

After his defeat in the Crimean War, Tsar Alexander II needed a port to shelter his damaged and demoralised fleet. In 1856 he convinced the Piedmont-Sardinian King Victor Emmanuel to give him free access to the port in Villefranche-sur-Mer. The Empress Féodorovna, horribly bored with freezing winters, promptly refused to go back to the ice and snow of her homeland and set up court around what later became the Parc Imperial off avenue Tzarewitch in Nice.

Thus began the Golden Age of the Riviera: a time of splendid *belle époque* villas and no-expense-spared Russian monuments, most impressive of which is the Russian Orthodox Cathedral. Inspired by St Basil's in Red Square, and inaugurated in 1912 by Tsar Nicolas II himself, the church is crowned by five gilded domes and is filled with artworks donated by long-dead Russian aristocrats, whose tombstones you can see at the large Russian cemetery (78 av Ste-Marguerite). Other churches went up on the Riviera, too, in Cannes, Menton and San Remo.

Five years later there were only a few aristocrats left in the region. The 1917 Russian revolution had effectively wiped out the monarchy and its court. However, successive waves of immigrants – refugees, soldiers of the defeated White Army, Jews and political dissidents – continued to stream in to Nice and the surrounding area.

The arts flourished. Marc Chagall and Boris Grigorleff thrived here, later donating many of their works to their adopted city; Nobel prize for literature Yvan Bounine wrote here until his death; and Diaghilev's Ballets Russes became famous in its adopted home of Monte Carlo.

After the collapse of the Soviet Union in 1991, wealthy Russians returned en masse to their Riviera playground, spending money like it was water. Certain visitors were known to shell out as much as €100 for a soft drink, indulging a taste for opulence that hadn't been seen since before World War I.

Today, Russians rank third in the number of visitors to the Côte d'Azur but first in per capita spending – which means a very gracious welcome in hotels, luxury stores, casinos and restaurants suffering from a recent drop in tourist dollars. This incipient longing for huge yachts, Dom Perignon and fur coats has created a nasty side to *la vida loca* as alleged money laundering, prostitution and crime rings now dog the reputations of many Russians on the Riviera – visitors and locals alike.

To discover Russian heritage, pick up a leaflet or a Russian cultural tour from Nice tourist office, visit the Maison Russe (7 rue St-Augustin, Vieux Nice, 04.93.62.61.58) where you can sample vodka, beer, borscht, and the traditional zakouskie platter, or check out Russian cultural organisations and history in France on www.russie.net/france.

The Riviera & Southern Alps

Thoroughly modernised since the days when Matisse had a seafront apartment here, this comfortable 1930s hotel has its own private beach.

Hôtel les Cigales
16 rue Dalpozzo (04.97.03.10.71/www.hotel-lescigales. com). **Double** €75-€180. **Credit** AmEx, MC, V.
This family-run hotel in a recently renovated *hôtel particulier* has cheerful, well-soundproofed rooms, some with small balconies looking over the garden.

Hôtel Excelsior
19 av Durante (04.93.88.18.05/www.excelsiornice. com). **Double** €70-€100. **Credit** AmEx, MC, V.
An impressive turn-of-the-century building on a quiet street, with clean, old-fashioned rooms and a small garden where breakfast is served.

Hôtel de la Fontaine
49 rue de France (04.93.88.30.38/www.hotel-fontaine.com). **Double** €82-€105. **Credit** AmEx, MC, V.
This immaculate, simply designed hotel has cheerfully tiled bathrooms and a lovely inner courtyard; your stay includes a substantial breakfast buffet.

Hôtel Le Floride
52 bd de Cimiez (04.93.53.11.02/www.hotel-floride.fr). Closed 3wks Jan. **Double** €44-€60. **Credit** AmEx, MC, V.
Only a ten-minute walk from the centre of town and right near the Chagall museum, this modest small hotel even has a view from the top floor.

Hôtel Gounod
3 rue Gounod (04.93.16.42.00/www.gounod-nice.com). Closed mid-Nov to mid-Dec. **Double** €95-€135. **Credit** AmEx, DC, MC, V.
A dusty-rose *belle époque* exterior hides chic but standard modern rooms with balconies. Guests can use the rooftop pool next door at Hôtel Splendid.

Hôtel Le Grimaldi
15 rue Grimaldi (04.93.16.00.24/www.le-grimaldi. com). **Double** €95-€175. **Credit** AmEx, MC, V.
This elegant, upmarket bed and breakfast offers the kind of personalised hospitality often lacking in the glitzy Riviera palaces. All the rooms are different, and tastefully decorated with Provençal fabrics.

Hôtel Massena
58 rue Gioffredo (04.92.47.88.88//www.hotel-massena-nice.com). **Double** €100-€190. **Credit** AmEx, MC, V.
An abundance of modern comforts lurk behind the splendid *belle époque* facade of this recently renovated building near place Massena. Rooms are bright, sunny Provençal; many have great people-watching balconies that look over the street. Large baths, Internet connection in most rooms, fluffy green rugs and a friendly welcome are bonuses.

Hôtel Mercure Marché aux Fleurs
91 quai des Etats Unis (04.93.85.74.19/ www.mercure.com). **Double** €75-€143. **Credit** AmEx, MC, V.

Never mind the basic decor and matching florals: the service is dynamic and attentive, the €10 breakfast buffet is all-you-can-eat, and the lovely views stretch out over the Baie des Anges.

Hôtel Oasis
23 rue Gounod (04.93.88.12.29/www.hotel-oasis-nice.com.fr). **Double** €60-€84. **Credit** AmEx, MC, V.
This tranquil, centrally located hotel once lodged illustrious Russians including Chekhov and Lenin. The biggest rooms (110, 124 and 210) look over a splendid, shady garden.

Hôtel du Petit Palais
17 av Emile Bieckiert (04.93.62.19.11/www.hotel-petit-palais.com). **Double** €74-€144. **Credit** AmEx, MC, V.
On a quiet street in Cimiez, this 25-room *belle époque* hotel where Sacha Guitry lived in the 1930s may not be the *dernier cri* in decor, but the panoramic view and lush garden make up for the rest.

Hôtel La Petite Sirène
8 rue Maccarani (04.92.14.41.50). **Double** €56-€74. **Credit** MC, V.
Situated near boulevard Victor Hugo, this hotel is cute and quiet. Rooms are clean and comfortable and the attentive reception is a lovely welcome.

Hôtel Solara
7 rue de France (04.93.88.09.96). **Double** €65-€75. **Credit** AmEx, MC, V.
Although the front entrance looks a bit dodgy, rooms at this good-value central place are bright and tidy with fresh Provençal fabrics.

Hôtel Windsor
11 rue Dalpozzo (04.93.88.59.35/ www.hotelwindsornice.com). **Double** €70-€120. **Credit** AmEx, MC, V.
This cult address is an arty oasis. Avoid the cheaper 'standard' rooms and insist on one that has been decorated by a contemporary artist, including Ben, Peter Fend and Lawrence Weiner; there's also an exotic garden, aviary, hammam and small gym.

Villa Victoria
33 bd Victor Hugo (04.93.88.39.60/www.villa-victoria.com). **Double** €85-€125. **Credit** AmEx, DC, MC, V.
This comfortably renovated *belle époque* villa has a spacious, colourful bar area with wrought-iron furniture. Rooms are decently sized if heavily floral, but the real treat is the luxuriant garden with tall palm trees and rose pergola.

Resources

Municipal museums are free the first and third Sunday of the month. **Passe-musées** (€8 one day; €15 three days; €25 seven days) gives free entrance.

Hospital
Hôpital St-Roch, 5 rue Pierre Dévoluy (04.92.03.77.77/www.chu-nice.fr).

Internet

Webstore, 12 rue de Russie (04.89.06.90.00). **Open** 9am-noon, 4-7pm Mon-Sat. **Wayne's** (*see p259*).

Police

Police Municipal, 10 cours Saleya (04.93.54.10.32). **Open** 8.30am-5pm Mon-Thur; 8.30am-3.45pm Fri.

Post office

21-23 av Thiers (04.93.82.65.00).

Tourist information

Office du Tourisme et des Congrès, 5 promenade des Anglais (08.92.70.74.07/ www.nicetourism.com). **Open** 9am-6pm daily.
Branches: Aéroport Nice Côte d'Azur, Terminal 1 (04.93.21.44.11); Gare SNCF, av Thiers (04.93.87.07.07).

Getting there

From the airport

Nice airport is 8km west of the city centre. Bus No.98 runs between the airport and the gare routière, No.99 between the airport and the main SNCF station (about every 30 mins), bus No.23 goes from terminal 1 only to St-Maurice via the station. A taxi costs about €35 to the city centre.

By car

You can leave the A8 at exit 54 or 55, but it's more scenic to take the N7 or N98 along the coast.

By train

The main SNCF station is at 3 av Thiers, served by frequent trains from Paris and Marseille. Local

A painterly palette in **Vieux Nice**. *See p248.*

services to Menton also stop at Gare Riquier, near to the port and the old town. The Gare St-Augustin is near the airport. The private Gare de Provence, just north of the main station, is the departure point for the narrow-gauge Var Valley Train des Pignes.

By bus

The *gare routière* (04.93.85.61.81) on promenade du Paillon is the hub for most Côte d'Azur coach services, including international buses running Rome-Nice-Barcelona and Venice-Milan-Nice. **Phocéens Cars** (04.93.85.66.61) runs buses between Marseille and Nice via Aix and Cannes (3 daily Mon-Sat, 1 on Sun), 2 buses daily Mon-Sat from place Masséna to Toulon, via Cannes and Hyères. **RCA** (04.93.39.11.39, www.rca.tm.fr) runs regular buses along the coast to and from Cannes and Menton.

Getting around

By bus

An extensive bus network including 4 Noctambus night buses is run by **Sunbus** (10 av Félix Faure & 29 av Massena (04.93.13.53.13, www.sunbus.com, 29 av Massena, open 7.15am-6.30pm Mon-Fri, 8am-6pm Sat). Tickets cost €1.30. Bus-hop passes cost €4 (1-day), €12.96 (5-day) and €16.77 (7-day), available from Sunbus, tobacconists and newsagents.

By taxi

Nice taxis are notoriously expensive. To order a taxi, call Central Taxi Riviera (04.93.13.78.78).

The Arrière Pays

Mere minutes from Nice, the backlands known as the Arrière-Pays are the farthest thing from fast-paced urban energy, a quietly delightful mini-wilderness of olive groves, pine woods, wild flowers and perched villages, offering spectacular panoramas, cool summer breezes and rustic cuisine.

Just 18km north of Nice on the D2204/D15, **Contes**, once a Roman settlement, juts out from a steep slope overlooking the Paillon de Contes torrent. This quiet village found itself in the limelight in 1508 when the bishop of Nice was called in to rid the place of a nasty plague of caterpillars. Legend has it that he succeeded through force of pious good will; giving the townsfolk good reason the build the **Chapelle Ste-Hélène** in 1525, remarkable today for its tiny Renaissance fountain in the courtyard. This area is also famous for all things olive: at the **Site des Moulins** olives are still pressed (Dec-Mar) in a 17th-century water-powered mill. Olive oil, salted olives and *tapenade* are on sale at **Gamm Vert** agricultural cooperative (rte de Châteauneuf, 04.93.79.01.51, closed Mon & Sun). In tiny **Châteauneuf-de-Contes**, 4.5km west, the 11th-century **Madone de la Vieille Ville** church is worth a look. A well-marked 30-minute walk leads to the atmospheric, abandoned ruins of Vieille Châteauneuf.

On the main square at **Coaraze**, self-styled *village du soleil* (village of the sun), the town hall bears dazzling modern sundials by Jean Cocteau and other artists. The village is a maze of vaulted passageways, cypress-lined gardens and fountains. Also of interest here is the unusual **Chapelle Notre-Dame de la Pitié**, otherwise known as the 'Blue Chapel' for its monochrome scenes depicting the life of Christ. At the top of the village is the old cemetery, with cement boxes for burials because the rocks are too hard even for pickaxes. The name Coaraze supposedly derives from *caude rase*

The Riviera & Southern Alps

(cut tail): wily medieval inhabitants caught Old Nick napping and grabbed hold of him, obliging him to shed his lizard-like tail to escape; a modern pavement mosaic illustrates the tale.

Only 16km from Nice on the D2204/D21, isolated on a rocky spur above olive groves, **Peillon** has not a single quaint boutique, the wise residents having banned all touristic upscaling. Instead there are narrow cobblestoned streets, pantiled roofs and an unbeatable panorama of the valley. Not to be missed is the minuscule **Chapelle des Pénitents Blancs** at the entrance to the village. The chapel is kept closed to protect the 15th-century frescoes of the Passion attributed to Giovanni Canavesio, but the works can be viewed through a grating with coin-operated lights. Further upstream – or a lovely one-and-a-half-hour ridge walk from Peillon – **Peille** is a quiet village with handsome Romanesque and Gothic doorways and a ruined feudal castle at the top. Peille's feisty inhabitants, who accepted numerous excommunications in the Middle Ages rather than pay taxes to the bishop, speak a dialect all their own known as *Pelhasc*.

At the bottom of the Peillon valley, the agricultural township of **L'Escarène** was once an important staging post on the Route du Sel (salt road) from Nice to Turin; for once, a piece of modern engineering – the viaduct of the Nice-Sospel railway – complements the view of the old town. Further up the Route du sel, the fortified medieval crossroads of **Lucéram** is worth a detour for the 15th-century **Eglise Stes-Marguerite-et-Rosalie** (rue de l'Eglise, closed Mon & Tue), which has a striking Italianate onion-domed yellow and pink belfry. Outstanding altarpieces by the Bréa school recount the story of St Marguerite, a shepherdess-martyr burned at the stake, who was one of Joan of Arc's favourite voices-in-her-head.

Where to stay & eat

In Contes, **Le Chaudron** (176 av Flaminius Raiberti, 04.93.79.11.00, double €34-€48 half-board obligatory, menu €15, closed Sun dinner & 2wks in Aug) has a good restaurant and six charming rooms – a discreet getaway in the centre of town. One of the most quietly celebrated Arrière-Pays destinations is the **Auberge du Soleil** (5 chemin Camin de la Beguda, 04.93.79.08.11, closed Nov to mid-Feb, double €62-€85, menus €18-€25) in Coaraze, where the bucolic vista is a treat for city-sore eyes. Try the *giboulette de lapin* (rabbit stew) and heavenly nougat ice cream. Rooms are simple but comfortable, and overlook the valley. At the edge of the village, five cosy rooms, a panoramic terrace and a pool are a nice surprise

at the **Relais de Feuilleraie** (04.93.79.39.90, double €43-€60, menus €15-€29). In Peillon, the **Auberge de la Madone** (2 pl Auguste Arnulf, 04.93.79.91.17, www.chateauxhotels.com/madone, closed 3wks Jan, mid-Oct to mid-Dec, double €95-€240, restaurant closed Wed, dinner by reservation, menus €45-€75) is a long-standing romantic hideaway with lovely antique-filled rooms, the best with loggias overlooking the village. The restaurant features refined Nissart specialities cooked up by chef Milo and his son Thomas, who trained under super-chef Alain Ducasse. The view from the flower-lined terrace is one of the best in the Arrière-Pays. In Peille, stop for a *pastis* and *pissaladière* at the café **Chez Cauvin** (5 pl Carnot, 04.93.79.90.41, closed dinner Mon, Thur & Sun, lunch Fri & Sat, all Tue & Wed, menu €18). Make yourself comfortable in the simple **Auberge de Peille Belvédère** (1 pl Jean Miol, 04.93.79.90.45, double €40, menus €14.50-€20), and dig in to a lovely meal, including excellent gnocchi. In l'Escarène, the **Auberge du Château** (26 rue du Château, 04.93.79.57.13, menu €12) serves homely country cuisine.

Resources

Tourist information

Coaraze *Office du Tourisme, 7 pl Ste-Catherine, 06390 Coaraze (04.93.79.37.47).* **Open** *Apr-Sept* 10am-noon, 2-5pm daily. *Oct-Mar* 10am-noon, 2-5pm Mon, Tue, Thur, Fri.
Contes *Syndicat d'Initiative, pl d'Albert Olivier, 06390 Contes (04.93.79.13.99/www.ville-contes.fr).* **Open** 2-5pm Mon-Fri.
Lucéram *Maison du Pays, la Placette, 06440 Lucéram (04.93.79.46.50).* **Open** 10am-noon, 2-5.30pm Tue-Sat.
Peille *Syndicat d'Initiative, Mairie, pl Carnot, 06440 Peille (04.93.91.71.71).* **Open** 9am-noon Mon-Fri.
Peillon *Syndicat d'Initiative, Mairie, 672 av de l'Hôtel de Ville, 06440 Peillon (04.93.79.91.04).* **Open** 8.30am-noon Mon, Tue, Thur; 8.30am-noon, 2-5pm Mon-Fri.

Getting there

By car

The starting point to get to the Arrière Pays is the D2204 Paillon Valley road, which begins at the Acropolis roundabout in Nice as bd J-B Verany.

By train/bus

The Nice-Sospel line (4-6 trains daily) stops at Peillon, Peille and L'Escarène, but only L'Escarène has a station in easy reach of the town; Peillon and Peille are a 5km walk from their respective stations. There are buses from Nice to Peillon and Peille (3 daily Mon-Sat), to L'Escarène and Lucéram (4 daily Mon-Sat), and to Contes and Coaraze (2 Mon-Sat); for details call the Nice *gare routière* (04.93.85.61.81).

The Corniches

Take the high road: the coast roads east of Nice offer beaches, donkey traffic, Roman victories and racing-driver thrills.

The three roads – high, middle and low – between Nice and Menton (and, by extension, the strip of coastline in between) conjure up visions of sun-bronzed boys and babes speeding along in convertible sports cars. Beware, however, as in summer the traffic often slows to a crawl – which at least gives you time to admire the glorious panoramas. The Basse Corniche (N98 – also known as the Corniche Inférieure) hugs the coast, passing through all the towns and resorts. To take some of the strain, the wider Moyenne Corniche (N7) was hacked through the mountains in the 1920s. The highest route – the Grande Corniche (D2564) – follows the ancient Roman Aurelian Way, and is the most spectacular of the three.

The glamour of the Corniches has its tragic side, too. On 13 September 1982, a car carrying Princess Grace of Monaco and her daughter Stéphanie swerved off the N53, a treacherous descent full of hairpin bends that leads from the Grande Corniche to the Moyenne Corniche. Stéphanie survived; her mother didn't. There's no memorial, but a bunch or two of fresh flowers can generally be seen by the roadside.

Basse Corniche: Villefranche-sur-Mer

Founded in the 14th century by Charles d'Anjou II as a duty-free port, Villefranche's stacked-up dusty-rose, ochre and apricot houses and trompe l'oeil frescoes redefine the term 'picturesque'. On the tiny cobblestoned port, you might still see old women mending fishing nets; in the old town rue Obscure, an eerie vaulted passageway, has changed little since the Middle Ages; and the Combat Naval Fleuri, held on the Monday before Ash Wednesday, is a surreal sight as dozens of fishing boats bedecked with flowers invade the harbour.

The deep harbour between the headlands of Mont Boron to the west and Cap-Ferrat to the east was used as a US naval base until France withdrew from the military wing of NATO in 1966. The quayside, lined with brasseries and overlooking a long sandy public beach, is a haven of high class compared to the days when it used to service sailors. At the western end of the port, the postage stamp-sized **Chapelle de**

St-Pierre-des-Pêcheurs, once a store for fishing nets, was covered in 1957 with lively frescoes by Jean Cocteau, depicting the life of St Peter. At the top of the old town, the **Eglise St-Michel** (04.93.01.73.13, open 9am-7pm daily) is a handsome 18th-century Italianate church. It boasts an impressive organ built in 1790 by the Niçois Grinda brothers, still played during Sunday mass. Wander through the old streets west of the church to the 16th-century Citadelle. It was built by the Dukes of Savoy and comes complete with a drawbridge. It now houses the voluptuous female figures of local sculptor Antoniucci Volti in the **Musée Volti** and 100 minor works by artists such as Picasso, Hartung, Picabia and Miró in the **Musée Goetz-Boumeester**. The citadel is also used for outdoor theatre and film, mainly in summer.

Chapelle de St-Pierre-des-Pêcheurs
quai Courbet (04.93.76.90.70). **Open** *Mar-June*
9.30am-noon, 3-7pm Tue-Sun. *July-Sept* 10am-noon,
4-6.30pm. *Oct-Feb* 9.30am-noon, 2.30-6pm Tue-Sun.
Closed 15 Nov-15 Dec. **Admission** €2; free under-
12s. **No credit cards.**

Musée Volti & Musée Goetz-Boumeester
Citadelle, av Sadi Carnot (04.93.76.33.27). **Open**
10am-noon, 2.30-6pm Mon, Wed-Sat; 2.30-6pm Sun
(July, Aug until 7pm). **Admission** free.

Where to stay & eat

The **Hôtel Welcome** (1 quai Amiral Courbet, 04.93.76.27.62, www.welcomehotel.com, closed 2wks Dec, double €132-€184) is a splendid yellow and blue portside establishment, and although it now bears little resemblance to the hotel of the same name where Jean Cocteau fraternised with young sailors amid opium fumes in the 1920s, the artist's spirit lives on. The airy rooms all have balconies, most of which overlook the port. Up a steep alley above several more casual eateries, **L'Echalote** (7 rue de l'Eglise, 04.93.01.71.11, open dinner only, closed Sun and Nov or Jan, menus €25-€36) serves locally inspired, often fruity, dishes in intimate surroundings. The **Fille du Pêcheur** (04.93.01.90.09, closed Wed, menu €27) and **l'Oursin Bleu** (04.93.01.90.12, closed Tue & 15 Jan-15 Feb, menu €32) sit side by side on quai

Courbet. *Tagliatelle aux fruits de mer* is a winner at the former, fish soup is spooned out at the table at the latter. The fisherman who supplies both restaurants moors his boat 20m away in the port. Next to the fountain, **Michel's** (04.93.76.73.24, closed Tue & Nov, average €30) is the pick of the restaurants in place Amélie Pollonais. Daily specials range from sea bream to *pissaladière* and some of the world's largest mussels. On the same square, friendly **Le Cosmo Bar** (04.93.01.84.05, average €20) offers a quality fish catch and some of the best *salade niçoise* on the Riviera and is also great for breakfast before the Sunday antiques market.

Resources

Tourist information

Office de Tourisme, Jardin François Binon, 06230 Villefranche-sur-Mer (04.93.01.73.68/ www.villefranche-sur-mer.com). **Open** *July, Aug* 9am-7pm daily. *Sept-June* 9am-noon, 2-6pm Mon-Sat.

Basse Corniche: Cap-Ferrat

The lush, secluded peninsula jutting out between Villefranche and Beaulieu is a millionaires' paradise of high-hedged, security-gated mansions. Part-time residents include Hubert de Givenchy and Andrew Lloyd Weber. The promontory is also a walker's dream, with a well-signed rocky 10km path that winds around the Cap en route to the Plage des Fosses, a pebbly beach ideal for small children. Swimmers can also drive or walk to tree-lined La Paloma beach, 500m south of Port St-Jean.

The approach to the Cap is dominated by the **Villa Ephrussi-de-Rothschild**, an Italianate extravaganza built for Béatrice de Rothschild in the early 1900s. Inside, Béatrice had appropriate settings recreated for her immense art collection, which focuses on the 18th century, along with Impressionist paintings and Oriental knick-knacks. The villa is surrounded by seven hectares of fountain-filled Spanish, Japanese and Italian gardens with arresting views.

On the eastern side of the peninsula, luxury yachts have replaced fishing boats at St-Jean-Cap-Ferrat, which remains a pleasant spot for an evening drink followed by a stroll along the marina and Port St-Jean. Further west, the **Zoo du Cap-Ferrat** has 300 species, from flamingos and talking cockatoos to Himalayan bears and Siberian tigers – all more likely to impress tots, however, than adult animal-lovers.

Villa Ephrussi-de-Rothschild

1 av Ephrussi-de-Rothschild (04.93.01.45.90/ www.villa-ephrussi.com). **Open** 10am-6pm daily (until 7pm July, Aug). **Admission** €8.50; €6.50 7-18s; free under-7s. **Credit** AmEx, MC, V.

Zoo du Cap-Ferrat

117 bd du Général de Gaulle (04.93.76.07.60/ www.zoocapferrat.com). **Open** *Apr-Oct* 9.30am-7pm daily. *Nov-Mar* 9.30am-5.30pm daily. **Admission** €10; €6.70 3-10s; free under-3s. **Credit** MC, V.

Where to stay & eat

You almost expect to see gentlemen in top hats strolling through the manicured gardens of the stately **Grand Hôtel du Cap-Ferrat** (71 bd Général de Gaulle, 04.93.76.50.50, www.grand-hotel-cap-ferrat.com, closed Jan & Feb, double €245-€1,100, menu €73), hidden near the tip of the peninsula. A new wing opens in 2004. Non-residents can eat at the classically elegant Le Cap restaurant or stop for a drink at the hotel's Somerset Maugham Bar, where the writer occasionally wandered from his nearby home to meet friends for gin tonics; for a €60 entrance fee, you can take the funicular to Le Club Dauphin, a spectacular spill-over pool. Set on a hill, the more affordable **Hôtel le Panoramic** (3 av Albert 1er, www.hotel-lepanoramic.com, 04.93.76.00.37, closed 11 Nov-20 Dec, double €105-€140) has airy rooms with terraces and a dazzling harbour view. **La Voile d'Or** (av Jean Mermoz, 04.93.01.13.13, www.lavoiledor.fr, closed mid-Oct to mid-Apr, double €215-€815, menus €45-€90) by Port St-Jean might be mistaken for an impressive family villa. The chintzy lounges are made up for by heavy wood finishes elsewhere, amazing balcony views, sauna, gym, private beach and a waterside pool. The small yet elegant menu at the restaurant brims with fresh fruit and seafood. **Capitaine Cook** (11 av Jean Mermoz, 04.93.76.02.66, closed Wed & lunch Thur, menus €22-€28), just 50m up the hill, cracks out lobster and oysters galore on its vine-covered terrace. In St-Jean itself, **Le Provençal** (2 av Denis Séméria, 04.93.76.03.97, menus €35-€150) prides itself on a seafood mêlée accompanied by figs. The **Hôtel Brise Marine** (58 av Jean Mermoz, 04.93.76.04.36, hotel-brisemarine.com, closed Nov-Jan, double €135-€148) is an ochre- and turquoise-trimmed villa with a tangled garden, near La Paloma beach. **Résidence Bagatelle** (11 av Honoré Sauvan, 04.93.01.32.86, double €75-€140), on a quiet backstreet between St-Jean and Beaulieu, has modestly priced rooms and an overgrown citrus garden.

Resources

Tourist information

Office de Tourisme, 59 av Denis Séméria, 06230 St-Jean-Cap-Ferrat (04.93.76.08.90). **Open** *June-Aug* 8.30am-6.30pm daily. *Sept-Apr* 8.30am-noon, 1-5pm Mon-Fri.

Villefranche-sur-Mer: free-trade in scenic views. *See p269.*

Basse Corniche: Beaulieu-sur-Mer

A charming *belle époque* resort that was long a favourite with holidaying Russian and British aristocrats, Beaulieu still has an old-world feel, with its genteel but non-designer boutiques and ubiquitous palms. Well-heeled Sunday strollers and their yapping dogs jostle for space on the scenic promenade Maurice Rouvier, which links the port of Beaulieu to St-Jean-Cap-Ferrat via the late David Niven's pink castle. Gustave Eiffel and Gordon Bennett, legendary director of the *New York Herald Tribune*, lived here. So did archaeologist Theodore Reinach, who was so enamoured of Ancient Greece that he built a fastidious and not-to-be-missed reconstruction of a fifth-century BC Athenian house. Situated in front of the Baie des Fourmis – so called because of the ant-like black rocks dotted about – the **Villa Kerylos** is now a museum, with sunken marble bath, reclining sofas and antique-looking frescoes galore (plus hidden modern amenities such as showers). Up the road towards the Port de Plaisance, the **Musée de Patrimoine Berlugan** covers local history since Palaeolithic times. The **Casino**, a turn-of-the-century jewel on the seafront offering roulette, blackjack and baccarat for the wealthy Cap-Ferrat crowd, is deliciously retro. So is

the **Tennis Club de Beaulieu-sur-Mer**, a quaint club with eight clay courts.

The Basse Corniche continues eastwards through the ribbon development of Eze-Bord-de-Mer and on to **Cap-d'Ail**, which would have little to recommend it were it not for a splendid pebbly beach, Plage la Mala, a democratic favourite equally prized by the Monaco jetset and Italian day-trippers. Be prepared for the weary trek down the steps (and up again).

Casino de Beaulieu-sur-Mer
4 rue Fernand Dunan (04.93.76.48.00/ www.partouche.com). **Open** *slot machines* 11am-4am daily; *gaming room* 8.30pm-4am daily. **Admission** (over-18s only) *slot machines* free; *gaming room* €11. **Credit** AmEx, DC, MC, V.

Musée du Patrimoine Berlugan
av des Hellènes (04.93.01.68.66). **Open** *Sept-July* 1-6pm Fri, Sat. **Admission** free.

Tennis Club de Beaulieu-sur-Mer
4 rue Alexandre 1er de Yougoslavie (04.93.01.05.19). **Open** *office* 9am-4pm daily (courts open 9am until late daily). **Admission** *1 hr* €10; *1 day* €16; *1 wk* €75. **No credit cards.**

Villa Kerylos
impasse Gustave Eiffel (04.93.01.01.44/www.villa-kerylos.com). **Open** *Feb-Nov* 10am-6pm daily. *Dec, Jan* 2-6pm Mon-Fri; 10am-10pm Sat, Sun & school holidays. **Admission** €7.50; €5.50 7-18s, students; free under-7s. **Credit** AmEx, MC, V.

Where to stay & eat

Relaxed yet stylish bistro **Les Agaves** (4 av Maréchal Foch, 04.93.01.13.12, open dinner only, closed mid-Nov to mid-Dec, menu €30), in the Palais des Anglais, once a grand hotel now apartments, is popular for its seasonal, creative cooking. Italianate **Le Métropole** (15 bd Leclerc, 04.93.01.00.08, www.le-metropole.com, closed Nov, double €170-€460) has gardens running down to the sea, floral rooms, heated pool and a restaurant (menus €55-€86) serving inspired seafood-heavy dishes. Celebrities and royalty once flocked to *fin de siècle* **Florentine Hôtel La Réserve** (5 bd Leclerc, 04.93.01.00.01, closed 15 Nov-15 Dec, double €160-€2,440), with spa and stunning pool, where refined but pricey Mediterranean cuisine (menus €98-€135) includes liberal sprinklings of caviar, foie gras and truffles. Blue and white **Hôtel Le Havre Bleu** (29 bd du Maréchal Joffre, 04.93.01.01.40, www.hotel-lehavrebleu.fr, double €52-€66) is a clean, simple villa. Lively retro-colonial **L'African Queen** (port de Plaisance, 04.93.01.10.85, average €35) offers carpaccios and a chance to rub elbows with stars like Jack Nicholson or Bono. Next door, **Marco Polo** (04.93.01.06.50, closed Wed & Thur lunch, average €40) offers marina-side seafood.

Resources

The daily food market (pl Charles de Gaulle) also has clothes and housewares on Saturday.

Tourist information

Office de Tourisme, pl Georges Clemenceau, 06310 Beaulieu-sur-Mer (04.93.01.02.21/www.ot-beaulieu-sur-mer.fr). **Open** *July-Sept* 9am-12.30pm, 2-6pm Mon-Sat; 9am-12.30pm Sun. *Oct-May* 9am-12.30pm, 2-6pm Mon-Sat.

Moyenne Corniche: Eze

Perched photogenically on a pinnacle of rock 430m above sea level, Eze started life as a Celto-Ligurian settlement, passing over the ages from Phoenicians to Romans, Lombards to Saracens. Its glorious vistas inspired Nietzsche, who would stride up here in the 1880s from his Eze-Bord-de-Mer home, composing the third part of *Thus Spake Zarathustra* in his head. The steep mule path he took (now called sentier Frédéric-Nietzsche) snakes through olive and pine groves. Allow an hour and a quarter for the uphill slog from the Basse Corniche.

During the Eze d'Antan Festival in the third week of July, the village is swamped by sword-toting knights and colourful pageantry. In what remains of Eze's castle, at the summit of the village, the **Jardin Exotique** is a prickly blaze of flowering cacti and succulents, offering a sweeping panorama over red-tiled roofs to the coast. Aside from the metal workshops, cutesy art gallery-cum-souvenir shops and perfectly rejuvenated Provençal lanes, there is little else of substance to actually see in Eze; but a place where donkeys still haul groceries up the steep lanes can't be entirely ruined.

Port St-Jean at **Cap-Ferrat** still has the allure of a fishing village. *See p270.*

Jardin Exotique

rue du Château, Eze (04.93.41.10.30). **Open** *Mar, Apr* 9am-6.30pm daily. *May, June* 9am-7pm daily. *July, Aug* 9am-8pm daily. *Sept-Feb* 9am-5pm daily. **Admission** €2.50; free under-12s. **No credit cards.**

Where to stay & eat

Nestling beneath the castle ruins, the **Nid d'Aigle** (rue du Château, 04.93.41.19.08, closed 8 Jan-8 Feb, menu €22) is an informal, family-run restaurant specialising in local dishes such as artichokes with goat's cheese and pasta pistou. Sumptuous rooms at the **Château de la Chèvre d'Or** (rue du Barri, 04.92.10.66.66, www.chevredor.com, double €260-€750) have sweeping coast views, and there's a pool too. New chef Philippe Labbé keeps up the gastronomic tradition at the restaurant (menus €60-€130) with classics such as sea bass, fillet of beef and local lamb. **Château Eza** (rue de la Pise, 04.93.41.12.24, www.chateza.com, closed Nov-Mar, double €230-€530), a mini-castle at the top of endless crooked steps, with quite feasibly one of the greatest views in the entire world, reopens after a change of ownership and renovation in April 2004. Its outdoor terrace restaurant has romantic balconies for two.

Resources

Tourist information

Office de Tourisme, pl Général de Gaulle, 06360 Eze (04.93.41.26.00/www.eze-riviera.com). **Open** *Apr-Oct* 9am-6.30pm daily. *Nov-Mar* 9am-5pm daily.

Grande Corniche: La Turbie

Built under Napoléon along the Aurelian Way (known in this stretch as the Via Julia Augusta), the Grande Corniche winds for 32km over breathtaking drops: a favourite with wannabe Formula One drivers, masochistic cyclists, scenery-lovers and *To Catch a Thief* fans.

Dominating the road is **La Turbie** (from *tropea*, Latin for trophy), a spectacularly located village that is often shrouded in mountain mist. Basking in sleepy charm, it consists of little more than a row of ancient ochre houses, two town gates and an 18th-century church, **St-Michel-Archange**, with a host of 'attributed to' and 'school of' works. What puts the village on the map is the Roman **Trophée des Alpes**, a partly restored curve of white Doric columns set in a hilltop park. The Trophée was erected in 6 BC to celebrate Augustus' victory over rowdy local tribes; a copy of an inscription praising Augustus can be seen on the trophy, though the huge statue of the victor that once adorned it has long since gone. Inside the

adjoining museum is a scale model of the original, and diverse artefacts unearthed on the site. Little pieces of history abound in the village as you wander around, from the odd carved doorway to bits of ancient city wall.

If it's sport, not history, you're after, the **Monte-Carlo Golf Club** is an 18-hole course with a vertiginous view. Star-gazers should head for **Eze Astrorama**, a wildly popular astronomical show (planetarium, telescopes, videos), north of La Turbie.

Eze Astrorama

rte de la Revere (04.93.41.23.04). **Open** *July, Aug* 6-11pm Mon-Sat. *Sept-June* 6-11pm Fri, Sat. **Admission** €10; €5 children; free under-6s.

Monte-Carlo Golf Club

rte du Mont Agel (04.93.41.09.11). **Open** 8am-6pm daily (until 8pm June Sept). **Admission** €90 Mon-Fri, €110 Sat, Sun. **Credit** MC, V.

Trophée des Alpes

18 av Albert 1er, La Turbie (04.93.41.20.84). **Open** *mid-May to mid-Sept* 9.30am-6pm daily. *mid-Sept to mid-May* 10am-1pm, 2.30-4.30pm Tue-Sun. **Admission** €4.60; €3.10 18-25s; free under-18s.

Where to stay & eat

Besides its rather sumptuous guestrooms La Turbie's **Hôtellerie Jérôme** (20 rue de Compte de Cessole, 04.92.41.51.51, doubles €89-€136) boasts a classy restaurant (closed Mon & Tue, menus €50-€90), giving regional recipes a Ligurian twist. Clinging to a precipice off the Grande Corniche, **Roquebrune Vista Palace** (04.92.10.40.00, www.vistapalace.com, closed Feb, double €203-€389) is a St-Moritz-style wedge of dated 1970s grandeur; the vast triangular rooms have a luxury-liner feel, and spellbinding views. Main restaurant **Le Vistaero** (closed lunch mid-May to Sept, menus €60-€90) cultivates classic French cuisine with a hint of Provençal whimsy; less stuffy **Le Corniche** (average €20) indulges in more Mediterranean fare.

Getting there & around

By train

Villefranche, Beaulieu, Eze-Bord-de-Mer and Cap-d'Ail are served by regular trains from Nice (*see p284-5*). Beaulieu is also served by faster Italian trains on the Nice-Genova run, but not by French TGVs. Shuttle buses connect Eze-Bord-de-Mer station and Eze village every hour or so.

By bus

RCA (04.93.85.61.81) No.100 bus runs along the Basse Corniche between Nice and Menton. No.112 Nice-Beausoleil stops in Eze (and ends there on Sun); No.116 runs Mon-Sat Nice and Peille via La Turbie.

The Riviera & Southern Alps

Monaco & Monte-Carlo

The Grimaldis' own theme park, Monaco makes entertaining viewing as you watch the ridiculously rich at play.

Controlled by the Grimaldi family since 1297, Monaco is the last remaining European state aside from the Vatican to have an autocratic ruler. The prince holds benevolent but absolute sway over 39,000 residents, of whom only 7,000 are Monégasque citizens, and they, in return, are happy to barter democracy for tax breaks.

Monaco has pizazz, thanks to its royal family, famous visitors, grand hotels and *belle époque* architecture, but it's losing its picture-perfect edge. The new concrete jetty is an eyesore in the once-glamorous, yacht-filled Port Hercule, along with the new Port Palace Hôtel, an aesthetically crude mass of white marble, gilt and blue glass.

One look, though, at the Casino and its square lined with Ferraris, Lamborghinis and Rolls-Royces (many hired just for the stay), with white-gloved *gendarmes* directing traffic, and you know this is a world apart. Here you can indulge your dress-code daydreams: from sables to labels, you can never be too ostentatiously rich, though the young and wealthy are more likely to be wearing Diesel. As for jewels, if they're real, never fear: there's a policeman for every 55 residents and some 250 surveillance cameras guard the 2km² realm.

It wasn't always like this. When Menton and Roquebrune were whisked away from Grimaldi control in 1848, Europe's poorest state lost its main source of revenue: a tax on lemons. Then-ruler Charles III called in financier François Blanc, who set up the Société des Bains de Mer (SBM) to operate a casino on a hill named after the prince: Monte-Carlo. The crown took 10% of SBM profits. Blanc gave the French government a 4.8-million-franc loan so it could finish building the Paris Opéra; in return, he got the Opéra's architect, Charles Garnier, to design the casino, plus a French-built railway to ship in gamblers. So fruitful was the venture that in 1870 the flourishing principality abolished taxes for nationals and residents, and for companies based and trading here. Since then, SBM (now 69% Grimaldi-family-owned, 31% by private shareholders) has expanded its folio and owns, or manages, the majority of the four-star, luxury slice of Monaco's tourism.

Nowadays, Monaco has a government of sorts, the 24-member National Council elected by Monégasque citizens (not residents). The Council's main job is to pass French legislation on to the reigning prince: if he approves, it becomes law in Monaco too; if he doesn't, it doesn't. Relations between the principality and its bigger neighbour run pretty smoothly. Much more smoothly, indeed, than the affairs of the Grimaldi family. Dapper Rainier III's fairytale 1956 marriage to Grace Kelly came to a tragic end when Princess Grace was killed in a car accident in 1982. Princess Caroline's first marriage ended disastrously, and her second husband was killed in a speedboat race; she since united the European blue-bloods by wedding Prince Ernst-August of Hanover. Her sister Stéphanie is a media magnet for her less-than-royal choice of suitors (after a former bodyguard husband and a Swiss elephant-trainer boyfriend, she recently married a trapeze artist). But the real pressure is on heir to the throne Prince Albert, who remains single.

Sightseeing

Glitzy Monte-Carlo is just one of Monaco's six districts. It packs in the **Casino**, with its **Salle Garnier** opera house (currently closed for renovation), designer-label shops, posh hotels and the **Café de Paris**. Fontvieille is a concrete sprawl of high-rise, high-price apartments and home to the **Stade Louis II**. Its small harbour has become a fashionable waterfront spot for lunch, apéritif or dinner while watching the yachts. Fontvieille's *pièce de résistance* is the divinely fragrant Rose Garden, dedicated to Princess Grace, and, in the park behind, a brilliantly curated Sculpture Trail of works by major international artists.

Further back from the sea, Monaghetti is mainly residential, but home to the cactus-filled **Jardin Exotique** and the **Monaco Tennis Club**. Le Rocher – or Monaco-Ville – is the medieval town, dominated by the **Palais Princier**. The neo-Byzantine **Cathédrale de Monaco** is the final resting place of many Grimaldi princes and of Princess Grace. More Grimaldis can be seen in the **Historial des Princes de Monaco** waxworks museum. Head for the infinitely more fascinating **Musée Océanographique** or the old masters in the **Musée de la Visitation**. La Condamine, the harbour area, has a good daily food market, the **Eglise Ste-Dévote** and industrial lofts that

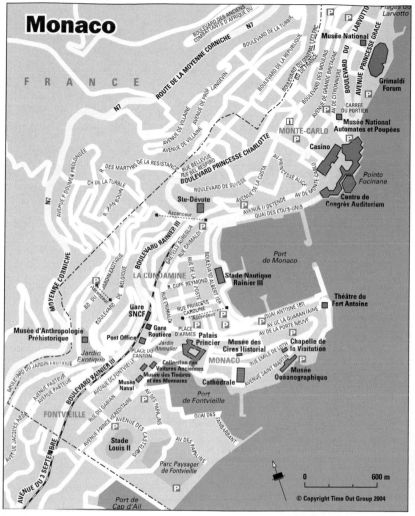

Monaco

have been turned into workshops for a select group of international artists (Arman, Botero, Sosno, Adami), whose work is often exhibited at the **Marlborough** (4 quai St-Antoine, 00.377-97.70.25.50), Monaco's best commercial gallery. Pedestrianised rue Princesse Caroline is becoming the fashionable place to hang out. If you're on the celebrity watch, Larvotto, the eastern strip where Monaco's beaches are located is your best bet: you may glimpse residents Boris Becker, Ringo Starr or Claudia Schiffer at **Le Sporting Club**.

Cathédrale de Monaco

av St-Martin (00.377-93.30.87.70). **Open** 8.30am-7pm daily, no entry during mass. **Admission** free. Built in 1875, the cathedral has a 15th-century altarpiece by Louis Bréa, tombs of the Monégasque princes and a simple slab for Princess Grace.

Collection des Voitures Anciennes

terrasses de Fontvieille (00.377-92.05.28.56). **Open** 10am-6pm daily. **Admission** €6; €3 8-14s; free under-8s. **No credit cards**.
Prince Rainier's vintage car collection, from a 1903 De Dion Bouton to a 1986 Lamborghini Countach.

Monaco: millionaires' rock.

Eglise Ste-Dévote

pl Ste-Dévote (00.377-93.50.52.60). **Open** 9am-7pm daily. **Admission** free.
This portside church was built in 1870 on the site where Monaco's patron saint was supposedly guided ashore by a dove after a shipwreck off Africa. Medieval pirates stole the saint's relics; they were caught and the ship was set on fire. A replica goes up in flames in front of the church every 26 January.

Jardin Animalier

terrasses de Fontvieille (00.377-93.25.18.31). **Open** *Mar-May* 10am-noon, 2-6pm daily. *June-Sept* 9am-noon, 2-7pm daily. *Oct-Feb* 10am-noon, 2-5pm daily. **Admission** €4; €2 under-14s. **No credit cards.**
Mini-zoo housing monkeys, wild beasts and exotic birds collected by Prince Rainier.

Jardin Exotique et Grotte de l'Observatoire/Musée d'Anthropologie Préhistorique

62 bd du Jardin Exotique (00.377-93.15.29.80, www.monte-carlo.mc/jardinexotique). **Open** 9am-6pm daily (till 7pm mid-May to mid-Sept). **Admission** €6.70; €3.40 6-18s; free under-6s. **Credit** MC, V.
This succulent wonderland has everything from giant Aztec agaves to ball-shaped 'mother-in-law's cushion' cacti. The grotto contains a stalactite- and stalagmite-lined Neolithic dwelling 60m underground. The museum traces Stone Age life on the Riviera, with bones of extinct animals and impressive Cro-Magnon skeletons found in the Grimaldi caves just over the border in Italy.

Jardin Japonais

av Princesse-Grace, Larvotto. **Open** 9am-sunset daily. **Admission** free.
This enchanting garden designed by Yasuo Beppu creates a Zen experience alongside the Mediterranean. Bridges, waterfalls, a tea-house and the neatly pruned vegetation are only surpassed by the wondrous poi carp languishing in their ponds.

Musée de la Chapelle de la Visitation

pl de la Visitation (00.377-93.50.07.00). **Open** 10am-4pm Tue-Sun. **Admission** €3; €1.50 6-14s; free under-6s. **No credit cards.**
The 17th-century chapel houses religious paintings by Rubens, Zurbaran and Italian Baroque masters.

Musée des Cires Historial des Princes de Monaco

27 rue Basse (00.377-93.30.39.05). **Open** 11am-5pm daily (till 6pm Mar-Sept). **Admission** €3.80; €2 8-14s; free under-8s. **No credit cards.**
Everything you've ever wanted to know (and probably rather more) about the Grimaldi dynasty writ in wax, with life-sized figures in full regalia.

Musée National Automates et Poupées

17 av Princesse Grace (00.377-93.30.91.26, www.monte-carlo.mc/musee-national). **Open** *Apr-Sept* 10am-6.30pm daily. *Oct-Mar* 10am-12.15pm, 2.30-6.30pm daily. **Admission** €6; €3.50 6-14s; free under-6s. **No credit cards.**

18th- and 19th-century dolls and mechanical toys, set in motion several times daily. It's worth checking if the Barbie designer collection is on show.

Musée Naval

terrasses de Fontvieille (00.377-92.05.28.48/ www.musee-naval.mc). **Open** 10am-6pm daily. **Admission** €4; €2.50 8-18s; free under-8s. **No credit cards.**
Prince Rainier's scale models of famous sea vessels.

Musée Océanographique

av St-Martin (00.377-93.15.36.00/www.oceano.mc). **Open** *Apr-Sept* 9am-7pm daily (till 7.30pm July, Aug). *Oct-Mar* 10am-6pm daily. **Admission** €11; €6 6-18s; free under-6s. **Credit** MC, V.
Albert I's aquarium contains nature's most bizarre creatures, plus bream circling endlessly like bored Monégasque millionaires. A live coral reef and a giant shark lagoon are a guaranteed thrill for kids.

Musée des Souvenirs Napoléoniens et Collection des Archives Historiques du Palais

pl du Palais (00.377-93.25.18.31). **Open** *June-Sept* 9.30am-6.00pm daily. *Oct, Nov* 10am-5pm daily. *Dec-May* 10.30am-noon, 2-4.30pm Tue-Sun. Closed 12 Nov-16 Dec. **Admission** €4; €2 8-14s; free under-8s. **No credit cards.**
Bonaparte buffs will enjoy the vast display of objects and documents from the First Empire, while the more Monaco-smitten can peruse an exhibit of historic charters and Grimaldi medals.

Musée des Timbres et des Monnaies

11 terrasses de Fontvieille (00.377-93.15.41.50). **Open** 10am-5pm daily (till 6pm July-Sept). **Admission** €3; €1.50 12-18s; free under-12s. **Credit** MC, V.
More conspicuous money in a coin and stamp display covering four centuries of Monégasque minting.

Palais Princier

pl du Palais (00.377-93.25.18.31). **Open** *June-Sept* 9.30am-6pm daily. *Oct* 10am-5pm daily. Closed Nov-May. **Admission** €6; €3 8-14s; free under-8s. **No credit cards.**
The sugary palace, built over a 13th-century Genoese fortress, is closed to the public when the prince is in residence (signalled by a red and white banner). The 30-minute tour takes in the frescoed gallery, sumptuous bedrooms, state apartments, throne room and mosaic courtyard. The changing of the guard takes place at 11.55am daily.

Arts & entertainment

Le Cabaret du Casino

pl du Casino (00.377-92.16.36.36). **Show** 10.30pm Wed-Sat. **Show & dinner** €60. **Credit** AmEx, DC, MC, V.
Slick cabaret shows offer an alternative to gambling. The 'Let's be Wild' show incorporates live animals and film music, in a red-velvety nightclub atmosphere with Hollywood murals.

Casino de Monte-Carlo

pl du Casino (00.377-92.16.20.00/www.casino-monte-carlo.com). **Open** (over-21s only, ID essential). *Salons européens* noon-late daily. *Slot machines* 2pm-late Mon-Fri; noon-late Sat, Sun. *Salons privés* 3pm-late daily. *Club anglais* 10pm-late daily. **Admission** €10 (€20 for Salons privés & Club anglais). **No credit cards.**
At the ornate Garnier-designed casino, old-fashioned precepts still apply: no clergymen or Monégasque citizens are allowed into the gaming rooms. For men, a sports jacket and tie are *de rigueur*. Roulette has a €5 minimum bet; stakes are higher in the Salons privés and the Club anglais.

Grimaldi Forum

10 av Princesse Grace (00.377-99.99.30.00/ www.grimaldiforum.com). **Open** noon-7pm Mon-Sat. **Admission** varies.
A modular glass and steel complex with everything from concert halls, art and trade shows to a cyber-café. It also hosts opera productions and innovative Ballet de Monte-Carlo productions while the Salle Garnier is under renovation.

Monte-Carlo Beach Club

av Princesse Grace (04.93.28.66.66). **Open** *Apr-Oct* 9am-6pm daily. *June-Sept* 9am-7pm. **Admission** €75; €50 mid-Sept to mid-May; €35/€45 guests at SBM-owned hotels. **Credit** AmEx, DC, MC, V.
The favoured summer playground for socialites is a concrete environment where you won't fit in if you're not in the latest designer casuals. Most of the action is by the huge heated seawater pool where Princess Stéphanie herself laps. Most facilities and restaurants are only open in July and August.

Monte-Carlo Country Club

155 av Princesse Grace (04.93.41.30.15/www.mccc.mc). **Open** *July, Aug* 8am-9pm daily. *Sept-June* 8.30am-8.30pm daily. **Admission** one-day €36; €26 under-18s. **Credit** AmEx, MC, V.
The swankiest club on the Riviera has clay tennis courts, squash, gym and a heated open-air pool (open May-Oct) with airjets, waterfalls and a counter-current basin for aquatic workouts.

The New Open Air Cinema

terrasses du Parking des Pêcheurs (00.377-93.25.86.80/ www.cinemasporting.com). **Open** mid-Aug to mid-Sept 9.30pm daily. **Admission** €10-€15. **No credit cards.**
On a warm summer evening, sit under the stars with a glass of rosé and watch the latest movie on top of the rock, at this Version Originale cinema with the largest open-air screen in Europe.

Stade Louis II

3 av des Castelans (00.377-92.05.40.11). **Open** guided tours at 2.30pm & 4pm Mon, Tue, Thur, Fri. **Admission** €4; €2 under-12s. **No credit cards.**
This unsightly circular concrete block houses a gigantic sports complex with gyms, an athletics track, a pool – and the soccer pitch where AS Monaco plays its home games (*see p255*).

Stade Nautique Rainier III

quai Albert I (00.377-93.30.64.83). **Open** 9am-6pm daily (till 8pm July & Aug). *Ice-rink Dec-Mar* noon-6.30pm Mon-Thur; noon-9pm Fri; 10am-9pm Sat; 10am-6.30pm Sun. **Admission** €4.30; *ice-rink* €5.30. **No credit cards.**
This beautiful Olympic-sized seawater outdoor pool is a great place for serious swimming. In winter it turns into an ice-rink.

Les Thermes Marins de Monte-Carlo

2 av de Monte-Carlo (00.377-92.16.40.40/ www.montecarlospa.com). **Open** 8am-8pm daily (no treatments Sun). **Credit** AmEx, DC, MC, V.
This temple of thalassotherapy has state-of-the-art fitness centre and heated seawater pool. A one-day package with four marine treatments costs €130.

Restaurants

Bar et Boeuf

av Princesse Grace (00.377-92.16.60.60/www.alain-ducasse.com). **Open** 8pm-1am Tue-Sun (daily July, Aug). **Average** €80. **Credit** AmEx, DC, MC, V.
Ducasse's conceptual contemporary food revolves around *bar* (sea bass) and *boeuf* (beef). High tables and bar stools allow you to be both visible and approachable: high priorities in Monaco.

Le Café de Paris

pl du Casino (00.377-92.16.25.54). **Open** noon-2am daily. **Average** €50. **Credit** AmEx, DC, MC, V.
The renowned turn-of-the-century brasserie has an outdoor terrace so perfect for people-watching that it compensates somewhat for the pricey espresso. Try the crêpe Suzette, inadvertently invented here in 1898 when a creation by Escoffier caught fire.

Castelroc

pl du Palais (00.377-93.30.36.68). **Open** noon-2.30pm, 7.30-10pm Mon-Fri, Sun (lunch only mid-Sept to mid-June). Closed Dec, Jan. **Menus** €20-€39. **Credit** AmEx, DC, MC, V.
Don't be put off by the touristy air of the outdoor terrace: this affordable bistro is an established local haunt for seafood such as stockfish and scampi.

L'Eden Bleu

32 port de Fontvieille (00.377-99.99.99.69/ www.lamouledor.com). **Open** noon-2.30pm, 7.30-11pm Tue-Fri, Sun; 7.30-11pm Sat. **Average** €25. **Credit** MC, DC, V.
This wonderfully friendly waterfront brasserie serves the freshest *moules* cooked in 15 styles with *frites*, or plates of home-made pasta with seafood.

Huit et Demie

4 rue Princesse Caroline (00.377-93.50.97.02). **Open** noon-2.30pm, 7-11pm Mon-Sat. **Average** €38. **Credit** AmEx, DC, MC, V.
Fellini-esque surroundings and a huge terrace harbour gaggles of Italians, English and Monégasques. Fresh Mediterranean fare includes *beignets de courgettes* and sea bream *en papillotte*; fresh fruit soup with homemade lemon sorbet is divine.

Louis XV

Hôtel de Paris, pl du Casino (00.377-92.16.29.76/ www.alain-ducasse.com). **Open** 12.15-2.30pm,

How to do Monaco

To be taken seriously in Monaco's snootiest establishments, not only do you have to wear labels stylishly but you really ought to be driving the latest Mercedes cabriolet – or even better, get the chauffeur to pick you up in one. Arriving by yacht at the **Beach Club**'s La Vigie restaurant gives the right cachet in the daytime, while driving a Ferrari and wearing Bulgari jewels stands you in good stead at the **Casino** and **Hôtel de Paris**. Unless you dress like an aristo, spend like a royal and mingle with jetsetters, you'll rarely feel completely at ease in these seriously rich hangouts. If you need to check the price, you can't afford it and would be much better off renting a sunlounger on **Larvotto Plage** or staying at a more casual hotel than feeling stressed about not having the right swimsuit for the **Thermes Marins** or the right luggage for the **Hermitage**. If money's short, drink at a bar, rather than a nightclub and if you do venture into Jimmy'z (at **Le Sporting Club**),

get a long drink and make it last all evening. Casual wear is acceptable, but it tends to be more Ralph Lauren than London-urban-street. If you wear jeans, wear designer jeans, a shirt or polo shirt, not a T-shirt, and avoid scuffed shoes or trainers. Don't attempt to dine in a smart restaurant or venture near the **Casino** without a jacket and tie (men) or smart evening wear (women), and don't approach nightclub doormen in large gaggly gangs – you won't get in, unless you're with David Coulthard. Aside from that, sunbathing on Larvotto's sandy beach, seeing an exhibition at the **Grimaldi Forum**, eating on the terrace at **Zebra Square**, catching a movie at the **New Open Air Cinema** and then sipping a nightcap at the **Café de Paris** is a blissful way to spend a day, and won't break the bank. If you really must catch a glimpse of a superstar, get tickets for a show at **Le Sporting Club**'s Sporting d'Eté – if it's a major artiste, there will probably be a Grimaldi in the audience.

Casino de Monte-Carlo. *See p277.*

8-10.30pm Mon, Thur-Sun (plus 8-10pm Wed in July, Aug). Closed two weeks late-Feb & all Dec. **Menus** €90-€160. **Credit** AmEx, DC, MC, V.
The ultimate Riviera gilt trip with one of the most glamorous outdoor terraces in the world, this was Alain Ducasse's first restaurant and is still his best. The food is a contemporary update of peasant food from Nice to Genoa, complemented by a great cellar.

Il Terrazzino

2 rue des Iris (00377-93.50.24.27). **Open** noon-2.30pm, 7-11pm Mon-Sat. **Menus** €17 lunch, €37 dinner. **Credit** AmEx, DC, MC, V.
Locals come here for a blowout meal of Italian (Campania) specialities. The *antipasti*, a veritable conveyor belt of grilled vegetables, is irresistible, as are the vast platters of three types of pasta – each. Wear elasticated trousers.

Bars & nightlife

Le Living Room

7 av des Speluges (00.377-93.50.80.31/ www.mcpam.com). **Open** 11pm-dawn Mon-Sat. **Credit** AmEx, DC, MC, V.
No entrance fee but this great little private club does charge €15 a drink. Still that's half the price and double the atmosphere of Jimmy'z. Great dance music, live musicians and a lively crowd of 18-50-somethings vetted at the door of this gently kitsch joint.

McCarthy's

7 rue du Portier (00.377-93.25.87.67/www.monte-carlo.mc/mccarthys). **Open** 6pm-5am, daily. Live music daily June-Aug, & Thur-Sat Sept-May. **Credit** AmEx, DC, MC, V.
Catch up with the locals at this friendliest of Irish bars where everyone hangs out, from the local carpenter to Bono. Foccacias and pizza are served to soak up the Guinness and the terrace-bar buzzes from June to September.

La Note Bleu

Plage Larvotto, av Princesse Grace (00377-93.50.05.02). **Open** *June to mid-Sept* daily 9am-11pm. *mid-Sep to May* 9am-7pm. Closed Mar & Thur in Nov. Live music Thur-Sun June to mid-Sept. **Average** dinner €60; tapas from €5. **Credit** DC, MC, V.
Dine on tapas on the jetty at sunset, or share a candlelit dinner on the sands of Larvotto Plage with jazzy blues tinkling from the bar behind. Alternatively, pitch up later and snuggle into thickly cushioned sofas with a drink.

Slammers

6 rue Suffren Reymond (00.377-97.70.36.56). **Open** 5pm-1am daily. **Credit** MC, V.
Join the 20-to-40-something afterwork and yachty crowd for happy-hour (5-8pm), when mama provides home-made nibbles, drinks are two for the price of one, and people actually talk to each other. The decor is cosy and candlelit with low-level seating.

Le Sporting Club + Jimmy'z

av Princesse Grace (00.377-92.16.22.77). **Open** 10.30pm late daily. **Admission** €46 (incl 1st drink). **Credit** AmEx, DC, MC, V.
This six-hectare seaside complex is frequented by royalty, models, pop stars, Middle Eastern princes and mini-skirted *demoiselles* in Cartier. Jimmy'z (00.377-92.16.36.36, open Apr-Nov 11.30pm-dawn Wed-Sun), the disco for beautiful people, requires chic dress and an ample wallet. Le Sporting d'Eté entertainment complex hosts big-name crooners.

Stars & Bars

6 quai Antoine 1er (00.377-97.97.95.95). **Open** *July, Aug* 10am-5am daily. *Sept-June* 11am-midnight Mon-Thur; 11am-2am Fri-Sun. **Credit** AmEx, MC, V.
This portside American-style sports bar is packed with locals, plus racing drivers and the odd rock or film star. There's Tex-Mex food, a kids' playroom, a video games room and a small upstairs club (admission €3-€8) with live bands.

Zebra Square

Grimaldi Forum, 10 av Princesse Grace (00.377-99.99.25.50). **Open** *Bar* noon-6am daily. *Restaurant* noon-3pm, 8pm-midnight daily. **Credit** AmEx, DC, MC, V
The hot new after-hours lounge and restaurant atop the Grimaldi Forum has lots of high-tech, low-light atmosphere and oversized cushioned booths. The nouveau-Provençal cuisine is rather good, and the terrace is a wonderfully romantic spot.

Shopping

Luxury knows no bounds in Monte-Carlo, from the rash of jewellery shops near the Casino to the boutiques along boulevard des Moulins and avenue Princesse Grace. In place du Casino, Galerie du Metropole is an upscale three-storey mall and home to the Fnac CD, book and hi-fi store. Rue Grimaldi offers the flip, hip side of fashion. True Monégasques shop in the Centre Commercial in Fontvieille, a large mall with a mega-supermarket.

Where to stay

Hôtel Columbus

23 av des Papalins (00.377-92.05.90.00/ www.columbushotel.com). **Doubles €240-€290. Credit** AmEx, DC, MC, V.
Launched by Ken McCulloch, founder of the wildly successful Malmaison chain, this hip lifestyle hotel on the Fontvieille harbour has given a contemporary spin to Monaco's stuffy, old-world image. The 153 rooms and 31 suites are decked out in soft lavenders and creamy beiges, with luxurious leather upholstered beds, CD player and Internet. The bar is a haunt of Formula One drivers, presided over by part-owner, David Coulthard.

Hôtel de France

6 rue de La Turbie (00377-93.30.24.64/www.monte-carlo/france). **Double €74-€90. Credit** MC, V.
In a backstreet of La Condamine, this small, welcoming hotel is bright and cheerful with fresh yellow and rust check fabrics in the bedrooms, some of which have a sofa-bed and balcony.

Hôtel Helvetia

1bis rue Grimaldi (00.377-93.30.21.71/www.monte-carlo.mc/helvetia). Closed 2wks Dec. **Double €77-€85. Credit** AmEx, MC, V
A stone's throw from the port, this clean, affordable hotel has unremarkable decor but friendly staff.

Hôtel Hermitage

sq Beaumarchais (00.377-92.16.40.00/www.sbm.mc). **Double €355-€750. Credit** AmEx, DC, MV, V.
The Hermitage is a *belle époque* landmark of understated elegance, with a stained-glass-domed *jardin d'hiver* designed by Gustav Eiffel. Rooms are comfortable and modern; the more expensive ones have balconies with harbour views. Its rooftop restaurant Le Vista Mar (00.377-92.16.27.72, menus €39-€55) serves up exquisite seafood.

Hôtel de Paris

pl du Casino (00.377-92.16.30.00/www.sbm.mc). **Double €365-€750. Credit** AmEx, DC, MC, V.
This rococo-style palace built in 1865 is the most luxurious of the three hotels owned by the Société des Bains de Mer and was frequented by everyone from Sarah Bernhardt to Churchill. If funds are short, soak up the atmosphere in its old-world bar.

Monte-Carlo Grand Hôtel

12 av des Spélugues (00.377-93.50.65.00/ www.montecarlograndhotel.com). **Double €245-€485. Credit** AmEx, DC, MC, V.
This high-rise hotel built over the sea may be glitzless and efficiently modern, but it's also family-friendly, with a choice of restaurants and bars, a fitness centre, rooftop swimming pool and casino.

Resources

The international phone code for Monaco is 00.377. From France, dial 00.377 then the number. When phoning a Monégasque number from inside the principality, omit the code. To call abroad from Monaco, use the international prefix 00 then the country code (33 for France) and omit the first zero. Letters from Monaco must bear Monégasque stamps. Although Monaco is not part of the European Union, the euro is now the official currency.

Hospital

Centre Hospitalier Princesse Grace, av Pasteur (00.377-97.98.99.00).

Internet

Stars & Bars, see p279.

Police

Police Municipale, pl Marie (00.377-93.15.28.26).

Post office

1 av Henri Dunant (00.377-97.97.25.25). **Open** 8am-7pm Mon-Fri; 8am-noon Sat.

Tourist information

Direction du Tourisme et des Congrès de la Principauté de Monaco *2A bd des Moulins, 98000 Monaco (00.377-92.16.61.16/www.monaco-tourisme. com).* **Open** 9am-7pm Mon-Sat, 10am-noon Sun.

Getting there & around

By helicopter

Heli-Air Monaco, Fontvieille (00.377-92.05.00.50). A seven-minute flight from Nice airport costs €84.35; €49.85 under-12s; free under-2s.

By car

Leave the A8 autoroute at exit 57 or 58 or by N98 (Basse Corniche), the coast road from Nice to the west and Cap Martin and Menton in the east.

By train

Monaco-Monte-Carlo station is served by regular trains on the Cannes-Nice-Menton-Ventimiglia line, as well as a few TGVs direct from Paris (around 6hr).

By bus

From Nice *gare routière*, **RCA** and **Broch** (04.93.21.30.83) run services every 15mins Mon-Sat (every 20mins Sun) along the Basse Corniche road between Nice and Menton, stopping at Monaco.

Roquebrune to Menton

Although studded with millionaires' hideaways, the secluded coves on the
Cap-Martin coast can be enjoyed by anyone.

Roquebrune-Cap-Martin

Wedged between Monaco and Menton, the
lovely **Cap-Martin** promontory is cloaked in
pines, firs, olive and mimosa trees, and studded
with luxury hideaways, most of them hidden
from mere mortals' view in the millionaires' row
of the Domaine privé du Cap-Martin. Empress
Eugénie, Churchill, Coco Chanel, Le Corbusier
and WB Yeats lived (and, in the case of the
latter two, died) here, as did a less-respectable
resident, African dictator Emperor Bokassa.

The well-maintained Sentier Douanier coast
path winds around the peninsula passing by **Le
Cabanon**, Le Corbusier's tiny modular beach
shack (call tourist office for visits, 10am Tue &
Fri), set just before the Pointe de Cabbé. West of
here, the curved Plage du Golfe Bleu beach is a
favourite landing spot for hang-gliders. The
architect, who drowned while swimming here in
1965, had the foresight to design himself an
impressive memorial in the cemetery (open
10am-7pm daily) in the handsome old, perched
village of **Roquebrune**, which rises above the
Cap-Martin peninsula. It started life in the tenth
century as a fortified Carolingian fiefdom. For
five centuries, from 1355, it belonged to the
Grimaldis, until it was incorporated into France
in 1860. Up the steep stairways at the top of the
village is the **Château de Roquebrune**,
which was almost fairytale-ified by an English
owner in the 1920s until the locals kicked up
a fuss. It now has four floors of historical
displays, lordly armour and a dungeon.

For the energetic, the Sentier Massolin is
little more than a giant staircase leading from
Roquebrune village down to the coast via
Carnolès, the much less exclusive but popular
seaside suburb that sprawls between the Cap
and Menton. It has a bustling shingle beach;
there are two more secluded beaches just below
Cap-Martin Roquebrune rail station, as well as
plenty of tiny paths into the water off the
Sentier Douanier.

Château de Roquebrune

pl William Ingram (04.93.35.07.22). **Open** *Feb,
Mar, Oct* 10am- 12.30pm, 2-6pm daily. *Apr-June,
Sept* 10am-12.30pm, 2-6.30pm daily. *July, Aug* 10am-
12.30pm, 3-7.30pm daily. *Nov-Jan* 10am-12.30pm,
2-5pm daily. **Admission** €3.50; €1.60 7-18s; free
under-7s. **No credit cards.**

Where to stay & eat

On the water's edge, the **Hôtel Westminster**
(14 av Louis Laurens, 04.93.35.00.68/
www.westminster06.com, closed mid-Nov to
mid-Feb except Christmas/NewYear, double
€70-€87) is a small, reasonably priced gem with
glorious views. A secluded shingle cove lies at
the end of a winding path just down the street.
On the eastern tip of Cap-Martin is the friendly
modern **Hôtel Alexandra** (93 av Winston
Churchill, 04.93.35.65.45, www.hotel-
alexandra.net, double €72-€108), where most
rooms have Jacuzzi baths and balconies with
views towards the bay of Menton and Italy. In
Roquebrune Village, **Au Grand Inquisiteur**
(18 rue du Château, 04.93.35.05.37, closed Mon
& Tue lunch and mid-Nov to mid-Dec, menus
€24.50-€36) serves up gastronomic beef and
fish dishes. For a breathtaking sea view, dine
on the terrace of the lovely **Hôtel-Restaurant
des Deux-Frères** (pl des Deux Frères,
04.93.28.99.00, www.lesdeuxfreres.com, closed
15 Nov-15 Dec, double €65-€101, menus €24-€45), an
impeccably run inn at the foot of the *vieux
village*. Its elegant restaurant serves generously
garnished, herb and garlic packed Provençal
cuisine. Across the square, atmospheric,
troglodyte café **La Grotte** (3 pl des Deux
Frères, 04.93.35.00.04, closed Wed and 1wk Oct)
offers salads, *plats du jour* and pretty good
pizzas. **L'Idée Fixe** (1 rue de la Fontaine,
04.93.28.97.25, closed Sun, menu €23) serves
tasty fish dishes and imaginative seafood.

Resources

Tourist information

*Office de Tourisme, 218 av Aristide Briand,
Carnolès, 06190 Roquebrune (04.93.35.62.87/
www.roquebrune.com).* **Open** *May-June, Sept* 9am-
12.30pm, 2-6.30pm Mon-Sat. *July, Aug* 9am-1pm, 3-
7pm daily. *Oct-Apr* 9am-12.30pm, 2-6pm Mon-Sat.

Menton

Claiming the mildest climate on the Riviera,
Menton, last stop before the Italian border, is
France's answer to the Costa Geriatrica. As well
as the elderly, lemon trees thrive here and the

humble fruit is juiced, iced, painted on plates or amassed in gigantic kitsch floats for the Fête du Citron each February. The town's festive calendar extends to a street theatre and young musicians fair in May, a volley of jazzy music evenings in July, the prestigious Festival de Musique every August and a Mediterranean garden event in mid-September.

After more than six centuries of Monégasque domination, Menton voted to become French in 1860. In the same year, British physician Henry Bennet recommended Menton for its healthy air. Before long, wealthy Britons and Russians began gracing its shores, bringing tea rooms and botanical gardens, and staying in grand *belle époque* hotels, now sadly all demolished or turned into flats. Writers, artists and musicians – among them Monet, Maupassant, Flaubert and Liszt – also sojourned here. The sea air wasn't always restorative. Tuberculosis sufferers Robert Louis Stevenson (who discovered opium in Menton) and Katherine Mansfield, in her tiny villa Isola Bella, found the seaside dampness worsened their condition.

The tone of present-day Menton is still set by its dilapidated *belle époque* villas. But there's modernity, too: artist-aesthete-poet Jean Cocteau left his mark, as did architect-designer Eileen Gray, whose minuscule 1930s cube-house, later owned by painter Graham Sutherland, is visible on the route de Castellar.

Menton has few nocturnal hotspots, and the gambling at the **Casino** is low-key. Year-round, however, smartly dressed Italians stroll the seafront promenade du Soleil, scooping up fruit in the excellent covered market behind the quays, or sunbathe topless on the uninspiring pebbly beach. Indeed, border-hopping is a favourite pastime with many Italian workers commuting into France daily, while Mentonnais head into Italy for bargains at Ventimiglia market on Friday or to load up on olive oil, Italian wine and Parmesan cheese at the supermarket. Beware of counterfeit goods though, they are liable to be confiscated by border guards and you could be fined.

The **Musée des Beaux-Arts** in the Palais Carnolès, the 18th-century summer retreat for the Princes of Monaco, has European paintings ranging from Italian primitives and a beautiful Virgin and Child by Louis Bréa to modern artists including Graham Sutherland. The palace is surrounded by the **Jardin des Agrumes**, an extravaganza of 400 citrus trees.

Just north towards Gorbio, the **Eglise Russe**, financed by rich Russian families in 1892, was built by Danish architect Tersling, who also built the grandiose Palais de l'Europe in 1909-10 (the former casino, now the tourist office and art gallery), which overlooks the Jardin Bioves, a municipal garden planted with orange trees, palms and statuary.

The Salle des Mariages in the **Hôtel de Ville** was decorated by Jean Cocteau in the 1950s. It features splendid murals of swirling seas, a fish-eyed fisherman and his straw-hatted bride, as well as kitsch palm tree candelabras and a mock panther-skin carpet. There's more Cocteau in a fortified stone bastion in the harbour, where the **Musée Jean Cocteau** contains works donated by the artist, ranging from beach-pebble mosaics and Aubusson tapestries to vases and pastels.

Two blocks north of the Hôtel de Ville, the **Musée de Préhistoire Régionale** shows what life was like on the Riviera a million years ago, with remains from Vallonet, Lazaret and the Grimaldi caves. East of here, the Italianate *vieille ville*, a largely pedestrian zone, climbs uphill to the Baroque **St-Michel** church (open 10am-noon, 3-5pm Mon-Fri), which has a gilded marble interior with a trompe l'oeil dome and an altarpiece of St Michael slaying the dragon.

Higher still in the *vieille ville* is the **Cimetière du Vieux-Château**, the terraced cemetery, where artist Aubrey Beardsley and the Reverend William Webb Ellis – credited with being the first person to pick up a soccer ball and run with it, thus inventing rugby – rest in peace, along with a lot of Russian dignitaries. Heading east, promenade de la Mer leads into Garavan, a leafy quarter of romantic villas. Just off the promenade, the **Jardin Val Rahmeh** is a tropical garden founded in 1905 by Lord Radcliffe. Rare trees from Easter Island, the Canaries and New Zealand can be found here. Towards Gorbio, Major Lawrence Johnston, designer of Hidcote Manor gardens, began the **Serre de la Madone** botanical garden in 1919. A vast breadth of species grow in the gardens landscaped with pools and fountains. Other gardens including the nearby Jardin des Colombières, planted with olives and cypresses, the Jardin de la Villa Maria Serena, around a villa designed by Charles Garnier, and the Jardin Fontana Rosa, can be visited through the Service du Patrimoine. Amateur botanists can also take in the **Giardino Botanico Hanbury** just across the Italian border, which has inspiring rose gardens and an Australian forest.

Casino de Menton

av Félix Faure (04.92.10.16.16). **Open** *slot machines* 10am-3am daily; *salle de jeux* 7pm-3am Mon-Thur, Sun; 7pm-4am Fri, Sat. **Admission** (over 18s only) *slot machines* free; *salle de jeux* €10. **Credit** AmEx, MC, V.

Eglise Russe

12 rue Paul Morillot (04.93.35.70.57). **Open** 5pm Sat; 10am Sun. **Admission** free.

Menton claims to have the mildest climate on the Riviera.

Hôtel de Ville
17 rue de la République (04.92.10.50.00). **Open**
Salle des Mariages 8.30am-12.30pm, 2-5pm Mon-Fri.
Admission €1.50. **No credit cards.**

Musée des Beaux-Arts
Palais Carnolès, 3 av de la Madone (04.93.35.49.71).
Open 10am-noon, 2-6pm Mon, Wed-Sun.
Admission free.

Musée Jean Cocteau
Le Bastion, quai Napoléon III (04.93.57.72.30).
Open 10am-noon, 2-6pm Mon, Wed-Sun.
Admission €3; free under-18s. **No credit cards.**

Musée de Préhistoire Régionale
rue Lorédan Larchey (04.93.35.84.64). **Open** 10am-
noon, 2-6pm Mon, Wed-Sun. **Admission** free.

Jardin botanique exotique du Val Rahmeh
av St-Jacques, Garavan (04.93.35.86.72). **Open**
May-Sept 10am-12.30pm, 3-6pm Mon, Wed-Sun.
Oct-Apr 10am-12.30pm, 2-5pm Mon, Wed-Sun.
Admission €4; €2 6-18s, students; free under-6s.
No credit cards.

Jardin des Colombières
372 rte des Colombières, Garavan (04.93.10.97.10).
Open by appointment. **Admission** €5. **No credit
cards.**

La Serre de la Madone
74 rte de Gorbio (04.93.57.73.90). **Open** ring for
details. **Admission** €8; free under-16s.

Giardino Botanico Hanbury
*Pont San Luigi, La Mortola, Vintimille, Italy (00-39-
01.84.22.95.07).* **Open** *Jan-Sept* 9.30am-5pm daily.
Oct-Dec 9.30am-5pm Mon, Tue, Thur-Sun.
Admission €6.50; €3 6-18s, students; free under-6s.
No credit cards.

Where to stay & eat

The *belle époque* **Hôtel Aiglon** (7 av de la
Madone, 04.93.57.55.55, www.hotelaiglon.net,
closed 5 Nov-15 Dec, double €83-€205), set back
from the beach towards Carnolès, is the epitome
of old Riviera charm. It has a garden with
towering banana palms, rooms with frescoes
and a pool. **Hôtel des Ambassadeurs** (3 rue
des Partouneaux, 04.93.28.75.75, double €180-
€430) is a mini-palace with a central location,
grand entrance and vast bedrooms. The **Hôtel
Chambord** (6 av Boyer, 04.93.35.94.19,
www.hotel-chambord-menton.cote.azur.fr,
double €100-€110) is smart and functional.

In the heart of the old town, stone-vaulted
Braijade Meridiounale (66 rue Longue,
04.93.35.65.65, closed lunch in July & Aug, and
Tue & Wed Sept-June, closed 15 Nov-8 Dec,
2nd wk in Jan, menus €25-€45) is a favourite
for local specialities, such as brochettes grilled
over an open fire, tripe and *aïoli*. Highly
recommended **Pistou** (9 quai Gordon Bennett,
04.93.57.45.89, closed Sun dinner & Mon and 15
Nov-15 Dec, menus €13-€20) sits on the Vieux

Port overlooking the Plage des Sablettes, and specialises in shellfish, *bouillabaisse* and paella. **La Coquille d'Or** (1 quai Bonaparte, 04.93.35.80.67, average €35) serves excellent Provençal-style seafood in glitzy surroundings.

Resources

Internet access
Café des Arts *16 rue de la République (04.93.35.78.67).* **Open** 7.30am-10pm Mon-Sat.

Tourist information
Office de Tourisme *Palais de l'Europe, 8 av Boyer, 06500 Menton (04.92.41.76.76, www.villedementon.com).* **Open** *June-Sept* 8.30am-6pm Mon-Sat; 10am-noon Sun. *Oct-May* 8.30am-12.30pm, 1.30-6pm Mon-Sat.
Service du Patrimoine *Hôtel d'Adhémar de Lantagnac, 24 rue St-Michel (04.92.10.97.10).* **Open** 10.30am-12.30pm, 2-6pm Mon-Sat.

North of Menton

From Menton, a series of narrow roads fans out through dramatic mountain scenery to a cluster of *villages perchés*. **Gorbio** sits on a hilltop due north of Roquebrune. A growing number of tourists are attracted to its narrow arched streets, especially for the Procession des Limaces (snails) on the feast of Corpus Christi in June. Don't expect a live snail race, however:

it's a procession of villagers carrying snail shells made into tiny oil lamps. From June to August the town's squares play host to a torrent of classical and folk bands.

Up the tortuous D22 from Menton, **Ste-Agnès** hangs from the rock at 780m above sea level and has spectacular panoramas of the coastline. The **Fort Maginot**, built in the 1930s when the village was a strategic point in Riviera defences, has some impressive cannons and tunnels. Local festivals include the lavender fête in June, Andean music in August and a celebration of the mushroom in mid-October.

High in the hills **Castillon**, the 'artists' village', is a regrettably prettified town with Disneylandish boutiques. Its redeeming feature, in fact, is an exit: the ancient mule trail to Ste-Agnès, which makes for a lovely two-hour hike over the Verroux pass and the Pas du Loup.

After skirting the *vieille ville* of Menton, the route de Castellar (D24) winds uphill towards the Italian border to fortified medieval **Castellar**, a tiny *village perché* without a trace of cute gentrification. It attracts walkers and lunchers from Menton. A free tour (in French) starts 2.30pm each Sunday opposite the Mairie.

Fort Maginot
Ste-Agnès (04.93.35.84.58). **Open** *July-Sept* 3-6pm daily. *Oct-June* 2.30-5.30pm Sat, Sun. **Admission** €3.05; €1.52 7-15s; free under-7s. **No credit cards**.

Cannes to Ventimiglia by train

The Riviera & Southern Alps

Heaven is a train line that runs from 6am until midnight cheaply, efficiently and regularly on one of the prettiest routes in the world. When you arrive at Nice airport, or at any of the 20 stations on the line, be sure to pick up a copy of the Cannes to Ventimiglia train timetable. Armed with this and an €11 Carte Isabelle unlimited day pass you can pretty much 'do' the Riviera, stopping off at leisure (avoid the stations either side of Nice-Ville if time is limited). Most attractions, except Eze and Roquebrune where the sights are a hike away, are within spitting distance of the often tiny railway stations.

Most of the half-hourly or so services are state-of-the-art double-decker affairs with big windows from which to watch the hotspots. The old blue trains are rare nowadays although they do have the advantage of manually operated doors which the locals pull right open when the train is in motion to cool passengers down – dangerous, but effective air-conditioning.

0 hour: Cannes Station right in town close to the shops and five minutes from the glamour of La Croisette.
7 min: Golfe-Juan Walk out to the harbour stocked with glitzy yachts and restaurants.
11 min: Juan-les-Pins Head down avenue Docteur Fabre to the Casino, shops and public beaches.
14 min: Antibes Lands you at the Port Vauban marina; Fort Carré and the old town are a five-minute stroll away.
18 min: Biot-sur-Mer For killer whales at Marineland, a public beach and buses to stunning hilltop Biot proper.
21 min: Villeneuve-Loubet-Plage Slightly tacky resort with a pebbly public beach.
27 min: Cagnes-sur-Mer Real French town with cracking daily market and fine old town Haut-de-Cagnes on the hill.
30 min: Cros-de-Cagnes: Very tacky resort with a pebbly public beach.
34 min: St-Laurent-du-Var For the gloriously inexpensive CAP3000 shopping complex.

Where to stay & eat

Les Terrasses in Gorbio (88 pl de la République, 04.93.35.95.78, average €25) serves refined Provençal platters, local pasta and salads. Friendly **Hôtel St-Yves** (76 rue des Sarrasins, 04.93.35.91.45, closed 20 Nov-20 Dec, double €30) in Ste-Agnès offers small but comfortable rooms with large beds. The half-board option (€40 per person) has country dishes served in the homely restaurant. For typical regional fare try the bar-restaurant **Le Logis Sarrasin** (40 rue des Sarrasins, 04.93.35.86.89, lunch only except July-Aug, closed Mon and mid-Oct to mid-Nov, menus €15-€28). In Castillon, **Hôtel La Bergerie** (chemin Strauss, 04.93.04.00.39, closed Nov, double €65, restaurant closed Mon-Fri from Sept to Easter, average €28) has rustic rooms, a small pool and a good restaurant. In Castellar, the **Hôtel des Alpes** (1 pl Clemenceau, 04.93.35.82.83, closed mid-Nov to mid-Dec, double €45, restaurant closed some Thur in Oct & Jan, menus €9-€19) has cheerful rooms, most with sea view; its restaurant serves regional fare.

Resources

Tourist information

Castillon *Syndicat d'Initiative, rue de la République, 06500 Castillon (04.93.04.32.03).*

Open 10am-noon, 1-5pm daily.
Gorbio *Mairie, 30 rue Garibaldi, 06500 Gorbio (04.92.10.66.50).* **Open** 8.30am-12.30pm Mon, Thur; 8.30am-12.30pm, 1.30-5.30pm Tue, Wed, Fri.
Ste-Agnès *Espace Culturel des Traditions, 51 rue des Sarrasins, 06500 Ste-Agnès (04.93.35.87.35).* **Open** 9.30am-1pm, 2-5pm Tue-Sun.

Getting there

By car

Leave the A8 at exit 58 and follow the Grande Corniche down to Roquebrune, exit 59 for Menton (last exit before Italy), or one of the three Corniches from Nice. Gorbio is 9km northwest of Roquebrune-Cap-Martin on the narrow D23. For Ste-Agnès, take rte des Castagnins from Menton, which becomes the D22 (13km). Castillon is 10km up the D2566 Sospel road from Menton. Castellar is 6km up the D24.

By train

Local trains on the Nice-Ventimiglia line stop at Roquebrune-Cap-Martin (just before the headland), Carnolès (just beyond), at Menton and Menton-Garavan stations. There are also daily TGV connections between Paris and Menton.

By bus

RCA Menton (08.20.42.33.33) runs a regular daily service from Menton Gare Routière (next to the train station) along the Basse Corniche to Nice, stopping at Carnolès, Roquebrune and Monaco, and hourly shuttle buses from Carnolès station to Roquebrune village.

village, buy a picnic from the market or proceed to walk around Cap-Ferrat via David Niven's old villa.
60 min: Eze Grab a waiting taxi to the arresting *village perché* or climb up the signposted pathway opposite the station.
64 min: Cap d'Ail Wonderful walking around the smallest of the rocky, herb-scented, sea-splashed Caps.
70 min: Monaco Brand new station bang in the centre of the Principality.
74 min: Roquebrune Cap-Martin Head up to the *vieux village*, down for the two beaches or east for a walk around the lovely Cap to Carnolès station.
78 min: Carnolès Family fun a few minutes away on the beach, otherwise wander down to avenue Winston Churchill for the coastal walk.
81 min: Menton Five-minutes on foot will grant you *belle époque* romanticism by the beach.
84 min: Menton-Garavan Still a beach and plenty of villas.
93 min: Ventimiglia Welcome to Italy. Cheap Parmesan, Ligurian cuisine and a fine daily market await just minutes from the station.

37 mins: Nice St-Augustin Nice airport is a (not signposted) five-minute walk away. Not a lot of people know that.
43 min: Nice-Ville Change for Paris, Milan and Turin. Brings you out on avenue Jean Médecin, Nice's shopping high street that leads to the beach, a 15-minute walk away.
50 min: Nice Riquier a stroll to the Vieux Port.
53 min: Villefranche-sur-Mer Picture-perfect seaside resort with long beach, excellent restaurants and a delightful castle.
56 min: Beaulieu-sur-Mer Walk into the

The Riviera & Southern Alps

Grasse & the Gorges du Loup

Flowers, not grass, made the fortune of this Provençal town, still the place for a whiff of the perfume industry before branching out into the mountainous wilds.

Grasse

Grasse's perfumed history dates back to the days of Catherine de Medici, who decided its balmy micro-climate, and the reputation of its tanning industry, would make it the perfect place to turn out the perfumed gloves that were the must-have item of every Renaissance It-girl. When these gloves went out of fashion, the Grassois continued to perfect the art of perfume-making and the town still boasts easily toured factories that continue to extract precious floral essences for the likes of Dior, Chanel and Yves Saint Laurent. Until a few decades ago this industry kept the fields of the Plan de Grasse below the town filled with flowers ready for harvest. Nowadays, the view of the valley is less romantic and less fragrant, with more factories than lavender and freesias: but Grasse itself retains plenty of old-world charm.

A train link to Cannes is being rebuilt, and this, combined with recent cultural subsidies and a determination to put Grasse firmly on the map, has resulted in a vibe of regeneration and optimism. Yet, unlike picture-perfect Valbonne and Mougins, Grasse's town centre has hung on to its earthy charm: paintwork peels, children play in the streets, washing hangs from the windows and men of all ages loiter in tiny squares. This is a rare phenomenon – a lived-in Old Town, rather than one prettied up for rich visitors and inhabitants. Grasse's wealthy prefer to hide out in the surrounding villages, leaving the centre to working families.

Steep staircases with hidden doorways jostle for space with the tacky glitz of the boulevard du Jeu de Ballon, which climbs up past the municipal casino. Much of the Old Town is pedestrianised, although some roads open to traffic are so narrow they hardly look wide enough for a baby's buggy. Cours Honoré Cresp, the main square, is home to a cluster of museums (park underneath the square to avoid getting stuck in traffic jams further up the hill). The rather fusty **Musée International de la Parfumerie** provides a useful, though not always easy to understand, introduction to the area's chief industry. Exhibits include perfume bottles from Antiquity to the present and Dior's 1947 New Look Bar Suit. The most interesting bit (and easily missed) is the greenhouse on the roof where you can smell different plants and herbs. Almost next door, in the 18th-century Hôtel Pontevès-Morel, is the **Musée de la Marine**, dedicated to Admiral François Joseph Paul (1722-88), Count of Grasse, whose defence of Chesapeake Bay during the siege of Yorktown helped bring the American War of Independence to an end. On the other side of the perfume museum, the **Musée d'Art et d'Histoire de Provence** gives an insight into the lives of the 19th-century Provençal bourgeoisie. From here, wander down through the touristy shops of rue Jean Ossola where, at No.2, the collection of the **Musée Provençal du Costume et du Bijou** is housed in the magnificent 18th-century home of the Marquise de Clapiers-Cabris, sister of flamboyant Revolutionary politician Mirabeau. Then turn right down rue Gazan into place du Petit Puy. The square is dominated by the **Cathédrale Notre-Dame-du-Puy**, a prime piece of Lombard-influenced Romanesque, much mauled in the 17th and 18th centuries. In its right aisle are several paintings by a young Rubens; it also houses *The Washing of the Disciples' Feet*, a rare religious subject by local boy Fragonard.

From here, head down the steps to the side of the Hôtel de Ville towards the place des Herbes, which was once Grasse's herb and vegetable market. Then head up the rue Droite (very crooked, despite its name), passing the Maison Doria de Roberti at No.24, which has a remarkable Renaissance stairwell. At the top look out for the portal and Gothic window of the old Oratory Chapel incorporated into the facade of Monoprix. Turn left here and head for cobbled place aux Aires with its fountain and street cafés. Every morning except Monday, the square hosts a flower and fresh produce market.

At the far end of the *jardin public* from the perfume museum stands the **Villa-Musée Fragonard**, the elegant 17th-century country house where artist Jean-Honoré Fragonard

(1732-1806) sought refuge when he fell from favour with the Revolutionary powers. The son of a not particularly successful glove-maker, Fragonard took himself to Paris at a young age. In the capital, he offered four paintings representing the steps of amorous conquest to Louis XV's favourite, the Comtesse du Barry. A virtuoso painter, Fragonard's chocolate-box works were all the rage, but were little liked by the children of the Revolution who, in any case, had decapitated most of his clients. The villa has *trompe l'oeil* murals by Fragonard's 13-year-old son and sketches and etchings by Fragonard himself.

Grasse's three big perfume houses, **Parfumeries Fragonard**, **Galimard** and **Molinard**, all offer factory tours, which let you see the process of distilling and blending. Fragonard's 1782 Historic Factory is in the centre of town and has a collection of stills and perfume bottles upstairs. Its modern Fabrique des Fleurs, opened in 1986, is where perfumes are made today. At Galimard's Studio des Fragrances, you can take an initiation course and, under the advice of Le Nez, mix up your own fabulous creation, to be funnelled into a charming glass bottle. The flowers at the heart of Grasse's perfume success are celebrated in the Expo-Rose in May and the Jasmine Festival the first weekend of August. The **Jardin de la Princesse Pauline** on avenue Thiers has a spectacular view and the scents of jasmine, roses and other aromatic plants. Further out in nearby Plascassier, the plants of the **Domaine de Manon** find their way into Chanel N°5, Guerlain's Jardin de Bagatelle and Patou's Joy.

If you've had enough of perfumeries, another good local buy is olive oil. After a decline following World War II, olive cultivation is on the increase and oil made from the local olive de Nice has been awarded an *appellation d'origine contrôlée*. Try the **Moulin à Huile Conti** (138 rte de Draguignan, 04.93.70.21.42, closed Sun, and Mon Feb-Oct) on the outskirts of Grasse. The shop is open year round, but to see the mill in action, visit during pressing season (Nov-Jan).

Domaine de Manon

36 chemin du Servan, Plascassier (04.93.60.12.76/ www.4acf.com/domaine_manon). Open May to mid-June roses 10am-5pm daily. late July to Oct jasmine 8am-11am daily. Admission 6; free under-12s. No credit cards.

Musée d'Art et d'Histoire de Provence

2 rue Mirabeau (04.93.36.80.20/ www.museesdegrasse.com). Open June-Sept 10am-6.30pm daily. Oct-May 10am-12.30pm, 2-5.30pm Mon, Wed-Sun. Closed Nov. Admission €3-€4; €1.50-€2 10-16s; free under-10s. Credit MC, V.

Musée International de la Parfumerie

8 pl du Cours Honoré Cresp ((04.93.36.80.20/ www.museesdegrasse.com). Open June-Sept 10am-7pm daily. Oct-May 10am-12.30pm, 2-5pm Mon, Wed-Sun. Admission €3-€4; €1.50-€2 10-16s; free under-10s. No credit cards.

Musée de la Marine

2 bd du Jeu de Ballon (04.93.40.11.11). Open June-Sept 10am-7pm daily. Oct-May 10am-5pm Mon-Sat. Closed Nov. Admission €3; €2 students; €1.50 12-16s; free under-12s. No credit cards.

Musée Provençal du Costume et du Bijou

2 rue Jean Ossola (04.93.36.44.65/www.fragonard.com). Open Feb-Oct 10am-1pm, 2-6pm daily. Nov-Jan 10am-1pm, 2-6pm Mon-Sat. Admission free.

Parfumerie Fragonard

Historic Factory, 20 bd Fragonard (04.93.36.44.65/ www.fragonard.com); Fabrique des Fleurs, Les Quatre Chemins, 17 rte de Cannes (04.93.77.94.30). Open Feb-Oct 9am-6.30pm daily. Nov-Jan 9am-12.30pm, 2-6.30pm daily. Admission free.

Parfumerie Galimard

73 rte de Cannes (04.93.09.20.00/www.galimard.com). Open usine May-Oct 9am-6pm daily. Nov-Apr 9am-12.30pm, 2-6pm Mon-Sat. Studio des Fragrances, rte de Pégonas. Open by appointment. Admission usine free; studio €34. Credit AmEx, MC, V.

Parfumerie Molinard

60 bd Victor Hugo (04.93.36.01.62/ www.molinard.com). Open Mar-Oct 9am-6pm. Nov-Feb 9am-12.30pm, 2-6pm. Admission free.

Villa-Musée Fragonard

23 bd Fragonard (04.97.05.58.00/ www.museesdegrasse.com). Open June-Sept 10am-7pm daily. Oct-May 10am-12.30pm, 2-6.30pm daily. Closed Nov. Admission €3.50; €1.90 12-16s; free under-12s. Credit MC, V.

Activities

Swimming

MJC Altitude 500 (57 rte Napoléon, 04.93.36.35.64) is an Olympic-size municipal outdoor pool, open July & Aug only, which offers breathtaking views and is less crowded than the beaches below. All year there is also a small pool at 73 av Antoine de St Exupéry (04.93.36.20.89), with roof that comes off in summer. Locals also swim in the Lac de St-Cassien (*see p214*).

Where to stay & eat

Jacques Chibois is one of the hottest chefs on the Riviera; his **Bastide St-Antoine** (48 av Henri Dunant, www.jacques-chibois.com, 04.93.70.94.94, double €182-€318, menus €47-€150) serves exquisite food (mushrooms are a speciality) with perfect service. Set in a century-

Cathédrale Notre-Dame-du-Puy.
See p287.

old olive grove below Grasse, it also has 11 elegant rooms. Near the *gare routière*, **Café Arnaud** (10 pl de la Foux, 04.93.36.44.88, menus €19-€28.50) offers classic Provençal fare in a low-lit ambience. **La Voûte** (3 rue du Thouron, 04.93.36.11.43, menus €22-€25) draws lots of locals for its Provençal specialities and French classics; from April to October it opens an outdoor annexe, **Côté Place**, on place aux Aires. **Le Moulin des Paroirs** (7 av Jean XXIII, 04.93.40.10.40, closed Mon & Sun, menus €25-€34) serves a superbly tender *pigeon à la royale* in a candlelit, converted olive mill. For those who can't survive without a good curry, there is **Le Punjab** (3 rue Fabreries, 04.93.36.16.03, closed lunch Mon, menus €18-€20), which also does deliveries, if you're firmly ensconced in your gîte and can't face the drive into town. **L'Indiana's** in the Casino de Grasse (bd Jeu de Ballon, 04.93.36.91.00, dinner only, closed Mon & Tue in winter, menu €22) has a certain Las Vegas style that's hard to ignore. The food is anything but Tex-Mex, offering weekly themes from Chinese to Indian, friendly service and a huge upstairs terrace. Have a drink in the kitsch bar before heading into the casino itself; for the latter remember you'll need your passport to get in. A short drive out of town, the **Moulin du Sault** (rte de Cannes, 04.93.42.25.42, closed Mon, dinner Sun, menus €28-€45), in Moulin Vieux near Auribeau-sur-

Siagne, is perfect for a special occasion, thanks to its stunning terrace, mill stream and wheel and the superb food. Five minutes on foot up the Route Napoléon towards Digne, the **Hôtel Ste-Thérèse** (39 av Yves Emmanuel Baudoin, 04.93.36.10.29, www.hotelsainte therese.com, double €60) is a former Carmelite hospice built on to an old chapel. Rooms are basic, but the terrace has views right to the sea. The quiet **Auberge La Tourmaline** (381 rte de Plascassier, 04.93.60.10.08, double €65) is a little out of the way but has great views, as does the friendly, recently renovated and central **Hôtel des Parfums** (bd Eugène Charabot, 04.92.42.35.35, www.hoteldesparfums.com, double €96-€112), which has a pool and gym. **Hôtel Le Victoria** (7 av Riou Blanquet, 04.93.40.30.30, www.le-victoria-hotel.com, closed Jan, double €58-€75) is a mid-sized hotel with pool, nice gym and reasonable restaurant.

Resources

Internet
Le Petit Caboulot, escalier Maximim Isnard (04.93.40.16.01). **Open** 8am-7.15pm Mon-Sat.

Tourist information
Office de Tourisme, 22 cours Honoré Cresp, 06130 Grasse (04.93.36.66.66/www.grasse-riviera.com). **Open** 9am-12.30pm, 2-5pm Mon-Sat.

West of Grasse

A surprising hinterland awaits along the Route Napoléon (N85, rte de Digne; *see p293* **Napoléon's long march**) north-west out of Grasse, as you soon find yourself climbing through grandiose but arid mountain scenery. About 12km along lies the medieval village of **St-Vallier-de-Thiey**, which sits on the flat plateau de Caussols, a good vantage point for spotting *bories*, dry-stone igloos once occupied by shepherds. Nearby is the **Souterroscope de Baume Obscure**, where underground waterfalls crash past stalactites, stalagmites and other natural phenomena. Bring a sweater, as it's a constant 12°C. Further north towards Castellane and the Gorges de Verdon (*see pp215-220*), the scenery gradually gets more Alpine, going through pine forests and crossing the 1,054m Col de Luens pass.

South of St-Vallier towards Cabris are the **Grottes des Audides**. This cave system, inhabited in prehistoric times, was discovered by a shepherd in 1988. In the adjoining Parc Préhistorique, dioramas illustrate the lives of the original inhabitants.

But the richest and most popular village in the area has to be **Cabris**, which boasts a large green upon which the Anglophone Cabris Cricket Club (04.93.77.56.99) plays its matches. There are numerous cafés and restaurants.

Perched above the river Siagne is the larger, unspoiled medieval village of **St-Cézaire-sur-Siagne**, famed for its fantastically preserved architecture and magnificent views. Look out for the Gallo-Roman sarcophagus in the entrance to the 12th-century cemetery chapel. Most visitors come to see the **Grottes de St-Cézaire** caves with their rusty red stalagmites and stalactites, some of which emit an eerie musical sound when struck.

Grottes des Audides

1606 rte de Cabris (04.93.42.64.15). **Open** *15 Feb-June, Sept* 2-5pm Wed-Sun. *July-Aug* 10am-noon, 12.30-6pm daily. Closed Oct to mid-Feb. **Admission** *Caves* (by reservation) €5; €3 4-11s; free under-4s. *Parc Préhistorique* €3; €2.50 4-11s; free under-4s. **No credit cards.**

Grottes de St-Cézaire

9 bd du Puit d'Amon (04.93.60.22.35/ www.lesgrottesdesaintcezaire.fr). **Open** *June, Sept* 10.30am-noon, 2-6pm daily. *July-Aug* 10.30am-6.30pm daily. *Oct-May* 2.30-4.30pm Sun. Closed Dec to early Jan. **Admission** €5; €2.50 5-11s; free under-5s. **No credit cards.**

Souterroscope de Baume Obscure

Chemin Ste-Anne, St-Vallier-de-Thiey (04.93.42.61.63). **Open** *May-Sept* 10am-5pm Mon-Sat; 10am-6pm Sun. *Oct-Apr* 10am-5pm Tue-Sun. Closed mid-Dec to mid-Feb. **Admission** €7.65; €3.80 4-12s; free under-4s. **Credit** MC, V.

Place aux Aires in Grasse. See p287.

Where to stay & eat

In St-Vallier-de-Thiey, **Le Relais Impérial**
(85 rte Napoléon, 04.92.60.36.36,
www.relaisimperial.com, double €34-€73) is
cosy and clean with a restaurant. **Le Préjoly**
(pl Cavalier Fabre, 04.93.42.60.86, closed mid-
Nov to Feb, double €30-€69, restaurant closed
Mon in winter, average €27) is a welcoming
country inn with 17 rooms and a restaurant
serving high-quality classical cuisine. Towards
St-Cézaire, **L'Hostellerie des Chênes
Blancs** (2020 rte de St-Vallier, 04.93.60.20.09,
www.chenes-blancs.com, closed 1-15 Jan,
double €49.50-€105, menus €15-€20) has a pool,
tennis courts and restaurant.

In Cabris, **L'Horizon** (100 promenade
St-Jean, 04.93.60.51.69, closed mid-Oct to Mar,
double €54-€106) has a pool, terrace and
renovated bedrooms. **Le Vieux Château**
(pl du Panorama, 04.93.60.50.12,
www.aubergeduvieuxchateau.com, restaurant
closed Mon & Tue, double €59-€98, menu €23-
€34) is a charming hotel-restaurant carved out
of the old castle, with Provençal food and four
double rooms: reserve well ahead. **Le Petit
Prince** (15 rue Frédéric Mistral, 04.93.60.63.14,
closed Dec to mid-Jan, menus €19-€28) serves
great Provençal fare and has a terrace
overlooking the green. The rabbit with lavender
and raspberry vinegar is recommended. **Le
Mini Grill** (5 pl du Puits, 04.93.60.55.58, closed
lunch Wed, menu €19), with its off-road terrace,
is handy for children on summer lunchtimes.

Resources

Tourist infomation

Cabris *Office de Tourisme, 4 rue Porte Haute,
06530 Cabris (04.93.60.55.63).* **Open** 9.15am-
12.15pm, 1.30-5.15pm Mon-Sat. Closed Dec.
St-Cézaire *Office de Tourisme, 3 rue de la République,
06530 St-Cézaire-sur-Siagne (04.93.60.84.30/
www.saintcezairesursiagne.com).* **Open** 10am-noon,
3-6.30pm Mon-Fri; 10am-noon Sat, Sun.
St-Vallier *Office de Tourisme, 10 pl du Tour,
06460 St-Vallier-de-Thiey (04.93.42.78.00/
www.saintvallierdethiey.com).* **Open** *Mar-Oct* 9am-
noon, 3-6pm Mon-Sat (and July, Aug 10am-noon Sun).
Nov-Feb 9am-noon, 3-5pm Mon-Sat.

The Gorges du Loup

Built on a rocky peak surrounded by precipices,
medieval **Tourrettes-sur-Loup** produces so
many violets (celebrated in the early-March
Fête des Violettes) that it has earned the name
'Violet Village'. In the 1920s it became a
meeting place for artists and writers. Today,
more than 30 workshops and galleries make
Tourrettes a high spot for arts and crafts. The
Grand'Rue is lined with earnest (and therefore
expensive) shops. The **Confiserie Florian** is a
visit for a rainy day, a factory using traditional
techniques to make sweets and chocolates
flavoured with violets, lemon verbena and
citrus. Tours are available in English.

Le Bar-sur-Loup has all the authentic
charm of a well-kept medieval village. The
Gothic church of St-Jacques contains a 15th-
century altarpiece, as well as a famous *Danse
Macabre*, which portrays tiny courtly dancers
being shot by Death, their souls being judged
unworthy by St Michael and hurled into hell.
When he's in the area, a less saintly Michael –
Schumacher – takes a spin at **Fun Kart**.

Tortuous bends and overhanging cliffs,
accompanied by the sound of crashing
waterfalls, lead you into the **Gorges du Loup**
where hiking and canyoning are a must. Along
the D6, amid lush vegetation, a huge monolith
marks the entrance to the spectacular **Saut du
Loup**. The waters of the Loup swirl furiously
through this enormous, eroded cauldron,
gushing down through moss and vegetation
petrified by the lime carbonate of the spray.

Perched between Grasse and the Loup valley
lies **Gourdon**, a medieval citadel which kept
watch against marauding Saracens. The 13th-
century **Château de Gourdon** blends French
and Italian Romanesque influences and has
gardens laid out in the 17th century by André
Le Nôtre. It houses the Musée Historique, with
the usual weaponry and torture implements
plus a Rembrandt and a Rubens, and the Musée
de la Peinture Naïve with Douanier Rousseau-
type daubs and one example of the real thing.

Château de Gourdon

(04.93.09.68.02). **Open** *June-Sept* 11am-1pm, 2-7pm
daily. *Oct-May* 2-6pm Mon, Wed-Sun. **Admission**
€4; €2.50 12-16s; free under-12s. **No credit cards.**

Confiserie Florian

Le Pont du Loup, Tourettes-sur-Loup (04.93.59.32.91).
Open 9am-noon, 2-6.30pm daily. **Admission** free.

Activities

Canyoning

Canyoning is dangerous so organise a private guide:
Destination Nature (69 rue Georges Clemenceau,
La Colle-sur-Loup, 04.93.32.06.93, www.loisirs-
explorer.com/destination-nature) is affordable and
reliable. Qualified guides organise half- to two-day
canyoning trips, as well as mountain hiking. If you
are experienced enough to do it on your own, consult
Les Guides Randoxygène, available at tourist offices.

Fun Kart

*Plateau de la Sarée, rte de Gourdon (04.93.42.72.27/
www.fun-karting.com).* **Open** 9.30am-dusk daily.
Rates €16/10 mins; children €6/5 mins. **Credit** MC, V.

The Riviera & Southern Alps

Where to stay & eat

In Tourrettes-sur-Loup, **Chez Grande Mère** (pl Maximin Escalier, 04.93.59.33.34, closed Wed, lunch Sat and Nov to mid-Dec, menus €16-€19.50) makes a fabulous lentil soup and has a cosy fireplace. **Le Petit Manoir** (21 Grand'Rue, 04.93.24.19.19, closed Mon & Tue and 15-30 Nov, menus €15-€34) is a local favourite for traditional Provençal dishes, and has a great vegetarian selection. **Le Mas des Cigales** (1673 rte des Quenières, 04.93.59.25.73, closed Nov-15 Mar, double €87-€92) is a lovely bed and breakfast with a pool and tennis courts. **Relais des Coches** (28 rte de Vence, 04.93.24.30.24, closed Mon & Tue and all Jan; July & Aug open every evening, closed lunch, average €40) offers traditional French fare, and Sunday roast or brunch cooked by a Yorkshire chef (noon-6pm, €25). The **Auberge de Tourrettes** (11 rte de Grasse, 04.93.59.30.05/ www.aubergedetourrettes.fr, closed end Nov to beg Feb except Christmas/New Year, double €65-€130, menu €45) has six cosy rooms, a lovely terrace and excellent restaurant.

Restaurant delights are slim in Le Bar: try **La Jarrerie** (av Amiral de Grasse, 04.93.42.92.92, closed Mon Oct-Apr, all Tue, dinner Wed May-Sept and all Jan, menus €19-€43), which serves hearty Provençal fare. In Gourdon, the **Auberge de Gourdon** (04.93.09.69.69, closed Nov, menu €15-€19.50) is a bar-tabac-restaurant with local charm, heavy Provençal accents and simple, honest dishes. If you have a tent, the **Camping Rives du Loup** (2666B rte de la Colle, Pont du Loup 04.93.24.15.65, two person tent €13.50; large tent/caravan €18.50) is a well-organised site in a lovely setting.

Resources

Tourist information

Le Bar *Office du Tourisme, pl Francis Paulet, 06620 Le Bar-sur-Loup (04.93.42.72.21/www.bar-sur-loup.com)*. **Open** 9am-12.20pm, 2-5pm daily.
Gourdon *Syndicat d'Initiative, pl de l'Eglise, 06620 Gourdon (04.93.09.68.25/www.gourdon-france.com)*. **Open** *July, Aug* 9am-7pm. *Sept-June* 10am-6pm.
Tourrettes-sur-Loup *Office de Tourisme, 2 pl de la Libération, 06140 Tourrettes-sur-Loup (04.93.24.18.93/www.tourrettessurloup.com)*. **Open** 9.30am-12.30pm, 2.30-6.30pm Mon-Sat (daily May-Aug).

Valbonne & Sophia-Antipolis

Unlike most villages in Provence, **Valbonne** was planned on a chequerboard design in the 17th century by the monks of Lérins, clearly inspired by the plans of Roman towns, as part of a bid by Augustin de Grimaldi, Bishop of

Grasse's multicultural restaurant scene on rue Fabreries. *See p288.*

Grasse, to repopulate a region that had been devastated by plague. The village is bordered by 'rampart houses' with an entrance gate on each of its four sides. Today it has several glass workshops, notably for perfume flasks. At the heart of the village is place des Arcades, where the Fête du Raisin celebrates the late-ripening servan grape at the end of January (and where the village's English pub is located). The parish church is part of the former Chalaisian Abbey which also contains the small **Musée des Arts et Traditions Populaires**.

In the shadow of Valbonne lies **Sophia-Antipolis** (www.saem-sophia-antipolis.fr), the Riviera's 15,000-hectare bid for hi-tech power and prestige, where 20,000 people from more than 60 countries work in R&D-intensive companies – keeping the already high property prices in the area bubbling over. Work on this perfectly landscaped, perfectly soulless science park, which has been described as the 'Milton Keynes of the Riviera', began in 1969; today 1,300 hi-tech companies share the site.

South-west of Valbonne, **Mouans-Sartoux** draws contemporary art pilgrims. The Renaissance château was converted into the **Espace de l'Art Concret** in 1990 by artist Gottfried Honegger. The permanent collection includes works by Honegger, Albers, André, LeWitt and Morellet, exhibited along with three- or four-month theme shows dedicated to geometrical abstraction and minimalist art.

Espace de l'Art Concret

Château de Mouans-Sartoux (04.93.75.71.50).
Open *June-Sept* 11am-7pm Mon, Wed-Sun. *Oct-May*
11am-6pm Mon, Wed-Sun. **Admission** €2.30; €1.15
students; free under-12s. **No credit cards.**

Musée des Arts et Traditions Popularires

rue Paroisse, Valbonne (04.93.12.96.54). **Open**
May-Sept 3-7pm Tue-Sun. *Oct-Apr* 2-6pm Tue-Sun.
Closed mid-Dec to mid-Jan. **Admission** €2; free
under-12s. **No credit cards.**

Where to stay & eat

The **Hôtel Les Armoiries** (pl des Arcades,
04.93.12.90.90, doubles €88-€158) occupies a
17th-century building. Just outside Valbonne,
Château la Bégude (rte de Roquefort Les
Pins, 04.93.12.37.00, closed mid-Nov to mid-Dec,
double €104-€164, restaurant closed dinner Sun
Nov-Mar) is a lovely restored manor with 34
beautifully decorated rooms and a restaurant
with a terrace overlooking the golf course. The
Bistro de Valbonne (11 rue de la Fontaine,
04.93.12.05.59, closed Mon & Sun, and Thur
lunch mid-June to mid-Sept, menus €16.80-€32)
serves French classics and superb smoked wild
Baltic salmon. If you like Moroccan food, try
low-lit and intimate **La Pigeot** (16 rue Alexis
Julien, 04.93.12.17.53, average €35). At **Lou
Cigalon** (4-6 bd Carnot, 04.93.12.27.07, closed
Mon & Sun, menus €38-€75) owner-chef Alain
Parodi gives a modern spin to Provençal cuisine.

Resources

Tourist information

Valbonne *Office de Tourisme 1 pl de l'Hôtel de Ville,
06560 Valbonne (04.93.12.34.50/www.tourisme-
valbonne.com).* **Open** *15 June-15 Sept* 9am-5pm
Mon-Fri; 9am-12.30pm, 3-5pm Sat; 9am-12.30pm Sun.
16 Sept-14 June 9am-5pm Mon-Fri; 9am-12.30pm Sat.

Getting there & around

By car

The N85 (route Napoléon) is dual carriageway
between Cannes and Grasse, before continuing
towards Digne via St-Vallier-de-Thiey. From Nice
take the D2085 at Cagnes towards Le Bar-sur-Loup
and Grasse. For Cabris, take the D4 out of Grasse,
then D13 to St-Cézaire. The D2210 winds from Vence
towards Grasse via Tourrettes-sur-Loup and Le Bar,
with side roads turning off up the Gorges du Loup.

By bus

Rapides du Côte d'Azur (RCA 04.93.36.37.37)
runs buses daily between Grasse and Cannes, Nice
Airport, Vence, Grasse and St-Cézaire, some of which
stop at Cabris, and between Grasse and St-Vallier-de-
Thiey (Mon-Sat). For the Gorges du Loup, take RCA's
No.511 from Grasse to Pont-sur-Loup. **TACAVL**
(04.93.42.40.79) operates several services (Mon-Sat)
between Grasse and Le Bar-sur-Loup. **STCAR**
(04.93.12.00.12) bus No.3VB runs from Cannes direct
to Valbonne about every hour (less on Sun) and the
No.5VB (4 buses Mon-Fri) goes via Sophia-Antipolis.
Sillages (04.92.28.58.68, www.sillages-stga.tm.fr)
also runs buses in the area.

Napoléon's long march

After the fall of Paris in April 1814 to allied
troops, Napoléon was forced to abdicate to
the Isle of Elba. On 1 March 1815, he
returned, landing at Golfe Juan (*see p233*) at
the head of a tiny army. 'The eagle, with the
national colours, will fly from steeple to
steeple until it reaches the towers of Notre-
Dame,' he proclaimed, as, braving the Alpine
winter, he set off to reclaim his imperial title,
choosing the mountain route to avoid royalist
Provençal troops. Napoléon bivouacked on
the beach at Cannes, before heading into the
mountains via Mouans-Sartoux and Grasse.
He paused at St-Vallier-de-Thiey (marked by a
column), crossed the Pas de la Faye in thick
fog, ate two eggs at Escragnolles, camped on
2 March at the mountain hamlet of Séranon
and lunched the next day at Castellane,
making his way north via Digne, Sisteron and
Gap. Napoléon may have been out of official
favour but he remained a popular hero and

symbol of justice for the peasantry, who
feared the return of high taxes under the
restored monarchy. As Napoléon approached
Grenoble the crowd of torch-bearing peasants
grew around him; on 6 March royal troops
deserted to his side and on 7 March, after
324km, he made a triumphal entry into
Grenoble. By the time he reached Paris on
20 March, he headed of an army of 20,000.
Louis XVIII fled into exile and Napoléon was
back (briefly) on centre stage. The six-day
march marked the start of the Hundred Days
that ended in his defeat at Waterloo.

Today the N85 road, or Route Napoléon
(www.route-napoleon.com), roughly follows the
old mule trail taken by the deposed emperor,
and imperial eagles and countless Auberge
Napoléons signal the points where he stayed
or ate. At Golfe Juan, on the first weekend of
March, the landing is re-enacted by 400 soldiers
in full Napoléonic regalia (*pictured, p6*).

The Riviera & Southern Alps

Vence & St-Paul

André Gide and DH Lawrence stayed here, Matisse created his masterpiece: arty Vence and St-Paul inject cultural kudos into the Côte d'Azur.

Vence

When the Emperor Augustus led his jack-sandalled hordes into what they were to call Vintium, it had long been inhabited by a Ligurian tribe. Set in a strategic position 10km back from the sea, Vence was a bishopric from the fourth to 19th centuries, and boasts two patron saints. The first was fifth-century bishop Véran, who organised the town's defences against Visigoth invaders (though Saracens would later succeed where the Barbarians had failed, razing the cathedral and much of Vence to the ground). The second, 12th-century bishop Lambert, defended the town's rights against its rapacious new baron, Romée de Villeneuve, setting a trend of rivalry between nobility and clergy that was to last until the bishopric was dissolved after the Revolution. Perhaps Vence's most popular prelate – though this one was never canonised – was 17th-century bishop Antoine Godeau, a gallant dwarf, poet and renowned wit who was a founding member of the Académie Française.

In the 1920s, Vence became a popular pitstop for artists and writers, including Paul Valéry, André Gide and D H Lawrence, who died here in 1930. A simple plaque in Vence cemetery marks the place where Lawrence lay for five years before he was cremated at the behest of his widow and his ashes shipped to Taos, New Mexico. However, Frieda Lawrence's lover, Ravagli, who was entrusted with the task, apparently boasted that he had dumped the ashes somewhere between Marseille and Villefranche to save himself the trouble.

Walls still encircle some of the medieval *vieille ville*, which manages to retain its old-world feel despite the modern sprawl outside. The boulevard Paul André follows the old ramparts and offers sweeping views to the Alps. Outside the western Porte Peyra, one of five original town gates, place du Frêne is named after its giant ash tree planted to commemorate Pope Paul III's visit to Vence in 1538. The *porte* leads into place Peyra, site of the Roman forum. Between the two squares, the 17th-century **Château de Villeneuve** now hosts modern art exhibitions. At the centre of the *vieille ville*, the **Ancienne Cathédrale Notre-Dame de la Nativité** (open 9am-6pm

daily) was built over a Roman temple of Mars, a column from which can be seen in place Godeau. A fifth-century church was replaced by a Romanesque one, which has itself been reworked over the centuries. The Roman legacy can be seen in inscriptions worked into the Baroque facade on place Clemenceau and in the pre-Christian sarcophagus (third chapel on the right) in which St Véran is said to have been buried. There's a Chagall mosaic of Moses in the bulrushes in the baptistry, and some charmingly irreverent 15th-century carvings by Jacques Bellot on the choir stalls.

Leave the medieval town through place du Grand Jardin, edged with cafés from which you can watch the *boules* players, and visit the daily morning farmers' market. The town never looks truly busy until July when the **Nuits du Sud** music festival brings four raunchy weeks of Latin, salsa, jazz and French-Arabic music, waking Vence from its slumber.

Vence's biggest tourist attraction, the **Chapelle du Rosaire**, designed by Matisse as a gift of thanks to the Dominican nuns who cared for him, lies slightly north of the *vieille ville* (*see p297* **Matisse's masterpiece**). Southwest of town, at the new-agey **NALL (Nature, Art & Life League) Art Association**, you can see artists in action. Students, some in rehab, others gaining credits towards their degree, work as assistants to Nall, the artist-founder, while painters, sculptors, writers and musicians hire cottages within the extensive grounds to work on their personal projects. The house, completely built and decorated by Nall, is a work of art in itself.

West of Vence on the Grasse road, the **Galerie Beaubourg** is more museum than private gallery, a gem of an exhibition of contemporary works housed in a château. Terraced sculpture gardens dotted with pieces by Niki de Saint Phalle, Arman and Julian Schnabel are part of a permanent collection assembled by former Parisian gallery owners Marianne and Pierre Nahon. The *pièce de résistance* is the Jean Tinguely chapel, featuring his weird and wonderful *Grande odalisque*.

To the north-east of Vence, **St-Jeannet** is a wine-making village dominated by the dramatic rock outcrop known as Le Baou, which can be ascended by a waymarked path. 15km east of

Vence, **La Gaude** is comparatively dull, but a well-preserved and friendly little perched village founded in 189BC. It's a good place to start a pedestrian exploration of the surrounding countryside: there are six marked walks, the one to Vence taking an hour and ten minutes, and the one to Le Baou an hour and a half. The tourist office has maps.

Chapelle du Rosaire
466 av Henri Matisse (04.93.58.03.26). **Open** 10-11.30am, 2-5pm Tue, Thur; 2-5.30pm Mon, Wed, Sat plus 2-5.30pm Fri during school holidays; mass 10am Sun. Closed mid-Nov to mid-Dec. **Admission** €2.50; €1 6-16s; free under-6s. **No credit cards.**

Château de Villeneuve Fondation Emile Hugues
2 pl du Frêne, Vence (04.93.24.24.23). **Open** *July-Sept* 10am 6pm Tue-Sun. *Oct-June* 10am-12.30pm, 2-6pm Tue-Sun. **Admission** €5; €2.50 12 18s; free under-12s. **No credit cards.**

Galerie Beaubourg
Château Notre Dame des Fleurs, 2618 rte de Grasse (04.93.24.52.00/www.galeriebeaubourg.com). **Open** by appointment. **Admission** €5; €2,50. 12-18s; free under-12s. **No credit cards.**

NALL (Nature, Art & Life League) Art Association
232 bd de Lattre, Vence (04.93.58.13.26/www.null.org). **Open** *May-Sept* 3-6pm Mon, Sat, Sun. **Admission** €3. **No credit cards.**

Where to stay & eat

Super-chef Jacques Maximin at **Restaurant Jacques Maximin** (689 chemin de La Gaude, Vence, 04.93.58.90.75, closed lunch July & Aug, and Mon & Tue Sept-June, menus €40-€95) is a Provençal legend and you'll see why once you tuck into a starter like his salad of artichoke hearts, broad beans, squid, penne and parmesan, or the classic autumnal salad of ceps and scallops. It's pricey, but worth it, especially when they're serving outdoors in the lush subtropical garden. Recently renovated **La Closerie des Genêts** (4 impasse Marcellin Maurel, 04.93.58.33.25, double €39-€69) has 12 chintz-draped rooms. **Hôtel Miramar** (167 av Bougearel, 04.93.58.01.32, double €78-€145), on the eastern edge of Vence, is a delightfully converted ancient manor with pool, terrace and lovely views of St-Jeannet, while the inexpensive **Hôtel Le Provence** (9 av Marcellin Maurel, 04.93.58.04.21, double €38-€69) has a central location and pretty rooms. Slightly out of the centre, **Hôtel Villa Roseraie** (av Henri Giraud, 04.93.58.02.20, closed 15 Nov-15 Feb, double €95-€146) has a magnificent garden with pool. The luxurious **Château du Domaine St-Martin** (av des Templiers, 04.93.58.02.02, www.chateau-st-martin.com, double €240-€590, menus €69-€92) offers elegant accommodation and

Fresh vegetables by the *panier* in **Vence**.

La Colombe d'Or.

Vence market Tuesday and Friday mornings.

Tourist information

La Gaude *Syndicat d'Initiative, 20 rue Centrale, 06610 La Gaude (04.93.24.47.26/www.mairie-lagaude.fr).* **Open** *mid-June to mid-Sept* 9am-12.30pm, 3-6pm Tue-Fri; 9am-4pm Sat. *mid-Sept to mid-June* 9am-12.30pm, 2.30-5.30pm Tue-Fri; 9am-4pm Sat. **St-Jeannet** *Syndicat d'Initiative, 35 rue de la Soucare, 06640 St-Jeannet (04.93.24.73.83/ www.saintjeannet.com).* **Open** *June-Sept* 9am-6pm daily. *Oct-May* 9.30am-noon, 2.30-5pm Tue-Sat. **Vence** *Office de Tourisme, 8 pl du Grand Jardin, 06140 Vence (04.93.58.06.38/www.ville-vence.fr).* **Open** *July-Aug* 9am-7pm Mon-Sat; 9am-1pm Sun. *Sept-June* 9am-6pm Mon-Sat.

St-Paul-de-Vence & La Colle-sur-Loup

St-Paul-de-Vence might have been just another picturesque *village perché*. Instead, it has become a *quartier général* of modern art, helped along by a heritage of illustrious artistic visitors and the presence of one of the most important modern art museums in France.

St-Paul flourished in the Middle Ages thanks to its vines, figs, olives and orange trees, as well as hemp and linen. The almost-intact ramparts were put up in 1540 by François 1er after the town helped him beat off arch-enemy, Emperor Charles V. The town went into a decline until the 20th century. Picasso, Matisse, Braque and Dufy were just some of the daubers who pitched up here after World War I, paying for their board and lodging at **La Colombe d'Or** with paintings that still adorn the hostelry's walls. In the 1960s, art dealer-collectors Aimé and Marguerite Maeght created the Fondation Maeght for their remarkable private collection.

St-Paul's narrow medieval lanes are filled with daytrippers in high season and lined with bougainvillea, jasmine and geraniums along with hard-sell artists' studios and shops selling antiques, crafts and souvenirs. Rue Grande, the main street, is well worth visiting for the fabulously smart foodie shops selling perfectly packaged olive oil and designer chocolates, in between chic boutiques and touristy tack. In the **Eglise Collégiale** on place de la Mairie (open 8am-8pm daily), only the choir remains from the original 12th-century building; later adornments include St Clément's chapel, a masterpiece of Baroque stucco, and a painting of St Catherine of Alexandria, attributed to Tintoretto. Sit at **Café de la Place** in place de Gaulle to observe France's most famous *terrain de boules*, shaded by plane trees. Celebrities line up to challenge local champions and Japanese players travel

stunning views plus an excellent restaurant. A new extension is being added for 2004. Best of all, you can cut out all those winding roads by availing yourself of the hotel's private helipad. **L'Auberge des Templiers** (39 av Joffre, 04.93.58.06.05, closed Mon, menus €39-€59) has great mod-Med cuisine cooked up by internationally trained (but Vence-born) chef Stéphane Demichelis in a pretty setting with tables in the garden in summer. Live and dine like a medieval lord in the 15th-century **Auberge des Seigneurs** (pl du Frêne, 04.93.58.04.24, closed Nov-Mar, double €75-€85, restaurant closed Mon and lunch Tue-Thur, menus €20-€39), an inn since 1895; its restaurant specialises in roast meats. In the heart of Vence's old town, **Le P'tit Provençal** (4 pl Clemenceau, 04.93.58.50.64, closed Wed, Thur and Nov, end Feb to early Mar, menus €22-€43) offers foie gras with figs and rabbit casserole with thyme. At the nearby **La Terrasse du Clemenceau** (22 pl Clemenceau, 04.93.58.24.70, closed Mon & dinner Sun, 3wks Nov, 2wks Mar, menu €24) vastly improved service makes dining a pleasure, and you can devour lamb cooked in a wood oven in the loveliest terrace on the square.

Rest up before or after a hike at the **Hôtel du Baou** (le plan du Bois, 04.93.59.44.44, double €59-€89, restaurant 04.93.24.40.49, menu €20) in La Gaude, which has a pool.

huge distances for regional tournaments, but rookies are welcome (*boules* can be rented from the tourist office at €3/hour per set). The walk around the ramparts affords spectacular views from the Alps to the sea. The Porte de Nice leads to the **cemetery** (open June-Sept 7.30am-8pm; Oct-May 8am-5pm) where Chagall lies beneath a slab of stone adorned with pebbles, coins, twigs and acorns, placed there by fans.

In a pinewood just north-west of St-Paul, the **Fondation Maeght** is one of the Côte's star attractions. Opened in 1964, this extraordinary low-slung construction set in grounds bristling

with artworks was designed by Catalan architect José Luis Sert to house Aimé and Marguerite Maeght's collection. The Fondation is a maze, with no fixed route and nothing resembling a hanging plan. Some works do have places of their own, by virtue of being part of the fabric of the place: Giacometti figures in the courtyard; a Miró labyrinth peopled with sculptures and ceramics, including the half-submerged *Egg*; mural mosaics by Chagall and Tal-Coat; the pool and stained-glass window by Braque; Pol Bury's fountain; Calder's bobbing mobiles. But the Fondation's more moveable

Matisse's masterpiece

The tiny Chapelle du Rosaire (*see p295* for opening details) in the hill town of Vence is all too easy to miss, but it would be your greatest oversight, as it's one of the most exquisite pieces of 20th-century artwork on the coast.

Not unlike a contemporary installation, this is the complete and final work of Matisse, who was architect and designer of the chapel from 1947 until its opening in 1951. While he wasn't a practising Christian, in the last years of his life he was cared for by Dominican nuns, in particular Sister Jacques-Marie, who encouraged him to design the chapel. He said, 'I regard it, despite all its imperfections, as my masterpiece... as an effort which is the culmination of a whole life dedicated to the search for truth.'

Although the chapel is white, it is saturated in colour. Matisse, renowned as 'the painter of light', used white reflective materials, such as Carrara marble and white tiles, as his canvases, which are dappled with the glowing, reflected colours of the stained glass windows that dominate the west and south walls. Best seen in the morning sunlight, the overall result perfectly creates the atmosphere that Matisse desired: 'I want those entering my chapel to feel themselves purified and lightened of their burdens.'

A vast black line drawing of St Dominic on white ceramic tiles is striking in its simplicity and you may recognise the original design from photographs of the elderly, bedridden Matisse in his Nice studio, painting with a brush strapped to the end of a long bamboo rod. Alongside it, an uplifting line drawing of Mary and Jesus is surrounded by flowers, while a simple, almost rough sketch of the Stations of the Cross covers the east wall.

Matisse chose every material and colour with precision, the green of the stained glass

represents nature, the blue the sky and the yellow the sun, while the central altar is made from pierre du Rogne, a rough, pitted warm stone, to represent bread and body. Atop the altar are golden candelabras and a stylised Jesus on the cross lit by an intricate filigree oil lamp, all designed by Matisse, and in the corner a confessional door, inspired by his visits to Morocco. Don't miss the original sketches and brightly coloured vestments on display in the room beyond the chapel, like silk versions of the familiar Matisse cutouts.

Braques and Légers, Kandinskys and Mirós, Bonnards and Chagalls disappear into storage to make way for temporary exhibitions, including the annual summer show.

The more modern, commercial **Galerie Guy Pieters** was opened by the Belgian gallery owner in 2000, showing American Pop and French *nouveau réalisme*, including Christo, Niki de Saint Phalle, Arman and Robert Indiana. For art which is truly state-of-the-art, head into town where **Galerie Catherine Issert** has a seriously contemporary feel and a fine line in installation.

Southwest of St Paul-de-Vence, unspoiled **La Colle-sur-Loup** has an attractive 17th-century church, but is best known for antiques. The main drag of antique shops on rue Yves Klein is open daily 4-6pm, and an antiques market is held every second Sunday of the month. The **Maison des Arts** offers residential art and 'creative thinking' courses in a beautiful 18th-century house and also puts on shows of local artists. What really puts La Colle on the map is **L'Abbaye**, a 12th-century monastery that is now a stunning hotel/restaurant (*see below*).

Fondation Maeght
chemin des Trious (04.93.32.81.63). **Open** *Oct-June* 10am-12.30pm, 2.30-6pm daily. *July-Sept* 10am-7pm daily. **Admission** €11; €9 10-18s; free under-10s. **Credit** AmEx, MC, V.

Galerie Catherine Issert
2 rte des Serres (04.93.32.96.92/www.galerie-issert.com). **Open** 11am-1pm, 3-7pm Mon-Sat.

Galerie Guy Pieters
chemin des Trious (04.93.32.06.46/ www.guypietersgallery.com). **Open** *June-Oct* 10am-7pm Mon-Sat. *Nov-May* 10am-1pm, 2-6pm Mon-Sat.

Maison des Arts
10 rue Maréchal Foch, La Colle-sur-Loup (04.93.32.32.50/www.maisondesarts.com). **Art courses** €1,384-€1,560/week.

Where to stay & eat

Accommodation is expensive in St-Paul, but the **Hostellerie les Remparts** (72 rue Grande, 04.93.32.09.88, closed mid-Nov to mid-Dec and mid-Jan to mid-Feb, double €39-€80, restaurant closed lunch Mon, and dinner Tue-Thur & Sun Nov-Mar, menu €30) in the centre of the old town combines style and value. Its nine charming rooms have a medieval feel and its restaurant serves regional specialities. Book well ahead for a meal or a bed at **La Colombe d'Or** (pl des Ormeaux, 04.93.32.80.02, www.la-colombe-dor.com, closed late-Oct to mid-Dec & 2wks in Jan, double €244-€260, restaurant average €57) if you want to get even a glimpse

inside – the artworks left here in lieu of payment by clients including then-unknowns Picasso, Modigliani, Miró, Matisse and Chagall are only on view to guests. A meal on the celebrated, fig-shaded terrace is still an occasion, with its combination of earthy food and jet-set clientele. **Le St-Paul** (86 rue Grande, 04.93.32.65.25, double €190-€300, menus €45-€85) is a 16th-century mansion with four-poster beds. Chef Frédéric Buzet offers modern Provençal gastronomy and a fine list of local wines. For light meals in cosy surroundings **Comme à la Maison** (montée de l'Eglise, angle rue Grande, 04.93.32.87.81, dishes €9-€20) is a poetry café with vegetarian tendencies. Reward yourself at the end of rue Grande with a hot chocolate with violet and ginger at **Joël Durand** (84 rue Grande), fave *chocolatier* of Princess Caroline and Inès de la Fréssange. Chagall once stayed at the pretty whitewashed **Hôtel le Hameau** (528 rte de La Colle, 04.93.32.80.24, www.le-hameau.com, closed mid-Nov to mid-Feb, double €94-€140), which oozes charm and has 16 attractive rooms, a pool and terraced garden with fruit trees. **La Ferme de St-Paul** (1334 rte de La Colle, 04.93.32.82.48, closed lunch Tue & Wed, average €40) serves fine, classic Provençal cuisine in a converted 18th-century farmhouse. Set in an eight-hectare park with views to the Med, **Le Mas d'Artigny** (20 rte de la Colle, 04.93.32.84.54, www.mas-artigny.com, double €150-€450, menus €43-€65) has rooms, self-catering apartments and a heated outdoor pool open all year, plus a venerable restaurant that has been given a new direction by chef Francis Scordel. It's the lounge, cloisters, pool and restaurant that make romantic medieval monastery **L'Abbaye** (541 bd Honoré Teisseire, La Colle-sur-Loup, 04.93.32.68.34, double €150-€250, restaurant closed all Mon, lunch Tue, menus €30-€80) so special; Protestant marriages can be arranged in the achingly beautiful chapel. Menus are good value for a special occasion, but the speciality of sea bass cooked in a salt crust will make you ditch the prix-fixe for the *à la carte*.

Resources

Tourist information
La Colle-sur-Loup *Office du Tourisme, 8 av Maréchal Foch, 06480 La Colle-sur-Loup (04.93.32.68.36/www.lacollesurloup.com).* **Open** *July, Aug* 9am-7pm Mon-Fri; 9am-12.30pm 3-7pm Sat, Sun. *Sept-June* 9am-12.30pm, 2-6pm Mon-Sat.
St-Paul-de-Vence *Office de Tourisme, 2 rue Grande, 06570 (04.93.32.86.95/www.stpaulweb.com).* **Open** *June-Sept* 10am-1pm, 2-7pm daily. *Oct-May* 10am-6pm Mon-Fri; 10am-1pm, 2-6pm Sat, Sun.

Into the Alps

In this giant slice of unspoiled nature, roads are vertiginous, forests thick with pine and rivers churning with white-water frenzy.

After the decadent glitter of the Riviera, high fashion makes way for the serious Alpine crags that dominate the deeply scored valleys of the Roya, the Vésubie, the Tinée and the Haut Var. When it's time to take a break, isolated mountain villages are warmly welcoming and justifiably proud of tiny Baroque chapels with frescoes worthy of the best museums. Walking, skiing, canyoning and mountain biking bring nature-lovers in droves; but even for the more sedate, the sheer natural power of the region makes it easy to toss out carefully planned vacation itineraries and just settle in and relax.

Running along a huge swathe of territory near the border with Italy, the Parc National du Mercantour has some 600km of waymarked footpaths. Here, as well as free-roaming, bell-clanking sheep and goats, are chamoix and marmots, rare imperial eagles, eagle owls, snow grouse, the recently reintroduced lammergeyer (a bearded vulture that lives mainly on bones), as well as Alpine ibex or bouquetin which roam between the Mercantour and the adjacent Parco Naturale delle Alpi Marittime in Italy (officially twinned with its French cousin since 1987). Less welcome to some locals are the wolves that have made their way back over the border from Italy and have been blamed for excessive sheep consumption (*see p304* **Who's afraid of the big bad wolf?**). The park is efficiently, even aggressively, run, with strictly enforced bans on dogs, camping, firearms, gathering of plants, fires and off-road driving. The Parc also has one of the area's more unusual sights – the rock-hewn Bronze Age engravings of the Vallée des Merveilles.

The Roya & Bévéra Valleys & the Vallée des Merveilles

When Savoy and the rest of the County of Nice officially became a part of France under the reign of Napoléon III in 1860, the upper valleys of the Roya and its tributary the Bévéra were granted to Vittorio Emanuele II, sovereign of the new kingdom of Italy. A nice little gesture between rulers, especially since they were Vittorio's favourite hunting grounds. The inhabitants of the valleys stayed essentially French, at least in spirit, but it was not until 1947 that they were allowed to decide which side of the border they wanted to be on. The Italian influence still makes itself felt in colourful village houses and churches.

Sospel, a sleepy, sprawling town beside the river Bévéra, is the mountain gateway to the Roya valley and a great place to stock up on the outstanding local olive oil. Sospel was the second largest city in the County of Nice in the 13th century, thanks to its crucial situation along the Mediterranean salt route; the 11th-century *Vieux Pont* (old bridge) still spans the river in two graceful arcs, its tower (now the tourist office) was once the tollgate that gave passage, for a price, to a steady stream of mules on the salt trail from Nice to Turin. The oldest house on the south bank (Palais Ricci) bears a plaque describing Pope Pius VII's stay here. The streets abound with charming squares and sculpted fountains, but the main highlight is the floridly Baroque **Eglise St-Michel** (open 3-6pm daily) on place St-Michel, with its stucco facade, trompe l'oeil murals and François Bréa's splendid early-16th-century Immaculate Virgin surrounded by angels. From the church you can hike up to the **Musée du Fort St-Roch**, a fascinating relic of the Maginot line. Built in 1932, this underground world was a marvel of 30s technology, and from what appears to be the entrance to a garage on the side of a cliff visitors embark on a trip through seemingly endless galleries, containing officers' quarters, munitions, a hospital, some impressive kitchens and even a wine cellar.

Northwest of Sospel, the narrow D2566 climbs alongside the Bévéra river through the Turini forest, rich in maple, beach, chestnut and spruce trees. Several roads meet at the 1,604m **Col de Turini**, a popular spot to start hiking or cross-country skiing (04.93.03.60.52) at the edge of the Parc National du Mercantour. For a wonderfully scenic drive, take the D68, which runs through the Authion Massif. The **Monument aux Morts**, a few kilometres along, pays tribute to those who died in the Austro-Sardinian war of 1793 and against the Germans in 1944. Further along are the **Cabanes Vieilles**, stark ruins of an old Napoleonic military camp that was damaged in the fighting of 1944. At the Pointe des Trois-Communes at the far edge of the camp, there is a marvellous panorama of the peaks of the Mercantour and the Pré-Alpes of Nice.

An alternative route north of Sospel, the D2204, climbs over the 879m Col de Brouis before dropping into the Roya valley proper at **Breil-sur-Roya**. A tranquil village of red-tiled pastel houses, Breil has several small industries – leather, olives, dairy farming. It has also become an internationally known centre for canyoning, rafting and kayaking. Visit the flamboyant 18th-century church of **Sancta-Maria-in-Albis** (open 9am-noon, 2-5pm daily), which has a fine gilded organ from the 17th century. This is but one of seven historic, finely decorated organs in the area which are put into service in **Les Baroquiales** Baroque music festival every summer (*see p39*). Also of note is the unusual and colourful A Stacada: a festival that takes place every four years (next in 2006) where villagers dressed in medieval costume parade through the town, periodically stopping to perform scenes portraying the abolition of the *droit du seigneur* (the rebellion of the local inhabitants against a tyrant's demand for tax).

Saorge lies in a rugged setting, its cluster of Italianate houses and bell towers with shimmering fish-scale-tile roofs clinging to the side of a mountain at the entrance to the breathtaking Roya Gorge. It is the most spectacular Roya village: a narrow cobbled street winds up to the 15th-century **Eglise St-Sauveur**, which was built by hauling stones up on the back of mules and contains another of those magnificent carved organs. This one was built in 1847 by the Lingiardi of Pavia, shipped by sea from Genoa and then carried to Saorge, also on the back of a mule. Despite these achievements, there are no boutiques and only one pizzeria and one restaurant. South of the village is the not-to-be-missed **Couvent des Franciscains**, whose lovely cloister is filled with painted sundials and 18th-century frescoes depicting the life of St Francis of Assisi. Beyond the monastery's cypress-lined terrace, a mule track leads to **Madone del Poggio**, a ruined Romanesque abbey (closed to the public).

As one approaches **Tende**, 20km on, the surrounding peaks become seriously Alpine. Tende is a market town where hikers and nature lovers gather to gear up before heading off into the Mercantour or the Vallée des Merveilles. Anyone intending to visit the Vallée des Merveilles should not miss the modern **Musée des Merveilles**, which has a diorama and interactive exhibits as well as an array of Bronze Age artefacts. It's dry stuff, but it clearly explains the prehistoric drawings in the valley – a topic easily subject to wild theories about voodoo or even prehistoric curses.

The **Vallée des Merveilles** itself is reached from St-Dalmas-de-Tende, 5km south of Tende (the Association des Taxis Accompagnateurs, 04.93.04.63.21, can provide transport), where a paved mountain road branches west to Casterino, jumping-off point for two waymarked footpaths – the direct route via the Refuge de Fontalbe, the only refuge accessible by car and then a 30-minute walk, or the longer northern route via the Refuge de Valmasque. Western access is from Madone de Fenestre in the Vésubie valley (*see p303*), via the high-altitude Refuge de Nice. A magnificent, rock-strewn valley dominated by the 2,872m Mont Bego, it contains at least 50,000 engravings, most dating from 2500BC to 500BC, although there are more recent interlopers (crucifixes, Napoleonic slogans, and local ritual signs made in the 16th to 18th centuries). Bronze and Iron Age shepherds chipped away at the red rocks to depict apparently familiar objects – cattle, ploughs, field systems. One of the most famous – and a symbol of the Vallée des Merveilles – is the so-called Sorcerer, a bearded giant who appears to be shooting lightning bolts from his hands. For guided 4WD tours of the valley contact Franck Panza (groups €55pp per day, 04.93.04.73.21, www.panzamerveilles.com).

Heading downstream from Tende, a side road leads east to picturesque **La Brigue**,which has three Baroque churches, of which the 15th-century **La Collégiale St-Martin** (La Place, open 9am-6pm daily), with some fine primitive paintings of the Nice school, is the only one open to the public. The real treat lies further east, where the mountain chapel of **Notre-Dame-des-Fontaines** (contact La Brigue tourist office to visit), a site of pilgrimage since antiquity, conceals a series of frescoes that has earned it the moniker of 'Sistine of the Alps'. The nave frescoes by Giovanni Canavesio push beyond the Gothic into a touching, though still primitive, foretaste of the Renaissance.

Couvent des Franciscains

Saorge (04.93.04.55.55). **Open** *Apr-Oct* 10am-6pm Mon, Wed-Sun. *Nov-Mar* 10am-noon, 2-5pm daily. **Admission** €4.60; free under-18s. **No credit cards.**

Musée du Fort St-Roch

16 pl Guillaume Tell, Sospel (04.93.04.00.70). **Open** *Apr, May, Sept, Oct* 2-6pm Sat, Sun. *June-Aug* 2-6pm Tue-Sun. **Admission** €5; €3 5-13s; free under-5s. **No credit cards.**

Musée des Merveilles

av du 16 Septembre 1947, Tende (04.93.04.32.50/ www.museedesmerveilles.com). **Open** *July, Aug* 10am-6.30pm daily. *Sept-June* 10am-5pm Mon, Wed-Sun. Closed 2wks Mar, 2wks Nov. **Admission** €4.55; €2.30 14-18s; free under-14s. **Credit** AmEx, MC, V.

Intense concentration for the serious sport of *pétanque* in **Sospel**. *See p299*.

Where to stay & eat

Just outside Sospel, the homely, wood-and whitewash interior of the **L'Auberge Provençale** (rte de Col de Castillon, 04.93.04.00.31, www.aubergeprovencale.fr, double €65, menu €21) makes for a cosy welcome, while in town the leisurely Bel Acqua restaurant of the **Hôtel des Etrangers** (7 bd de Verdun, 04.93.04.00.09, closed Nov-Feb, double €65-90, restaurant closed Mon & lunch Wed, menus €21-€32) is a local institution and the food, including a tank of justifiably worried trout, is first-class. Right in the centre of Sospel is the charming **Le St-Pierre** (14 rue St-Pierre, 04.93.04.00.66, www.sospello.com, double €64-€86), which has five wonderfully rustic rooms and provides a copious breakfast.

At the Col de Turini, the modern, log-cabin-like **Les Trois Vallées** (04.93.04.23.23, double €48-€91, breakfast included) has a restaurant (menus €15-€22), a sauna and a first-class gym. Friendly **Les Chamois** (04.93.91.58.31, double €50-€55, menus €20) has basic, comfortable rooms in ski-lodge style and quite good food.

Out of Breil-sur-Roya, beside the Roya on the N204, the **Hôtel Restaurant Castel du Roy** (146 rte de l'Aigora, 04.93.04.43.66, www.castelduroy.com, closed Nov-Easter, double €56-€66, restaurant closed Mon, menus €23-€26) has comfortable rooms and exquisitely

served regional cuisine (try sea perch with a Provençal *tian* or local trout). A youthful, sporty, and friendly option is the **Gîte d'Etape** (392 chemin du Foussa, 04.93.04.47.64, www.aetcanyoning.com, double €29-€36 incl. breakfast and dinner).

In Saorge, the restaurant **Le Bellevue** (5 rue Louis Périssol, 04.93.04.51.37, closed Wed and end Nov to mid-Dec, menus €16-€22) has a panoramic view. There are no hotels in Saorge but trekkers flock to the **Gîte Bergiron** (04.93.04.55.49, €11 per person in a dorm, €28 with dinner) behind the Franciscan monastery.

In Tende, **L'Auberge Tendasque** (65 av du 16 Septembre 1947, 04.93.04.62.26, menus €13-€20) serves the famous *truite au bleu*, where the fish hardly pauses from tank to plate. In nearby St-Dalmas-de-Tende, **Hôtel Restaurant Le Prieuré** (av Jean Médecin, 04.93.04.75.70, double €44-€64, restaurant closed Mon & dinner Sun Nov-Mar, menus €10-€22) offers pristine rooms and immaculate grounds – a comfortable stop for those allergic to mountain refuges. If you want to try one of the Vallée des Merveilles refuges contact **Club Alpin Nice** (04.93.62.59.99, www.cafnice.org, bed in dorm €13.50).

At La Brigue, **La Cassoulette** (20 rue du Général de Gaulle, 04.93.04.63.82, closed Mon & dinner Sun and Mar, menus €14-€27) is a tiny, convivial bistro, chock-a-block with statuettes of barnyard birds. It offers divine foie gras, duck confit and mouthwatering desserts (book). **Hôtel Restaurant Le Mirval** (3 rue Vincent Ferrier, 04.93.04.63.71, closed Nov-Mar, double €50-€59, restaurant closed lunch Fri, menus €15-€23) has utilitarian but quite spacious modern accommodation; it also organises 4WD excursions into the surrounding valleys.

Resources

Market day in Breil is Tuesday, in Sospel is Thursday, in Tende is Wednesday.

Tourist information

Breil-sur-Roya *Office de Tourisme, 17 pl Bianchéri, 06540 Breil-sur-Roya (04.93.04.99.76/ www.breil-sur-roya.fr).* **Open** *Apr-Sept* 9am-noon, 1.30-5pm Mon-Fri; 9am-noon Sat. *Oct-Mar* 9am-noon, 2-4pm Mon-Sat; 9am-noon Sun.
La Brigue *Office de Tourisme, Mairie, pl St-Martin, 06430 La Brigue (04.93.04.60.04).* **Open** 9am-noon, 1.30-5pm Mon-Sat. Closed mid-Jan to mid-Feb.
Sospel *Office de Tourisme, Le Pont-Vieux, 06380 Sospel (04.93.04.15.80).* **Open** *July, Aug* 9am-noon, 2-7pm daily. *Sept-June* 9am-noon, 2-6pm daily.
Tende *Office de Tourisme, av du 16 septembre 1947, 06430 Tende (04.93.04.73.71).* **Open** *June-Oct* 9am-noon, 2-6pm daily. *Nov-May* 9am-12.30pm, 2-5.30pm Mon-Wed, Fri, Sat; 9am-12.30pm Sun.
Parc National du Mercantour Bureau d'Information *23 rue d'Italie, Nice (04.93.16.78.88/www.parc-mercantour.fr).* There are also local information offices at Tende (103 av du 16 Septembre 1947, 04.93.04.67.00), St-Martin-Vésubie (pl Félix Faure, 04.93.03.23.15) and St-Etienne-de-Tinée (Ardon, 04.93.02.42.27).

The Vésubie valley

The Vésubie river is fed by the snows of the Alpine ranges and flows through one of the most beautiful valleys above Nice. The best way into the upper valley is the D19 out of Nice, which rises almost imperceptibly past villas and pastures to the village of **Levens**, an atmospheric cluster of stone houses with an excess of burbling fountains. Beyond Levens the mountains begin with a vengeance as the road clings to the side of the **Gorges de la Vésubie** – which can also be negotiated on the lower D2565 route. Soon after the two roads meet is the turn-off for **Utelle**, a village which projects like a balcony over the Vésubie valley below. This isolated village has managed to keep its original character: old houses with sundials and a church with a pretty Gothic porch and doors carved with scenes from the life of local boy St Véran. The nearby **Chapelle des Pénitents-Blancs** has a carved wooden version of Rubens' *Descent from the Cross*,

while the shrine of **Madone d'Utelle** stands on a barren peak 6km further on; try to visit in the morning, as the clouds often roll up here later in the day. A plain terracotta barn of a church, it owes its existence to a ninth-century shipwreck on the patch of sea that, on a clear day, can be seen far below. Believing they had been saved from drowning by the Virgin, who appeared on the mountainside bathed in light, grateful Spanish mariners climbed up here to set up a shrine.

The road up to St-Martin-Vésubie continues past Lantosque to **Roquebillière**, a crumbling old village with a modern offshoot opposite, built after a landslide in 1926 that claimed 17 lives. Down by the river on the same side as the modern village is the unusual church of **St-Michel-de-Gast-des-Templiers**. Built by the Knights Templars and later taken over by the Knights of Malta, it is full of abstruse Templar symbolism; on one capital there is a carving of the Egyptian baboon god Thot. The key is kept by the voluble Madame Périchon, who lives in the house opposite the church.

At **Berthemont-les-Bains** you'll find a modern spa. The sulfurous, 30°C waters were used by the Romans to treat respiratory diseases and rheumatism. Today, they are funnelled into various indoor pools where clients relax after a

Sospel, where time stands still. *See p299.*

therapeutic massage at the **Station Thermale de Berthemont-les-Bains** (04.93.03.47.00, closed Oct-Apr, rates €33-€44, weekly rate €210).

St-Martin-Vésubie is a good place to refuel and pick up supplies and information. The pocket-sized place Félix Faure links the main valley road with rue Cagnoli, St-Martin's pedestrian backbone. A little paved channel of water, known as a *gargouille*, runs the whole way down the steeply inclined street.

The road west to the church of **Madone de Fenestre** criss-crosses a mountain stream. Push on to the end, where a large mountain refuge and a tin-roofed church are surrounded by a cirque of high peaks. The church is only two centuries old, but its miraculous icon of the Madone de Fenestre (kept down in St-Martin in winter) dates from the 12th century. Allow at least an hour and a half for the rewarding walk up past a lake to the Col de Fenestre on the Italian border. Madone de Fenestre also gives access to the Vallée des Merveilles.

Perched on a rocky spur that overlooks St-Martin, **Venanson** is home to the tiny **Chapelle Ste-Claire** on place St-Jean, which has lively 15th-century frescoes of the life of St Sebastian. If it's closed, collect the key from the Hôtel Bellavista (04.93.03.25.11) opposite.

West of St-Martin, the D2565 continues up to the Col St-Martin (1,500m), which links the Vésubie and Tinée valleys. Just right from the Col is a *via ferrata*, a protected climbing route with handrail, that will certainly do its best to get your pulse racing. There are three routes, blue, black and red depending on their difficulty, and even the easiest takes an hour and a half. Ask at the tourist office for details and equipment. Just below the pass is the aspiring resort of **La Colmiane**, where, in June and July, you can career down the mountain on a *trottinerbe*, a sort of kid's scooter with huge soft tyres, from the top of the Pic de Colmiane lift. In winter, it's a small ski resort. The charms of **St-Dalmas-de-Valdeblore**, the first village over the pass, are more sedate. The **Eglise de l'Invention de la Ste-Croix**, a fine Romanesque church with its very own piece of the Holy Cross, once belonged to a powerful Benedictine priory.

Where to stay & eat

Just above Utelle on the Madone d'Utelle road, **Le Bellevue** (04.93.03.17.19, hotel only open July & Aug, double €35-€48, restaurant closed Mon, menus €12-€26) has a pool and views that live up to the name. Its restaurant is open all year serving traditional home cooking. In Lantosque, **L'Ancienne Gendarmerie** (Le Rivet, 04.93.03. 00.65, closed Nov-Feb, double

€78-€115, restaurant closed Mon & dinner Sun except July-Aug, menus €19-€25) really was a police station – hence the sentry box outside – and offers eight rooms and a small swimming pool perched above the river. Up in the village, the **Bar des Tilleuls** (04.93.03.05.74) is a good place for a *pastis* or light lunch under the eponymous lime trees.

In Roquebillière, the friendly *chambres d'hôtes* **Ferme les Cartons** (Quartier Gordon, 04.93.03.47.93, double €45, including breakfast) has lovely views and charmingly rustic rooms.

In St-Martin-Vésubie, **La Treille** (68 rue Cagnoli, 04.93.03.30.85, closed Wed & Thur except in school holidays, and Dec to mid-Feb, menus €17-€22), towards the top of the main street, is a friendly restaurant with good wood-fired pizzas (dinner only), classic meat and fish dishes and a panoramic terrace at the back. **La Taverne du Pelago** (Lac du Boeron, 04.93.03.22.00, menu €20.50) looks over the lake and serves lovely roast lamb and great local cheeses. For breakfast with homemade jam, or a quick lunch, head to the **Café-Boulangerie La Maverine** (34 rue Cagnoli, 04.93.03.35.08, closed Wed). **La Bonne Auberge** (La Place, 04.93.03.20.49, closed 15 Nov-15 Feb, double €38-€47, menus €18-€25) lives up to its name, offering solid mountain hospitality in a cheerful building overlooking the valley. The slightly more luxurious **Edward's Parc Hôtel La Chataigneraie** (04.93.03.21.22, closed Oct-May, double €55 €69), is a little frayed but still a good place to relax, with the aid of a heated outdoor swimming pool and mini-golf.

Resources

Tourist information

St-Martin-Vésubie *Office de Tourisme, pl Félix Faure, 06450 St-Martin-Vésubie (04.93.03.21.28/ www.stmartinvesubie.fr).* **Open** *June-Sept* 9am noon, 3-7pm daily. *Oct-May* 10am-noon, 2.30-5.30pm Mon-Sat.

Bureau des Guides du Mercantour

pl du Marché, St-Martin-Vésubie (04.93.03.31.32). **Open** *July, Aug* 10.30am-12.30pm, 4-5.30pm daily. Organises guided mountain hiking expeditions, climbing lessons and canyoning. Call in winter for ice-fall canyoning and ski excursions.

The Tinée valley

Most Niçois see this road as a bit of scenery on the way to the ski resorts of Isola 2000 or Auron, but the upper reaches of the Tinée valley are worth a visit in their own right, though less precipitous than the Vésubie. The Tinée flows into the Var just where the latter changes direction to head south to Nice. A few side roads wind their way up to the *villages perchés* of **La Tour** and **Clans**. The former has some vivacious 15th-century scenes of vices and virtues in the Chapelle des Pénitents-Blancs and an ancient but working oil mill. In well-preserved medieval Clans, the Chapelle de St-Antoine features frescoes of the life of the saint. On the east side of the valley, **Marie** is a pretty hamlet of only 60 inhabitants with an excellent hotel/restaurant, Le Panoramique (*see below*).

Approaching **St-Sauveur-sur-Tinée**, the iron-rich cliffs turn a garish shade of puce – quite a sight at sunset. St-Sauveur is a one-horse town, with little to retain the visitor, but it is also the jumping-off point for a spectacular route west via the ski resort of Valberg into the Haut Var valley, whose source lies just below the Col de Cayolle, one of the most rewarding of all the gateways into the Mercantour.

Above St-Sauveur, the Tinée valley heads north through the Gorges de Valabre before broadening out below Isola, a siesta of a village amid chestnut groves, with a solitary 15th-century bell tower and, rather incongruously given the pace of life around these parts, **Aquavallée** (04.93.02.16.49, 11am-8pm Mon-Fri, 10am-8pm Sat, Sun), a covered fun pool with sauna, gym, steam room and squash courts. Further incongruities lie in wait up the side road that ascends the Chastillon torrent to the ski resort of **Isola 2000**. The 1970s British design of this blight on the landscape has not aged well, but from here you can walk into the surrounding high peaks or continue by car over the Col de la Lombarde pass into Italy.

St-Etienne-de-Tinée, near the head of the valley, is a surprisingly lively market town of tall, pastel houses and Gothic portals, which celebrates its shepherding traditions in the Fête de la Transhumance on the last Sunday in June. It has a cluster of interesting frescoed churches, though you need to go on a tour organised by the Office de Tourisme to see them.

Who's afraid of the big bad wolf?

Ignoring country borders with carefree indifference, the intrepid wolf has been slipping over the Franco-Italian frontier in increasing numbers since 1992, happily setting up camp in the wilds of the Mercantour. Since then, a bitter battle has been raging between ecologists and shepherds. The latter are terrified that their flocks will be killed, the former thrilled that the approximately 27 wolves in the park are thriving against earlier odds predicting extinction. In the ecologists' scientific opinion, '*les chiens errants*' (stray dogs) are to blame for recent attacks since, contrary to dogs, wolves only kill to eat. The shepherds, on the other hand, are not nearly so philosophical – they just want the attacks on their sheep to stop.

A first investigative report was ordered by the French government, with little practical effect except to agree that the wolves really were in the Mercantour. Sheep continued to die, wolves continued to roam, and the conflict continued to simmer. It reached boiling point in 2002, when the Minister for Ecology and Sustainable Development released provisional numbers relating to flock damage: 2,304 sheep killed by vicious wild dog/wolf attacks. Bad enough from a shepherd's point of view, but what triggered the explosion was an unexpectedly gory event in the *commune* of Moulinet. A flock of sheep was attacked by two wolves, resulting in 407 dead animals. Only six were actually bitten, but the rest, reacting in mass terror, flung themselves off a cliff to their deaths in the ravine below.

Tensions started to run high and Parliament instantly ordered another investigation to try and come up with some sort of solution. The resulting report, published in June 2003, gives ambiguous advice: wolf-friendly zones ought to have borders. Outside these borders wolves can be shot. It is an impractical solution at best as the wolf is protected by international agreements and fencing mountains is not the easiest thing to do. The committee also suggested better regulation of subsidised enclosures, financial compensation and specially trained dogs ('*patou*') to fight off wolf attacks.

Today, there are fewer than 500 wolves in Italy, and about 1,500 in Spain, plus the 27 that officially live in French territory. They are an endangered species. And yes, they do attack sheep as their nature dictates. So what to do? Solutions – more shepherds, sheep dogs, protected enclosures for the nights – do exist, but they are expensive. And encouraging the simple 'exterminate them all!' option would certainly further endanger the already fragile survival of the species. It's a tricky question for the big, bad wolf – and the answer, unfortunately, is nowhere in sight. Find more information on the Mercantour at www.parcsnationaux-fr.com.

The prize for the most unexpected sight in the Alpes-Maritimes must go to the **Chapelle de St-Erige** (collect the key from the tourist office) in the lively ski resort of **Auron**. This little wooden chapel – commissioned by wealthy parishioners in the 15th century, when this upland plain was covered in summer cornfields – is almost overwhelmed by the faux-Swiss-chalet hotels that surround it. Inside, it's another story – a series of stories, in fact, told in vivid frescoes dating back to 1451. Scenes of the life of Mary Magdalene alternate religious mysticism with the secular spirit of the troubadour poets.

North of St-Etienne the D2205 soon becomes the D64 to Barcelonnette, the highest paved road in Europe. When the pass is open (June-Sept) bikers, motorists and even cyclists slog up to the Col de la Bonette, where the road loops to encircle the bare peak of Cime de la Bonette. From the highest snack bar in Europe (2,802m), a short path takes you up to the viewing table at 2,860m for a spectacular 360° panorama.

Alternatively, leave the D2205 north of St-Etienne and head left to the ravishingly pretty mountain village of **St-Dalmas-le-Selvage**, the highest in the Alpes-Maritimes. Most of the houses still have their original larchwood roofs, open under the eaves where the corn was traditionally laid out to dry. The parish church has two early 16th-century altarpieces, and inside the tiny **Chapelle de Ste-Marguerite** in the centre of the village are frescoes by Jean Baleison, which were discovered behind the altar in 1996.

Activities

Skiing

The two main resorts with widest choice of options are Auron and Isola 2000. **Auron**, at 1,600m altitude, offers 130km of pistes and 25 assorted téléphériques, télésièges and téléskis to get to them, as well as Surf-land, a huge playground for snowboarders, with a half-pipe and runs for beginners. Purpose-built resort **Isola 2000** offers 48 runs, including five blacks, heli-skiing, and one of the largest snowboarding and mini-skiing clubs in France. Passes cost around €19-€22. And if 70s concrete is not your style, try the rustic chalets north of the station. Smaller **St-Dalmas-le-Selvage** mainly offers cross-country skiing, with over 35km of pistes, plus snowshoe and skidoo excursions.
For weather conditions call Météo des Routes et des Pistes (04.93.59.70.12) or Météo Neige (08.36.68.10.20).

Where to stay & eat

It's worth planning a lunch or dinner stop in Marie, where the relaxing family-run hotel-restaurant **Le Panoramique** (pl de la Mairie,

The Tinée valley. *See p303.*

04.93.02.03.01, double €40, restaurant closed Thur, menus €16-€30) provides five scenic rooms and fine meals, including seasonal game. In Isola (the village, not the ski resort), **Au Café d'Isola** (pl Jean Gaïssa, 04.93.02.17.03, menus €14-€23) does decent pizzas and snacks. The comfortable **Hôtel Le Régalivou** (8 bd d'Auron, 04.93.02.49.00, double €40-€58) has a summer restaurant (July, Aug only) serving solid regional dishes (menus €17-€32). The town also has a well-run municipal **campsite** on a small watersports lake, a three-minute walk from the centre (Plan d'Eau, 04.93.02.41.57, €10 two people). The **Hôtel Chastellares** (pl Central, 04.93.23.02.58, closed Apr-June, double €68-€90 with half-board) in the centre of Auron has lovely balconies and a good restaurant. **L'Auberge de l'Etoile** (04.93.02.44.97, closed mid-Oct to mid-June, open Sat & Sun and school holidays Dec to mid-June by reservation, average €25) in St-Dalmas-le-Selvage hides not a little sophistication beneath its rustic decor, which is enlivened by fake Van Goghs. Booking is essential. There is also a homely **Gîte d'étape** (04.93.02.44.61, dormitory €10) in the village, designed for walkers doing the GR5 long-distance path, but open to all comers.

The Riviera & Southern Alps

Resources

Tourist information

Auron *Office de Tourisme, Grange Cossa, 06660 Auron (04.93.23.02.66/www.auron.com).* **Open** 9am-noon, 2-5.30pm daily.
Isola 2000 *Chalet d'Acceuil, 06420 Isola (04.93.23.15.15/www.isola2000.com).* **Open** school holidays 8.30am-7pm daily. *rest of year* 9am-noon, 2-6pm Mon-Fri; 8.30am-7pm daily.
St-Etienne-de-Tinée *Maison du Tourisme, 1 rue des Communes de France (04.93.02.41.96).* **Open** 9am-noon, 2-5.30pm daily.

The Upper Var valley

The river Var flows into the Mediterranean just next to Nice airport at St-Laurent-du-Var, but in the upper reaches it offers Alpine scenery and perilously perched villages. Although you can follow the route by N202 from Nice airport, this is one place where the train trip on the **Train des Pignes** is worth the journey in itself. Built in 1891-1900 between the Gare de Provence in Nice and Digne-les-Bains in the sparsely populated Alpes de Haute-Provence, it was part of an ambitious plan to provide a direct rail link between the Alps and the Côte d'Azur. The one-metre narrow-gauge railway runs over 31 bridges and viaducts and through 25 tunnels, climbing to an altitude of 1,000m.

Beyond **Plan du Var** the mountains close in on either side at the forbidding **Défilé de Chaudan**, beyond which the Var abruptly changes direction, heading west. **Villars-sur-Var** is a *village perché* with some good Renaissance art in the church of St-Jean-Baptiste, but its main claim to fame is as the centre of the tiny Bellet wine appellation, which occupies a mere 31 hectares; the white is definitely worth trying. At **Touët-sur-Var**, space is so tight that the village church straddles a mountain stream. The valley opens out a little at **Puget-Théniers**, an old Templar stronghold and the birthplace of Auguste Blanqui, one of the leaders of the Paris Commune of 1870, who is commemorated by a stirring Aristide Maillol monument on the main road.

Cradled in a curve of the river, **Entrevaux** is a handsome fortified village. Perched way above on a perilous ridge is a fortress built by Louis XIV's military architect Vauban in the 1690s. Until 1860, this was a border town between France and Italy. The twin towers that guard the entrance to the village across a single-arched bridge are almost Disney-picturesque, but once inside it is a sturdily practical place, with tall houses, narrow lanes and a 17th-century cathedral built into the defensive walls. The castle itself is a steep, appetite-building climb from the town up a zigzag ramp; it's an atmospheric old pile, with dungeons and galleries to explore.

Beyond Entrevaux, the Train des Pignes continues towards Digne-les-Bains via the old town of **Annot**, where the houses are built right up against huge sandstone boulders, and **St-André-les-Alpes** on the Lac de Castellane. The Var valley backtracks again in a route that can be traced by the D2202 along the dramatic red-schist Gorges de Dalious to its source way north in the Parc de Mercantour.

Resources

Tourist information

Puget *Maison de Pays, 2 rue Alexandre Borety, 06260 Puget-Theniers (04.93.05.05.05).* **Open** *Mar-Oct* 9am-noon, 2-7pm daily. *Nov-Feb* 9am-noon, 2-5pm daily.

Train des Pignes

(04.97.03.80.80). Trains depart from the Gare de Provence in Nice (4bis rue Alfred Binet) and arrive at the Gare Digne-les-Bains. There are four daily departures in each direction; Nice to Digne takes just over three hours and costs €17.65 (€8.82 4-12s) one-way; Nice to Entrevaux takes an hour and a half and costs €9. Trains are modern, with two carriages, but steam trains complete with staff in costume still ply the route on Sunday from May to October.

Getting there & around

By car

For the Roya and Bévéra valleys take the D2566 from Menton to Sospel, then the D2204 north for Breil-sur-Roya. Alternatively, the Roya valley can be ascended from Ventimiglia in Italy on the S20, which crosses into France at Olivetta San Michele, 10km before Breil. The N202 follows the Var valley from Nice airport; the D2565 branches off here along the Vésubie valley (also reached by D2566/D70 from Sospel via the Col de Turini), the D2205 follows the Tinée valley.

By train

Around five trains a day travel the picturesque Nice-Cuneo line stopping at Menton, Sospel, Breil-sur-Roya and Tende. For the Train des Pignes from Nice to Digne, see left, Upper Var valley.

By bus

Bus travel is limited in this area; **Autocars Rey** (04.93.04.01.24) runs services between Menton and Sospel and between Sospel and other destinations in the Roya valley. **TRAM** (04.93.89.47.14) buses run twice daily between Nice and St-Martin-Vésubie, Mon-Sat, and once daily Sun. In summer, one a day continues to La Colmiane, only Sunday in winter. Infrequent buses also serve Le Boréon and Madone de Fenestre in summer. **Santa-Azur** (04.93.85.92.60) runs daily services between Nice, St-Etienne-de-Tinée and Auron, and between Nice, Isola and Isola 2000.

Directory

Directory

Getting There & Around

By air

Airlines from the UK

The arrival of low-cost airlines has greatly increased air travel options to the South of France.

Air France (UK 0845 084 5111/USA 1-800 237 2747/France 08.20.82.08.20/www.airfrance.com). London Heathrow to Nice. Also Paris to Avignon, Marseille, Montpellier, Nice, Nîmes.

bmibaby (UK 0870 264 2229/France 01.41.91.87.04/www.flybmi.com/ bmibaby). East Midlands to Nice.

British Airways (UK 0845 773 3377/US 1-800 247 9297/France 08.25.82.54.00/www.britishairways.com). London Gatwick to Marseille, Montpellier, Toulon. Heathrow, Gatwick, Birmingham and Manchester to Nice.

British Midland (UK 0870 607 0555/France 01.48.62.55.65/www.flybmi.com). Heathrow and East Midlands to Nice.

Easyjet (UK 0870 600 0000/France 08.25.08.25.08/www.easyjet.com). Gatwick, Stansted, Aberdeen, Bristol, Liverpool and Luton to Nice, and Gatwick to Marseille.

Ryanair (08.92.55.56.66/www.ryanair.com). Stansted to Nîmes.

Airlines from the USA

From the USA, most flights involve a Paris connection.

Delta (US 1-800 241 4141/France 08.00.35.40.80/www.delta.com) flies daily from New York JFK to Nice.

Airports

Marseille and Nice are the two main airports.

Aéroport Avignon-Caumont (04.90.81.51.51). Served by Air France from Paris Orly.

Aéroport Marseille-Provence (04.42.14.14.14/www.marseille. aeroport.fr). Situated in Marignane,

28km NW of town. Buses run every 20 mins to Marseille rail station, every 30 mins to Aix-en-Provence.

Aéroport Montpellier Méditerranée (04.67.20.85.00/recorded times 04.67.20.85.85/www.montpellier.aeroport.fr).

Aéroport Nice-Côte d'Azur (08.20.42.33.33/recorded times www.nice.aeroport.fr). 7km W of the centre, Nice is France's second airport. Most airlines use Terminal 1; Air France flights use Terminal 2.

Aéroport de Nîmes-Arles-Camargue (04.66.70.49.49). 10km SE of Nîmes; 20km from Arles.

Aéroport de Toulon-Hyères (04.94.00.83.83). Near Hyères port.

Helicopter services

Air St-Tropez (04.94.97.15.12). Between Nice and St-Tropez €765 for five plus tax.

Héli-Air Monaco (00.377-92.05.00.50). Nice to Monaco costs €84.35 per person.

Nice Hélicoptères (04.93.21.34.32). Cannes-Nice return approx €130/person plus tax.

By train

One of the quickest and most efficient ways to travel within France is by train. French trains are run by the SNCF state railway (www.sncf.com).

Train lines

Mainline services

The French TGV (high-speed train) runs to the South from Paris Gare de Lyon and Lille, via Lyon to Avignon, where it splits west to Nîmes and east to Aix-en-Provence, Marseille, Toulon, Draguignan-Les Arcs, St-Raphaël, Cannes, Antibes, Nice, Monte-Carlo and Menton (not all trains stop at all stations). Note that the highest-speed track currently only reaches Marseille and Nîmes. It takes around 2hrs 40min to Avignon, 3 hrs to Aix, Marseille and Nîmes, 5hrs 30 mins to Nice. On slower long-distance trains from Menton and

Nice, you can travel overnight by *couchette* (bunk-bed sleeping car shared with up to five others) or *voiture-lit* (more comfortable sleeping compartment for up to three). Both are available in first- and second-class, and must be reserved ahead.

Eurostar (UK 01233-617575/France 08.92.35.35.39/www.eurostar.fr). For the Eurostar to the South of France, change at Lille or Paris for the TGV. From late May to late Oct a weekly Eurostar goes direct from London Waterloo to Avignon Central in just 6hrs 15mins.

Local trains

The local train network is most extensive in the Rhône valley and along the coast. Out-of-town stations usually have a connecting *navette* (shuttle bus) to the town centre. Sometimes SNCF runs buses (indicated as Autocar in timetables) to stations where the train no longer stops; rail tickets and passes are valid on these. Métrazur runs along the coast, stopping at all stations between Marseille and Ventimiglia in Italy. There's also a Marseille-Aix-Gap line and two mountain lines from Nice: the Roya valley line via Sospel, and the privately run Train des Pignes (from Gare de Provence).

Fares & tickets

You can buy tickets in all SNCF stations from counters or by French-issued credit card at automatic ticket machines; some travel agents also sell tickets. Phone bookings can be made on 3635 or 08.92.35.35.35 (open 7am-10pm daily). For information in English call 08.36.35.35.39. Internet bookings can be made on www.sncf.com or www.tgv.com, and paid online or at ticket machines; certain tickets can be printed out directly at home. The TGV can be booked up to two months ahead. You must have seats reserved for the TGV. For all train journeys you must 'composter votre billet' - date-stamp your ticket in the orange *composteur* machine on the platforms before starting the journey.

In the UK, tickets for through travel can be booked from any mainline station or travel centre. Or try the International Rail Centre (08.707.515.000/www.international-rail.com) or the Rail Europe Travel Shop 179 Piccadilly, London W1V OBA (0870 584 8848/ www.raileurope.co.uk).

Fares & discounts

Fares vary according to whether you travel in normal (*période normale*) or peak (*période de pointe*) hours; discounts are sometimes still available within these times; first-class travellers pay the same rate at all times. 'Découverte à deux' gives a 25% reduction for two people travelling together on a return journey, and there are discounts for up to four adults travelling with a child under 12. Every Tuesday www.sncf.com advertises special *dernière minute* offers, while Prem's (available every day) gives low prices for selected cities bought in advance. You can also save 25-50% by purchasing special discount cards for under 12s, 12 25 yr olds and over-60s. Children under four travel free.

International passes

A Eurodomino pass allows unlimited travel on France's rail network for a 3-8 day duration within 1 month, but must be bought before travelling to France. Discounted rates are available for children aged between 4 and 11, young people between 12 and 25 and for the over-60s. Passes for North Americans include Eurailpass, Flexipass and Saver Pass, which can be purchased in the USA.

Bicycles on trains

For long-distance train travel bicycles need to be transported separately, and must be registered and insured. They can be delivered to your destination, though this may take several days. On Eurostar bikes can be transported as hand luggage in a bike bag, or checked in at the station's goods depot up to 24 hours in advance of your journey. Bikes can be transported on many local trains (indicated by a bicycle symbol in timetables). See also the *SNCF Guide Train + Vélo*.

By bus & coach

Travelling round France by bus takes determination.

Eurolines

(*UK 01582 404511/France 08.92.69.52.52/www.eurolines.fr/*) runs regular coaches from London Victoria to Avignon, Marseille, Toulon and Nice.

Local buses

The coastal area is reasonably well served by buses, especially around the main towns, and city centres

have good regular services. In the country, services are more limited and generally run by a galaxy of small local companies. Most towns of any size have a *gare routière* (bus station), often near the train station. In rural areas buses are often linked to the needs of schools and working people, so there may well be only one bus in the morning, one in the evening and none on Sunday or during school holidays.

By car & motorbike

Much of Europe heads south during July and August, when motorways and coast roads, especially around St-Tropez or between Cannes and Menton, crawl at snail's pace. Roads are at their worst on Saturdays and around the 14 July and 15 August public holidays. Look for BIS (Bison Futé) signs, which attempt to reduce summer traffic by suggesting diversions on backroads.

Car ferries & Eurotunnel

Brittany Ferries (*08.03.82.88.28/ www.brittanyferries.fr*). Poole to Cherbourg, Plymouth to Roscoff, Portsmouth to St-Malo or Caen.

Eurotunnel (*UK 08705-353535/ France 03.21.00.61.00/ www.eurotunnel.com*). Takes cars through the Channel Tunnel Folkestone-Calais.

Hoverspeed (*UK 0800 1211 1211/France 08.20.00.35.55/ www.hoverspeed.com*). High-speed seacats from Dover to Calais and Newhaven to Dieppe.

P&O Stena Line (*UK 08705-202020/France 01.55.69.82.28/ www.posl.com*). Ferries from Dover to Calais, and Portsmouth to Cherbourg or Le Havre.

Sea France (*UK 08705-711711/ France 08.03.04.40.45/ 03.21.46.80.00/www.seafrance.com*). Ferries from Dover to Calais.

Driving in France

Roads

French roads are divided into *autoroutes* (motorways, marked A8, A51, etc), *routes nationales* (national 'N' roads, marked N222, etc), *routes départementales* ('D' roads) and tiny rural *routes communales* ('C' roads).

Autoroutes & tolls

From Calais to Nice is 1,167km; from Caen to Nice 1,161km. Dieppe to Avignon is 854 km, Calais to Avignon 965km. For Provence, the quickest route from Calais is via Paris (though avoid the Périphérique ring road at rush hour) and the A6 Autoroute du Soleil to Lyon and the Rhône valley. A less-trafficked route to western Provence is the A10-A71-A75 via Bourges and Clermont-Ferrand. www.iti.fr, www.mappy.fr, www.viamichelin.com and www.autoroutes.fr can help you plan your route. 08.92.68.10.77 and Radio 107.7 FM give information on motorway traffic.

French autoroutes are toll (*péage*) roads, although some sections – especially around major cities – are free. At *péage* toll-booths, payment can be made by cash or credit card. From Calais to Menton, expect to spend around €80 on tolls, Nice airport to Monaco costs €3.20, Aix-en-Provence to Nice €14.

There are *aires* approximately every 20-30km; simple ones offer picnic tables and toilets; larger ones have 24-hr petrol stations, cafés, shops and sometimes summer activities and tourist information.

Motorail

A comfortable though pricey option is the Motorail; put your car on the train in Calais or Paris and travel overnight down to the coast, though services do not run every day except in high summer and you may travel on a different day to your car. Couchettes are mandatory. For UK bookings, contact Rail Europe (0870 584 8848/www.frenchmotorail.com).

Paperwork

If you bring your car to France, you will need to bring the relevant registration and insurance documents, and, of course, your driving licence. New drivers need to have held a licence for at least a year.

Speed limits

In normal conditions, speed limits are 130km/hr (80 miles) on autoroutes, 110km/hr (69 miles) on dual carriageways, and 90km/hr (56 miles) on other roads. In heavy rain and fog, these limits are reduced by 20km on autoroutes, by 10km on other roads. Speed limits are also reduced on days of heavy air pollution. The limit in built-up areas is 50km/hr (28 miles), with 30km/hr (17 miles) in some districts. Recent government policy has been to rigorously enforce speed limits; automatic radars have been installed all over France since autumn 2003, which can automatically send off a speeding fine for as little as 6km/hr over the speed limit.

Breakdown services

The AA or RAC do not have reciprocal arrangements with French organisations, so it's best to take out additional breakdown insurance cover, for example with **Europ Assistance** (UK 01444 442211). Local 24-hr breakdown services include **Dépannage Côte d'Azur** (04.93.29.87.87). Autoroutes and routes nationales have emergency telephones every 2km. *See also p315* **Emergencies**.

Driving tips

• At intersections where no signposts indicate the right of way, the car coming from the right has priority. Roundabouts follow the same rule, though many now give priority to those on the roundabout: this will be indicated either by stop markings on the road or by the message 'Vous n'avez pas la priorité'.
• Drivers and all passengers must wear seat belts.
• Children under ten are not allowed to travel in the front, except in special baby seats facing backwards.
• You should not stop on an open road; pull off to the side.
• When drivers flash their lights at you, this means that they will not slow down and are warning you to keep out of the way. Oncoming drivers may also flash their lights to warn you when there are gendarmes lurking on the other side of the hill.
• Carry change, as it's quicker to head for the exact-money line on *péages*; but cashiers do give change and *péages* accept credit cards.
• Motorbikes must have headlights on while in motion; cars must have their headlights on in poor visibility.
• All vehicles have to carry a full spare set of light bulbs and drivers who wear spectacles or contact lenses must carry a spare pair.
• The French drink-driving limit is 0.5g alcohol per litre of blood (about two glasses of wine). Above 0.8g/l and you can have your licence confiscated on the spot.
• Cédez le passage = give way.
• Vous n'avez pas la priorité = you do not have right of way.
• Passage protégé = no right of way.
• Rappel = reminder.

Fuel

Only unleaded (*sans plomb*) and diesel (*gasoil*) are available, but a special unleaded petrol is available for cars that run on leaded fuel. Petrol tends to be most expensive on autoroutes; many drivers fill up at supermarkets. Petrol stations can be scarce in rural areas, especially on Sunday, though some supermarket stations have 24-hr pumps that accept Carte Bleue.

Parking

In high season, you have to get up very early to get a parking space at the beach. Inland, some highly touristed villages now have compulsory car parks. Car parks are often the best option in the main cities. Parking meters have now largely been replaced by *horodateurs*, pay-and-display machines, which take either coins or cards, available from *tabacs*. Parking may be free over lunch-time, on Sunday and public holidays. Check exact details on the machine or display panels.

Vehicle hire

To hire a car you must normally be 25 or over and have held a licence for at least a year. Some hire companies will accept drivers aged 21-24, but a supplement of €8-€15 per day is usual. Remember to bring your licence and passport with you.

Car hire companies

ADA 01.41.27.49.00/www.net-on-line.net/ada

Avis 08.02.05.05.05/www.avis.com

Budget 0800.472 3325/www.budget.com

Europcar 08.25.352.352/www.europcar.com

EasyCar (No phone reservations) www.easycar.com

Hertz 01.39.38.38.38/www.hertz.com

Interrent 08.99.70.02.92/www.interrent.fr

Rent A Car 08.92.69.46.95/www.rentacar.fr

Car hire rates

Hiring a car in France is expensive. Consider fly-drive packages, or arranging car hire before leaving home, which can work out cheaper. SNCF offers a train/car rental scheme, in association with Avis. There are often good weekend offers (Fri evening to Mon morning). Week-long deals are better at the bigger hire companies – with Avis or Budget, for example, it's around €250 a week for a small car with insurance and 1,700km included. Most international companies will allow the return of a car in other cities or even countries. Low-cost operators, such as Ada, may have a high excess charge for dents or damage. Rates with EasyCar vary according to demand when you book.

Motorbike hire

Harley-Davidson Factory 8 rue Boyer, Nice (04.92.00.08.41/ *www.hdrentals.com*). Fancy tearing around Provence on a Harley? Go on,

indulge. You must be over 21 and a licence holder for at least two years. Prices start at around €225/day.

By bicycle

Cycling is an excellent way to see Provence. If you have a foreign-made bike, bring spare tyres with you, as French sizes are different.

Bike hire

Holiday Bikes (*www.holiday-bikes.com*). Franchise network with 20 branches along the Côte d'Azur, between Bandol and Menton, plus Avignon and Forcalquier. Bicycles, scooters and mopeds can be hired at individual agencies or on the web. Prices start at €21/day. Note that prices vary from branch to branch.

SNCF Bikes can be rented from some SNCF stations (around €11/day plus €150 deposit), and returned to any station in the scheme. *See also p309* **Bicycles on trains**.

On foot

Provence is crossed by several well-signposted long-distance *sentiers de grande randonnée* (GR), as well as local footpaths, all described in *Topo* guides, available from bookshops and newsagents. On the coast, some of the most beautiful *caps* (headlands) have waymarked paths, while walking in the Calanques gives access to spectacular unspoilt beaches. The best periods for walking are spring and autumn; access may be limited in high fire-risk areas in high summer. Be sure you have plenty of water and sun protection. *See also p317* **Maps** and *p319* **Sport & activity holidays**.

Hitch-hiking

Allô-Stop

8 rue Rochambeau, Paris (01.53.20.42.42). Safer than just taking a chance on the kerbside. This agency puts hitchhikers in touch with drivers. You should call several days ahead. There's a fee of €4.50-€10.50 depending on distance; you then pay €0.33/10km to the driver (Paris to Nice costs around €31).

Accommodation

There is a huge variety of accommodation available in the South, from the grandest seafront Palace hotel to the simplest mountain refuge; in between you can rent villas or gîtes, camp, or stay in a wide range of country auberges and *chambres d'hôtes*. In summer it is advisable to book ahead, and essential if you want to stay on the coast, but outside the peak period of mid-July to mid-August, you should not have too much trouble finding accommodation. Many hotels and most campsites close from November to around March, some reopen just for the Christmas break. Some tourist offices offer a free booking service and, if you arrive in peak season without accommodation, most will know which hotels have last-minute vacancies.

Camping

French campsites (*les campings*) can be surprisingly luxurious. Many are run by local councils. Prices range from €6 to around €22 per night for a family of four, with car, caravan or tent. Camping rough (*camping sauvage*) is discouraged but you may be given permission if you ask. Be very careful camping in areas that may have a fire risk.

Campsites are graded from one-star (minimal comfort, water points, showers and sinks) to four-star luxury sites that offer more space for each pitch and above-average facilities. To get back to nature look out for campsites designated 'Aire naturelle de camping' where facilities will be absolutely minimal, with prices to match. Some farms offer camping pitches under the auspices of the Fédération Nationale des Gîtes Ruraux –

these are designated 'Camping à la ferme', and again facilities are usually limited.

Information

The *Guide Officiel* of the French Federation of Camping and Caravanning (FFCC) lists 11,600 sites nationwide. The *Michelin Green Guide – Camping/Caravanning France* is also informative.

Chambres d'hôtes

Chambres d'hôtes are the French equivalent of bed and breakfasts, in private homes with a maximum of five bedrooms. Sometimes dinner *en famille* is also available. It is often an upmarket (and pricey) option; many are beautifully decorated rural farmhouses or even châteaux.

The following guides, available from French Government Tourist Offices, provide listings, and most tourist offices will have a local list, but it is also worth simply looking out for roadside signs, especially in rural areas (we also list selected *chambres d'hôtes* in the **Where to stay** sections). Gîtes de France (*see below*) has some *chambres d'hôtes* on its books as well as self-catering accommodation.

Chambres et tables d'hôtes – listings for 14,000 French B&Bs.
Chambres d'hôtes Prestige – a selection of 400 luxury B&Bs, plus 100 luxury gîtes.
Châteaux Accueil – a selection of B&Bs in private chateaux.
Thomas Cook Welcome Guide to Selected Bed & Breakfasts in France – 500 personally inspected B&Bs.

B&B Abroad 5 Worlds End Lane, Orpington, Kent BR6 6AA (01689 857838/www.hotelsabroad.com). A straight-forward B&B booking service; can include ferry bookings.

Gîtes & holiday rentals

If you want to live as a local, there are plenty of

opportunities to rent self-catering accommodation. Properties range from simple farm cottages to grand manor houses and even the odd château. On the coast, holiday rentals range from luxury villas near St-Tropez to purpose-built (and often cramped) flats or Résidences de Tourisme in the newer coastal resorts. Rentals are usually by the week or month and normally run Saturday to Saturday; book well ahead for July and August. Weekend rentals may be possible in winter. Individual tourist offices usually also have lists of rental properties. Alastair Sawday's *Special Places to Stay French Holiday Homes* (www.specialplacestostay.com) is a selective guide to holiday rentals all over France.

Fédération des Gîtes Ruraux de France

Maison des Gîtes de France, 59 rue St-Lazare, 75009 Paris (01.49.70.75.85/www.gites-de-france.fr). France's best-known holiday cottage organisation was set up after World War II to stimulate the rural economy by offering grants to owners to restore rural properties and let them out as holiday homes. Note that some will be off the beaten track and the use of a car, or at the very least a bicycle, is usually essential. You will often be expected to supply your own bed linen, but most have owners living nearby who will tell you where to buy local produce (or will even provide it). Prices average €250-€400 per week in August for a two- to four-person gîte. Properties are inspected by the Relais Départemental and given an épi (ear of corn) classification from one to five according to level of comfort. Prices tend to be much lower than for UK-based agencies, but many properties are also correspondingly more basic; check carefully for details such as an independent entry or garden or whether the gîte is in the same building as the owner. **Brittany Ferries** (Brittany Centre, Wharf Road, Portsmouth PO2 8RU, 0870 536 0360) is the UK agent for Gîtes de France, although its brochure only lists a small selection.

Directory

Clévacances (05.61.13.55.66/ www.clevacances.com). A more recently established association of holiday flats, houses and *chambres d'hôtes*, which exists in some *départements* and is reputed for its more up-to-date rating system.

UK-based agencies

Upmarket agencies can lay on all sorts of extras from maid service to helicopters.

Balfour France (020 8878 9955/www.balfourfrance.com). Top of the market rentals along the Côte d'Azur and Luberon, often grand villas with endless terraces and views over the Med. Expect to pay £2,000-£3,500/wk.

French Affair (UK 020 7381 8519/www.frenchaffair.com). A long-established company that lets out privately owned villas and houses in Provence and other parts of France (notably Dordogne), including refurbished stone farmhouses and recently built *mas* and bungalows; most have swimming pools. Prices go from around £500 to £2,800/wk, including ferry crossing, depending on size and location of the property.

Riviera Retreats/Kestrel Travel (UK 01672 520651/ France 04.93.24.10.70/ www.kestreltravel.com). Specialists in well-equipped upmarket villas and yachts on the coast between St-Tropez and Monaco, or the chic hinterland around Vence and Grasse. Prices from around £2,000 to a money-is-no-object £25,000/wk.

Gîtes d'Etape & refuges

Gîte d'Etape accommodation – which is often found in mountain areas, or along long-distance footpaths – is intended for overnight stays by hikers, cyclists, skiers or horse-riders. These gîtes are often run by the village and tend to be spartan, with bunks and basic facilities. Booking is recommended. *Gîte de neige*, *Gîte de pêche* and *Gîte équestre* are all variations on the *Gîte d'étape*, for skiers, anglers and horse riders respectively.

Mountain *refuges* (shelters) range from large and solid stone houses to basic huts. All have bunk beds; many offer food – often of surprisingly

high quality. Many are open only June-September; they should always be booked in advance. Prices vary between €6 and €14 per person. Lists are available from local tourist offices or from the Club Alpin Français (see p319).

Hotels

Hotels in France are generally reasonably priced in relation to much of western Europe, though the South of France is the most expensive French region along with Paris. Hotels are graded from no stars to four star and four star luxe, according to factors such as room size, lifts and services, but the star system does not necessarily reflect quality or welcome, nor facilities such as air conditioning or computer sockets: an old building may lack a lift but be otherwise charming. For this reason we do not list star-ratings. The majority of French hotels are small, family-run affairs. Many close in winter.

Prices & reservations

You can usually get a decent room with an adequate bathroom from around €45 for two, though prices are higher on the coast. Prices are usually given per room rather than per person, and will be posted on the back of the door. We quote the price for double rooms, but many hotels will also have triples, quadruples or suites suitable for families, or can provide an extra bed or cot for a child (there may be a supplement). Breakfast is not normally included: expect to pay from €6 in a budget hotel to €25 in a luxury hotel. In the peak season hotels often insist on *demi-pension* (with lunch or, more usually, dinner included). All hotels charge an additional room tax (*taxe de séjour*) of €0.15-€1 per person per night. When booking, you may be asked for a deposit; most will accept a credit card number; some may be satisfied with a confirming fax. When booking a room, it is normal to look at it first; if it doesn't suit, ask to be shown another (rooms can vary enormously within the same hotel).

Hotel groups & chains

Best Western (08.00.90.44.90/ www.bestwestern.fr/

www.bestwestern.com). Huge international grouping of privately owned, mainly three-star hotels of varying styles from historic coaching inns to modern constructions.

Châteaux & Hotels de France (01.40.07.00.20/ www.chateauxhotels.com). A group of independent, upmarket hotels, ranging from moderate to luxury, plus a few B&Bs in private châteaux.

Concorde Hôtels (UK 0800 0289 880/France 08.00.05.00.11/ www.concorde-hotels.fr). French luxury group includes the Martinez, Cannes, Palais de la Méditerranée, Nice, and Belles-Rives, Juan-les-Pins.

Logis de France (*Fédération Nationale des Logis et Auberges de France, 83 av d'Italie, 75013 Paris, 01.45.84.70.00/www.logis-de-france.fr*). France's biggest hotel network acts as a sort of quality-control stamp for over 5,000 private, often family-run, hotels, all with restaurant, in the countryside or small towns; most are one- or two-star.

Groupe Accor (www.accorhotels.com). This is the biggest hotel group in the world, ranging from the luxury Sofitels to budget Etap and Formule 1 chains (which may be in industrial estates or by motorways) via the mid-range Hôtel Ibis and Novotel and upmarket Mercure, generally situated in towns.

Relais & Châteaux (01.45.72.90.00/ www.relaischateaux.com). A consortium of luxury hotels with upmarket restaurants, often in châteaux, in France and abroad.

Relais du Silence (01.44.49.79.00/ www.silencehotel.com). A grouping of peaceful independent hotels in châteaux or grand houses.

Special offers

The **Bon Week End en Villes** (www.bon-week-end-en-villes.com) scheme offers two nights for the price of one at weekends at selected hotels in participating cities, including Aix-en-Provence, Avignon and Marseille, usually from November to March. **Les Escapades Provençales** pass offers three nights for the price of two in hotels in the Vaucluse (excluding Avignon) in winter.

Youth hostels

To stay in most *auberges de jeunesse* you need to be a member of the International YHA or the **Fédération Unie des Auberges de Jeunesse** (27 rue Pajol, 75018 Paris, 01.44.89.87.27, www.fuaj.org).

Resources A-Z

Addresses

All addresses in France have a five figure postcode before the name of the town or village, starting with two numbers that indicate the administrative *département*. This may be the only address in small rural communes; bigger villages and towns have street names and numbers; Marseille is divided into 16 arrondissements.

Age restrictions

You must be 18 or over to drive and 16 to consume alcohol in a public place. The age of consent is 15.

Beauty spas

Thalassotherapy

Biovimer Spa *Marina Baie des Anges, Cros-de-Cagnes (04.93.22.71.71/www.biovimer.fr).*
Thalassa Hyères *allée de la Mer, La Capte, Hyères (04.94.58.00.94).*
Thalazur Antibes *770 chemin des Moyennes Bréguières, Antibes (04.92.91.82.00).*
Thermes Marins de Monte-Carlo *2 av de Monte-Carlo (00.377-92.16.40.40).*
Seawater spas are popular with the French, who will often devote an entire holiday to thalassotherapy–therapeutic seawater massage and seaweed treatment. Six days is the recommended stay, though you can usually just visit for the day. The atmosphere is health-focused, and children are generally not welcome (although some offer babysitting services and postnatal packages). Expect to pay €46-€75/day depending on treatments and facilities.

Thermal spas

Thermes de Gréoux-les-Bains *av des Thermes, Gréoux-les-Bains (04.92.70.40.01).*
Thermes Sextius *55 cours Sextius, Aix-en-Provence (04.42.23.81.81).*
Inland there are thermal spas on the site of natural springs exploited since

Roman times. Aix is aimed at beauty and fitness, Gréoux more geared to medical treatments.

Grape cures are also available in the Vaucluse wine region (contact Avignon Office de Tourisme on 04.90.82.65.11). Most spas have associated hotels offering treatment and accommodation packages.

Business

The most important thing to know about doing business in France, especially in the South, is that people will invariably prefer to meet you in person. You will often be expected to go in and see someone, even if it's to discuss something that could easily have been dealt with over the phone. Shake hands and remember that French is a more formal language than English: use the *vous* form in business dealings, unless with someone you know well.

Most major banks can refer you to lawyers, accountants and tax consultants; several US and British banks provide expatriate services. The standard English-language reference is *The French Company Handbook*, a list of all companies in the 120 Index of the Paris Bourse, published by the *International Herald Tribune* (01.41.43.93.00). It can be ordered for £50 from Paul Baker Publishing, 37 Lambton Road, London SW20 OLW (0176 568 8236).

Business media

For business and financial news, the French dailies *La Tribune* and *Les Echos*, and the weekly *Investir*, are the tried and trusted sources. *Capital*, its sister magazine *Management* and the weightier *L'Expansion* are worthwhile monthlies. *Défis* has tips for the entrepreneur, *Initiatives* is for the self-employed. BFM on 96.4 FM is an all-news business radio station. *Les Echos* gives stock quotes on www.lesechos.com, as does **www.boursorama.com**. Business directories *Kompass France* and *Kompass Régional* also give

company details and French market profiles on **www.kompass.fr**.
English Yellow Pages
English Yellow Pages is a free A-Z directory of English-speaking businesses from banks and interpreters to plumbers and gardeners in the Alpes-Maritimes and Var *départements*, aimed mainly at expats. Also on 08.92.68.83.97/ www.englishyellowpages.fr

Congress centres

Acropolis
1 esplanade Kennedy, Nice (04.93.92.83.00).
Centre des Congrès Auditorium
bd Louis II, Monte-Carlo, Monaco (00.377.93.10.84.00).
Centre de Rencontre Internationale
13 bd Princesse Charlotte, Monte-Carlo (00.377.93.25.53.07).
Palais des Congrès
Parc Chanot, 2 bd Rabatau, Marseille (04.91.76.16.00).
Palais des Festivals
La Croisette, Cannes (04.93.39.01.01).

Useful addresses

Banque Populaire de la Côte d'Azur
International Branch, 22 bd Victor Hugo, 06000 Nice (04.93.82.81.81/ www.cotedazur.banquepopulaire.fr). Banking advice in English.
British Chamber of Commerce
25 bis bd Carnot, Nice (04.97.08.11.30). By appointment.
Centre de Ressources Côte d'Azur
Chambre de Commerce et d'Industrie Nice Côte d'Azur, 20 bd Carabacel, Nice (04.93.13.74.36/ www.businessriviera.com). Information centre.

Services

Computer services
Gale Force *13 av St-Michel, Monte-Carlo (00377.93.50.20.92/ www.galeforce.com).* In English.
Loca Centre *1330 av Guilbert de la Lauzière, Europarc de Pichaury, Batiment B5, 13865 Aix-en-Provence (04.88.71.88.35/www.locacentre.com).* Rentals of laptops, PCs, printers and scanners. Branch in Marseille.

International couriers

DHL (*Freephone 0800.20.25.25/ www.dhl.com*).
FedEx (*Freephone 0800.12.38.00*).

Translation services

Accents *Pauline Beaumont, 120 chemin des Serres, 06510 Gattières (04.93.08.38.38/pauline.beaumont@ worldonline.fr)*.

Children

France is a child-friendly country. Plenty of kids' activities are laid on, children are normally welcome in restaurants, and many hotels have family rooms or can add a cot (*lit bébé*) or folding bed. Disposable nappies (*couches jetables*) are easy to find, and French baby food is often of gourmet standard.

Activites & Sightseeing

The beach and the sea are the easiest way to amuse children, and private beach concessions with sunloungers and parasols are the easiest of all; just book your parasol close to the shore and watch the kids make sandcastles. Inflatables are often provided and there are sometimes bouncy castles, too. Main resorts and beaches have monitored beaches with lifeguards in summer. But do be careful with the intense midday sun – most French families leave the beach between noon and 3pm. There's a stream of touring circuses at beach resorts in July and August. If you're visiting main cities in the rest of the year many theatres and museums organise activities and performances for children, especially on Wednesday and Saturday. Even small villages often have a playground with a slide or climbing frame, and this can be a good place to meet other families. Sightseeing is only likely to be difficult in steep hill villages, which can be hard to negotiate with a pushchair. Museums and monuments generally have reduced rates for children: under-18s are free at state museums. Other popular family attractions include zoos at Fréjus and La Barben, Marineland at Antibes and the Aquarium in Monaco.

Eating out

Eating out with children is a normal part of the French lifestyle, and children, as long as they are

reasonably well behaved, are generally welcome. It's especially easy during the day, at cafés or restaurants with a terrace. Many restaurants offer a children's menu or will split a *prix-fixe* menu between two children or let a child eat just a starter or even give you an extra plate to share your own meal.

Transport

When hiring a car, be sure to book baby and child seats in advance – though larger hire companies usually have a few ready to go. For train fares *see p309*.

Customs

There are no limits on the quantity of goods you can take into France from another EU country for personal use, provided tax has been paid on them in the country of origin. However, Customs still has the right to question visitors. Beware bringing in fake goods from the markets at Ventimiglia and San Remo just across the border in Italy as the goods may be confiscated and you may be fined. Quantities accepted as being for personal use are:

● up to 800 cigarettes, 400 small cigars, 200 cigars or 1kg loose tobacco.

● 10 litres of spirits (over 22% alcohol), 90 litres of wine (under 22% alcohol) or 110 litres of beer.

For goods from outside the EU:

● 200 cigarettes or 100 small cigars, 50 cigars or 250g loose tobacco.

● 1 litre of spirits (over 22% alcohol) and 2 litres of wine and beer (under 22% alcohol).

● 50g perfume.

Visitors can carry up to €7,600 in currency.

Tax refunds (Détaxe)

Non-EU residents can claim a refund on VAT (TVA) if they spend over €175 in one day. At the shop ask for a *bordereau de vente à l'exportation* form and when you leave France have it stamped by customs. Then post the form back to the shop. *Détaxe* does not cover food, drink, antiques or works of art.

Disabled travellers

Travel & transport

Location de Véhicules Equipés et Automatiques

51 rue Celony, 13100 Aix-en-Provence (04.42.93.54.59/ www.lvea.fr). Rents specially adapted cars for disabled drivers; around €100/day.

Eurotunnel (*UK 0870 535 3535/France 03.21.00.61.00/ www.eurotunnel.com*). The Channel Tunnel car-on-a-train is good for disabled passengers; you may stay in your vehicle and get a 10% discount.

Groupement pour Insertion des Handicapés Physiques (GIHP) (*04.91.11.41.000*). Information on disabled transports.

Taxis Taxi drivers cannot legally refuse to take disabled people or guide dogs, and must help them get into the taxi.

Trains Eurostar (UK special requests 020 7928 0660) trains give wheelchair passengers 1st-class travel for 2nd-class fares. For SNCF information call 08.00.15.47.53. People accompanying handicapped passengers get free or reduced rates, as do guide dogs.

Holidays & accommodation

Tourist offices should be able to provide information on sights and hotels accessible to the disabled. Look at *départemental* websites (*see p324*) for lists of hotels with disabled access. In bigger cities there is usually reasonably good provision – especially in newer museums and modern hotels and restaurants. Disabled parking is indicated with a blue wheelchair sign; the international orange disabled parking disc is also recognised. Even if places claim to have disabled access, it's wise to check beforehand and specify your needs. To hire a wheelchair or other equipment, enquire at the local pharmacy. In Nice, part of the public beach has been adapted for wheelchairs with ramp access and a concrete platform on the shingle.

Gîtes Accessibles à Tous (Gîtes de France, 59 rue St-Lazare, 75009 Paris, 01.49.70.75.85/www.gites-de-france.fr) lists holiday rentals equipped for the disabled. The *French Federation of Camping and Caravanning Guide* (available from Deneway Guides & Travel Ltd, Manor Garden, Burton Bradstock, Bridport, Dorset, DT6 4QA, 0130 889 7809, price £9 + p&p) and the

*Michelin Green Guide –
Camping/Caravanning France* both
list campsites with disabled facilities.

Useful addresses

**Association des paralysés de
France** (01.40.78.69.00).
**Comité national de liaison
pour la réadaptation des
handicapés (CNRH)**
(01.53.80.66.85/www.handitel.org).
**RADAR (Royal Association for
Disability & Rehabilitation)**
*Unit 12 City Forum, 250 City Road,
London EC1V 8AF (0207 250
3222/Minicom 0207 250
4119/www.radar.org.uk)*.
Ulysse *23 bd Carlone, 06200 Nice
(04.93.96.09.99)*. Can help with
transport, tourist visits and hotels.

Drugs

Possession of drugs is illegal in
France. Officially there is no
legal distinction between 'hard'
and 'soft' drugs and possession
of even a small amount of
cannabis for personal use
could land you in jail and incur
a large fine.

Electricity & gas

Electricity in France runs on
220V, so visitors with British
240V appliances can simply
change the plug or use a
converter (*adaptateur*),
available at hardware shops.
For US 110V appliances, you
will need a transformer
(*transformateur*), available at
Fnac and Darty chains.
    Gas and electricity are
supplied by the state-owned
EDF-GDF (Electricité de
France-Gaz de France). Contact
them about supply, bills, or
in case of power failures or
gas leaks (*see below*
Emergencies).
    Butane gas is widely used
for cooking (and sometimes
water and heating) in towns
and villages without mains gas
supply. If you stay in rented
accommodation, you may need
to change the cylinder and buy
new ones, from a garage or
supermarket.

Embassies & consulates

For general enquiries,
passports or visas, you usually
need the consulate rather than
the embassy. Always phone to
check opening hours first, you
may need to make an
appointment. The
answerphone will usually give
an emergency contact number.
There's a full list of embassies
and consulates in the *Pages
Jaunes* under *Ambassades et
Consulats* or on line at
www.pagesjaunes.fr.

Consulates in the South

British *24 av du Prado, 13006
Marseille (04.91.15.72.10)*.
USA *12 bd Paul Peytral, 13286
Marseille (04.91.54.92.00)*.
*7 av Gustave V, 06000 Nice
(04.93.88.89.55)*.
Canadian *10 rue Lamartine,
06000 Nice (04.93.92.93.22)*.
Irish *152 bd JF Kennedy, 06160
Cap d'Antibes (04.93.61.50.63)*.

Paris embassies & consulates

Australian Embassy
(01.40.59.33.00/www.austgov.fr).
British Embassy
*(01.44.51.31.00/www.amb-
grandebretagne.fr)*. **Consulate**
(01.44.51.33.01/ 01.44.51.33.03).
Canadian Embassy
*(01.44.43.29.00/www.amb-
canada.fr)*.
Irish Embassy
(01.44.17.67.00/).
New Zealand Embassy
*(01.45.01.43.43/www.nzembassy.com
/france)*.
South Africa *(01.53.59.23.23/
www.afriquesud.net)*.
USA Embassy *(01.43.12.22.22/
www.amb-usa.fr))*.

Emergencies

See also below, **Health**.
Police 17.
Fire (Sapeurs-Pompiers) 18.
Ambulance (SAMU) 15.
EDF/GDF 08.10.12.61.26

Emergencies from mobile
phone 112.

Gay & lesbian

France is a generally gay-
tolerant country and the
Riviera has long been a
stomping ground for pink
people – plenty of beach
cruising, sun to soak up and
same-sex action. Gay bars,
saunas and discos abound in
Nice, Toulon, Marseille, Nîmes,
Aix and Avignon, there are
Gay Pride marches in Marseille
and Cannes, and an
infrastructure of groups is
slowly developing, especially
in Avignon and Marseille.
    Gay beaches are eye-
popping day-trip destinations.
Nice's **Coco Beach** is a 24-
hour cruising point. Other gay
beaches include the ritzy
Plage de St-Laurent-d'Eze
and Plage St-Aygulf at Fréjus.
La Batterie, just outside
Cannes towards Antibes, is a
straight and gay nude beach.

Associations & information

Centre Gai et Lesbien *11 rue
Regal, 30000 Nîmes
(04.66.67.10.59)*. **Open** 7-9pm Thur.
Support and advice.

www.gay-provence.org
Useful website lists gay-friendly
hotels and B&Bs, activities and
associations such as **Des ils et des
elles** in Avignon or the **Marseille
Frontrunners**, gay and lesbian
sports club in Marseille.

www.france.qrd.org France-wide
directory of gay and lesbian
associations and events.

Health

All EU nationals staying in
France are entitled to use the
French Social Security system,
which refunds up to 70% of
medical expenses (but
sometimes much less, for
example for dental treatment).
To get a refund, British
nationals should obtain form
E111 before leaving the UK
(or E112 for those already in

Directory

treatment). Nationals of non-EU countries should take out insurance before leaving home. Fees and prescriptions have to be paid for in full, and are reimbursed, in part, on receipt of a completed *fiche* (form).

If you undergo treatment in France, the doctor will give you a prescription and a *feuille de soins* (statement of treatment). The medication will carry *vignettes* (stickers) that you must stick on to your *feuille de soins*. Send this, the prescription and form E111 to the local Caisse Primaire d'Assurance Maladie (in the phone book under *Sécurité Sociale*). Refunds can take over a month to come through.

Accident & emergency

See also p315. Note that in the case of accidents the Sapeurs-Pompiers, fire brigade who are also trained paramedics. will usually be called rather than the SAMU.

Complementary medicine

Most pharmacies also sell homeopathic medicines and can advise on their use. For alternative medicine practitioners, ask in the pharmacy, or look them up in the *Pages Jaunes* (www.pagesjaunes.fr).

Contraception & abortion

For the pill (*la pilule*) or a coil (*stérilet*) you will need a prescription. Visit a GP (*médecin généraliste*) or gynaecologist (*gynécologue*), look in the *Pages Jaunes* (www.pagesjaunes.fr) or ask at a pharmacy for a recommendation. You can buy condoms (*préservatifs*) and spermicides from pharmacies. French pharmacies also dispense the morning-after pill (*pilule du lendemain*) without a prescription. Abortion (*avortement* or *interruption volontaire de la grossesse*) is legal up to 12 weeks and can be reimbursed by French social security; consult a gynaecologist or look for the local *Planning Familial* centre in the telephone directory.

Doctors & dentists

A complete list of practitioners is in the *Pages Jaunes* under *Médecins Qualifiés*. To get a Social Security refund, choose a doctor or dentist registered with the state system; look for *Médecin Conventionné* after the name. Consultations cost at least €20 of which a proportion can be reimbursed – if you are entitled to use the French Social Security system (*see above*). A *médecin généraliste* is a general practioner, though you are also free to go to the specialist of your choice – who may also be *conventionné* but whose fees may be two or three times higher.

Helplines & house calls

In cases of medical emergency, dial 15 to call an ambulance or ring the Service d'Aide Médicale d'Urgence (SAMU), which exists in most large towns and cities – the numbers will be given at the front of telephone directories. The fire brigade (sapeurs-pompiers) also have trained paramedics.

Alcoholics Anonymous South of France (*04.93.82.91.10*). Local contacts and meetings.

Centre Anti-Poisons (*04.91.75.25.25*).

Nice Médecins (*04.93.52.42.42*). Local doctor service for home visits.

SOS Help (*01.46.21.46.46*). **Open** 3-11pm daily. Paris-based English-language helpline.

SOS Médecins (*08.10.85.01.01*). Covers the whole region and will give another number for another locality if necessary. Can send a doctor on a house call. A home visit before 7pm starts at €38 if you don't have French Social Security, €23 if you do; the fee rises after 7pm.

Hospitals

For a complete list, consult the *Pages Blanches* (www.pagesblanches.fr) under *Hôpital Assistance Publique*.

Opticians

Any optician can make small repairs and will be able to supply new glasses, but remember to bring your prescription. Drivers are required by law to carry a spare pair.

Pharmacies

Pharmacies sport a green neon cross.

They have a monopoly on issuing medication, and also sell sanitary and beauty products. Most open from 9am or 10am to 7pm or 8pm. Staff can provide basic medical services such as disinfecting and bandaging wounds, attending to snake or insect bites (for a small fee) and will indicate the nearest doctor on duty. French pharmacists are highly trained; you can often avoid visiting a doctor by describing your symptoms and seeing what they suggest. They are also qualified to identify mushrooms, so you can take in anything you aren't sure about. Towns have a rota system of *pharmacies de garde* at night and on Sundays. Any closed pharmacy will have a sign indicating the nearest open pharmacy. Otherwise, you can enquire from the *Gendarmerie*. Toiletries and cosmetics are usually cheaper in supermarkets.

STDs, HIV & AIDS

SIDA Info Service (*08.00.84.08.00*). **Open** 24hrs daily. Confidential AIDS information in French; some bilingual counsellors.

ID

You need to be able to prove your identity to the police at all times, so keep your passport or *Carte de séjour* with you.

Insurance

See also **Health**. Insurance is often required for sporting activities but is sometimes included with the fee.

Internet

After a slow start, the use of Internet has skyrocketed. Big youth and student-oriented cities such as Aix and Marseille abound in cybercafés, but availability in rural areas and villages is much more variable. WiFi is now available in some hotels and airports, often using prepaid cards.

ISPs

America Online (*08.26.02.60.00/www.aol.fr*).
Club-Internet (*08.26.02.70.28/ www.club-internet.fr*).

Wanadoo *(France Télécom)*
(08.10.63.34.34/www.wanadoo.fr).
Free *(www.free.fr).*

Language

See p323 **Essential
Vocabulary,** *p24-25* **Provençal
menu lexicon,** for food terms,
and p320 for courses.

Legal advice

Mairies (town halls) may be
able to answer legal enquiries.
Phone for details and times of
free *consultations juridiques.*
Or they will be able to
recommend an *avocat* (lawyer)
or *notaire* (solicitor), both are
addressed as *'Maître'.* The
*English Language Yellow
Pages* can give names of
English-speaking lawyers in
the Côte d'Azur by phone
(08.92.68.83.97) but not in its
published version.

Lost & stolen property

To report a crime or loss of
belongings, visit the local
gendarmerie or *commissariat de
police (see p318* **Police &
crime).** If you want to make
an insurance claim, you will
need a police report anyway.
Telephone numbers are given
at the front of local directories;
in an emergency dial 17. If you
lose a passport, report it first
to the police, then to the
nearest consulate *(see p315*
Embassies & consulates).

Maps

Tourist offices can usually
provide free town maps *(plans).*
The large-format Michelin
Atlas or 1:1,000,000 (1cm:1km)
989 sheet map *(carte routière et
touristique)* for the whole of
France are good for driving.
Michelin Carte Régionale 528
Provence, Côte d'Azur is a
good 1:200,000 (1cm:2km) all-
purpose map of the region. For
walking or cycling, the Institut

Géographique National (IGN)
maps are invaluable. Top 100
(1:100,000, 1cm to 1km) and
Top 50 (1:50,000, 2cm to 1km)
maps mark all roads and most
footpaths, the IGN blue series
1:25,000 (4cm:1km) has even
greater detail.

Media

English-language press

Most of the major British and a few
American papers, including the
Paris-based *International Herald
Tribune,* can be picked up from
newsagents *(maisons de la presse)* in
the centre of the major towns, at train
stations and airports, and along most
of the coast in summer and in
cosmopolitan inland areas such as
Les Alpilles, Luberon and inland Var.

Local English Press
Riviera Reporter (04.93.45.77.19) is a
glossy magazine aimed at foreign
residents, carrying local information,
news and small ads, it can be picked
up at English bookshops and other
outlets. Monthly newspaper *Riviera
Times* (www.rivieratimes.com) has
local news, events and classifieds.
The *Connexion* is an A4-sized news
and ads freebie.

French press

As well as the French national dailies
Le Monde (centre-left), *Libération*
(left), *Le Figaro* (right), and sports
daily *L'Equipe,* the French are
attached to their local papers: *Nice
Matin* (www.nicematin.fr), *La
Provence* (www.laprovence-presse.fr),
Var Matin (www.varmatin.com), *Le
Dauphiné Vaucluse* and *La
Marseillaise* cover most of Provence
and the Côte d'Azur. Free news
dailies are booming in Marseille with
local versions of *20 Minutes* and
Metro, plus free *Le Marseillaise*
offshoot *Marseille Plus.*
A vast range of magazines includes
news weeklies *L'Express, Nouvel
Observateur, Le Point* and *Marianne,*
women's mags *Elle* (weekly), *Marie-
Claire, Jalouse, Vogue,* gossip
essentials *Paris Match, Gala* and
Voici, and countless arts, deco, TV
and travel publications.

Radio

FM radio
Note that for many stations
wavelengths vary from area to area.

87.8 France Inter State-run, MOR
music and international news.
91.7/92.1 France Musique State
classical music with concerts
and jazz, and lots of talk.
93.5/93.9 France Culture
Highbrow state culture station.
105.5 France Info 24-hour news,
economic updates and sports.
Repeated every 15 minutes, so good
for learning French.
BFM Business and economics. Wall
Street in English every evening.
RTL Most popular French station
mixing music and talk.
Europe 1 News, press reviews,
sports, business and interviews.
NRJ very popular pop channel.
Nostalgie golden oldies.
Rire et chansons French comedy
acts mixed with pop.

Local FM stations
88.8 FM Radio Grenouille.
Marseille station, with hip coverage
of culture, events and new music.
98.8 FM Radio Monte Carlo.
106.3 & 106.5 FM Riviera Radio
parochial English-language radio
with small ads and local gossip.

BBC World Service
Between **6.195** and **12.095** MHz
shortwave.

Television

Terrestrial channels
France has six terrestrial channels.
The biggest, **TF1,** features movies,
reality shows, soaps and news with
star anchors Patrick Poivre d'Arvor
and Claire Chazal. **France 2** is a
similar state-run version minus the
reality shows. **France 3** has
regional news, sports, documentaries
and Sunday's *Cinéma de Minuit* with
classic films in the original language
(VO). **Canal+** is a subscription
channel with recent movies,
exclusive sport and late-night porn.
Arte is a Franco-German hybrid
specialising in intelligent arts
coverage and films and themed
evenings. Its wavelength is shared
with educational channel **La
Cinquième** (6.45am-7pm). **M6**
rotates music videos, imported series
and some excellent magazine
programmes.

Cable TV & satellite
The cable and satellite network is
well-established. Channels include
LCI for 24-hour news and business
bulletins, documentary **Planète,**
Histoire and **Voyages, Téva** for
women's programmes and good
sitcoms in VO, **Mezzo** for classical

Directory

music and dance, **Eurosport** for sport, and **Canal Jimmy**, **13e Rue**, **Série Club**, **RTL9** for sitcoms and police series, **TMC** for sitcoms and classic movies; there are also several specialist film channels. Foreign-language channels include **BBC World**, **BBC Prime** and **CNN**.

Money

The euro (€)

The euro (€) is the official currency in France and the ten other participating European Union nations. Coins exist in 1, 2, 5, 10 and 50 centime denominations and 1 and 2 euros; notes in 5, 10, 20, 50, 100, 200 and 500 denominations. Try to avoid €200 and €500 notes as few shops are willing to accept them. A useful website for converting to or from euros is www.xe.com/ucc.

ATMs

If your cash withdrawal card carries the European Cirrus symbol, withdrawals can be made from bank and post office cash machines by using your card's PIN. The specific cards accepted are marked on each machine, and most give instructions in English. Credit card companies charge a fee for cash advances, but rates are often better than bank rates. Note that cash machines are widespread in major cities and towns, but can be few and far between in rural areas.

Banks

French banks usually open 9am-5pm Monday-Friday (some close for lunch 12.30-2.30pm); some also open on Saturday. All close on public holidays (usually from noon on the previous day). Not all banks have foreign exchange counters and not all accept travellers' cheques. Commission rates vary between banks.

Bank accounts

To open an account (*ouvrir un compte*), you need proof of identity, regular income and an address in France. You'll probably have to show your passport or *Carte de séjour*, a utility bill in your name and a payslip or a letter from your employer. Students need a student card and may need a letter from their parents. French banks are tough on overdrafts, so try to anticipate any cash crisis in advance and work out a deal for an authorised overdraft (*découvert autorisé*) or you risk being

blacklisted as *interdit bancaire* – forbidden from having a current account for five years. Depositing foreign-currency cheques is slow, and incurs high charges, so use wire transfer or a bank draft in euros to receive funds from abroad.

Credit cards

Major international credit cards are widely used in France, especially Visa (linked to the French Carte Bleue), though there may well be a minimum sum (often €15 in shops or restaurants). American Express and Diners Club coverage is more patchy. French-issued cards have a security microchip (*puce*) in each card. The card is slotted into a card reader; the holder keys in a PIN to authorise the transaction. Non-French cards generate a credit slip to sign.

In case of credit card loss or theft, call the following 24-hour services, which have English-speaking staff:

- **American Express** *01.47.77.72.00*
- **Diners' Club** *08.20.00.07.34*
- **MasterCard** *01.45.67.84.84*
- **Visa** *08.92.69.08.80.*

Natural hazards

See also p321 **Climate** on heat and floods.

Insects

For every tourist there is at least one mosquito in the South, particularly in the Camargue. Plug-in vaporisers are a good defence and are available in most supermarkets. Campers should beware of a spider that bites exposed skin at night, producing a scratchy rash. Black scorpions are sometimes found from late spring to autumn.

Fire

Fire is a major risk during the dry summer period, and each year there are usually several serious fires, some of them caused deliberately. Always be careful when walking or cycling on open mountain or in woodland; campfires are strictly banned and certain paths are closed in high summer or on windy days.

Opening times

Shops generally open 9.30am-7pm, earlier for food shops. The sacred lunch hour is still largely observed, which means that many shops and offices

close at noon or 1pm and reopen at 2pm or later. Many shops also close on Monday morning or all day Monday. Hypermarkets (*grandes surfaces*) usually stay open through lunch. Most shops close on Sundays, though *bureaux de tabac* (cigarettes, stamps) and newsagents are often open Sunday mornings, and *boulangeries* (bakers) may be open every day.

Banks usually open 9am-noon and 1.30-5pm Mon-Fri. Public offices and *mairies* (town halls) usually open 8.30am-noon, then 2-6pm.

Except in peak season, many museums also close for lunch. They also close on certain public holidays, notably 1 January, 1 May and 25 December. National museums usually close on Tuesday.

Police & crime

Police in urban and rural areas come under two different governmental organisations. The **Gendarmerie nationale** is a military force serving under the *Ministère de la Défense* and its network covers minor towns and rural areas. The **Police nationale** serve under the *Ministère de l'Intérieur* in main cities. Some cities also have Police municipale.

Beware of crime from cars. Police advise leaving nothing visible in parked cars. In Nice, there has also been a spate of 'car jackings' – car theft as people are parking; petrol theft is not unknown in rural areas.

If you are robbed, you need to make a statement at the police station or gendarmerie for your insurance claim.

Postal services

Postes (post offices) generally open 9am-noon, 2-7pm Monday-Friday, 9am-noon Saturday. In main post offices, individual counters are marked according to the services they

provide; if you just need
stamps, go to the window
marked *Timbres*.

If you need to send an
urgent letter or parcel
overseas, ask for it to be sent
through Chronopost, which is
faster but more expensive.
Chronopost is also the fastest
way to send parcels within
France; packages up to 25kg
are guaranteed to be delivered
within 24 hours.

For a small fee, you can
arrange for mail to be kept
poste restante, addressed to
Poste Restante, Poste Centrale
(for main post office), then the
town postcode and name.
You will need to present your
passport when collecting mail.

Stamps are also available at
tobacconists (*bureaux de tabac*)
and other shops selling
postcards and greetings cards.
For standard-weight letters or
postcards (up to 20g within
France and 10g within the EU),
a €0.50 stamp is needed.

Telegrams can be sent
during post office hours or by
telephone (24-hrs); to send a
telegram abroad, dial
08.00.33.44.11.

Fax and photocopying
facilities are often available at
post offices and newsagents.
Many supermarkets have coin-
operated photocopiers.

Religion

The presence of the British in
the South of France over the
past two centuries means there
are several Anglican churches.
For more information contact:

**Intercontinental Church
Society** *1 Athena Drive, Tachbrook
Park, Warwick CV34 6NL (0192
643 0347/www.ics-uk.org).*

Holy Trinity Church *rue du
Canada, Cannes (04.93.94.54.61).*
Service 10.30am Sun.

Monaco Christian Fellowship
*9 rue Louis Notari, Monaco
(00.377.93.30.60.72).* Service
11am Sun.

St Michael's Anglican Church
*11 chemin des Myrtes, Beaulieu
(04.93.01.45.61).* Service 10am Sun.

Removals

For international removals, use
a company that is a member of
the International Federation of
Furniture Removers (FIDI) or
the Overseas Moving Network
with experience in France.

Overs International *Unit 8, Abro
Development, Government Rd,
Aldershot GU11 2DA (01252 343646).*
Weekly service to the Côte d'Azur.

Tooth Removals *107 rte du Plan,
06130 Le Plan de Grasse
(04.93.77.90.15/UK 01784 251
252).* Between London and the Côte
d'Azur.

Smoking

Despite health campaigns and
a law that insists restaurants
provide non-smoking areas
(*zones non-fumeurs*), the
French remain enthusiastic
smokers. Cigarettes are
officially only on sale in *tabacs*,
which tend to close at 8pm,
and 2pm on Sundays.

Sport & activity holidays

Enquire at local tourist offices
about swimming and tennis
facilities; there is also useful
sports information on the
regional tourist board website
(www.crt-paca.fr). Many UK
tour operators offer holidays
tailored to specific activities.

Climbing

Les Guides Randoxygène (available
from main tourist offices) are
excellent guides for climbers and
walkers with detailed trails in the
region. Dozens of climbing clubs
provide courses, plus guides and
monitors for day outings.
Club Alpin Français *14 av
Mirabeau, Nice (04.93.62.59.99/
www.cafnice.org) or 3 rue St-Michel,
Avignon (04.90.82.34.82).*

Cycling

Taking your own bike (*vélo*) to
France is relatively easy (*see p309*).
Some youth hostels also rent out
cycles and arrange tours, contact the
YHA. Package cycling holidays are
offered by various organisations;

luggage is normally transported each
day to your next destination. It is
advisable to take out insurance
before you go. The IGN 906 Cycling
France map gives details of routes,
cycling clubs and places to stay. The
Cyclists Touring Club (Cotterell
House, 69 Meadrow, Godalming,
Surrey GU7 3HS; 01483 417217,
www.ctc.org.uk) can provide
members with cycle and travel
insurance, detailed touring itineraries
and general information sheets about
France; its tours brochure lists trips
to the region, organised by members
The club's French counterpart is the
**Fédération Française de
Cyclotourisme** (01.56.20.88.88,
www.ffct.org).

Golf

Provence has some excellent golf
courses. For more information,
contact the **Fédération Française
de Golfe** (01.41.49.77.00/
www.ffg.org). Most clubs can
provide lessons with resident
experts. **Cordon Rouge Villas**
(01253 739749) and **French Golf
Holidays** (01277 824100, www.golf-
france.co.uk) offer golf holiday
packages out of the UK.

Horse riding

Horse riding and pony trekking are
popular activities, with *centres
équestres* all over the region. See also
p76 on riding in the Camargue.
Equestrian Travellers Club
(0208 3878076) and **Foxcroft
Travel** (01509 813252) offer French
equestrian holidays out of the UK.
For further information, contact the
Association Drôme à Cheval
(04.75.45.78.79/www.drome-a-
cheval.com) or the **Ligue Régionale
de Provence de Sports
Equestres** (298 av du club
Hippique, 13090 Aix-en-Provence,
04.42.20.88.02, www.provence-
equitation.com).

Skiing

There are several ski resorts in the
Alpes-Maritimes; the three with the
best facilities are Auron, Valberg and
Isola 2000 (*see p305*).
Fédération Française de Ski
(04.50.51.40.34/www.ffs.fr).

Watersports

All along the coast you can water-ski,
windsurf or scuba dive; surfing, too,
is possible on certain beaches.
Antibes and Cannes are major
watersports centres, and the Iles de

Directory

Lérins, the Iles de Hyères and the *calanques* offer some of the best diving in the Mediterranean. Inland, canoeing and rafting are popular in the Gorges de Verdon (*see p217*) and river Argens (*see p202*). For detailed listings pick up the *Watersports Côte d'Azur* brochure from main tourist offices or go online to www.france-nautisme.com.

Comité Régional de Voile Alpes-Provence *46 bd Kraemer, Marseille (04.91.11.61.78).*

Comité Régional de Voile Côte d'Azur *Espace Antibes, 2208 rte de Grasse, Antibes (04.93.74.77.05).*

Fédération Française de Canoë-Kayak et des Sports Associés en Eau-Vive *(01.45.11.08.50/www.ffck.org).*

Fédération Française d'Etudes et de Sports Sous-Marins *24 quai Rive-Neuve, Marseille (04.91.33.99.31/ www.ffessm.com).*

Ligue Régionale Canoë Alpes-Provence *14 av Vincent Auriol, Bagnols-sur-Cèze (04.66.89.47.71/ www.canoe-alpesprovence.com).*

Travel info

For up-to-date information on travel to a specific country – including the latest news on safety and security, health issues, local laws and customs – contact your home country government's department of foreign affairs. Most have websites packed with useful advice for would-be travellers.

Australia
www.dfat.gov.au/travel

Canada
www.voyage.gc.ca

New Zealand
www.mft.govt.nz/travel

Republic of Ireland
www.irlgov.ie/iveagh

UK
www.fco.gov.uk/travel

USA
www.state.gov/travel

Walking

Each *département* has its own ramblers' organisation that arranges guided walks. The Club Alpin Français in Nice (*see above* Climbing) organises day-long hikes at various levels with coach/minibus transport from Nice. See also p317 **Maps**.

Fédération Française de Randonnée Pédestre *(01.44.89.93.93/www.ffrp.asso.fr).*

Study & students

For cookery courses *see p22*.

Language courses

Actilangue *2 rue Alexis Mossa, 06000 Nice (04.93.96.33.84/fax 04.93.44.37.16/www.actilangue.com).*

Alliance Française *310 rue de Paradis, 13008 Marseille (04.96.10.24.60); 2 rue de Paris, 06000 Nice (04.93.62.67.66).*

Azurlingua *25 bd Raimbaldi, 06000 Nice (04.97.03.07.00)/ www.azurlingua.com).*

Centre International d'Antibes *38 bd d'Aguillon, Antibes 06600 (04.92.90.71.70/ www.cia-France.com).*

ELFCA *(Institut d'Enseignement de la Langue Française sur la Côte d'Azur) 66 av de Toulon, 83400 Hyères (04.94.65.03.31/ www.elfca.com).*

International School of Nice *15 av Claude Debussy, 06200 Nice (04.93.21.04.00/04.93.21.84.90).*

Student discounts

A wide range of student discounts are on offer. To claim discounts in museums, cinemas and theatres you need an **International Student Identity Card**. ISICs are only valid in France if you are under 26. Under-26s can also get discounts of up to 50% on trains with the **Carte 12/25**. The **Carte Jeune** (€18.29 from **Fnac**) also gives discounts.

Universities

The **Université d'Aix-Marseille** has faculties in the two cities (arts, humanities, law in Aix; science, mathematics in Marseille); Aix-Marseille III *(04.42.21.59.87/ 04.91.28.81.18/www.u-3mrs.fr)* is the most international part. Contact the **Institut d'Etudes Françaises pour Etudiants Etrangers** *(23 rue Gaston de Saporta, Aix-en-Provence,*

04.42.21.70.90) about courses for foreign students. *See also p165.* Other universities include **Avignon** *(04.90.16.25.00/www.univ-avignon.fr)*, **Nice-Sophia Antipolis** *(04.92.07.67.07/www.unice.fr)* and **Toulon** *(04.94.14.20.00/www.univ-tln.fr)*.

Useful organisations

Central Bureau for Educational Visits & Exchanges *10 Spring Gardens, London SW1A IBN (020 7389 4004).*

Centre des Échanges Internationaux *1 rue Golzen, 75006 Paris (01.40.51.11.71).* Sporting and cultural holidays and educational tours for 15-to-30-year-olds. Non-profit-making organisation.

Socrates-Erasmus Programme In Britain *UK Socrates-Erasmus Council, RND Building, The University, Canterbury, Kent CT2 7PD (0122 776 2712/ www.erasmus.ac.uk*. This scheme enables EU students with a reasonable standard of written and spoken French to spend a year of their degree taking appropriate courses in the French university system. The UK office publishes a brochure, but applications must be made through the Erasmus co-ordinator at your home university.

Souffle *Espace Charlotte, La Crou, 83260 (04.94.00.94.65).* An umbrella organisation for courses in French as a foreign language.

Telephones

Telephone numbers are always ten figures, written and spoken in sets of two, for example – 01.23.45.67.89. If you want numbers to be given singly rather than in pairs as is customary, ask for *chiffre par chiffre*. Regional telephone numbers are prefixed as follows **Paris & Ile de France** 01; **North-west** 02; **North-east** 03; **South-east and Corsica** 04; and **South-west** 05. **Mobile phones** start 06. When calling from abroad, omit the zero. The code for dialling France is 33; for Monaco it is 377.

Public phones

Public phone boxes use phone cards (*télécartes*),which are available from post offices, stationers, stations, *tabacs* and some cafés. To make a call from a public phone box, lift the receiver, insert the card, then dial the number. To make a follow-on call, do not replace the receiver but press the green *'appel suivant'* button and dial.

International calls

Dial 00 followed by the country's international code.

International codes

Australia *00 61*
Canada *00 1*
Ireland *00 353*
Monaco *00 377*
New Zealand *00 64*
South Africa *00 27*
UK *00 44*
US *00 1*

Special rate numbers

Numbers starting with the following prefixes have special rates:
0800 Numéro vert freephone.
0801 Numéro azur €0.11 first 3 mins, then €0.04/min.
0802 Numéro indigo I €0.15/min.
0803 Numéro indigo II €0.23/ min.
0867 €0.23/min.
0836/0868/0869 €0.34/min.

Cheap rates

Within France, cheap rates apply weekdays 7pm to 8am and weekends.

Mobile phones

France has three mobile phone operators (Bouygues, France Telecom/Orange and SFR) offering myriad subscriptions and prepaid card systems.

Misterrent

(01.44.88.76.80/ www.misterrent.com). Internet-based company finds the nearest franchise outlet in a nationwide network,which will then bike the phone to you.

Rentacell

(08.10.00.00.92/www.rentacell.com). Mobile phone rental for €8/day, €30/wk; calls in France cost €0.75/min, international €1.22/min; incoming calls are free. Phones can be delivered to hotels, airports or salons the same day in Cannes or Nice, reserve 2 days ahead elsewhere.

Phone directories

Phone directories are found in post offices and in most cafés. The *Pages Blanches* lists people and businesses alphabetically. *Pages Jaunes* lists

businesses and services by category. Both are available on www.pagesjaunes.fr.

24-hour services

French directory enquiries (*renseignements*) **12**.
International directory enquiries **32 12** then country code (eg. 44 for UK, 1 for USA).
Telephone engineer **13**.
International news (French recorded message, France Inter) dial **08.36.68.10.33** (€0.34/min).
To send a telegram (all languages): international **08.00.33.44.11**, within France **36.55**.
Speaking clock **36.99**.

Time

France is one hour ahead of Greenwich Mean Time (GMT) and six hours ahead of New York. The clocks change between summer and winter time on the same date as the UK. The 24-hour clock is frequently used in France when giving times: 8am is *8 heures*, noon (*midi*) is *12 heures*, 8pm is *20 heures*, and midnight (*minuit*) is *0 heure*.

Tipping

By law a service charge of 10-15% is included in the bill in all restaurants; leave a small extra tip of €0.50-€2 on the table if you are particularly pleased, more in a grand establishment. In a taxi, rounding up to the nearest €0.50 or €1 is appreciated. €1-€2 are also appropriate for doormen, porters, guides and hairdressers. In bars and cafés, it is usual just to leave small change as a tip.

Toilets

Anyone may use the toilet in a bar or café, although it's polite to at least have a café at *le zinc*. (Ask for *les toilettes* or *le WC* – pronouced 'vay say'.) You may have to get a token (*jeton*) from the bar. Public toilets vary; some are old-fashioned squat jobs.

Tourist information

France has an efficient network of tourist information offices (Office de Tourisme or Syndicat d'Initiative), often present in even tiny villages, with information on accommodation, sporting facilities, cultural attractions and guided visits; some also have hotel booking and ticket reservation services.

For information before you travel, there are French Government Tourist Offices in the UK (178 Piccadilly, London W1; 0906 824 4123) and USA (444 Madison Avenue, NY NY 10022; 212 838 7800), or consult the French Government Tourist Office's official Internet site, www.franceguide.com.

Visas

To visit France, you need a valid passport. Non-EU citizens require a visa, although USA, Canada, Australia or New Zealand citizens do not need a visa for stays of up to three months. If in any doubt, check with the French consulate in your country. If you intend to stay in France for more than 90 days, then you are supposed to apply for a *Carte de séjour*.

Weights & measures

France uses the metric system. Remember that all speed limits are in kilometres. One kilometre is equivalent to 0.62 mile (1 mile = 1.6km). Petrol, like other liquids, is measured in litres (one UK gallon = 4.54 litres; 1 US gallon = 3.79 litres).

When to go

Climate

The climate is generally hot and dry, except for spring, when there may be heavy rainfall, and November, which can be blustery, cold and wet. The coast has a gentle Mediterranean climate with mild winters, daytime temperatures rarely lower than 10°C/50°F degrees, and hot summers with temperatures often rising above 30°C/86°F. Temperatures can rise into the 40s in the middle of the day. Try to stay in the shade, wear a sunhat and drink plenty of water.

In Provence, the mistral – a harsh, cold wind – blows down the Rhône Valley and howls through the streets of Arles, Avignon and Marseille, bringing temperatures down dramatically. It usually lasts three or four days, but can go on as long as ten days. The area has also seen dramatic storms in recent years, causing flash floods in autumn. The high mountains usually have snow November to March. Although summer is generally dry, there are often dramatic thunderstorms along the Riviera in late August. Average sunshine on the French Riviera is six hours in January, 12 hours in July.

Information

For local forecasts dial 08.92.68.12.34 followed by the *département* number, look at websites www.meteo.fr, www.lachainemeteo.com, www.meteoconsult.com, or dial 3201.

Public holidays

On public holidays, banks, post offices and public offices will be closed. Food shops – in particular *boulangeries* (bread shops) – will still open, even on Christmas Day. It is common practice, if a public holiday falls on a Thursday or Tuesday, for French businesses to *faire le pont* (bridge the gap) and take Friday or Monday as a holiday, too. The most fully observed holidays are 1 Jan, 1 May, 14 July, 15 Aug and 25 Dec.

1 Jan New Year's Day (Nouvel an). **Easter Monday** (Lundi de Pâques). **1 May** Labour Day (Fête du Travail). **May** Ascension Day (Ascension), on a Thursday 40 days after Easter. **8 May** Victory Day (Fête de la Libération) end of World War II. **May/June** Pentecost (Pentecôte), ten days after Ascension (holiday possibly to be cancelled). **14 July** Bastille Day (Quatorze Juillet). **15 Aug** Assumption Day (Fête de l'Assomption). **1 Nov** All Saints' Day (Toussaint). **11 Nov** Armistice Day (Fête de l'Armistice). **25 Dec** Christmas Day (Noël).

Women

Women need feel no more threatened in the South of France than in any other

European country; indeed women alone will be more comfortable than in many places. The usual safety precautions should be taken in big cities at night. Be careful on trains, especially sleepers. You may receive compliments – more a cultural difference than sexual harrassment. A polite 'N'insistez pas!' (don't push it) should turn off any unwanted attention. For contraception and abortion *see p316*.

International Women's Club of the Riviera (*04.93.14.93.62*). Coffee mornings for newcomers.

SOS Viol Informations *08.00.05.95.95.* Freephone in French dealing with rape.

Working in the South of France

Anyone coming to work in France should be prepared for bureaucracy. Documents regularly required include a passport and a legally approved translation of your birth certificate (embassies have lists of translators).

Carte de séjour

Officially, all foreigners, both EU citizens and non-Europeans, in France for more than three months, must apply at the local *mairie* (town hall) for a *Carte de séjour*, valid for five years. Those who have had a *Carte de séjour* for at least three years, have been paying French income tax, can show proof of income and/or are married to a

French national can apply for a *Carte de résident*, valid for ten years.

Job-hunting

All EU nationals can work legally in France, but must apply for a *Carte de séjour* (*see above*) and a French social security number from the *Caisse Primaire d'Assurance Maladie*. Some job ads can be found at branches of the *Agence National Pour l'Emploi* (ANPE, www.anpe.fr), the French national employment bureau. This is also the place to sign up as a *demandeur d'emploi*, to be placed on file as available for work and to qualify for French unemployment benefit. Britons can claim unemployment benefit after having worked a minimum period in France. Offices are listed under *Administration du Travail et de l'Emploi* in the *Pages Jaunes*. In the UK, the Employment Service (Overseas Placing Unit, Level 2, Rockingham House, 123 West Street, Sheffield S1 4ER, 0114 259 6051) publishes information on working in France. Opportunities include the technopark of **Sophia-Antipolis** near Valbonne, where a number of international hi-tech companies are based.

Seasonal employment

Seasonal work is available mainly in the tourist industry, in hotels, restaurants, bars, ski resorts and outdoor activity centres. You will need to speak decent French. Other possibilities are gardening, house-sitting and teaching English, which can be well paid, especially if you have a TEFL qualification. Foreign students in France can get a temporary work permit (*autorisation provisoire de travail*) for part-time work in the holidays. Grape and fruit picking is another possibility, but very difficult to set up in advance. A good Internet job search engine is www.pacajob.com.

Temperatures in Nice

MONTH	AVG	MIN	MAX
Jan-Mar	11°C	6°C	15°C
Apr-May	14°C	10°C	18°C
June	19°C	15°C	23°C
July-Aug	24°C	19°C	29°C
Sept	23°C	18°C	27°C
Oct	18°C	14°C	22°C
Nov-Dec	12°C	7°C	18°C

Directory

Essential Vocabulary

In French, as in other Latin languages, the second person singular (you) has two forms. Phrases here are given in the more polite *vous* form. The *tu* form is used with family, friends, young children and pets; you should be careful not to use it with people you do not know sufficiently well. You will also find that courtesies such as monsieur, madame and mademoiselle are used much more than their English equivalents. See p320 for information on language courses and p24-25 for Provençal menu terms.

General expressions

good morning/good afternoon, hello *bonjour*
good evening *bonsoir*
goodbye *au revoir*
yes *oui*; no *non*; OK *d'accord/ça va*.
hi (familiar) *salut*
How are you? *Comment allez vous?/vous allez bien?*
How's it going? *Comment ça va?/ça va?* (familial)
Sir/Mr *monsieur (M or Mr)*;
Madam/Mrs *madame (Mme)*
Miss *mademoiselle (Mlle)*
please *s'il vous plaît*;
thank you *merci*; thank you very much *merci beaucoup*
sorry *pardon*; excuse me *excusez-moi*
Do you speak English? *Parlez-vous anglais?*
I don't speak French *Je ne parle pas français*
I don't understand *Je ne comprends pas*
Speak more slowly, please *Parlez plus lentement, s'il vous plaît*
Leave me alone *Laissez-moi tranquille*
how much?/how many? *combien?*
Have you got change? *Avez-vous de la monnaie?*
I would like... *Je voudrais...*
I am going *Je vais*; I am going to pay *Je vais payer*
it is *c'est*; it isn't *ce n'est pas*
good *bon(ne)*; bad *mauvais(e)*
small *petit(e)*; big *grand(e)*
beautiful *beau/belle*
well *bien*; badly *mal*
expensive *cher*; cheap *pas cher*
a bit *un peu*; a lot *beaucoup*; very *très*; with *avec*; without *sans*; and

et; or *ou*; because *parce que*
who? *qui?*; when? *quand?*; which? *quel?*; where? *où?*; why? *pourquoi?*; how? *comment?*
at what time/when? *à quelle heure?*
forbidden *interdit/défendu*
out of order *hors service/en panne*
daily *tous les jours (tlj)*
except Sunday *sauf le dimanche*

On the phone

hello (telephone) *allô*; Who's calling? *C'est de la part de qui?/ Qui est à l'appareil?*
Hold the line *Ne quittez pas/ Patientez s'il vous plaît*

Getting around

When is the next train for...? *C'est quand le prochain train pour...?*
ticket *un billet*; station *la gare*;
train station *gare sncf*; platform *le quai*; bus/coach station *gare routière*; bus/coach *autobus/car*
entrance *entrée*; exit *sortie*
left *gauche*; right *droite*;
interchange *correspondence*
straight on *tout droit*; far *loin*;
near *pas loin/près d'ici*
street *la rue*; street map *le plan*;
road map *la carte*
bank *la banque*; is there a bank near here? *est-ce qu'il y a une banque près d'ici?*
post office *La Poste*; a stamp *un timbre*

Sightseeing

beach *une plage*; bridge *pont*; cave *une grotte*; wine cellar *une cave*;
church *une église*; protestant church *un temple*; market *marché* or *les halles*; museum *un musée*;
mill *un moulin*; town hall *l'hôtel de ville/la mairie*; exhibition *une exposition*; ticket (for museum) *un billet*; (for theatre, concert) *une place*;
free *gratuit*; reduced price *un tarif réduit*; open *ouvert*; closed *fermé*

Accommodation

Do you have a room (for this evening/for two people)? *Avez-vous une chambre (pour ce soir/pour deux personnes)?* full *complet*; room *une chambre*; bed *un lit*; double bed *un grand lit*; (a room with) twin beds *(une chambre) à deux lits*; with bath(room)/shower *avec (salle de bain/douche*; breakfast *le petit déjeuner*; included *compris*
lift *un ascenseur*; air-conditioned *climatisé*; swimming pool *piscine*

At the café or restaurant

I'd like to book a table (for three/at 8pm) *Je voudrais réserver une table (pour trois personnes/à vingt heures)*
lunch *le déjeuner*; dinner *le dîner*
coffee (espresso) *un café*; white coffee *un café au lait/café crème*;
tea *le thé*; wine *le vin*; beer *la bière*;
a draught beer *une pression*
mineral water *eau minérale*; fizzy *gazeuse*; still *plate*; tap water *eau du robinet/une carafe d'eau*
the bill, please *l'addition, s'il vous plaît*

Behind the wheel

give way *céder le passage*
it's not your right of way *vous n'avez pas la priorité*; no parking *stationnement interdit/ stationnement gênant*; deliveries *livraisons*; residents only *sauf riverains*.
pedestrian *piéton*;
toll *péage*; speed limit 40 *rappel 40*
petrol *essence*; unleaded *sans plomb*; diesel *gasoil*.
traffic jam *embouteillage/bouchon*;
speed *vitesse*
dangerous bends *attention virages*

Numbers

0 *zéro*; 1 *un, une*; 2 *deux*; 3 *trois*;
4 *quatre*; 5 *cinq*; 6 *six*; 7 *sept*;
8 *huit*; 9 *neuf*; 10 *dix*; 11 *onze*;
12 *douze*; 13 *treize*; 14 *quatorze*;
15 *quinze*; 16 *seize*; 17 *dix-sept*;
18 *dix-huit*; 19 *dix-neuf*; 20 *vingt*;
21 *vingt-et-un*; 22 *vingt-deux*;
30 *trente*; 40 *quarante*;
50 *cinquante*; 60 *soixante*;
70 *soixante-dix*; 80 *quatre-vingts*;
90 *quatre-vingt-dix*; 100 *cent*;
1,000 *mille*; 1,000,000 *un million*.

Days, months & seasons

Monday *lundi*; Tuesday *mardi*;
Wednesday *mercredi*; Thursday *jeudi*; Friday *vendredi*; Saturday *samedi*; Sunday *dimanche*.
January *janvier*; February *février*;
March *mars*; April *avril*; May *mai*;
June *juin*; July *juillet*; August *août*; September *septembre*;
October *octobre*; November *novembre*; December *décembre*.
Spring *printemps*; summer *été*;
autumn *automne*; winter *hiver*.

Directory

Further Reference

Books

Non-fiction

Maurice Agulhon, Noël Coulet
Histoire de la Provence A short
political and economic history, in
French. Que sais-je? PUF, 2001.

James Bromwich *The Roman
Remains of Southern France* No
stone unturned. Routledge, 1996.

Alain Ducasse *Flavours of France*
By the star chef. Artisan, 1998.

**Noëlle Duck, Christian
Sarramon** *Provence Style* How to
get the sun-bleached look in your
home. Flammarion, 2002.

Kenneth Frampton *Le Corbusier:
Architect and Visionary* Corb's ideas
and work. Thames & Hudson, 2001.

Andrew Jefford *New France: A
Complete Guide to Contemporary
French Wine* Mitchell Beazley, 2002

Ed. Hugh Johnson *Touring in
Wine Country: Provence* Vineyard
companion. Mitchell Beazley, 1993.

Louisa Jones, Vincent Motte
*Gardens of Provence; Gardens of the
French Riviera.* Flammarion, 2002.

Ed. Ronald de Leeuw *Letters of
Van Gogh* Vincent writes to beloved
brother Theo. Penguin, 1997.

John Richardson *The Sorcerer's
Apprentice: Picasso, Provence and
Douglas Cooper* Gossipy account of
Picasso and his dealer. Cape, 1999.

Fiction & literature

J G Ballard *Super-Cannes* Expat
couple mixed up in murder in Riviera
business park. Flamingo, 2001.

Sybille Bedford *Jigsaw* Wry
account of childhood and neighbours
in Sanary-sur-Mer. Penguin, 1999.

Carol Drinkwater *The Olive Farm*
British actress and a Frenchman fall
for an olive farm. Abacus, 2001.

Alexandre Dumas *The Count of
Monte Cristo* Ripping yarn of prison,
treasure and revenge. Various eds.

F Scott Fitzgerald *Tender is the
Night* Wealthy American socialites
on the Riviera. Various eds.

Jean Giono *The Man who Planted
Trees* Eco-fable for grown-ups by
gritty Southern writer. Harvill, 1992.

Jean-Claude Izzo *One Helluva
Mess* The first in Izzo's Marseille
detective trilogy. Arcadia, 2001.

Peter Mayle *A Year in Provence*
Former ad man copes with the
Luberon locals. Penguin, 1989.

Tobias Smollett *Travels through
France and Italy* Cantankerous letters
of novelist and doctor on his travels.
Oxford World's Classics, 1999.

Patrick Süskind *Perfume* A
smelly thriller set in the 18th-century
Grasse perfume trade. Picador, 1989.

Emile Zola *La Fortune des Rougon*
The first of Zola's Rougon-Macquart
saga is set in Plassans, a loosely
disguised Aix-en-Provence. Plassans
also features in *L'Oeuvre* about a
struggling artist. Penguin Classics.

Films

La Baie des anges (1963) Jeanne
Moreau plays a compulsive gambler
in Jacques Demy's ravishing New
Wave film in Nice and Monte-Carlo.

To Catch a Thief (1955) Cary
Grant and Grace Kelly in Hitchcock
crime riddle on the Riviera.

Et Dieu créa la femme (1956)
Director Roger Vadim's classic
launched the teenage Brigitte Bardot,
with St-Tropez in the background.

The French Connection (1971)
Gene Hackman stars as a tough New
York cop brought to the Riviera on
the trail of a drug smuggling ring.

**Les Gendarmes et les
extraterrestres** (1978) Aliens
land in St-Tropez, a classic comedy
with Louis de Funes.

Goldeneye (1995) James Bond
tears along the Corniche, then cashes
in his chips at Monte-Carlo casino.

Herbie Goes to Monte-Carlo
(1977) Disney's VW beetle all tuned
up for the Paris to Monte-Carlo road
race but falls for a pert little Lancia.

**Jean de Florette and Manon
des Sources** (1986) Depardieu and
Auteuil battle it out over water,
based on Pagnol's *L'Eau des Collines.*

Marius, Fanny and César (1931,
1932, 1936) Sentimental homage to
Marseille, scripted by Pagnol.

Marius et Jeanette (1997) Robert
Guédiguian's portrait of a working-
class friendship in L'Estaque.

La Piscine (1968) Alain Delon and
Romy Schneider hang out around the
pool above St-Tropez.

Swimming Pool (2002) Charlotte
Rampling and Ludivine Sagnier hang
out around the pool in the Luberon.

Taxi (1998) Stunts galore in the Luc
Besson-scripted and -produced car
chase caper through Marseille.

Two for the Road (1967) Albert
Finney and Audrey Hepburn in
marital crisis on the Riviera.

Music

Bizet *L'Arlésienne Suite* the
Provençal signature tune.

Gounod *Mireille* Camargue opera.

IAM *Revoir au Printemps* soul-
infused Marseille rappers joined by
Redman and Beyoncé.

Poulenc *La Dame de Monte-Carlo*
soprano monologue, lyrics by Cocteau.

Rolling Stones *Exile on Main
Street* Recorded in 1971 at Keith
Richard's Côte d'Azur villa.

Troublemakers *Doubts &
Convictions* Marseille electro trio.

Websites

Official tourist sites

For local tourist office sites, see
individual destinations.

**www.alpes-haute-
provence.com**

www.crt-paca.fr PACA region.

www.drome-tourisme.com

www.franceguide.com France-
wide official government tourist site.

www.guideriviera.com The
Alpes-Maritimes.

www.provenceguide.com The
Vaucluse.

www.tourismevar.com The Var.

www.visitprovence.com The
Bouches-du-Rhône.

Unofficial & media

www.cityvox.com city guides.

www.cote.azur.fr What's on and
tourist information in the Var and
Alpes-Maritimes.

www.documentsdartistes.org
Contemporary artists in the South.

**www.festivals.laregie-
paca.com** Summer festivals.

www.luberon-news.com
Bilingual guide to villages, hotels,
rentals, restaurants, wine, markets,
events and property.

www.nicematin.fr Regional daily.

www.pitchoun.com What's on
between Antibes and Nice.

www.provenceweb.fr Good
bilingual guide covers hundreds of
villages and towns.

www.riviera-reporter.com
English-language expat mag online,
community events and small ads.

Directory

Index